Who's Who in Hockey

Other Books by Stan and Shirley Fischler

Stan and Shirley Fischlers' book collaboration began in 1971 with the publication of *Up From The Minor Leagues of Hockey*, followed in 1973 by *Action Sports Hockey*, a compilation of their writings from a magazine the Fischlers edited for three seasons.

In more than three decades of together, the Fischlers have written or edited nearly 100 books, including:

Fischler's Hockey Encyclopedia, 1975

Best, Worst and Most Unusual Moments In Sports, 1977

The Hockey Encyclopedia, 1983

Everybody's Hockey Book, 1983

Breakaway, 1986, 1987, 1988

Champions with Kevin Lowe, 1988

Thunder and Lightning (with John Ferguson), 1989

Red Line, 1990

Great Book of Hockey, 1991, 1992

All-Time Book of Hockey Lists, 1993

More All-Time Book of Hockey Lists, 1994

Heroes of Hockey, 1994

20th Century Hockey Chronicle, 1994.

Who's Who in Hockey

By Stan and Shirley Fischler

Research Editor:
Brian L. Schiazza

Andrews McMeel Publishing

Kansas City

Book design by Aimee Eckhardt
Book composition by Just Your *Type*

ISBN: 0-7407-1904-1

02 03 04 05 06 RR4 10 9 8 7 6 5 4 3 2 1

Library of Congress Catalog Control Number on file.

To all my favorite hockey players, referees, executives . . .
and most of all, my favorite coach, Shirley.

—Stan Fischler
New York City
May 2002

To Josh Lentin, the ultimate hockey fan, who endured three
heart transplants waiting for his Islanders to get better.

To Mom and Dad, who still know the score. To son Ben,
mate Kine, and their newest hockey fan, not even born yet. To
son Simon and betrothed Danielle, keeping score by Internet
from Israel.

But most of all, to my coauthor, husband, and friend, Stan,
who has dragged me kicking and screaming into these projects
for 35 years. Bless them all.

—Shirley Walton Fischler
New York City
May 2002

Table of contents

c-g

g-l

n-s

S-Z

Acknowledgments

The authors wish to thank the following for their valuable help in the preparation of this book: Vanessa White, Josh Samuelsson, John Marino, Angela Panzarella, Daniel Rice, Jeff Klein, Max Feinberg, Eric Reich, Debbie Elicksen, Bob Matuszak, Stephanie Bechky, and Josh Liebman.

Special gratitude to our editor, Patrick Dobson, for his patience, fortitude, and understanding in guiding us through the project. And, finally, to our agent and good friend, John Wright, our eternal gratitude for his orchestration of the book.

Introduction

A person's reach should exceed his grasp, Robert Browning once suggested, or what's a heaven for?

Obviously, Robert Browning never tried to compile a Who's Who of hockey!

Reach we did, from Sid Abel to Sergei Zubov. After years of collecting, filing, collating, and writing, lo and behold—our grasp, unlike Browning's experience, exceeded our reach.

We had so many names, so many subjects, that volumes would have been required to find room for everyone. As a result, a lot of good hockey people, funny subjects, and, perhaps, favorites of yours, made their exit. It was as painful as telling a rookie or an aging veteran in training camp that he wasn't good enough to make the team, even though the reject believed otherwise.

Our objective, nonetheless, was to produce the most comprehensive A to Z list of hockey subjects, from players to teams to curses, ever attempted. We believe we succeeded.

Producing detail was the biggest obstacle. Because of space limitations, we omitted statistical matter on owners and managers, but provided at least the basics, as thoroughly as possible, on players. In some cases, especially turn-of-the-century players and other pre-NHL aces, details and information were, at best, limited.

More than anything, we attempted to make this project as entertaining, readable, and fun as it was comprehensive. In that sense we sincerely hope our reach at least equaled our grasp.

Who's Who in Hockey

SID ABEL

BORN: Melville, Saskatchewan, February 22, 1918
DIED: February 8, 2000
POSITION: Center, Detroit Red Wings, 1938–43, 1945–52; Chicago Blackhawks, 1952–53; Coach, Chicago Blackhawks, 1952–54; Detroit Red Wings, 1957–70; St. Louis Blues, 1971–72; Kansas City Scouts, 1976; General Manager, Detroit Red Wings, 1963–71; St. Louis Blues, 1972–73; Kansas City Scouts, 1973–76
AWARDS/HONORS: Hart Memorial Trophy, 1949; NHL First Team All-Star, 1949, 1950; NHL Second Team All-Star, 1951; NHL All-Star Game, 1949–51; Hockey Hall of Fame, 1969

There may have been better centers in the National Hockey League than Sid Abel (alias "Ole Bootnose" because of his prominent proboscis), but few were more productive in all the vital areas. He was a dogged and creative playmaker, the balance wheel between Gordie Howe and Ted Lindsay on Detroit's Production Line. He could score as well as develop goal-making plays for others.

Sid Abel (left) in action against the Rangers' Red Sinclair

Reared in the wheat fields of Melville, Saskatchewan, Abel became a member of the Red Wings in 1938–39, remaining in the Motor City until 1952 when he was released to become player-coach of the Chicago Blackhawks in 1952–53. Curiously, that season has been overlooked by hockey historians, although it underlined Abel's insatiable drive.

Sid inherited one of the worst collections of ragtag major-leaguers in NHL history, a team that had finished last in five out of the previous six seasons, and somehow he made them winners. The difference was his spirited play at center coupled with the extraordinary goaltending of angular Al Rollins, who emerged with the Hart (MVP) Trophy at season's end.

Abel not only drove his charges into the playoffs, but very nearly scored a stunning semifinal Stanley Cup playoff victory over the Montreal Canadiens. The Blackhawks lost the series in the seventh and final game when rookie goalie Jacques Plante, imported from Buffalo, bailed out the Canadiens.

However, Abel is best remembered for his exploits in Detroit. "Sid," said hockey historian Ed Fitkin, "will go down in the Red Wings' history as the greatest competitor and inspirational force the Red Wings ever had." Few would have bet on that when he arrived in Detroit as a 19-year-old in the fall of 1937.

A six-footer who weighed only 155 pounds, Abel was greeted by manager-coach Jack Adams. "You got a future, kid," Adams told him, "but you have to build yourself up."

After watching Abel dazzle in workouts, Adams suggested he stick around Detroit and play in the Michigan-Ontario League, which was flourishing then. Abel demurred and returned to western Canada to play with the Flin Flon (Manitoba) Bombers, one of the better Senior Division clubs in the Dominion.

The year of seasoning was just what Abel needed. When he returned to the Red Wings' camp in the fall of 1938–39, the Red Wings tried him at left wing for a while, but he didn't achieve meaningful recognition until 1941–42, playing on a line with Eddie Wares and Don "the Count" Grosso.

Abel was named alternate All-Star left wing for 1941–42, but he ended up a thoroughly distraught young man by April 1942. His Red Wings took on the Toronto Maple Leafs in the Stanley Cup finals. The Red Wings were a distinct underdog, yet Detroit won the first three games of the best-of-seven series and appeared certain to win the Cup. When it appeared the Red Wings would wrap up the series at Detroit's Olympia Stadium, Toronto rallied for a victory and then won the next three games and the championship. "To Abel," said a friend, "it was the greatest disappointment of his life."

The balm was administered the following autumn when manager-coach Adams named Sid captain of the Red Wings. Detroit finished first and won the Stanley Cup. Significantly, Detroit defeated Boston, 6–2, in the opening game of the finals, and Abel enjoyed the most productive night of his career to that point with 1 goal and 3 assists. He finished the playoffs with 5 goals and 8 assists for 13 points in 10 games.

Prior to the 1943–44 campaign, Abel enlisted in the Royal Canadian Air Force, but not before marrying Red Wings secretary Gloria Morandy. He was away from hockey for almost three years, serving as a physical training instructor for the RCAF both in Canada and overseas.

Sid returned to the Red Wings in February 1946. He was 28 years old and there were suspicions that he, like many returning war veterans, was too old and had been away too long. Still, he stayed with the Red Wings and survived the training camp cuts, scoring 19 goals in 1946–47.

At the start of the 1947–48 race, Abel was installed as center between galloping youngsters Gordie Howe (right wing) and Ted Lindsay (left wing), a pair he had worked with only occasionally in previous years.

It wasn't until the 1948–49 season, at age 31, that Abel realized his dream of a 20-goal season. He scored 28 that year, with a little help from his friends, Lindsay and Howe. "It just seemed," said Sid, "that every time I shot, I scored. I kept telling my wife to pinch me. I felt sure that one day I'd wake up and find that I was just dreaming."

The Lindsay-Abel-Howe combine developed into the dreadnoughts of the ice lanes. Abel had the savvy, and both Howe and Lindsay percolated along with style, explosiveness, and aggression that terrorized opposing teams. With The Production Line orchestrating the wins, Detroit captured the first of seven consecutive Prince of Wales Trophies (first place) in 1949. The Red Wings won the Stanley Cup in 1950 and again in 1952, whereupon Abel decided to try coaching—and playing—with the Blackhawks.

Abel eventually returned to Detroit, becoming coach of the Red Wings in January 1958, when Jimmy Skinner was forced by illness to retire. He remained until 1962–63, when he became the Red Wings' general manager. Despite friction between Abel and the aging Jack Adams, Sid remained in command and stayed on the Detroit payroll in one way or another through part of the 1970–71 season.

Abel signed as coach of the St. Louis Blues in 1971–72. He was named general manager of the Blues in October 1971 and remained until April 17, 1973, when he was appointed general manager of the Kansas City Scouts.

Clearly, Abel's major contribution to hockey was as a player, and he was named to the Hockey Hall of Fame in June 1969. As a manager-coach, Sid never achieved the success he enjoyed as a player. He left hockey in 1976 to become a Red Wings broadcaster.

TAFFY ABEL

BORN: Sault Ste. Marie, Michigan, May 28, 1900
DIED: August 1, 1964
POSITION: Defenseman, New York Rangers, 1926–29; Chicago Blackhawks, 1929–34

Bunyanesque Taffy Abel, imported from Minneapolis's minor-league club in 1926 along with Ivan "Ching" Johnson, was one of the original members of the New York Rangers, who fielded their first team that year. Abel and Johnson teamed on the Rangers' back line to give the Blueshirts' defense a fortification that averaged 225 pounds and menaced enemy forwards at every turn. Built like a skating dirigible, Taffy played three full seasons with the Rangers, including the 1928 Stanley Cup–winning sextet, before being traded to Chicago. He was the first U.S.-born skater in the NHL. Abel played five full seasons with the Blackhawks, all of them alongside Lilliputian Harold "Mush" March, with whom he developed an astonishing Mutt and Jeff goal-scoring routine.

It worked this way: Abel would carry the puck over the enemy blue line with the tiny March following close behind. Once Taffy was about ten feet inside the opponent's defensive zone, he would pass the puck to March and

skate toward the net. March would then fire the puck through an opening in Abel's legs. Never has such a screened shot been seen before or since.

KEITH ACTON

BORN: Stouffville, Ontario, April 15, 1958
POSITION: Center, Montreal Canadiens, 1979–83; Minnesota North Stars, 1983–88; Edmonton Oilers, 1988–89; Philadelphia Flyers, 1989–93; Washington Capitals, 1993; New York Islanders, 1993–94; Assistant Coach, Philadelphia Flyers, 1995–98; New York Rangers, 1998–2000; Toronto Maple Leafs, 2000–

Many small players have survived in NHL action because they played much taller than their size. Keith "Woody" Acton was a perfect example. Standing five feet eight and weighing 170 pounds, Acton enjoyed more than a dozen active major-league seasons, starting with the Montreal Canadiens, and finishing with the New York Islanders. By far his best campaign was 1981–82, when he tallied 36 goals and 52 assists for 88 points in 78 games.

His tops in the playoffs was 1984–85 with the Minnesota North Stars. Acton totaled 11 points on 4 goals and 7 assists in 15 games. His tours of duty also included the Edmonton Oilers, Philadelphia Flyers, and Washington Capitals.

Acton then moved behind the bench as an assistant coach with several teams including the New York Rangers, and, most recently, the Toronto Maple Leafs. Keith survived a bout with cancer during the 2001–02 season, returning to help the Leafs advance in the playoffs.

Clarence "Taffy" Abel, Rangers defenseman

CHARLES ADAMS

BORN: Newport, Vermont, October 18, 1876
DIED: 1947

The Boston Bruins franchise was conceived as the result of a Stanley Cup playoff in Montreal! After Charles Adams saw his first playoff, this former grocery boy solicited the help of Art Ross, and the Beantown Bruisers were born in 1924.

Desperately in need of strong players, Adams purchased the entire Western Canada League from the Patrick family in 1926, and followed this move by guaranteeing $500,000 to help build Boston Garden. Adams was inducted into the Hockey Hall of Fame prior to his death in 1947.

JACK ADAMS

BORN: Fort William, Ontario, June 14, 1895
DIED: May 1, 1968
POSITION: Forward, Toronto Arenas, 1917–19; Toronto St. Patricks, 1922–26; Ottawa Senators, 1926–27; Coach, Toronto St. Patricks, 1922–23; Detroit Red Wings, 1927–47; General Manager, Detroit Red Wings, 1927–63; President, Central League, 1963–68
AWARDS/HONORS: Lester Patrick Trophy, 1966; Hockey Hall of Fame, 1959

Without Jack "Jovial Jawn" Adams there might never be a Detroit Red Wings franchise today. Adams played NHL hockey with the Toronto Arenas, the Toronto St. Patricks, and the Ottawa Senators, as manager-coach. He was an exceptionally galvanic personality who would do anything to win and rarely concerned himself with the consequences.

Always confident, Jack walked into the NHL office prior to the 1927–28 season and asserted to NHL president Frank Calder that he was the man for the vacant Detroit NHL coaching job. When Calder agreed and sent Adams to meet with Detroit club president Charlie Hughes,

Adams again revealed the same brashness to Hughes. "I'd been involved in winning the Stanley Cup in Ottawa," he said, "so I told Hughes he needed me more than I needed him."

Hughes signed Adams to a contract and told him to get started building a winner. A year later Hughes knew he had taken the right course. From a dismal 12–28–4 record, the Detroiters climbed to the .500 mark, winning 19, losing 19, and tying 6 games. It wasn't a good enough record for a Stanley Cup berth, but there was no question that the road to the Cup had opened for the team, then known as the Detroit Cougars. The following season, Detroit, newly nicknamed the Falcons, finished third in the American Division.

The turning point occurred when James Norris Sr., a grain millionaire with a fervent love of hockey, bought the team in 1932, and changed the nickname to the Red Wings. A no-nonsense type, Norris was even brasher than Adams. He laid it on the line with the manager. "I'll give you a year on probation," Norris warned, "with no contract."

Adams may not have had a written pact with Norris, but he quickly gained the millionaire's confidence as well as access to his bankroll to sign superior players like Syd Howe, who became a Hall of Famer.

Jack Adams (right) with another Hall of Famer, Mervyn "Red" Dutton

By the 1935–36 season, the Adams-Norris combine was the best in hockey. The manager was not only off probation, but had become so friendly with his awesome boss that he referred to Norris as "Pops."

By March 22, 1936, the final day of the 1935–36 season, Detroit was perched atop the American Division with a record of 24 wins, 16 losses, and 8 ties for 56 points, the best record in either division.

To win the Cup in 1936, the Red Wings were first required to dispatch the strong Montreal Maroons in the opening playoff round that began March 24, 1936, at the Forum in Montreal. To this day, the game remains a classic among classics. It was the longest hockey match ever played in the NHL. Exactly 116 minutes and 30 seconds of sudden-death overtime was required, almost two additional full games. The winning goal was scored by Modere "Mud" Bruneteau of the Red Wings at 16:30 of the sixth overtime.

The Red Wings plummeted in 1937–38. Not only did they fail to retain their hold on first place, they didn't even gain a playoff berth. It took six years for Adams's Red Wings to win another Stanley Cup, in the 1942–43 season, when they finished first.

Without question, 1946 was the most important year in the history of Adams and his Detroit hockey club. It was then that a muscular youngster named Gordie Howe arrived in Detroit. He was accompanied by another young player, Ted Lindsay, who had joined the Red Wings two years before. When Adams placed captain Sid Abel, the center, on a line with Howe on right wing and the truculent Lindsay on left, no three forwards ever jelled more firmly. As they began to pump goal after goal into the enemy nets it was rather appropriate that the city that developed the automobile production line should name Abel, Lindsay, and Howe "The Production Line."

Even with other stars like defensemen "Black Jack" Stewart, Bill Quackenbush, and Leonard "Red" Kelly, and Harry Lumley in

goal, it wasn't until 1949–50 that the Red Wings were ready once again for a serious assault on the championship. After Adams brought them to first place for the second year in a row, the Wings' first objective was the Maple Leafs, whom they defeated in seven games, but only after Howe had sustained a near-fatal head injury in the opening match. That put Detroit in the finals against the New York Rangers, whom they also beat in seven games.

Adams's clubs went on to win three more Stanley Cups, and finished first six more times until Jack stepped down in 1962–63 to become president of the Central League. His longevity inspired the NHL to annually honor a coach in his name with the Jack Adams Award beginning in 1974.

Adams is the only Hall of Famer to have won the Stanley Cup as a player, general manager, and coach.

ANDREW AITKENHEAD

BORN: Glasgow, Scotland, March 6, 1904
DIED: 1968
POSITION: Goaltender, New York Rangers, 1932–35

Blond, blue-eyed goaltender Andrew Aitkenhead was hired by New York Rangers manager-coach Lester Patrick in the 1932–33 season as a replacement for John Ross Roach. Aitkenhead's addition to the New York sextet was a pivotal one at the time, particularly since Roach had played mediocre goal for the Rangers during the previous season.

With Andy starting in the nets, the Rangers defeated Toronto three games to one in the best-of-five Stanley Cup finals in April 1933 to win the world championship. That, however, was the acme of Andy's success. He played one more full season and only ten games of the 1934–35 campaign before making his exit from the major leagues.

DANIEL ALFREDSSON

BORN: Gothenburg, Sweden, December 11, 1972
POSITION: Right Wing, Ottawa Senators, 1995–
AWARDS/HONORS: NHL All-Rookie Team, 1996; Calder Memorial Trophy, 1996; NHL All-Star Game, 1996–98

During the Alexei Yashin years in Ottawa, which began in 1993–94 and ended in 2000–01, it was difficult to put a spotlight on any other Senators forward.

But when Yashin was traded to the New York Islanders in the summer of 2001, Daniel Alfredsson became the unequivocal star of a team that accented speed. The redhead from Gothenburg, Sweden, clearly was one of the fastest skaters in the National Hockey League, and proved to be one of the best finds in NHL history.

In the 1994 Entry Draft, Alfredsson was selected 133rd overall (Ottawa's fifth choice). He was an immediate hit in his rookie year of 1995–96 with a Calder Trophy win, and provided Ottawa fans with a glimmer of hope for their emerging franchise. In the 1997–98 playoffs, he scored 7 goals and 2 assists in 11 games, proving he could deliver in the clutch.

Standing five feet eleven and weighing 195 pounds, Alfredsson was susceptible to injury and never played a full season after his rookie year. Nevertheless, his value to the Senators transcended points, and his leadership skills prompted the high command to name him captain for the 2001–02 campaign.

Alfredsson was a key factor in the 2002 postseason, as Ottawa stunned the Philadelphia Flyers in round one, then succumbed to Toronto in round two.

KEITH ALLEN

BORN: Saskatoon, Sasketchewan, August 21, 1923
POSITION: Defenseman, Detroit Red Wings, 1953–55; Coach, Philadelphia Flyers, 1967–69; General Manager, Philadelphia Flyers, 1969–83
AWARDS/HONORS: NHL All-Star Game, 1954; Lester Patrick Trophy, 1988; Hockey Hall of Fame, 1992

A defenseman for the Red Wings in 1953–54 and 1954–55, Allen is best remembered for coaching the expansion Philadelphia Flyers in its first two years of existence, 1967–68 and 1968–69. With an impressive 31–32–11 mark in their first year of NHL existence, the Flyers earned their first West Division championship and a spot in the playoffs in their debut year, a remarkable feat for an expansion team.

Allen helped persuade reluctant Flyers honcho Bud Poile to draft a high-scoring diabetic named Bobby Clarke in 1969, and eventually evolved into general manager. His moves resulted in their Stanley Cup championships in 1974 and 1975, with Fred Shero behind the bench. Also responsible for drafting Flyer luminaries Bill Barber, Paul Holmgren, Ron Hextall, and Bill Clement, he stepped into the executive vice president's role after 1982–83, and actively held the post into the next century.

Allen's leadership in the Flyers' first years helped get him elected into the Hockey Hall of Fame in 1992.

JASON ALLISON

BORN: North York, Ontario, May 29, 1975
POSITION: Center, Washington Capitals, 1993–97; Boston Bruins, 1997–2001; Los Angeles Kings, 2001–
AWARDS/HONORS: NHL All-Star Game, 2001

It is a measure of Jason Allison's potential that when he slumped during the 1999 Stanley Cup playoff series against Buffalo—which the Bruins lost, four games to two—president–general manager Harry Sinden publicly ripped him. Sinden questioned the "dedication" and "sacrifice" of his top-scoring center. He also claimed Allison had become a fat cat and that his multimillion-dollar contract had diminished his drive.

The criticism, which some observers considered excessive, nevertheless demonstrated that the six-feet-three, 205-pounder from North York, Ontario, commanded attention: If he wasn't scoring to Sinden's standard, it was worthy of comment. On paper, at least, the boss had little to complain about—either in 1997–98 or 1998–99—when it came to performance.

In his first full campaign with Boston, Allison registered the most improvement of any NHL player with a plus-55 differential. He averaged more than a point a game (81 games, 33–50–83), which led the team in scoring. Jason not only established career-season highs in all categories but finished ninth overall in the scoring race. After a 95-point season in 2000–01, in which he was the NHL's fifth leading scorer, a contract dispute and subsequent holdout with the Bruins triggered a trade of Allison (along with Mikko Eloranta) to Los Angeles for ex-Bruins Glen Murray and Josef Stumpel. In California, Allison's game was revived to a point-per-game clip. He helped a struggling Kings team into the Western Conference elite.

By the end of the 2001–02 season, Allison was regarded as one of the NHL's premier scorers.

TONY AMONTE

BORN: Hingham, Massachusetts, August 2, 1970
POSITION: Right Wing, New York Rangers, 1990–94; Chicago Blackhawks 1994–2002; Phoenix Coyotes, 2002–
AWARDS/HONORS: NHL All-Rookie Team, 1992; NHL All-Star Game, 1997–2001

Tony Amonte emerged as the foremost forward of the new millennium to play for Chicago. He followed in the exalted tradition of Stan Mikita, Bobby Hull, and Max Bentley. To become a Blackhawk, Amonte first was involved in a controversial deal on March 21, 1994.

At the time, Amonte was a budding star on Broadway, having played three seasons as a Ranger. But then coach Mike Keenan redesigned his roster and elected to obtain Stephane Matteau and Brian Noonan in exchange for the colorful right wing.

Matteau and Noonan were significant contributors to the Rangers' 1994 Stanley Cup drive while Amonte gradually developed into a star in the Windy City. His four-goal game in the playoffs against Toronto on April 21, 1994, endeared him to his new fans. By 1999–2000, Amonte reached his productive peak, scoring 43 goals and 41 assists for 84 points, following a 44-goal campaign one year earlier. His eight seasons of 30-plus goals or more (including six consecutive) easily marked him as a bona fide American scorer, with berths on Team USA for the 1998 and 2002 Olympics, as well as the 1996 World Cup champions, for whom he scored the series-clinching goal versus Canada.

Amonte's forte was breakaway speed, a lethal shot, and generally superior offensive instincts, which made Chicago heavily reliant on the Massachusetts native. Amonte helped the 2001–02 edition of the Blackhawks to the Western Conference elite. After the playoffs, Amonte became a free agent and signed a long-term deal with the Phoenix Coyotes.

GLENN ANDERSON

BORN: Vancouver, British Columbia, October 2, 1960
POSITION: Right Wing, Edmonton Oilers, 1980–91, 1996; Toronto Maple Leafs, 1991–94; New York Rangers, 1994; St. Louis Blues, 1994–95, 1996
AWARDS/HONORS: NHL All-Star Game, 1984–86, 1988

When the Edmonton Oilers became the highest-scoring team of the 1980s, their most famous sharpshooters were Wayne Gretzky and Mark Messier. But the Stanley Cup champions of 1984, 1985, 1987, 1988, and 1990 were supported by a number of lesser, yet noteworthy, snipers.

One of the most underrated of that group was an exceptionally speedy forward named Glenn Anderson. The six-feet-one, 190-pound right wing exemplified the clever drafting that enabled Glen Sather to build a near-dynasty in Alberta.

Anderson was not drafted until 69th overall after a season playing for the University of Denver and the 1980 Canadian Olympic team.

As an Oiler, it took him only two seasons to average more than a point a game. In 1981–82, he tallied 38 goals and 67 assists, for 105 points. During the early to mid 1980s, Anderson had three 100-point seasons and held a plus/minus rating of over plus-40 for three consecutive years. He not only scored during the regular season, but also when it counted the most. The playoffs were when Anderson played at his peak: 93 goals and 121 assists over the course of 225 playoff games easily ranked Glenn as a clutch performer. Moreover, his three overtime playoff goals were an Oilers record.

With age, Anderson no longer performed at his best, but still was productive for the Maple Leafs after they acquired him in 1991. In 1994, he became a Ranger in time for their long-awaited Stanley Cup victory, joining old friend Messier on Broadway for that single spring before finishing in 1996 with St. Louis.

While the small winger never reached the status of his teammates, Messier and Gretzky, he was an integral member of the Oilers in the 1980s.

DAVE ANDREYCHUK

BORN: Hamilton, Ontario, September 29, 1963
POSITION: Left Wing, Buffalo Sabres, 1982–93, 2000–01; Toronto Maple Leafs, 1993–96; New Jersey Devils, 1996–99; Boston Bruins, 1999–2000; Colorado Avalanche, 2000; Tampa Bay Lightning, 2001–
AWARDS/HONORS: NHL All-Star Game, 1990, 1994

For a man who thought he would never make it to the National Hockey League, Dave Andreychuk surprised himself and a lot of other people.

He reached the 20-year mark in the big leagues during the 2001–02 season and seemed virtually assured of eventual entrance into the Hockey Hall of Fame.

The numbers tell the story. At age 38 in the 2001–02 season, his 20th in the NHL, Andreychuk had played 1,405 games, a record for the most games of any active player who has never won a Stanley Cup.

During the same season, the six-feet-four, 220-pound left wing took his place in the record books as number two in career and season power-play goals, number three among left wings in career points, goals, and assists, tied for number five for most consecutive 20-goal seasons, number six among active goal scorers, and number 14 all-time.

The numbers show that "Andy" has passed Hall of Famers like Mike Bossy and Stan Mikita in his lengthy career.

"It's hard to believe I'm actually going by these guys," Andreychuk said. "Someday I'm going to sit back and realize the accomplishments, but right now it's tough to swallow."

After a decade flourishing with Buffalo,

Andreychuk was traded to Toronto, New Jersey, Boston, and Colorado, before re-signing in 2000 with his old team, the Sabres. All too soon, Buffalo management was muttering that Andy had become "lazy." Shortly thereafter, the lumbering forward found a new home in Tampa Bay. Lightning coach John Tortorella saw something different and Andreychuk became an asset, a father figure and role model to Tampa Bay's young roster.

"People consider him a lazy guy if he can't get down the ice," said Tortorella. "He's not a young guy anymore, and everybody in the league knows he can't skate a lick. His skating is a liability. But get Andy around the net, get him in offensive situations and face-offs and penalty-killing, and he's one of the best."

A pretty high appraisal for someone who thought he might not make it to the league.

SYL APPS

BORN: Paris, Ontario, January 18, 1915
DIED: December 24, 1998
POSITION: Center, Toronto Maple Leafs, 1936–43, 1945–48
AWARDS/HONORS: Calder Memorial Trophy, 1937; Lady Byng Memorial Trophy, 1942; NHL First Team All-Star, 1939, 1942; NHL Second Team All-Star, 1938, 1941, 1943; NHL All-Star Game, 1939, 1947; Hockey Hall of Fame, 1961

Syl Apps was the Bobby Orr of the pre–World War II era (except, of course, Orr was a defenseman), and for some time beyond. The original "All-Canadian Boy," Syl was born in the tiny town of Paris, Ontario. His father believed he should become well educated and proficient in sports, and helped young Syl on both counts. The name Apps soon became prominent in both the classroom and the athletic field, where he eclipsed others in his age group.

Long and lean, Syl developed a graceful skating style, which later was to inspire Montreal author Vincent D. Lunny to call him "a Rembrandt on the ice, a Nijinsky at the goalmouth." By the time Syl was 14 years old, the village team found a center ice spot for him, and his hockey career began.

"His dazzling bursts of speed," wrote Ron McAllister, "and great sweeping strides made him an exciting player to watch, and he soon discovered that he was gaining quite a reputation among sports fans in his hometown."

Apps betrayed one "weakness" that alarmed his coach, Russell Sandercock of the Paris Juniors. He showed no inclination to retaliate when fouled by the opposition; and since he was easily the best player on his team, the enemy constantly tried to reef him along the boards or behind the net. Syl would take his blows and return to action as if nothing had happened.

Later, other "obstacles" blocked Apps's climb to the NHL: pole-vaulting and football. At the age of 17, Syl entered McMaster University in Hamilton, Ontario, on a scholarship, majoring in political economy, and turned out for the track team. His specialty was pole-vaulting, and he became so adept at it that in 1934 he was invited to represent the Dominion of Canada at the British Empire Games in London, England.

Syl Apps of the Toronto Maple Leafs

Apps won his event and returned home, became captain of the McMaster football team, and spearheaded its march to the Intercollegiate Championship. Syl also played for McMaster's hockey team and was as impressive among the collegians as he had been in junior hockey. He was so skilled that Bill Marsden, a former Toronto hockey coach who had moved to the University of Western Ontario, told his friend Conn Smythe about the big kid with the long strides.

When Smythe and Apps finally met, Syl made it clear that before he considered the NHL he wanted to complete his college education and compete in the Olympic Games, to which he had been invited. He also wasn't sure he was capable of playing big-league hockey. Smythe nursed some doubts, too, and they agreed that a year in the tough Ontario Hockey Association Senior A League would provide a good indication of Syl's NHL potential.

The answer was supplied at the end of the season. Apps had led the league in scoring. He then headed for Berlin, Germany, and the Eleventh Olympiad. There, before 100,000 spectators, including Adolf Hitler, Syl vaulted to a sixth-place tie for Canada.

He returned to Canada with the world at his feet. He could move on to graduate school, or he could accept Smythe's offer to attend the Maple Leafs' training camp. Throughout late summer and early autumn, speculation mounted about Syl's choice between hockey and advanced education. A September meeting with Smythe sealed his fate with the Maple Leafs.

Coach Dick Irvin put Apps at center between Busher Jackson and Gordie Drillon. Although veteran Jackson was no longer noted for his diligence, the two younger players remained on the ice long after regular work-outs, perfecting Drillon's "secret weapon," the tip-in shot. Apps was vital to the play since he was to deliver the pass. Drillon, of course, would get credit for the goals, but as *Toronto Globe and Mail* reporter Bill Roche pointed out,

"The serious-minded Apps was the one who proposed they do the experimenting."

Results came immediately, and by mid-season Apps was hailed as a shoo-in for Rookie of the Year. "He's a better player than Howie Morenz was at the same age," said Detroit manager Jack Adams, always grudging in his acclaim for a Toronto player.

Smythe, who remarked from time to time that he didn't want any Lady Byng (good conduct) hockey players on his team, tried to goad Apps into some form of belligerence. Syl finished the season with only 10 minutes in penalties, but, more important, he scored 16 goals and 29 assists for 45 points, second to Dave "Sweeney" Schriner of the Americans. Apps had missed the scoring championship by only a point. In the balloting for the Calder Trophy, Apps polled 79 out of a possible 81 votes and easily won rookie honors.

The aging Busher Jackson didn't last long on the Apps line. Irvin replaced him the following season with Bob Davidson, a husky, hard-checking winger, and the D-A-D (Drillon-Apps-Davidson) Line was born.

Thanks to Syl's crisp passes, Drillon led the NHL in scoring during the 1937–38 season, with 26 goals and 26 assists for 52 points. The unselfish Apps finished second again, with 21 goals and 29 assists for 50 points. Injuries began taking their toll in the next season, especially torn shoulder muscles, yet Apps still managed to lead the Maple Leafs in scoring, improving every month.

While earning his place among hockey greats, Syl also managed to take his first turn in the political arena. He was nominated as the conservative candidate for the federal election in North Brant. He was defeated in the election, however, and once again he concentrated full-time on his hockey campaign. In 1948, he led the Leafs to first place and the Stanley Cup.

Apps retired from pro hockey in 1948 and went on to become a member of the Ontario Legislature for Kingston and a member of the Cabinet.

AL ARBOUR

BORN: Sudbury, Ontario, November 1, 1932
POSITION: Defenseman, Detroit Red Wings, 1953–54, 1955–58; Chicago Blackhawks, 1958–61; Toronto Maple Leafs, 1961–66; St. Louis Blues, 1967–71; Coach, St. Louis Blues, 1970–73; New York Islanders, 1973–86, 1988–94
AWARDS/HONORS: NHL All-Star Game, 1969; Jack Adams Award, 1979

**Al Arbour,
Islanders coach**

One of the greatest coaches in NHL history, Al Arbour began as an unspectacular defenseman for the Detroit Red Wings in 1953–54. He did not make rink-length dashes, nor did he bash oncoming forwards with bone-rattling checks. He simply frustrated the opposition with timely stick-checks and blocked shots, epitomizing the term "defensive defenseman."

Arbour, one of the few players ever to wear glasses, played 16 seasons for four different teams, including, in order, Detroit, Chicago, Toronto, and the St. Louis Blues during their inaugural season. In 1970, he coached 50 games for the Blues before returning as a player, and was appointed assistant general manager the following year, only to take over the bench again on Christmas, 1971. Unable to tolerate front office interference, Al left St. Louis to become a scout for the Atlanta Flames.

Arbour became the head coach of the New York Islanders in 1973–74, to mentor a team that had set virtually every record for futility in its maiden season, 1972–73.

He established his grip on the young team early with rigorous curfews, punishing drills,

and fines for lateness. Arbour's firm hand on the adversity-laden team soon cultivated a "never-say-die" spirit in the Islanders. By 1975, the hardworking "Cinderella" Islanders defeated their crosstown rivals, the Rangers, in the preliminary round, came back from 0–3 to defeat the Pittsburgh Penguins in the quarterfinals, and took the eventual Stanley Cup winners, the Philadelphia Flyers, to seven games before bowing out. But it was the start of something humongous.

"When Al first came," recalled goalie Glenn "Chico" Resch, "he had to instill everything in us: a winning attitude, the defensive attitude you need to win, his system, his discipline, what he expects from each player. It was inbred in the team, strict discipline in your play. Al achieved it; Vince Lombardi achieved it."

After stellar seasons in the late 1970s, Arbour's troops finally completed their journey and seized four straight Stanley Cups, from 1979–80 through 1982–83. They nearly had a fifth Cup in 1983–84, but the Islanders, after winning an all-time record 19 straight playoff rounds, relinquished the Cup to the Edmonton Oilers.

Arbour's championship teams included an impressive list of players. The names of Bryan Trottier, Mike Bossy, Denis Potvin, Clark Gillies, Bob Nystrom, and Billy Smith will be forever remembered by Islanders fans. But it was under Arbour's tutelage that they grew as players and produced their Stanley Cup experiences, unprecedented for an American-based team in the NHL.

Arbour coached the Islanders in two different stints. The first, from 1972–73 through 1985–86, produced 552 victories, 317 defeats, and 169 ties. After successor Terry Simpson couldn't get the rebuilding team off the ground, Al returned from 1988 through 1993–94 for 187 more wins.

Though the Islanders would not always qualify for the postseason during that period, Arbour engineered a sweet, vintage performance out of his 1992–93 squad, when a new generation, led by Pierre Turgeon, Ray Ferraro, and rookie Darius Kasparaitis, surged unexpectedly to the Wales Conference finals after a victorious overtime-filled opening round versus the Washington Capitals. They dethroned the defending Cup champion Pittsburgh Penguins, shepharded by Scotty Bowman and Mario Lemieux, in round two. Following 1993-94, Arbour permanently retired, finishing with 739 victories, and a terrific playoff record of 123 wins and 86 losses. He remained close to the Islander organization into the twenty-first century.

In 1996, his overdue induction into the Hockey Hall of Fame capped the career of a man who crafted a dynastic Islander team capable of playing any style of hockey demanded of them en route to ultimate victory—again and again.

GEORGE ARMSTRONG

BORN: Skead, Ontario, July 6, 1930
POSITION: Center, Toronto Maple Leafs, 1949-50, 1951-71
AWARDS/HONORS: NHL All-Star Game, 1956-57, 1959, 1962-64, 1968; Hockey Hall of Fame, 1975

George Armstrong, a First Nation Canadian lad, was the choice to be groomed by the Toronto Maple Leafs' owner Conn Smythe as a replacement at pivot once Syl Apps retired in April 1948. Tall and awkward, Armstrong climbed through the Leafs' hockey system, playing for the Toronto Marlboros in both the Ontario Hockey Association's Junior and Senior Divisions. He had a two-game trial with the Leafs in 1949-50 and played 20 NHL games with them in 1951-52, after which he was signed on as a regular.

It was clear, despite Armstrong's relentless improvement, that he'd never be another Syl Apps, Max Bentley, or Ted Kennedy, the best of the NHL centers in the late 1940s, although he most resembled the latter. Like Kennedy,

Armstrong—nicknamed "Chief"—was a plodding skater with a bland shot. But he played a persistent two-way game and eventually was named the Leafs' captain after Kennedy's retirement. However, it wasn't until Punch Imlach's reign as Toronto coach that Armstrong reached his apex as a player. During his captaincy, the Leafs won four Stanley Cups and finished first once.

The Chief remained with Toronto throughout his career, ultimately retiring at the conclusion of the 1970-71 season after playing 1,187 games for the Maple Leafs. He then became coach of the Toronto Marlboros of the OHA Junior A League, and eventually, albeit briefly, got to run the bench for his beloved Leafs in 1988-89 for 47 matches before joining the scouting ranks.

He was elected to the Hall of Fame in June 1975.

JASON ARNOTT

BORN: Collingwood, Ontario, October 11, 1974
POSITION: Center, Edmonton Oilers, 1993-98; New Jersey Devils, 1998-2002; Dallas Stars, 2002-
AWARDS/HONORS: NHL All-Rookie Team, 1994; NHL All-Star Game, 1997

Originally a high-draft pick of the Edmonton Oilers in 1993, Jason Arnott will forever be remembered for his Stanley Cup-winning double-overtime goal in the 2000 playoffs that gave the Devils their second Stanley Cup in six years.

After impressing the Oilers as an 18-year-old with an impressive 68-point freshman year, Arnott failed to improve that total in any of the following four years. Eventually Edmonton fans soured on him, forcing a trade to the Devils.

Arnott arrived in New Jersey from Edmonton in a 1998 deal for Bill Guerin and eventually found his size a complementary component for Czech linemates Patrik Elias and Petr Sykora. They clicked almost immediately, and the result was one of the National Hockey League's most potent forward units—the "A-Line." For two straight seasons the A-Line powered the Devils to the finals in 2000 and 2001. The line combined for 50 points in 23 games in the 2000 playoffs.

Often injured in his last two New Jersey seasons, Arnott struggled with his role as assistant captain, and, at age 26, found himself changing teams again in 2002. The Devils unexpectedly dealt Arnott and Randy McKay to the same Dallas team he thwarted two springs earlier, for Joe Nieuwendyk and Jamie Langenbrunner.

LARRY AURIE

BORN: Sudbury, Ontario, February 8, 1905
DIED: December 11, 1952
POSITION: Right Wing, Detroit, 1928–39
AWARDS/HONORS: NHL First Team All-Star, 1937; NHL All-Star Game, 1934

His full monicker was Harry Lawrence Aurie, but soon after coming to Detroit in 1927, the skillful right wing was nicknamed "Little Dempsey," as in heavyweight champ Jack Dempsey.

Larry Aurie was hardly a heavyweight, but he was a champion. And by the mid 1930s, he had become one of the most popular Red Wings. The five-feet-six Aurie weighed in at 148 pounds, but his grit weighed a ton.

As the Red Wings developed into a powerhouse in the mid 1930s, coach Jack Adams fortuitously teamed Aurie with center Marty Barry and left wing Herbie Lewis. As a unit, the Aurie-Lewis-Barry trio became the first

great line in Red Wing history. It might have been Detroit's greatest ever were it not for the advent of The Production Line of Gordie Howe, Ted Lindsay, and Sid Abel 15 years later.

At a time when low scoring was the norm, Aurie excelled in the 1934–35 season, scoring 17 goals along with 29 assists for a career high 46 points in a 48-game season.

But it was a year later when Aurie and his two pals put Detroit on the hockey map. The Red Wings not only finished first in the American Division but also established their supremacy by sweeping the Montreal Maroons in the Stanley Cup semifinal round, three games to nothing. They then whipped Toronto three games to one to win the Stanley Cup for the first time on April 11, 1936.

The next season, Aurie made headlines by leading the NHL in goal-scoring with 23 red lights in 45 games. By today's standards, that may not seem like an overwhelming number, but it was phenomenal enough then to earn Larry a place on the first NHL All-Star team.

Once again, the Aurie-Lewis-Barry line helped Detroit to first place and the playoffs, where the Wings won another Stanley Cup. Detroit thus became the first NHL team ever to finish first and win the Cup in two straight seasons.

Aurie, however, had reached the end of his hockey rope and the Red Wings sagged terribly in seasons to come. Detroit manager Jack Adams always regretted not trading Aurie after the 1936–37 season.

"Instead of standing pat," said Adams, "I should have traded. I'll never hesitate to bust up a champion team again."

But Larry Aurie was an integral part of the Detroit Red Wings' first glory years.

PETE BABANDO

BORN: Braeburn, Pennsylvania, May 10, 1925
POSITION: Left Wing, Boston Bruins, 1947–49; Detroit Red Wings, 1949–50; Chicago Blackhawks, 1950–52; New York Rangers, 1952–53

Like Dusty Rhodes of baseball fame, Pete Babando was a journeyman who might never have achieved acclaim except that he came through, as did Rhodes, in a clutch situation.

At Olympia Stadium in Detroit on April 23, 1950, the Rangers and Red Wings were tied at three games apiece and the scored tied, 3–3, in the Stanley Cup final. Babando, a short, chunky skater who had played two seasons with the Bruins (1947–48, 1949) before being traded to Detroit, took a face-off pass from George Gee and beat New York goalie Chuck Rayner with a screened shot at 8:31 of the second overtime. Babando's reward was a ticket to the lowly Chicago Blackhawks the following season. He played two seasons in the Windy City before being traded, ironically, to the Rangers during the 1952–53 season, his last in the majors.

RALPH BACKSTROM

BORN: Kirkland Lake, Ontario, September 18, 1937
POSITION: Center, Montreal Canadiens, 1956–70; Los Angeles Kings, 1971–73; Chicago Blackhawks, 1973; Chicago Cougars (WHA), 1973–75; Denver Spurs-Ottawa Civics (WHA), 1975–76; New England Whalers (WHA), 1976–77
AWARDS/HONORS: Calder Memorial Trophy, 1959; NHL All-Star Game, 1958–60, 1962, 1965, 1967; Paul Daneau Trophy (Most Sportsmanlike Player, WHA), 1974

When the Montreal Canadiens' dynasty was in the process of winning five consecutive Stanley Cups between 1956 and 1960, Ralph Backstrom had the misfortune of being low man on the totem pole of centers behind Jean Beliveau and Henri Richard. On any other team, Backstrom would have been the first center. He was faster than most players, had a good shot and excellent hockey sense, and was good enough to play for more than a decade.

He was named Rookie of the Year in 1958–59, and would ultimately be a member of six Stanley Cup championship teams.

After twelve years, Backstrom decided to retire in 1970 but was talked into returning, then traded to the Los Angeles Kings. In 1973, he was sent to the Chicago Blackhawks. He later became disenchanted playing behind Stan Mikita and signed with the Chicago Cougars of the rival WHA. With his Canadiens background—classy skating and excellent stickhandling—Backstrom helped the Cougars to an upset and a spot in the WHA playoff finals in 1974, the same year he also became the uncontested star of the WHA-Russia series.

A symbol of Backstrom's hard-earned success was a letter he received from one of hockey's living legends, Conn Smythe: "I have never believed in the statement that it doesn't matter whether you win or lose, but how you play the game. However, with your example in the Russian series, I have to say that it has some merit."

One of Backstrom's other claims to fame was the fact that he was an early pioneer of in-line roller skates, which led to the roller hockey boom of the late-twentieth century. By 2001, Backstrom had become a scout for the St. Louis Blues.

ACE BAILEY

BORN: Bracebridge, Ontario, July 3, 1903
DIED: April 7, 1992
POSITION: Left Wing, Toronto Maple Leafs, 1926–34
AWARDS/HONORS: Art Ross Trophy, 1929; Hockey Hall of Fame, 1975

Ace Bailey, a superb puck carrier and penalty killer, was one of the few skaters ever to come very close to getting killed during a hockey game. On the night of December 12, 1933, Bailey was skating for the Maple Leafs against the Bruins at Boston Garden. As Toronto nursed a lead in the fateful match, the Bruins grew more and more frustrated, especially when Bailey expertly killed a penalty against the Leafs. It was during that sequence that Boston defenseman Eddie Shore was tripped by King Clancy of the Leafs.

Many observers insist that Shore mistakenly believed Bailey had tripped him, asserting that Shore then pursued Bailey to get even. At the time Bailey had his back to Shore, who was skating fiercely at the Toronto forward. Shore impacted Bailey across the kidneys, sending him head over heels until he landed on his head with terrifying force.

Bailey was badly hurt and was removed to a hospital, where he was given little hope of surviving. Doctors performed two brain operations to save him. Eventually he recovered enough to return to a normal life, although he never played pro hockey again. Weeks later Bailey minimized Shore's role in the fracas. "We didn't see each other coming," Ace said graciously.

Shore, who had been suspended by the NHL, was sent on a recuperative vacation by the Bruins. A month later, the governors decided that since the Bruin had never before suffered a match penalty for injuring an opponent he would be reinstated. He returned to the Boston lineup in January 1934, and later shook hands with Bailey at a special All-Star game benefit in Ace's behalf. In later years, Irvine Wallace Bailey became a minor NHL official at Maple Leaf Gardens in Toronto.

HOBEY BAKER

BORN: Wissahickon, Pennsylvania, January, 1892
DIED: 1918
POSITION: Rover, played entirely on amateur teams in the United States (Princeton, New Jersey, and St. Nicholas Club, New York City)
AWARDS/HONORS: Hockey Hall of Fame, 1945

Improbable as it may seem, one of the most respected hockey players in Canada before World War I was Hobey Baker, an American, who never played professionally and never played for a Canadian team.

Born in a small Pennsylvania town, Hobart Baker learned to skate effortlessly and stick-handle with remarkable finesse. Hobey first played organized hockey in Concord, New Hampshire, at St. Paul's School. By 1910, he was at Princeton, where he captained his team to two intercollegiate titles. He also kicked a field goal in football that earned the Tigers a tie with Yale.

In the Ross Cup series in Montreal against the Montreal Stars, he led his amateur St. Nicholas (New York City) team to victory and the press commented in astonishment: "Uncle Sam has the cheek to develop a first class hockey player—who wasn't born in Montreal!"

Baker died in 1918, testing a plane as a combat pilot in the United States Armed Forces. He was posthumously inducted into the Hockey Hall of Fame. Further recognition would arrive in the form of the Hobey Baker Award, given to the top U.S. collegiate hockey player in the nation every year since 1981. Considered hockey's answer to football's Heisman Trophy, the Baker Award was bestowed on several players who went on to NHL success, including 1980 Olympians Neal Broten and Paul Kariya.

HOWARD BALDWIN

BORN: New York City, New York, May 14, 1942

Few American hockey magnates have accomplished as much in as short a time as Howard Baldwin. An original founder of the World Hockey Association in 1972, Baldwin helped develop the New England Whalers (now the Carolina Hurricanes) into a championship team in one season.

Baldwin later became WHA president and helped win National Hockey League respect for the budding league. In 1979, Baldwin helped engineer an unexpected merger of the two leagues. As a result four WHA clubs—the Whalers, the Jets, the Oilers, and the Nordiques—became part of the NHL. The WHA dissolved following the 1978–79 season.

Baldwin served as the managing general partner of the Whalers until their sale in 1988. At the time, the $31 million price tag was the highest in league history—this on the heels of three straight seasons of record crowds in Hartford.

Baldwin became an adviser to several NHL teams after leaving Hartford. Continuing his role as a builder in the NHL, he helped create the expansion San Jose Sharks in 1990. After establishing the Sharks franchise, Baldwin traded his interest in the Sharks for a controlling interest in the Minnesota North Stars—for a time keeping them from moving out of the state.

After divesting himself of the North Stars, Baldwin joined Morris Belzberg and Thomas Ruta in purchasing the Pittsburgh Penguins in 1991, subsequently leading them to their second consecutive Stanley Cup.

With a desire to focus on the developmental aspect of the game, Baldwin sold his interest in the Penguins in 1998. After successfully developing the AHL Wilkes-Barre/Scranton Penguins, Baldwin sought other opportunities on the minor league level, eventually establishing the Manchester Monarchs. Both teams rank among the top three in AHL attendance.

Currently, Baldwin is president and CEO of Crusader Entertainment, a motion picture production company that has produced such titles as *Mystery, Alaska* and *Sudden Death*. Baldwin has also served on the NHL board of governors, participating in the league's advisory, finance, forward planning, pension, and television committees.

HAROLD BALLARD

BORN: Toronto, Ontario, July 30, 1903
DIED: April 11, 1990
POSITION: Hockey Hall of Fame, 1977

Harold Ballard, the colorful, outspoken president of Maple Leaf Gardens, had more than his share of headaches after assuming control of the venerable Ontario arena in 1961.

In July 1969, Ballard and his sidekick on the Maple Leaf franchise, Stafford Smythe, were charged with income tax evasion. If that wasn't enough, the duo was arrested less than two years later, this time charged with fraud, theft, and mismanagement of Maple Leaf Gardens funds. Ballard served time at a minimum security prison in Ontario, but Smythe died unexpectedly before his trial was completed.

Ballard's time in the "sin bin" didn't mellow his outspoken approach to his hired help. When asked to explain his team's lack of oomph in the 1974–75 season, Ballard wasn't hesitant to name names. "Inge Hammarstrom," he spouted, "could go into the corner with six eggs in his hip pocket and not break one of them."

Ballard's acid tongue wasn't restricted to players either. "Red Kelly," he observed, "is too nice a guy to coach." Kelly responded to his boss's needle the next night by patrolling the Leafs' bench brandishing an imposing-looking bullwhip.

A cynical view of Ballard was taken in December 1974 by Montreal *Gazette* columnist John Robertson, who said of the Leaf boss: "I can't remember the exact crime Harold Ballard was convicted of—theft, fraud, tax evasion or a combination of all three—but whatever it was shapes up as a simple misdemeanor when compared to the $13 he's charging for 'gold seats' at the Gardens for Toronto Maple Leaf hockey games."

In 1979, with his team playing so-so hockey, Ballard dismissed coach Roger Neilson after a Thursday night game. But on the following Saturday night, with fans and a national TV audience watching, Neilson was still behind the bench. What happened? Well, according to Ballard, he had not really fired Neilson, it was a joke—Ballard's way of shaking up the club. He claimed he had no intention whatsoever of letting Roger go. Insiders, however, believe that Ballard did, most certainly, want to get rid of Neilson and replace him with Ed Johnston, coach of the New Brunswick Blackhawks, an AHL team affiliated with both the Maple Leafs and the Chicago Blackhawks. Johnston was the property of the Blackhawks and they would not release him, thus leaving Ballard without a coach. Roger Neilson didn't exactly buy Ballard's public statement. "If my firing was a joke," said Neilson, "I was the only one who didn't know anything about it." Ballard fired him anyway, weeks later.

Ballard's reputation as a solid hockey man had reached its apex in the 1977–78 season, when his Maple Leafs upset the favored New York Islanders in a brutally played seven-game playoff series, climaxed by a sudden-death overtime goal by Lanny McDonald at Nassau Veterans Memorial Coliseum. From that point on, Ballard allowed his emotionalism to overwhelm rationality, both as it pertained to his hockey club and his social life. His quirky behavior was excellent fodder for the Toronto media, but distracted his hockey people and negatively affected his club, which slid out of

serious playoff contention on four occasions during the 1980s. And when underpaid Leafs record-holder and star Darryl Sittler asked for a raise, Ballard refused and let him go to Philadelphia, outraging fans.

At times, Ballard proved an embarrassment to the league, but on other occasions, his sound hockey mind took over, and he would enthrall reporters with his tales of the old NHL and minor-league hockey.

Despite ill health, Ballard remained steadfastly involved with his hockey club until his death in April 1990.

BILL BARBER

BORN: Callander, Ontario, July 11, 1952
POSITION: Left Wing, Philadelphia Flyers, 1972–84; Coach, Philadelphia Flyers, 2000–02
AWARDS/HONORS: NHL First Team All-Star, 1976; NHL Second Team All-Star, 1979, 1981; NHL All-Star Game, 1975–76, 1978, 1980–82; Hockey Hall of Fame, 1990; Jack Adams Award, 2001

Bill Barber was Philadelphia's first choice in the 1972 NHL amateur draft. One of five brothers, he was encouraged to play hockey by his father, who hoped at least one of his sons would make it to the NHL.

"Just to make sure we had everything going for us," said Barber, "Dad built us a rink that was almost regulation size, had hydro poles put up, and lights strung out."

A high-scorer in Junior Division play, Barber made the Flyers in 1972–73 after improving his checking abilities, and went on to become a key ingredient of the 1974 and 1975 Stanley Cup–winning Flyer teams.

Although he was disparaged as the most outrageous "swan diver" in the NHL, he often paired with hard-nosed captain Bobby Clarke on a top-line offense that enabled Bill to score 420 goals over his career, an all-time mark in the Flyers organization, as well as accumulate 883 points, second only to Clarke.

Consistent and intense, Barber was also a clutch performer at playoff time, recording 108 points and 109 penalty minutes in 129 playoff games. Barber's stellar career came to an end in 1983–84 when he retired with four 40-goal seasons (1977–78, 1979–82), and one 50-goal mark (1975–76), admirable credentials for his Hockey Hall of Fame enshrinement in 1990.

A loyal soldier, Barber continued his career in a smorgasbord of roles for the Flyers, including assistant coach, director of pro scouting, and head coach of the Flyers' top affiliates, the AHL's Hershey Bears and Philadelphia Phantoms. With enormous success coaching youngsters in the Flyers' stables, resulting in four first-place finishes and an AHL Calder Cup in 1997–98, Barber finally was given his shot when Flyers general manager Bobby Clarke rewarded Bill's loyalty with a head coaching berth behind the Flyer bench in December 2000. The result was an eight-game undefeated string to begin his tenure, en route to a 31–16–7 run that put his powerful Philadelphia team into a second-place finish in the Atlantic Division in 2000–01, despite the constant distraction fueled by trade rumors involving exiled star Eric Lindros and his feud with Clarke. When Barber won the Jack Adams Award that summer, it was evident he was on the way to further NHL excellence.

In 2001–02, the Flyers acquired Jeremy Roenick via free agency, and dealt Lindros for Kim Johnsson, Jan Hlavac (later dealt for Donald Brashear), and Pavel Brendl, creating tremendous depth for Barber to supplement returning stars Keith Primeau, Simon Gagné, and Mark Recchi. Predictably, the Flyers' deluxe lineup enjoyed the Atlantic Division lead for most of 2001–02. However, Philly fell to the Ottawa Senators in the first round of the playoffs, due to a severe lack of scoring that infiltrated even their formidable power play. Amid shocking criticism from his players after the series ended, Barber became the sixth Flyers coach fired in seven seasons, and was replaced by Ken Hitchcock.

BILL BARILKO

BORN: Timmins, Ontario, March 25, 1927
DIED: April 24, 1951
POSITION: Defenseman, Toronto Maple Leafs, 1946–51
AWARDS/HONORS: NHL All-Star Game, 1947–49

Bill Barilko died in a plane crash at the height of his career, shortly after he had scored the winning goal in sudden-death overtime to clinch the Stanley Cup for the Toronto Maple Leafs in April 1951.

Barilko was respected around the NHL for his fearsome "snake-hip" body checks and his ability to block dangerous enemy shots on goal along with his partner Garth Boesch. Barilko became a Maple Leaf during the 1946–47 season, elevated from the Hollywood Wolves of the Pacific Coast League. It was no coincidence that he played on four Stanley Cup championship teams in five years prior to his untimely death at 24.

TOM BARRASSO

BORN: Boston, Massachusetts, March 31, 1965
POSITION: Goaltender, Buffalo Sabres, 1983–88; Pittsburgh Penguins, 1988–2000; Ottawa Senators, 2000; Carolina Hurricanes, 2001–02; Toronto Maple Leafs, 2002–
AWARDS/HONORS: Calder Memorial Trophy, 1984; Vezina Trophy, 1984; William M. Jennings Trophy (shared with Bob Sauve), 1985; NHL All-Star Game, 1984–85, 1993

Tom Barrasso had an extraordinary NHL career, but almost all observers would agree it's a shame he couldn't seem to enjoy it more.

The evidence of Barasso's talent was everywhere, from his direct jump from high school to the NHL, to his Vezina Trophy and his part in the Penguins' two Cups.

However, his longevity may be the clearest sign of his ability, as a player who displayed Barrasso's arrogance and petulance could not have survived 17 seasons in the NHL unless he was very good at his job.

Barrasso started as a classic butterfly-style goalie, but as he gained experience, he stayed on his feet more to take advantage of his excellent skating and puckhandling skills, which allowed him to act almost as a third defenseman.

Mental edges such as confidence, anticipation, and concentration were also Barrasso specialties, as was an excellent glove hand. In his top years, his only real vulnerabilities were shots low to the glove-hand side, and five-hole shots, which are a common foe of butterfly goalies.

Barrasso was traded to the Penguins by the Sabres for Doug Bodger and Darrin Shannon in 1988, just in time to help the Penguins on their ride to the top of the NHL.

As backstop of the strong Penguin teams, Barrasso reached the pinnacle of his career during the Penguins' Cup years of 1991 and 1992, when it was generally acknowledged that he was the man you'd want in the nets for the big save in Game Seven. Dogged by shoulder injuries until 1998, Barrasso did not reach such heights again in the 1990s.

In 2000, he was traded to the Ottawa Senators for Ron Tugnutt and Janne Laukkanen. Ottawa hoped Barrasso would be the key to a long playoff run, but when this did not pan out, the Senators and Barrasso parted company.

Barrasso did not retire, and let it be known that he would only consider offers where he would be the starting goaltender. But by 2001–02, Tom joined the Carolina Hurricanes to bolster their netminding behind Arturs Irbe, and accompanied Team USA to the 2002 Olympic Games at Salt Lake. Later on in the season, Barrasso would find himself in a vital role for the Toronto Maple Leafs, after being acquired to compensate for the loss of the injured Curtis Joseph. Joseph returned in time for the postseason, however, and Barrasso was out of the picture.

MARTY BARRY

BORN: St. Gabriel, Quebec, December 8, 1905
DIED: August 20, 1969
POSITION: Center, New York Americans, 1928; Boston Bruins, 1930–35; Detroit Red Wings, 1936–39; Montreal Canadiens, 1940–41
AWARDS/HONORS: Lady Byng Memorial Trophy, 1937; NHL First Team All-Star, 1937; Hockey Hall of Fame, 1965

What Tinker-to-Evers-to-Chance was to baseball, Marty Barry-to-Larry Aurie-to-Herb Lewis was to hockey in the mid 1930s. The Detroit Red Wings' best forward combination, until The Production Line of Sid Abel-Ted Lindsay-Gordie Howe evolved, the Barry-Aurie-Lewis line led the Wings to NHL glory beginning in 1935–36.

Originally a Boston Bruin, Marty was one of the most productive players in Beantown from his rookie year of 1929–30 through 1934–35, when he was dispatched to Detroit.

Until that time, Detroit had never won an NHL championship. But that all changed when Barry lined up with Aurie and Lewis.

How the deal came about is a story in itself. During the 1935 playoffs, Detroit general manager Jack Adams and his Boston counterpart, Frank Patrick, got into a trading conversation. "If I had Cooney Weiland," Patrick said, mentioning Detroit's crack center, "Boston would be in this final." To which Adams shot back, "If I had Marty Barry, Detroit would win the Stanley Cup."

A few minutes later the exchange was made and ultimately the Lewis-Aurie-Barry line paced Detroit to a first-place finish in the American Division in 1935–36. That spring, the Red Wings took a serious run at the Stanley Cup and began by dispatching the Montreal Maroons in the opening round. The highlight, by far, was the longest hockey match ever played in the NHL: exactly 116 minutes and 30 seconds of sudden-death overtime was required, almost two additional full games.

The winning goal was scored by Modere "Mud" Bruneteau of Detroit at 16:30 of the sixth overtime. Adams coached Detroit to a three-games-to-one victory in the finals to annex the silver mug.

Winning two consecutive championships was considered a virtual impossibility in the highly competitive NHL of the mid 1930s, and despite injuries, the Red Wings were poised, finishing first in the American Division for the second consecutive year. The Red Wings' superiority extended into the playoffs, where they first disposed of the pesky Montreal Canadiens three games to two, concluded by another sudden-death classic that lasted until 12:45 A.M., when Hec Kilrea beat Habs goalie Wilf Cude after 51 minutes and 49 seconds of overtime.

As the favorites to defeat the New York Rangers in the 1937 Stanley Cup finals, Detroit, forced to use substitute goalie Earl Robertson, went to five games with the Blueshirts, and on April 15, 1937, at Olympia Stadium, Barry delivered his finest clutch performance. He scored two goals in a 3–0 victory over the Rangers. Thus, Detroit became the first team to finish first and win the Stanley Cup in consecutive seasons.

Marty skated for the Wings through the 1938–39 season before being traded to the Montreal Canadiens. He concluded his playing career with Montreal after the 1940–41 season.

ANDY BATHGATE

BORN: Winnipeg, Manitoba, August 28, 1932
POSITION: Right Wing, New York Rangers, 1953–63; Toronto Maple Leafs, 1963–65; Detroit Red Wings, 1965–67; Pittsburgh Penguins, 1967–68, 1970–71; Vancouver Canucks (WHL), 1968–70; Vancouver Blazers (WHA), 1974
AWARDS/HONORS: Hart Memorial Trophy, 1959; NHL First Team All-Star, 1959, 1962; NHL Second Team All-Star, 1958, 1963; NHL All-Star Game, 1957–64; Hockey Hall of Fame, 1978

Andy Bathgate at first appeared too much the pacifist for the NHL jungle. But he raised his dukes when necessary, licking such notorious hockey cops as Howie Young, then of the Red Wings, and Vic Stasiuk of the Bruins. By 1954–55, Andy was in the NHL to stay, and soon was being favorably compared with the greatest Ranger right wing, Bill Cook.

While it's never been firmly established who invented the slap shot—Bernie "Boom-Boom" Geoffrion and Bobby Hull are often mentioned—Bathgate was among the earliest practitioners. It was Andy's shot at Madison Square Garden in November 1959 that smashed Montreal

Andy Bathgate of the Rangers

goalie Jacques Plante's face and inspired Plante to don a face mask permanently, thus ushering in the era of the goalie mask. Bathgate was also among the first to develop a curved "banana" blade. By the end of the 1961–62 season, during which Andy scored 84 points in 70 games, he had become the most popular Ranger, team captain, and seemingly a permanent fixture on Broadway. He also was prime trade bait, and he was dealt to Toronto in February 1964 in a huge trade. Don McKenney accompanied Bathgate to Toronto. In exchange, the Leafs sent Dick Duff, Bob Nevin, Rod Seiling, Arnie Brown, and Bill Collins to New York.

As a result of the trade, the Leafs won the 1964 Stanley Cup. Bathgate scored five important playoff goals and said getting traded to the Leafs was the biggest break of his life. But just a season later, Bathgate had a falling-out with manager-coach Punch Imlach. "There's a limit to an athlete's endurance," said Bathgate. "Imlach has pushed a few of the players past that limit physically and mentally."

Furious, Imlach snapped back at his ace. "There's no limit to what you can do," Imlach told Bathgate. "Who says there's a limit? Only you! I live by the creed that you can always be better than you are."

Imlach unloaded Bathgate to Detroit in 1965–66. His play declined sharply and in 1967–68 he was dealt to the expansion Pittsburgh Penguins. He returned to form in Pittsburgh, but appeared more and more disenchanted and departed the NHL in 1968. Andy played briefly in Switzerland, returning to Canada to become coach of the Vancouver Blazers in the WHA in 1974. An eye injury suffered in a home accident in 1973 limited the vision in Andy's right eye by 80 percent. Despite the impaired vision, Bathgate returned temporarily to active play with the Blazers in December 1974 before retiring.

BOBBY BAUER

BORN: Waterloo, Ontario, February 16, 1915
DIED: September 16, 1964
POSITION: Right Wing, Boston Bruins, 1936–42, 1945–52
AWARDS/HONORS: Lady Byng Memorial Trophy, 1940–41, 1947; NHL Second Team All-Star, 1939–41, 1947

Although moderns may think of Bobby Bauer as the man who helped devise a hockey skate of the same name, Bauer the hockey player gained early stardom in the early 1930s while attending St. Michael's College in Toronto. In 1934–35, Bauer graduated to Kitchener of the Ontario Hockey League, a junior league for players under 21. He teamed with Milt Schmidt and Woody Dumart, both pals from Kitchener, and the "Sauerkraut Line" was born.

A right-winger, Robert Theodore Bauer was signed by the Boston Bruins in the spring of 1935. The NHL got its first look at "The Krauts" in 1937–38 as the Bruins began to maul opponents. Thanks to Bauer, Schmidt, and Dumart, Boston finished first four successive times and won the Stanley Cup twice. In 1942, Bauer enlisted along with his buddies in the Royal Canadian Air Force. He returned to the NHL in 1945–46 and retired after the following season, although Bobby made one more appearance, in 1951–52, to play at Boston Garden in a "night" to honor the Kraut Line. He scored a goal and an assist on that occasion and then retired permanently.

BOBBY BAUN

BORN: Lanigan, Saskatchewan, September 9, 1936
POSITION: Defenseman, Toronto Maple Leafs, 1956–67, 1971–73; Oakland Seals, 1967–68; Detroit Red Wings, 1968–71; Coach, Toronto Toros (WHA), 1975–76
AWARDS/HONORS: NHL All-Star Game, 1962–65, 1968

Among hockey pros, Bob Baun was recognized as one of the hardest—and cleanest—bodycheckers in the game. Players respected Baun for his respect of the rulebook. Billy Harris, Baun's teammate at Toronto and later at Oakland, once put it this way: "His duels with Bobby Hull are legend now. And the respect they showed each other was evident every time they collided. You seldom saw an elbow or a raised stick. Just a brutal test of strength between two fine athletes."

When Baun was sitting on the bench, or when shelved by injury, opponents took a completely different view of the Oakland team. "The night Baun missed a game in Chicago, we started taking liberties," said then-Blackhawk Bobby Hull. "We realized he wasn't in town, so we could get away with a lot more. When Baun was around, that right side was like an obstacle course."

Sometimes Baun got caught in his own obstacles, as he did in March 1961, in New York. Camille Henry of the Rangers ran into Baun and in the entanglement Henry's skate sliced through the skin of Baun's neck. It appeared to be a routine injury and Bobby returned in the third period. But seconds after he boarded the team bus following the game, he began to gasp desperately. He attempted to yell for help but couldn't squeeze out a sound. Neck muscles cut by the skate had started to hemorrhage. Bobby gagged as his tongue slipped down his throat.

Baun waved his arms, groping for attention. When his teammates realized the trouble, they rushed him to a hospital, where doctors performed an emergency operation to permit breathing. Less than a week later Bobby was taking a regular turn on the Leaf defense in the Cup playoffs.

"Baun was a marvel," said Leaf trainer Bobby Haggert. "I remember one weekend when he hurt his ankle on a Saturday night, kept an ice pack strapped to it for twenty-four hours, then played a game on Sunday. On his first shift he stepped into Reg Fleming with a check that rattled Reggie's wishbone. Next minute he stopped a shot on the same foot. Instead of crying 'uncle,' he stayed out there, didn't miss a shift, and handed Fleming two more bruising checks."

Among his achievements, Baun's most stirring heroics came during the Leafs' comeback victory over Detroit in the 1964 Cup finale. With the Leafs down three games to two, Bobby suffered a broken ankle blocking a wicked shot. Riddled with painkillers, he scored the winning goal in overtime and contributed through the series for Toronto's third straight Cup. When expansion came in 1967, Baun was claimed by the Oakland Seals. He played only one season in California, three for the Detroit Red Wings, and three more for the Leafs before retiring in 1973. He spent 1975–76 as coach of the WHA's Toronto Toros.

BARRY BECK

BORN: Vancouver, British Columbia, June 3, 1957
POSITION: Defenseman, Colorado Rockies, 1977–80; New York Rangers, 1980–86; Los Angeles Kings, 1989–90
AWARDS/HONORS: NHL Challenge Cup All-Star, 1979; NHL All-Star Game, 1978–82

Few players enter the National Hockey League with more promise but leave with more disappointment than Barry Beck, who launched his career with the Colorado Rockies in 1977, but received more attention after being dealt to the New York Rangers in 1980.

Centerpiece of one of the league's biggest player exchanges (Colorado received Pat Hickey, Lucien Deblois, Mike McEwen, Dean Turner, and Bobby Crawford), Beck arrived on Broadway as the so-called savior of a Rangers team in search of the Stanley Cup.

Instead, Beck's stay with the Blueshirts was marked by misery. Injuries sidelined him at key moments, such as the 1984 playoffs versus the Islanders, and controversy surrounded his performance. In one incendiary practice session, coach Herb Brooks withered Beck with criticism. On other occasions, Rangers television analyst Bill Chadwick constantly harped on Beck's reluctance to use his vaunted slap shot.

"Shoot the puck, Barry, shoot the puck!" was Chadwick's mantra, which soon became a chant around Madison Square Garden.

Unfortunately for Beck, he never came close to achieving the level expected of him, and he finally retired in 1986. A brief comeback with the Los Angeles Kings in 1989-90 was laudable, if not productive.

Six feet three and 215 pounds, "Bubba" was a crunching hitter who scored 22 goals and 60 points as a rookie in 1977-78, breaking Denis Potvin's record for most goals by a rookie defenseman. He finished second to Mike Bossy in Calder Trophy voting that same year.

The number one selection of the Rockies in the 1977 Amateur Draft, Beck would score 59 points for the Rangers in 1979-80, but his offensive output dwindled by the time his career closed.

ED BELFOUR

BORN: Carmen, Manitoba, April 21, 1965
POSITION: Goaltender, Chicago Blackhawks, 1988-97; San Jose Sharks, 1997; Dallas Stars, 1997-2002; Toronto Maple Leafs, 2002–
AWARDS/HONORS: Calder Memorial Trophy, 1991; Vezina Trophy, 1991, 1993; William M. Jennings Trophy, 1991, 1993; NHL First Team All-Star, 1991, 1993; NHL Second Team All-Star, 1995; NHL All-Star Game, 1991, 1993, 1995, 1998

Many things get better with age, and Eddie "The Eagle" Belfour's career was definitely one of them; he reached his peak at an age when goaltenders are often on the decline.

Belfour took an unusual route to the NHL. Relegated to his high school junior varsity, he worked his way to junior hockey and through the University of North Dakota at least partly on dogged determination.

Eddie was signed by the Chicago Blackhawks in 1987 as an undrafted free agent. Soviet goaltending great Vladislav Tretiak, the Blackhawk goaltending coach, worked extensively with Belfour, who credits Tretiak with his maturation as a goalie and a person.

Belfour's style, a butterfly/stand-up hybrid, relied on quickness, aggressiveness, and technical strength. Excellent at controlling rebounds, he took away the lower portion of the net and also had good puckhandling and skating skills. He never quite overcame his vulnerability to top corner shots, and his aggressiveness and determination were often accompanied by a volatile temper.

The high point of Belfour's tenure in Chicago came in 1992, when the Mike Keenan–coached Blackhawks faced the Penguins in the Cup finals. Unfortunately, the Hawks were swept in four games.

In 1997, Belfour, no longer in Chicago's plans, was traded to San Jose for Chris Terreri, Michal Sykora, and Ulf Dahlen; after the season, he signed as a free agent with the Dallas Stars. Belfour benefited from Dallas's tight defense, and he outplayed both Colorado's Patrick Roy and Buffalo's Dominik Hasek in backstopping the Stars to the Cup in 1999.

The Eagle put on another goaltending exhibition in the 2000 playoffs, again outdueling Roy before finally falling to the New Jersey Devils in a finals series in which the last two games went to triple and double overtime, respectively.

By the 2001–02 season, Belfour was thought to be on the decline. Although named to the gold medal–winning Canadian Olympic team, it was Marty Brodeur who would play nearly all of Canada's key games. Further, Belfour's temper was beginning to run amok again, as he trashed an NHL dressing room one night in a fit of pique upon learning his Dallas coach, and sometime nemesis, Ken Hitchcock, would start emerging backup goaltender Marty Turco for a second consecutive game. Belfour, a free agent in 2002, was signed by the Toronto Maple Leafs, replacing Curtis Joseph, who had been obtained by Detroit.

JEAN BELIVEAU

BORN: Trois-Rivières, Quebec, August 31, 1931
POSITION: Center, Montreal Canadiens, 1951–71
AWARDS/HONORS: Hart Memorial Trophy, 1956, 1964; Art Ross Trophy, 1956; Conn Smythe Trophy, 1965; NHL First Team All-Star, 1955–57, 1959–61; NHL Second Team All-Star, 1958, 1964, 1966, 1969; NHL All-Star Game, 1953–60, 1963–65, 1968–69

A day after the Montreal Canadiens clinched first place in the National Hockey League in March 1968, Sid Abel, general manager–coach of the Detroit Red Wings, made it quite clear how important captain Jean Beliveau was to the Canadiens. "If Beliveau stays healthy," Abel predicted, "the Canadiens are a cinch to win the Stanley Cup, too."

Two months later, Abel's forecast was realized. The Flying Frenchmen of Montreal defeated the Boston Bruins in four straight games; the Chicago Blackhawks in five; and finally, the St. Louis Blues in four. Beliveau, known in the French-speaking province of Quebec as *Le Gros Bill* (Big Bill), as always, led the team to victory.

Remaining injury-free was never easy for Beliveau. Throughout his 18-year National Hockey League career, the princely, six-feet-three, 205-pound center was hobbled by an assortment of problems. One of the worst occurred during the 1966–67 season, when he was hit in the eye by a wildly swung stick and his sight was imperiled.

"The pressure on my nerves bothered me more than the pain," said Beliveau. "The first thing I did, naturally, was to open my eye to see if I had vision. I couldn't even see the big, bright lights. The next day, I could see a little bit. I'm a lucky man. But all the time I kept wondering how I would react when I started playing again. Would I instinctively pull back when a stick was raised in a corner? If I did, it would be the end for me."

He soon recuperated and the fear reflex evaporated and he was the Beliveau of old. This facet of Beliveau was never more evident than during the 1967–68 season when the Canadiens were lodged in the subterranean depths of last place in the East Division as late as December 27, 1967. On that night, the Canadiens trailed the Red Wings by two goals with four minutes remaining in the game. Then rookie Jacques Lemaire scored and Beliveau tied the contest. According to former Montreal coach Toe Blake, Beliveau's goal turned the tide for the Canadiens.

But that goal was more symbolic. The following highlights are only part of Beliveau's contribution to Montreal's 1967–68 championship:

• Only ten of his 31 goals were scored against the weaker teams in the NHL's Western Division, demonstrating that Beliveau played more solidly in clutch games.

- He went over the 1,000-point mark and was the only player in the NHL at the time to do it, with the exception of Gordie Howe.

- He totaled 68 points (31 goals, 37 assists) in only 59 games, scoring on 15.1 percent of his shots, surpassing NHL scoring champion Stan Mikita's 13.2 percent average.

- He scored nine of the 50 goals compiled by the Habs' effective power play.

- His wingmen enjoyed productive seasons: Yvan Cournoyer scored 28 goals and Gilles Tremblay made 23.

When votes were tabulated for the Hart Memorial Trophy (MVP) at midseason, Mikita accumulated 34 points to Beliveau's 4. But in the second-half poll, Beliveau outscored Mikita, 39–18, which gave the Chicago center the overall prize, 52–43—a decision that, incidentally, did not wear well with all critics. "To me," said Red Sullivan, then the Pittsburgh Penguins' coach, summing up the case for Beliveau, "Big Jean was more important to the Canadiens than Mikita was to the Hawks."

A typical Beliveau team-first gesture, which endeared him to his colleagues, occurred late in December 1967, when the Canadiens were playing the Leafs at Maple Leaf Gardens in Toronto. The Leafs were carefully guarding a 2–1 lead with less than three minutes remaining in the game when Beliveau tied the score after teammate John Ferguson had relayed the puck to Claude Provost who, in turn, passed to Beliveau. Instead of accepting congratulations for his effort, Beliveau lamented the fact that Ferguson was not given an assist on the play. "What's wrong with the official scorer here?" Beliveau asked. "Fergy made the big play on our goal and they refuse to give him an assist. I was shocked when I didn't hear a correction after I had brought the matter to the attention of referee Art Skov and the fellows at the timer's bench. But if not for Fergy we would have lost the game. All I had to do was put the puck in."

As a captain, Beliveau was surprisingly diffident. He rarely, if ever, shouted to his teammates on the bench and he was hardly the rah-rah type in the dressing room. Yet, somehow, he managed to inspire grand efforts from the men who wore the red, white, and blue uniforms of the Canadiens. More than anything it seemed to come from Beliveau's quiet charisma; his teammates were inspired by how he acted more than by what he said. "It's hard to put into words how we felt about Jean," former teammate Ralph Backstrom once explained. "It's just that we were so damned proud to have him as our captain."

"It was his quiet dignity," added ex-teammate Dick Duff. "He was so unassuming for a guy of his stature. He was a very unselfish player. He had great moves, that great range, and anybody playing on a line with him was certain to wind up with a lot of goals. If you got there, the puck would be there. He had so much courage, so much determination." The results are all there in the record book.

Beliveau retired from the ice in 1971, his jersey number 4 with him. He continued with the Canadiens organization for many years as an ambassador to the Montreal community.

GORDIE BELL

BORN: Portage La Prairie, Manitoba, March 13, 1925
DIED: November 3, 1980
POSITION: Goaltender, Toronto Maple Leafs, 1945–46; New York Rangers, 1956

From time to time, journeymen goaltenders are handed a big-league baton and sprint with it successfully to the finish line. Gordie Bell (along with Alfie Moore, Joe Miller, et alia) was one such goalie. Bell bounced around the minors for years, playing everywhere from Buffalo to Washington. Gordon got his NHL chance in 1955–56 when regular Rangers goalie Gump Worsley was injured during the Stanley Cup semifinal round with the heavily favored Montreal Canadiens. Playing at the hostile Montreal Forum, Bell thwarted the Flying Frenchmen in a splendid display of goalkeeping while his Rangers triumphed, 4–2. In time, the Rangers were wiped out, Worsley returned to the nets, and Gordie Bell never was heard from again in the NHL.

BRIAN BELLOWS

BORN: St. Catharines, Ontario, September 1, 1964
POSITION: Left Wing, Minnesota North Stars, 1982–92, Montreal Canadiens, 1992–95, Tampa Bay Lightning, 1995–97, Anaheim Mighty Ducks, 1997; Washington Capitals, 1998–99
AWARDS/HONORS: NHL All-Star 1984, 1988, 1992

The Minnesota North Stars may have hoped they were getting a superstar when they drafted Brian Bellows second overall in 1982; they had to settle for a star instead, a pure finisher who gave them ten years of yeoman service.

In 1982, Bellows jumped straight from junior hockey to the NHL, and over the next 12 seasons with Minnesota and Montreal he became something of a scoring machine, netting 30 or more five times, 40 or more three times, once even reaching 50 goals.

In his ten seasons with the North Stars, he averaged almost a point a game, and, although he stopped playing for the franchise in 1992, as of 2000, Bellows remained the third-highest point getter in the Dallas/Minnesota franchise's history.

Brian was a strong, balanced skater with quick hands, dangerous around the net, who was willing to take a hit and drive to the net to score.

Traded to Montreal before the 1992–93 season for Russ Courtnall, Bellows was a key part of the surprise Canadiens Cup winner in 1993. Montreal coach Jacques Demers paired Bellows with center Kirk Muller, who was willing

to do the dirty work to get Brian the puck, allowing him to do what he did best, finish.

Bellows displayed great heart and courage in the 1993 playoffs, contributing 15 points while playing through fractured ribs and only missing two out of Montreal's 20 playoff games.

Although he spent two more seasons with Montreal, his point production began to decline and in 1995 Bellows was traded to Tampa Bay for Marc Bureau. He moved to Anaheim in 1997.

Bellows spent the 1997–98 season in Europe, returning to the NHL to join the Washington Capitals for the stretch run; he was with the team for their trip to the Stanley Cup finals that spring and then stayed with the Capitals for the 1998–99 season before retiring.

CLINT BENEDICT

BORN: Ottawa, Ontario, September 26, 1892
DIED: November 12, 1976
POSITION: Goaltender, Ottawa Senators (NHA and NHL), 1913–24; Montreal Maroons, 1924–30
AWARDS/HONORS: Hockey Hall of Fame, 1965

While the consensus through the years points to the legendary Georges Vezina as the first great goalkeeper of pro hockey, a bit of investigation reveals Clint Benedict had a better overall goals-against average and was also single-handedly responsible for introducing the practice of flopping to the ice to stop a shot. He also was one of the first goalies to use a face mask.

Believe it or not, prior to 1918, it was a penalty for the goalie to leave his feet in order to block the puck. Benedict would have none of this nonsense and, rather than call a penalty on the maverick netminder every few minutes, the league capitulated and changed the rule.

Benedict was in goal on four Stanley Cup winners during his 18-year career, winning the centerpiece three times with the Ottawa Senators and once with the Montreal sextet near the end of his playing days. A flamboyant showman, Benedict is a member of the Hockey Hall of Fame.

DOUG BENTLEY

BORN: Delisle, Saskatchewan, September 3, 1916
DIED: November 24, 1972
POSITION: Left Wing/Center, Chicago Blackhawks, 1939–44, 1945–52; New York Rangers, 1953–54
AWARDS/HONORS: Art Ross Trophy, 1943; NHL First Team All-Star, 1943–44, 1947; NHL Second Team All-Star, 1949; NHL All-Star Game, 1947–51; Hockey Hall of Fame, 1964

It is amazing how alike the Bentley brothers were on the ice. Max, a center for his 12-year career, finished with 544 points, while Doug, a left wing and center who often teamed with his sibling on the same line in Chicago and New York, totaled 543. After three failures in attempts to make NHL squads, Doug finally made it to the big leagues with the Blackhawks. He teamed with Max in 1942–43, and both reached stardom.

Doug led the NHL in scoring with 73 points that year. The next season he scored the most goals, 38, and was second in league scoring. He then joined his younger brother in the army and missed the 1944–45 campaign.

The brother act was broken up in 1947 when Max was dealt to Toronto. "I thought of quitting," Doug stated about his feelings concerning the deal. "But I felt I still had a good year left in me."

He was wrong. Bentley had four seasons remaining as an NHLer. He quit the Hawks in 1951 to coach Saskatoon of the Western League.

Doug was coaxed out of retirement to help the Rangers, and brother Max, in their drive toward a playoff spot in 1954. In his first game with New York after two years in retirement, Doug registered a goal and three assists, Max had two goals and a pair of setups, and the Rangers won, 8–3. Doug stayed with New York for the rest of the season as the Rangers fell short in their playoff bid.

Doug went back to coaching Saskatoon the next year. Max joined him there in 1954. Doug made a brief comeback in 1962 with the Los Angeles Blades of the WHL. He succumbed to cancer in 1972.

MAX BENTLEY

BORN: Delisle, Saskatchewan, March 1, 1920
DIED: January 19, 1984
POSITION: Center, Chicago Blackhawks, 1940–43, 1945–47; Toronto Maple Leafs, 1947–53; New York Rangers, 1953–54
AWARDS/HONORS: Hart Memorial Trophy, 1946; Art Ross Trophy, 1946–47; Lady Byng Memorial Trophy, 1943; NHL First Team All-Star, 1946; NHL Second Team All-Star, 1947; NHL All-Star Game, 1947–49, 1951; Hockey Hall of Fame, 1966

The original "Dipsy Doodle Dandy from Delisle," Max Bentley is regarded by some purists as the most exciting—if not the best—center who ever lived. Kid brother of Doug Bentley, Max originally starred on the Pony Line with brother Doug and Bill Mosienko at Chicago. All lightweights, "The Pony Boys" were extraordinary stickhandlers and

Max Bentley as a Ranger

playmakers who could only be thwarted by rough play.

Max won the NHL scoring championship in 1946 and 1947 before being involved in one of the NHL's biggest trades. Despite the Bentleys' prolific scoring, the Blackhawks were a hopelessly weak team, short on goalkeeping and equally weak on defense, so Max was shipped to Toronto with Cy Thomas for Gus Bodnar, Bud Poile, Gaye Stewart, Ernie Dickens, and Bob Goldham.

After being traded to Toronto, it took a while for Max to adjust to his new surroundings. He went ten straight games without a goal, but once he got going, there was no stopping him. With Bentley in the lineup, the Leafs became the supreme NHL power. They finished first in 1948 and then went on to win their second consecutive Stanley Cup. Never before had a team won three straight world championships, but Max led the Leafs to the third Cup in a row in April 1949, and a fourth in five years in April 1951.

After that, age began to erode Max's talents, and the Leafs began losing more and more frequently. In the 1952 Cup semifinals against Detroit, Toronto was routed in four straight games.

Rangers general manager Frank Boucher had his eye on Max, and in the summer of 1953 he persuaded him to make a comeback after Bentley had retired following the 1952–53 season. Max drove a hard bargain. In addition to his $15,000 contract, extraordinary for those days, Max persuaded Boucher to bring his wife and kids and his nephew, Bev, as spare goaltender, as well as Bev's wife and a family friend, who served as a companion and babysitter, to New York.

Boucher was delighted, because with Max in the fold he believed he could persuade brother Doug to come out of retirement. That took a bit longer, but by midseason Doug agreed and he flew to Manhattan amid the fuss and fanfare normally accorded a conquering hero.

At last the Bentleys were reunited for the first time since November 1947 when Max had been traded to the Leafs. In their first game as a team again, Max and Doug played on a line with Edgar Laprade, whose unique stickhandling and skating talents melded perfectly with the Bentleys'. The Rangers played the Bruins, routing them, 8–3, mostly because of the Bentleys and Laprade. "It was one of those wonderful moments in sports," said Boucher, "when everything comes together, when the juices truly flow, and in this fleeting moment, late in their careers, Doug and Max shed the years as they piled up eight scoring points between them."

Max was a hypochondriac of the first order, important ammunition for enemy skaters during the homestretch of the 1953–54 season. "Before one game," said former Bruins coach Lynn Patrick, "I told my center, Cal Gardner, who had once played with Max, to strike up a conversation with Bentley on the ice before the game started. I wanted Cal to tell Max how terrible he looked and that he should see a doctor immediately after the game."

Gardner fulfilled his mission. By the opening face-off, Max had become terribly concerned about his health. He played a poor game, and the Bruins won and gained a playoff berth while the Rangers finished fifth. Max and Doug returned to Delisle, this time to stay. Doug died of cancer in 1972, while Max continued to operate the family wheat farm and tell stories about the great days of long ago, until his own death in 1984.

BRYAN BERARD

BORN: Woonsocket, Rhode Island, March 5, 1977
POSITION: Defenseman, New York Islanders, 1996–99; Toronto Maple Leafs, 1999–2000; New York Rangers, 2001–02; Boston Bruins, 2002–
AWARDS/HONORS: Calder Memorial Trophy, 1997

Bryan Berard is an example of a player whose return to the NHL after what appeared to be a career-ending injury bordered on the miraculous.

Berard, originally a high first-round draft pick of the Ottawa Senators in 1995, was unable to come to terms with the Senators, and was traded in 1996 to the Islanders for their young defenseman, Wade Redden, before he ever played an NHL game.

There were high expectations for Berard, and he met them as he stepped into the NHL with a weak team and won the Calder Trophy as Rookie of the Year.

Berard created sorely needed excitement on the Island, as his speed, creativity, and willingness to take risks reminded people he had the potential to be an elite offensive defenseman. Although he was still learning the defensive aspect of the game, he was becoming a force.

In 1999, Berard was traded to the Toronto Maple Leafs for goalie Felix Potvin, joining an offensive-minded team on the rise. He became more consistent, and his skating, point shot, and ability to carry the puck with confidence were key components in the Toronto offensive attack.

Then, in March 2000, tragedy struck, literally. Berard was struck in the eye by the stick of Ottawa forward Marian Hossa as the forward followed through on a shot.

Berard suffered a cut cornea, a detached retina, and a fractured orbital bone. The accident triggered intense discussion regarding whether shields should be made mandatory, as Berard was not wearing one at the time of the incident.

He underwent myriad surgeries and was fitted for a special contact lens that would act like a functioning iris. It would take the better part of two seasons, but eventually these surgeries would provide just enough vision to allow Bryan to meet the minimum NHL standards. Bryan made a comeback by joining the 2001–02 New York Rangers. He played the entire season but was released by the Rangers after the campaign.

RED BERENSON

BORN: Regina, Saskatchewan, December 8, 1939
POSITION: Center, Montreal Canadiens, 1961–66; New York Rangers, 1966–67; St. Louis Blues, 1967–71, 1974–78; Detroit Red Wings, 1971–74; Assistant Coach, Buffalo Sabres, 1982–84; Coach, St. Louis Blues, 1979–82; Michigan Wolverines (CCHA), 1984–
AWARDS/HONORS: Team Canada, 1972; NHL All-Star Game, 1965, 1969–72, 1974; Jack Adams Award, 1981

When Gordon "Red" Berenson, the scholarly center with the educated stick, was traded by the New York Rangers to the St. Louis Blues in November 1967, the deal was largely ignored. But when Berenson was dealt from St. Louis to the Detroit Red Wings early in February 1971, the news resounded with the impact of a thunderclap. In less than four years the anonymous redhead emerged as the Babe Ruth of St. Louis hockey, the man who put the Blues on the ice map—and into the Stanley Cup finals.

It was Berenson who scored six goals in a single game against the Philadelphia Flyers and who became the first superstar of the National Hockey League's expansion West Division. "The Red Baron" of the Blues, as he came to be known, was in a class with Bobby Hull, Gordie Howe, and Jean Beliveau.

Then, without warning, he was traded away by the very team that had coveted him so dearly. It was the shot heard round the hockey world. Precise reasons for the trade may never be known, but repercussions lasted for years. Berenson claimed the deal was simply a union-busting move on the part of the Blues' front office. "I think the Blues traded me because I was president of the NHL Players' Association," said Berenson. "I don't know why the Blues should be uptight about the association, but I'm convinced I was dealt because of that. I was shocked and disappointed." So were the hockey fans in St. Louis.

Red found himself at home in Detroit in more ways than one. He had BA and MA degrees from the University of Michigan and had played much of his college hockey in that area. When Berenson made All-America at Michigan, Detroit's vitriolic manager Jack Adams attempted to lure him to Detroit. But the Montreal Canadiens owned his rights at the time and had no intention of parting with them. Curiously, the Canadiens seemed indifferent to Berenson once he moved up to the majors in 1961–62.

Montreal's Toe Blake underplayed Red and Berenson insists he never got a good chance to prove himself. But Berenson hardly saw more ice when traded to the Rangers. At first it seemed he'd be the number one center, but an injury sidelined him and his place was taken by Orland Kurtenbach. Every time he made a comeback he'd suffer another injury and word made the rounds that he was brittle.

Red was traded to St. Louis by the Rangers in 1967, where he became an instant star. But by the 1970–71 season, Berenson had worn out his welcome with St. Louis and the Salomon family owners, probably because of his deep involvement in the burgeoning Players' Association. In Detroit, Red temporarily came back to life and productivity, but by January 1975 he was back in St. Louis, where he played through the 1977–78 season.

Incredibly, Red accomplished a feat in 1968 that even Wayne Gretzky or Mario Lemieux never touched, when he scored six goals in one game against the Philadelphia Flyers, the first since 1944 to do so. Those six goals established an NHL record for a road game, with four of them scored in one period, also tying an NHL record.

Red remained with the Blues as an assistant coach, assuming the head coaching duties in 1979. His .669 winning percentage for the 1980–81 season earned him the Jack Adams Award.

Upon migrating back to his alma mater, the University of Michigan in 1984, Berenson proceeded to energize the sagging hockey program into a powerhouse model, guiding so many NCAA championships (a record nine) and Frozen Four appearances that his coaching prowess became legend. With over 400 wins to his credit, the former Wolverines' captain, as the first collegiate player to step right onto NHL ice, blazed a significant path that elevated the role and relevance of college hockey.

TODD BERTUZZI

BORN: Sudbury, Ontario, February 2, 1975
POSITION: Right Wing, New York Islanders, 1995–98; Vancouver Canucks, 1998–

For several years, Todd Bertuzzi loomed as one of the biggest busts of any first-round pick ever made by the NY Islanders (23rd overall, 1993). The Islanders were so desperate to release Bertuzzi's potential that they assigned legendary left wing Clark Gillies to work with the youngster.

It was to no avail. From time to time, Bertuzzi showed flashes of brilliance and the ability to use his powerful body (six feet three, 235 pounds) to bull past opposing defensemen. But after two and a half seasons on Long Island, Bertuzzi was dealt to the Vancouver Canucks in a deal that involved him and Bryan McCabe heading west as Trevor Linden headed to the Islanders.

After arriving in British Columbia, Todd remained in a mediocre mode until the arrival of Mike Keenan as coach, after which he began a slow and steady improvement. But it wasn't until the 2001–02 season that Todd climbed to a starry level. Playing on a line with Brendan Morrison and Markus Naslund, Bertuzzi racked up 36 goals and 49 assists for 85 points, all of which were career highs. His 85 points ranked third in the league, behind only teammate Naslund, who finished with 90 points and Jarome Iginla, who finished with 96 points. Interestingly, Todd scored more points than anyone in the NHL after January 1st.

Bertuzzi also became a threat on the power play in the 2001 season, notching 14 goals, then matched it with 14 the next season as well. In the 2001 and 2002 playoffs, Bertuzzi finally began to be the inexorable force everyone had expected him to be, checking mightily and notching four points each year, as the Canucks were eliminated in four by Colorado in 2001, in six by Detroit in 2002.

GARY BETTMAN

BORN: New York City, New York, June 2, 1952

When the National Hockey League decided to replace John Ziegler as its leader in the early 1990s, it looked to the highly successful National Basketball Association for candidates.

The original hope was to lure NBA commissioner David Stern to the NHL, but when Stern declined, hockey owners opted for one of the NBA's top legal minds, Gary Bettman.

New York–born and raised Bettman was given the title of commissioner, one never designated in the NHL before. A hockey fan since his youth, the new commissioner immediately instituted significant changes, some of which annoyed hockey purists. He eliminated division names such as Norris, Patrick, Adams, and Smythe, eventually changing them into Atlantic, Northeast, Southeast, Central, Northwest, and Pacific.

Shortly after taking office, Bettman had to deal with a controversial episode in which Dale Hunter of the Washington Capitals clubbed New York Islander scoring ace Pierre Turgeon from behind in the final game of a Washington Capital–New York Islander playoff series in Nassau Coliseum. Bettman suspended the Washington forward for 21 games, unprecedented in the league.

Under Bettman, the league recorded significant gains in attendance and teams. The league expanded to 30 franchises, as well as negotiating long-term television deals in Canada and the United States.

Although some critics asserted that Bettman was brought into the league to establish NBA-style salary caps, none was delivered and in 1994, Bettman and his owners imposed a lockout on the National Hockey League Players' Association that lasted until the middle of January 1995, after which an abridged season was played.

Asked about his accomplishments during an interview in March 2002, Bettman said: "[The NHL] is more widely viewed, better attended, [has] more franchises, and [has] more business partners. The research tells us our fans are overwhelmingly satisfied with the game and so I think we've embarked upon an effort to grow the fan base, increase the fan base and make the game stronger."

Bettman was so successful that he won the coveted Lester Patrick Trophy in 2001.

One idea Bettman instituted was the Olympic break every four years, in order to give players a chance to play for their homelands as well as to give the game more exposure. However, with players getting injured in the tournament, as well as disrupting the season, the idea will be reconsidered for 2006. Looming on the commissioner's horizon is another marathon battle with the NHLPA, to formulate another Collective Bargaining Agreement by 2004, hopefully without another lockout.

LES BINKLEY

BORN: Owen Sound, Ontario, June 6, 1936
POSITION: Goaltender, Pittsburgh Penguins, 1967–72; Ottawa Nationals (WHA), 1972–73; Toronto Toros (WHA), 1973–76

When goalie Les Binkley played in Philadelphia, Hugh Brown of the *Evening Bulletin* observed: "Binkley looks somewhat like he sounds, meaning he could pass for a near-sighted, narrow-chested bird watcher." After nine seasons in the minors, Les was plucked by the Pittsburgh Penguins to be second-string goalie behind Hank Bassen in the NHL's first big expansion in 1967–68. But as soon as the campaign got under way, it became apparent that Binkley not only was better than Bassen, but better than a lot of other goaltenders in the National Hockey League.

"I know of only one man who had the edge on Binkley," said Red Sullivan in the middle of that season, "and that was Johnny Bower of Toronto. There are one or two others who were Bink's equal. There are several who get more publicity. But there is no one outside of Bower who had more ability as a goaltender than Binkley."

But if Binkley was so good, what kept the NHL bosses from finding him? One factor was the pre-expansion six-team league, then loaded with good goalies. When expansion came, six openings developed, and goaltenders were sought by every new club. According to Les, another problem was his eyesight. "The contact lenses, that's what kept me back," he said. "They [the managers] knew I had good reflexes, but they were afraid I couldn't see."

Binkley jumped to the WHA in 1972, joining the Ottawa Nationals, and remained active through 1975–76 with the Toronto Toros. He became a scout in the 1980s, including a stint as chief scout for the Winnipeg Jets (Phoenix Coyotes).

WREN BLAIR

BORN: Lindsay, Ontario, October 2, 1925
POSITION: Coach, Minnesota North Stars, 1967–70; President, Pittsburgh Penguins, 1975–77

Wren Blair, otherwise known as the Bird of hockey, was a milkman who made it big in the NHL. Blair became disenchanted with his Ontario milk route at an early age and turned to coaching and managing amateur teams. He is one of a dozen hockey people who have taken personal credit for discovering Bobby Orr when the wunderkind was a 12-year-old playing Junior C level amateur hockey in the Ontario Association. (Lynn Patrick, Milt Schmidt, and God are among the others who have taken bows for finding Orr and signing him to a Bruins contract.)

When the NHL expanded from six to 12 teams in 1967–68, Blair was named general manager and coach of the Minnesota North Stars. He frequently relinquished the coaching because of ill health, but retained the managerial post. In 1970–71, the Blair-developed North Stars reached a high point in their young life by reaching the semifinal round of the Stanley Cup playoffs before being eliminated by Montreal in six games. From there

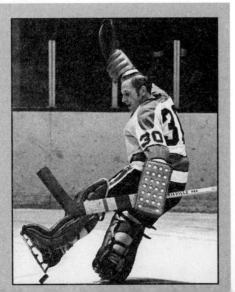

Les Binkley of the Pittsburgh Penguins

it was all downhill for the Bird and he left in 1974. In 1975, Blair became president of the Penguins, the owners hoping he could turn the struggling franchise around. He faded, departing Pittsburgh in 1977.

ROB BLAKE

BORN: Simcoe, Ontario, December 10, 1969
POSITION: Defenseman, Los Angeles Kings, 1990–2000; Colorado Avalanche, 2000–
AWARDS/HONORS: James Norris Memorial Trophy, 1998; NHL All-Rookie Team, 1991; NHL First Team All-Star, 1998; NHL Second Team All-Star, 2000–01; NHL All-Star Game, 1994, 1999–2002

For a player elected as low as the fourth round, 70th overall, in the 1988 National Hockey League Entry Draft, Rob Blake became an extraordinarily successful major-leaguer.

Only one year after being drafted, the tall (six feet four, 225 pounds) versatile defenseman was a playing regular on the Los Angeles Kings blueline.

By the late 1990s, he would emerge as the team's best defenseman, captain of the Kings, and one of the top defenders in the majors with his crunching hits, offensive prowess, and booming slap shot.

The one element that eluded Blake was playing for a Stanley Cup winner, and it took an extraordinary trade to change that. The Colorado Avalanche picked up Blake and Kings teammate Steve Reinprecht during the 2000–01 season in exchange for Adam Deadmarsh, Aaron Miller, and a first-round pick. Then, most appropriately, the teams battled in a thrilling seven-game second-round playoff series that spring.

Not only did the Avalanche beat Blake's old mates, but they conquered the New Jersey Devils for their second Stanley Cup. Blake finished the season tied with fellow first-time Cup-winner Ray Bourque for third in scoring among defensemen, as well as finishing

second in blueliner goals and power-play goals. Through 2001–02, Blake had scored over 20 goals twice in his career.

The Simcoe, Ontario, native was quoted as saying that if he didn't play hockey he would be a farmer. His success at the NHL level, as well as at the 2002 Olympic Games in which he helped Team Canada take home the gold medal, showed he definitely made the right decision.

TOE BLAKE

BORN: Victoria Mines, Ontario, August 21, 1912
DIED: May 17, 1995
POSITION: Left Wing, Montreal Maroons, 1934–35; Montreal Canadiens, 1935–48; Coach, Montreal Canadiens, 1955–68
AWARDS/HONORS: Hart Memorial Trophy, 1939; Art Ross Trophy, 1939; Lady Byng Memorial Trophy, 1946; NHL First Team All-Star, 1939–40, 1945; NHL Second Team All-Star, 1938, 1946; Hockey Hall of Fame, 1966

A hard-nosed left wing who scored enough goals to be nicknamed "the Old Lamplighter," Hector "Toe" Blake remained a Montreal hockey player from his rookie year— and only season—with the Maroons (1934–35) to his retirement following the 1947–48 campaign with the Canadiens, for whom he played during all his other NHL years.

Blake played hard and talked loud, something that didn't endear him to referees around the NHL. That's why to this day it remains a mystery how Blake won the Lady Byng Trophy for good sportsmanship in the 1945–46 season.

But Toe had been a trophy winner long before that. While the Canadiens were finishing sixth in 1938–39, Blake led the league in scoring. His awards included the Hart Trophy as the most valuable player, not to mention an All-Star nomination. "When Dick Irvin became Canadiens coach in 1941," wrote hockey historian Charles L. Coleman, "his rebuilding job was done around Blake."

At the start of the 1940s, Blake was used on a line with Johnny Quilty and Joe Benoit, but Irvin soon changed that with the insertion of Elmer Lach at center. The Canadiens were improving, with Blake leading the way, but they didn't reach maturity as a championship club until the 1943–44 season, when Irvin inserted young, fiery Maurice "Rocket" Richard on right wing on the line with Blake and Lach.

The trio, named the Punch Line, finished one-two-three (Lach, Blake, Richard) in scoring on the team, and the Canadiens finished first and won the Stanley Cup. The Punch Line became one of the classiest units in league annals and helped the Canadiens to another Stanley Cup in 1946. Blake scored 29 regular season goals that year, but then began a decline in his playing fortunes. He scored only nine goals in 1947–48, a year in which the Canadiens missed the playoffs, and then made his exit from the NHL.

Regarded as surefire coaching timber, Toe broke in as a bench boss in the minors with stints in such unlikely places as Houston, Buffalo, and Valleyfield, Quebec. When Dick Irvin resigned as Canadiens coach after the 1954–55 season, several names were tossed in the hopper, but the only serious contender was Blake.

The Old Lamplighter had studied coaching well in the Quebec Senior League. He was partially French Canadian, and he was admired by all the players, particularly Maurice Richard. Kenny Reardon, who had moved up to a key front-office position with the Canadiens, was a strong advocate of Blake, and ultimately the opinions of manager Frank Selke and Reardon prevailed. On June 8, 1955, the signing of Blake was officially announced before a standing-room crowd at the Forum, and Les Canadiens were ready to become the greatest team in hockey history.

Toe Blake wielded a dictator's baton over Les Canadiens, but at first ruled them like a benevolent despot. This was easy because the players, to a man, respected Blake, and vice versa. The pivotal personality on the team was the Rocket. He went out of his way to assure the Canadiens' hierarchy that he backed Blake to the hilt, and he meant every word of it.

Now it was up to the Old Lamplighter to produce. All the ingredients were there: a competent young goaltender, a strong, intelligent defense, and the most explosive collection of scorers in history.

His scrubs, such as defenseman Jean-Guy Talbot and Bob Turner, were good enough to be first-liners on almost any other team, which was a credit to Selke's superb farm system. It was, indeed, a galaxy that dazzled nobody more than it did Blake. "I couldn't help [but] be amazed once we started holding our first workouts," said Toe. "I was glad I was as young as I was. Otherwise I would have been killed. All those great shots. The puck was flying around with such speed I thought I was in a shooting gallery."

Blake's success at Valleyfield in the Quebec Senior League was well known to management, but it hardly made an impression on the rank-and-file fan who had as many doubts about Blake as Toe himself. "I was nervous," the rookie coach allowed. "I felt I had to produce with a club like that. So much potential. And it was a big test for me. But the Rocket went out of his way to help me. So did Kenny Mosdell and Floyd Curry and Butch Bouchard.

"Sometimes it's tough to coach players you once had as teammates. But these fellas went out of their way to make it easy for me. Even from the beginning we were like one big happy family."

Blake was so successful with his "happy family" that he helped to engineer the arrival of eight Stanley Cups in his 13-year tenure.

Before his retirement in 1968, Blake's Habitants had finished first nine times and Toe was regarded by many experts as the finest all-around coach in NHL history. Toe died in 1995 after a long illness.

GUS BODNAR

BORN: Fort William, Ontario, August 24, 1925
POSITION: Center, Toronto Maple Leafs, 1943–47; Chicago Blackhawks, 1947–54; Boston Bruins, 1954–55
AWARDS/HONORS: Calder Memorial Trophy, 1944

GARTH BOESCH

BORN: Millestone, Saskatchewan, October 7, 1920
DIED: May 14, 1998
POSITION: Defenseman, Toronto Maple Leafs, 1946–50

When Gus Bodnar was promoted to the Toronto Maple Leafs in the fall of 1943 at age 20, coach Hap Day quipped: "It appears that we have reached the Children's Hour in the NHL." But Bodnar, a slick center, immediately proved he was a winner. In his first NHL game, October 30, 1943, against the Rangers, Bodnar scored 15 seconds after the opening face-off against goalie Ken McAuley. Gus thus set a record for "fastest goal scored by a rookie." He finished his first season with 22 goals and 40 assists for 62 points in 50 games. His total set a league record for rookies and he was named the outstanding freshman in the league.

Surprisingly, his play never again reached that standard, although he played on Stanley Cup winners in 1945 and 1947 with the Leafs. As a member of the Chicago Blackhawks in 1952, Gus worked for a while with Bud Poile and Gaye Stewart, also from the same city. Their unit, the Flying Forts, went en masse along with Ernie Dickens and Bob Goldham to the Chicago Blackhawks in a trade for Max Bentley and Cy Thomas in November 1947. Bodnar played capably for Chicago and set another NHL speed record for the fastest three assists, when Bill Mosienko netted his own record of three goals in 21 seconds against the New York Rangers in a March 23, 1952 game.

Gus was traded to the Bruins in 1953–54 and finished his NHL career in Boston in 1954–55.

Only two players wore mustaches in the NHL during the 1940s: Don "Bones" Raleigh of the Rangers and Garth Boesch of the Maple Leafs. Raleigh's was only a temporary fixture; Boesch's remained permanent and complimented his cool defensive style. A Saskatchewan wheat farmer, Boesch was a cog in the Toronto dynasty launched by Conn Smythe in 1946. From the 1947 playoffs through April 1949, the

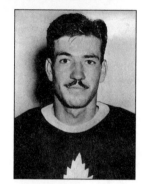

Garth Boesch, Toronto defenseman (and the only one with a mustache in 1947)

Leafs won three Stanley Cups in three tries, aided by the superb play of Boesch. His defense partner was Bill Barilko and together, they perfected the Maginot Line knee drop, in which they would simultaneously fall to their knees to block enemy shots, as if they were connected by invisible rods. During the 1949–50 season, when Smythe conducted his notorious fight against fat on his team, Boesch was one of the few Leafs to check in on the scale under his established weight. As defensemen go, Boesch was one of the most underrated quality backliners ever to play in the majors.

LEO BOIVIN

BORN: Prescott, Ontario, August 2, 1932
POSITION: Defenseman, Toronto Maple Leafs, 1951–55; Boston Bruins, 1955–65; Detroit Red Wings, 1966–67; Pittsburgh Penguins, 1967–69; Minnesota North Stars, 1969–70; Coach, St. Louis Blues, 1975–76, 1977–78
AWARDS/HONORS: Hockey Hall of Fame, 1986

A low center of gravity (he stood five feet seven), a firepluglike build and nearly 200 pounds of muscle were Leo Boivin's major assets. Breaking in with the Maple Leafs, Leo was traded to Boston, where he spent nine colorful seasons before moving to Detroit. Boivin closed out his career skating for Pittsburgh and Minnesota after expansion. Leo had two short tenures as coach of the Blues, but found out coaching was not for him.

When Leo was enshrined in the Hockey Hall of Fame in 1986, his admission was challenged by some analysts who believe he was not that qualified, despite his hitting, whereas others claim that the league does not have an award for defensive defensemen. Boivin represented the most flamboyant, but no less effective type of checker, and therefore qualified.

PETER BONDRA

BORN: Luck, Ukraine, February 7, 1968
POSITION: Right Wing, Washington Capitals, 1990–
AWARDS/HONORS: NHL All-Star Game, 1993, 1996–99

The Washington Capitals have enjoyed precious few natural scorers from the inception of the franchise in 1974 through the club's first decade of play in the National Hockey League. It wasn't until American-born Bobby Carpenter scored 50 goals in 1985 that the Caps found such an offensive threat.

But in 1990, the Capitals got lucky in more ways than one. Peter Bondra was selected 156th overall by Washington in the eighth round of the June Entry Draft.

Within five years, he had become a big-league scoring sensation, hitting a personal record level of 52 goals in 1995–96 and again in 1997–98, often paired with playmaker Adam Oates. By the millennium, Bondra held second place in Capitals' career goal scoring with 382, just 15 short of number one Mike Gartner, and held the Capitals' career records for power-play goals (99), game-winning goals (57), shorthanded goals (29), and hat tricks (17). The sniper was also second among the NHL's top goal scorers from 1993 to 2001 with 305, just 41 shy of Jaromir Jagr, with whom the sniper formed a formidable scoring tandem upon Jagr's summer 2001 trade to the Caps.

Bondra also played for his home country in the 1998 and 2002 Olympics and the 1996 World Cup.

DICKIE BOON

BORN: Belleville, Ontario, January 10, 1878
DIED: May 3, 1961
POSITION: Defenseman, Montreal (CAHL), 1900–03; Montreal Wanderers (FAHL), 1904–05
AWARDS/HONORS: Hockey Hall of Fame, 1952

A Hall of Famer who never played professional hockey, Dickie Boon played junior hockey with the talented Mike Grant on the Young Crystals team of Montreal.

He played with the Monarch Hockey Club in 1897, followed by a two-year stint with the Montreal A.A.A. Juniors. In 1901, Boon made the senior club, which went on to win the Stanley Cup against the Winnipeg Victorias in 1902. Boon and his teammates were so small they became known as "the Little Iron Men."

In 1903, Boon became manager of the Montreal Wanderers and, until his retirement in 1916, piloted the Wanderers to three Stanley Cups.

MIKE BOSSY

BORN: Montreal, Quebec, January 22, 1957
POSITION: Right Wing, New York Islanders, 1977–87
AWARDS/HONORS: Calder Memorial Trophy, 1978; Lady Byng Memorial Trophy, 1983–84, 1986; Conn Smythe Trophy, 1982; NHL First Team All-Star, 1981–84, 1986; NHL Second Team All-Star, 1978–79, 1985; NHL Challenge Cup All-Star, 1979; Canada Cup All-Star Team, 1981; NHL All-Star Game, 1978, 1980–83, 1985–86; Hockey Hall of Fame, 1991

Among right wing sharpshooters, Mike Bossy ranks at the top with Maurice "The Rocket" Richard and Gordie Howe.

Alongside Bryan Trottier, Denis Potvin, Bill Smith, and Clark Gillies, Bossy was an integral part of the four-time Stanley Cup–winning New York Islanders who put together a record 19 consecutive playoff-series victories between 1980 and 1984.

Mike Bossy of the New York Islanders

Surprisingly, Bossy was selected 15th overall in the 1977 Amateur Draft because scouts were dubious about his defensive skills. "I need a natural goal scorer," said Islanders coach Al Arbour. "I can teach Mike how to play defense."

Arbour did just that, while Bossy immediately displayed a quick release shot that produced 53 goals in his rookie season, 1977–78, during which he won the Calder Trophy as Rookie of the Year. From his first year, Bossy reeled off nine consecutive seasons in which he scored 50 or more goals.

For most of his career, Bossy played on a line with Trottier at center and Gillies on the left. The Trio Grande helped cement the Islanders' dynasty and Bossy reached his peak in 1982 when he won the Conn Smythe Trophy as the playoffs' most valuable player.

During the 1982 Stanley Cup finals against the Vancouver Canucks, Bossy scored one of the most spectacular goals in playoff history, rapping the flying puck past goalie Richard Brodeur while Mike was in midair.

A thoughtful, insightful athlete, Bossy made headlines when he publicly declared he would not fight. It was a courageous statement at a time when brawling was more prevalent than after the turn of the twenty-first century. The NHL awarded him the Lady Byng Trophy, for combining high skill with clean play, in 1983, 1984, and 1986.

Nevertheless, at the very peak of his productivity, Bossy was overshadowed by the prodigious Wayne Gretzky, who had emerged as the top point-getter of the 1980s with the Edmonton Oilers.

Bossy's career went into abrupt decline during the 1986–87 season when chronic back problems braked his skills. He was able to play only 63 games and managed to score 38 goals and 37 assists. The 75 points was a dramatic drop for a sharpshooter who never before had scored less than the 91 points he amassed in his rookie year.

A perfectionist by nature, Bossy retired in 1987 and to this day remains one of the most underappreciated superstars ever to come down the pike. Elected to the Hockey Hall of Fame in 1991, Bossy's number 22 was retired by the Islanders that same year.

PIERRE BOUCHARD

BORN: Montreal, Quebec, February 20, 1948
POSITION: Defenseman, Montreal Canadiens, 1970–78; Washington Capitals, 1978–82

The Montreal Canadiens were hoping Pierre Bouchard would be a chip off the old block. His father, Emile, alias Butch, was a star defenseman on Stanley Cup-winning teams in the 1940s for the Habs and a member of the Hockey Hall of Fame.

During a career that spanned a dozen NHL seasons, Pierre played a solid game on the blueline, while a member of Stanley Cup–winning teams himself in 1975–76, 1976–77, and 1977–78.

Generally a calm individual, Bouchard was an excellent fighter when aroused. Among his more memorable victories was his knockdown of Ranger toughie Ted Irvine at Madison Square Garden.

After concluding his playing career, Bouchard turned to broadcasting, and was one of the most popular francophone NHL analysts into the new century.

FRANK BOUCHER

BORN: Ottawa, Ontario, October 7, 1901
DIED: December 12, 1977
POSITION: Center, Ottawa Senators, 1921–22; New York Rangers, 1926–38, 1943–44; Coach, New York Rangers, 1939–48; General Manager, New York Rangers, 1948–55
AWARDS/HONORS: Lady Byng Memorial Trophy, 1928–31, 1933–35 (trophy awarded to him in perpetuity, 1935, and second trophy donated); NHL First Team All-Star, 1933–35; NHL Second Team All-Star, 1931; NHL All-Star Game, 1937; Hockey Hall of Fame, 1958

One of the classiest players in NHL history, Frank Boucher gained acclaim first as a member of the Royal Canadian Mounted Police, then as a sparkling Ranger on the "A-Line" with the Cook brothers, Bill and Bun.

There were many scintillating skaters on that first Ranger team, but none captured the imagination of the Garden crowd like the brothers Cook and Frank Boucher. They moved with the grace of figure skaters and passed the puck with radarlike accuracy. Bill was the crackerjack shot, Bun had the brawn, and Boucher had all the class in the world.

Without question, Boucher was the cleanest player ever to lace on a pair of skates in the

NHL; he finished his career with only 119 penalty minutes. He won the Lady Byng Trophy so many times—seven times in eight seasons—the league finally gave it to him in perpetuity and a new trophy was struck in 1936.

The one fight Boucher had in his entire NHL career took place in the Rangers' very first game in Madison Square Garden, November 16, 1926, against the Montreal Maroons, the Stanley Cup champions. "They were big," wrote *New York Times* columnist Arthur Daley, "and they were rough. Every Maroon carried a chip on his shoulder."

The chips became heavier when Bill Cook took a pass from brother Bun and scored what proved to be the only goal of the night. Fortified with a one-goal lead, the Rangers began counterattacking with their bodies and fists. Balding Ching Johnson would drop a Maroon to the ice, then grin his special trademark smile that delighted the Garden crowd. Huge Taffy Abel hit every Montreal skater in sight, and soon the rink was on the verge of a riot. Up until then the gentlemanly Boucher had minded his business and stayed out of trouble. But "Bad" Bill Phillips, one of the most boisterous of the visitors, worked Boucher over with his elbows, knees, and stick at every opportunity. "The patient Boucher," wrote Daley, "endured the outrages until a free-for-all broke out."

At that point Boucher discreetly dropped his stick, peeled off his gloves, and caved in Phillips's face with a right jab. The Maroon badman slumped to the ice, whereupon Boucher politely lifted him to his feet and belted him again. When Boucher lifted Phillips for the second time, the Montrealer grabbed his stick and bounced it off Boucher's head, whereupon referee Lou Marsh interceded. Miraculously, both men escaped injury, acquiring only five-minute penalties for scrapping.

When he retired as a player, Boucher turned to coaching and management, where he made many lasting marks. He popularized the strategy of pulling the goaltender in favor of an extra attacker as coach of the Rangers, and helped incorporate the center red line into the NHL while serving on the rules committee. His first season as mentor to the New York Rangers would result in the 1940 Stanley Cup championship, the last time the team would win until 1994. He became their general manager and eventually fostered various Junior leagues until his death in 1977.

GEORGE BOUCHER

BORN: Ottawa, Ontario, 1896
DIED: October 17, 1960
POSITION: Defenseman, Ottawa Senators, 1917–28; Montreal Maroons, 1929–31; Chicago Blackhawks, 1931–32; Coach, Boston Bruins, 1949–50

Frank Boucher's older brother, George "Buck" Boucher, starred as a defenseman for the Ottawa Senators in the NHL from 1917–28. During the 1928–29 season, he was traded to the Montreal Maroons and finished his NHL career with Chicago in 1931–32. He coached the Boston Bruins briefly in 1949–50, leaving rather abruptly after a front-office tiff.

BOB BOURNE

BORN: Kindersley, Saskatchewan, June 21, 1954
POSITION: Left Wing/Center, New York Islanders, 1974–86; Los Angeles Kings, 1986–88
AWARDS/HONORS: Bill Masterton Memorial Trophy, 1988; NHL All-Star Game, 1981

Bob Bourne only got lucky once in his career. He had been the property of the expansion Kansas City Scouts but never played for them. The Scouts traded him to the up-and-coming New York Islanders, before he ever skated in an NHL game. Bourne made his own luck through the rest of his career, on a combination of speed, versatility, determination, attitude, and heart.

By Bourne's own reckoning, it took him about four years to lose his initial awe at playing

in the NHL, but his contributions to the Islanders grew steadily. His speed, defense, and penalty-killing skills made him extremely valuable even if he was not as well-known as many of his teammates.

Bourne's career peaked just when the Islanders began their Cup dynasty, and he was stellar in both the 1980 and 1983 Cup runs, piling up 20- and 28-point performances, respectively.

In the 1983 Cup quarterfinals, Bourne scored a spectacular goal in Game Five against the Rangers—skating through the entire Rangers team from one end of the rink to the other. It is considered one of the 50 greatest goals in Stanley Cup history. Even better, it crushed the Rangers' hopes of an upset and set the Isles on the road to their fourth consecutive Stanley Cup.

Bourne played for the Islanders for several more years before being traded to the Los Angeles Kings prior to the 1986–87 season. He retired from the Kings and the NHL in 1989.

Bourne's post-NHL life included a stint as the coach and general manager of the Utah Grizzlies of the IHL before its demise in 2001, as well as the promotion of fantasy hockey tournament camps.

RAY BOURQUE

BORN: Montreal, Quebec, December 28, 1960
POSITION: Defenseman, Boston Bruins, 1979–2000; Colorado Avalanche, 2000–01
AWARDS/HONORS: Calder Memorial Trophy, 1980; James Norris Memorial Trophy, 1987–88, 1990–91, 1994; King Clancy Memorial Trophy, 1992; NHL First Team All-Star, 1980, 1982, 1984–85, 1987–88, 1990–1994, 1996, 2001; NHL Second Team All-Star, 1981, 1983, 1986, 1989, 1995, 1999; Canada Cup All-Star Team, 1987; NHL All-Star Game, 1981–94, 1996–99

There was something extraordinarily deceptive about Raymond Bourque that tended to ever-so-slightly cloud the glitter that was his due. One part of it had to do with his subdued personality; another was rooted in the historic fact that two decades of Bourque's stardom failed to produce a Stanley Cup for Boston. Finally, there was a style that was well-honed in all aspects, but conspicuously less than sensational. Nevertheless, the Montrealer's name would be inscribed in the books as a nonpareil best called a blueline version of Gordie Howe: artistic, indestructible, and menacing when challenged.

Raymond Jean Bourque's sparkling career began with Verdun of the Quebec Major Junior Hockey League. Drafted eighth overall in the first round of the 1979 Entry Draft by Boston, Bourque was touted as the turn-around player of the Bruins' defense corps. He won the Calder Trophy as the NHL's top rookie in 1980, as well as making the NHL First All-Star Team. He would be a member of the team 12 more times and also earned six spots on the Second All-Star Team.

What made Bourque unique, among many factors, was his durability. The French-Canadian played one of the most trying positions in sports at the highest level for two decades. In tribute to that durability and top-level consistency, during the 1998–99 season he was nominated for the Norris Trophy as the NHL's best defenseman for the 14th time.

Bourque won the Norris five times. Those credentials are testimony to the man's ability to take the ice night after night and deliver a vigorous, inspiring performance with little fuss or fanfare.

For instance, at the age of 38, during the 1999 playoffs, the defenseman was unsparing of his body. Facing the rugged Sabres in the second round, Bourque played more minutes than stars who were 15 years younger. In one match, he logged 35 minutes and 19 seconds. Ray worked equally hard, if not harder, in the 2001 playoffs, but the outcome was different. The former Bruin won his first and only Stanley Cup, as a Colorado Avalanche.

Even the best players have to lose steps to Father Time sooner or later. That Bourque

had been able to keep pace over two decades was an unending source of amazement to teammates and foes alike.

JOHNNY BOWER

BORN: Prince Albert, Saskatchewan, November 8, 1924
POSITION: Goaltender, New York Rangers, 1953-55, 1956-57; Toronto Maple Leafs, 1958-70
AWARDS/HONORS: Vezina Trophy, 1965 (shared with Terry Sawchuk); NHL First Team All-Star, 1961; Hockey Hall of Fame, 1976

Goaltending was the Toronto Maple Leafs' big weakness before manager Punch Imlach arrived. When the club finished last in 1957–58, Ed Chadwick, goaltender in all 70 games, finished the season with a 3.23 goals-against average, worst of all the league regulars.

Billy Reay, Imlach's predecessor, scouted the minors for a replacement. His first choice was Al Rollins, who had starred for the last Leaf Cup winner. Rollins was playing for Calgary in the Western League, but he played poorly the night Reay scouted him, losing his return ticket to the NHL. Reay's second choice was Johnny Bower, a veteran who had bounced around the minors for years. Bower played one full season with the Rangers in 1953–54 and parts of two other campaigns, 1954–55 and 1956–57, in New York before returning to the bushes.

Cynical about past treatment and uncertain about his NHL future, Bower rejected Reay's first offer. "I was happy in Cleveland," he said. "I'd had my fling at the NHL, and besides, I didn't think I could help Toronto."

Another consideration was that he was almost 34 years old, ancient for a goaltender in those days. Then something changed Bower's mind, and he decided to sign with the Leafs. Bower's play during the 1958–59 season made him the Leafs' regular goaltender. Bower was a glutton for punishment, especially during practice sessions, during which he performed as diligently as the rawest of rookies. "I've always had to work hard," Bower explained. "I don't know any other way to play the game."

Bower led the Leafs to the Stanley Cup finals six out of nine years and won the Cup four times, in 1962, 1963, 1964, and 1967.

Johnny hung up his skates and pads for the last time in 1969–70 and became a scout for his beloved Leafs.

RUSSELL BOWIE

BORN: August 24, 1880
DIED: April 8, 1959
POSITION: Center/Rover, Winnipeg Victorias (CAHL, ECAHA), 1899–1908
AWARDS/HONORS: Hockey Hall of Fame, 1945

Russell Bowie, who toiled at center ice for the turn-of-the-century Victorias, has been called, by hard-line old-timers, the greatest pivotman to play the game.

A quick glance at Bowie's stats shows that he was indeed the Phil Esposito of his day. Throughout his ten seasons with Winnipeg, from 1899–1908, he amassed 234 goals in 80 games, almost three goals per game!

He led the league in scoring for five years, and was a perpetual All-Star. Oddly, Bowie remained an amateur throughout his career, and although there were allegations that he had accepted a retainer from the professional Montreal Wanderers in 1907, he was finally cleared. While the Wanderers went on to win a string of championships, the Victorias, starring Russell Bowie, never drank Stanley Cup champagne.

SCOTTY BOWMAN

BORN: Montreal, Quebec, September 18, 1933
POSITION: Coach, St. Louis Blues, 1967–71; Montreal Canadiens, 1971–79; Buffalo Sabres, 1980–87; Pittsburgh Penguins, 1991–93; Detroit Red Wings, 1993–2002
AWARDS/HONORS: Jack Adams Trophy, 1977, 1996; Hockey Hall of Fame, 1991

Early in the year 2001, when Scott Bowman was presented with the Lester Patrick Trophy for "service to hockey in the United States," it surprised absolutely no one in the civilized ice world.

Unquestionably, the Montreal native is regarded as *the* coach of the half-century, if not the greatest NHL bench boss of all time.

Scotty Bowman

The ultimate living legend among coaches, Bowman won 1,500 games overall (including playoffs) from 1967 into the twenty-first century, a record that surely will never be broken.

A severe head injury, suffered in 1951–52 while playing junior hockey, completely altered Scotty Bowman's career. He joined the Montreal Canadiens' organization, where he spent 16 years scouting, troubleshooting throughout the farm system, and coaching at the Junior and minor-league professional level.

In 1967, Scotty was hired as the first coach of the expansion St. Louis Blues and led them to the Stanley Cup finals in each of his first three seasons. Worsening relations with the Blues' owners forced Bowman to leave Mound City for Montreal, where in seven seasons his club won five Stanley Cups—1973 and successively in 1976, 1977, 1978, and 1979.

Bowman's trademark was the one expression he wore during a game, appearing to give him an air of arrogance. To those who knew him, however, the jutting jaw was misleading, for Scotty was a likable, direct man, serious about his job, who performed without theatrics, and was himself at all times.

Bowman was irked at the beginning of the 1978–79 season when the general manager's job, vacated by Sam Pollock, was not offered to him. After collecting his fourth consecutive Stanley Cup, his fifth in six years as coach of the Habs, Bowman accepted an offer to manage the Buffalo Sabres starting in 1980.

Although the Sabres finished first in 1979–80, Bowman could not win a Cup during his Buffalo stint, which became less successful than anticipated. He left the Sabres in 1987 to become a television analyst and, for all intents and purposes, his coaching career came to a halt.

To everyone's surprise, the Pittsburgh Penguins hired Bowman in June of 1990 to become director of player development and recruitment. But when Penguins coach Bob Johnson became ill shortly before the 1991–92 season, Bowman moved behind the bench once more and directed Pittsburgh to its second consecutive Stanley Cup.

The Penguins were favored to make it three straight in 1993 but were upset by Al Arbour's New York Islanders in a Patrick Division final series. Bowman was criticized for being too aloof and hands-offish in his orchestration of the champions.

Whatever the case, Scott moved on to Detroit, where he signed a lucrative contract with the Red Wings. Owner Mike Ilitch made it abundantly clear that he expected Bowman to do what he had done six times before: Produce a Stanley Cup winner.

Bowman responded by first leading the Red Wings to a respectable (46–30–8) finish in the regular 1993–94 race. After a shaky start, Detroit moved into a contending position and emerged as a perennial elite NHL team. Nevertheless, Bowman did not achieve the ultimate goal right away. Unhappy with Tim Cheveldae's goaltending, Bowman finally prevailed upon general manager Bryan Murray to

obtain Bob Essensa from Winnipeg. Essensa was less than superb upon his settling in Detroit, but Bowman brought his club to the playoffs, where the Red Wings opened against the little-respected San Jose Sharks and suddenly found themselves behind the eight-ball. What was expected to be a breeze turned into a death struggle. Armed with such stars as Sergei Federov, Steve Yzerman, and Paul Coffey, Bowman nevertheless could not firmly establish Detroit superiority. Ultimately, he gambled on rookie Chris Osgood in goal and Osgood blew the deciding game. Bowman and his favored Red Wings were humiliated in the first round.

But in 1997, Bowman delivered. At Joe Louis Arena on a Saturday night, June 7, 1997, Bowman's club broke the Motor City schneid. The Red Wings, backstopped by the experienced Mike Vernon, defeated the Philadelphia Flyers, 2–1, to win the Stanley Cup. The 42-year championship drought—dating back to May 1955, when Alex Delvecchio ignited a seventh-game win over Montreal—was over. And in 1998, Bowman, with Osgood as his ace in the net, sealed another Cup for Hockeytown.

Scotty inspired admiration from all angles.

"What really impressed me," said Larry Robinson, "is that he did the job so long and so well and that the kids still listened to him. After three or four years, you've pretty well said everything you've got to say. That's when players tune you out. Scotty continued to coach and get results."

Osgood, who won a Stanley Cup with Bowman in 1996–97 and 1997–98, but fell into the coach's disfavor and was eventually waived, still commended his former mentor.

"The thing that made Scotty so successful," said Osgood, "is that he was always on top of everything. Ask him about any team in the league—their penalty killing, their power play, which player has how many blocked shots—and he'd know exactly how many. When I was in Detroit, we were always prepared for every team that we played, and he would know exactly what they would do. It's impossible to get anything by him."

By 2001–02, with Bowman still strongly at the helm, Detroit—newly seeded with future Hall-of-Famers Luc Robitaille, Brett Hull, and Dominik Hasek—coasted through the season, easily taking the President's Trophy for the best record in the league. With the ballyhoo surrounding the team in the modern media-rich NHL, Bowman was the perfect man to handle it.

"The most impressive thing about Scotty is his ability to adjust over the years," Capitals coach Ron Wilson said during the 1998 Stanley Cup finals. "A lot of coaches are very regimented. I think if you look at all of Scotty's teams from St. Louis, Montreal, Buffalo, Pittsburgh, and Detroit, every one of his teams have been different. And he was flexible enough to start in the sixties, go through the seventies, eighties, and into the nineties." Bowman guided the Red Wings to another Stanley Cup in 2002. Following the final game, he announced his retirement.

CARL BREWER

BORN: Toronto, Ontario, October 21, 1938
DIED: August 25, 2001
POSITION: Defenseman, Toronto Maple Leafs, 1957–65; Detroit Red Wings, 1969–70; St. Louis Blues, 1970–72; Toronto Toros (WHA), 1973–74; Toronto Maple Leafs, 1979–80
AWARDS/HONORS: NHL First Team All-Star, 1963; NHL Second Team All-Star, 1962, 1965, 1970; NHL All-Star Game, 1959, 1962, 1964

Carl Brewer had an unusual hockey career, to say the least. At the age of 26, in the prime of his ice life, Brewer quit the Maple Leafs to study at the University of Toronto. He campaigned successfully to regain amateur status, then performed with the Canadian National team. Carl coached in the International Hockey League and also the Helsinki IFK sextet in Finland. "The funny part of it," he says, "is

Carl Brewer as a Maple Leafs defenseman

that I didn't have any master plan in mind when I made the changes."

His professional tenure included ten NHL seasons with the Leafs, Red Wings, and Blues, and a year in the WHA with the Toronto Toros, sandwiched around stints with the IHL Muskegon Mohawks and AHL New Brunswick Blackhawks. He was a four-time All-Star, and an all-time philosopher.

"The game of hockey itself is very easy," he professes. "It's the thinking about it that makes it hard."

Brewer retired in 1974 to do TV color commentary for the Toros, but briefly came back for a 20-game revisit with the Maple Leafs in 1980. Twelve years later, Carl was instrumental in leading former players in a landmark lawsuit against the NHL Players' Association for improper use of player pension funds, which netted a $40 million payout and a prison sentence for Players' Association figurehead Alan Eagleson.

MEL BRIDGMAN

BORN: Trenton, Ontario, April 28, 1955
POSITION: Forward, Philadelphia Flyers, 1975–81; Calgary Flames, 1981–83; New Jersey Devils, 1983–87; Detroit Red Wings, 1987–88; Vancouver Canucks, 1987–88; General Manager, Ottawa Senators, 1992–93

The Flyers traded two players and a number one draft pick to the Washington Capitals for the right to choose Mel Bridgman first overall in the 1975 Amateur Draft.

A prolific scorer with the Victoria Cougars, Bridgman was named Western Canadian Hockey League (Junior) Most Valuable Player in 1975, after leading the league in scoring with 157 points.

As a major-leaguer, Bridgman became one of the toughest players on a rough Philadelphia team, and captained the Flyers from 1979 until his 1981 arrival in Calgary for Brad Marsh. In his first 63 games as a Flame, Mel potted 75 points, totaling a career-high 87.

The bruising forward never shied away from body contact. "I'm a little aggressive with my gloves," Bridgman admitted. But consistency became his forte. Later on, his leadership qualities shone brightly as captain of the New Jersey Devils in their early years, with 68 goals from 1983–84 through 1985–86, before twilighting in Detroit and Vancouver. A solid performer and ferocious fighter, the Trenton, Ontario, native reliably excelled along the boards and in both zones, routinely contributing 50-plus points to the offense.

Educated at the Wharton School of Business, Bridgman was appointed general manager of the all-new Ottawa Senators in 1992. He drafted Alexei Yashin and an overburdened squad of AHLers, but was fired after their avoidably abysmal inaugural season of 10–70–4, which barely missed being the worst season in NHL history, before becoming a player agent.

FRANK BRIMSEK

BORN: Eveleth, Minnesota, September 26, 1915
DIED: November 11, 1998
POSITION: Goaltender, Boston Bruins, 1938–43, 1945–49; Chicago Blackhawks, 1949–50
AWARDS/HONORS: Calder Memorial Trophy, 1939; Vezina Trophy, 1939, 1942; NHL First Team All-Star, 1939, 1942; NHL Second Team All-Star, 1940–41, 1943, 1946–48; NHL All-Star Game, 1939, 1947–48; Hockey Hall of Fame, 1966

For years, Bruins manager Art Ross received excellent service from goalie Tiny Thompson, so it was no surprise when Tiny started the 1938–39 campaign in the Boston nets. But Ross was unhappy, not so much about Thompson as about a young goalkeeper, Frank Brimsek, who was impressing scouts at nearby Providence in the International American League. Brimsek was not only a good hockey player but he was that rare breed—a good American-born, American-developed player, who had learned the game in the cold wastes of Eveleth, Minnesota. Also, the Detroit Red Wings had revealed their willingness to spend

Frank "Mister Zero" Brimsek as Boston goalie

$15,000, at that time a respectable sum, for Thompson.

Ross put one and one together: Thompson was aging; Brimsek was ready. Late in November 1938, the Bruins announced that their veteran goalie had been sold to Detroit. Brimsek would henceforth start in the Boston goal. Neither Thompson, his teammates, nor most of the Bruin fans could believe the news. After all, Tiny had won the Vezina Trophy four times and was still considered one of the finest goalies around, even after ten years in the NHL.

Nothing about Brimsek initially altered the prevailing opinion that he could be a flop. Those who remembered him in Providence recalled he had a habit of not really appearing to be "in" the game when the action picked up. Others decided an American kid just couldn't make it in the Canadian-dominated NHL.

Brimsek did nothing to enhance his image. He had an idiosyncrasy of wearing a pair of old red hockey pants instead of the then-traditional gold, brown, and white Bruins' outfit, and his footwork was less than sparkling. But his glove hand was amazingly fast and his confidence enormous.

Doubts about Brimsek's potential were eliminated within his first dozen games. In a stretch of three weeks, he scored six shutouts in seven games, was immediately dubbed "Mister Zero," and went on to win both the Calder Trophy and the Vezina Trophy as top goalie.

Brimsek permanently secured the affection of Bruins fans after his first two shutouts. When Boston faced Montreal in the next game at the Garden, the kid goalie appeared destined for still another superb goalless game, as the second period ticked to a close. But the visitors organized a two-on-one rush late in the period. Herb Cain, who was later to star for the Boston club, broke free and beat Brimsek from directly in front of the net. Once the home fans had digested the momentary tragedy, they suddenly broke into

an unremitting chorus of applause for "Mister Zero," whose record had reached 231 minutes and 54 seconds of shutout goaltending.

ROD BRIND'AMOUR

BORN: Ottawa, Ontario, August 9, 1970
POSITION: Center/Left Wing, St. Louis Blues, 1988–91; Philadelphia Flyers, 1991–2000; Carolina Hurricanes, 2000–
AWARDS/HONORS: NHL All-Star Game, 1992

If one were asked to select the best trade the Philadelphia Flyers ever made, there would be several choices from which to pick. But among the less obvious, yet most meaningful, was one that evolved on September 22, 1991. The Flyers acquired Rod Brind'Amour, who over a period of time revealed himself as one of the most durable and dependable skaters ever to wear the Philadelphia colors. In Rod's first season in Philly, he scored 33 goals, doubling his figure for St. Louis, with 44 assists and totaling 77 points along with 100 penalty minutes.

Although born in Ottawa, Brind'Amour moved with his family to Campbell River, British Columbia, when he was a youth. As a teenager, he enrolled at the revered Notre Dame College (actually a high school) in Wilcox, Saskatchewan. A long-time feeder for pro players, Notre Dame won a Canadian Midget-level title with Brind'Amour aboard. That, plus some starry moments with Canada's Spengler Cup (world university) team in Europe inspired the Blues to make him the ninth-overall draft choice in 1988.

His reaction was to enroll at Michigan State University, where he played in 1988–89. A season later, he was in Missouri scoring 26 goals alongside some distinguished linemates. Even though he was the Blues' fifth-leading scorer, his plus-minus total was a handsome plus-23. He combined offense and defense better than Oates, MacLean, Zezel, and Brett Hull.

By 1997–98, Brind'Amour was in his prime, and it was his all-around game that impressed both friend and foe. Dealt to the Carolina Hurricanes for Keith Primeau in 2000, Rod's first season with Carolina combined 36 assists with 20 goals. As the Canes finally rose to NHL prominence with a memorable run to the Stanley Cup finals, Brind'Amour remained steadfast as a leader, although the Hurricanes were defeated four games to one in the end.

PUNCH BROADBENT

BORN: Ottawa, Ontario, 1893
DIED: March 6, 1971
POSITION: Right Wing, Ottawa Senators (NHA and NHL), 1913–15, 1919–24, 1927–28; Montreal Maroons, 1924–27; New York Americans, 1928–29
AWARDS/HONORS: Art Ross Trophy, 1922; Hockey Hall of Fame, 1962

Right-winger Harry Broadbent rightfully deserved his nickname Punch, because he packed plenty of it with his fists as well as his scoring prowess. In fact, Punch holds a scoring record that still stands today. In 1922, a year that saw Harry lead all NHL scorers, Broadbent lit the red lamp in 16 consecutive contests. This feat has never been duplicated, even in today's faster, higher scoring games.

A Hall of Famer, Broadbent played on four Stanley Cup winners, three with the Ottawa Senators and one with the 1926 Montreal Maroons. Punch finished his career in 1929 with the New York Americans.

TURK BRODA

BORN: Brandon, Manitoba, May 15, 1914
DIED: October 17, 1972
POSITION: Goaltender, Toronto Maple Leafs, 1936–43, 1945–52
AWARDS/HONORS: Vezina Trophy, 1941, 1948; NHL First Team All-Star, 1941, 1948; NHL Second Team All-Star, 1942; Hockey Hall of Fame, 1967

Any similarity between Walter "Turk" Broda and a big-league goaltender was a mirage. Pudgy and slow on his feet, Broda appeared the antithesis of a goaltender.

They called him "Turkey Egg" in the wheat country surrounding Brandon, Manitoba. During a history lesson, an instructor told his class that an English king was given that nickname because of the huge freckles covering his face. Since nobody had more freckles than Broda, Walter was immediately hailed as Turkey Egg. Eventually he was called just plain "Turk."

Although his skating was poor, Broda earned a spot on the school team by default. Luckily, his principal noticed that Turk betrayed an unusual enthusiasm. The principal began working privately with his student, teaching him the finer points of goaltending, until Broda's game began to improve. He soon caught on with a local club called the Brandon North Stars, and played goal for them in a one-game playoff with the Elmwood Millionaires. Broda's club lost 11–1!

One spring the Red Wings were on exhibition in western Canada. One of their stops was Winnipeg, and it was there that Broda made his presence known. He discovered Detroit manager Jack Adams's downtown hotel, learned Adams's room number, and, accompanied by his teammate Modere "Mud" Bruneteau, nervously went up to see the boss of the Red Wings. Adams was surprisingly hospitable, and after some mental gymnastics he finally remembered the name Broda. When Turk asked if he could meet some Red Wings, Adams was impressed with his enthusiasm and provided him with a ticket for the exhibition game that night.

"They were like two kids on a picnic," said Adams after watching Broda and Bruneteau at the Winnipeg Amphitheater that night. "They took in every move. Once in a while they would excitedly talk to each other, pointing out some particularly good play. I figured if two kids were that interested in becoming hockey players, they would certainly be worth a look."

Minutes after the game ended, Adams invited Broda and Bruneteau to the Detroit Red Wings' training camp the following autumn. Turk was 20 years old when he showed up at the Red Wings' base, an exuberant, naive hayseed who immediately became the butt of veterans' jokes. Detroit boasted two splendid goalkeepers at the time, John Ross Roach, a veteran, and Normie Smith, a young and gifted goalie destined to start in the minors with the Detroit Olympics. Broda was around for laughs.

There were plenty of laughs. One afternoon, Roach and Smith approached Turk with a sheaf full of papers. "Broda," said Roach, "don't you think it's time you joined the union?"

Turk was baffled, a not uncommon reaction for him in those days. "What union?" "Are you kidding?" snapped Roach. "Don't you know that we goalies have our own association—the Goaltenders' Union? You should become a member." Oozing with pride, impressed that so distinguished a player as John Ross Roach had invited him to join the association, Turk quickly peeled off the $25 "dues" requested by his elder. The ploy ended when veteran goalie Alex Connell, who was looking on, nearly fell over backward with laughter.

Turk was returned to the minors, and Conn Smythe bought his contract from the Detroit organization in 1936. Leaf fans wondered who Broda was, but they soon found out.

Turk finished his critical rookie year as a Maple Leaf with a 2.32 goals-against average, fifth best in the eight-team league, but so close

to pacesetters Davey Kerr, Norm Smith, Wilf Cude, and Tiny Thompson that Broda had proved he belonged with the best, at least for the moment.

The Maple Leafs' accent-on-offense style of play made it enormously difficult for Broda to win the Vezina Trophy, but carefree Turk didn't seem to mind. "Sure those goal-hungry forwards can make life tough for me," he said, "but I don't mind as long as Mr. Smythe and the fans don't expect me to lead the league in shutouts."

Broda did win the goaltender's acme, however; in fact, he won the Vezina twice (1941 and 1948), helped the Leafs to six Stanley Cups, and eventually earned immortality in the Hall of Fame.

MARTIN BRODEUR

BORN: Montreal, Quebec, May 6, 1972
POSITION: Goaltender, New Jersey Devils, 1993–
AWARDS/HONORS: Calder Memorial Trophy, 1994; William M. Jennings Trophy (shared with Mike Dunham), 1997–98; NHL All-Rookie Team, 1994; NHL Second Team All-Star, 1997–98

By the 2000–01 season, Marty Brodeur had two Stanley Cup rings, several years of miniscule goals-against averages, and a reputation as one of the best puckhandling goaltenders to ever play in the NHL.

Martin Brodeur, New Jersey Devils goalie

However, Brodeur's greatest contribution to hockey may be that he disproved the old adage that all goaltenders were high-tension nuts.

Amiable, good-humored, and almost completely unflappable, Brodeur rarely let on-ice incidents get to him, remaining calm amidst the chaos around him, while still mustering the intensity necessary to win consistently at the most demanding position in hockey.

Martin had unique access to the NHL world when growing up, as father Denis, himself once an Olympic goaltender for Canada, was the team photographer for the Montreal Canadiens. As he grew older, Martin was influenced by goaltenders such as Patrick Roy, but was even more impressed by Ron Hextall, due to his puckhandling skills. He was also influenced by Soviet great Vladislav Tretiak, and Brodeur's style, a butterfly/stand-up hybrid, with an emphasis on puckhandling, reflected all these men.

As a child, Brodeur played both forward and goal, and his experiences as a forward helped him develop his puckhandling skills, which made him almost a third defenseman.

Drafted in the first round by the Devils in 1990, he joined New Jersey for good in the 1993–94 season. He started the season alternating with Devils veteran Chris Terreri, but by the time the playoffs rolled around, Brodeur was the man.

Few goaltenders had such a playoff experience in their rookie year, as the Devils won in seven games against the Sabres, including a quadruple-overtime loss in Game Six, and lost to the Rangers in the epic seven-game Eastern Conference finals, this time in double-overtime.

In the lockout-shortened 1995 season, the Devils won it all for the first time in their history. Brodeur went 16–4, with a 1.67 goals-against average in backstopping New Jersey to the Cup.

Over the next few years, Brodeur's regular season numbers would look better and better, but the Devils would experience postseason heartache year after year. In 1996, they did not even qualify for the postseason, and three subsequent years of early exits left the Devils organization embarrassed and somewhat frustrated.

There was particular criticism that Brodeur's regular season numbers were meaningless when he could not encore the big one. Although the team was unable to score sufficiently, some games—particularly Game Seven against the Penguins in 1999—could be fairly laid at Brodeur's door.

But a retooled Devils team entered the 2000 playoffs having fired their coach with eight games left in the season, and proceeded to eradicate memories of recent postseason ineptitude.

After an astounding rebound from being down three games to one against the Flyers in the Eastern finals, Brodeur outdueled the Dallas Stars' Eddie Belfour in the Cup final, backstopping the Devils to the Cup in a double-overtime win in Game Six. Before that overtime win, Brodeur and the Devils had lost their last seven overtime playoff games.

But in 2001, the defending champion Devils lost their hold on the Cup in a seven-game showdown with the Ray Bourque-led Colorado Avalanche, after leading the series three games to two and losing Game Six at home.

Through it all, Brodeur consistently worked to improve his game. His stickhandling and poke checks around the net were some of the best in the game and he even scored two goals, one each in the regular season and the playoffs.

Martin Brodeur was not the perfect goaltender; he could still be beaten on the occasional wraparound or the odd, soft long shot. But the unflappable French-Canadian also became the youngest netminder ever to reach 300 career wins and succeeded in garnering at least 30 wins every single regular season, through 2001–02.

HERB BROOKS

BORN: St. Paul, Minnesota, August 5, 1937
POSITION: Olympic Coach, Team USA, 1980, 2002; Coach, New York Rangers, 1981–85; Minnesota North Stars, 1987–88; New Jersey Devils, 1992–93; Pittsburgh Penguins, 1999–2000

As American hockey icons go, Herb Brooks ranked as *the* man.

Brainy, yet brash, politically incorrect, yet powerfully intellectual, the Minnesota native put the most powerful imprint on Uncle Sam's hockey map of any homebred talent.

Brooks's signature accomplishment was coaching the overwhelmingly underdog U.S. Olympic hockey team to a gold medal in 1980. Yet two decades and two years later, Herb continued to exert his spell over American hockey as head coach of the Star-Spangled team at Salt Lake City. It was a daunting task to say the least but those who knew Brooks best— among them, his aide, Lou Vairo—insisted that Herbie was the man for the job.

"Herb is one coach who does not have to earn the respect of his players," says Vairo. "They all know what he's accomplished in the hockey arena."

Vairo had the unfortunate timing to coach the American Olympians in 1984, four years after Brooks had orchestrated the "Miracle on Ice" at Lake Placid in 1980. Brooks and Vairo were teamed to go for another gold in 2002. Unfortunately for Brooks, his team fell short of another gold, but settled for a respectable silver, after Canada came alive at the end of the Olympic Games.

Most critics agree America's win over the vaunted—and thoroughly professional—Soviet team in 1980 ranks as the greatest single hockey upset of all time.

"I didn't want an 'I, me, myself' organization," said Brooks. "There is a wealth of hockey expertise around the country, so I wanted to get those people involved."

One of those who knew Brooks better than most was USA Hockey's senior director of International Administration, Art Berglund, who observed the evolution of Brooks for more than 40 years.

"Herb has both a great love and spirit for the game of hockey," said Berglund. "He also appreciates the American tradition going back to the Jack Rileys, Bill Clearys, and Dave Christians who made a name for Uncle Sam in the past," said Berglund.

Art even remembered Herb when Brooks tried out for the 1960 Olympic team, winding up as the last cut on the squad.

"Herb was a real good player," Berglund recalls. "I remember his energy driving down the right wing. He played the game like a fat man likes to eat. And the spirit he had as a player rolled over into his coaching."

Disdaining the philosophy of the "politically correct," the St. Paul native tilted with "the establishment," while vigorously advancing ideas to improve the ice game.

As coach of the New York Rangers in 1981, Herb startled traditionalists with his use of the long pass and a European style accenting artistry and individuality along with the North American aggressive style of forechecking. Brooks said: "What I introduced in New York was atypical of general coaching then. Craig Patrick, who was general manager, and I brought a different approach. We introduced such things as body fat tests, which had been ignored by the teams, and we tried new ways of playing the game. My idea was to 'stretch' the zones; to get more out of the available space."

Brooksian techniques helped a smallish Rangers team upset Philadelphia's Broad Street Bullies in a stunning 1982 playoff. "The Flyers had one of their big teams then," Brooks said, "and made it seem like the series would be easy for them. In fact, they referred to our club as 'The Smurfs' because, as a group, we were so much smaller. But our skilled players prevailed and we wound up beating their big men, dazzling them with our footwork and skill." He also stirred a cauldron of controversy for allegedly calling top defenseman Barry Beck a coward, not contributing at his peak.

Brooks-watchers said it was a classic case of the coach playing mind games.

"Mind games? Of course I play mind games," said Herb. "What else am I going to do? What is a coach supposed to do? I'm supposed to tug everything I can out of the team. This is a tough business. It's show business. I am not going to be your friend; nobody's guaranteed anything here."

Brooks's NHL tour of duty also included stints behind the bench in New Jersey, Minnesota, and, most recently, Pittsburgh. Following in his tradition of upsets, the Brooks-led Penguins upended the favored Washington Capitals in the first playoff round of 2000. By 2002, Brooks assumed the role of director of player personnel for the Pens.

To Midwest hockey fans, Herb was best known as the man who turned the University of Minnesota into a collegiate powerhouse. Not surprisingly, the 1980 Olympic team was well-sprinkled with Minnesota natives. "I had a lot of Minnesota kids on the team and I didn't want to display favoritism," said Brooks. "By design, I was withdrawn, I didn't want their personalities to influence the decision I had to make. So I treated them all the same, all bad!"

Some of the Brooks alumni, such as 1980 hero Steve Janaszak, would agree; with a chuckle, of course.

"Every team I played on for five years always felt a common bond," said Janaszak. "Twenty guys who all hated Herb. You knew that the guy sitting next to you had been through the same crap."

In seven seasons with the University of Minnesota Gophers, he won three NCAA championships. Brooks would tell his varsity candidates, "The best compliment I can give you is a jersey."

MUD BRUNETEAU

BORN: St. Boniface, Manitoba, November 28, 1914
DIED: April 15, 1982
POSITION: Right Wing, Detroit Red Wings, 1935–46

On March 24, 1936, the Detroit Red Wings and the Montreal Maroons played the longest NHL game ever. By the time the Maroons and Red Wings had played through the second overtime without a goal, the crowd began to get restless. The players, of course, were laboring on badly chopped ice that didn't have the benefit of modern resurfacing machines. Nevertheless, they plodded on past midnight with no end in sight.

When the sixth period began, a cascade of cheers went up from the previously numbed crowd. Perhaps they hoped to inspire the Maroons to a spirited rush and a score, but this didn't happen. Despite the hour, the majority of spectators remained in their seats. The monumental contest had become an obsession with both players and fans. Everyone was determined to see it through to a conclusion.

Four minutes and 46 seconds after the ninth period began, the teams had broken the longest-game record set by Toronto and Boston and, still, there was no end in sight. It was past 2 A.M. and many spectators were fighting to keep their eyes open, not wanting to miss the decisive goal if it ever was to be scored.

By this time the veterans of both teams were fatigued beyond recovery. It was essential to employ the players with the most stamina left, and, naturally, those were the inexperienced younger skaters. One of them was Modere "Mud" Bruneteau, a native of St. Boniface, Manitoba, who had played the previous season for the Wings' minor-league team, the Detroit Olympics.

As a rookie on a loaded first-place club, Bruneteau had seen little action. But he was young, and at the 12-minute mark of the ninth period, Mud Bruneteau was in better shape than most of his teammates—or opponents.

Bruneteau gathered the puck in the Detroit zone and passed it to Hec Kilrea. They challenged the Montreal defense, Kilrea faking a return pass, then sliding it across the blue line. Bruneteau cut behind the defense and retrieved the puck. "Thank God," he said, "Chabot fell down as I drove it in the net. It was the funniest thing. The puck just stuck there in the twine and didn't fall on the ice."

Referee Nels Stewart put up his hand as a signal, and after 116 minutes and 30 seconds of overtime the Red Wings had defeated the Maroons, 1–0.

Bruneteau continued as a second-stringer with Detroit, and it wasn't until the war years, 1941–46, with the Red Wings depleted, that he saw regular action. His career-high 35 goals came in 1943–44, but by 1948–49, "Mud" retired into the coaching ranks.

JOHN BUCYK

BORN: Edmonton, Alberta, May 12, 1935
POSITION: Left Wing, Detroit Red Wings, 1955–57; Boston Bruins, 1957–78
AWARDS/HONORS: Lady Byng Memorial Trophy, 1971, 1974; NHL First Team All-Star, 1955, 1963–65, 1970–71; NHL Second Team All-Star, 1968; Lester Patrick Trophy, 1977

John Bucyk, one of the most unobtrusive players on a strong and flashy Bruin squad, spanned two decades of Boston hockey history, performing his tasks on left wing through some of the best and the worst years that team ever witnessed.

Bucyk played junior hockey with the Edmonton (Alberta) Oil Kings, came to the NHL with the Detroit Red Wings in 1955, and two years later was traded to Boston for goaler Terry Sawchuk.

In Boston, Johnny was reunited with Bronco Horvath and feisty Vic Stasiuk, with whom he had played in Edmonton, and the Uke Line (for Ukrainian) came into being. The world looked rosy that season, with the Bruins making the Stanley Cup finals in 1958. It was Horvath who coined Bucyk's nickname, "the Chief," after his straight ebony hair, swarthy complexion, and stoic visage.

In 1958–59, Bucyk was so good at digging the puck out of the corners for linemate Horvath that Bronco came within two points of winning the scoring title, behind Bobby Hull.

But the goals of the Uke Line were to no avail, for Boston dropped to fifth place that year, and when Horvath was drafted by Chicago and Stasiuk traded to Detroit, the Uke Line became a thing of the past.

Bucyk continued his efficient ways, but the Bruins mopped up the basement for six years, and were next-to-last another two. It wasn't until 1967–68 that Boston, with Orr, Esposito, Hodge, Cashman, and, of course, John Bucyk, once again climbed to the top of the NHL.

Bucyk's life then became one of setting records while his more spectacular teammates, Orr and Esposito, broke bigger ones or more of them, leaving the Chief in the shadows, which he seemed to prefer.

In 1978, after 23 seasons and 1,540 games, Bucyk retired with 556 goals and 813 assists for a total of 1,369. That placed the Chief in fourth place on the NHL list of all-time career point leaders—quite an achievement.

Johnny continued his loyalty to the Bruins organization both in public relations and in the broadcast booth.

HY BULLER

BORN: Montreal, Quebec, March 15, 1926
DIED: August 3, 1968
POSITION: Defenseman, Detroit Red Wings, 1943–45; New York Rangers, 1951–54
AWARDS/HONORS: NHL Second Team All-Star, 1952; NHL All-Star Game, 1952

During the six-team era of the NHL, several outstanding skaters remained buried in the minors. When Rangers manager Frank Boucher finally acquired Hy Buller—one of the few Jewish skaters in the NHL—in 1951 from the Cleveland Barons' farm club, he was a seasoned pro who could play a solid defense yet bolster the attack with his hard shots from the blue line.

His value was proven in his rookie season with election to the second All-Star team. He retired prematurely after the 1953–54 campaign. The reasons behind Buller's retirement always have remained enshrouded in mystery. One theory had it that a series of debilitating injuries had caused Buller to lose his playing edge and rather than play mediocre defense, he chose to gracefully leave the NHL. Another theory was that Buller had become disenchanted with the game's violence and was depressed over a series of dangerous collisions with some NHL headhunters, and that he decided to retire rather than risk serious injury.

BILLY BURCH

BORN: Yonkers, New York, November 20, 1900
DIED: December 1950
POSITION: Defenseman/Forward, Hamilton Tigers, 1922–25; New York Americans, 1925–32; Boston Bruins, 1932; Chicago Blackhawks, 1932–33
AWARDS/HONORS: Hart Memorial Trophy, 1925; Lady Byng Memorial Trophy, 1927; Hockey Hall of Fame, 1974

A star with the Hamilton Tigers of the National Hockey League, Billy Burch led a revolt of players against management in the spring of 1925. During the playoffs, Hamilton players complained that they were underpaid. They went on strike, whereupon the NHL suspended the franchise. When the Hamilton sextet was transferred to New York to become the Americans, Burch and teammate Jackie Forbes each got $20,000 for three-year contracts. Burch starred for the Amerks through the 1931–32 season. He split the following season between Boston and Chicago. That was his last season in the NHL. Despite his lengthy NHL career (11 years), Burch appeared in only one playoff, 1928–29, but scored neither a goal nor an assist.

PAVEL BURE

BORN: Moscow, USSR, March 31, 1971
POSITION: Right Wing, Vancouver Canucks 1991–97, Florida Panthers, 1997–2002; New York Rangers, 2002–
AWARDS/HONORS: Calder Memorial Trophy, 1992; Maurice "Rocket" Richard Trophy, 2000–01; NHL First Team All-Star, 1994; NHL Second Team All-Star, 2000; NHL All-Star Game, 1993–94, 1997–98, 2000–01

In the late 1980s, the Soviet Central Red Army Team (CSKA) thought it had its line of the future, with Sergei Fedorov centering for wings Alexander Mogilny and Pavel Bure.

Instead, Mogilny landed in Buffalo, Fedorov in Detroit, and Bure, "The Russian Rocket," took his jet-powered skates and magnificent scoring touch to the Vancouver Canucks.

Although Bure's NHL career was a rollercoaster ride of exaggerated ups and downs, the appeal of the most exciting goal scorer in the NHL more than made up for the hiccups that came along.

Bure first put on skates at age six, and was trained unceasingly during his childhood by father Vladimir, a former Olympic swimmer. By age 16, Pavel was accomplished enough to join CSKA, practicing against established stars more than ten years his senior.

He was the Soviet National League Rookie of the Year in 1988–89, but gradually lost his linemates as Mogilny defected in 1989, and Fedorov slipped away from the Goodwill Games in 1990.

Meanwhile, in Vancouver, tremendous expectations had built up, and when Pavel joined the Canucks in 1991, he entered a world that was part hockey and part hype. Vancouver literally went crazy for the kid.

His on-ice performance gave fans good reason to go nuts; Bure was a small, but extremely strong, quick, and fearless player. His skill and ability to control the puck recalled his idols, Boris Mikhailov and Valeri Kharalmov, and his goals were often of the highlight-reel variety. Although he wasn't much for defensive play, the offensive upside almost always had fans coming out of their seats.

Bure didn't disappoint in the early years in Vancouver, winning the Calder Trophy in his rookie year, netting 60 goals in his second, and leading the Canucks to the seventh game of the Stanley Cup finals in 1994.

That, however, is when the weirdness began.

Rumors circulated that Pavel had threatened not to play in Game Five of the finals unless his contract was torn up and immediately renegotiated. Pat Quinn, then Canuck general manager and coach, verified later that one of Bure's agents did make the threat. Bure said he knew nothing of it and, in any case, didn't believe it.

Whatever the truth, relations were now strained between Bure and Canucks management, and they would never again be the same.

The next few years were frustrating for Bure, as he blew out a knee in 1995 and wasn't truly back on form until 1997–98, when he scored 51 goals. On top of that, new rumors— about his connections to the Russian Mob— were circulating, disturbing both the Canucks and the NHL.

Then the other shoe dropped: Bure demanded to be traded and swore he'd never play for the Canucks again. He held out for five months before he was dealt to the Florida Panthers for Ed Jovanoski, Dave Gagner, Kevin Weekes, Mike Brown, and a first-round draft choice in January 1999.

Bure delighted Florida fans with 11 goals in 12 games before blowing out his knee again, ending his season. In 1999–2000, he was back with a vengeance, scoring 58 goals without a regular centerman and capturing the first ever "Rocket" Richard Trophy. However, both Bure and the Panthers disappeared in the first round of the playoffs versus New Jersey, and team attendance dwindled despite Bure's billing.

In 2000–01 and 2001–02, the Panthers continued to grossly underachieve, leading to a March 2002 trade with the Rangers for Igor Ulanov and a package of prospects and draft picks. Bure, reenergized and delighted by moving to Broadway, was not enough to help New York attain a postseason berth, but managed to electrify the Madison Square Garden crowd by scoring 11 goals in his first ten games as a Blueshirt, including one in his first game at the arena.

SEAN BURKE

BORN: Windsor, Ontario, January 29, 1967
POSITION: Goaltender, New Jersey Devils, 1987–91; Hartford Whalers, 1992–97; Carolina Hurricanes, 1997–98; Vancouver Canucks, 1998; Philadelphia Flyers, 1998; Florida Panthers, 1998–99; Phoenix Coyotes, 1999–
AWARDS/HONORS: NHL All-Star Game, 1989, 2001–02

What Sean Burke did best since his rookie National Hockey League season was to bail out seemingly hopeless teams. In one magnificent campaign, he actually lifted the New Jersey Devils into the franchise's first playoff (1988).

Since then, Burke has been a netminder singularly underblessed by performers in front of him; one who could have been treated for "rubberitis," the affliction that confronts goalies who face too many pucks in too short a time.

Drafted by New Jersey in 1985, Burke starred for the Canadian Olympic team and was regarded as one of the most promising young goalies on the continent. When he arrived at East Rutherford after the 1988 Olympics, the Devils were going nowhere fast and appeared destined to miss another playoff berth.

En route to the playoffs, Burke posted a 10-1-0 record and a 3.05 goals-against average. His mental toughness was remarkable, considering that he joined a club that literally could not afford to lose more than one game. He played his angles confidently and skated fluidly in the crease.

Sean's bubble eventually burst in the seventh game of the 1988 Wales Conference finals against the Boston Bruins, which the outmanned Devils lost 6–2, but he had become New Jersey's main man in goal. In 1988–89, his first full year in the NHL, he became the first NHL rookie and first Devil to start an NHL All-Star game. Over two seasons, Sean set a team record with 54 career victories.

However, in the 1989–90 playoffs Burke played two games, lost them both, and came out of it with a 3.84 goals-against average. Meanwhile, the Devils' second goalie, Chris Terreri, had shown enough improvement to earn more playing time, at Burke's expense. After the 1990–91 season, Burke decided not to return to Jersey and signed with the minor league San Diego Gulls of the former International League as well as the Canadian Olympic team. Burke won a silver medal with the Olympians. The Devils still owned his NHL rights and eventually Sean was traded by New Jersey to the Hartford Whalers for Bobby Holik and Jay Pandolfo.

For five straight years Hartford missed the playoffs, yet Burke remained the workhorse when not sidelined by injury. Then, in the spring of 1997, owner Peter Karmanos moved the team out of Hartford to Carolina, where they became the Hurricanes. The changes did not instantly make the transformed club a playoff contender, but Sean's focus remained unchanged.

In 1998, Sean bounced to Vancouver and Philadelphia and finally to Florida, where he played for two seasons. He was then traded to Phoenix in 2000, where he led the Coyotes to a playoff run. By the the 2001–02 season, when the Wayne Gretzky-owned Coyotes were decimated by the previous trades of stars Jeremy Roenick and Keith Tkachuk, it was Sean Burke who turned in an MVP-caliber performance in leading a young pack of Coyotes to an unexpected berth in the Western Conference.

PAT BURNS

BORN: St. Henri, Quebec, April 4, 1952
POSITION: Coach, Montreal Canadiens, 1988–92; Toronto Maple Leafs, 1992–96; Boston Bruins, 1996–2000; New Jersey Devils, 2002–
AWARDS/HONORS: Jack Adams Award, 1989, 1993, 1998

His steely eyes, car-bumper mustache, and flaming hair set Pat Burns apart from his peers. By a lot.

The Montreal native was the quintessential bench cop, figuratively and literally, as he moved with extraordinary speed through the coaching ranks after years of undercover work for the Gastineau, Quebec, police force.

As a rookie NHL mentor, he led the Montreal Canadiens through the playoffs to a 1989 six-game final series before capitulating to the Calgary Flames.

For a time, it appeared that Burns would be a fixture on St. Catherine Street West as long as the Forum was intact. He originally arrived in the Habs dressing room upon the departure of Jean Perron's regime and immediately made sense out of the chaos.

"That's one place where my police background comes in because I really don't give a damn," said Burns. "I'm just an ordinary person who has been on the street and worked nine to five. It wouldn't bother me to go back to my police work."

The hard-line approach worked in Burns's favor when, as a part-time coach of the Hull Olympiques, he was offered the full-time gig by then-team owner Wayne Gretzky, who thought Burns was NHL material. Sure enough, after making it to the Canadiens' top affiliate in Sherbrooke, Burns assumed the reins in Montreal in 1988, and seized the Adams Division title with a .719 winning percentage, as well as the Jack Adams Award. For four straight years (1988–89 through 1991–92), Burns was the NHL's top bench boss with a 174–104–42 record.

Pat orchestrated the best one-season turnaround ever in Toronto, when the Leafs went from 67 points in 1991–92 to 99 points in 1992–93, and also captured the Jack Adams Award in 1993, becoming the second man to win the honor for two different teams. In 1993–94, he guided the Leafs past Detroit and San Jose before bowing to the Vancouver Canucks.

The ex-cop's grinding coaching style, although effective, did not arrest the imagination in terms of offensive creativity, and infuriated opponents and observers who preferred more excitement to The Game. Even after twice guiding the Maple Leafs to the Conference finals in 1992–93 and 1993–94, Pat was out of a job again by 1996.

But the mercurial Burns soon found himself coaching in another Original Six city—Boston—by 1997–98, where he pushed the Bruins into identical records of 39–30–13 in his first two seasons, earning himself another Jack Adams Award. Although instrumental in helping many rising young Bruins, like Joe Thornton, elevate their game, Burns was dismissed during the 2000–01 in favor of contemporary Mike Keenan, as the team struggled to win. However, during the summer of 2002, Burns was back in the majors as head coach of the New Jersey Devils.

WALTER BUSH

BORN: Minneapolis, Minnesota, September 25, 1929

Walter L. Bush Jr. was involved in hockey most of his life, serving as a player, coach, manager, administrator, and team owner. He played at the high school, college, and senior levels and his senior team won three Minnesota state championships. After playing amateur hockey for 22 years, Bush got into team management, starting with the 1959 U.S. National team, leading them to the IIHF World Championship in Prague, Czechoslovakia.

In 1964, Bush served as general manager of the U.S. Olympic team. He was also special assistant to United States Olympic Committee president Bill Hybl for the U.S. delegation at the XVIII Olympic Winter Games in Nagano, Japan. He later became a member of the board of directors of the United States Olympic Committee and secretary of the U.S. Olympic Foundation.

On the international level, Bush served as one of 11 members of the International Ice Hockey Federation Council and, in June 1998, was reelected to a second consecutive term as vice president of the IIHF. Bush was also active with numerous committees within the IIHF, having served as chairman of the IIHF Women's Ice Hockey Committee, the IIHF In-Line Hockey Committee, and the Selection Committee for the newly-created IIHF Hall of Fame. As chairman of the IIHF Women's Ice Hockey Committee, Bush was instrumental in organizing the first IIHF Women's World Championship, held in 1990 in Ottawa, Ontario, Canada. He also led the successful campaign to make women's ice hockey a medal sport in the Olympic Winter Games beginning in 1998 in Nagano, Japan. Bush was president of the Minnesota Amateur Hockey Association for three years, owner and president of the minor-league Minneapolis Bruins from 1963–65, and led a group of businessmen in securing a National Hockey League franchise— the Minnesota North Stars—for the Twin Cities area. He became the North Stars' first president, from 1967–76, and a chairman of the board. For 17 years, Bush worked with various institutions within the NHL, later moving to the American Hockey League to become one of two principal owners of the Kentucky Thoroughblades.

Bush was given hockey's highest honor when he was elected to the Hockey Hall of Fame in Toronto in 2000, for which he also served as a governor and vice chairman. He was also given the NHL's Lester Patrick Award in 1973 in recognition of his outstanding service to ice hockey in the United States. He entered the U.S. Hockey Hall of Fame in 1980, where he was also a director and member of the selection committee, and was elected to the Minnesota Sports Hall of Fame in 1989.

One of the most recognized and respected leaders in the sport, Bush became president of USA Hockey in June 1986 after serving as a member of the organization's board of directors since 1959. In 2002, Bush was honored with the Olympic Order, the highest possible individual award for international athletics.

HERB CAIN

BORN: Newmarket, Ontario, December 24, 1912
DIED: September 15, 1982
POSITION: Left Wing, Montreal Maroons, 1933–38; Montreal Canadiens, 1938–39; Boston Bruins, 1939–46
AWARDS/HONORS: Art Ross Trophy, 1944; NHL Second Team All-Star, 1944

Herb Cain is best remembered for leading the NHL in scoring with Boston during the 1943–44 season (82 points in 48 games), and least remembered for nearly killing himself accidentally during a practice one afternoon when he played for the Canadiens (1938–39) while ebullient Tommy Gorman was Montreal's creative manager. At the time, Gorman was obsessed with the idea that too many of his veterans were lugging the puck behind the net before heading for enemy territory. His lectures on the subject proved fruitless, and finally Tommy decided that more drastic measures had to be taken. So, just prior to a practice session, he walked out onto the ice armed with a couple of hundred yards of thick rope. With the help of some rink attendants, Gorman attached the rope to the goal net and then extended it to each of the sideboards, thereby creating what amounted to a roadblock from the goal line to the end boards. The players were not to skate behind the net before starting a rush.

Unfortunately, Gorman neglected to inform all his players of the scheme, and Herb Cain, who was the first on the ice, had no idea a barricade had been erected. Typical of an enthusiastic skater, Cain leaped on the ice and pursued the puck, which happened to be sitting a few feet behind the rope. Herb's interest was so consumed with the puck he completely ignored the rope. By this time Cain had picked up speed and was hurtling at about twenty miles an hour when he started what was to be a circling of the net with the puck. Before the startled rinksiders could shout a warning, Cain struck the rope at neck level, became enmeshed in the twine, and, with the momentum behind him, began whirling upside down like a miniature Ferris wheel. He ultimately landed on his back and was knocked unconscious when his head struck the hard ice. Luckily, his injuries proved not to be serious. The rope was never seen again at the Forum.

FRANK CALDER

BORN: Bristol, England, November 17, 1877
DIED: February 4, 1943

Originally secretary of the old National Hockey Association, Frank Calder was named the first president of the National Hockey League when it was formed in 1917. A nonplayer, it may well have been the fact that Calder was a calm Scotsman that helped him form the solvent, strong base that is today's wealthy NHL. The league presented the Calder Trophy and later the Calder Memorial Trophy for rookie-of-the-year honors to commemorate the service of this avid hockey fan. Calder, a member of the Hall of Fame, died February 4, 1943.

CLARENCE CAMPBELL

BORN: Fleming, Saskatchewan, July 7, 1905
DIED: June 24, 1984
POSITION: Referee, 1929–40; President of NHL, 1946–77; Honorary Chairman of the Board of the NHL, 1977–84
AWARDS/HONORS: Lester Patrick Trophy, 1972; Clarence S. Campbell Bowl in his honor, 1973; Hockey Hall of Fame, 1966

President of the National Hockey League from 1946 through 1977, Clarence Campbell was one of sport's more maligned figures. He also brought the game into the public eye on both sides of the border, led the league through numerous expansions, and survived many an owner's and player's tirade.

When Campbell returned from World War II, he immediately went to work for Red Dutton, then head man of the NHL. Campbell had been close to the sport. "Although I wasn't ever much good at hockey, I was good enough to play in Europe when a Rhodes scholar." He had refereed in the NHL, and Dutton had a specific job in mind for the 41-year-old bachelor as they headed to a league governors' meeting.

"As we were walking out of the office, Red turned to me and said, 'By the way, when we get to the meeting, I'm going to resign and recommend you for president of the league.' That was the first I heard of it, or anybody did for that matter. The owners voted on it and they gave me a raise to $10,000 and put me in charge.

"Being a referee was enormously valuable. As a referee, you condition yourself to accept criticism. You learn to live in an atmosphere of hostility. As a commissioner, you are almost like an official. From the start everything is against you, and you'd better understand that."

The NHL endured many changes under Campbell. It went from a solid, six-team organization to twice that size in one swoop in 1967. The advent of the slap shot and the increase of fighting were big revisions from the game Campbell once officiated. It was

Campbell's misfortune to be best remembered for suspending Maurice Richard just before the 1955 playoffs. Richard had just been the instigator (or victim, as the Rocket claimed) in a bloody ruckus in Boston.

"I had warned him after an almost identical incident in Toronto," Clarence said, "that I would suspend him if it ever happened again. He had been making a profit out of every fine I laid on him. If I fined him $250, he would get $2,500 in donations. You can't tolerate such a frustration of league authority.

"The violence in the league then had reached an alarming stage. The blood had to stop. I'd drive to games with the owners, and they were petrified at what might happen on the ice. But they were also frightened that I would monkey with a good product."

Richard was suspended for the remainder of the season and the playoffs, and Montreal fans erupted. "You've got to remember," Campbell remembered, "this was the time of an enormous sociological upheaval. It was just the beginning of the French movement, and the only man in Quebec better known than Richard was the prime minister."

Campbell claimed he never thought twice about attending the next Canadiens game at the Forum. Escorting his secretary, Phyllis King, who later became his wife, and two other women, the league president calmly strode to his seat, despite the hatred and ugly catcalls emanating from the Forum fans. Bottles and vegetables were hurled at the NHL boss during the opening period. In the intermission, a fan threw a punch at him. Eventually, the Forum erupted into a riot and the game was forfeited.

Perhaps Campbell could have avoided much of the uproar at the Forum that night by simply staying home. But his presence at that contest, and his firmness in the Richard decision, established his authority once and for all.

"It's funny," he once said, "but until I made that decision, I was never really acknowledged as the head of the NHL."

In 1977, Clarence Campbell stepped down and turned the presidency over to John A. Ziegler Jr., and became Honorary Chairman of the Board. After 31 years of distinguished service, respect and dignity are the best words to describe what Clarence Campbell meant to the NHL. The league honored him with the naming of the Campbell Conference in 1974–75 (renamed the Western Conference in 1994), as well as the creation of the Clarence S. Campbell Bowl, awarded to the playoff champion from that conference.

GUY CARBONNEAU

BORN: Sept-Îles, Quebec, March 18, 1960
POSITION: Center, Montreal Canadiens, 1982–94; St. Louis Blues, 1994–95; Dallas Stars, 1995–2000
AWARDS/HONORS: Frank J. Selke Trophy, 1988–89, 1992

When Guy Carbonneau was drafted by Montreal in 1979, the Canadiens were undergoing transformation. The retirement of key players such as scorer Yvan Cournoyer and two-way forward Jacques Lemaire meant the Habs were looking for replacements.

Based on Carbonneau's prolific scoring for Chicoutimi of the QMJHL, fans in Montreal probably expected another Cournoyer, but they got a player in the mold of long-time Montreal captain Bob Gainey—a defensive expert who was never afraid to do the dirty work.

So how did a player who lit up junior hockey become the ultimate defensive weapon? Through hard work, heart, courage, and dedication to being the ultimate team player.

In the end, Carbonneau always put the team before himself and his statistics.

Guy did not change into a two-way player overnight; the QMJHL was never known for defensive play and he never had been expected to provide it before. Although his coaches were working with him on the defensive aspects of the game, in his first minor-pro season, Carbonneau was still mainly an offensive player.

After a second impressive year in the minors, Guy moved up to the NHL for good.

Guy started as the Habs' fourth line center and got little ice time. However, injuries gave him the chance to show his penalty-killing skills, and soon he was matched with Gainey to shut down the opposition's top lines. They stayed together for the next six years, and Carbonneau sharpened his skills playing beside Gainey, then the NHL's premier defensive forward.

Over the next few years, the Canadiens became more and more defensively oriented, and Carbonneau's ability to check, block shots, and win face-offs, combined with his speed, skill, and incredible pain threshold, made him a key building block of the Montreal system. Although he was a steady point contributor, defense came first.

In 1986, Carbonneau helped lead a very young Canadiens team to the club's first Cup since 1979. As usual, his defensive work was stellar, plus he scored 7 goals and 12 points in 20 postseason games.

Guy was recognized three times in a five-year period with the Selke Trophy as the NHL's premier defensive forward. In 1989, the Canadiens bestowed the team's ultimate honor on Carbonneau, making him their captain.

The 1992–93 regular season was not kind to Carbonneau, as he played the least games and had the lowest goal, assist, and point total of his career to that point. There was some speculation that he might be done, at least in Montreal.

An unexpected trip to the Cup finals, propelled by Patrick Roy's goaltending heroics, changed everything. Carbonneau was given the important role of shadowing Wayne Gretzky and the Habs won it all when it was least expected.

Guy stayed in Montreal and had a good 1993–94 season, but mounting tensions with Canadiens management eventually came to a head in the summer of 1994, when he was traded to the St. Louis Blues for Jim Montgomery. General manager Serge Savard, who had never appreciated Carbonneau's candor with the press, refused to forgive him for a public incident with a photographer and took the opportunity to move him.

A year later, Carbonneau was moved to the Dallas Stars for Paul Broten. Dallas must have seemed like Montreal with a Texas drawl, since his general manager was Bob Gainey, and many of the players and coaching staff were ex-Habs.

Dallas was acquiring players who knew how to win, and in 1999, it all paid off with a Stanley Cup, the first for Dallas, and the third for Carbonneau.

Carbonneau retired in 2000, after one more trip to the finals with the Stars. He moved to the Montreal organization, becoming an assistant coach, but was lured back to the Dallas organization as an aide to new coach Dave Tippett.

BOBBY CARPENTER

BORN: Beverly, Massachusetts, July 13, 1963
POSITION: Center, Washington Capitals, 1981–87; New York Rangers, 1987; Los Angeles Kings, 1987–89; Boston Bruins, 1989–92; Washington Capitals, 1992–93; New Jersey Devils, 1993–99
AWARDS/HONORS: NHL All-Star Game, 1985

Dubbed the "Can't Miss Kid" when he broke into the NHL with the Washington Capitals in 1981–82, Bobby Carpenter was glorified as the first American-born sharp-shooter who could compete on equal footing with Canadian counterparts.

Son of a Beverly, Massachusetts, policeman, Carpenter was the Washington Capitals' first choice (third overall) in the 1981 Entry Draft. His move from New England high-school hockey directly to the NHL was considered

astonishing at the time. As it happened, Carpenter proved to be a worthwhile choice, scoring 53 goals for the Capitals in the 1984–85 season, and netting at least 27 in each of his first four seasons.

The bubble burst in 1986 when Carpenter was included in what became a lopsided deal when the New York Rangers acquired him for Mike Ridley, Kelly Miller, and Bob Crawford. Ridley and Miller became longtime Caps, while Carpenter struggled on Broadway. Soon Bob was dealt with Tom Laidlaw to Los Angeles for the aging Marcel Dionne, and produced his usual numbers during his only full season for the Kings, 1987–88: 71 games, 19 goals, 33 assists, and 52 points.

In 1989, a deal sent Carpenter home to play for the Bruins, and while there, Carpenter helped the B's with two 25-goal seasons, as well as a trip to the Stanley Cup finals and the President's Trophy in 1990.

As a free agent, Bob returned to Washington in 1992–93 before signing with the New Jersey Devils the following year. While offensive production declined, Carpenter gained new fans for stellar face-off and defensive work. He later helped the 1994–95 Devils to their Stanley Cup championship over Detroit, and the "Can't Miss Kid" continued to produce until the end of his career after the 1998–99 season. Carpenter finished with a respectable 320 goals and 728 points.

Carpenter then turned to coaching. In the 1999–2000 season, he was assistant coach for the Devils when New Jersey won its second Stanley Cup. He also worked behind the New Jersey bench in 2000–01 when the club reached the seventh game of the Stanley Cup finals against the Colorado Avalanche.

He finally achieved his goal of becoming a head coach in 2001–02 when named to that position with the Albany River Rats, the Devils' top farm team in the American Hockey League.

LORNE CARR

BORN: Stoughton, Saskatchewan, July 2, 1910
DIED: Date unknown
POSITION: Right Wing, New York Rangers, 1933-34; New York Americans, 1934-41; Toronto Maple Leafs, 1941-46
AWARDS/HONORS: NHL First Team All-Star, 1943-44

One never would have figured Lorne Carr as an NHL star by his rookie season (1933-34) with the Rangers. In 14 games, he scored no goals and no assists and was traded to the New York Americans in the following campaign. It was then that he emerged as a star. Carr played excellently for the Amerks until 1941-42, when he was traded to the Toronto Maple Leafs.

In his first season with Toronto, Lorne was a vital factor in the Leafs' conquest of the Stanley Cup, as he was again in 1944-45. Carr completed his career in 1945-46 with the Maple Leafs, retiring with a total of 204 goals at a time when that was considered a very big total.

JOE CARVETH

BORN: Regina, Saskatchewan, March 21, 1918
DIED: August 15, 1985
POSITION: Forward, Detroit Red Wings, 1940-46, 1950-51; Boston Bruins, 1946-48; Montreal Canadiens, 1948-50
AWARDS/HONORS: NHL All-Star Game, 1950

The advent of World War II spelled the end of several big-league careers, as stickhandlers joined the armed forces and returned with skills dimmed beyond redemption. On the other hand, the war provided opportunities to lesser-skilled skaters who blossomed in the diluted brand of wartime hockey.

One such player was Detroit Red Wings right wing Joe Carveth, who, after several trials,

played his first full season with the Red Wings in 1942-43 and remained in the Motor City through the 1945-46 season. His best year was 1943-44, when he scored 21 goals and 35 assists for 56 points. A year later he compiled 54 points.

He was traded to Boston in 1946-47 for Roy Conacher and in 1947-48 dealt to Montreal for Jimmy Peters. He finished his NHL career back in Detroit, after being traded back to the Wings in the 1949-50 season for Calum MacKay. Carveth helped the Detroiters to a Stanley Cup championship in his NHL swan song.

WAYNE CASHMAN

BORN: Kingston, Ontario, June 24, 1945
POSITION: Left Wing, Boston Bruins, 1964-65, 1967-83; Assistant Coach, New York Rangers, 1987-92; Tampa Bay Lightning, 1992-96; San Jose Sharks, 1996-97; Philadelphia Flyers, 1998-2000; Head Coach, Philadelphia Flyers, 1997-98; Boston Bruins, 2001-
AWARDS/HONORS: NHL Second Team All-Star, 1974; Team Canada, 1972

Wayne Cashman came as close to being the distilled essence of a big, bad Bruin as anybody else on the Boston roster. No one pushed him around. What's more, no one pushed the other Bruins around whenever Wayne was on the ice. Wayne's temperament often resembled that of an aroused loan shark, but he insisted the rough stuff was a strategy, not a vendetta. "If you can get a guy to alter his game by half a step, then you've created an advantage for your team," he said.

During the second half of the 1972-73 season, a back injury prohibited him from playing his customary hard-hitting brand of hockey. Before each game and practice he was taped "like a mummy." But he never considered sitting it out. "We had won the Stanley Cup the year before," he explained. "Once you win it, you don't ever want to let it get away.

I wanted to keep playing. I wasn't going to sit back and watch some other team take it away from us."

Montreal, of course, did eventually take it away, and Cashman began a summer of extensive medical therapy for his injury. Perhaps he hadn't won the Stanley Cup, but he certainly won his private battle, not to mention added respect from a roomful of guys who had watched him win so many fights before.

Once scoring 89 points (in 1973–74), Cashman consistently contributed offense over the years, with 793 points in 1,027 games as a lifelong Bruin, serving as captain from 1977 through his retirement in 1983.

Shortly thereafter, Wayne entered the NHL coaching brotherhood, beginning as a New York Rangers assistant in 1987–88. After similar turns in Tampa Bay and San Jose, Cashman landed the head coaching post of the Philadelphia Flyers in 1997–98, and steered them to a 32–20–9 mark before stepping aside into his familiar assistant's role in favor of Roger Neilson in March of that season. Following a stint as Director of Hockey Operations for the East Coast League's Pensacola Ice Pilots, the longtime Bruin returned to Beantown as part of Robbie Ftorek's coaching staff in 2001–02.

LORNE CHABOT

BORN: Montreal, Quebec, October 5, 1900
DIED: October 10, 1946
POSITION: Goaltender, New York Rangers, 1926–28; Toronto Maple Leafs, 1928–33; Montreal Canadiens, 1933–34; Chicago Blackhawks, 1934–35; Montreal Maroons, 1935–36; New York Americans, 1936–37
AWARDS/HONORS: Vezina Trophy, 1935; NHL First Team All-Star, 1935

In the mid 1920s, it was fashionable to sign goaltenders who were small in stature on the theory that a half-pint goalie was more agile than a taller man. Montreal-born Chabot was the exception. He stood six feet one, weighed 185 pounds, and joined the original Rangers after playing for the Port Arthur (Ontario) Allan Cup champions. His goals-against averages in two seasons with New York were 1.56 and 1.79. In his second year (1928), Chabot and the Rangers won the Stanley Cup, although he suffered a serious eye injury and was replaced by coach Lester Patrick halfway through the series.

In melting-pot New York, Chabot briefly was known to fans as Lorne "Chabotsky" after the Blueshirts' press agent, Johnny Bruno, decided to attract more Jewish and Italian fans and changed Lorne's last name to Chabotsky, as well as Finnish forward Oliver Reinikka's name to Ollie Rocco. Once Canadian hockey writers caught on to the stunt and lampooned it, the players were relieved of their *noms dé glace* and Bruno was canned.

LORNE CHABOTSKY

See CHABOT

BILL CHADWICK

BORN: New York, October 10, 1915
POSITION: NHL Referee, 1940–55
AWARDS/HONORS: Lester Patrick Trophy, 1975; Hockey Hall of Fame, 1964

Bill Chadwick was unique among NHL referees, not because he was the only one ever to come from the streets of New York City, but because he was the first and only NHL zebra who only had vision in one eye!

Chadwick was a New York Rangers prospect when he suffered the hockey mishap that changed his career. It was March 1935 and he was going to play in an all-star game at Madison Square Garden.

As Chadwick stepped on the ice to start the game, he was hit in the eye by a puck accidentally fired by an opponent. After hospitalization,

Chadwick was informed he now had only one good eye.

Amazingly, he returned to play the following season with the Rangers' farm club, the New York Rovers, and this time was hit in the good eye. He quit playing at that point, although he recovered full vision in his left eye.

A few weeks later he was pressed into emergency service as an Eastern League referee, when the regular official was snowbound. He soon became a regular arbiter, then an NHL linesman, and finally an NHL referee. Bill refereed through the World War II years and then the turbulent postwar period against such irksome characters as Ted Lindsay and Gordie Howe. According to Chadwick, his disability turned out to be useful in its own way. "Because I knew about my problem," he explained, "I made it a point to be on top of the play. I skated harder and was involved in the game at all times.

"Having only one good eye didn't hamper me at all. In those days I had twenty-twenty vision in my left eye, so it was no problem. I was never far away when there was a play on the net.

"I really don't know if any of the players really knew about it," said Chadwick. "But this much I do know; in all my years I refereed and was an NHL linesman nobody said anything to me about my eye. If anybody had done it, I certainly would have remembered because I was very sensitive about it.

"On the other hand, I know that the NHL governors knew about it and I'm pretty damn sure that some of the managers like Conn Smythe, Art Ross, and Jack Adams knew."

Chadwick was regarded as one of the most competent referees ever to skate in the NHL, although some fans might take exception to that statement as they took exception to his calls. Once, in a game between Toronto and the Bruins at Boston, Chadwick called a misconduct penalty against Jimmy Thomson of the Maple Leafs. A period later he called a similar penalty against a Bruin. A Boston Garden fan was so angry he wrapped up several newspapers and swung at Chadwick.

"He knocked me cold," Chadwick recalled. "When I finally came to my senses Thomson was standing next to me and pointed out the guy who had hit me. I had him ejected from the building. A week later I got a letter from the fan apologizing for hitting me.

"I really liked what Thomson did. It proved what I already knew—that players can disagree with you all the way, but they won't let anyone interfere with your game."

Although he believed he had a few years left in his legs, Chadwick retired at the age of 39. A year later, an amazing thing happened: Bill Chadwick, a referee, was given a "night" in his honor at Madison Square Garden, probably the first and only time a referee was so honored in the NHL.

For many years, Chadwick became a favorite of Ranger fans during his stints as a radio and television analyst.

His Rangers sidekick Marv Albert nicknamed Chadwick "The Big Whistle," a nickname that remained with him for the rest of his career. Chadwick remained a popular figure in the New York Metropolitan area, frequently attending Rangers events through the late 1990s. He retired and lived on Long Island.

GERRY CHEEVERS

BORN: St. Catharines, Ontario, December 7, 1940
POSITION: Goaltender, Toronto Maple Leafs, 1961–61; Boston Bruins, 1965–72, 1976–80; Cleveland Crusaders (WHA), 1972–76
AWARDS/HONORS: NHL All-Star Game, 1969; Hockey Hall of Fame, 1985

Although Gerry Cheevers never won a Vezina Trophy, it's unlikely he was ever bothered by the omission. In Cheevers's mind, it was all about the Stanley Cup, and he got two with the Boston Bruins.

The offense-first Bruins played an attacking game that often left Cheevers on his own to stop the opponent's counterattack. Although this style drove up his goals-against average, it suited Cheevers's competitive and combative on-ice nature.

Originally drafted by Toronto, Cheevers was stuck behind several quality netminders in the Leafs' system, and Boston grabbed him in 1964 for the $30,000 waiver price.

A trip to the minors allowed Gerry to work with Harry Sinden, who supported the young goaltender, gradually rebuilding his confidence and allowing his talent to blossom.

Cheevers joined the Bruins for good in 1967 and teamed with Eddie Johnston for Boston's 1970 and 1972 Cup wins.

Although his off-ice personality was surprisingly laid-back, Cheevers was intensely competitive and he hated to lose. In fact, he hated to lose so much that he refused to stay on-ice for the traditional handshake line when the Canadiens upset the Bruins in 1971. Not that the Bruins did all that much losing with him in net; Cheevers set an NHL record in 1971–72 by playing goal through 32 unbeaten games.

In 1972, Cheevers jumped to the Cleveland Crusaders of the WHA. The move proved Cheevers was one of the best goaltenders in hockey (the Bruins suffered mightily without him) and that Cheevers had plenty of nerve, gambling with the new circuit. When Cheevers returned to Boston Garden on November 27, 1972, with the Crusaders, the 9,000 spectators knew immediately that the Bruins would never be the same without the man they called "Cheesie." He won the WHA's award for best goaltender in 1973. In 1974, he was the number one goalie for Team Canada in the series against the Soviet All-Stars.

Gerry returned to the Bruins in 1976, immediately improving the Bruins' record and putting them back into contention. He remained in Boston until his retirement in 1980.

Upon retirement, Cheevers assumed head-coaching duties for the Bruins, and served for four and a half successful seasons (1980–85) in which he recorded a .604 winning percentage and lost the Conference finals in 1983 to the New York Islanders. He joined the Bruins' broadcasting team, and remained there into the new century, where he began scouting for the B's.

For his talent, competitiveness, and durability, Cheevers was elected to the Hockey Hall of Fame in 1985.

CHRIS CHELIOS

BORN: Chicago, Illinois, January 25, 1962
POSITION: Defenseman, Montreal Canadiens, 1983–90; Chicago Blackhawks, 1990–99; Detroit Red Wings, 1999–
AWARDS/HONORS: James Norris Memorial Trophy, 1989, 1993, 1996; NHL All-Rookie Team, 1985; NHL First Team All-Star, 1989, 1993, 1995–96; NHL Second Team All-Star, 1991, 1997; NHL All-Star Game, 1985, 1990–98, 2000, 2002

For the first few years of his career, Chris Chelios was definitely a work in progress. The finished product, a three-time Norris Trophy winner, was well worth the wait.

Chelios started his career under the legendary Badger Bob Johnson at the University of Wisconsin. After finishing a tour of duty with the U.S. Olympic Team in 1984, he joined the Canadiens and was part of the Cup-winning team in 1986.

Chris was definitely still raw and, like many defensemen, needed work to develop a complete game. He had the offensive skills, especially good playmaking abilities, but still didn't have a handle on his defensive responsibilities. Too eager to get involved in the rush or pinch at the blue line, Chelios was often caught up-ice and out of position.

Chelios was schooled by some of the best, including Larry Robinson and Rick Green, learning when to gamble and when to play it safe. Once he put together the complete game, he was able to rack up the points and win a Norris Trophy in 1989.

Chris was also known for the physical aspect of his game, although it was often controversial. Some observers claimed Chelios never went after the tough guys, but targeted the opponent's skill players so he would never have to pay the price. Others, including Chelios, claim it was his job to intimidate the opponent's best players. Throughout his career, Chelios continued to pile up penalty minutes while intimidating opponents, whether through physical play on the ice, or not-so-veiled threats off the ice.

However, the Canadiens had coveted Denis Savard for ten years since skipping over him in the draft. In 1990, Montreal traded Chelios and a second-round draft pick to Chicago for Savard, ultimately one of the worst deals in recent Montreal history. Savard lasted three more mediocre years in Montreal, while Chelios was still a top NHL defender a decade later.

For many players, returning to play in their hometown is a recipe for disaster. For Chelios, it was a match made in heaven. He was part of one of the NHL's best blueline corps, and in 1992 the Hawks went to the Cup finals before being swept by Pittsburgh.

Chelios was a hometown hero, and he loved it. His high level of play netted him two more Norris Trophies in 1993 and 1996. In the mid to late 1990s, the Hawks' stubborn refusal to pay their players competitive salaries cost the team most of their talent, while Chelios grimly hung on, hoping for a turnaround in the club's fortunes.

By 1999, no turnaround was in sight. Chelios, who never imagined he'd play anywhere but Chicago, was traded to rival Detroit for the playoff run.

Detroit paired him with Niklas Lidstrom, and Chelios was asked to do less offensively. A true team player, Chelios willingly took on the less glamorous role, and the pair developed into one of the best blueline combinations in the NHL. Although he suffered a major knee injury in the 2000–01 season, Chelios returned to vintage form in 2001–02, leading the NHL in plus/minus and powered Detroit's deluxe team to the Stanley Cup in 2002.

As a three-time Norris Trophy winner, and one of the best defensemen of his generation, Chelios became a free agent in the summer of 2002, but immediately re-signed with Detroit.

DON CHERRY

BORN: Kingston, Ontario, February 5, 1934
POSITION: Defenseman, Boston Bruins, 1954–55; Coach, Boston Bruins, 1974–79; Colorado Rockies, 1979–80
AWARDS/HONORS: Jack Adams Award, 1976

Don Cherry earned the opportunity to coach the Boston Bruins after two seasons as Coach of the Year in the American Hockey League. His Rochester clubs, with no major-league affiliations, still managed to challenge for the Calder Cup, and finished first in 1973–74 in the divisional race.

His job with the Bruins was a difficult one, especially for a man who played in only one

Chris Chelios as a Chicago Blackhawks defenseman

NHL game and spent most of his playing days in the AHL. He led men like Bobby Orr and Phil Esposito, top stars for years, with only a minor-league background—a background that included four minor-league championships in his last five years as a player.

Don "Grapes" Cherry as Boston Bruins coach

Don, who was considered a top NHL coach, consistently iced winning teams. While he didn't win a Stanley Cup, he led his Bruins to the finals in 1977 and 1978.

Popular with players and fans alike, Cherry was never on any "Good Guy" list as far as officials were concerned. A chronic referee baiter, Cherry was fined on a number of occasions and during one regular season game in 1979 was banished from the bench for his actions.

A colorful spokesman and never at a loss for words, Don frequently guested as an analyst on NHL telecasts. No matter how controversial a remark, Cherry spoke his mind at the "drop-of-a-puck," and with his terrific sense of humor, became a favorite with viewers.

Although Cherry led the injury-plagued Bruins to the seventh game of the semifinals in 1978–79, the flamboyant coach and Boston management became equally disenchanted with one another when Cherry sought a substantial salary increase. Unable to come to terms, Cherry bid a sad good-bye to his players and signed a lucrative contract with the Colorado Rockies, taking on the challenge of coaching the team with the worst record in the NHL in 1979.

Cherry was relieved of the Colorado job after a dispute with general manager Ray Miron, but this proved to be a sweet use of adversity. At the behest of *Hockey Night in Canada* producer Ralph Mellanby, Cherry was invited to become an television analyst. The show, "Coach's Corner," cohosted by Ron McLean, became an instant smash on Canadian television. Thanks to Cherry, ratings soared and Cherry became a national Canadian hero. His popularity grew further after Don offered his autobiography, *Grapes,* which sold out in both hardcover and paperback.

Cherry's feuds also became legendary. One of his longest lasting battles involved his former boss, Bruins general manager Harry Sinden, whom Cherry reviled both in print and on the air. An ultimate Canadian chauvinist, Cherry was widely critical of European players until 2001, when he accepted foreign-born players on his own Junior team, the Mississauga Ice Dogs.

Among Cherry's many trademarks were his wildly unorthodox suits and tight-buttoned shirts, not to mention unabashedly critical remarks about general managers such as the Ottawa Senators' Marshall Johnston, of whom Grapes said late in the 2001–02 season, "He wouldn't know a hockey player if he tripped over Bobby Orr."

Despite critics' charges that Cherry was losing his touch and popularity in the late 1990s, the fans remained dedicated to his banter and "Coach's Corner" remained a *Hockey Night in Canada* staple into the new century.

DINO CICCARELLI

BORN: Sarnia, Ontario, February 8, 1960
POSITION: Right Wing, Minnesota North Stars, 1980–89; Washington Capitals, 1989–92; Detroit Red Wings, 1992–96; Tampa Bay Lightning, 1996–98; Florida Panthers, 1998
AWARDS/HONORS: NHL All-Star Game, 1982–83, 1989, 1997

For a player whose career was judged finished before he ever graduated from junior hockey to the professionals, Dino Ciccarelli did more than commendably as a big-leaguer.

A serious leg injury almost doomed a teenage Dino. Despite the mishap—and the fact that he was one of the smallest players in the NHL at five feet eight—Ciccarelli matured into a big-time scorer and one of the most prolific point-getters of the late twentieth century.

The diminutive-but-sturdy right-winger will forever be remembered as a grinder with soft hands who earned his living in front of the opposition's net, where he often was pummeled, and where he scored most of his 608 career goals.

Undrafted, Ciccarelli signed with the Minnesota North Stars as a free agent. As a rookie in 1980, Dino recorded 30 points in his first 32 games with the North Stars. But he would astound the hockey world by setting a playoff rookie record of 21 points (which still stands), as the North Stars reached the Stanley Cup finals and lost to the dynastic New York Islanders.

The next season, Ciccarelli trumped his early numbers and exploded for a 55-goal, 106-point season, his career high. For nine years, Dino was the shining Star of Minnesota, earning multiple All-Star berths, always ensconced in the list of top goal scorers—and biggest nuisances.

"He's like a fly that won't go away," said former NHLer Neil Sheehy. "He's buzzing around your nose and mouth, you keep swatting at him, but he won't go away."

Dino was dealt to Washington along with Bob Rouse for fellow goal-gobbler Mike Gartner and Larry Murphy in 1989. Although he would average nearly a point per game with the Caps, he would be dealt again after three seasons of playoff nonsuccess to the Detroit Red Wings. He enjoyed a resurgent 97-point season in 1992–93, but never came close to that mark again.

Dino next toiled for the Tampa Bay Lightning and Florida Panthers, neither of which made the postseason during his stay, before retiring in 1999.

With a record boasting 1,200 points, 608 goals, 118 playoff points, most power-play playoff hat tricks (two), and 1,000 games played, Ciccarelli demonstrated that a little man could be a consistent scorer in the NHL.

KING CLANCY

BORN: Ottawa, Ontario, February 25, 1903
DIED: November 8, 1986
POSITION: Defenseman, Ottawa Senators, 1921–30; Toronto Maple Leafs, 1930–37; NHL Referee, 1937–49; Coach, Toronto Maple Leafs, 1953–56; Vice President, Toronto Maple Leafs, 1967
AWARDS/HONORS: NHL First Team All-Star, 1931, 1934; NHL Second Team All-Star, 1932–33; NHL All-Star Game, 1934, 1937; Hockey Hall of Fame, 1958

Some good old Irish luck intruded to help Maple Leafs manager Conn Smythe obtain one of the most genuinely colorful characters hockey has known, Francis "King" Clancy, whose ancestors lived among the peat bogs and rich grassy fields of Ireland.

Frank "King" Clancy, Toronto Maple Leafs defenseman

The son of Thomas Clancy, Frank was born in Ottawa and was practically pushed into sports by his burly father. Unfortunately, young Frank was slightly built and it was not uncommon to hear a despairing neighbor complain: "Tom's youngster will never be the athlete his father is; he's just too small."

But Frank developed an indefatigable spirit, which was complemented by his natural hockey talent. Despite his size, he joined the best amateur club in Ottawa, and, according to one observer, "His courage and speed and nervy play began to gain him a reputation among fans and players alike." When young Clancy was only 18, he decided he was ready for the NHL.

So did Thomas Gorman, manager of the NHL Ottawa Senators, who heard about Clancy's exploits in the city league. He sent an invitation to Clancy to visit the Senators' office for a conference. But Gorman had difficulty suppressing his laughter when he saw the 125-pound Clancy. "And you want to play defense?" chortled Gorman with amazement. "Okay, put on your skates and come out to practice. If you make the team, I'll sign you for three years at $800 per season."

The Ottawa skaters were not merely good; they represented the cream of Canada's hockey players, Stanley Cup champions in 1920 and 1921, with such legendary stickhandlers as George Boucher, Eddie Gerard, Sprague Cleghorn, and Frank Nighbor. When they realized what a surplus of gutsiness Clancy possessed, even to dare to skate with them, they obliged by passing him the puck to see what the kid could do.

Ron McAllister wrote in *Hockey Heroes:* "Everyone who watched his debut marveled at the confidence of the Irish lad as he sailed into the Stanley Cuppers as though they were all kids together playing shinny on a local rink!"

When practice concluded, Clancy received the equivalent of a standing ovation; the veteran Senators patted him generously on the back and wished him well. Gorman was among the first to congratulate Clancy, but he remarked that his size was more suited to the library than the hockey rink. He handed Clancy a contract as a substitute player and said: "We'll put fifty pounds of rock salt in your shirt to weigh you down!"

The two shook hands, and Clancy became a Senator substitute, collecting splinters on the bench during his rookie season. But irrepressible Frank was destined to crack the big team, and soon he was pressed into service as a utility skater, even playing goal. His weight leaped to 147 pounds, and before Gorman could shake his head in disbelief, Clancy had earned a spot on the first team. As a member of the Ottawa club, Clancy played on four Stanley Cup winners and appeared to be a fixture in the capital city. Then the Depression began, and the Senators' attendance dropped off at an alarming rate. By the time the 1930–31 season approached, the Ottawa management needed money fast. There was only one thing to do: Peddle a star to a wealthier club.

The most attractive star on the club was none other than "King" Clancy. Thus the Senators played right into Conn Smythe's hands. Conn was looking for a colorful superstar, and the moment he heard about Clancy's availability, he decided to get him. There was only one problem—Smythe didn't have the money. He knew he would lose Clancy to the Rangers or Blackhawks if he didn't find the cash somehow. Always a gambler, Smythe pulled off yet another daring move.

Smythe had become a horse racing buff, and he owned a colt named Rare Jewel, who just happened to be running at Woodbine Racetrack in Toronto at that time. The odds were 100–1 against Rare Jewel (optimistic odds at that), yet Smythe put his bankroll on his horse and then cheered him on to an astonishing victory. With the winnings he had enough money to purchase Clancy.

Smythe bought Clancy from Ottawa for $35,000 and threw in two extra players, Art

Smith and Eric Pettinger, who were worth a total of $15,000 on the NHL market. Clancy cost Smythe $50,000 but he proved to be worth every penny of it. "King" would help Toronto get to the Stanley Cup finals four times, with a Stanley Cup win in only his second year with them, 1931–32. He later became an NHL referee and ultimately a vice president of the Maple Leafs.

To honor the noble Clancy, the NHL Board of Governors instituted the King Clancy Memorial Trophy in 1988, two years after Clancy's death, which was awarded each season thereafter to a player who "best exemplifies leadership qualities, on and off the ice, and has made a noteworthy humanitarian contribution in his community."

DIT CLAPPER

BORN: Newmarket, Ontario, February 9, 1907
DIED: January 20, 1978
POSITION: Right Wing/Defenseman, Boston Bruins, 1927–47; Coach, Boston Bruins, 1945–49
AWARDS/HONORS: NHL First Team All-Star, 1939–41; NHL Second Team All-Star, 1931, 1935, 1944; NHL All-Star Game, 1937, 1939; Hockey Hall of Fame, 1947

Aubrey "Dit" Clapper played his first ten years in the NHL as a star forward and last ten years as a top-flight defenseman, all with the Boston Bruins.

Dit Clapper, a tower of strength whether playing right wing or defense, labored for the Boston Bruins for 20 consecutive seasons. During his long and distinguished career with the powerhouse Bruins, he helped them to six championships and three Stanley Cups. Clapper scored well over 200 goals and was named to the All-Star team six times.

Clapper's most memorable seasons as a forward came when he, Cooney Weiland, and Dutch Gainor combined to form the feared Dynamite Line. This trio swept the Beantowners to the 1929 Stanley Cup. With Dit's aid, the Bruins lost only five games in the entire 1930 season, but they were defeated in the playoffs by the Montreal Canadiens.

In 1939, after ten years as one of the premier forwards in the league, Clapper made the switch to defense. Paired with the legendary Eddie Shore, Dit made First Team All-Star and the Bruins again won the Stanley Cup.

Clapper saw double duty as a player-coach during his last three years with the Bruins until his retirement as a player in 1947. He continued on as a coach of the Bostonians from 1945–46 through 1948–49 and was elected to the Hall of Fame in 1947.

WENDEL CLARK

BORN: Kelvington, Saskatchewan, October 25, 1966
POSITION: Left Wing, Toronto Maple Leafs, 1985–94, 1996–98, 2000; Quebec Nordiques, 1994–95; New York Islanders, 1995–96; Tampa Bay Lightning, 1998–99; Detroit Red Wings, 1999; Chicago Blackhawks, 1999
AWARDS/HONORS: NHL All-Rookie Team, 1986

Wendel Clark's job was to wreak havoc, and he did it very well. Throwing his five-feet-ten body into the fray as if he were a foot taller, Clark became a folk hero to Leafs fans.

Drafted first overall by Toronto in 1985, Clark had been an award-winning defenseman in junior hockey. He joined the Leafs for the 1985–86 season as a left wing and abandoned all pretense of playing defense for the rest of his career.

Although Clark would never score more than 80 points in a season, to Toronto fans, his wrecking-ball playing style was worth losing a few points. Unfortunately for Wendel, it also led to continual absences due to injury.

In his prime, Clark scorched wicked wrist shots past goaltenders, hit anything that moved, and willingly dropped the gloves with all comers. When he hit, whether with his body or his fists, he hit hard and he hit to hurt.

Clark was no playmaker and got many assists when teammates, trailing in his wake, picked up his rebounds as he caused havoc in front of the net. His actual passing skills were practically nonexistent, nor did he look to improve them.

The most successful playoff years for Wendel, named Leafs captain in 1991, were 1992–93 and 1993–94. The Leafs went to the Western Conference finals both years, but were eliminated by Los Angeles and Vancouver.

Clark's "take no prisoners" approach to the game was a heavily-desired quality, and after the 1993–94 season, Toronto traded Clark, Sylvain Lefebvre, Landon Wilson, and a first-rounder to Quebec for Mats Sundin, Garth Butcher, Todd Warriner, and Quebec's first-rounder.

Clark's game deteriorated as his body began to break down even more often. He was traded to the Islanders in 1995 for Claude Lemieux, then went back to Toronto in 1996 for Kenny Jonsson and a first-round pick. On his return to Toronto, Clark scored on his first shift, while delirious Leafs fans screamed, "Wendel, Wendel."

Clark wandered through the NHL between 1998 and his retirement in 2000, playing for Tampa Bay, Chicago, and returning briefly to the Leafs before hanging them up for good.

Toronto fans would always remember Clark in his prime, intimidating opponents with his shot, his hits, and his heart. He worked as a community representative for the Leafs after retirement, epitomizing the club to fans who always adored him.

BOBBY CLARKE

BORN: Flin Flon, Manitoba, August 13, 1949
POSITION: Center, Philadelphia Flyers, 1969–84; Vice President/General Manager, Minnesota North Stars, 1990–92; Florida Panthers, 1993–94; President/General Manager, Philadelphia Flyers, 1984–90; 1994–; General Manager, Team Canada, 1998
AWARDS/HONORS: Hart Memorial Trophy, 1973, 1975–76; Bill Masterton Memorial Trophy, 1972; NHL First Team All-Star, 1975–76; NHL Second Team All-Star, 1973–74; Team Canada, 1972; NHL Challenge Cup, 1979; Lester Patrick Trophy, 1980; Frank J. Selke Trophy, 1983; Hockey Hall of Fame, 1987

In a roundabout way it could be said that the Philadelphia Flyers' 1974 Stanley Cup was won on the ice of Moscow's Sports Palace in September 1972. That was when Team Canada defeated the Soviet National Hockey Club, and Robert Earle "Bobby" Clarke, the diabetic kid from northerly Flin Flon, Manitoba, emerged as the most sought-after player, according to Russian hockey experts. "Clarke is the one NHL hockey player we like watching the most," said a Soviet hockey official. "We have rarely seen [a man] work so hard on the ice."

The Russian bigwig echoed a sentiment that was often repeated on the North American continent, where Clarke was regarded as one of the finest centers in the NHL. Clarke returned from the Russian series to win the coveted Hart Trophy, as the league's most valuable player, for the 1972–73 season—a feat he repeated in 1975 and 1976. After 15 seasons as the team's franchise player, Clarke became the team's all-time leader in games (1,144), assists (852), points (1,210), shorthanded goals (32), playoff points (119), and playoff games (136).

The hockey-mad town of Flin Flon, one of the coldest spots in Canada—not surprisingly, since it's not all that far from the Arctic Circle—is a major mining area in the province of Manitoba and one of the foremost producers of young hockey talent. Like many crack stickhandlers, Clarke played junior hockey for the Flin Flon Bombers.

However, professional scouts were aware that Bobby was a diabetic and, not surprisingly, scorned him as a potential NHL prospect. Even the Flyers overlooked him at first. But, under the prodding of bird dog Gerry Melnyk, they decided to take a gamble. Three years after Melnyk's recommendation, Bobby was voted Flyers' captain, the youngest leader in the NHL. He was also a prime architect in the ascendency of Philadelphia as a hockey power. In the spring of 1973, the Flyers reached the Stanley Cup semifinals for the first time, before being eliminated by Montreal in five tough games. It was during this series that Clarke first gained attention as a less-than-dainty combatant.

The Canadiens said he was downright dirty; the Flyers countered, he was tough, not dirty. This much was clear: Clarke played the game extraordinarily hard, and by 1973–74 everybody knew it.

"Forget the baby face," said *Philadelphia Inquirer* columnist Frank Dolson, "the easy smile, the refreshing modesty. When the game begins, the face grows hard, the young man grows mean. For a couple of hours a night, 78 nights a year—plus playoffs—the sweet, lovable guy who scores all those goals and kills all those penalties and wins all those games for the Flyers turns into one of the meanest so-and-so's in the NHL." And that from a home-town critic.

As for his coach at the time, Fred Shero said, "Bobby's like a leech. Check, check, check.

Bobby's the ultimate competitor. He'll fight everybody and beat 'em."

Clarke, like other Flyers, grew to resent accusations that his club reached the top at the point of a hockey stick. Quite the contrary. "You don't have to be a genius to figure out what we do on the ice," said Clarke. "We take the shortest route to the puck, and arrive in ill humor!"

Such was Clarke's deportment during the 1973–74 season as he captained his troops to the Clarence S. Campbell Bowl, emblematic of the West Division championship, and into the astonishing 1974 Stanley Cup playoffs. He was a tower of strength as Philadelphia breezed past Atlanta in four straight games and knocked out tough Rangers center Walt Tkaczuk in the opening game of the semifinals. "My defenseman, Moose Dupont, pushed me," said Clarke, "and my shoulder accidentally hit Tkaczuk in the head."

Clarke went about the business of knocking the Rangers out of the playoffs. Against Boston in the finals, he went head-to-head with rival center Phil Esposito, and won so many face-offs from the Boston ace that Beantown papers wondered if Phil had lost his touch.

That, of course, was not the case; it was merely that Clarke had become so much better. Likewise, his Flyers had become so strong that they eliminated Boston in six, capped by a stirring 1–0 victory at the Spectrum. When the game ended, Clarke, who figured the Flyers could do it all along, cradled the Stanley Cup to his chest and skated proudly around the ice with hockey's number one prize.

The Clarke-led Flyers captured the Stanley Cup again in 1975 against the Buffalo Sabres and reached the finals the following year, where they lost to the Canadiens. It appeared that after their two Cup victories, many of the Flyers lost their hunger and hustle. In 1980, Clarke's Flyers lost to the New York Islanders in a classic Stanley Cup final series that concluded in six games.

Clarke finally retired in 1984 to become the Flyers' vice president and general manager, a role that would bring him near-success on numerous occasions. He gave Mike Keenan his first NHL stint as head coach, but the Flyers lost in the 1985 and 1987 finals to the dynastic Edmonton Oilers. Clarke departed in 1990 to become general manager of the Minnesota North Stars, who overachieved their way to the 1991 finals against the Mario Lemieux-led Pittsburgh Penguins, but lost in six games.

In 1993, Clarke was hired as the Florida Panthers' head honcho. Icing a competitive team of veteran grinders, Clarke's tenure resulted in a record .494 winning percentage for an expansion franchise, which narrowly missed a playoff berth in the last week of the season. But two years later, the Panthers made the Stanley Cup finals, with Bryan Murray in Clarke's place running the team.

Returning to the general manager's post in Philadelphia in 1994, Bobby built the Flyers into the Eastern Conference's most consistent challenger. The additions of Eric Desjardins, John LeClair, and wunderkind Eric Lindros, a mean, hulking player in Clarke's image, transformed the Flyers into a formidable playoff foe. Led by Lindros, Philly came close to a Cup again in 1997, but were swept by the Detroit Red Wings.

Problems in key areas at the most critical moments appeared to prohibit Clarke's team from advancing farther in the playoffs, despite three first-place Atlantic Division titles in 1994–95, 1995–96, and 1999–2000 and finishing no lower than second in Clarke's tenure. Coaches (Terry Murray, Wayne Cashman, Craig Ramsey, and Roger Neilson) and goaltenders (John Vanbiesbrouck, Garth Snow, Ron Hextall, and Sean Burke) came and went. But when Lindros feuded with Clarke during the 1999–2000 season over the team's medical practices, Clarke responded by stripping Lindros's captaincy, and ultimately sat on his asset until the right deal came along.

With both sides trading verbal barrages in the press, Clarke, incensed with the situation and feeling his organization had been hurt, finally dealt Lindros to the New York Rangers in the summer of 2001 for Kim Johnsson, Jan Hlavac, Pavel Brendl, and a draft pick. Meanwhile, with the tremendous additions of Jeremy Roenick at center and ex-linemate Bill Barber behind the bench in 2001, Clarke resiliently remained a general manager who was as potent behind the scenes as he had been on the ice.

The Flyers made an embarrassingly quick exit to Ottawa in 2002's first-round playoff, and while Clarke's position was intact, Barber was replaced by Ken Hitchcock by mid May.

ODIE CLEGHORN

BORN: Montreal, Quebec, 1891
DIED: July 13, 1956
POSITION: Forward/Goaltender, Montreal Canadiens, 1918–25; Pittsburgh Pirates, 1925–26, 1927–28; NHL Referee, 1930s

Few big-leaguers can make Odie Cleghorn's claim of having been a forward, goaltender, and referee in the National Hockey League. The Montreal-born skater played for the Canadiens from 1918–19 through 1924–25 and completed his NHL career spending the next two seasons with the Pittsburgh Pirates.

Cleghorn attained notoriety of sorts in Boston, when he was a referee, as the culprit in a strange Stanley Cup episode between the Maple Leafs and Bruins in the mid 1930s. The clubs were matched in a short two-game series, total goals to count. Boston won the opener, 3–0, in Boston Garden. The second match, at Maple Leaf Gardens in Toronto, saw Boston lead, 1–0, in the first period. Toronto now was behind four goals to none and the Leafs' ace Charlie Conacher was being effectively checked by Boston's Red Beattie. Toronto defenseman King Clancy suggested a strategy to help turn things around:

"Why don't you go out and belt Beattie?" Clancy asked. "Give it good to the sneaky bastard."

"I'd get a penalty," Conacher said.

"So what's a penalty?" asked Clancy, who later became a referee. "Look, I'll get the puck and pass it to you just when Beattie's near you. When he gets close, whack him!"

Conacher obeyed the instructions of his Irish playmate. He jammed an elbow into Beattie's flushed features, but Odie Cleghorn, a tolerant referee, overlooked the foul. A few minutes later Clancy tripped Eddie Shore, the meat and sinew of the Boston team. Cleghorn also missed that infraction, to Shore's very vocal chagrin: "Trip, Odie! I was tripped!"

Clancy, skating in malicious circles, stimulated Shore's wrath. "The man's blind, Eddie! He's robbin' you, sure as hell! Look how he blew the call on Beattie!"

Then Red Horner, a few minutes later, deflected a shot from Art Jackson past Tiny Thompson in the Boston goal. The Bruins, led by Shore, clamored around Cleghorn, vehement in their insistence that Horner had been illegally standing inside the goal crease.

Clancy's urchin sense of opportunity stoked the turmoil. "Eddie," he bawled at Shore, "what a lousy decision! You're bein' robbed blind. Blind!"

Shore's temper came untied. He shot the puck at Cleghorn, hitting that distinguished gentleman in the middle of his ample rear.

"You're gone!" the referee hollered. "That'll cost you a two-minute penalty!"

Injustice fanned Shore's indignation. He picked up the puck and pitched it into a delighted Toronto crowd.

"And that'll be ten minutes more!" the referee said, as he added a misconduct penalty to the minor.

While Shore was gone, fuming, the Leafs scored four goals to grab a 5–4 lead on the round. They kept scoring after he returned, finally winning the game, 8–3, and the series, 8–6. Conacher scored three goals and assisted on two others, but on most scorecards Clancy and Cleghorn were responsible for needling the Bruins into elimination.

SPRAGUE CLEGHORN

BORN: Montreal, Quebec, 1890
DIED: July 11, 1956
POSITION: Defenseman, Ottawa Senators, 1919–21; Toronto St. Patricks, 1921; Montreal Canadiens, 1922–25; Boston Bruins, 1926
AWARDS/HONORS: Hockey Hall of Fame, 1958

Sprague Cleghorn was a Montreal native and a big, capable leader. "He was a product of a rough neighborhood," said the late Bobby Hewitson, then curator of hockey's Hall of Fame, "where everything you got you had to fight for. He played hockey the same way. You could be sure that Sprague was well fitted for it."

Anyone who had doubts about Cleghorn's toughness should have been in the Ottawa rink on the night of February 1, 1922. Sprague had played three years for the Senators and saw no reason why the Ottawa sextet had dealt him to Montreal. He made no effort to conceal his hatred for the Senators' management, and on this night he took out his hostility on any member of the opposition who happened to get in his way, injuring Eddie Gerard, Frank Nighbor, and Cy Denneny in the process. Referee Lou Marsh said in his report that he considered Sprague and his brother Odie "a disgrace to the game."

Nonetheless, the "disgrace to the game" played well enough to be inducted into the Hockey Hall of Fame in 1958.

BILL CLEMENT

BORN: Buckingham, Quebec, December 20, 1950

POSITION: Center, Philadelphia Flyers, 1971–75; Washington Capitals, 1975–76; Atlanta Flames, 1976–80; Calgary Flames, 1980–82

AWARDS/HONORS: NHL All-Star Game, 1976, 1978

As a Flyer, Bill Clement usually remained in the shadow of his more ostentatious teammates, but this didn't prevent him from ripening to stardom and helping Philadelphia win the Stanley Cup against the Boston Bruins in 1974, nor did it block his outstanding career as a top hockey analyst.

He was traded to the Washington Capitals in 1975 for a first-round draft choice, but during the 1975–76 season was on the move once again, this time to the Atlanta Flames for Gerry Meehan, Jean Lemieux, and a first-round draft choice. There, in 1978, Bill registered a career-high 50 points.

A good, hard skater, and an excellent defensive specialist, Clement concluded his playing career with the Calgary Flames in 1982 and moved to broadcasting. By the 1990s, Bill became the top NHL hockey color commentator for ESPN. Paired often with Gary Thorne, the duo eventually would work the 2002 Olympics, as well as call the Stanley Cup finals each season for ESPN. Bill's voice and sharp commentary became so recognizable that he was included on interactive hockey video games and ESPN's on-line chat rooms, where fans would seek his expert analysis.

PAUL COFFEY

BORN: Weston, Ontario, June 1, 1961

POSITION: Defenseman, Edmonton Oilers, 1980–87; Pittsburgh Penguins, 1987–92; Los Angeles Kings, 1992–93; Detroit Red Wings, 1993–96; Hartford Whalers, 1996; Philadelphia Flyers, 1996–98; Chicago Blackhawks, 1998; Carolina Hurricanes, 1998–2000; Boston Bruins, 2000

AWARDS/HONORS: James Norris Memorial Trophy, 1985–86, 1995; NHL First Team All-Star, 1985–86, 1989, 1995; NHL Second Team All-Star, 1982–84, 1990; NHL All-Star Game, 1982–86, 1988–94, 1996–97

Along with Mark Messier, Wayne Gretzky, Grant Fuhr, Jari Kurri, and Kevin Lowe, Paul Coffey was an integral element in the Edmonton Oilers' run to three Stanley Cups from 1984 through 1987.

Watching Paul Coffey play was like viewing pieces at an Art Nouveau exhibition: He was flowing, graceful, and natural. It didn't hurt that he also skated at supersonic speed. A lyrical skater in the Bobby Orr mode, Coffey was one of the best offensive defensemen of the post–WHA/NHL merger era.

His effortless style propelled him from one end of the rink to the other on offensive forays and also enabled him to sprint back on defense when necessary.

Although he will never be remembered for pure defensive skills, Coffey was spectacular when playing for a team that didn't need him to play basic defense in the regular season. Unfortunately, only three of his teams—Edmonton, Pittsburgh, and Detroit—could afford that luxury.

Coffey was drafted sixth overall by Edmonton in 1980, and joined the team that fall. He had only 9 goals and 32 points in his rookie year, but that was the calm before the scoring storm. Over the next few years, the Oilers' high-powered offense was driven more and more by the defense jumping up into the play. This evolution in style, along with Coffey's role as the Oilers' power-play quarterback, sent his point totals into the stratosphere.

In 1985 and 1986, Coffey won the Norris Trophy, which was somewhat controversial, since some felt that Coffey wasn't really a defenseman, but a center who happened to call himself a defenseman. Truly, in 1986 there was no way to deny him the award, as his 139 points were the second most in history for a defenseman, and his 48 goals were the most ever scored by a blueliner.

Coffey was a huge part of the Oilers' Cup winners in 1984, 1985, and 1987. He became disenchanted when the Oilers refused to renegotiate his contract (as they had done for other key cogs in the Oiler machine) in 1987 and held out for a trade.

In 1987, the Oilers dealt Coffey, Dave Hunter, and Wayne Van Dorp to the Pittsburgh Penguins for Craig Simpson, Dave Hannon, Moe Mantha, and Chris Joseph. Pittsburgh was a team on the rise, featuring a high-powered offense anchored by Mario Lemieux. Coffey fit right in, and helped the team win the Cup in 1991.

However, Coffey was traded to Los Angeles in 1992 for Brian Benning, Jeff Crychrun, and a 1992 first-round draft pick. The situation in LA looked promising, as he joined several of his old Oiler teammates, including Wayne Gretzky. However, the Kings' offense was not good enough to cover Coffey's lack of defensive play, and he moved to Detroit in 1993.

Over the next few years, Detroit grew into a powerhouse. Although Coffey's defensive play didn't improve, Detroit's overall excellence hid his flaws. Coffey had an excellent offensive year in the lockout-shortened 1995 season, and again won the Norris Trophy. However, before Detroit annexed the Cup, Coffey was traded again.

In 1996, he was traded to Hartford with Keith Primeau for Brendan Shanahan, and after a few months, Coffey, who was displeased by the trade, was moved to Philadelphia.

Over the next few years, Coffey played for the Flyers, Blackhawks, Hurricanes, and Bruins. Although he could still skate like the wind, he rarely played a full season, playing on teams that needed well-rounded defensemen, never Coffey's forte.

In 2000, Boston released Coffey. Although he did not immediately retire, no one had knocked on his door begging to sign him by the end of the 2001–02 season.

For his magnificent offensive contributions to the game, Paul will no doubt find the Hall of Fame knocking on that door.

ERIK COLE

BORN: Oswego, New York, November 6, 1978
POSITION: Left Wing, Carolina Hurricanes, 2002–

Stanley Cup history has shown that players who have remained in obscurity during the regular season suddenly emerge as major factors in the playoffs.

This was never more evident than in the 2001–02 season. Rookie Erik Cole was not even one of the three finalists for the Calder Trophy as NHL Rookie of the Year at the end of the regular campaign. But once the playoffs started—Carolina vs. New Jersey in round one—the six-feet, 185-pound left wing emerged as a dominant force.

Going head-to-head with crack defensemen such as Scott Stevens of the Devils, Cole displayed the savvy of a veteran power forward and was regarded by critics as a key factor in the Hurricanes six-game triumph over New Jersey.

Cole, the first NHL star product to come from Oswego, New York, continued his stellar play in round two and round three victories over Montreal and Toronto, respectively.

By the Stanley Cup finals—Carolina versus Detroit—Cole had become so dangerous that the eventual champion Red Wings gave him special attention. When the playoffs were over,

Cole had a total of six goals and three assists, by far the best of any rookie in the playoffs, including a game-winning tally.

NEIL COLVILLE

BORN: Edmonton, Alberta, August 4,1914
DIED: December 26, 1987
POSITION: Defenseman/Center, New York Rangers, 1935–49; Coach, New York Rangers, 1950–51
AWARDS/HONORS: NHL Second Team All-Star, 1939–40, 1948

Although he was the elder Colville (older than Mac by two years), Neil Colville remained in the NHL longer than his kid brother. After a one-game trial in 1935–36, Neil became a regular in 1936–37 and a star with Mac and Alex Shibicky, giving the Rangers one of the NHL's strongest lines—until the linemates enlisted in the Canadian Armed Forces. When the war ended, the Colvilles reacted differently to the competition, in 1946–47. Mac played 14 games and then retired. Neil scored 4 goals in 60 games but did not retire.

He was switched to defense, teaming with Frankie Eddolls. The change worked so well that Neil won a spot on the NHL's Second All-Star team. He remained a Ranger until 1949, playing 14 games and then calling it quits. In the fall of 1950, he became the Rangers' coach, but failed to deliver a playoff team, and soon his ulcer caught up with him and Neil retired.

CHARLIE CONACHER SR.

BORN: Toronto, Ontario, December 10, 1909
DIED: December 30, 1967
POSITION: Right Wing, Toronto Maple Leafs, 1929–38; Detroit Red Wings, 1938–39; New York Americans, 1939–41; Coach, Chicago Blackhawks, 1948–50
AWARDS/HONORS: Art Ross Trophy, 1934–35; NHL First Team All-Star, 1934–36; NHL Second Team All-Star, 1932–33; Hockey Hall of Fame, 1961

There are those who insist even today that Charlie Conacher was the most exciting player they had ever seen and that his shot was the hardest of its day, when slap shots were unheard of and a player beat a goaltender with a quick snap of his wrist.

Scouting Conacher was easy. Charlie learned his hockey on Toronto's Jesse Ketchum Public School rink, and he learned all other sports from his older brother, Lionel, who would be voted Canada's Athlete of the Half-Century. Charlie broke in as a goalie, but he soon moved to the front line. However, his career was nearly ended at the age of ten when he developed a passion for mountain climbing, a rather illogical choice in Toronto, where the elevation rarely climbs much above sea level. To overcome this problem Charlie would find bridges on which to practice his mountaineering techniques.

One day in 1920, he challenged the Huntley Street span in Toronto, which crossed a ravine. Young Conacher was proceeding smartly through the iron supports on the underside of the bridge when he missed a steel stepping area, lost his balance, and plummeted some 35 feet to the ground below.

At this point fate intervened, and Charlie was intercepted by a pine tree, which cushioned his blow so perfectly that he escaped with only minor scratches, or so it seemed. Unknown to him at the time, his kidney was damaged, but that injury was not to affect him until much later in his life.

When autumn came, Conacher was able to play hockey, and he continued to improve each winter. He eventually became captain of Selke's Marlboros in 1926, a club that won the Memorial Cup for Canada's Junior championship.

Conacher's booming shot was his forte, but his skating still left something to be desired. Thus, when Smythe announced that Charlie had made the team for 1929–30, straight out of Juniors, there was considerable surprise.

Charlie made his NHL debut on November 14, 1929, at the Mutual Street Arena. Chicago's Blackhawks, with the redoubtable Charlie Gardiner in goal, were the opponents, and fans filling the old Toronto ice palace were frankly skeptical of Conacher's ability to skate and shoot with the pros, especially since he had never had basic hockey training in the minor leagues.

The game was close, but Charlie was never out of place. At one point the puck came to him as he skated over the blue line. Conacher caught it on the blade of his stick and in the same motion flung the rubber in Gardiner's direction. Before the Chicago goalie could move, the red light had flashed, and Charlie Conacher was a Leaf to stay.

Not long after that he once again proved himself, this time against brother Lionel, who skated defense for the New York Americans. In no time, Charlie left his brother befuddled with a series of "dekes," skated past Lionel's belated attempt at a body check, and fired the puck past goalie Roy Worters.

At first, Smythe used Conacher on a line with Joe Primeau at center and Harold "Baldy" Cotton on left wing. Just before Christmas, 1929, Smythe pulled Cotton off the line and inserted Busher Jackson in his place on right wing. Hockey's first and most renowned "Kid Line" was born.

Success was as dramatic as a volcanic eruption. Toronto defeated the Blackhawks, the Canadiens, and the Maroons right after Christmas and went undefeated until January

23 of the new year. Charlie went on to become one of the most dynamic of NHL forwards. He later took a turn at coaching the Chicago Blackhawks with considerably less success than he had had as a player.

LIONEL CONACHER

BORN: Toronto, Ontario, May 24, 1901
DIED: May 26, 1954
POSITION: Defenseman, Pittsburgh Pirates, 1925–26; New York Americans, 1926–30; Montreal Maroons, 1930–33, 1934–37; Chicago Blackhawks, 1933–34
AWARDS/HONORS: NHL First Team All-Star, 1934; NHL Second Team All-Star, 1933, 1937; NHL All-Star Game, 1934; Hockey Hall of Fame, 1994

An amazing specimen of a man, Lionel Conacher was chosen Canada's Athlete of the Half-Century (1900–50). He was a superstar in hockey even before that word was invented, despite the fact that shinny was only his third or fourth best game.

Lionel "Big Train" Conacher turned pro in 1926 as a defenseman with the Pittsburgh Pirates of the NHL. During his second season in Steel City, Lionel was traded to the New York Americans, where he shuttled back and forth from defense to forward for the next three seasons. Conacher developed into a dangerous scoring threat with the Amerks, but really preferred blue line duty.

In 1931, Conacher was traded to the Montreal Maroons for Red Dutton, but couldn't shake the bad habits he had picked up on the Gay White Way. After three seasons with Montreal, Conacher was again traded, this time to the Chicago Blackhawks and the watchful eyes of coach Tommy Gorman.

Lionel settled down to some serious hockey playing with the Hawks and led them to the 1934 Stanley Cup while making First Team All-Star. Through a complex, three-cornered deal, Big Train found himself back with the

Maroons the following season where he was on another Cup-winning squad.

Conacher played two more years with the Maroons, making the All-Star team in 1937, his last year as a player. Later in life he was elected to a seat in Parliament, where he died of a heart attack during his term of office.

ROY CONACHER

BORN: Toronto, Ontario, October 5, 1916
DIED: December 29, 1984
POSITION: Left Wing, Boston Bruins, 1938–42, 1945–46; Detroit Red Wings, 1946–47; Chicago Blackhawks, 1947–52
AWARDS/HONORS: Art Ross Trophy, 1949; NHL First Team All-Star, 1949; NHL All-Star Game, 1949; Hockey Hall of Fame, 1998

There were five boys—and five girls—in the famed Ben Conacher clan in Toronto as the Roaring Twenties unfolded. Some of them became bywords in Canadian sport. Lionel was the best-rounded of the group and Charlie was the most exciting on ice. Dermott was a fine football player, but later gave up sports for a regular job. Roy and Bert, younger twin brothers, appeared destined for NHL stardom, but Bert was blinded in his left eye when he was 16 and never had a pro career.

Roy did, however, make it to the top. He first starred for the Bruins from 1938–39 through 1945–46. Boston traded him to Detroit in 1946–47. Roy had a productive season scoring 30 goals in 60 games for the Red Wings, but was always considered a rather unpredictable athlete.

He was especially close with brother Bert, and when Detroit traded Roy to Chicago in 1947 he refused to join the Blackhawks unless Bert moved with him to Chicago. Roy paid the rent and Bert agreed. Roy's wife, Fran, was philosophical. "When I married Roy," she said, "I married them both." Roy finished his career in the middle of the 1951–52 season with Chicago.

ALEX CONNELL

BORN: Ottawa, Ontario, February 8, 1902
DIED: May 10, 1958
POSITION: Goaltender, Ottawa Senators, 1924–31, 1932–33; Detroit Falcons, 1931–32; New York Americans, 1933–34; Montreal Maroons, 1934–35, 1936–37
AWARDS/HONORS: Hockey Hall of Fame, 1958

An excellent goaltender with Ottawa, then Detroit, Ottawa again, and finally the Montreal Maroons, Alex Connell played in the National Hockey League from 1924–25 through 1936–37, recording 193 victories and a lifetime 1.91 goals-against average.

He also held the record for longest shutout sequence, going six consecutive games without allowing a goal, which he achieved in the 1927–28 season. His sparkling play helped both the Ottawa Senators and Montreal Maroons win Stanley Cups in 1926–27 and 1934–35, respectively.

He had an unusual brush with death during the 1931–32 season. Playing for Detroit, Connell tended goal at Madison Square Garden against the New York Americans. The Amerks were owned by notorious Prohibition rumlord William "Big Bill" Dwyer, one of the richest

Alex Connell, Montreal Maroons goaltender

bootleggers in the country. During the game, Connell engaged in a keen argument with the goal judge and tried to hit the judge with his large goalie stick. Unknown to Connell, the goal judge was a "hit man" for Dwyer. Members of the gang tried unsuccessfully to rub out Connell after the game and only quick thinking by a cordon of police saved the goaltender's life.

Connell's career later took him to the Americans and Montreal Maroons before he retired in 1937.

BILL COOK

BORN: Brantford, Ontario, October 9, 1896
DIED: April 6, 1986
POSITION: Right Wing, New York Rangers, 1926–37; Coach, New York Rangers, 1951–53
AWARDS/HONORS: Art Ross Trophy, 1927, 1933; NHL First Team All-Star, 1931–33; NHL Second Team All-Star, 1934; Hockey Hall of Fame, 1952

Bill Cook, Rangers

Many old-timers regard William Osser "Bill" Cook as the finest right-winger of all time. Certainly he ranks among the greatest, past or present, including Gordie Howe, Bernie Geoffrion, and any number of other old goldies. What set Cook apart from the others, ironically, was his inseparability from brother Bun and Frank Boucher. Together, the Cook brothers and Boucher were the cornerstones of the sensational Ranger teams, starting in 1926–27, when the Blueshirts opened on Broadway, and through the mid 1930s. It was impossible to talk of Bill Cook without mentioning brother Bun, or their close friend and linemate, Boucher.

When the Rangers won the Stanley Cup in 1928 and again in 1933 it was Bill Cook leading the way with Bun and Boucher alongside to supply, or receive, the passes. Although he originally made his mark in Canadian pro hockey, Bill became a legendary part of the New York sporting scene and remained a Ranger until his retirement after the 1936–37 season. With Boucher as manager, he returned to New York as coach for a brief term from December 1951 through the 1952–53 season.

But Bill was best remembered as a player, and nobody remembered him better than his old pal Boucher, who described him this way:

"Bill would do most of the talking. He'd say, 'Now look, Bunny (and I knew that although he was addressing his words to Bunny he damned well meant me too), when I want that puck, I'll yell for it, and you get that damn puck to me when I yell.' On the ice, Bill's cry was the most amazing half-grunt, half-moan, half-yell that I ever heard. He'd let this weird sound out of him, meaning that he was in the clear. And he'd say in these skull sessions of ours, 'When I yell, I want the puck then; don't look up to see where I am; just put it there and I'll be there.'

"So I'd be carrying the puck and hear that goddamned crazy noise from Bill, and I'd be sure to put the puck at an angle, in advance of the sound, sort of leading him because I knew he'd be cutting in on the goal, going like hell, and I'd angle the pass, not fast or it would lead him too far, but slow so he would take it in full stride, and a lot of times I'd be lying on my back, knocked down by a defenseman just as I released the puck, and although I couldn't see anything, I'd hear the roar of the crowd and know that he'd banged it past the goaltender."

BUN COOK

BORN: Kingston, Ontario, September 18, 1903
DIED: March 19, 1988
POSITION: Left Wing, New York Rangers, 1926–36
AWARDS/HONORS: NHL Second Team All-Star, 1931; Hockey Hall of Fame, 1995

The rugged member of the famed Cooks-Boucher Line, Frederick Joseph "Bun" Cook was frequently overshadowed by his more spectacular older brother, Bill, and the smoothy, Frank Boucher. But Bun himself was a deft passer who could muck his way in the corners with the best of them. He was an original Ranger, playing on two Cup-winning teams. He was forced out of the lineup during the 1935–36 season by a recurring throat problem.

JACK KENT COOKE

BORN: October 25, 1912
DIED: April 6, 1997

They all laughed at Christopher Columbus when he said the world was round," so says the song. And they all laughed at Jack Kent Cooke when he said the hockey world would revolve around his Los Angeles Kings.

Given to braggadocio under normal circumstances, Cooke was up against a conservative board of governors when he first applied for a franchise in the expanded National Hockey League. But his salesmanship worked. The owners took his $2 million and then, almost as an afterthought, asked Cooke where he proposed to have his team play its games during 1967–68. "I'm going to build the most beautiful arena in the world," Cooke told them, "and it'll be ready sometime in the opening season."

Armed with a franchise and plans for an arena, Cooke then went about the business of building a hockey team. He hired Leonard "Red" Kelly, the former Detroit Red Wing and

Toronto Maple Leaf star, as his coach. Then, he and Kelly attended the NHL draft meeting at Montreal in June 1967, and came away with a collection of players who were conspicuous by their lack of big-league credentials. All that the Kelly-Cooke combine appeared to have in its favor was Terry Sawchuk, the onetime leading goaltender in hockey, but who, in his twilight years, was, at best, a question mark.

The Kings ended their first season in the new expansion West Division only one point out of first place. Needless to say, Cooke was voted Top Executive of the Year by the *Hockey News*.

The irrepressible Cooke always was less concerned with his opponents than they were with him. But the onetime orchestra leader and radio-station owner managed to capture more newspaper space than all eleven of his NHL owner colleagues combined; a feat that delighted him no end. "What's the fun of laying out five million dollars," demanded Cooke, "if you can't get excited about what you've bought."

Cooke had been excited as a team owner before. He had a good chunk of the Toronto Maple Leafs baseball club in the International League, until it became apparent the Leafs were losing their grasp on the public. Besides, the Leafs were minor-league and Cooke was never satisfied with anything less than the top drawer. Eventually he moved on to buy a quarter share of the Washington Redskins football team, and he paid $5,175,000 for the Los Angeles Lakers of the National Basketball Association.

By January 1968, the apologies began flowing into Cooke's office. Obviously, he had pulled a coup. Whereas the Pittsburgh Penguins had gone with jaded veterans who appeared to be "playing their last two years to entitle them to full pensions," as Cooke pointed out, the Kings' youngsters were outsprinting their rivals and just about any established team that chose to match them in speed.

On top of that was Cooke's real frosting, his monument to himself, the Los Angeles

Forum. "It must be seen to be believed," commented Eric Hutton in *Maclean's* magazine, "and maybe not even then. It is the gaudiest sports palace this side of the heyday of the Colosseum of Ancient Rome, of which the Forum is, in fact, a modernized copy."

Cooke eventually sold the team after having firmly established big-league hockey in Southern California.

SHAYNE CORSON

BORN: Barrie, Ontario, August 13, 1966
POSITION: Left Wing, Montreal Canadiens, 1986–92, 1996–2000; Edmonton Oilers, 1992–95; St. Louis Blues, 1995–96; Toronto Maple Leafs, 2000–
AWARDS/HONORS: NHL All-Star Game, 1990, 1994, 1998

Like a solid baseball player who regularly averages about .280 at bat and fields with near-impeccable precision, Shayne Corson was similarly valuable to every hockey team for which he played.

Never to be confused with a superstar, Corson nevertheless was a superior foot soldier who often delivered in the clutch. Players of his caliber were always in demand, and brought a cupboard of intangibles that inspire honors, such as Corson's selection to the 1998 Canadian Olympic team in Nagano.

Corson's boardwork and crease-crowding were an impressive part of his game that prompted the Montreal Canadiens to draft him eighth overall in 1984. By the 1986–87 season, Shayne made the team and steadily increased his output in each successive season, while building his reputation as a power forward by piling on the penalty minutes. He has never had less than 108 in a season.

In 1989–90, Corson scored a career-high 75 points and earned an All-Star selection. He later brought his physical brand of play to the rebuilding Edmonton Oilers, and then the St. Louis Blues, where he signed as a free agent

and earned the captaincy under then-coach Mike Keenan.

After a productive playoffs in 1995–96 in which he led the Blues in goals (eight, with an NHL-leading six on the power play), Corson was dealt once again to the Montreal Canadiens with Murray Baron and a draft pick for Pierre Turgeon, Craig Conroy, and Rory Fitzpatrick.

With injuries and a struggling team limiting his production, the fan-favorite, also serving as the Habs' captain, exercised his free-agent rights and signed with the Toronto Maple Leafs in the summer of 2000. The Leafs had courted Corson, along with Gary Roberts, to provide muscle and no-nonsense leadership after trailing the New Jersey Devils in those areas during the playoffs.

Paired often on an effective two-way line with his brother-in-law, Darcy Tucker, the left wing helped transform Toronto into a more formidable postseason threat, as witnessed by the Leafs' near dethroning of the Devils in round two of the 2001 Stanley Cup playoffs, and their battering seven-game triumph over the New York Islanders in round one of the 2002 playoffs, followed by an equally gritty win over the Ottawa Senators in seven games of round two.

GERRY COSBY

BORN: Roxbury, Massachusetts, May, 15, 1909
DIED: November 26, 1996

A Boston-bred goaltender who wound up playing for the Rovers, a New York Rangers farm team, Gerry Cosby is best known for developing the most famous hockey store in North America, located in Madison Square Garden. The Cosby enterprise began while he was playing for the Rovers, whose manager was Tommy Lockhart.

"Lockhart called me into his office to ask a simple question: 'Can you get me a gross of hockey sticks?' If I'd said no, I wouldn't be running the biggest hockey equipment company in the world today. But the answer was yes, and the next thing I knew I was on the phone with a company in Erie, Pennsylvania, and I managed to get Lockhart a gross of sticks at a very good price. It must have been good because he came back to me right away for more. Then he wanted some gloves and pads and that started me in the hockey equipment business in 1940.

"Next I was equipping the Rangers, the Americans, and all the Eastern League teams. The crazy thing about it was that I didn't have a penny of capital. I can gratefully remember when Lockhart once wrote me a check for the merchandise before it even arrived."

Cosby eventually developed an enterprise that brought hockey people from the world over to his shops, first at Rockefeller Center, then at the old Madison Square Garden. When the current Garden opened in 1968, Gerry moved his establishment there.

Since Cosby's death, the Gerry Cosby outfit has been ably run by his son Michael.

LES COSTELLO

BORN: South Porcupine, Ontario, February 16, 1928
DIED: Date unknown
POSITION: Left Wing, Toronto Maple Leafs, 1947–49

Just when it appeared that Les Costello would make it as a hockey pro, he abruptly quit to become a Roman Catholic priest. "I could have continued to play professionally," said Costello, "but I had a strong inclination to go into the priesthood. It was my call in life."

In the late 1940s, Costello was a highly regarded Toronto Maple Leafs prospect who played briefly on a line with Hall of Famer Max Bentley and Fleming Mackell. "Cos played the game hard," said Mackell. "He had more than his share of fights and always came to my aid when I got into one. Once, when we were playing in Pittsburgh, Cos made a point

of getting even with the veteran defenseman Ott Heller, who was with Indianapolis. Well, that night Cos really gave Heller a taste of his own medicine and Heller didn't bother us much after that."

Costello also had a good sense of humor on ice. "Once in Cleveland," Mackell recalled, "Cos was belted six times and each time fell flat on his back. After a while I skated over and asked him what the trouble was. 'I'm just testing these big guys to see how strong they are,' he told me. And then he laughed."

Costello played 15 games for the Maple Leafs in 1948–49 and scored two goals and three assists. He played on Toronto's 1948 Stanley Cup winners.

"There may have been better players," said Mackell, "but few with Cos's grit and determination."

BALDY COTTON

BORN: Nanticoke, Ontario, November 5, 1902
DIED: September 9, 1984
POSITION: Left Wing, Pittsburgh Pirates, 1925–28; Toronto Maple Leafs, 1928–35; New York Americans, 1935–37

A competent left-winger, Harold "Baldy" Cotton broke into the National Hockey League with the Pittsburgh Pirates in 1925–26, but gained fame years later as a member of the "Gashouse Gang" Toronto Maple Leafs of the early 1930s. Toronto manager Conn Smythe bought Cotton from Pittsburgh for the 1928–29 season and used him on a number of lines.

Cotton inadvertently played a part in the formation of one of the NHL's most spectacular units—the Kid Line of Joe Primeau, Busher Jackson, and Charlie Conacher—when Smythe placed Baldy alongside Primeau and Conacher. Just before Christmas, 1929, Cotton was pulled off the line and replaced by the more talented Jackson. Immediately, the line became the hit of the NHL.

During the 1932–33 campaign, Cotton fell victim to a prank that has since gone down in the annals of superb but dangerous hockey lessons. The prank had its origins in a Saturday night game at Maple Leaf Gardens. Cotton was playing an especially competent game for Toronto that night, diligently working himself into scoring position. But whenever it was time for him to receive the puck, his teammates failed to deliver. It appeared Hal was not going to reap dividends no matter what he did, and he became more and more unhappy about the turn of events.

By the time the game ended and the Maple Leafs returned to their dressing room, Cotton had reached a high state of pique, which grew in intensity as the players headed for the railroad station and the overnight trip to New York City for a match against the Rangers. Eventually Cotton got his frustration out of his system and began belaboring his linemates with assorted adjectives regarding their failure to pass the puck.

The only trouble was that Hal didn't know when to stop. His peroration continued through the night and extended to the next day, when the hockey club checked into the old Hotel Lincoln. Cotton and his roommate, Charlie Conacher, took the elevator up to their suite on the twentieth floor. Charlie was tired, and he went right to bed. Still mulling over his misfortune, Cotton walked back and forth in the room, berating each teammate who had failed to deliver.

During the first minutes of the diatribe Conacher pretended not to hear a word. But when Cotton suddenly announced in a fit of rage that he would obtain retribution by refusing to pass the puck to any of his teammates who were in scoring position, Conacher rose from his pillow and wondered whether he had heard Cotton correctly. Hal repeated his threat.

That did it. Conacher, a man with a physique reminiscent of Paul Bunyan, leaped out of bed and grabbed Cotton. Charlie

knew—as did all the Leafs—that Cotton had an obsessive fear of high places. Out of the corner of his eye Conacher noticed an open window. He carried Cotton to the window sill, gripped him firmly about the ankles, and held Cotton out the open window. Head down, screaming frantically, Cotton could do nothing but stare at the sidewalk 20 floors below.

While all this was going on, Conacher delivered his ultimatum by asking Cotton whether he was or was not going to pass the puck. Without waiting for an answer, Charlie carefully lowered Cotton another inch toward the street. Sheer terror brought Hal to his senses, and he hurriedly canceled his earlier threats. Whereupon Conacher calmly lifted him up and back into the room. It was the last time Cotton ever threatened to be a one-man team.

After his retirement from hockey in 1937, following a season with the New York Americans, Baldy drifted into scouting and broadcasting. He became a regular fixture on the Canadian Broadcasting Corporation's *Hot Stove League* programs between periods of the Toronto Maple Leafs' Saturday night games, and soon became renowned as a storyteller.

ART COULTER

BORN: Winnipeg, Manitoba, May 31, 1909
DIED: October 14, 2000
POSITION: Defenseman, Chicago Blackhawks, 1931–35; New York Rangers, 1935–42
AWARDS/HONORS: NHL Second Team All-Star, 1938–40; Hockey Hall of Fame, 1974

Considering the little ink he received, it was amazing that Arthur Edmund "Art" Coulter, the former Blackhawks and then Rangers defenseman ever made it to the Hall of Fame. But Coulter was a quiet gem, a man who became the Rangers' captain during their second golden era at the end of the 19030s.

"He was a superb ice general," said his coach Frank Boucher. "He lent strength to our smaller players, always on the spot if opposing players tried to intimidate them, responding beautifully to new responsibilities. He was a well set up fellow, quite tall, very muscular without an ounce of fat."

Art was nicknamed "the Trapper" because he would talk fishing and hunting by the hour. Coulter teamed with Muzz Patrick to give the Rangers a fearless, bruising defense. He also was the linchpin of the Rangers' offensive penalty-killing team, an innovation the New Yorkers introduced in 1939. Coulter was the anchor man, working with forwards Alex Shibicky, Neil and Mac Colville. Over the season, the Rangers outscored their opponents almost two to one when they were short-handed. Coulter remained a Ranger through the 1941–42 campaign.

Art "Trapper" Coulter, Rangers captain in 1940

YVAN COURNOYER

BORN: Drummondville, Quebec, November 22, 1943
POSITION: Right Wing, Montreal Canadiens, 1963–79
AWARDS/HONORS: Conn Smythe Trophy, 1973; NHL Second Team All-Star, 1969, 1971–73; Team Canada, 1972; NHL All-Star Game, 1967, 1971–74, 1978; Hockey Hall of Fame, 1982

Montreal's Canadiens are known as "the Flying Frenchmen" and nobody wearing the "*bleu* [blue], *blanc* [white], *et rouge* [red]" uniform flew faster than Yvan Cournoyer, the compact right wing.

Shooting and skating were Cournoyer's main interest in life since he was a kid in the French-speaking town of Drummondville, Quebec. When he was 14, his family moved to Montreal and he quickly climbed hockey's sandlot ladder, winding up with Lachine, a powerful team in the Canadien-sponsored Metropolitan Junior League.

NHL scouts had heard good things about the little kid with the big part in his hair, but they really took notice after the final game of a Lachine-Verdun series. Yvan's club was trailing by one goal with less than a minute remaining when he captured the puck behind his own net. Bobbing and weaving, he skated around the opposition and shot the puck past the Verdun goalie. Then he scored the winning goal in sudden-death overtime.

Cournoyer soon graduated to the Junior Canadiens, a regal teenage version of the parent club. Claude Ruel was his coach then as he was later with the NHL Canadiens. "I could tell right away," says Ruel, "that he had the same scoring knack as the Rocket. I told him to shoot even more, to strengthen his shot."

Yvan went home to his father's machine shop, probed around for some scrap steel, and designed some shot-improvers. "I made a couple of steel pucks," he recalls, "about two pounds each. Then I went down to the basement and shot them at heavy carpets lined up against the wall." The exercise may have weakened the foundations of the house, but it strengthened his wrists. By the following winter he had a much better shot.

This improvement was well timed. The Canadiens were scanning the junior hockey horizon for future heirs to Henri Richard and Jean Beliveau, the reigning French-Canadian scoring titans. They called Yvan up for a five-game tryout in the 1963–64 season and he scored in his first game. "He pounced on the puck like a cat," said Beliveau. However, coach Toe Blake was less enthused. He gave Yvan part-time work during his rookie year, 1964–65, and Cournoyer scored only seven goals. "But I never let down," says Yvan, "because when you let down you're finished."

In time, he became one of the most productive Canadiens scorers with 863 lifetime points. Cournoyer would become a Canadiens icon, finishing his career with the Habs in 1979, and epitomizing the Flying Frenchmen by no better means than his nickname, "The Roadrunner."

GEOFF COURTNALL

BORN: Duncan, British Columbia, August 18, 1962
POSITION: Left Wing, Boston Bruins, 1983–88; Edmonton Oilers, 1988; Washington Capitals, 1988–90; St. Louis Blues, 1990–91, 1995–2000; Vancouver Canucks, 1991–95

In a game of speed, Geoff Courtnall was one of the fastest players in the National Hockey League for more than a decade, starting with his first full season as a Boston Bruin in 1984–85.

He was signed as a free agent by the Bruins on July 6, 1983, after he had starred in junior hockey for the Victoria Cougars of the Western Hockey League. After four full seasons with Boston, he was traded to Edmonton, but played only briefly for the Oilers before moving on to the Washington Capitals.

If there was one knock against Geoff, it was his inability to remain a fixture with any one team—until 1991, when the St. Louis Blues dealt him to the Vancouver Canucks. Courtnall remained in Vancouver through the 1994–95 season, coming close to a Stanley Cup win in 1994, when the Canucks were defeated in seven by the New York Rangers. He then finished his career with the St. Louis Blues.

Courtnall achieved success in his time with the Blues, ranking 23rd on their all-time scoring list with 216 points. He scored 20 or more goals ten times in his career, and even had one 40-plus goal season.

Known for physical fitness, Geoff was a member of the Stanley Cup champion Edmonton Oilers team of 1987–88.

RUSS COURTNALL

BORN: Duncan, British Columbia, June 2, 1965
POSITION: Right Wing, Toronto Maple Leafs, 1984–88; Montreal Canadiens, 1988–92; Minnesota North Stars, 1992–93; Dallas Stars, 1993–95; Vancouver Canucks, 1994–97; New York Rangers, 1997; Los Angeles Kings, 1997–99
AWARDS/HONORS: NHL All-Star Game, 1994

Toronto's first choice (seventh overall) in the 1983 entry draft, Russ Courtnall made his NHL debut in 1983 after playing for Canada's national team and then the Olympic squad.

Speedy like older brother Geoff, Russ wore the royal blue and white of the Maple Leafs until 1988, when he was dealt to the Montreal Canadiens. He then became an itinerant right wing, skating in turn for the Minnesota North Stars, Dallas Stars, Vancouver Canucks, New York Rangers, and Los Angeles Kings.

Russ's most productive year was 1992–93, when he surpassed the 30-goal mark for the only time in his life, tallying 36 red lights. A year later, he set his personal record for points with 23 goals and 53 assists for 80 points.

BILL COWLEY

BORN: Bristol, Quebec, June 12, 1912
DIED: December 31, 1993
POSITION: Center, St. Louis Eagles, 1934–35;
Boston Bruins, 1935–47
AWARDS/HONORS: Hart Memorial Trophy,
1941, 1943; Art Ross Trophy, 1941; NHL First
Team All-Star, 1938, 1941, 1943–44; NHL
Second Team All-Star, 1945; Hockey Hall of Fame
1968

Overshadowed during most of his National Hockey League career by his teammate, center Milt Schmidt, Bill Cowley nevertheless became regarded as one of the classiest playmakers. He entered the NHL during the 1934–35 season with the St. Louis Eagles, but became a Bruin to stay the following year. He starred for the Boston sextet through the 1946–47 season. Smaller than Schmidt, Cowley relied on guile more than strength, emphasizing subtlety over Schmidt's accent on sock. Many critics later opined that if Cowley had been blessed with linemates such as Woody Dumart and Bobby Bauer, who complemented Schmidt on the Kraut Line, then Bill would have been the more productive Bruin.

JIM CRAIG

BORN: North Easton, Massachusetts, May 31,
1957
POSITION: Goaltender, Boston University,
1976–79; U.S. National Team, 1979, 1982–83;
U.S. Olympic Team, 1979–80; Atlanta Flames,
1980; Boston Bruins, 1980–81; Minnesota North
Stars, 1983–84
AWARDS/HONORS: NCAA East All-American,
1979; ECAC First All-Star, 1979

Although his goaltending never was in the same class as Ken Dryden, Patrick Roy, and Glenn Hall, Jim Craig remains in the netminders' pantheon because of his performance for the United States Olympic team during its gold medal achievement in 1980 in Lake Placid. Craig's emotional display, wrapping an American flag around his uniform after the upset victory was a classic vignette topping an improbable run.

A star at Boston University, the New Englander played for the United States national team before being selected by coach Herb Brooks to start for Uncle Sam's skaters at Lake Placid. Following the gold medal run, Craig was signed by the Atlanta Flames and that's where the Cinderella story ended.

As a big-league goalie, Craig failed after four games with Atlanta and was no more impressive a season later with the Boston Bruins, who eventually sent him to the minors.

In 1983–84, Craig got one more shot at The Show. He played three games for the Minnesota North Stars, finishing with a 4.91 goals-against average. With that, Craig's big-league career ended. Nevertheless, his Olympic performance was enough to ensure that he would be an American hockey icon forever.

JACK CRAWFORD

BORN: Dublin, Ontario, October 26, 1918
DIED: January 19, 1973
POSITION: Defenseman, Boston Bruins, 1938–50
AWARDS/HONORS: NHL First Team All-Star,
1946; NHL Second Team All-Star, 1943

A defenseman's defenseman, John Shea "Jack" Crawford was a Boston Bruins mainstay from 1938–39 until his retirement at the conclusion of the 1949–50 season. Crawford played for both the 1939 and 1941 Stanley Cup winners as well as the Prince of Wales Trophy winners in 1938, 1939, 1940, and 1941. For a decade, Crawford was unique among NHL regulars as being the only skater to wear a helmet. Curiously, Crawford's helmet was worn not so much for reasons of health, but rather for cosmetic purposes. Jack was very, very bald. The helmet did a very, very good job of concealing his pate.

MARC CRAWFORD

BORN: Belleville, Ontario, February 13, 1961
POSITION: Left Wing, Vancouver Canucks, 1981–87; Coach, Quebec Nordiques, 1994–95; Colorado Avalanche, 1995–98; Vancouver Canucks, 1998–
AWARDS/HONORS: Jack Adams Award, 1995

The American Hockey League has produced innumerable coaches who graduated from the minors to the NHL and became successful. One of the best was Marc Crawford, who moved from St. John's of the AHL to the Quebec Nordiques.

When the Quebec franchise was transferred from the east to Denver in 1995, Crawford directed the Colorado Avalanche to the highest levels of the National Hockey League. In 1996, the Avalanche reached the Stanley Cup finals and with Crawford behind the bench routed the Florida Panthers in four straight games.

Crawford seemed set for a long career in Denver, but his tenure ended after the 1997–98 season, after which he became a color commentator for CBC's *Hockey Night in Canada*. Late in the 1998–99 season, he was hired by the Vancouver Canucks as their head coach.

In his second full season at Vancouver, Crawford directed the Canucks back into the playoffs demonstrating that he had not lost his touch, while helping players such as Todd Bertuzzi, Ed Jovanovski, and Markus Naslund improve their skills.

TERRY CRISP

BORN: Parry Sound, Ontario, May 28, 1943
POSITION: Center, Boston Bruins, 1965–66; St. Louis Blues, 1967–72; New York Islanders, 1972–73; Philadelphia Flyers, 1973–77; Coach, Calgary Flames, 1987–90; Tampa Bay Lightning, 1992–97

The other guy from Parry Sound," Bobby Orr's hometown, is how Terry Crisp was referred to. He was best known for digging the puck out of corners and onto the sticks of teammates in front of the net, and former Flyers' coach, Fred Shero, dubbed Terry, "a coach on the ice." In a sense, Shero was a prophet because when Terry retired after a 201-point career, he became an assistant coach with the Flyers.

One of the original St. Louis Blues and New York Islanders, Crisp knew about a learning atmosphere. He coached 391 games with the expansion Tampa Bay Lightning from its inception through 1997, leading the franchise to its first playoff berth in 1996.

Colorful, direct, and intense, Crisp clashed with a young Brett Hull over the winger's offense-only style when Terry coached the powerhouse Calgary Flames of the late 1980s. His team, led by Lanny McDonald, Doug Gilmour, and Mike Vernon, overpowered the Montreal Canadiens in 1989 in six games for Calgary's only Stanley Cup.

Terry moved into the broadcasting field after his Tampa Bay tenure, and joined the expansion Nashville Predators as a color analyst in 1998–99 after similar turns with TSN and FOX Sports.

ROGER CROZIER

BORN: Bracebridge, Ontario, March 16, 1942
DIED: January 11, 1996
POSITION: Goaltender, Detroit Red Wings, 1963–70; Buffalo Sabres, 1970–76; Washington Capitals, 1977
AWARDS/HONORS: Calder Memorial Trophy, 1965; Conn Smythe Trophy, 1966; NHL First Team All-Star, 1965

If Glenn Hall was the first goaltender to popularize the "butterfly" style of puckstopping, Roger Crozier was the first puckstopper to take that form to the next, more advanced, level of perfection.

Roger Crozier is never mentioned in the same breath as Glenn Hall when it comes to the all-time top goaltenders. But, had constant ill-health not bedeviled Crozier, there is every possibility he would have been ranked with the likes of Hall, Terry Sawchuk, and Jacques Plante of the pre-Expansion era.

A compulsive worrier, Crozier developed an ulcer at age 17. Many times he could not eat before a game, or afterward. But despite the many troubles that faced Roger—illness, excessive nerves, and often being forced to backstop for mediocre clubs—he was nonetheless one of The Game's premier puckstoppers during his career, several seasons of which were with the Detroit Red Wings.

Crozier followed a line of great Detroit goaltenders, beginning with Johnny Mowers, Harry Lumley, and Terry Sawchuk, and rose to continue the tradition.

Initially, however, scouts and critics weren't fans of Crozier, who was small at five feet eight and 155 pounds. Although Roger would ultimately perfect and refine the emerging butterfly style, initially minor-league coaches tried to rid him of his sprawling style, thinking it would never succeed in the NHL. Crozier spent most of the 1963–64 season with Pittsburgh in the minors, but, unlike the youngster's detractors, Detroit coach Sid Abel had faith in him.

Roger broke into the National Hockey League in 1964–65 season at the tender age of 21. "The Dodger" played extremely well, winning the Calder Trophy as the league's best rookie and helping the Wings finish first with a remarkable 40 wins. Crozier's rookie performance also justifiably earned him a slot in goal as a First Team All-Star in 1965.

The following season, in the 1966 Stanley Cup finals, Roger won the Conn Smythe Trophy as the MVP for his team in the playoffs, even though Detroit lost the final to the Montreal Canadiens, after a two-games-to-zero Red Wing lead in the series.

Roger Allan Crozier was one of 14 children. Starting his ice career in goal at age six, by the time Roger was 14, he was playing goal on an intermediate team with men twice his age. It was then that Bob Wilson, the scout who discovered Bobby Hull, spotted Roger. The difference was that, while Wilson knew immediately Hull would be a star, with Crozier he figured the youngster was too small to ever make it to the National Hockey League. Still, the Blackhawks were in desperate need of a goalie for their Junior team in St. Catharines, so Wilson signed Crozier.

Next up was St. Louis of the Central Pro League for the 1962–63 season, where Roger figured he would remain. But the antics of Detroit defenseman Howie Young were grating the Red Wings and they decided to unload him—for any offer. They sent Young to Chicago for Crozier and a minor-league defenseman. Roger then spent the 1963–64 season playing for Pittsburgh, doing such a good job that Abel decided he belonged in the NHL.

Crozier justified Abel's faith in 1964–65, the only goaltender in the NHL to play all of his team's games (70). The young rookie allowed only 2.42 goals per game and led the NHL in shutouts that year, with six. The Wings' first-place showing was due in large part to the excellent goaltending of Crozier.

Roger went home with $9,000 of bonus money, proof that he belonged in the National

Hockey League. Although his self-confidence should have been growing by now, Crozier instead found himself worrying more than ever. The world-class fretter once recollected life as a National Hockey League goaltender. "I like everything about hockey: the traveling, the friends I've met, the interviews. Everything but the games. They're pure torture."

Acquired by the expansion Buffalo Sabres in 1970–71, Crozier helped lead Buffalo to the Stanley Cup finals in 1974–75, where the Sabres succumbed to Philadelphia in a memorable six-game series. Then, traded for cash to Washington on March 3, 1977, Crozier would hang up his pads after only three games, finishing with a respectable lifetime goals-against average of 3.04 and 30 shutouts. Crozier remained with the Capitals' organization as assistant general manager until a major club shake-up in 1982. Crozier died in 1996.

WILF CUDE

BORN: Barry, Wales, Great Britain, July 4, 1910
DIED: May 5, 1968
POSITION: Goaltender, Philadelphia Quakers, 1930–31; Boston Bruins, 1931–32; Detroit Red Wings, 1933–34; Montreal Canadiens, 1934–41
AWARDS/HONORS: NHL Second Team All-Star, 1936–37; NHL All-Star Game, 1937, 1939

Wilf Cude was a solid NHL goaltender who had his best years with the Montreal Canadiens of 1935–38. He was the Second Team All-Star goalie in 1936 and 1937 and provided living proof of the frustrations that can consume a goaltender.

It happened one night while the Canadiens were playing their neighboring rivals, the Montreal Maroons. Maroon forward Dave Trottier had the puck at center ice and was bearing down on Wilf in the Habitant nets. Suddenly, Trottier snapped off an unexpected long shot that whizzed past the startled Cude and into the cage.

With his stick raised triumphantly in the traditional "I just scored a goal" pose, Trottier circled the net, paused at the goalmouth and laughed in Cude's ever-reddening face. That did it. Swinging his heavy goalie's lumber like a medieval mace, Cude chased the still giggling Trottier all the way to center ice until the frenzied netminder was forcibly restrained by his teammates and led back to the confines of his goal crease.

FLOYD CURRY

BORN: Chapleau, Ontario, August 11, 1925
POSITION: Right Wing, Montreal Canadiens, 1947–48, 1949–58
AWARDS/HONORS: NHL All-Star Game, 1951–53, 1956–57

Floyd "Busher" Curry was a solid, workmanlike winger. One of the lesser lights on the power-packed Montreal Canadiens squad of the mid 1950s, Curry's specialty was stopping the opposing teams' big scorers. Busher went about his task without complaint, forsaking the offensive duties and backchecking like a demon to blunt his opposite number. Called a coach's "dream player" during his days in the NHL, Busher went on to coach and generally assist in the Habs' system.

CULLY DAHLSTROM

BORN: Minneapolis, Minnesota, July 3, 1913
POSITION: Center, Chicago Blackhawks, 1937–45
AWARDS/HONORS: Calder Memorial Trophy, 1938

A native of Minneapolis, Minnesota, Cully Dahlstrom was one of the American-born players Major Frederic McLaughlin signed with the Blackhawks in his quest during the 1930s for an All-American team. The major wasn't all that crazy about Dahlstrom and, in fact, preferred Oscar Hanson, but American-born coach Bill Stewart (the baseball umpire) preferred Dahlstrom. It turned out that Stewart was right. Dahlstrom justified his coach's faith in him by winning the Calder Trophy as the NHL's Rookie of the Year. Dahlstrom later emerged as the Blackhawks' playoff hero in March and April 1938, when Chicago upset Toronto for the Stanley Cup. Dahlstrom remained a Blackhawk his entire career, retiring after the 1944–45 season.

VINCENT DAMPHOUSSE

BORN: Montreal, Quebec, December 17, 1967
POSITION: Center, Toronto Maple Leafs, 1986–91; Edmonton Oilers, 1991–92; Montreal Canadiens, 1992–99; San Jose Sharks, 1999–
AWARDS/HONORS: NHL All-Star Game, 1991–92

The list of topflight French-Canadian players who have made their mark in the NHL as top scorers is long; Maurice Richard, Jean Beliveau, Bernie Geoffrion, and Guy Lafleur rank among the best.

In the post-Expansion era, the name Vincent Damphousse will join that top echelon.

Vincent Damphousse

Damphousse was drafted by Toronto in 1986, and made his first significant impact in his rookie season, when he played in all 80 games and tallied 21 goals, 25 assists, and 46 points.

But the true breakout year would come in 1989–90, when Vincent scored 33 goals and finished second in team scoring with 94 points. In 1990–91, he paced the team with 26 goals and 73 points and was named the MVP of the NHL All-Star game in Chicago, thanks to a four-goal effort.

In one of the biggest trades in NHL history, Damphousse was traded with Peter Ing, Scott Thornton, Luke Richardson, and cash to the Edmonton Oilers for Grant Fuhr, Glenn Anderson, and Craig Berube in 1991. The move to northern Alberta seemed to agree with him, as he led the Oilers with 38 goals, 51 assists, and 89 points. In the playoffs, he scored 14 points in 16 games as the team reached the Campbell Conference finals before losing to the Chicago Blackhawks.

Damphousse was then traded with a fourth-round draft pick to the Montreal Canadiens for Shayne Corson, Brent Gilchrist, and Vladimir Vujtek. Playing in his hometown, Damphousse responded with 39 goals, 58 assists, and 97 points for the Habs and the playoffs were even better. A smooth-skating forward whose durability matched his skills, Damphousse starred for the Montreal Canadiens Stanley Cup–winning team in 1993, when he had 23 points in 20 games as the Canadiens won the Cup, defeating

Wayne Gretzky and the Los Angeles Kings four games to one.

Damphousse led the Canadiens with 40 goals, 51 assists, and 91 points during 1993–94. In the lockout-shortened 1994–95 campaign, he played all 48 games and scored 40 points. A season later, he co-led the Canadiens with 38 goals and finished second in team scoring with 56 assists and 94 points, tying his career high. In 1996–97, he led the Canadiens with 54 assists and 81 points and finished second in team scoring with 59 points the following year.

It seemed Damphousse, a natural favorite in French Montreal, would be a Hab for the rest of his career. But no, Vincent was moved to his fourth NHL club when he was traded to the Sharks for three draft picks. In 2000–01, he was limited to just 45 games, but still scored 37 assists as the Sharks set a franchise record with 40 wins and 95 points.

Often paired with either Teemu Selanne or Owen Nolan, Damphousse patrolled center ice admirably for the Sharks as they came to prominence in the Western Conference at the beginning of the twenty-first century.

LEO DANDURAND

BORN: Bourbonnais, Illinois, July 9, 1889
DIED: June 26, 1964

It is quite possible that there would not be a Montreal Canadiens hockey club today were it not for the efforts of Leo Dandurand. A French-Canadian sportsman, Dandurand was a partner with Joe Cattarinich and Louis Letourneau in a Cleveland, Ohio, racetrack when the Canadiens were put on the auction block in October 1921. Since the Musketeers, as the trio was known, were occupied with their thoroughbred venture, they were unable to be in Montreal at the time of the sale, but Dandurand was consumed with a desire to obtain the hockey team. He phoned a friend, Cecil Hart, in Montreal and asked if he would stand in and bid as high as possible for the Canadiens.

Hart agreed and went to the auction, where he found himself in competition with Tom Duggan, who was representing both himself and the Mount Royal Arena Company. Duggan opened with a bid of $8,000 and Hart countered with $8,500. The auction was abruptly halted when NHL president Frank Calder revealed he was representing an Ottawa group intent on purchasing Les Canadiens. Calder said he wanted to contact his party for further instructions. At that point the bidding was postponed for a week.

When the auction was reopened, Duggan startled the audience by placing ten $1,000 bills on the table. Calder said he would top that. Now it was Hart's turn. He asked for time and dashed into the next room where he phoned Leo in Cleveland. Unfortunately, neither Letourneau nor Cattarinich was around when Hart called Dandurand. But Leo decided to gamble and instructed Hart to go the limit.

The emissary returned to the room and raised the bid to $11,000, catching both Duggan and Calder unaware. The two adversaries looked at each other and conceded the decision to Hart who, in turn, ran out and phoned Dandurand with the news. Leo didn't know whether to be jubilant or crestfallen, but he had no choice but to tell his partners they had just acquired a professional hockey team. The investment paid off immediately, because Les Canadiens collected a $20,000 profit the first year they owned it.

KEN DANEYKO

BORN: Windsor, Ontario, April 17, 1964
POSITION: Defenseman, New Jersey Devils, 1983–
AWARDS/HONORS: Bill Masterton Memorial Trophy, 2000

Ken Daneyko never had any illusions of being an offensive force from the blue line. He did become the prototypical defensive defenseman and the heart and soul of the Devils franchise.

By the 2001–02 season, Daneyko was starting his 19th season with the Devils organization, never having scored more than six goals or 21 points in any season, although his substantial penalty minute totals highlighted his reputation as a defensive force.

Daneyko's exceptional competitive drive, which often led to emotional penalties in his younger years, made him a valuable and beloved teammate as he matured and learned to harness it to help the team. He played in every one of the Devils' playoff games and was with the team for the 1995 and 2000 Cup wins.

Perhaps Daneyko's greatest contribution to the NHL came in the fall of 1997, when he walked into the office of Devils general manager Lou Lamoriello and admitted that he was losing his battle with alcohol abuse. The Devils and Daneyko agreed he would enter the NHL's substance abuse program, and Daneyko missed 45 games in alcohol rehab.

Daneyko was the first player to publicly, voluntarily enter the program during the season. Most players waited until the off-season, and only when forced due to legal troubles.

To many NHL players and their families, Daneyko's recovery and continued sobriety made it easier for others to ask for help. In 2000, the NHL honored Daneyko with the Masterton Trophy for perseverance, sportsmanship, and dedication to hockey. He was a truly deserving recipient, and in turn, continued to thrive as a Devil. Entering the 2001–02 Stanley Cup playoffs, Daneyko had played in every single playoff game in New Jersey Devils history.

GARY DAVIDSON

Gary Davidson, who with Dennis Murphy founded the World Hockey Association in 1972, was no newcomer to professional sports rivalry, having been instrumental in the formation of the now defunct American Basketball Association in 1967.

"It has been conclusively proved by the players themselves that there is room in hockey for a second major league," declared Davidson. "That those players had the courage to follow the leadership of the WHA's equally courageous owners is ample testimony to our credibility."

Davidson, who also created the new and unique nonreserve clause in the standard player contract of the new league, never saw the WHA become a stable entity, and he departed in 1974 to try his hand in other sports. All of Davidson's attempts to set up these rivalries turned out to be colossal failures for the investors but not for himself. From all accounts, Davidson did very well financially and went on to be a successful banker in California.

The WHA remained shaky, with franchises moving from city to city or folding. On many occasions, the league tried desperately to merge with the NHL but it never materialized. Finally, in 1979, four of the more solvent franchises—the Hartford Whalers (Carolina Hurricanes), Winnipeg Jets (Phoenix Coyotes), Edmonton Oilers, and Quebec Nordiques (Colorado Avalanche)—were invited to join the NHL as expansion teams before the league disbanded altogether after the completion of the 1978–79 season.

JOHN DAVIDSON

BORN: Ottawa, Ontario, February 27, 1953
POSITION: Goaltender, St. Louis Blues, 1973–75; New York Rangers, 1975–83

John Davidson, just like his pop-singing namesake, made the big time as a youngster, but unlike the showbiz Davidson, who rarely faced a hostile gathering, goalie Davidson went up against tough opponents every night before taking the microphone himself as a broadcaster.

A first-round draft pick of the Blues in 1973, Davidson became a regular immediately, at the tender age of 20. In 1975, the six-feet-three goalie was dealt to the New York Rangers.

With the exception of his first year on Broadway, John battled injuries every season. In 1979, an injury again slowed the big, easy-going fellow and it appeared his career was going the way of a TV repeat. Coach Fred Shero, however, had faith in "J.D.," as fans and teammates called him, and announced that, no matter what, Davidson was his number one goalie. John came back a few weeks prior to the playoffs and looked simply dreadful. But then, as if by magic, the playoffs began and Davidson delivered the goaltending performance of a lifetime.

His heroic saves and 2.28 goals-against average enabled the Rangers to defeat the Islanders in the second round of the 1979 playoffs and move on to the finals, where the Blueshirts lost to Montreal. He retired after 1982–83 and almost immediately put his mark on the broadcasting field with exceptional commentary for Madison Square Garden Network, *Hockey Night in Canada* (1984 to 1986), and ABC/ESPN.

Davidson became a television star after permanently joining partner Sam Rosen as part of the New York Rangers' television broadcast team in 1986–87. J.D. emerged as the preeminent color analyst for virtually every major hockey event ever since. His television credits include stints on the NHL All-Star games, the 1992, 1994, 1998, and 2002 Olympic games, and the Stanley Cup finals.

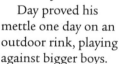

HAP DAY

BORN: Owen Sound, Ontario, June 14, 1901
DIED: February 17, 1990
POSITION: Defenseman, Toronto St. Patricks, 1924–26; Toronto Maple Leafs, 1926–37; New York Americans, 1937–38; Coach, Toronto Maple Leafs, 1940–50
AWARDS/HONORS: NHL Second Team All-Star (Coach), 1944; NHL All-Star Game, 1934, 1937; Hockey Hall of Fame, 1961

Clarence "Hap" Day learned his hockey in a small Ontario village near Owen Sound. At times, he would plod miles through the snow to find a place to play hockey, and he eventually became a leader with the Midland Juniors.

Day proved his mettle one day on an outdoor rink, playing against bigger boys.

Clarence "Hap" Day, Toronto Maple Leafs coach

The afternoon was bitter cold, heightened by an icy wind cutting across the hockey rink. In order to protect himself, Day mistakenly donned a second sweater, considerably longer than he should have worn. Drooping down his body, the sweater gave Day the look of a larger skater and encouraged the enemy to take hefty charges at him from every angle. Day was constantly being smashed to the ice.

To the amazement of his foes, Day clambered back to his feet over and over again until a blow late in the game left him lying in a state of semiconsciousness along the sideboards. By then even the enemy had grown to respect young Day, and a group of players skated over to the fallen defenseman. "Y'know, kid," one of the bigger players on the opposition remarked, "you must be a lot lighter than you look." Day had come to his senses. He quickly dusted the ice shavings off his jersey. "Oh, no," he replied, "I'm really quite heavy. I must have slipped!"

Hap Day's courage and ability enabled him to climb the long, hard hockey ladder in Ontario. He moved from the Midland Juniors to the Intermediate sextet and then to the Hamilton Tigers. Hockey was not the only subject on his mind; Day wanted very much to be a pharmacist, and he enrolled at the University of Toronto, where he eventually obtained a degree. While attending the university he played for the varsity club. It was then that Charlie Querrie spotted Day and persuaded him, not without a considerable battle, to turn pro instead of applying for a job in the nearest drugstore.

When Querrie signed him, Day was a left-winger. However, Conn Smythe believed that Hap's potential was more suited to defense, and he moved him back to the blue line when he took control of the Maple Leafs. Day was right at home in the defense slot and emerged as a superb, hard-checking defenseman who specialized in skating opponents out of the play. Later, as Leaf coach, he won Stanley Cups in 1942, 1947, 1948, and 1949.

ERIC DAZÉ

BORN: Montreal, Quebec, July 2, 1975
POSITION: Left Wing, Chicago 1995–
AWARDS/HONORS: NHL All-Rookie Team, 1996; NHL All-Star Game, 2002 (MVP)

For the first few years of his career, Eric Dazé looked like a power forward in the making. However, he never quite mastered the "power" part.

Dazé started out on a high note: He led all rookies in goals in the 1995–96 season and was a finalist for the Calder Trophy.

Due to Dazé's size (six feet four, 200-plus pounds), his decent speed, and his excellent puckhandling skills, the Blackhawks thought they had a man who could run people over,

drive to the net and score. Some were predicting many 40-goal seasons to come.

However, over the years Dazé appeared not eager to pay the price night in and night out to do the things that make a true power forward. His goal total only topped 30 once, in 1997–98.

However, the Blackhawks underwent a renaissance in 2001–02, hovering near the top of the Western Conference for much of the season, and Eric's performance rose accordingly, as he tallied 38 goals and 32 assists to lead the Hawks in scoring. His newfound success was put to the test in the 2002 playoffs as Chicago opened the first round against St. Louis, where, unfortunately, they were ousted rapidly in five games, three via shutouts by Blues goalie Brent Johnson.

ADAM DEADMARSH

BORN: Trail, British Columbia, May 10, 1975
POSITION: Right Wing, Quebec Nordiques/Colorado Avalanche, 1994–2001; Los Angeles Kings, 2001–

Foot soldiers are essential to any championship hockey team, yet they rarely command All-Star status, with their names on a marquee.

But every so often a foot soldier—Bob Nystrom of the New York Islanders is a classic example—climbs to a higher level, and thereby finds himself in the company of superstars.

Adam Deadmarsh is just such a performer.

The lean years in Quebec during the early 1990s seeded a strong foundation of youth, and Deadmarsh led the never-ending parade of excellent prospects who would play a key role for the franchise.

A 14th overall draft pick in 1993, Adam stormed onto the Nordiques midway through the 1995 season, and blossomed while skating with the likes of Joe Sakic and Peter Forsberg. His willingness to drop the gloves and muck in the corners added a needed power element to create room for his star teammates.

At a solid six feet, 200 pounds, Adam brought speed, skill, and havoc-wreaking intensity to the team, which departed for Colorado following his rookie year, 1994–95.

Deadmarsh helped the new Avalanche christen their inaugural season with a defeat of Detroit in the 1996 semifinals and, ultimately, fellow first-time finalist Florida for the Stanley Cup. His mark of 17 playoff points that spring was a sign he could take the post-season pressures.

Adam became a mainstay on the NHL list of top power forwards, compiling around 20-plus goals and over 100 penalty minutes each season. He was also named twice to the U.S. Olympic Team, in 1998 and 2002.

Adam proved himself a prime-timer after a devastating trade from his Stanley Cup favorite Avalanche for Los Angeles Kings superstar Rob Blake at the 2001 trading deadline. After having been injured much of the season, Adam quickly recovered, regained focus, and delivered. When the Kings shocked the hockey world by vanquishing heavily-favored Detroit in round one that spring, Deadmarsh netted a dramatic overtime series-winning rebound goal in Game Six.

Even though his Kings lost a nail-biting second round to Adam's alma mater Avalanche in seven games, Deadmarsh was instrumental in LA's successful post-Blake endeavors.

The 2001–02 season was another example of what would be a long and productive NHL career. Deadmarsh netted 29 goals while skating on an LA top line with Jason Allison and Ziggy Palffy, which helped propel the Kings to a playoff berth, where they succumbed again to the Avs, this time in a first-round face-off.

ALEX DELVECCHIO

BORN: Fort William, Ontario, December 4, 1931
POSITION: Center, Detroit Red Wings, 1950–73; Coach, Detroit Red Wings, 1973–75; General Manager, Detroit Red Wings, 1974–77
AWARDS/HONORS: Lady Byng Memorial Trophy, 1959, 1966, 1969; Lester Patrick Trophy, 1974; NHL Second Team All-Star, 1953; NHL All-Star Game, 1953–59, 1961–65, 1967; Hockey Hall of Fame, 1977

The eternal Red Wing. One would think such a title would best fit Gordie Howe, or perhaps Ted Lindsay. Certainly, of the moderns, it has been worn well by Steve Yzerman.

But unlike Howe and Lindsay, who played on other National Hockey League teams in the twilight of their careers, Alex "Fats"

Alex Delvecchio, a career Red Wing as player, coach, and general manager

Delvecchio was a Red Wing from start (1950) to finish (1974), two decades plus four years in Red and White!

Peter Alexander Delvecchio made the Red Wings varsity at the tender age of 19, contributing 15 goals in his rookie campaign as the Wings swept to the Stanley Cup championship. Alex went on to roll up impressive statistics: 1,549 games, 1,281 points, and 825 assists. He also potted 456 goals.

He also was one of the finest centers ever to skate down the pike and a member of three Stanley Cup–winning teams, including the 1954–55 squad, the last Detroit sextet to win the championship before the Expansion of 1967.

Everything about Delvecchio was likeable, from his gregarious personality to his delightfully clean play. If ever a major-league hockey player could be called a gentleman, scholar, and artist, Fats was that man.

Ironically, there was nothing fat about Alex except his cherubic face. He measured six feet and 195 pounds, big for his era, but moved around the rink with a lyrical style that sometimes suggested nonchalance.

How good was Delvecchio?

Perhaps the best way to put it was that he had an awfully tough act to follow in Detroit and he not only followed captain Sid Abel as top center, he eventually out-performed his predecessor.

In the late 1940s and during the 1949–50 season when the Red Wings beat the New York Rangers to win the Stanley Cup, Abel centered the famed Production Line with Ted Lindsay at left wing and Gordie Howe on the right. The trio's gears meshed so well together that most observers doubted another center could work as well with Lindsay and Howe. But when Abel left Detroit after the 1951–52 season, to become player-coach of the Chicago Blackhawks, Delvecchio stepped in without missing a beat.

Less abrasive than Abel, Delvecchio nevertheless was a stylist in the clean, competent manner of such respected centermen as Syl Apps and Jean Beliveau. Delvecchio was a three-time winner of the Lady Byng Trophy (1959, 1966, and 1969) and was voted to the Second All-Star Team in 1953. He was also one of the few players to gain All-Star acclaim at two different positions, also being named to the All-Star squad as a left wing in 1959.

There was good reason why Fats never made the First Team during his 23-year National Hockey League career, as he played mostly in the shadow of such classic centers as Beliveau, Stan Mikita, and Henry Richard. Nevertheless, Delvecchio's high-grade credentials are abundant. He played on three Stanley Cup championship teams and seven first-place clubs. He became captain of the Red Wings in 1961, and scored 20 or more goals in 13 of his campaigns.

Also blessed with durability, Delvecchio missed only 43 games in 22 full seasons; from 1957 to 1964, Fats played in 490 consecutive games.

His calm but firm demeanor eventually made Fats one of the most suitable candidates to take over the chores behind the bench of a struggling Red Wings team in 1973, and in November of that year, Delvecchio was officially named coach of the 2–9–1 club. His controlled discipline, laced with a healthy respect for his players as individuals, made Fats successful at his new craft, raising the comatose Detroiters to a level of respectability, and at the same time making life pleasurable for his troops. He was not averse to picking up some cold cuts and beer after a game or taking the team out to dinner after a practice. But rather than being taken advantage of because of his good nature, Delvecchio gained the respect of his entire team, allowing them to simply go out and do what they were paid to do: play hockey. His tenure as general manager lasted from 1974 to 1977.

But Alex Delvecchio, one of Detroit's finest skaters, purest centers, and most diligent of coaches, was obviously missed after he left the NHL scene. His appearances at NHL Heroes of Hockey and Old-Timers Games delighted faithful fans who missed his playing days.

JACQUES DEMERS

BORN: Montreal, Quebec, August 25, 1944
POSITION: Coach, Quebec Nordiques, 1979–80; St. Louis Blues, 1983–86; Detroit Red Wings, 1986–90; Montreal Canadiens, 1992–96; Tampa Bay Lightning, 1997–99; General Manager, Tampa Bay Lightning, 1998–99
AWARDS/HONORS: Jack Adams Award, 1987–88

In the spring of 1975, a French-Canadian assistant coach rode the bus out of Springfield with his Chicago Cougars (WHA).

The Windy City sextet had just scored a major upset over the New England Whalers and Jacques Demers felt he was on the way up. After incremental stints in the International Hockey League and the WHA, Demers did indeed make it to the NHL, first as the coach of the Quebec Nordiques in 1979–80.

Jacques Demers as St. Louis coach

Once the driver of a Pepsi-Cola delivery truck in Quebec, Demers's blend of smarts and affability endeared him to players and fans alike, although he was out of an NHL coaching job again after just one season.

Then, when Harry Ornest bought the St. Louis Blues in 1983, his general manager, Ron Caron, picked Demers to run the team. Jacques pressed all the right buttons and St. Louis soon became one of the most endearing underdog clubs in the NHL. After Jacques guided the Blues to upset wins in the 1986 playoffs, he was sought by other NHL clubs, and eventually signed with the Detroit Red Wings.

Demers became a major Motor City hero—winning 137 games and appearing in two Conference finals—although he never won a Stanley Cup for the Winged Wheelers, where he remained until 1990. Jacques received the Jack Adams Award in 1987 and 1988, the first man to win it consecutively.

Joining the Montreal Canadiens in 1992–93, Demers instantly reached his apex as a coach with a band of overachieving players, which included Kirk Muller as captain, that won 48 games and captured the 24th Stanley Cup championship for the storied franchise. His last three years with the Habs did not produce the same results, and he was fired in 1995–96 after opening the season 0–5.

Demers continued to serve the Canadiens as a scout until the Tampa Bay Lightning hired him as coach in November 1997. He replaced Phil Esposito as general manager at the start of the 1998–99 season, but the team floundered to 19 wins and was sold to Palace Sports and Entertainment in June of that year. The new owners revamped management by replacing Demers with Rick Dudley upon assuming control of the Lightning.

Demers thereafter worked in the broadcasting business and also wrote newspaper columns critiquing hockey.

CORBETT DENNENY

BORN: Cornwall, Ontario, January 25, 1894
DIED: January 16, 1963
POSITION: Left Wing/Center, Toronto Shamrocks (NHA), 1915; Toronto Arenas (NHA), 1916–17, 1918–19; Ottawa Senators (NHA), 1917; Toronto St. Patricks, 1919–23; Vancouver Millionaires (PCHA), 1923; Hamilton Tigers, 1924; Toronto Maple Leafs, 1926–27; Chicago Blackhawks, 1927–28

Corbett and his brother Cy both started their hockey careers with the Toronto Shamrocks back in 1915. After the Shams folded, Cy settled down with the Ottawa Senators, but Corbett roamed around the ice-hockey world, getting in on two Stanley Cup acts with Toronto in 1918 and 1922.

A forward who could play either center or left wing, Corbett's best years were with Toronto, when he pivoted a line with Reg Noble and Babe Dye. In 1923, he was traded to Vancouver and never truly regained his scoring touch. He helped Saskatoon reach the playoffs in 1925 and 1926, but never was on a Cup winner again. He finished his career with Chicago in 1928.

CY DENNENY

BORN: Farrow's Point, Ontario, December 23, 1891
DIED: October 12, 1970
POSITION: Left Wing, Toronto Shamrocks (NHA), 1915–16; Ottawa Senators, 1917–28; Boston Bruins, 1928–29
AWARDS/HONORS: Scoring leader (prior to NHL's Art Ross Trophy), 1924; Hockey Hall of Fame, 1959

After the Toronto Shamrocks caved in financially, the Denneny brothers were signed by the Toronto Arenas, where they skated together on a line centered by Duke Keats. This awesome threesome accounted for 66 goals during the 1916 season, tops in the league for scoring by a single line. There was only one problem, though; the Arenas finished dead last.

Happily, Cy was rescued when the Ottawa Senators pulled off the coup of the season by sending $750 and a player named Sammy Herbert to Toronto in return for Denneny's services. It took only one season for Cyril to establish himself as the regular left-winger on the powerful Senator squad. No one would unseat him for the next nine years.

A rough-and-tumble type player despite his small stature, Denneny was sometimes cast into an enforcer's role when looking out for smaller, mild-mannered linemates. The rugged Harry Broadbent was a tough cop on the beat as well, and when this duo was paired together, they were gleefully referred to as "The Gold Dust Twins" by the delirious Senator faithful.

Cy skated for five Stanley Cup teams in his long and illustrious career, four with the Senators and the fifth with the 1929 Bruins. He was a fantastic scoring machine, and although he only led the league once in total points, he never dropped below fourth in the standings for ten consecutive years.

After retiring in 1929, Cy saw service as a referee and hockey coach. He became a member of the Hockey Hall of Fame in 1959.

JIMMY DEVELLANO

BORN: Toronto, Ontario, June 18, 1943
POSITION: Scout, St. Louis Blues, 1968–72; New York Islanders, 1972–79; Assistant General Manager, New York Islanders, 1981–82; General Manager, Indianapolis (CHL), 1979–81; Detroit Red Wings, 1982–90; Senior Vice President, Detroit Red Wings, 1990–

When it comes to hockey executives with a golden touch, Jimmy Devellano belongs in a select circle.

He broke in as an aide to St. Louis Blues general manager Lynn Patrick in 1968, as St. Louis reached the Stanley Cup finals in its first three years of existence.

When Devellano moved to Long Island to help Isles general manager Bill Torrey in 1972, the Islanders—thanks in part to Devellano's decisions—were en route to a dynasty.

Among the players Devellano helped acquire were Bryan Trottier, Ken Morrow, Stefan Persson, Adam Graves, Steve Yzerman, Mike Bossy, Bob Probert, Dave Langevin, and Randy McKay, to name just a few.

After Red Wings owner Mike Ilitch bought the Motor City sextet in 1982, he hired Devellano to rebuild the hapless hockey club.

One of hockey's most beloved figures, Devellano was promoted to senior vice president of the Red Wings and held a similar title with the Detroit Tigers, also owned by Ilitch.

Among Devellano's managerial protégés were Neil Smith, whose Rangers won the Stanley Cup in 1994, and Ken Holland, who succeeded Devellano in Detroit and led the Wings to three Cup victories in six years.

"Jimmy had no problem hiring young people if he felt they had a passion for the game and a work ethic," said Holland. "Not only does he have a great eye for hockey players, but he's got a real keen eye for spotting and developing young coaches and managers."

BILL DINEEN

BORN: Arvida, Quebec, September 18, 1932
POSITION: Forward, Detroit Red Wings,
1953–57; Chicago Blackhawks, 1957–58; Coach,
Houston Aeros (WHA), 1972–78; New England
Whalers (WHA), 1978–79; Philadelphia Flyers,
1991–93; General Manager, Houston Aeros
(WHA), 1975–78; New England Whalers (WHA),
1978–79
AWARDS/HONORS: Schmertz Trophy (WHA
Outstanding Coach), 1977–78

During an NHL career that spanned 1953–58, Dineen played for Detroit and then Chicago. In his rookie season, 1953–54, Bill scored an impressive 17 goals in 70 games. His manager Jack "Jolly Jawn" Adams promised Dineen a bonus in his contract from $6,000 to $6,500 for the 1954–55 season. "I thought I was getting a raise of $500," Dineen recalled. "What I didn't know at the time was that the NHL had raised its minimum salary from $6,000 to $6,500. So all Adams did was give me the minimum once again!"

After retiring as a player, Bill Dineen stepped behind the players' bench. He coached the WHA's Houston Aeros to the Avco Cup in 1974 and 1975 before moving to the New England Whalers, who fired him in 1979.

Bill then bounced around the minor-league hockey coaching circuit until getting a shot at helming the Philadelphia Flyers in 1991. His two seasons in Philadelphia did not yield a playoff spot.

Bill also raised a hockey family; sons Kevin, Gord, and Jerry all were involved with the NHL.

KEVIN DINEEN

BORN: Quebec City, Quebec, October 28, 1963
POSITION: Right Wing, Hartford Whalers,
1984–91, 1995–97; Philadelphia Flyers,
1991–95; Carolina Hurricanes, 1997–99; Ottawa
Senators, 1999–2000; Columbus Blue Jackets,
2000–
AWARDS/HONORS: NHL Man of the Year,
1991; NHL All-Star Game, 1988–89

Few hockey players made a greater impact in a shorter time at The Spectrum than Kevin Dineen. The ebullient right wing spent five years wearing the orange and black of the Flyers. Philadelphia fans appreciated his zest for The Game. Dineen's competitive nature came natu-

Kevin Dineen

rally. His father, Bill Dineen, had been a teammate of Gordie Howe's on some mighty Detroit Red Wings squads. The elder Dineen blended talent with hustle. Kevin's trademarks were diligence and smarts, since he was neither a particularly good skater nor shooter. But he was a fan favorite because of his natural affability and untiring years of community service.

Kevin broke in with the Hartford Whalers in 1984–85, teaming with Ron Francis for most of his tenure, which yielded a career best 89-point breakout in 1988–89. Dealt to the Flyers in 1991–92, he averaged slightly under a point per game in his new milieu. A full season on Broad Street in 1992–93 found the rejuvenated Dineen churning out 63 points and 201 penalty minutes.

Though his numbers dropped steadily afterward, the gritty Dineen was particularly effective in the 1994–95 playoffs during which he helped the Flyers reach the third round with 10 points in 15 games before being eliminated by the New Jersey Devils. Kevin returned to the Whalers in 1995 to captain his old team for two years.

The five-feet-eleven, 190-pound right wing then played a season with Ottawa in 1999 before going to the Columbus Blue Jackets, who selected him in the 2000 Expansion Draft as a pillar of professionalism for their new franchise. With Dineen mentoring the young players, Colombus sold out all of their home games in their second season, 2001–02.

MARCEL DIONNE

BORN: Drummondville, Quebec, August 3, 1951
POSITION: Center, Detroit Red Wings, 1971–75; Los Angeles Kings, 1975–87; New York Rangers, 1987–89
AWARDS/HONORS: Lady Byng Memorial Trophy, 1975, 1977; Lester B. Pearson Award, 1979–80; Art Ross Trophy, 1980; NHL First Team All-Star, 1977, 1980; NHL Second Team All-Star, 1979, 1981; NHL All-Star Game, 1975–78, 1980–81, 1983, 1985; Hockey Hall of Fame, 1992

At one point during the early 1970s, it seemed as if Marcel Dionne would enjoy a long career as a Red Wing as both captain and top scorer.

Despite a diminutive physique some believed would hamper his survivability in the rugged National Hockey

Marcel Dionne as a New York Ranger

League, Dionne exploited his speed and savvy to a point where size really didn't matter.

At five feet nine, 170 pounds, Marcel was able to dart around the ice like a water bug on a pond, and was called the "Little Beaver" of the NHL.

Dionne also was one of the league's most accurate shooters. Dionne's 1976–77 totals of 53 goals and 69 assists for 122 points placed him second in scoring behind the Montreal Canadiens' gifted Guy Lafleur.

Marcel grew up in the steel mill town of Drummondville, in the mostly French-speaking province of Quebec. He began skating at the age of two on a makeshift rink in his backyard. His parents encouraged young Marcel to play hockey, aware that if he didn't make a career of hockey, he would inevitably spend his life working in the steel mills, like his father.

When Marcel was 15, he had established himself as a professional prospect, and after wowing scouts with his years in Drummondville, the Montreal Junior Canadiens, and St. Catharines, he was selected second in the 1971 NHL Amateur Draft by the Detroit Red Wings; only Guy Lafleur of the Canadiens was chosen before Dionne.

Desperate for help, the Red Wings expected instant miracles from Marcel. Detroit general manager Ned Harkness sought a replacement for the legendary Gordie Howe, who had quit the Wings following the 1970–71 season. But Gordie Howe replacements were seldom found, and the unprecedented attention from the Detroit press and the fans, along with a six-figure contract, created a pressure cooker atmosphere before Dionne even put on a Red Wings uniform.

Marcel overcame the pressures of his freshman year, and completed his rookie season with 28 goals and 49 assists for 77 points, a new NHL record for points in a season by a rookie at the time. Thus, it hardly was surprising that he received a veteran's responsibility.

Despite the presence of Marcel, the Red Wings managed to miss the playoffs that year, as well as each of the four years Dionne remained in Detroit. As Red Wings' losses mounted throughout Marcel's second and third seasons in the Motor City, Dionne was singled out by management as *"l'enfant terrible"* of the team. The bosses accused him of "not giving one hundred percent" and not being a team player.

Marcel himself fanned the flames of dissension with such comments as: "There were only three NHL-caliber players on that team," and "I was not going to give one hundred percent in practice." This philosophy put Dionne on a collision course with manager Harkness and coach Johnny Wilson. Before a night game against the Vancouver Canucks, the coach noticed Dionne skating in a relaxed way and demanded he speed it up.

Dionne recalled, "I told him I felt there wasn't really any reason for me to break my chops in practice. Well, he told me to leave and not to come back. I left the ice, and I *didn't* come back!"

Indeed, Marcel missed that night's game and was promptly suspended.

Despite such dilemmas, Dionne enjoyed an outstanding offensive year, with 40 goals and 50 assists for 90 points. Detroit management could not argue with such statistics, but Marcel remained subject to harsh criticism.

The 1974–75 season, Dionne's fourth in the majors, brought a new head coach, former Detroit superstar Alex Delvecchio. More importantly, it was Marcel's option year; by not signing a new contract, Dionne would be free to go to the team of his choice at the end of the campaign. Knowing this, the Red Wings attempted to placate Marcel by giving him more responsibility and named him team captain.

Marcel responded with his finest season as a Red Wing, amassing 47 goals and 74 assists for 121 points. But Dionne's productive campaign failed to erase the scars of bygone years and, once the season ended, Dionne's agent Eagleson informed Delvecchio that Marcel would be taking his services elsewhere.

Six teams were in the early running: the Montreal Canadiens, St. Louis Blues, Buffalo Sabres, Toronto Maple Leafs, Los Angeles Kings, and Edmonton Oilers. Ultimately, the Kings, whose owner Jack Kent Cooke had just acquired Kareem Abdul-Jabbar for his basketball Lakers, offered the most money.

The Kings won the bidding war, and surrendered veteran defenseman Terry Harper and rugged forward Dan Maloney to Detroit. Cooke signed Marcel to a five-year, $1.5 million pact, though the Kings didn't always make the playoffs during Dionne's 12 years there.

Dionne played 17 prolific seasons for an assortment of teams, but he became a superstar with Los Angeles, scoring 137 and 135 points in his first two seasons there (1979–80 and 1980–81). His 1,771 career points were firmly fourth all time entering 2001–02.

He completed his career in 1988–89 with the New York Rangers and went on to become a successful businessman, often appearing at NHL rinks for Heroes of Hockey events and Old-Timers Games.

KEN DORATY

BORN: Stittsville, Ontario, June 23, 1906
DIED: April 4, 1981
POSITION: Forward, Chicago Blackhawks, 1926–27; Toronto Maple Leafs, 1932–35; Detroit Red Wings, 1937–38
AWARDS/HONORS: NHL All-Star Game, 1934

Even the severest of hockey critics acknowledged that the Toronto-Boston playoff confrontation on April 3, 1933, remains one of the classic sports events of all time. It was marked by robust body checks, superlative goaltending by Lorne Chabot of Toronto and Tiny Thompson of Boston, and not a single goal in regulation time.

The clubs battled through period after period of sudden-death overtime and the game went on into the early morning. Early in the sixth overtime, Bruins defenseman Eddie Shore attempted a clearing pass that was intercepted by Andy Blair of Toronto. Blair spotted Ken Doraty and slipped a pass to the little forward, who raced in and scored the winning goal, at 4:46 of the sixth overtime—164:46 of the game, the longest game played in the NHL for many years. Doraty's feat was eclipsed by Modere "Mud" Bruneteau, who scored the winning goal in the sixth overtime period for Detroit against the Montreal Maroons on March 24, 1936.

GARY DORNHOEFER

BORN: Kitchener, Ontario, February 2, 1943
POSITION: Right Wing, Boston Bruins, 1963–67; Philadelphia Flyers, 1967–78

It is amazing that Gary Dornhoefer missed only 25 contests in the Flyers' Stanley Cup season of 1973–74. The big right-winger was plagued by torn knee ligaments and a broken wrist during the regular campaign, yet still managed to total 50 points. His best season was 1972–73, when Dorny accounted for 30 goals and 49 assists.

Originally the property of the Boston Bruins, Gary derived as much pleasure as anyone in beating the Bruins for the Cup in 1974, even though sidelined in Game Three of the final series with a shoulder separation.

Dornhoefer remained an NHL player with the Flyers through 1978. Following retirement, he turned to broadcasting, working as a Flyers TV analyst into the twenty-first century.

GORDIE DRILLON

BORN: Moncton, New Brunswick, October 23, 1914
DIED: October 22, 1986
POSITION: Right Wing, Toronto Maple Leafs, 1936–42; Montreal Canadiens, 1942–43
AWARDS/HONORS: Art Ross Trophy, 1938; NHL First Team All-Star, 1938, 1939; NHL Second Team All-Star, 1942; Hockey Hall of Fame, 1975

One of the best NHL scorers was a six-feet-two, 178-pound right-winger from Moncton, New Brunswick. Hefty and handsome, Drillon alarmed Leaf manager Conn

Smythe in one way: He seemed disinclined to fight, and that left Conn wondering whether Gordie could fill Charlie Conacher's skates. In his rookie year, 1936–37, Drillon scored 16 goals and 17 assists for 33 points in 41 games. A season later, he had established himself as a first-rate forward with 26 goals, 26 assists, and 52 points. He led the league in goals and points.

Unfortunately, Drillon had two raps against him. He was following the beloved Conacher, and he had a habit of scoring the kind of goals that lacked spectator appeal. The public considered Drillon more lucky than skillful and tended to label his efforts "garbage goals."

Those who followed Drillon and studied his craft soon realized there was a subtle secret to Gordie's goal-scoring. Drillon would park himself in front of the net, angle his stick, and allow passes to ricochet off the blade and into the cage before the goalie could move. This skill was accomplished after long weeks of practice with Turk Broda, his goaltender.

Opponents kept ribbing Gordie about his "luck." Once he was severely withered by veteran players on the New York Americans, who happened to steal a look at Drillon in a private workout with Broda.

Just then, Red Dutton, manager and coach of the Americans, drifted by and heard the carping. He admonished his athletes that they'd do better to study Drillon than to scorn him. That night Gordie scored two of his "garbage goals," the Maple Leafs won, and Dutton lost not only the game but a hat he had thrown on the ice in utter disgust after his players allowed Gordie's second goal.

Drillon was named to the Hockey Hall of Fame in 1975.

JUDE DROUIN

BORN: Mont-Louis, Quebec, October 28, 1948
POSITION: Center, Montreal Canadiens,
1968–70; Minnesota North Stars, 1970–75;
New York Islanders, 1975–78; Winnipeg Jets,
1979–81

Like many Quebecois youngsters, Jude Drouin dreamed of someday playing center for the Montreal Canadiens. Unlike most French-Canadian boys, Drouin got the chance to do precisely that—for 12 games—in which he registered one assist. Drouin's break came when he was dealt to Minnesota in 1970, a year in which he set a mark for rookies with 52 assists. Despite his size, or lack of it, Drouin, one of the best stickhandlers in the game in his era, became an important cog in the North Star machinery.

In the middle of the 1974–75 season, he was traded to the Islanders, where he starred in the Isles' miracle playoff performances, before they succumbed to the Flyers in a seventh semifinal game.

Drouin's career concluded in Winnipeg in 1981.

CHRIS DRURY

BORN: Trumbull, Connecticut, August 20, 1976
POSITION: Left Wing/Center, Colorado
Avalanche 1998–
AWARDS/HONORS: Hobey Baker Award
1997–98; Calder Memorial Trophy, 1998; NHL
All-Rookie Team, 1998

When the Colorado Avalanche won the Stanley Cup in 2001, they were able to beat the New Jersey Devils in a seven-game series without their ace scorer Peter Forsberg.

However, the Avalanche did have the benefit of Chris Drury, one of the finest American products ever to play in the NHL.

Many observers would attest that without Drury's clutch performance, the Cup win in Denver would have never been possible. Overshadowed by the likes of Joe Sakic, Patrick Roy, and Forsberg, Drury nevertheless was the heart of the Colorado hockey club.

Since his Calder Trophy–winning rookie season of 1998, Drury managed to combine the elements of an indomitable foot soldier and finesse stickhandler.

Hardworking in all areas of the rink and unwavering in journeys to the front of the net, Drury left the mark of a winner upon all of his athletic endeavors. At age 13, he pitched his Little League team to a World Series victory over Taiwan.

Following in the footsteps of older brothers, Chris made the Boston University hockey squad, earning all imaginable accolades ever given to a single player by the school, including multiple NCAA All-American and All-Star selections. By winning the Hobey Baker Award as college hockey player of the year in 1998, Chris became the only player in history to win both the Hobey and the Calder Trophy.

Silencing any doubters of smallish players, Drury's point production increased dramatically in his sophomore NHL effort to 67 from 44 as a rookie.

Drury surprised the eventual champion Dallas Stars with an OT goal in Game Four of the 1999 Western Conference finals, and a regulation-winning tally in Game Five. The ex-collegian punctuated that playoff season with four game-winning goals, tying a record for rookies set by Claude Lemieux in 1986. Two years and a Stanley Cup later, Drury already had eight postseason game-winning goals.

The former All-American translated his success into sharing. His 2001 Stanley Cup run was dedicated to Travis Roy, his fellow teammate at BU, paralyzed during their first game together as freshmen.

KEN DRYDEN

BORN: Hamilton, Ontario, August 8, 1947
POSITION: Goaltender, Montreal Canadiens, 1970–73, 1974–79; General Manager, Toronto Maple Leafs, 1997–99; President, Toronto Maple Leafs, 1997–
AWARDS/HONORS: Conn Smythe Trophy, 1971; Calder Memorial Trophy, 1972; Vezina Trophy, 1973, 1976, 1977–79 (all shared with Michel Laroque); Team Canada, 1972; NHL First Team All-Star, 1973, 1976–79; NHL Second Team All-Star, 1972; NHL Challenge Cup, 1979; NHL All-Star Game, 1972, 1975–78; Hockey Hall of Fame, 1983

The bombshell of September 1973—"Ken Dryden quits hockey for the law books"—was obliterated by the bombshell of May 1974, when the elongated goaltender signed a record contract with the Montreal Canadiens, returning to the nets after a season that saw the Canadiens collapse in his absence.

Dryden began his National Hockey League career in the NHL limelight. Elevated by the Canadiens late in the 1970–71 season, from the Montreal Voyageurs of the American Hockey League, Dryden played in only six regular-season games. Then, as the Canadiens captured the Stanley Cup under coach Al MacNeil, Dryden won the Conn Smythe Trophy as the most valuable player in the playoffs. Dryden posted a 2.24 goals-against average in 1971–72, his official rookie season (he was still considered a rookie because he had played less than 26 games in the previous season) and was awarded the Calder Trophy as the best NHL freshman. The next season, his average climbed a hair to 2.26, as he played in 54 games, ten less than his rookie year. Dryden carted home the Vezina Trophy for this effort.

It was then that Ken dropped the big verbal bomb. He announced he was quitting pro hockey to take a $7,000-a-year job as a law clerk in Toronto. Money was, and wasn't, his object. He was willing to work for peanuts as a law clerk because the Habs weren't willing to meet his financial terms.

Dryden's replacements were three relative novices: Wayne Thomas, Michel Plasse, and Michel "Bunny" Larocque. Many observers felt the Canadiens would fold without extra competence between the crossbars. Ultimately, they were right.

Meanwhile, Ken enjoyed several activities, among them, playing defense in a Toronto industrial league. He also did television commentary for the Toronto Toros of the World Hockey Association.

Naturally, the rumor mill flourished. Would Dryden jump to the WHA in 1974–75? It was no secret that he and Pollock had had their differences. Toros president John Bassett wanted to build a new arena and would need a drawing card. All was resolved on May 24, 1974, when Dryden returned to Montreal to sign his new NHL contract. The McGill Law School graduate employed an old Cornell classmate, Arthur Kaminsky, as his agent. The contract was one of the highest ever for goalies, estimated at well over $100,000 a year. But Ken had a mediocre year in 1974–75 as the Canadiens were wiped out of the Stanley Cup playoffs by Buffalo.

That loss was eradicated when the Canadiens won four consecutive Stanley Cups from 1976–79, with Dryden capturing the Vezina—shared with Larocque—in 1977, 1978, and 1979—after each season. He retired in 1979 with a .758 winning percentage and immersed himself in writing and education.

Armed with a law degree, Dryden returned to the NHL as president of the Toronto Maple Leafs in 1997, and briefly served as general manager until appointing Pat Quinn in 1999. He remained an active proponent of clean and speedier hockey and also campaigned for better television coverage.

RICK DUDLEY

BORN: Toronto, Ontario, January 31, 1949
POSITION: Left Wing, Buffalo Sabres, 1972-75, 1979-81; Winnipeg Jets, 1981; Coach, Buffalo Sabres, 1989-92; General Manager, Ottawa Senators, 1998-99; Tampa Bay Lightning, 1999-2002; Florida Panthers, 2002-

Rick Dudley developed into one of those rare professional athletes who excelled at two sports, ice hockey and lacrosse. He turned hockey pro with the Minnesota North Stars organization, but was shelved by a leg injury in less than two seasons. Buffalo obtained the rights to Dudley after a tip from an old lacrosse coach. Dudley made his NHL debut in 1972-73 with the Sabres, but didn't achieve eminence until the 1974-75 season, when he became the team's fifth leading scorer with 31 goals. He hurt his knee during the 1975 Stanley Cup playoffs against Montreal and missed the first two contests of the Cup finals against Philadelphia. When he returned, the Sabres won the next two.

Following the Sabres' elimination in six games, Dudley announced he had joined Cincinnati's new team in the rival WHA. But he would jump back to the NHL and the Sabres in 1979 before finishing his playing career as a Winnipeg Jet in 1981.

A hands-on kind of man, Dudley entered the management realm and became owner-general manager-coach of Carolina of the ECHL before becoming that league's president in 1983. Coaching became his main focus when he helmed the Buffalo Sabres from 1989-92, and he followed that with stints in the AHL and IHL, including the San Diego Gulls, New Haven Nighthawks, Phoenix Roadrunners, and extensive work with the Detroit Vipers.

Developing a penchant for scouting players, Dudley was appointed general manager of the Ottawa Senators in 1998 and guided them to a 103-point season. In 1999, he became general manager of the floundering Tampa Bay Lightning and helped replenish their stock of players. When star center Vincent Lecavalier feuded with management in 2002, and could not be traded, Dudley took the fall, although he had improved the Lightning in his short tenure there.

In May 2002, Dudley rebounded and reappeared in Florida, this time as the Panthers general manager.

DICK DUFF

BORN: Kirkland Lake, Ontario, February 18, 1936
POSITION: Left Wing/Defenseman, Toronto Maple Leafs, 1954-64; New York Rangers, 1964; Montreal Canadiens, 1964-70; Los Angeles Kings, 1970; Buffalo Sabres, 1971-72
AWARDS/HONORS: NHL All-Star Game, 1956-58, 1962-63, 1965, 1967

Dick Duff may not be in the Hockey Hall of Fame, but he certainly did many famous things on the ice. For one, he was a prime catalyst in the Toronto Maple Leafs' 1962 Stanley Cup win, propelling the Leafs to a three-straight Cup dynasty, although he only played on two of the Cup winners. In addition, Duff was a centerpiece for one of the biggest deals in NHL history. He was traded to the New York Rangers with Arnie Brown, Bob Nevin, Bill Collins, and Rod Seiling for Andy Bathgate and Don McKenney on February 22, 1964.

A splendid two-way player, Duff came to the NHL via the vast Toronto Junior farm system. A graduate of St. Michael's College in Toronto, Duff made his NHL debut in the 1954-55 season, but became a regular the next year. In 1958-59, he was a major force, helping the Leafs to the greatest homestretch drive in league annals.

With two weeks left to the season, Toronto trailed the Rangers by seven points, but caught New York on the final night of the season.

It coincided with Duff's career year—29 goals, 24 assists for 53 points. When Toronto won its Stanley Cup in 1961–62, Dick averaged more than a point-per-game, with 3 goals and 10 assists in a dozen games in the postseason. While his stint with the Rangers was a disappointment, Duff found a new life when he was traded to the Montreal Canadiens during the 1964–65 season. Once again, Duff proved how valuable he could be in a championship drive. He was a key figure on no less than four Montreal Stanley Cup–winning teams: 1964–65, 1965–66, 1967–68, and 1968–69. In 1968–69, he recorded a career-high 6 play-off goals and 8 assists for 14 points in 14 playoff games.

Duff concluded his career with the Los Angeles Kings and Buffalo Sabres, and became a scout.

WOODY DUMART

BORN: Kitchener, Ontario, December 23, 1916
DIED: October 19, 2001
POSITION: Left Wing, Boston Bruins, 1936–54
AWARDS/HONORS: NHL Second Team All-Star, 1940–41, 1947; NHL All-Star Game, 1947–48; Hockey Hall of Fame, 1992

The Boston Bruins' crack Kraut Line usually spotlighted center Milt Schmidt or right-winger Bobby Bauer. But its left-winger, Woodrow Wilson Clarence "Woody" Dumart, packed a hard shot and did the less flashy checking that kept him more in the shadows than his pals.

Dumart and Schmidt originally played together—without Bauer—for Kitchener in the Ontario Hockey League, a junior league for players under 21. Dumart made his debut with the Bruins in 1936–37 and played his entire career in Boston, culminating with the 1953–54 campaign. One of Dumart's least-publicized but most effective performances occurred during the 1953 Stanley Cup semifinals against the first-place Detroit Red Wings. Woody,

an aging veteran, was asked to shadow the inimitable Gordie Howe, Detroit's crack right wing. Dumart accomplished his task so well that the Bruins upset the Red Wings in six games and Howe was limited to only two goals.

After serving in the Royal Canadian Air Force from 1941 through 1946, Dumart had his best season in 1946–47 with 24 goals and 28 assists.

Dumart retired in 1959 and spent his retirement years in the Boston area, frequently appearing at Bruins games until his death in 2001.

MOOSE DUPONT

BORN: Trois-Rivières, Quebec, July 27, 1949
POSITION: Defenseman, New York Rangers, 1970–71; St. Louis Blues, 1971–73; Philadelphia Flyers, 1973–80; Quebec Nordiques, 1980–83
AWARDS/HONORS: NHL All-Star Game, 1976

Rejected by the Rangers and Blues, Andre "Moose" Dupont was a boisterous defenseman reclaimed by Flyers coach Fred Shero during the 1972–73 season and turned into a first-rate backline. "Dupont," said *Philadelphia Bulletin* writer Jack Chevalier, "is one of a handful of players who give the fans $8 worth of entertainment every night." The rap against the French-Canadian toughie in New York and St. Louis was that he turned overemotional in many games, took foolish penalties, and hurt rather than helped his team.

Dupont was a Flyers hero in their 1974 Stanley Cup triumph over the Bruins and turned into an All-Star in 1976 when he potted 36 points in 75 games. The man they call "Moose" completed his career with the Quebec Nordiques in 1983, but remained one of the most beloved characters in Flyers history.

BILL DURNAN

BORN: Toronto, Ontario, January 22, 1915
DIED: October 31, 1972
POSITION: Goaltender, Montreal Canadiens, 1943–50
AWARDS/HONORS: Vezina Trophy, 1944–1947, 1949–50; NHL First Team All-Star, 1944–47, 1949–50; NHL All-Star Game, 1947–49; Hockey Hall of Fame, 1964

Bill Durnan's approach to goal-tending suggested Georges Vezina. Like Vezina, Durnan played without a pair of skates until his teens, when a friend "borrowed" his father's unused blades and urged Bill to wear them. Durnan protested that it made little sense wearing

**Bill Durnan,
Canadiens goalie**

the blades even if he was playing goal because he really couldn't skate. Skater or no, in time young Durnan made it to Montreal.

"We weren't impressed with Durnan at first," said Canadiens manager Tommy Gorman, "but he seemed to get better with every game. As goaltenders go he was big and hefty, but nimble as a cat and a great holler guy."

Les Canadiens assumed that Durnan would fit right into the lineup for the 1943–44 season, especially when it was learned that Paul Bibeault had received his call from the Canadian army. Gorman invited Bill to the Canadiens' training camp at Ste. Hyacinthe, Quebec, and the elderly "rookie" quickly impressed Irvin with his ability to glove shots.

"Sign him up," Irvin urged, "and we'll open the season with Durnan in the nets." They did and Les Habitants were off and running to one of the most extraordinary seasons any team ever enjoyed in the NHL. Durnan, in

turn developed into one of the NHL's finest goaltenders, leading the NHL in wins from 1943–44 through 1946–47. His 208 victories in just seven seasons assured his election into the Hall of Fame in 1964.

RED DUTTON

BORN: Russell, Manitoba, July 23, 1898
DIED: March 15, 1987
POSITION: Defenseman, Montreal Maroons, 1926–30; New York Americans, 1930–36; President of the NHL, 1943–46
AWARDS/HONORS: Hockey Hall of Fame, 1958

Red Dutton, a great defenseman of the early NHL, broke into pro hockey with Calgary of the old WCHL. After five years with the Tigers, Mervyn "Red" Dutton signed with the Montreal Maroons where he spent four years gleefully bouncing opposing forwards off the boards.

In 1931, Red was traded to the New York Americans in exchange for the great Lionel Conacher. Red was one of the leading badmen of the day, but the Americans were a hapless bunch of skaters with no real leadership to speak of.

It was not until 1936, when Red became player-manager of the Americans, that they began to approach respectability. Dutton's leadership got the Amerks into the playoffs, but he suffered a painful back injury and was forced to watch from the sidelines as the Toronto sextet bounced the Americans back to Broadway in the semifinal round.

After Dutton retired as a player, he served as manager for six more seasons. The Redhead remained very active on the pro hockey scene and was president of the NHL from 1943 to 1946. Dutton was elected to the Hall of Fame in 1958, and died in 1987 at the age of 89.

BABE DYE

BORN: Hamilton, Ontario, May 13, 1898
DIED: January 3, 1962
POSITION: Right Wing, Toronto St. Patricks, 1919–21, 1921–26; Hamilton Tigers, 1921; Chicago Blackhawks, 1926–27; New York Americans, 1928–29
AWARDS/HONORS: Art Ross Trophy, 1923, 1925; Hockey Hall of Fame, 1970

A right-winger with limitless potential, Cecil "Babe" Dye was unique among young athletes who learned their trade in the renowned Jesse Ketchum School playground in Toronto. Raised by his mother on Boswell Avenue, Babe lost his father only a year after he was born. Esther Dye vowed her son would not lack athletic instruction and proceeded to follow through. "Essie" Dye was an exceptional woman, and nobody appreciated her more than her son. "Mom knew more about hockey than I ever did," Babe once remarked, "and she could throw a baseball right out of the park. She could even cook—as a pinch-hitter!"

Esther Dye's first order of business when the first winter frost arrived was to flood the back-yard rink adjacent to their house; then she would lace on the skates with Cecil. She taught her son until Babe knew everything there was to know about handling a puck, especially the art of shooting it at blinding speed.

"Babe could shoot the puck from any length or from any spot on the rink," said Canadian author Ron McAllister. "He could score with his back turned, or from any side at all. In time, he played with the older boys of the neighborhood, who were forced to welcome him, in spite of his size, for young Dye had a shot like a thunderclap and an astounding accuracy. His light weight became only secondary for Dye because he could snap a two-inch plank with one of his drives."

Babe could pitch and hit a baseball as well as he could manipulate a puck. In 1919, he was invited to sign with the Baltimore Orioles, but he refused in favor of a contract with the Toronto baseball club. Babe's heart was torn between baseball and hockey. His compromise was to play both sports, but his name was to become a household word because of his exploits on the ice, starting with the 1921–22 season, when he donned the Toronto colors.

The Babe played magnificently, scoring 30 goals in 24 games to tie for the league lead with Harry Broadbent of Ottawa. In the play-offs, Babe Dye didn't assert himself to the utmost until the Stanley Cup finals reached the second game. Vancouver, with Lester Patrick behind the bench, edged the St. Pats 4–3 in the first contest, but a goal by the Babe at 4:30 of sudden-death overtime gave Toronto a 2–1 win in the second game. Vancouver went ahead for the last time in the series with a 3–0 triumph in the third match.

Dye continued to sparkle in the Toronto colors. He scored 17 goals in 19 games during 1923–24 and still hadn't reached his peak. Thanks to the Babe's 38 goals in 29 games, Toronto finished a close second to Hamilton in the 1924–25 race. League arrangements called for the second-place Toronto team to meet the third-place Canadiens for the right to play Hamilton in the NHL finals. However, the

Toronto St. Pats ace Cecil "Babe" Dye

Hamilton players staged a surprise strike, demanding more money. League president Frank Calder angrily rejected their demands and ordered the winner of the Montreal-Toronto series to be declared league champions.

This time, Dye was overshadowed by a new star on the NHL horizon. Howie Morenz outshone Dye, leading Montreal to a 3–2 victory in the opening playoff game in Montreal and a 2–0 return match at Toronto. The Babe, meanwhile, was held scoreless and the St. Pats lost possession of the Stanley Cup.

Dye played one more season, 1925–26, with Toronto and scored 18 goals. However, he was traded to Chicago the following year, scoring 25 goals for the Blackhawks. His swan song was played in 1928–29 when the Babe played briefly and ingloriously for the New York Americans. That ended an illustrious NHL career.

ALAN EAGLESON

BORN: St. Catharines, Ontario, April 24, 1933

A bittersweet hockey story, Alan Eagleson was recognized in 1989 for his contributions to hockey when he was entered into the Hockey Hall of Fame as a builder.

An alumni of the University of Toronto, where he graduated with a law degree in 1957, Eagleson was a member of the Provincial Parliament of the Ontario government from 1963 to 1967. He was known to the hockey world as the mastermind behind the 1966 contract with the Boston Bruins, making Bobby Orr worth $75,000 over two years (which, in 1966, was a whopping sum).

In 1967, Eagleson introduced the National Hockey League Players' Association, an institution key to increasing player salaries and one that helped to stabilize relations between players and management.

Eagleson helped organize a Summit Series between Canadian professional hockey players and the Soviet national team in 1972. That success inspired him to form the Canada Cup tournament, which was held for the first time in 1976.

However, Eagleson's meteoric success story and powerful reputation crumpled when he was convicted of embezzlement (taking money from the players' pension fund) and fraud (in organizing international hockey events). Eagleson was sent to jail and was heavily fined for his sins. In 1998, The Eagle, wings thoroughly clipped, became the first Honored Member ever removed from the Hall of Fame.

FRANK EDDOLLS

BORN: Lachine, Quebec, July 5, 1921
DIED: August 13, 1961
POSITION: Defenseman, Montreal Canadiens, 1944–47; New York Rangers, 1947–52
AWARDS/HONORS: NHL All-Star Game, 1951

He didn't know it at the time, but defenseman Frank Eddolls was the cause of a breakup between two old friends and associates—Lester Patrick, the Rangers' vice president and Frank Boucher, the club manager. In trying to rebuild the Rangers during the summer of 1947, Boucher dealt youngsters Hal Laycoe, Joe Bell, and George Robertson to Montreal for Eddolls and center Buddy O'Connor. Patrick, who was being phased out of the Madison Square Garden hierarchy, opposed the deal, but Boucher overruled him.

"Lester," said Boucher, "stopped speaking to me."

The deal was a beauty for Boucher. Eddolls became one of the NHL's best defensemen and O'Connor won the Hart and Lady Byng trophies. Thanks to Eddolls, the Rangers made the playoffs in 1947–48 for the first time in six years. Frankie played for the Rangers through the 1951–52 season and starred for the New Yorkers in the 1950 playoffs when the Rangers took the Red Wings to the seventh game of the finals before losing. He later became a popular and successful minor-league coach before his untimely death of a heart attack in the middle of a round of golf on August 13, 1961.

PATRIK ELIAS

BORN: Trebic, Czechoslovakia, April 13, 1976
POSITION: Left Wing, New Jersey Devils, 1994–
AWARDS/HONORS: NHL All-Rookie Team, 1998; NHL First Team All-Star, 2001; NHL All-Star Game, 2000, 2002

At the end of the twentieth century and into the twenty-first, one of the most productive forward units in the NHL was called the A-Line. It comprised Patrik Elias, Petr Sykora, and Jason Arnott. Those who watched the New Jersey Devils considered Elias the most talented of the three.

It was Patrik's pass to Arnott that produced the Stanley Cup–winning goal against the Dallas Stars at Reunion Arena during the 1999–2000 finals. And it was Elias who helped the Devils to the Stanley Cup finals again in 2000–01.

"He's one of the most gifted players in the league," said Larry Robinson, who was his coach when the Devils won the Cup in June 2000.

Elias came to North America from his native Czechoslovakia in 1994. He was drafted 51st overall and his NHL career took off in 1996–97. He quickly became the Devils' leading scorer, both in the regular season and playoffs in 1999–2000 and 2000–01.

The six-feet-one, 195-pound left wing proved a complete goal scorer whose speed and efficient skating techniques made him one of the most recognized players in the league. These assets also landed him a spot on the Czechoslovakian Republic Olympic team during the 2002 Winter Olympics.

With the third-highest NHL point total and the highest plus/minus in the 2000–01 season, Elias recorded career highs in goals (40), assists (56), and points (96). But 2001–02 was not as stellar a season, for the Devils or for Elias. The A-Line continued to lead the team in scoring, but the team as a whole was struggling.

Finally, at the March 2002 trade deadline, the A-Line was disassembled, when Jason Arnott was traded, along with Randy McKay and a first-round draft pick, to Dallas for forwards Joe Nieuwendyk and Jamie Langenbrunner. Elias finished the season on a line with the two new linemates.

After the 2001–02 season, Sykora was traded to Anaheim. Elias, in turn, was signed to a new long-term contract by the Devils.

RON ELLIS

BORN: Lindsay, Ontario, January 8, 1945
POSITION: Right Wing, Toronto Maple Leafs, 1963–75, 1977–81
AWARDS/HONORS: NHL All-Star Game, 1964–65, 1968, 1970; Team Canada, 1972, 1977

Perhaps the greatest compliment ever paid Ron Ellis, the steady, unspectacular winger for the Toronto Maple Leafs, was afforded by Ace Bailey, the legendary Leaf of years past. It seems that Ron wore jersey number eight for his first four seasons with the Leafs, until Bailey himself

Ron Ellis as a Maple Leaf

suggested that Ellis be given number six. Six, by the way, happened to be Ace's very own numeral that had been retired along with him when Bailey hung up his skates in 1934.

Ellis was a model of consistency and unselfishness with the Leafs from the day he broke in as a regular in 1964. An honest, two-way hockey player, Ellis was one of the unsung heroes of the 1972 Team Canada–Soviet Union series.

After the 1975 season, Ellis said he had had it with the game and went into retirement.

The Maple Leafs' management kept on Ron and finally, in 1977, he succumbed to their pleas and returned to the team for four more seasons, until 1980–81, retiring with 640 points in 1,034 games.

Ellis turned to the management side of the business, and eventually became head of the Hockey Hall of Fame in Toronto.

BRIAN ENGBLOM

BORN: Winnipeg, Manitoba, January 27, 1957
POSITION: Defenseman, Montreal Canadiens, 1976–82; Washington Capitals, 1982–84; Los Angeles Kings, 1984–86; Buffalo Sabres, 1986; Calgary Flames, 1986–87
AWARDS/HONORS: NHL Plus/Minus Leader, 1981; NHL Second Team All-Star, 1982

A solid defensive defenseman who was mostly overlooked during his days with the Montreal Canadiens, Brian Engblom didn't enjoy the limelight until after he retired to become an active television analyst. Engblom inauspiciously began his career with the Habs during the 1976 season, playing six years for Montreal, and he got in on three Stanley Cup victories before his career swerved headlong into the trade winds.

Over his five remaining years in the NHL, he played for four different teams. He joined the Washington Capitals in 1982 as part of their deal for Rod Langway, then moved on for stints with the LA Kings, the Buffalo Sabres, and, finally, the Calgary Flames, where he was forced to retire in 1987. A serious neck injury involving bone spurs required career-ending surgery to repair.

Engblom moved on to television work at ESPN/ABC and his vast knowledge of the game and sideline reporting became familiar trademarks to viewers.

PHIL ESPOSITO

BORN: Sault Ste. Marie, Ontario, February 20, 1942
POSITION: Center, Chicago Blackhawks, 1963–67; Boston Bruins, 1967–75; New York Rangers, 1975–81; Coach, New York Rangers, 1989; General Manager, New York Rangers, 1986–89; Tampa Bay Lightning, 1992–98
AWARDS/HONORS: Hart Memorial Trophy, 1969, 1974; Art Ross Trophy, 1969, 1971–74; NHL First Team All-Star, 1969–75; NHL Second Team All-Star, 1968, 1975; Team Canada, 1972; Lester Patrick Trophy, 1978; Hockey Hall of Fame, 1984

There are pundits who aver that Phil Esposito was the finest center ever to skate in the National Hockey League. They point to the indisputable fact that he regularly led the NHL in scoring; that he was consistently voted to the First All-Star Team and that the Boston Bruins' renaissance directly coincided with his arrival in Beantown at the start of the 1967–68 season. For further emphasis, the Esposito Marching and Chowder Society will quickly point out that Phil was chief architect of Team Canada's pulsating

Tony (left) and Phil Esposito on Team Canada

four-games-to-three (one tie) victory over the Russian National Team in September 1972.

"That series," said *Toronto Globe and Mail* columnist Dick Beddoes, "would not have been won without Esposito's big rough, relentless leadership. I saw him make what will become a hockey heirloom, passing down through the generations."

Others insist that discussing Esposito must occur in the past perfect tense; that something left the hulking centerman in 1973, never to return. Phil-knockers mention that he was knocked out of the 1973 Stanley Cup playoffs with a body check from Ron Harris, a third-string New York Rangers defenseman. The anti-Esposito clan then emphasize that Phil seemed to have lost his scoring touch in the clutch when Boston skated in the 1974 and 1975 playoffs.

Which proves, more than anything, that there are at least two sides to the Esposito controversy. There is, however, absolutely no doubt he was a superstar. Just the fact that he was able to recover from the near-crippling 1973 knee injury to win the 1973–74 scoring title—his fifth in six years—is testimony to the man's superiority and gumption. Because he worked with two burly and gifted wingmen, Ken Hodge and Wayne Cashman, Esposito was virtually unstoppable in his favorite camping ground outside the face-off circle, about 15 feet from the net.

"I'll tell you how good Phil Esposito is," said Maple Leaf manager Punch Imlach. "When you're playing against Espo, you start at least one goal down."

Many experts had a considerable problem defining the Esposito style. Unlike ex-teammate Bobby Orr and the flamboyant Bobby Hull, Esposito relied more on subtle skills.

"You can't compare Orr and me or Hull and me," said Phil. "They brought people to their feet. They are spectacular players. Orr was the best player in the game; I know it and I admit it. I also know that my role is to score goals, to pick up loose pucks and put them behind the goaltender any way I can. So that's what I try to do—and the people still call me a garbage collector."

While Phil's ex-teammate, Bobby Hull, built his reputation on a booming slap shot, Esposito concentrated on a quick wrist drive that was deadly accurate, though Phil rarely looked directly at the net.

On November 7, 1975, the unusually sensitive and highly emotional Esposito was shaken right out of his skates when he learned that, after eight seasons with the Bruins, he was being traded to the hated New York Rangers with Carol Vadnais for Brad Park, Jean Ratelle, and Joe Zanussi.

Hurt to the quick, Esposito's problems, including his hatred of New York City, were compounded when he was injured in his second game with New York and was forced to struggle the rest of that season.

The following year, he was named captain, much to the dismay of fans and some veteran Rangers who felt Rod Gilbert should have worn the "C." New responsibilities failed to ignite Phil, either that season or the next.

In 1978–79, the Rangers made a shift, bringing in Fred Shero as manager-coach, and the former Flyers' leader did two things at the start. First, he took the captaincy away from Esposito and, second, put in a system to which Phil could adapt. He made a remarkable turnaround, playing like the Phil Esposito of old, as he helped the Rangers to a winning season and an appearance in the 1979 playoffs.

Phil retired in 1981 with 717 career goals (fourth all-time) and 1,590 points (seventh all-time heading into 2001–02). The Hall of Fame instantly beckoned Phil in 1984 and his Boston Bruins number 7 jersey was retired—after Ray Bourque graciously relinquished that number. Bourque tore off his own number 7 sweater to reveal his new 77 sweater at an emotional ceremony at Boston Garden in 1987.

Espo headed to the Rangers' broadcast booth as color analyst before ascending to general manager of the Blueshirts in 1986. He coached the team briefly after his many trades and firing of bench boss Michel Bergeron failed to spark the team out of the first round of the 1989 playoffs.

In 1992, "Trader Phil" became the original general manager of the Tampa Bay Lightning, which he helped cofound. His tenure featured high attendance, many trades, and one playoff appearance (1996) before Espo left after an ownership shakeup in 1998. He returned to broadcasting, offering analysis for FOX Sports.

TONY ESPOSITO

BORN: Sault Ste. Marie, Ontario, April 23, 1943
POSITION: Goaltender, Montreal Canadiens, 1968–69; Chicago Blackhawks, 1969–84; General Manager, Pittsburgh Penguins, 1988–89; Director of Hockey Development and Scouting, Tampa Bay Lightning, 1991–98
AWARDS/HONORS: Calder Memorial Trophy, 1970; Vezina Trophy, 1970, 1972 (shared with Gary Smith), 1974 (shared with Bernie Parent); Team Canada, 1972; NHL First Team All-Star, 1970, 1972; NHL Second Team All-Star, 1973–74; NHL Challenge Cup, 1979; NHL All-Star Game, 1970–74, 1980; Hockey Hall of Fame, 1988

One thing the National Hockey League has never lacked is brother acts—the Bentley boys, Rocket and Pocket Rocket Richard, and the high-scoring Hulls, to name a few—all of them first-rate forwards and stars of their day. So when Tony Esposito, 14 months the junior of brother Phil, made his big-league debut in goal against the Oakland Seals on November 29, 1968, hockey followers did not take special notice. No fanfare, no big buildup; Phil's "kid brother" was just another rookie netminder about to be painfully indoctrinated into the frozen world of ricocheting rubber.

Tony played sparingly for the Habs. In June 1969, the Canadiens left him unprotected in the intraleague draft and he was picked up by Chicago.

Tony fit right into the Hawks' scheme. Coach Billy Reay displayed a lot of confidence in him by starting Espo in the 1969–70 season opener at St. Louis. Tony was bombed, 7–2, but Reay continued to give him the lion's share of the work while veteran goalie Denis DeJordy was relegated to a backup role.

Although the Hawks and Bruins finished in a virtual tie for first place in the East with identical point totals, Chicago was awarded that honor on the basis of most wins. That meant the Blackhawks would face the Detroit Red Wings in the opening round of the 1970 Stanley Cup playoffs, while Boston drew the New York Rangers.

Both the Hawks and the Bruins advanced to the semifinal round with relatively little trouble. The stage was set for one of the all-time classic grudge matches. The Boston players felt they deserved first place since they had finished with the best won-lost percentage, while Chicago was determined to prove that they were the rightful heirs to the Prince of Wales Trophy, emblematic of first place in the East Division.

Needless to say, the Espositos had their own personal affair to settle. Tony was determined to keep his older brother off the scoresheet. But Phil put his seven-year NHL savvy to use and led the Bruins to the Stanley Cup by way of a four-game sweep of the Hawks. Poor Tony manned the goal in each game. Even with Tony's outstanding goaltending and amount of minutes played over the years, the Hawks were unable to nail down the big prize during his tenure.

He finally retired in 1984 after 16 seasons, 423 wins (only Patrick Roy, Terry Sawchuk, and Jacques Plante had more), a lifetime 2.92 goals-against average, and 76 career shutouts, which remained seventh all-time.

Tony briefly assumed the vice president and

general manager's role with the Pittsburgh Penguins from April 1988 to December 1989 before a stint with Tampa Bay as director of Scouting and Development—while brother Phil co-owned and ran the team until 1998.

JACK EVANS

BORN: Garnant, South Wales, Great Britain, April 21, 1928
DIED: November 10, 1996
POSITION: Defenseman, New York Rangers, 1948–58; Chicago Blackhawks, 1958–63; Coach, California Seals, 1975–76; Cleveland Barons, 1976–78; Hartford Whalers, 1983–88
AWARDS/HONORS: NHL All-Star Game, 1961–62

There have been few players with more raw strength than Jack "Tex" Evans, who split his NHL career between the Rangers (1948 through 1958) and the Blackhawks (1958 through 1963). Tex also was renowned for his "lantern jaw" and his reluctance to speak. When Evans roomed with the equally shy Andy Hebenton, their entire daylong conversation went as follows:

"Tex, do you wanna see a movie today?"
"Yup!"

End of twelve-hour Evans-Hebenton dialogue.

After retiring as a player, Tex coached in the NHL after expansion, with stints in California and Cleveland, before some mild success in Hartford in the 1980s. Evans died in 1996.

BILL EZINICKI

BORN: Winnipeg, Manitoba, March 11, 1924
POSITION: Right Wing, Toronto Maple Leafs, 1944–50; Boston Bruins, 1950–52; New York Rangers, 1954–55
AWARDS/HONORS: NHL All-Star Game, 1947–48

Wild Bill" Ezinicki had sinewy arms and a body that bulged from daily weightlifting. A right-winger for the grand Toronto Cup winners (1947–48, 1948–49), he had a passion for free-skating that was outdone only by his passion for bodychecking. He also had a passion for tape, winding reams of it around his stick and around his knees and legs until they bulged grotesquely.

Once, Wild Bill had four teeth knocked out in a key homestretch game, but despite pain and nervous shock, he returned to score the winning goal. He would collide with opponents—usually bigger opponents—from any direction. Sometimes he would wait for an opponent to speed in his path, then bend forward, swing his hips, and send his foe flying over him. If Ezzie got the worst of a fracas, which did not happen often, he could still get consolation from his insurance policy; the policy paid him $5 for every stitch resulting from a hockey injury. "It's just like double indemnity," he'd say.

Ezinicki was adored in Toronto and despised everywhere else. The Red Wings charged him with deliberately injuring goalie Harry Lumley. *Boston Globe* writer Herb Ralby said, "Toronto has the leading candidate for the most hated opponent in Ezinicki." In New York, a woman in a front row seat jammed a long hatpin in Ezinicki's derriere as he bent over to take a face-off. On November 8, 1947, Ezinicki crumpled Ranger center Edgar Laprade to the ice with a body check. Laprade suffered a concussion, and Ranger coach Frank Boucher protested to league president Clarence Campbell with a scathing telegram.

Leafs coach Conn Smythe counterattacked the charge by urging Campbell to fine Boucher $1,000 for "acting in a manner prejudicial to the league." Smythe's trump card was a movie of the action. He offered to have a special screening for Boucher and six New York writers visiting Toronto. Boucher refused, and Smythe chortled: "They don't want to see a legal body check. It might give their players a bad habit."

Eleven days after the incident Campbell completed his investigation and said, "Reports of the officials show that the check by Ezinicki was perfectly legal and not a charge. The injury to Laprade was not caused by Ezinicki's stick but by Laprade striking the ice as he fell."

Ezinicki played on Toronto Cup winners in 1947, 1948, and 1949. He later was traded to Boston. After retiring from hockey he became a successful golf pro in Massachusetts.

SERGEI FEDOROV

BORN: Pskov, USSR, December 13, 1969
POSITION: Center/Defenseman, Detroit Red Wings, 1990–
AWARDS/HONORS: Frank J. Selke Trophy, 1994, 1996; Lester B. Pearson Award, 1994; Hart Memorial Trophy, 1994; NHL All-Rookie Team, 1991; NHL First Team All-Star, 1994; NHL All-Star Game, 1992, 1994, 1996, 2001

Rare is the athlete in any sport who can single-handedly change the nature of how a game is played. But Sergei Fedorov not only changed what hockey became in the 1990s, he also was paramount in the transformation of the fiscal policies that governed it during that decade.

With his shiny white skates and golden-brown hair flowing from his helmet, Sergei Fedorov hit the NHL at a time when it was being dominated by boorishness both inside and outside the rink.

This native of Pskov truly brought a breath of fresh air to a league that was becoming stale. Trained by the best coaches and teachers in the Soviet Union, and playing with the likes of future NHLers Alexander Mogilny and Pavel Bure, Fedorov defected to the United States in order to play in the NHL, an action that few had the courage to take, due to the political ramifications. He was taken in the fourth round of the 1989 draft by the Detroit Red Wings.

He broke into the league with fire in his eyes and jets in his skates. On October 4, 1990, Sergei Fedorov made his NHL debut in New Jersey. He promptly scored his first goal on the power play. He finished his rookie year with 31 goals and 48 assists, and was selected to the NHL All-Star Rookie Team in 1991. He also finished second in the Calder Trophy voting

for Rookie of the Year honors, losing out to Chicago goaltender Ed Belfour.

As the Red Wings rose to the top of the league in the mid 1990s with the likes of captain Steve Yzerman and goaltender Mike Vernon, Sergei Fedorov continued his ascent into stardom.

In 1993–94, Fedorov had the kind of magical season players dream about. Playing in all 82 games, Sergei scored 56 goals and added 64 assists, becoming only the fourth Red Wing ever to win the Hart Trophy as Most Valuable Player in the NHL. Additionally, he won the Lester B. Pearson Award as MVP of the league as voted by his peers, and the Frank J. Selke Trophy as best defensive forward. He was also an NHL First Team All-Star.

In 1997, Fedorov and the Red Wings entered the playoffs looking to end a 42-year Stanley Cup drought. Detroit began the playoffs in the unfamiliar position of being a slight underdog.

The previous three seasons, Detroit had posted outstanding regular season records, only to falter in the postseason. However, this year was going to be different, as the Wings actually finished the regular season just 12 games over .500.

During the latter part of the season, Coach Scotty Bowman even began to experiment with Sergei, using him as a defenseman during certain portions of a game

Proving his all-around worth, Sergei led the club with 20 postseason points, 12 assists, and 4 game-winning goals en route to helping Detroit win their first Stanley Cup since 1955.

That summer, Sergei became a restricted free agent while basking in the silver glow of Lord Stanley's chalice. Fedorov was free to sign with any club in the league; the stipulation, however, was that his new club would have to surrender a maximum of five first-round draft picks to the Wings.

But Fedorov's agent Mike Barnett and Red Wing general manager Ken Holland could not hammer out a deal. In February, the NHL for the first time allowed players to participate in the 1998 Winter Olympics in Nagano, Japan. Fedorov was invited to play for the Russian team. They would soon pick up the silver medal, losing to the upstart Czech Republic in the gold medal game.

But on February 18, 1998, Carolina Hurricane owner Peter Karmanos authorized his general manager, Jim Rutherford, to submit an offer sheet to the Fedorov camp that was of astronomical and seemingly insurmountable proportions. The offer was for a six-year contract worth $38 million, an amount that would signal the end to any type of fiscal sanity inherent among any hockey team's financial decision-makers.

The Red Wings would match the Hurricanes' offer, and Sergei Fedorov would be in a Detroit uniform for five more seasons.

After a tumultuous season, the Red Wings and Sergei Fedorov were finally ready to defend their 1997 Stanley Cup championship. By playing in only 21 regular season games, Sergei looked stronger than ever as the Wings prepared for their first-round opponents, the Phoenix Coyotes. He took off like a rocket, as Detroit defeated Phoenix in the first round, four games to two. Sergei had five goals in the first five games of the series and Coyotes coach Jim Schoenfeld deemed him the best Detroit player on the ice.

For the second year in a row, Detroit advanced to the Stanley Cup finals, where they were to meet the Washington Capitals.

The Wings came in a prohibitive favorite, and promptly swept the Capitals away in four games, winning the Stanley Cup for the second straight year. Again showing why he will be remembered as one of the best playoff performers in the history of the NHL, Fedorov scored the game-winning goal in Game Three of the series, and helped open the scoring in the deciding Game Four after curling away

from a would-be defender to whistle a perfect pass to Doug Brown, who lifted the puck into the net. The goal was indeed vintage Fedorov.

In the spring of 2002, Fedorov helped the Red Wings to get another Stanley Cup. There is no disputing that Fedorov not only helped liberate his peers back in the former Soviet Union, but also earned the reputation of being one of the best clutch performers during a time when it means the most: the playoffs.

JOHN FERGUSON

BORN: Vancouver, British Columbia, September 5, 1938
POSITION: Right Wing, Montreal Canadiens, 1963–71; General Manager/Coach, New York Rangers, 1976–77; General Manager, New York Rangers, 1977–78; General Manager, Winnipeg Jets, 1979–89; Front Office, Ottawa Senators, 1992–95; Senior Professional Scout, San Jose Sharks, 1996–
AWARDS/HONORS: NHL All-Star Game, 1965, 1967

When the third-place Boston Bruins took on the first-place Montreal Canadiens in the opening round of the Eastern Division's Stanley Cup playoffs in April 1968, there were whispers that the Canadiens were in for an upset. "You watch the Bruins' tough guys go after the smaller

John Ferguson as general manager of the Winnipeg Jets

Montrealers early in the game, soften 'em up, and then you'll see the game turn in Boston's favor," one newsman prophesied.

In the first game of the series, Canadian "policeman" Johnny Ferguson detected the Bruins' strategy on his radarscope and went after Ted Green. With one hand he grabbed Green's jersey and lifted it high over the Boston player's head so that Green was both blinded and partly handcuffed. With the other hand, Ferguson pummeled Green about the head until there was little doubt that the Montrealer had scored a decisive victory over a man who rarely lost fights.

Just how decisive the victory was soon became evident. The Bruins turned pussycats and, tails between their legs, lost the series in four straight games. While Ferguson didn't exactly win the round for Montreal, he turned the psychological lever in their direction and the Canadiens roared on to win the Stanley Cup.

Respect was the key prize Ferguson earned after joining Montreal in the 1963–64 season, and not merely for his fighting ability. During the Stanley Cup playoffs with the Rangers in 1967, it was Fergy who lifted the Canadiens into the finals by scoring the winning goal in sudden-death overtime of the fourth game. But scoring certainly was not his forte. A lumbering skater, he often suggested a rhinoceros galumphing up and down the rink. His shot was average at best, and he was not exactly known for his stickhandling ability.

Fergie's intense hatred for the opposition extended beyond the ice, and he was known to snub rivals even during the off-season, when he indulged his other great love, horse racing. In 1976, Fergy was coaxed back to hockey as general manager–coach of the New York Rangers. His stay was less than successful.

After the 1978 season, Ferguson was given his walking papers, but not before he completed a huge deal. He was responsible for the Swedish tandem of Ulf Nilsson and Anders Hedberg leaving the Winnipeg Jets of the WHA and signing with the Rangers. The irony was that when Ferguson left New York, he became general manager of the Jets, where he could well have used the services of the flashy Swedish pair.

Fergy remained active in hockey into the new century in a variety of roles, which included professional scouting for the San Jose Sharks and as an aide to general manager Dean Lombardi. His son, John Ferguson Jr., enjoyed a successful college playing career and eventually became the vice president and director of Hockey Operations with the St. Louis Blues.

RAY FERRARO

BORN: Trail, British Columbia, August 23, 1964
POSITION: Center, Hartford Whalers, 1984–91; New York Islanders, 1991–95; New York Rangers, 1995–96; Los Angeles Kings, 1996–99; Atlanta Thrashers, 1999–2002; St. Louis Blues, 2002
AWARDS/HONORS: NHL All-Star Game, 1992

The general feeling that hockey is a big-man's game has been refuted over the years by many stars, from Aurel Joliat to Bill Mosienko to Theo Fleury.

Another relatively small player was Ray Ferraro, who starred for Hartford, both New York teams, Los Angeles, Atlanta, and St. Louis. The five-feet-nine, 200-pound Ferraro finally earned the captain title with a club in his second year with the Thrashers.

"Ray is the type of captain who sets a great example for our younger players," said Don Waddell, general manager of the club. "He always gives his all and is the type of player we want to lead us into battle every night."

The highlight of Ferraro's career was his work in the 1993 Stanley Cup playoffs, where his inspired play and two overtime goals in round one against the Washington Capitals helped lead an upstart Islander team all the way to the Conference finals before they lost to Montreal. Just the season before, Ray had his career-best 40 goals and 40 assists in an All-Star season on Long Island.

Ferraro made stops for the Rangers and the Los Angeles Kings before signing as a free agent with expansion Atlanta in 1999.

In the 2000–01 season, Ray led the Thrashers in points (76) playing on a line with veterans Andrew Brunette and Donald Audette. He was named as one of three finalists for the Masterton Trophy in the same season, as well as given the Thrashers MVP Award by the fans.

An aspiring broadcaster, Ray was unexpectedly dealt to the Cup-contending St. Louis Blues in March 2002 but could not help them to a title. He retired to become a full-time broadcaster.

SLAVA FETISOV

BORN: Moscow, Russia, April 20, 1958
POSITION: Defenseman, Central Red Army, 1975–89; Soviet Junior National Team, 1975–77; Soviet National Team, 1976–90; New Jersey Devils, 1989–95; Detroit Red Wings, 1995–98; Coach, 2002 Russian Olympic Hockey Team
AWARDS/HONORS: Best Defenseman ELC-A, 1976; WJC-A All-Star, 1978, 1982–83, 1985–87, 1989–91; Best Defenseman WJC-A, 1978; Best Defenseman, WEC-A, 1978, 1982, 1985–86, 1989; USSR First Team All-Star, 1979–80, 1982–88; USSR Player of the Year, 1982, 1986; Leningradskaya-Pravda Trophy (Top Scoring Defenseman), 1984, 1986–88; NHL All-Star, 1997–98; Hockey Hall of Fame, 2001

Russian-born players long were renowned for their world-class play, but it wasn't until the New Jersey Devils broke the Iron Curtain barrier that kept Soviet aces from playing in North America that NHL audiences could appreciate their talent.

Viacheslav (Slava) Fetisov generally was regarded as the pioneer Russian who made the transition possible; but it wasn't easy.

After years of prodding by New Jersey Devil general manager Lou Lamoriello, Fetisov finally was granted—along with fellow countryman Sergei Starikov—permission to sign with the New Jersey outfit.

Fetisov made his NHL debut during the 1989–90 season at the age of 31. Considered the best of the Russian defensemen, he had lost a step by the time he came to North America, but still played a reasonably effective game as the Devils ascended the NHL ranks.

However, in the second sudden-death overtime period of the seventh game of the Rangers-Devils playoff in 1994, Fetisov delivered a fatal cross-ice pass that was intercepted by the Rangers. New York counterattacked and Stephane Matteau put the puck behind Martin Brodeur for the series-clinching goal.

Fetisov obtained a measure of glory after being traded to the Detroit Red Wings in 1995. He played on two Stanley Cup–winning teams, eventually retiring to become an assistant coach in New Jersey. He was dismissed late in the 2001–02 season but managed and coached the Russian Olympic Team in Salt Lake City for the 2002 Winter Games. The Russians were beaten by the United States in the semifinal round, but won the bronze after crushing Belarus in the third-place game. After being accepted into the Hockey Hall of Fame (2001), Slava became overseer of Russian sports in late spring of 2002.

FERNIE FLAMAN

BORN: Dysart, Saskatchewan, January 25, 1927
POSITION: Defenseman, Boston Bruins, 1944–51, 1954–61; Toronto Maple Leafs, 1951–54
AWARDS/HONORS: NHL Second Team All-Star, 1955, 1957–58; NHL All-Star Game, 1952, 1955–59; Hockey Hall of Fame, 1990

Before Bobby Orr and the Big Bad Bruins came along in the late 1960s, the Boston hockey club was notorious as a bashing sextet. From 1954 through 1961, its chief basher was defenseman Ferdinand Charles Flaman, a smooth-skating defenseman who broke into pro hockey as a teenager during World War II.

Flaman developed his hard-hitting style with the Eastern League Boston Olympics, playing briefly with the Bruins in 1944–45 and 1945–46. A year later he became a permanent NHL skater with Boston. In 1950–51, he was traded to the Maple Leafs where his style was less appreciated than in Beantown. He returned to the Bruins at the start of the 1954–55 campaign.

"Fernie was a solid bodychecker," said Hall of Famer Milt Schmidt, who coached Flaman in Boston, "and was at his best when things were rough."

Rare was the night when Flaman lost a fight. He decisioned Rangers' badman Lou Fontinato at Madison Square Garden and once nearly killed Montreal's Henri Richard with a devastating but legal body check during a game at Boston Garden.

Following his playing days, Flaman became a coach, first with the pros, later in the collegiate ranks for Northeastern. In the latter years of his career, Flaman was a trusted scout for the New Jersey Devils.

CLIFF FLETCHER

BORN: Montreal, Quebec, August 16, 1935
POSITION: General Manager, Atlanta Flames, 1972–80; Calgary Flames, 1980–91; CEO/President/General Manager, Toronto Maple Leafs, 1991–97; Senior Advisor, Tampa Bay Lightning, 1997–2000; General Manager, Phoenix Coyotes, 2000–02

Shrewd and with a flair for the dramatic move, Cliff Fletcher was one of the top NHL general managers for the better part of four decades.

Fletcher started his hockey career as a scout for the Montreal Junior Canadiens and St. Louis Blues, where he eventually moved into the assistant general manager position.

Fletcher then became general manager of the Calgary Flames for the club's first 19 years in the NHL. He managed the induction of the Atlanta Flames in 1972 and organized the franchise's move to Calgary in 1980. During

the club's first 11 seasons in Calgary, the team got two President's Trophies, two Campbell Conference titles, two Smythe Division titles, and a Stanley Cup in 1989. Fletcher's deal for Doug Gilmour in September of 1988 deftly accelerated his Calgary Flames' 1989 Cup march.

From 1991–97, Fletcher was the chief operating officer, president, and general manager of the Toronto Maple Leafs, with the Leafs making the Conference finals twice (1993 and 1994).

After Toronto, Fletcher was senior adviser to the general manager of the Tampa Bay Lightning for two years before moving to Phoenix in 2001 to become executive vice president and general manager of the Coyotes. The following season, when Wayne Gretzky joined the Coyotes' management and Michael Barnett became general manager, Fletcher became senior executive vice president of hockey operations, helping to rebuild the team into a playoff contender.

Fletcher's 25-plus years of experience as an NHL general manager and respect around the league led him to an appointment to the Hockey Hall of Fame's selection committee.

THEO FLEURY

BORN: Oxbow, Saskatchewan, June 29, 1968
POSITION: Right Wing, Calgary Flames, 1988–99; Colorado Avalanche, 1999; New York Rangers, 1999–2002; Chicago Blackhawks, 2002–
AWARDS/HONORS: NHL Second Team All-Star, 1995; NHL All-Star Game, 1991, 1992, 1996, 1997, 1998, 1999, 2001

Fiery, feisty, and often ferocious, Theo Fleury nonetheless had to overcome several obstacles to achieve stardom in the NHL. For one, he was—at five feet six—one of the smallest players in The Game. For another, early in his career, he was diagnosed with a chronic medical condition called Crohn's disease, which is controllable, but incurable.

However, from the moment he stepped on NHL ice, Fleury established the fact that his short stature would not be a problem, for himself at any rate. Theo's "in-your-face-even-though-his-face-is-level-with-your-chest" attitude defined the way he immediately played the game. He wasn't afraid to fight and when he couldn't fight, he'd harass the opposition unremittingly.

Theoren Fleury as a Calgary Flame

A ninth-round pick, 166th overall in 1987, Fleury immediately helped the Flames as a rookie, as Calgary walked away with the Cup that year, 1988–89. After coming up from the Salt Lake Golden Eagles, he scored 34 points in 36 games, and soon became a mainstay in the Flames' everyday lineup. However, Calgary's triumphant era of the 1990s was short, as free agents fled the team, making Fleury the only superstar on a team full of youngsters. With three 40-goal seasons and one 50-goal season to his credit, Fleury proved he had NHL mettle, and his eight seasons of 100-plus penalty minutes emphasized the point.

But, in 1999, it would be Fleury's turn to test the free agent waters, so Calgary shipped him to Colorado for the remainder of the season. After finishing the year with Colorado, Fleury signed as a free agent with the New York Rangers and began a second career, of sorts, on Broadway. Unfortunately, his first year was a disappointment, as he scored only 15 goals in the 1999–2000 season, the lowest total since his rookie season of 14 goals; but he rebounded with 30 goals in only 62 games in his next year.

Theo's 2000–01 season ended abruptly, however, as he checked himself into the NHL's substance abuse program and missed the final 20 games of the season. He was released and returned to the Rangers for 2001–02.

Joined by newly acquired Eric Lindros and speedy Mike York on the top line, Fleury delivered admirably in the Rangers' early-season drive to first place, but nose-dived when the team faded out of the playoff picture; again his personal, off-ice issues took a stranglehold. His effectiveness on the scoreboard stunted, Fleury's overall behavior spiraled out of control, overshadowing his 2002 Olympic gold medal win at Salt Lake with Team Canada, as well as his attaining 1,000 NHL points. By the time the Rangers had missed the postseason for a fifth consecutive year, Fleury's future in Gotham looked doubtful. He was released by New York in the summer of 2002. As a free agent, Theo was signed by the Chicago Blackhawks for the 2002–03 season.

LOU FONTINATO

BORN: Guelph, Ontario, January 20, 1932
POSITION: Defenseman, New York Rangers, 1954–61; Montreal Canadiens, 1961–63

In many ways, Lou Fontinato portrayed the best and worst aspects of pro hockey. He was lionized as a Broadway hero during most of his Ranger career and was feared throughout the league from his rookie season, 1954–55, until the day Gordie Howe destroyed his effectiveness with a flurry of lethal punches at Madison Square Garden.

On the day in question, Fontinato had a couple of scores to settle with Howe. For one thing, the Detroit superman had nearly sliced Fontinato's ear off with his stick in an earlier game; for another Fontinato was anxious to erase any doubts about who was the toughest man in the league. Besides, he felt obliged to assist Eddie Shack, who had started a fracas and seemed to be losing his bout with Howe on points.

Fontinato moved swiftly from his outpost at the blue line. The distance from the blue line to the bout was about 70 feet, which the Ranger policeman negotiated in a few seconds. The circumstances were perfect for Fontinato. In most of his fights he would defeat opponents by a surprise attack, raining blows on them before they could muster a defense. Howe, who was concentrating on Shack, didn't see Fontinato coming.

The Ranger knocked him off balance and discharged a flurry of punches that normally would have sent an opponent reeling for cover. Howe stared down the blows without flinching. He seemed to be sizing up Fontinato. Then, the counterattack began. Howe's short jabs moved like locomotive pistons, striking the Ranger around the nose and eyes. Clop! Clop! Clop! At about this time the linesmen moved in to halt the bout, but nobody wanted to get near the punches. Fontinato returned with a few drives to Howe's midsection, but Howe ignored them.

The once fearsome Ranger had been mashed almost beyond recognition. His nose was broken at a right angle to his face, which was dripping with blood. Only one factor saved him from complete disaster: He wasn't knocked down. The defeat ruined Fontinato. His air of braggadocio vanished. His play deteriorated and so did the Rangers. Coach Phil Watson traced the team's amazing end-of-season collapse and last-day ouster from a playoff berth to the Fontinato disaster.

Fontinato was traded by New York to the Montreal Canadiens prior to the 1961–62 campaign and was playing his second season in Montreal when he nearly was killed in a freak accident during a game, ironically, with the Rangers at the Montreal Forum. Racing with New York's Vic Hadfield for a loose puck at the end boards, Fontinato got there first. The Canadiens' defenseman then attempted to upend Hadfield by crouching low as his foe was about to hit Lou into the boards. Fontinato did manage to crouch, but Hadfield

bodied Lou in such a way that the defenseman's neck was broken. His career ended on the same violent note with which it had begun.

Prior to the accident Lou had built a reputation on hard checks and fast fists. He once bloodied Maurice Richard in New York, inspiring columnist Red Smith to describe the game as a "Roman circus." Fontinato had rarely lost a bout although he took on the NHL's toughest skaters; then Howe came along!

Forced into retirement, he became a successful farmer near Guelph, Ontario.

ADAM FOOTE

BORN: Toronto, Ontario, July 10, 1971
POSITION: Defenseman, Quebec Nordiques, 1991–95; Colorado Avalanche, 1995–

It would not be a stretch to say that Adam Foote, a defensive defenseman, energized the Colorado Avalanche to its 2001 Stanley Cup triumph. In Game Six of the finals with the New Jersey Devils, the score tied 0–0 late in the first period, Foote unleashed a long shot from the right side that beat Martin Brodeur, putting the Avalanche ahead 1–0. They never trailed after that in Game Six nor in Game Seven at Denver.

Foote originally gained attention playing junior hockey for a team in Sault Ste. Marie, Ontario, and was selected as Quebec's second choice—22nd overall—in the 1989 Entry Draft.

Foote established himself as a solid full-time defenseman in 1992–93 with the Nordiques. He followed the team to Denver when the franchise was Americanized into the Colorado Avalanche. Foote also was a member of the 1996 Stanley Cup winner in Colorado's inaugural season. Foote was respected as a clean but tough defender. Interestingly, in the 2001–02 season, he recorded 55 penalty minutes in 55 games.

PETER FORSBERG

BORN: Ornskoldsvik, Sweden, July 20, 1973
POSITION: Center, Quebec Nordiques, 1994–95; Colorado Avalanche, 1995–2001
AWARDS/HONORS: Calder Memorial Trophy, 1995; NHL All-Rookie Team, 1995; NHL First Team All-Star, 1998–99; NHL All-Star Game, 1996, 1998–99, 2001

When first-round draft pick Eric Lindros refused to report to the Quebec Nordiques in one of hockey's most controversial episodes, a massive trade took place instead, with a lesser-known Swedish player named Peter Forsberg.

Nobody could have imagined it at the time, but over almost a decade, from 1995 to 2001, Forsberg would become a more effective player—and a Stanley Cup winner to boot—than Lindros.

Some critics argued Forsberg developed into the best all-round player in professional hockey. He possessed breakneck speed, magnificent stickhandling skills, creativity, and a shot that terrorized goaltenders.

In just his second season, Forsberg exploded for 116 points during Colorado's inaugural season, helping the former Nordiques to win the 1996 Stanley Cup. He scored 580 points in his first 466 NHL games, often finishing among the top ten scorers in the NHL, and 108 points in his first 95 playoff games, clearly a world-class performer. Complementing teammate Joe Sakic as the NHL's best one-two punch at the center ice position throughout the late 1990s, Forsberg helped young Avalanche forwards such as Adam Deadmarsh to elevate their game on a deep and talented team.

But his career was marred by injury after injury. His worst was a splenectomy that caused him to leave the 2000–01 playoffs after 11 games, while his Avalanche went on to win their second cup.

But regardless of injuries, no one could say that Forsberg wasn't a complete asset when healthy. The Swedish center, at six feet, 205 pounds, appeared in the All-Star game each of his first six NHL seasons, played the Olympics twice—earning a gold medal in 1994—and had two Stanley Cup championships under his belt.

The prospects of a third Cup intrigued Forsberg enough to return to the Avalanche in time for the 2001–02 Stanley Cup playoffs after his yearlong sabbatical helped heal worn down feet and other injuries accumulated throughout his hard-nosed career.

EMILE FRANCIS

BORN: North Battleford, Saskatchewan, September 13, 1926
POSITION: Goaltender, Chicago Blackhawks, 1946–48; New York Rangers, 1948–52; General Manager, New York Rangers, 1964–76; Coach, New York Rangers, 1965–68, 1969–73, 1974–75; General Manager/Coach, St. Louis Blues, 1976–77; President/General Manager, St. Louis Blues, 1978–83; President/General Manager, Hartford Whalers, 1983–89
AWARDS/HONORS: Lester Patrick Trophy, 1982; Hockey Hall of Fame, 1982

Emile Francis, one of the winningest coaches in Rangers history (but without ever winning the Stanley Cup!), was also a much-traveled goaltender who got his first break in 1943–44, playing in the old Eastern League for Redvers MacKenzie and the Philadelphia Falcons. Francis was as happy about playing in Philadelphia as the Philadelphians were delighted to have him on their side.

Francis made it to the NHL in 1946–47, appearing in 19 games for the Chicago Blackhawks. The following season he guarded the cage 54 times. At best, "the Cat" (nicknamed for his catlike moves in the cage) was a so-so netminder for a rather poor Chicago outfit.

Emile eventually found his way to New York, where he occasionally tended goal for Frank Boucher's Rangers.

"On a few occasions when Chuck Rayner was sidelined," Boucher said, "we got some excellent work from Francis, whom we'd acquired from Chicago. Mostly, Emile worked up at New Haven, but he had fourteen games with us in 1951 to 1952. I had been in the stands one night at Providence watching his New Haven club, looking for players who might help the Rangers, when Emile took a terrible cut.

"He was just a little fellow, five-foot-seven or so, and weighing maybe 155. He didn't see a shot from the point and the puck hit the Cat in the mouth and nose. It knocked six teeth loose and cut his nose badly. I went down to the dressing room to see how he was. He was the only New Haven goaltender so he knew he'd have to go back into the net when the doctor finished patching him up.

"'Has anybody got any brandy?' I asked. Somebody produced a bottle and I poured a stiff slug for Emile. He downed it, shook his head, climbed to his feet, and went back to the padded cell.

"Emile had more guts than most. He lost eighteen teeth during his career, had his nose broken five times, and needed something like 250 stitches to close up the cuts. He had ligaments torn in both knees, and required surgery on his right ankle. Dr. Kazuo Yanagisawa, another Ranger doctor, operated on his shoulder, in 1951, because of chronic pain after a shoulder separation. It's not any wonder that Cat Francis was a success as a coach and general manager of the team in later years; he'd been through it all. My friend, Gene Ward, columnist for the *New York Daily News*, once remarked to me that he'd never seen anyone in sports with courage to match that of the goaltenders."

The Cat ended his playing career at Spokane of the Western League, after having dislocated both shoulders, in 1960. He immediately began coaching at Guelph, Ontario, a junior team with Rod Gilbert and Jean Ratelle, who would later star for Francis with the Rangers.

The road to the top of the Ranger organization was quickly traversed, and by 1964 he was New York's general manager. The next season, he took over as coach, and his career was the most successful of any Ranger mentor. Although his teams never captured a Stanley Cup, Francis coached more Ranger games than anyone. In 1976, the Rangers' management decided to dismiss Francis. He was a strict disciplinarian, able to elicit fierce loyalty from his players, but it just seemed his team could never win that "big one."

Emile signed with the ailing St. Louis Blues that same year, where he assumed his familiar role of general manager–coach. After his first season, he relinquished the coaching job to concentrate on managing and was the first to give New York City native Joe Mullen a chance when the undrafted forward signed in 1979. The Blues would not move past the second round in Francis's tenure, and he was dismissed as Blues general manager in 1983 in favor of Ron Caron.

Assuming the stewardship of the lukewarm Hartford Whalers franchise, Emile kept the Whalers competitive, and engineered deft moves for stalwarts Mike Liut, Dave Babych, and Doug Jarvis. Credited with bringing an element of respectability to the franchise, Francis stayed in the Hartford organization and presided over its only NHL playoff series win in 1986, as well as the only first-place finish the following season.

Retiring from the rigors of the NHL in 1993, the Cat eventually moved to Florida, but remained a member of the Hockey Hall of Fame selection committee. His son, Bob, would briefly make the NHL with the Red Wings in 1982 after playing college hockey. As coach of the upstart Phoenix Coyotes in 2001–02, Bobby Francis won the Adams Award as NHL Coach of the Year.

RON FRANCIS

BORN: Sault Ste. Marie, Ontario, March 1, 1963

POSITION: Center, Hartford Whalers, 1981–91; Pittsburgh Penguins, 1991–98; Carolina Hurricanes, 1998–

AWARDS/HONORS: Alka-Seltzer Plus Award, 1995; Frank J. Selke Trophy, 1995; Lady Byng Memorial Trophy, 1995, 1998, 2002; King Clancy Memorial Trophy, 2002; NHL All-Star Game, 1983, 1985, 1990, 1996

In an accurate assessment of the graying center during the 2001–02 season, *Hartford Courant* sports columnist Jeff Jacobs described Ron Francis as "the most underrated player in hockey history."

Virtually guaranteed entrance into the Hockey Hall of Fame, Francis excelled at the center ice position both

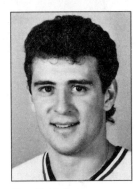

Ron Francis as captain of the Hartford Whalers

defensively and offensively, during a career that included stops in Hartford, Pittsburgh, and ultimately Raleigh, where he became captain of the Carolina Hurricanes.

The angular Italian-Canadian had the distinction of playing for Pittsburgh when the Penguins won two straight Stanley Cups (1991–98). Invariably he was overshadowed by flashier performers, such as Mario Lemieux and Jaromir Jagr. However, Francis's all-round talents always were appreciated by his coaches and managers.

During the 2001–02 season, Francis ranked fifth in league history in points (1,624) and third in assists (1,137). He trailed only New York Rangers captain Mark Messier among active players in points, and led the Carolina

franchise in games played (956), goals (323), assists (688), points (1,011), hat tricks (9), game-winning goals (50), and power-play goals (105).

By the 2001–02 season, the six-feet-three, 200-pound Ontario native had achieved 20 consecutive 50-point seasons, one of only two players in NHL history to do so—the other being Mr. Hockey, Gordie Howe.

It's no wonder why Carolina fans loved their captain, who held some of the most elite records on the team, nor is it surprising why Jacobs described him in such a manner. Though Francis's name may not be one of the first to be uttered around the league as a memorable player, he will definitely be remembered for his extraordinary career.

FRANK FREDERICKSON

BORN: Winnipeg, Manitoba, 1895
DIED: April 28, 1979
POSITION: Center, Detroit Cougars, 1926; Boston Bruins, 1927–28; Pittsburgh Pirates, 1929–30; Detroit Falcons, 1930–31
AWARDS/HONORS: Hockey Hall of Fame, 1958

One of the few National Hockey League players of Icelandic extraction to gain a niche in the Hockey Hall of Fame, Frank Frederickson had been a World War I pilot and hero before making a name for himself in professional hockey.

Frank captained the Winnipeg Falcons team that won the gold medal in the 1920 Winter Olympics at Antwerp (the first Winter Olympics to include ice hockey) and later enjoyed an NHL career that spanned 1926–27 through 1930–31.

He was a stylish center who scored 41 goals in 30 games for Victoria during the 1922–23 season, and helped the club win the Stanley Cup two years later. There have been better centers, to be sure, but not many with Frederickson's grace both on and off the ice.

Frank's parents came from Iceland and spoke only Icelandic in the house. Frank couldn't speak a word of English until age six. The target of schoolyard insults, Frederickson found an outlet in sports.

"My best outlet was hockey," said Frank. "I played well and captured the attention of two attorneys. They took an interest in me, not just as a hockey player, and urged me to go to school. So in 1914, I enrolled at the University of Manitoba and was named captain of the hockey team."

Not long after the outbreak of World War I, Frank enlisted in the 223rd Scandinavian Battalion, then the Royal Flying Corps, and remained an airman until the end of the conflict, miraculously surviving close calls.

After joining the Canadian Air Force in 1920, Frederickson was dealt a life-altering surprise.

"Out of the blue I received a letter from Lester Patrick, the Old Silver Fox, who had a Pacific Coast League team in Victoria, British Columbia," recalled Frank. "It was top-notch hockey, and Lester offered me what was a substantial contract in those days—$2,500 for twenty-four games. I call it substantial because the rest of the boys were playing for $800 and $900. I couldn't resist the offer and found myself right back in hockey again."

Although Frederickson did not play in the NHL as long as other members of the Hockey Hall of Fame, he was an eminent center in the years he skated for Detroit, Boston, Pittsburgh, and Detroit again, scoring 73 points in 161 games.

Following the conclusion of his playing days, he coached and managed Pittsburgh in 1930–31 and later returned to his home in Vancouver. He remained a vigorous citizen even in retirement, and followed the modern game with great interest until his death in 1979.

ROBBIE FTOREK

BORN: Needham, Massachusetts, January 2, 1952

POSITION: Center, Detroit Red Wings, 1973–74; Phoenix Roadrunners (WHA), 1975–77; Cincinnati Stingers (WHA), 1977–79; Quebec Nordiques, 1979–82; New York Rangers, 1982–85; Coach, Los Angeles Kings, 1987–89; New Jersey Devils, 1998–2000; Boston Bruins, 2001–

AWARDS/HONORS: All-Star (WHA Second Team), 1976, 1978; All-Star (WHA First Team), 1977, 1979; Howe Trophy (WHA Most Valuable Player), 1977; U.S. Hockey Hall of Fame, 1991

Massachusetts-born Robbie Ftorek represented the United States on their 1972 Olympic team before joining the NHL's Detroit Red Wings. Ftorek did not blossom into a major-league star, however, until he jumped to the WHA in 1975 and won Most Valuable Player honors a season later. A diminutive center, Ftorek entered the 1978–79 WHA season with the longest consecutive game streak in league history—a string of 276. In the three years Ftorek worked on that streak, he scored over 100 points each season for the Phoenix Roadrunners.

The next season, Ftorek was sent to the WHA Cincinnati Stingers, but the Stingers were dispersed when the four strongest WHA franchises merged with their former NHL rivals and Ftorek was one of six players picked by the Quebec Nordiques in 1979. His NHL career was brief the second time around, despite a 73-point season in 1980–81, and he retired after a stint with the AHL New Haven Nighthawks in 1986.

Ftorek turned to coaching, eventually landing the Los Angeles Kings' bench in 1987–88, where he recorded a .534 winning percentage in two seasons. After a brief tenure with the Quebec organization, Ftorek became a top man with New Jersey for ten years. He coached their top affiliate in Albany to a Calder Cup in

1994–95 and helped develop the Devils' rich crop of young players. He replaced Jacques Lemaire after 1997–98 and restored the Devils to a first-place finish, notwithstanding a first round playoff exit in spring 1999.

In 2000, with the Devils losing their grip on first place in the Atlantic Division, Ftorek was fired with eight games to go in the season. His replacement, Larry Robinson, guided the Devils to their second Stanley Cup in the subsequent postseason.

In a surprise move, the Boston Bruins, who had missed the playoffs with Mike Keenan behind the bench for half of 2000–01, hired local boy Ftorek to mentor the team. With a slew of free agent signings, Robbie's Bruins, led by Brian Rolston, Joe Thornton, and Bill Guerin, surged to an Eastern Conference title, but fell in the first round to the eighth-seeded Montreal Canadiens. But the Bruins' fabulous turnaround from playoff outsiders to Conference champs merited Ftorek a nomination for the Jack Adams Award, awarded to the NHL's top bench boss. He didn't win it—Bobby Francis of Phoenix did—but Ftorek had reestablished his credentials as a big-league bench boss.

GRANT FUHR

BORN: Spruce Grove, Alberta, September 28, 1962

POSITION: Goaltender, Edmonton Oilers, 1981–91; Toronto Maple Leafs, 1991–93; Buffalo Sabres, 1993–95; Los Angeles Kings, 1995; St. Louis Blues, 1995–99; Calgary Flames, 1999–2000

AWARDS/HONORS: Vezina Trophy, 1988; William M. Jennings Trophy (shared with Dominik Hasek), 1994; NHL First Team All-Star, 1988; NHL Second Team All-Star, 1982; NHL All-Star Game, 1982, 1984, 1985–86, 1988–89

Grant Fuhr didn't have to be perfect to backstop the Edmonton Oilers to four Stanley Cups in the mid to late 1980s. He just had to be what his general manager, Glen Sather, believed he was when Sather drafted him in 1981: acrobatic and unafraid.

Many goaltenders play with the constant knowledge that they can't give up more than one or two goals and expect to win. Fuhr knew he'd have five or six goals to work with on most nights, and his job was to make sure the other guys didn't get more than four or five into the Oilers' net.

Fuhr's job was more difficult than it sounds. The Oilers were a tremendously talented offensive team whose wide-open style pushed goals-per-game up by over a goal in the 1980s. Goaltenders' goal-against average rarely dropped below three during the decade, when they were regularly below three in the years before and after the Oiler juggernaut's dominance. During the regular season, the Oilers simply had no interest in playing much defense.

Fuhr could expect to see 35 to 40 shots on most nights, many coming on odd-man rushes. Although the Oilers would clamp down in the playoffs, the team's game plan was fairly simple: the rest of the team was trying to score as often as possible, and it was Fuhr's job to keep the puck out of the net.

From 1981 through 1989, Fuhr did his job exceedingly well. In addition to winning four Cups, he was voted to two end-of-season All-Star teams, and won the Vezina for best goaltender in 1988. He was the winning goaltender for Canada against the USSR in the classic and unforgettable 1987 Canada Cup. His acrobatic style was well suited to facing many shots and to making spectacular saves off of odd-man rushes. At the peak of his brilliance, Fuhr's glove saves and reflexes were without peer in the NHL. He worked best when given a heavy workload and the more games he played, the better he performed.

Unfortunately, toward the end of the 1980s, Fuhr's career took a downward turn. He was suspended for cocaine use, and suffered from weight gain and injuries. Although he was an Oiler for their fifth Cup in 1990, he did not play in the playoffs.

Eventually traded to Toronto in 1991, Fuhr suffered a knee injury, and lost the Toronto starting job to rookie Felix Potvin. He was traded to Buffalo, where he eventually lost out to the goaltending sensation of the 1990s, Dominik Hasek. A short stint with the Los Angeles Kings was nothing short of a disaster.

Mike Keenan and the St. Louis Blues rescued Fuhr off the scrap heap in 1995, and, after a shaky start and some serious fitness training, Fuhr looked like the goalie he'd been in the 1980s, only thinner. Fuhr was an excellent backstop for the Blues and then moved on to join an old adversary, the Calgary Flames. Fuhr retired from the Flames in 2000, after spending a few years tutoring young Fred Brathwaite—a small, acrobatic goalie whose style reminded some of a young Fuhr—and became Calgary's full-time goaltending coach.

BILL GADSBY

BORN: Calgary, Alberta, August 8, 1927
POSITION: Defenseman, Chicago Blackhawks, 1946–54; New York Rangers, 1954–61; Detroit Red Wings, 1961–66; Coach, Detroit Red Wings, 1968–69
AWARDS/HONORS: NHL Second Team All-Star, 1953–54; NHL First Team All-Star, 1956, 1958–59; Hockey Hall of Fame, 1970

No NHL player has ever contributed more in terms of blood, sweat, and tears without collecting a Stanley Cup than defensemen William Alexander "Bill" Gadsby, who spent two decades in the NHL and whose motto might have been, "Close, but no cigar."

Bill Gadsby as Detroit defenseman

Early in his career, Gadsby was a blueline ace for the Chicago Blackhawks (1946–55) and then the New York Rangers (1955–1961). But it was not until he was traded to Detroit in June 1961 for Les Hunt, that Gadsby achieved the level of excellence that eventually earned him entrance to the Hockey Hall of Fame.

He also appeared destined to win his first Stanley Cup during the 1964 playoffs, particularly after the Red Wings dispatched Chicago 4–3 in the semifinals. Detroit then took on the defending champion Maple Leafs in the finals. With Gadsby playing the best defense of his life, the Red Wings moved into a three-games-to-two lead. The Cup was only one win away from Bill.

Game Six was at Olympia Stadium in Detroit and Motown fans were primed for the knockout blow. Late in the second period, Gadsby appeared to have helped deliver that punch with a pass that enabled Gordie Howe to put Detroit ahead 3–2. But Toronto rallied to tie the count, sending the game into sudden-death overtime.

Detroit still appeared to be in the driver's seat, because Toronto's solid defenseman, Bob Baun, had broken an ankle stopping a shot late in regulation time. Nevertheless, when the first overtime began, Baun reappeared on the Toronto defense, his ankle shot up with painkiller. As luck would have it, it was not Gadsby, but Baun who scored the game-winning goal, enabling Toronto to take the next game and the Stanley Cup. It was the closest Gadsby ever came to sipping championship champagne.

Bill Gadsby broke in with the Blackhawks during the 1946–47 season and remained in the big time until 1965–66, when he retired from the Red Wings. During that span he was a three-time (1956, 1958, and 1959) member of the NHL First All-Star Team and was equally comfortable as a defensive or offensive defenseman. Gadsby next played for Chicago until the 1954–55 season, when he and Pete Conagher were traded to the Rangers for Al Stanley and Nick Mickoski a day before Thanksgiving. In his first game as a Ranger, Gadsby dove in front of a Bruins shot, preventing a goal, but breaking several bones in the process. The play symbolized the gutsy style that made Bill a hit on Broadway until 1961–62, when the Rangers' general manager Muzz Patrick dealt him to the Red Wings, where he continued to excel.

After retirement, Gadsby remained in the Detroit area, and was frequently seen at the Wings' home games, and often donned his skates for Old-Timers Games.

SIMON GAGNÉ

BORN: Ste. Foy, Quebec, February 29, 1980
POSITION: Left Wing, Philadelphia Flyers, 1999–
AWARDS/HONORS: NHL All-Rookie Team, 2000; NHL All-Star Game, 2001

Among the better aspects of a successful Flyers team during the 2001–02 campaign was the consistently high-grade play of forward Simon Gagné.

The Quebec native was drafted 22nd overall in the first round of the 1998 NHL Entry Draft. Gagné—unlike many top picks—fulfilled his notices in a remarkably short time.

A product of the Quebec amateur hockey leagues, Gagné was like many francophone stickhandlers before him—speedy and creative with a special offensive touch.

During Gagné's rookie season (1999–2000) he netted 20 goals and 28 assists. The Flyers went to the Eastern Conference finals, losing to eventual Cup champion New Jersey.

A sophomore slump in 2000–01 wasn't in the cards for Gagné, as he improved to 27 goals and 32 assists playing in just 69 games. In the All-Star game he played on Mario Lemieux's line.

As the Flyers strengthened their forward line with the signing of veteran Jeremy Roenick in 2001–02, Gagné improved to 33 goals and earned a berth on the gold medal–winning Canadian Olympic team at Salt Lake.

By the start of the 2002–03 season, Gagné was regarded as one of the NHL's most gifted young aces.

JOHN "BLACK CAT" GAGNON

BORN: Chicoutimi, Quebec, June 8, 1905
DIED: Date unknown
POSITION: Forward, Montreal Canadiens, 1930–34, 1935–39; Boston Bruins, 1934–35; New York Rangers, 1939–40
AWARDS/HONORS: NHL All-Star Game, 1937, 1939

Johnny Gagnon was nicknamed "the Black Cat" because of his swarthy complexion and jet-black hair, which always appeared to be pasted down with a gluelike pomade, as well as his quick, darting moves and natural puck sense. He developed into one of the most formidable scorers in Montreal Canadiens history and earned a place on the Canadiens' first line in 1931 with Howie Morenz and Aurel Joliat. The new line led the way to the Canadiens' Stanley Cup victory that year.

Gagnon last played in the NHL in 1939–40 with the New York Americans, after ten years and 252 points with Montreal. He returned to his alma mater, the Providence Reds of the AHL, to close out his playing days and even took a season off to coach the team in 1943–44.

BOB GAINEY

BORN: Peterborough, Ontario, December 18, 1953
POSITION: Forward, Montreal Canadiens, 1973–89; Coach, Minnesota North Stars, 1990–93; Dallas Stars, 1993–96; Vice President of Hockey Operations/General Manager, Dallas Stars, 1996–2002
AWARDS/HONORS: Frank J. Selke Trophy, 1978–81; Team Canada, 1978; Conn Smythe Trophy, 1979; NHL Challenge Cup All-Star, 1979; NHL All-Star Game, 1977–78, 1980–81; Hockey Hall of Fame, 1992

If Robert Michael "Bob" Gainey were an overcoat, he couldn't cover his defensive assignments any better. Generally known as the best defensive forward in the NHL during the 1970s, Bob Gainey was honored with the Frank J. Selke Trophy on four occasions.

"If I had a headache," said former New York Ranger Rod Gilbert after Bob had frustrated him throughout a playoff game, "Gainey would have taken the aspirin."

Bob Gainey

Captaining the Habs from 1981 through his retirement in 1989, the astute Gainey won five Stanley Cups with the Montreal Canadiens. He never had more than 47 points in a season, but Gainey earned respect around the NHL for his unparalleled leadership.

The Minnesota North Stars, who later landed in Dallas, hired Gainey as coach in 1990, and by 1992, Bob added the general manager's title. Under his wing, the North Stars reached the Stanley Cup finals in 1991, but lost to the Pittsburgh Penguins. Finally, following their 1993 relocation to Dallas, they won the Cup in 1999, after years of excellent regular seasons and disappointing playoff performances.

Gainey's team, shepherded by Ken Hitchcock, underwent many personnel changes in 2001–02. Summer acquisitions Pierre Turgeon, Jyrki Lumme, Rob DiMaio, Valeri Kamensky, and Donald Audette were complete busts on a defensive-oriented team, and chemistry issues forced Gainey to dispatch all but Turgeon by midseason. When the team faltered, Hitchcock was fired by Gainey, who then relinquished his duties to Doug Armstrong. All of the talent assembled by Gainey, which dominated in years past, did not make the playoffs, as Gainey assumed a consulting role with the team.

DON GALLINGER

BORN: Port Colborne, Ontario, April 10, 1925
POSITION: Center, Boston Bruins, 1942–44, 1945–48

Don Gallinger might have gone down in the annals of the NHL purely as a good-shooting, swift-skating forward of considerable respectability. Instead, he and teammate Billy Taylor were banished from hockey—the only players ever punished in that manner—for betting on games during the 1947–48 season.

According to league president Clarence Campbell, then in office for only two years, the two were given "life suspensions for conduct detrimental to hockey and for associating with a known gambler." Although Campbell kept the details of the scandal quiet, mostly in deference to Taylor's wishes, Gallinger tried years later to have the banishment lifted.

Gallinger once told his story to *Toronto Globe and Mail* reporter Scott Young. He admitted that he had, in fact, bet on games, although when the original scandal broke in February 1948, Gallinger had vehemently denied everything to Campbell and Bruins owner Art Ross. Eighteen months later, however, Gallinger confessed to the betting in an emotional meeting held in Campbell's office.

With the assistance of the Detroit police, the NHL was able to obtain evidence against Taylor and Gallinger through the use of illegal wiretaps. The records showed that the two had frequently talked with one James Tamer, a noted Detroit gambler and paroled bank robber.

Gallinger later admitted the details of the operation. "My bets varied from $250 to $1,000 a game," Gallinger said. "My instructions from the guy," he continued, meaning Tamer, "were to bet on what I knew of the team's attitude and our injuries." Gallinger insisted that while he began to bet three months before the scandal was disclosed, only eight or nine games were actually involved.

Although details of Gallinger's involvement were kept confidential in deference to his father, the ex-Bruin center made pleas for reinstatement after his father died in 1951, but his efforts only won him criticism.

The campaign by Young to get Taylor and Gallinger reinstated in 1963 was met with even harsher criticism by the NHL bosses and by Campbell. In fact, the celebrated Campbell cool went out the window, when he snapped, "If Scott Young was on fire, I wouldn't spit on him!"

Both Taylor and Gallinger were finally reinstated in the summer of 1970. Taylor returned to hockey in the coaching ranks.

CHARLIE GARDINER

BORN: Edinburgh, Scotland, December 31, 1904
DIED: June 13, 1934
POSITION: Goaltender, Chicago Blackhawks, 1927–34
AWARDS/HONORS: Vezina Trophy, 1932, 1934; NHL First Team All-Star, 1931–32, 1934; NHL Second Team All-Star, 1933; NHL All-Star Game, 1934; Hockey Hall of Fame, 1945

Chicago Blackhawk Charlie Gardiner developed into one of the finds of the 1930s. Whenever he stepped between the goal pipes, he usually wore a broad smile. At first, this seemed the height of presumptuousness, since his goalkeeping was scarcely flawless. But he worked diligently at his trade.

"He would come far out of the nets and sprawl on the ice in an effort to stop a score," reported Canadian writer Ron McAllister. "And even when his own team had folded up, he fought on and tried to defend his goal."

By 1929, Gardiner had improved so much that he finished second to the immortal George Hainsworth of the Montreal Canadiens in the race for the Vezina Trophy for the goalie whose team has the fewest goals scored against it. In 1932, he finally won the coveted prize and was named to the All-Star team.

In 1932–33, the Hawks finished fourth, out of the playoffs. They rallied the following year and launched their most serious assault on first place. That they failed by seven points and finished second to Detroit was no fault of Gardiner's. His goaltending had reached new degrees of perfection. He allowed only 83 goals in 48 games and scored ten shutouts. In 14 other games, he permitted just one goal.

But astute Gardiner watchers perceived that there was something unusual about the goalie's deportment, and they couldn't quite figure out what it was. Gardiner had lost his jovial manner and appeared melancholy.

Unknown to everyone, Gardiner was suffering from a chronic tonsil infection. However, the goaltender pressed on. Winning the Stanley Cup became an obsession with him, and the Blackhawks responded by defeating first the Canadiens and then the Montreal Maroons. This put them in the Cup finals against the awesome Detroit Red Wings, whose firepower included Ebbie Goodfellow, Larry Aurie, and Cooney Weiland.

The best-of-five series opened in Detroit and the Blackhawks won the first game, 2–1, in double overtime. In the second, also at Detroit's Olympia Stadium, the Hawks ran away with the game, 4–1. When the teams returned to Chicago for the third, and what appeared to be the final game, all hands were prepared to concede the Stanley Cup to the Blackhawks.

But it was not to be Charlie Gardiner's night. His body was wracked with pain and he prayed to recapture his physical condition of seasons past. By this time, coach Lionel Conacher and manager Tommy Gorman realized they had a weary and tormented player. "He's bad," said Gorman, turning to Conacher in the dressing room before the teams took the ice. "What do you think we should do?"

Gardiner knew the bosses were discussing him. With great effort, he lifted himself off the bench and walked over to them. "Listen," he insisted in tremulous tones, "I want to play. Let me play—for the Cup."

Gardiner took command at the Chicago fortress for two periods. But weariness and pain overcame him in the third, and he wilted before the Detroit attack. When the final buzzer sounded Detroit had won the game, 5–2.

When the team returned to the dressing room, Gardiner collapsed on a bench. But he wasn't totally done in. "Look," he said to his depressed teammates, "all I want is one goal next game. Just one goal and I'll take care of the other guys."

As he took his place in the goal crease on April 10, 1934, Gardiner's body was already numb with fatigue; self-hypnosis alone was enabling him to overcome the challenge of his ailment. For two periods, the game remained scoreless.

Early into the third period he began shouting encouragement to his players, even though it cost him valuable energy. Then Detroit captured the momentum and the Red Wings seemed to be headed for victory. But Gardiner's flailing arms and jabbing legs held them at bay.

When regulation time ended, the score remained tied, 0–0. Now the game would go into sudden-death overtime. But every minute more meant less chance for the disabled Gardiner to prevail against his well-conditioned foe, Wilf Cude, in the Detroit nets.

The referee finally whistled the teams back to the ice for the overtime. Gardiner's teammates feared he might collapse at any moment under the strain, as he had in the preceding four periods. But when he tapped his pads in front of the net for the face-off, he was wearing a broad smile, as if he knew something. And as the players began swirling at center ice, he waved his stick to the crowd.

Red Wings and Blackhawks crunched against each other for another period, and still there was no result. Another intermission was called, and then they returned to the ice for the second sudden-death overtime period. By now, Gardiner was beside himself with pain, but he would fight it as long as he could stand on his skates.

At the ten-minute mark, tiny "Mush" March of the Blackhawks moved the puck into Detroit territory and unleashed a shot at Wilf Cude. Before the goalie could move, the puck sailed past him, the red light flashed, and the Blackhawks had won their first Stanley Cup. Gardiner hurled his stick in the air and then just barely made it back to the dressing room under the thick backslaps of his mates.

He died in a Winnipeg hospital less than two months later.

HERB GARDINER

BORN: Winnipeg, Manitoba, May 8, 1891
DIED: June 13, 1934
POSITION: Defenseman, Montreal Canadiens, 1926–28, 1929; Chicago Blackhawks, 1928
AWARDS/HONORS: Hart Memorial Trophy, 1927; Hockey Hall of Fame, 1958

Herb Gardiner, who was signed to manage the Philadelphia Arrows in October 1929, emerged as a minor-league "Mister Hockey" in Philadelphia. He delivered a championship to the city of Brotherly Love in the 1932–33 season, when the Arrows compiled a record of 29 victories, only 12 losses, and 7 ties to finish in first place, seven points ahead of runner-up Providence.

Unfortunately, the Depression had hit the United States and there was talk of folding Philadelphia's sextet prior to the 1934–35 season because of losses at the gate. But the club was saved when the Arrows' receivers decided to run the team. Gardiner was retained as manager and members of the defunct NHL Philadelphia Quakers were lent to the Arrows.

This tenuous arrangement had its pitfalls, mostly on the ice where the Arrows stumbled around, looking more like the old Quaker team than anything else. Attendance at the Arena remained low and it was obvious that some transfusion of talent was necessary to save pro hockey in Philadelphia.

The SOS sign was detected in New York City, where Rangers manager Lester Patrick decided he would pump new life into Gardiner's club by making them a farm team of the New York NHL club. The Arrows name was changed to Ramblers and Gardiner did his usual competent job operating the club. In fact, Gardiner's 1935–36 Philadelphia sextet was one of the most accomplished teams ever assembled in professional hockey.

Unfortunately for Herb, the advent of World War II caused a severe drain on minor-league talent. Pro hockey was temporarily discontinued in Philadelphia and Gardiner's glory years came to an end.

CAL GARDNER

BORN: Transcona, Manitoba, October 30, 1924
DIED: Date unknown
POSITION: Center, New York Rangers, 1945–48; Toronto Maple Leafs, 1948–52; Chicago Blackhawks, 1952–53; Boston Bruins, 1953–57
AWARDS/HONORS: NHL All-Star Game, 1948–49

In their searches for the big, starry center, the New York Rangers, Boston Bruins, Toronto Maple Leafs, and Chicago Blackhawks each thought they had found him in Cal Gardner, a tall redhead who was quickly nicknamed "Ginger" in his amateur hockey days. Gardner learned his hockey in the Winnipeg area and was signed by the Rangers' Eastern League affiliate, the New York Rovers. Gardner played center on the Atomic Line with Rene Trudell and Church Russell on the wings. The trio devastated the Eastern League and was elevated en masse for the 1945–46 season. Of the three, Gardner prevailed longest. He was traded to Toronto for the 1948–49 season and was supposed to be the Leafs' replacement for their retired center, Syl Apps, but never quite cut the ice as well. In 1952–53, Gardner played for Chicago and in the next four seasons

finished his major-league career in Boston. His son, Dave Gardner, made his NHL debut in 1972–73 with the Montreal Canadiens and was regarded briefly as being as bright an offensive prospect as his father had once been.

DANNY GARE

BORN: Nelson, British Columbia, May 14, 1954
POSITION: Right Wing, Buffalo Sabres, 1974–81; Detroit Red Wings, 1981–86; Edmonton Oilers, 1986–87
AWARDS/HONORS: NHL All-Star Game, 1980

One of the most pleasant surprises of the Buffalo Sabres' 1974–75 season, right-winger Dan Gare supplied pugnacity—despite his smallish stature—and goals (31) in the Sabres' march to the Stanley Cup finals. In 1979–80, Gare tied for the league lead in goals with 56, also playing in the All-Star game that year. Because of his youthful appearance, Gare also was the butt of barbs in the Buffalo dressing room. Once, when he asked a teammate for shaving cream, the answer shot back was: "What would you want that for, Danny?" To which peach-faced Gare responded: "Oh, I have to shave regularly—every week!"

Over a span of 13 seasons, Gare was one of the all-time favorite Buffalo scorers. He finished his career in 1987 with Edmonton with a 354-career goal mark, but remained an idol of Sabres fans in a television capacity. Into the twenty-first century, he covered all Buffalo games as a rinkside-sideline reporter and analyst.

MIKE GARTNER

BORN: Ottawa, Ontario, October 29, 1959
POSITION: Right Wing, Washington Capitals,
1979–89; Minnesota North Stars, 1989–90;
New York Rangers, 1990–94; Toronto Maple
Leafs, 1994–96; Phoenix Coyotes, 1996–98
AWARDS/HONORS: NHL All-Star Game,
1981, 1985–86, 1988, 1990, 1993, 1996;
Hockey Hall of Fame, 2001

Since hockey is the fastest team game on earth, it is only appropriate that one of its most accomplished players of the post-Expansion era was one of its fastest, if not *the* fastest.

Mike Gartner graced the majors for two decades and had only one debit against his record: In those 20 graceful years, he never played for a Stanley Cup winner.

What Gartner did do was enhance the quality of the NHL spectacle with hard but clean play, an extraordinarily potent shot, and a positive attitude.

The sniper originally made his mark with the Washington Capitals for whom he played ten years, whipping up 397 goals, a career-high 50 of which came in 1985–86. He was dealt with Larry Murphy to the Minnesota North Stars for Dino Ciccarelli and Bob Rouse in 1989, where he had 34 goals in 1989–90 before being dealt again to the New York Rangers in March 1990 for Ulf Dahlen.

Mike remained on Broadway for four seasons until the Mike Keenan–led Blueshirts opted for more grit and dealt Gartner to Toronto for Glenn Anderson in a slew of March 1994 trade deadline moves designed to fortify the Rangers' Stanley Cup run.

In 1994–95, Mike only played 38 games, with a total of 12 goals, thereby breaking his string of 15 consecutive 30-or-more goal seasons, a daunting NHL record. His Leafs would not make it far in the playoffs during his stay, nor did the Phoenix Coyotes, who acquired Gartner in 1996. Mike finished his career in

1998, having netted 30-plus goals in 17 of his 19 seasons, also a record through the millennium. Only Wayne Gretzky, Gordie Howe, Marcel Dionne, and Phil Esposito scored more goals in their careers than Gartner, who held firm at 708 entering 2001–02.

A stalwart NHL Players' Association representative throughout his career, Mike became their director of business relations upon retirement, as well as serving on the board of directors in the NHL Alumni Association. In 2001, Gartner's career was enshrined in the Hockey Hall of Fame.

GEORGE GEE

BORN: Stratford, Ontario, June 28, 1922
POSITION: Center, Chicago Blackhawks,
1945–48, 1951–54; Detroit Red Wings,
1949–51
AWARDS/HONORS: NHL All-Star Game, 1950

If, as many critics have argued, the winning goal of the seventh game of the 1950 Stanley Cup finals between the Red Wings and Rangers was one of the biggest scores of all time, then the man who delivered the key pass on Pete Babando's shot rates credit. That man was George Gee.

Gee played three and a half seasons for Chicago before being dealt to Detroit. Always reliable, Gee centered a line with Babando and Gerry "Doc" Couture against the Rangers until just past the eight-minute mark of the second sudden-death period of the seventh game in April 1950 at Detroit's Olympia Stadium. Opposing Gee at the face-off was the Rangers' center Buddy O'Connor. Gee made one vital move. He turned to Babando before the face-off. "Move over behind me," Gee instructed, "you're too far to the left." Gee then won the face-off and delivered the puck to Babando whose shot beat the Rangers' goalie Chuck Rayner to win the Stanley Cup for Detroit. Gee returned to the Blackhawks in 1951–52 and ended his career in Chicago after the 1953–54 season.

BOOM-BOOM GEOFFRION

BORN: Montreal, Quebec, February 14, 1931
POSITION: Right Wing, Montreal Canadiens, 1950–64; New York Rangers, 1966–68; Coach, New York Rangers, 1969; Atlanta Flames, 1972–75
AWARDS/HONORS: Calder Memorial Trophy, 1952; Hart Memorial Trophy, 1961; Art Ross Trophy, 1955, 1961; NHL First Team All-Star, 1961; NHL Second Team All-Star, 1955, 1960; Hockey Hall of Fame, 1972

Nicknamed "Boom-Boom" because of the reverberation of his stick hitting the puck and the puck hitting the endboards (although it often went directly into the net), Bernie Geoffrion had many of the incendiary qualities of Maurice "Rocket" Richard.

But the Geoffrion character had one ingredient missing from the Richard psyche—a flamboyant sense of humor. For the most part, the Rocket was a quiet, introverted sort, even when life was agreeable; but when Geoffrion was scoring easily he became an opera-singing clown who led the Canadiens' laugh parade. He began delighting teammates late in the 1950–51 season after scoring 103 goals in 57 Montreal Junior League games. Geoffrion was under great pressure to turn pro with Les Canadiens and he resisted until there were only 18 games remaining in the 1950–51 schedule. Geoffrion realized that the Calder Trophy for rookie of the year was given to players who had skated in 20 or more games. By waiting until there were fewer than 20 games in the 1950–51 schedule, he thus became eligible to win it the following season.

The Boomer was no fool. He opened the 1951–52 season with two goals, including the winner, against Chicago in a 4–2 Montreal victory and immediately established himself as the newest Canadiens hero. It was relatively easy for Geoffrion. And not only was he an excellent young prospect, but he had recently married figure skater Marlene Morenz, the attractive blonde daughter of the legendary Howie Morenz.

Geoffrion went into orbit in 1952 and remained one of the most flamboyant and productive right-wingers in the NHL, playing right wing on a line with center Jean Beliveau and left-winger Dickie Moore. During the 1954–55 season, Geoffrion became the center of controversy in the last week of the schedule when teammate Maurice "Rocket" Richard was suspended for the remainder of the season by NHL president Clarence Campbell.

Richard was leading the league in scoring at the time and appeared certain to win his first points title. But once the Rocket was suspended, Geoffrion—despite the wishes of pro-Richard fans—moved ahead of Richard and the Boomer won his first scoring championship. As a result of the triumph, Geoffrion was vilified for years by his hometown fans. However, he continued to play superbly and won the scoring championship and the most valuable player award (Hart Trophy) in 1960–61.

Geoffrion retired temporarily after the 1963–64 season to become coach of the American League Quebec Aces and coached them to two consecutive championships. Then he made a remarkable comeback with the New York Rangers, playing two full seasons on Broadway.

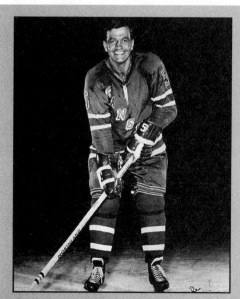

Bernard "Boom-Boom" Geoffrion as a Ranger

When he finally retired at the conclusion of the 1967–68 season, Geoffrion had scored 393 career goals, placing him behind only a handful of players, including Gordie Howe, Maurice Richard, Bobby Hull, and Jean Beliveau. He was the second man, after Maurice Richard, ever to score 50 goals in one season, accomplishing that feat in 1960–61.

Geoffrion reached another milestone on August 24, 1972, when he was inducted into the NHL Hall of Fame. That same year, the Boomer was named coach of the expansion Atlanta Flames and led them to the playoffs in 1974, their second full year. He quit for health reasons in the homestretch of the 1974–75 season and left hockey. But Boom-Boom couldn't stay away, and he returned to the organization as vice president of promotion and color man on Flames broadcasts.

Even after the Flames left Atlanta for Calgary, he remained a popular figure in the Georgia sports community, and was there when NHL hockey returned to Atlanta with the Thrashers in 1999.

EDDIE GERARD

BORN: Ottawa, Ontario, February 22, 1890
DIED: December 8, 1937
POSITION: Left Wing/Defenseman, Ottawa Senators (NHA and NHL), 1914–22, 1923; Toronto St. Patricks, 1922–23
AWARDS/HONORS: Hockey Hall of Fame, 1945

Eddie Gerard, defensive player par excellence, was afforded his highest compliment as a player while skating for the 1922 Toronto St. Pats in their Stanley Cup series against Vancouver.

Normally Eddie was a brilliant forward/defenseman for the Ottawa Senators. But when St. Pat ace defenseman Harry Cameron tore up his shoulder during the crucial series, an urgent SOS went out to Gerard to man Cameron's spot on the Toronto blue line.

Personnel loans such as these were commonplace in the early days of hockey, the one requirement being that you secure an okay from your opponents. As primitive as were the rules of the day, so must have been the sports media because Vancouver's usually wily Lester Patrick saw no harm in the eleventh-hour replacement. After one game of Gerard's puck-hawking and body checks however, Lester gave the thumbs-down to Gerard's stand-in act.

It was too late for Vancouver, however, and Toronto rolled to the Cup with no small thanks due to Gerard. Eddie played on three other Cup winners with his own Senators before retiring prematurely in 1923. He remained in hockey as a coach and manager and is a member of the Hockey Hall of Fame.

EDDIE GIACOMIN

BORN: Sudbury, Ontario, June 6, 1939
POSITION: Goaltender, New York Rangers, 1965–75; Detroit Red Wings, 1975–77
AWARDS/HONORS: Vezina Trophy (shared with Gilles Villemure), 1971; NHL First Team All-Star, 1967, 1971; NHL Second Team All-Star, 1968–70; NHL All-Star Game, 1967–71, 1973

When Rollie Giacomin was invited by Peanuts O'Flaherty, the coach of the Washington (Eastern League) Lions, to come down for a tryout, he was working a shift at the lumber mill, and asked his brother Eddie to stand in for him.

Upon Eddie's arrival in Washington, the coach looked at him, discovered he was not Rollie, and was unimpressed. The Lions, however, lost their next three games. With nothing to lose, and only six games left in the season, Eddie was given the go-ahead to play. The Lions won all six.

The following year, Giacomin was invited to the training camp of the American League Providence Reds and then spent the season playing for various minor-league teams in the East.

In 1960–61, Giacomin was called back to the Reds in midseason and toiled over the next four years for them. Finally, on May 17, 1965, he was signed by the New York Rangers.

Eddie played 36 games for the dreadful Ranger team of 1964–65. He was hardly impressive and the Ranger management sent him to the Baltimore Clippers of the AHL, a Ranger farm club. Giacomin took his demotion as a competitor with equanimity, and determined to come back.

In 1966, the Ranger brass staked everything they had on Giacomin. The team had finished out of the playoffs for the previous five years, and weak goaltending and poor defense were big factors. General manager and coach Emile Francis was impressed with Giacomin despite his poor rookie showing. Giacomin got the assignment and finished the season with a 2.61 goals-against average and a league-leading total of nine shutouts. The Rangers made the playoffs and Giacomin was given a berth on the First Team All-Star squad.

In 1970, the Rangers lost the Stanley Cup quarterfinals for the fourth straight year. People said that the reason the Rangers wilted in May was because Giacomin was dog-tired, the result of playing in excess of 60 games in an era of coast-to-coast scheduling.

When Giacomin returned to the Rangers' training camp in Kitchener, Ontario, the following season, he learned that he would be sharing the goaltending chores with Gilles Villemure, a veteran of seven minor-league seasons and a few stints with the Rangers. Giacomin disapproved of the two-goalie system. He insisted that he needed the extra work to stay at his sharpest. He vehemently denied charges that he was tired at season's end, and that he had failed in the playoffs. He had no choice, however, except to abide by Francis's decision. After 11 years of being the intrepid barefaced goalie, Giacomin also decided to wear a face mask.

The two-goalie system worked and by the end of the 1970–71 campaign, Giacomin had captured the coveted Vezina Trophy along with Villemure. Eddie Giacomin finished with a goals-against average of 2.15, the best of his professional career.

The Rangers clambered past the quarterfinals as they beat the Toronto Maple Leafs in a hard-fought six-game series. They then carried the Blackhawks to the full seven games before losing in the semifinals. Giacomin was splendid.

A year later Giacomin's average was a respectable 2.70. He starred in the victorious quarterfinal series against the defending champion Montreal Canadiens. But he damaged his knee in the first game of the semifinals against the Blackhawks. Villemure replaced him, and played so well that the Rangers reached the finals for the first time in 20 years. Next came the classic confrontation between New York and Boston. Giacomin couldn't stop the Bruins—it was simply a case of too much Bobby Orr for the Blueshirts. The Rangers were eliminated in six games.

Eddie suffered early season problems in 1972–73, but midway through the year he found himself and played a stretch of several games in which he allowed less than a goal a game. He also recorded his 41st career shutout, a Rangers record, surpassing that of Hall of Famer Chuck Rayner.

In the preliminary round of the 1975 playoffs, disaster struck the Rangers as they were upset by their arch rivals, the Islanders, a team hardly out of diapers. The Rangers' troubles continued as the 1975–76 campaign started and general manager Francis, in a panic move, put Giacomin on waivers. Eddie was claimed by Detroit on October 31, 1975, and the following night skated onto Madison Square Garden ice in a Red Wings uniform.

No one at the Garden that night would forget the sight of Eddie wiping away the tears as his loyal fans, in an expression of pure love, cheered their hero from the moment they saw him. They even cheered for the Red Wings against the Rangers, and for the first time in anyone's memory, the Rangers were treated like the visiting team.

The Red Wings, a team in turmoil, began making wholesale changes and released Giacomin in 1977. His career over, Eddie joined the New York Islanders as goalie coach and broadcaster in 1978. Giacomin became a popular figure after leaving Long Island, but eventually retired from the hockey scene.

GREG GILBERT

BORN: Mississauga, Ontario, January 22, 1962
POSITION: Left Wing, New York Islanders, 1982–89; Chicago Blackhawks, 1989–93; New York Rangers, 1993–94; St. Louis Blues, 1994–96; Coach, Calgary Flames, 2001–

After a series of outstanding draft picks in the early-to-mid 1970s, Islanders general manager Bill Torrey maintained his standard in the 1980 Entry Draft when he selected left-winger Greg Gilbert 80th overall.

Gilbert won two Stanley Cups with the Isles after joining the team in 1982, and posted his career zenith of 31 goals and 35 assists, with a plus-51 rating, in 1983–84. As the years passed, the redheaded Ontario native became a solid defensive forward for Mike Keenan's Chicago Blackhawks and New York Rangers teams. In 1994, Gilbert became the only player ever to win a Stanley Cup with both New York teams when the Rangers defeated the Vancouver Canucks in seven games.

After his playing career ended in 1996, Gilbert immediately took over as coach of the AHL Worcester Ice Cats, and got them to the playoffs each season before joining the Calgary Flames' coaching staff in 2000. Gilbert was promoted to head coach at the end of the 2000–01 season, and guided the Flames to a tremendous start—led by NHL scoring champ, Jarome Iginla—the following season before the team slowed out of contention by midseason. Nonetheless, Gilbert was regarded as one of the brightest young coaches on the NHL scene.

ROD GILBERT

BORN: Montreal, Quebec, July 1, 1941
POSITION: Right Wing, New York Rangers, 1960–77
AWARDS/HONORS: NHL First Team All-Star, 1972; NHL Second Team All-Star, 1968; Team Canada, 1972; Bill Masterton Trophy, 1976; Hockey Hall of Fame, 1982

Rod Gilbert's NHL career almost ended before it started. Playing for the Guelph Royals in the Ontario Hockey Association, he skidded on an ice-cream container top thrown to the ice by a fan and injured his back. A few days later, an opponent leveled him with a strong check, and Gilbert fell to the ice, his back broken. The first operation on his spine was a near disaster; his left leg began to hemorrhage and amputation was considered. During the summer of 1965, the bone grafts in his back weakened, and another operation was needed. Rod's career was in jeopardy; he played 34 games in a restrictive brace and then submitted to another operation. Happily, Rod's story was uphill to fame after that.

On February 24, 1968, at the Montreal Forum, Gilbert scored four goals against Rogatien Vachon, and established an NHL record, 16 shots on goal. In 1971–72, he hit for 43 goals, finished fifth in the NHL scoring race, and was named right wing on the First All-Star Team. He was the first Ranger in eight years to get a First Team nomination. In 1974, Gilbert passed Andy Bathgate as the Rangers' all-time leading scorer. His milestone goal was celebrated by a five-minute, deafening ovation.

Gilbert teamed with Jean Ratelle and Vic Hadfield to form the Rangers' number one line, the GAG Line (goal-a-game), which amassed 139 goals and 312 points in 1971–72. But Ratelle broke his ankle and Rod was hindered by pinched nerves in his neck that year; otherwise the Rangers might have taken the Cup from the Bruins.

In 1976, Rod's former on-ice nemesis John

Ferguson took over the Rangers, and the two men continued as enemies, with Ferguson doing everything to put Gilbert down, including passing him over for captain. Gilbert retired in 1978 and moved to the front office, where, it is believed, he was instrumental in Ferguson's dismissal.

Many thought that when Fred Shero came to the Rangers in 1978, Gilbert would play again. When that became known, Ferguson was reported to have asked an NHL club for a one-game contract so he could face Gilbert on the ice one last time. Gilbert, however, had retired for good.

But Rod remained a popular member of the Rangers organization, admirably serving the club as an ambassador into the new century. He was inducted into the Hockey Hall of Fame in 1982.

CLARK GILLIES

BORN: Moose Jaw, Saskatchewan, April 4, 1954
POSITION: Left Wing, New York Islanders, 1975–86; Buffalo Sabres, 1986–88
AWARDS/HONORS: NHL Challenge Cup All-Star and Most Valuable Player, 1979; NHL First Team All-Star, 1978–79; NHL All-Star Game, 1978; Hockey Hall of Fame, 2002

A Hall of Fame candidate for years, Clark Gillies was finally inducted in 2002. He was not only one of the NHL's most prominent power forwards but also a left wing who effectively rode shotgun for gifted linemates Bryan Trottier and Mike Bossy.

Together, they helped deliver four consecutive Stanley Cups for the New York Islanders starting in 1980.

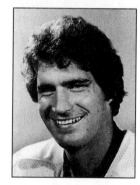

Clark "Jethro" Gillies as an Islander

Gillies symbolized general manager Bill Torrey's philosophy of building through the draft.

He was selected in the first round, fourth overall, in 1974 and quickly won a berth on an up-and-coming Islanders team. The hulking, hard-shooting Western Canadian made his presence felt during the 1975 playoffs, the first for the Islanders, when he was a pivotal offensive force in the first-round upset of the Rangers.

Some experts believe the Islanders never would have won the 1980 Stanley Cup had Gillies not successfully fought Boston's Terry O'Reilly in the second round. In fact, for years Gillies was considered the unofficial heavyweight "champion" of the league—so much so that opponents would simply decline to fight the Bunyanesque portsider.

After 12 seasons on Long Island, Gillies wound up his big-league career in Buffalo, but kept Long Island as his primary residence, where he went into business after retirement.

DOUG GILMOUR

BORN: Kingston, Ontario, June 25, 1963
POSITION: Center, St. Louis Blues, 1983–88; Calgary Flames, 1988–92; Toronto Maple Leafs, 1992–97; New Jersey Devils, 1997–98; Chicago Blackhawks, 1998–2000; Buffalo Sabres, 2000–01; Montreal Canadiens, 2001–
AWARDS/HONORS: Frank J. Selke Trophy, 1993; NHL All-Star Game, 1993–94

Unobtrusively, and without fuss or fanfare, a smallish center signed a contract with the St. Louis Blues in 1982.

Little was known about his ability to withstand the rigors of tough big-league hockey or of his skills as a potential

Doug Gilmour

offensive threat. But in just a few years, Doug Gilmour would establish himself as one of the premier "Little Men" ever seen.

When he came to St. Louis, entrepreneur Harry Ornest had just saved the Blues from collapse. Building around a nucleus that included coach Jacques Demers, general manager Ron Caron, and goaltenders Greg Millen and Rick Wamsley, Ornest saw his franchise grow from hapless to healthy within a couple of seasons. The Blues' captain, Brian Sutter, nicknamed Gilmour "Killer" for his intensity and for his vague resemblance to Charles Manson.

After three full seasons hovering around 50 points and concentrating on checking, Gilmour put on weight. In his words, he "ballooned" to 165 pounds, and began to play a more open game. In the 1986 playoffs, he had 21 points in 19 games when the Blues came within a game of advancing to the Stanley Cup finals. The next season, 1986–87, he finished the regular schedule with a career-high 42 goals and 105 points and was selected to play for Team Canada in the Canada Cup. He scored two important goals in the series against the Soviet Union and was named the tournament's most valuable player. After another solid season in St. Louis, Gilmour was traded to the Calgary Flames at the beginning of the 1988–89 campaign.

In Calgary, Gilmour continued his strong play in the playoffs, adding 22 points in 22 games as the Flames won the Stanley Cup in 1989. Gilmour scored the series-winning goal in Game Six of the finals against Montreal. Halfway through the 1991–92 season, Gilmour became disenchanted with his Flames salary and an arbitrator's decision increased his salary less than he expected. He decided to leave the team, but only a few hours later he was traded to the Toronto Maple Leafs in a blockbuster deal involving 10 players, the largest trade in league history.

Gilmour played his best hockey with the Leafs. He was a pesky defensive forward who was fearless in his checking. Offensively, he

was the focal point of an improving team, setting a franchise record with 127 points in his first full season with Toronto, 1992–93. He became only the second Leaf after Darryl Sittler to register over 100 points in a season and also led the team to within a game of the Stanley Cup finals, placing second in playoff scoring and leading the league with 25 playoff assists. Gilmour won the Selke Trophy as the top defensive forward, a remarkable achievement for a player with such offensive numbers.

Gilmour had 111 points the next season, earned his second consecutive spot in the All-Star Game, and once again led the Leafs to the semifinals in the playoffs. Gilmour was named team captain in 1994–95, before the lockout-shortened season, and remained a popular player in Toronto even as the team began to struggle.

When the Leafs began rebuilding, Gilmour was sent to the New Jersey Devils midway through the 1996–97 campaign. He spent one full season with the defense-oriented Devils, then was signed as a free agent by the Chicago Blackhawks in the summer of 1998. In the spring of 2000, he was traded to the Buffalo Sabres, where his productivity slackened and he contemplated retirement.

But he reconsidered and instead signed as a free agent with the Montreal Canadiens in October 2001. A revitalized Gilmour helped a renascent Habs squad to gain the postseason for the first time in four years.

FRED GLOVER

BORN: Toronto, Ontario, January 5, 1928
POSITION: Forward, Detroit Red Wings, 1949–50, 1951–52; Chicago Blackhawks, 1952–53; Coach, California Seals, 1968–71, 1972–74; Los Angeles Kings, 1971–72

During his 16 seasons with the American League's Cleveland Barons, Fred "No Kid" Glover virtually rewrote the American Hockey League record book. During this time he set records for most career goals (522), most career assists (815), most total career points (1,337), and most career penalty minutes (2,402).

In six years as player-coach of the Barons, he led the team to the American Hockey League's playoffs five times, winning the championship twice. He never quite clicked in the NHL despite trials with the Red Wings and Blackhawks and coaching stints with Oakland and Los Angeles.

Following retirement, he was honored by Cleveland hockey fans as the greatest scorer in history for the American League Barons.

BOB GOLDHAM

BORN: Georgetown, Ontario, May 12, 1922
DIED: November 6, 1991
POSITION: Defenseman, Toronto Maple Leafs, 1941–42, 1945–47; Chicago Blackhawks, 1947–50; Detroit Red Wings, 1950–56
AWARDS/HONORS: NHL All-Star Game, 1947, 1949–50, 1952, 1954–55

Bob Goldham turned hero immediately in his rookie NHL season (1941–42), playing defense for the Toronto Maple Leafs in the Stanley Cup finals against the Detroit Red Wings. Goldham, who had been elevated from the American League's Hershey Bears, was among several green, young players inserted into the Maple Leafs' lineup to replace aging veterans Bucko McDonald and Bingo Kampman as the Leafs fell behind three games to none. The Toronto sextet, sparked by the youthful Goldham, Ernie Dickens, Don Metz, and Wally Stanowski, rallied to win the next four games and the Cup.

In time, Goldham matured into an effective defenseman who was especially good at dropping to the ice to block enemy shots. During the 1947–48 season, he was part of a package—including teammates Gus Bodnar, Bud Poile, Gaye Stewart, and Ernie Dickens—that the Leafs sent to Chicago for ace center Max Bentley and utility forward Cy Thomas. Goldham was

dealt to Detroit in 1950–51 and finished his career with the Red Wings in 1955–56.

He later became a popular hockey commentator in Toronto, and was considered a potential Hall of Famer but never obtained sufficient votes.

SCOTT GOMEZ

BORN: Anchorage, Alaska, December 23, 1979
POSITION: Center, New Jersey Devils 1999–
AWARDS/HONORS: Calder Memorial Trophy, 2000; NHL All-Star Game, 2000

The first-ever Hispanic player drafted in the first round (1998, second choice, 27th overall) and the 18th Alaskan ever drafted, Scott Gomez burst onto the National Hockey League in 1999 as an instant headliner.

He was the only Devil to play in all 82 games during his rookie season (1999–2000), and played in the first 58 games of the 2000–01 season, setting a New Jersey Devils record for most consecutive games played at the start of a career.

This was only the beginning.

His 1999–2000 season with New Jersey brought him an All-Star game appearance, a Stanley Cup, and a Calder Trophy as the NHL's top rookie. He was tied for first in scoring among NHL rookies in both the regular season and the playoffs, only the third player to do so in the Expansion era.

Gomez quickly evolved into an effective, speedy player with charisma, although he slumped his sophomore year.

Though still effective, Gomez's numbers again fell in 2001–02 (48 points in 76 games) as the Devils struggled through much of the season. Just when the team had regrouped in time to make the playoffs, Scott suffered a broken hand that kept him out of action through the end of the regular season and the playoffs.

BOB GOODENOW

BORN: October 29, 1952

The National Hockey League's Players' Association was founded by Toronto-based lawyer Alan Eagleson in 1967. Eagleson dominated the NHLPA until the early 1990s, when a series of articles authored by Russ Conway, sports editor of the *Lawrence-Eagle Tribune,* a suburban daily outside Boston, challenged Eagleson's stewardship of the union. Eagleson, who eventually was jailed, was succeeded by Bob Goodenow, a former player who had become a successful player's representative.

After studying Eagleson's *modus operandi,* Goodenow revamped the NHLPA into a formidable operation.

"Everything with Bob was disclosure-disclosure, and was informational," said goalie Andy Moog, a prominent member of the NHLPA. An obvious result was the average player's salary. In 2001–02, it had reached an all-time high of $1.5 million.

Goodenow was notorious as well for his hard-nosed style, which became evident in 1992 during the NHL players' strike when he challenged NHL president John Ziegler. Goodenow's triumph was said by some observers to be a prime reason for Ziegler's resignation.

When Gary Bettman became the first NHL commissioner in 1993, he vowed to bring fiscal sanity to the league. Bettman and Goodenow collided head-on in September 1994, when the union and league battled over a new collective bargaining agreement. Goodenow's belligerent style pleased some of the union members.

"The players don't look at Mr. Goodenow as being the same as Mr. Eagleson," said Marty McSorley, an intense foe of Eagleson during the latter's reign. "They see Mr. Goodenow sitting on our side of the table this time." Neither side would budge, with the result that the league remained inactive for 103 days until the middle of January 1995.

In a sense, Goodenow was victorious. Average salaries climbed at least 59 percent after 1995. Meanwhile, Bettman and Goodenow worked out an extension of the CBA through 2004 to allow NHLers to participate in 1998 Olympics. In the early 2000s, many league executives demanded that Bettman get tougher with Goodenow when the 2004 CBA expiration loomed.

Unlike Eagleson, Goodenow survived any challenges from his critics, and appeared more powerful than ever in the new century.

EBBIE GOODFELLOW

BORN: Ottawa, Ontario, April 9, 1907
DIED: September 10, 1965
POSITION: Center/Defenseman, Detroit Red Wings, 1930–43; Coach, Chicago Blackhawks, 1950–52
AWARDS/HONORS: Hart Memorial Trophy, 1940; NHL First Team All-Star, 1937, 1940; NHL Second Team All-Star, 1936; NHL All-Star Game, 1937, 1939; Hockey Hall of Fame, 1963

Before Gordie Howe came along, Ebenezer Ralston "Ebbie" Goodfellow marauded the ice lanes for Detroit's Red Wings. Ebbie played NHL hockey in Detroit from 1929–30 until he retired in 1942–43. During that time he played on Stanley Cup winners in 1936 and 1937.

Ebbie Goodfellow, an early Detroit hockey star

In his later years, Ebbie switched to defense and actually coached the Wings when regular coach Jack Adams was suspended following an outburst during the 1942 Stanley Cup finals with Toronto. At the time, the Red Wings were leading the series three games to one, but the Leafs rallied and won the Cup four games to three. Ebbie took a turn at full-time coaching with the Chicago Blackhawks following World War II before quitting hockey altogether for business pursuits in Detroit.

BUTCH GORING

BORN: St. Boniface, Manitoba, October 22, 1949
POSITION: Center, Los Angeles Kings, 1969–80; New York Islanders, 1980–85; Boston Bruins, 1985; Coach, Boston Bruins, 1985–86; New York Islanders, 1999–2001
AWARDS/HONORS: Lady Byng Memorial Trophy, 1978; Bill Masterton Memorial Trophy, 1978; Conn Smythe Trophy, 1981

Butch Goring, at five feet nine, 170 pounds, was proof that size is no measure of skill when it comes to hockey. With his bowlegged, choppy skating style and ancient hockey helmet, he might have been laughable to fans, but his peers knew better. The classy center proved his prowess in the 1977 playoffs, when he scored 7 goals in 9 games, including a hat trick against the Atlanta Flames.

But his most significant impact would occur in 1979–80 when the New York Islanders acquired Butch at the trade deadline, as the quintessential final piece of their championship team. The team did not lose once in their final 12 games, and Goring's presence in the dressing room eased the burden on the Islanders' young stars Bryan Trottier and Mike Bossy. As their second-line center, Goring helped New York win 19 straight playoff rounds and four straight Stanley Cups, registering a Conn Smythe–winning performance in 1981.

Once his playing days were over, Goring took on coaching, beginning with the Bruins in 1985, and taking on some minor-league teams throughout the late 1980s and 1990s while winning two IHL championships with the Denver/Utah Grizzlies.

When the Islander franchise struggled in the late 1990s with unsteady ownership and young minor-league-quality teams, management looked to recapture the glory days by having Goring coach the team in 1999–2000. After a losing, but promising, season, Goring returned for 2000–01 with revitalized ambitious ownership and a batch of new players to aide his stewardship, but fared worse as the Isles finished dead last with 52 points.

Freely stating that he had lost the team, Goring was fired in March 2001. He continued coaching in the minor leagues through 2002.

JOHNNY GOTTSELIG

BORN: Odessa, Russia, June 24, 1905
DIED: May 15, 1986
POSITION: Left Wing, Chicago Blackhawks, 1929–45; Coach, Chicago Blackhawks, 1945–48
AWARDS/HONORS: NHL Second Team All-Star, 1939; NHL All-Star Game, 1937, 1939

The only NHL star to turn coach and then club press agent was Johnny Gottselig, born in Odessa, Russia. He became a Blackhawk in 1928–29 and remained one after he retired in 1944–45.

Gottselig was skating for the Hawks in 1933–34, their first championship year, and again when Chicago won its second Cup in 1938. Johnny coached Chicago in the mid 1940s when tiny Max and Doug Bentley led the Hawks in scoring. "It's the same damn story every winter," Gottselig once lamented. "Nobody is fast enough to catch the Bentleys, so they try to knock 'em out." Gottselig solved that problem by having big defenseman John Mariucci beat up on anyone who beat up the Bentleys.

MICHEL GOULET

BORN: Peribonka, Quebec, April 21, 1960
POSITION: Left Wing, Quebec Nordiques, 1979-90; Chicago Blackhawks, 1990-94
AWARDS/HONORS: NHL First Team All-Star, 1984, 1986-87; NHL Second Team All-Star, 1983, 1988; NHL All-Star Game, 1983-86, 1988; Hockey Hall of Fame, 1998

If ever there was a high-scoring forward who remained obscure for ages, it was Michel Goulet. Despite his scoring accomplishments, Goulet was hidden from the media centers because he spent much of his career in Quebec City, the smallest town in the NHL.

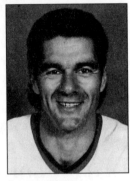

Michel Goulet as a Blackhawk

Deadly around the net, Goulet was a key member of successful Quebec Nordiques teams, which also featured offensive aces such as Peter and Anton Stastny.

Goulet's skills enabled him to remain a productive big-leaguer for 15 years and eventually won him entrance into the Hockey Hall of Fame. One of the most opportunistic scorers in league history, Michel Goulet was an elite left-winger. He managed to score at least 20 goals in all but his last NHL year and once enjoyed a stretch of seven consecutive seasons of at least 40 goals. Although he wasn't considered a rough player, Goulet wasn't intimidated by aggressive play on the part of the opposition.

As one of the former WHA clubs, the Quebec Nordiques had to wait until the established NHL teams chose in the 1979 Entry Draft before they could make their first selection at the 20th slot. Fortunately for them, Goulet was still available and they wasted no time in calling out his name. The youngster put up excellent numbers as a rookie with 22 goals and held up well over the grind of an 80-game NHL schedule. Over the next three years, his goal-scoring increased to 32, 42, and a personal high of 57. His 13 points in 16 games helped the Nordiques surprise many onlookers by reaching the Stanley Cup semifinals in 1982.

By the late 1980s, the Nordiques were in decline and many veterans were traded as part of a rebuilding and cost-cutting strategy. Just prior to the trading deadline in March 1990, Goulet was sent to the Chicago Blackhawks. He adjusted well to his first new team in a decade, but this change required his veteran poise; he was now playing on a tight-checking team that needed him to play a defensive role, while providing timely scoring. Goulet thrived in this new environment, though in the summer of 1990 he was diagnosed with a condition that causes a rapid heartbeat. A complicated procedure saved his career.

On February 16, 1992, he scored his 500th goal on a breakaway against the Calgary Flames in front of a thrilled audience at the old Chicago Stadium, and played well when the Hawks reached the Stanley Cup finals that year, although they lost to the defending champion Pittsburgh Penguins.

Goulet was in the midst of another solid year in the Windy City when his life changed suddenly. While playing the Canadiens at the Montreal Forum on March 16, 1994, he crashed into the end boards and struck his head. This resulted in a severe concussion that forced the veteran to retire and begin a difficult battle with the post-trauma symptoms. A year to the day after the accident, Goulet's number was retired by the Nordiques before a cheering crowd at Le Colisée. The popular winger eventually recovered from his injury to lead a normal life and was thrilled when he was voted into the Hockey Hall of Fame along with former teammate Peter Stastny in 1998.

Goulet stayed in hockey, becoming the Colorado Avalanche's vice president of player personnel through the 2001-02 season.

PHIL GOYETTE

BORN: Lachine, Quebec, October 31, 1933
POSITION: Center, Montreal Canadiens, 1956–63; New York Rangers, 1963–69, 1972; St. Louis Blues, 1969–70; Buffalo Sabres, 1970–72; Coach, New York Islanders, 1972–73
AWARDS/HONORS: Lady Byng Memorial Trophy, 1970

A veteran of 16 National Hockey League playing seasons, Phil Goyette made one key mistake: He agreed to coach the newborn New York Islanders in the 1972–73 season, when the expansion club was one of the worst ever to skate in the majors. Goyette had become accustomed to class hockey since breaking in with the Montreal Canadiens in 1956–57. He played on four straight Stanley Cup championship teams before being traded to the New York Rangers after the 1962–63 season. Goyette continued to star on Broadway, spending six years with the New Yorkers before being traded to the St. Louis Blues prior to the start of the 1969–70 season.

A slick, clean playmaker, Goyette enjoyed his single greatest year in St. Louis, scoring 29 goals and 49 assists for 78 points while winning the Lady Byng Trophy. He was drafted by the newborn Buffalo Sabres the following summer in the Expansion Draft and played for Buffalo for half a season before retiring as a player. But the Rangers persuaded him to return briefly that year for the homestretch.

He then became the Islanders' coach, was fired in midseason, and gradually disappeared from the hockey scene.

DANNY GRANT

BORN: Fredericton, New Brunswick, February 21, 1946
POSITION: Left Wing, Montreal Canadiens, 1965–66, 1967–68; Minnesota North Stars, 1968–74; Detroit Red Wings, 1974–78; Los Angeles Kings, 1978–79
AWARDS/HONORS: Calder Memorial Trophy, 1969; NHL All-Star Game, 1969–71

W hen Danny Grant won the Calder Trophy in 1969, hockey experts figured he would become one of the highest-scoring left-wingers in history. Traded to the Red Wings in 1974, Grant did hit the magic number of 50 goals in 1974–75 and was well on his way to the NHL "Iron Man" record in 1975–76, when a torn thigh muscle ended Grant's consecutive-game streak at 556.

When Danny returned to the lineup for Detroit's last six games, he proved he hadn't lost his touch by scoring a goal-per-game.

Grant was traded to Los Angeles in 1978, and retired after the 1978–79 season.

ADAM GRAVES

BORN: Toronto, Ontario, April 12, 1968
POSITION: Left Wing, Detroit Red Wings, 1988–89; Edmonton Oilers, 1989–91; New York Rangers, 1991–2001; San Jose Sharks, 2001–
AWARDS/HONORS: King Clancy Memorial Trophy, 1994; Bill Masterton Memorial Trophy, 2001; NHL Second Team All-Star, 1994; NHL All-Star Game, 1994

A dam Graves was not the original NHL power forward, but he did redefine that style of play from the time he came to the New York Rangers in 1991 to a Blueshirts victory over the New Jersey Devils in the 1997 playoffs, when he scored an overtime winning goal.

The quintessential gentleman off the ice, Graves became one of the most beloved athletes in New York history for his unparalleled charity work and noble effort on the ice.

In his early years as an Oiler, Graves was part of a youth movement that followed the dynastic Edmonton teams of the 1980s, which featured the likes of Wayne Gretzky, Grant Fuhr, and Mark Messier. As an Oiler, Graves played for a Stanley Cup–winning team in 1989–90, but was to enjoy even greater success after being dealt to New York.

His scoring touch, which was evident in Edmonton, climbed to a new level after he became a Ranger via free agency in 1991. In 1993–94, Graves tallied 52 goals, breaking the previous record set by Vic Hatfield in 1971, helping the Rangers electrify New York en route to a President's Trophy and the club's first Stanley Cup since 1940.

"Gravy" would not score at that rate again, but he consistently delivered 22 or more goals in each season from 1995–96 through 1999–2000 while earning respect across the NHL.

In 1997–98, Adam coled the Rangers with 23 goals in 72 games. In 1998–99, he delivered 162 hits and paced the team with 38 goals and 14 power-play markers. On January 14, 2001, he scored his 300th goal in a 4–2 win over the Minnesota Wild.

On a day that broke the hearts of Ranger fans everywhere, Adam was traded at the 2001 Entry Draft on June 24 to the San Jose Sharks for Mikael Samuelsson and Chris Gosselin. Graves's career was renewed on a veteran Sharks team that challenged Western Conference perennial powerhouses Detroit and Colorado for league supremacy.

SHORTY GREEN

BORN: Sudbury, Ontario, July 17, 1896
DIED: March 1960
POSITION: Forward, Hamilton Tigers, 1923–25; New York Americans, 1925–27; Coach, New York Americans, 1927–28
AWARDS/HONORS: Hockey Hall of Fame, 1962

Shorty Green was a tiny, intense player whose zeal for the game was not lessened one bit by the fact that he was an epileptic. Sometimes the violent seizures would overtake the slight forward during a game and it took up to four players to restrain him.

After playing a few seasons for Hamilton, Wilfred "Shorty" Green moved East with the New York Americans, where he was one of the most popular players on a dismal conglomeration of losers. After one particularly violent game with the rival New York Rangers, Shorty was rushed to the hospital, suffering from internal bleeding.

The New York tabloids sadly announced that Green was dying and possibly wouldn't make it through to morning. As it turned out, reports of Green's untimely death were slightly exaggerated, but he was finished as a player. He did, however, inherit the Amerk coaching duties, but suffering through a losing season from the sidelines was too much for a fierce competitor like Green. After one season behind the American bench, he stepped aside. Shorty Green is a member of the Hockey Hall of Fame.

TED GREEN

BORN: Eriksdale, Manitoba, March 23, 1940
POSITION: Defenseman, Boston Bruins,
1960-72; New England Whalers (WHA),
1972-75; Winnipeg Jets (WHA), 1975-79;
Assistant Coach, Edmonton Oilers, 1989-91,
1997-2000; Coach, Edmonton Oilers, 1991-93;
Assistant Coach, New York Rangers, 1999-
AWARDS/HONORS: NHL Second Team All-
Star, 1969

For almost eight years, Edward Joseph "Ted" Green epitomized the style of the Boston Bruins, bruising, roughhousing, and intimidating members of the opposing team every time he stepped out for a shift.

Then came the infamous stick-swinging incident with the late Wayne Maki, then of the St. Louis Blues, on September 21, 1969.

Former teammate Derek Sanderson recalls that Maki hit Ted from behind as Green was clearing the puck from the Boston zone. Green turned to knock Maki down, but Maki speared him as he rose from the ice. Green swung his stick at Maki, again knocking him down, and fell off-balance. Maki then swung his stick and hit Green across the top of his head. Green went down in a heap, his brain embedded with chips from his skull. Two operations were required to save his life. Green's left side was paralyzed. It was a question of whether or not he could live a normal life, much less skate or play hockey. Maki had two successful NHL seasons (1970-71 and 1971-72) after being claimed by Vancouver from St. Louis in the Expansion Draft.

Green sat out the 1969-70 campaign and watched as his team went on to win the Stanley Cup. Then, with his doctor's permission, he made a comeback the following year and was a key contributor when the Bruins won the Cup again in 1972.

When the WHA opened for business in 1972, Green accepted an offer to join the New England Whalers, where he remained until 1975, when he was traded to his hometown team, the Winnipeg Jets.

Toward the end of the 1978-79 season, Green decided to retire and at the time of the announcement made a plea to the powers that be to put an end to all violence in hockey. It seemed strange indeed to hear this from Teddy Green, a man who lived by violence on the ice.

But he turned to coaching and served in a variety of capacities for the Edmonton Oilers for 14 seasons. After co-coaching Edmonton to a 1990 Stanley Cup victory, Green assumed their head mentor position as the franchise began a rebuilding phase following the departures of Mark Messier, Jari Kurri, and other Oiler dynasty figures. After the 1993 campaign, Green moved to the front office, and then behind the bench again as an assistant to Ron Low in 1997, until former Oilers general manager Glen Sather beckoned both to New York to take on the same roles in 2000. Green became an assistant coach specializing in defense for the Rangers. Although Low was fired in 2002, Green remained on the Rangers staff.

TRAVIS GREEN

BORN: Castlegar, British Columbia, December
20, 1970
POSITION: Center, New York Islanders,
1992-98; Anaheim Mighty Ducks, 1998-99;
Phoenix Coyotes, 1999-2001; Toronto Maple
Leafs, 2001-

Unobtrusively, Travis Green blossomed into one of the NHL's best defensive centers after a decade of mostly average play. During the 2001-02 season, Green climbed to his highest level, spearheading the injury-riddled Toronto Maple Leafs to playoff victories over the New York Islanders, followed by a spirited effort against the Ottawa Senators.

A face-off winner without peer, the amiable Green broke in with the New York Islanders in 1992-93, playing on a youthful line with wingers Marty McInnis and Brad Dalgarno.

Dubbed the Kid Line, the unit helped the Islanders to a marvelous playoff run, during which Green tallied three goals and one assist in a dozen games. His most productive season on Long Island came in 1995–96; Travis had 70 points in 69 games as the Isles' top center.

He remained an Islander until 1998, when he was dealt to Anaheim—with Doug Houda and Tony Tuzzolino—for J. J. Daigneault, Mark Janssens, and Joe Sacco. After slipping for a couple of years, Green returned to top form with the Phoenix Coyotes in 1999–2000 with 25 goals before another move, this time to Toronto as part of a deal for Danny Markov, secured his two-way talent on a contending team. As the Leafs' checking line center for the 2001–02 season, Green scored 11 goals and 23 assists.

When Tornoto moved into the postseason, first defeating Green's old Isles, then Ottawa, Travis was leading the league in percentage of face-offs won and had either set up or scored key goals in both series. Before Toronto was eliminated by Carolina in the third playoff round, Green had been hailed as one of the better postseason performers.

RON GRESCHNER

BORN: Goodsoil, Saskatchewan, December 22, 1954
POSITION: Defenseman, New York Rangers, 1974–90
AWARDS/HONORS: NHL Challenge Cup All-Star, 1979; NHL All-Star Game, 1980

When handsome Ron Greschner was on the ice for the New York Rangers, the swift-skating, smooth stickhandling defenseman was the general for the Blueshirts' attack. Ron held the Blueshirt record for assists by a rookie defenseman until 1989. Greschner's all-out style of playing made him a Garden icon during his career, and he became the highest scoring Ranger defenseman when he assisted on a Dave Silk goal in 1981, a record held

until Brian Leetch appeared on the blueline. The popular Greschner also won the Ranger's "Good Guy" award for the 1985–86 season.

Ron grew up in the backwoods community of Goodsoil, where at the age of 12 he played in a senior league with skaters in their twenties and thirties. Gresch's father owned the local hotel in the small town. "It's farm country," Ron said, "and the hotel caters to moose hunters and oil well drillers."

Greschner remained an NHL fixture until 1990 before retiring for a brief broadcasting career. He remained a New York resident through the twenty-first century and often could be seen at Rangers alumni functions.

WAYNE GRETZKY

BORN: Brantford, Ontario, January 26, 1961
POSITION: Center, Edmonton Oilers, 1979–88; Los Angeles Kings, 1988–96; St. Louis Blues, 1996; New York Rangers, 1996–98; Part Owner, Phoenix Coyotes
AWARDS/HONORS: Hart Memorial Trophy, 1980–87, 1989; Lady Byng Memorial Trophy, 1980, 1991–92, 1994; Art Ross Trophy, 1981–87, 1990–91, 1994; Lester B. Pearson Award, 1982–85, 1987; Conn Smythe Trophy, 1985, 1988; NHL Plus/Minus Leader, 1982, 1984–85, 1987; Chrysler-Dodge/NHL Performer of the Year Award, 1985–87; Dodge Performance of the Year Award, 1989; Lester Patrick Trophy, 1994; NHL First Team All-Star, 1981–87, 1991; NHL Second Team All-Star, 1980, 1988–90, 1994, 1997–98; NHL All-Star Game, 1980–86, 1988–92, 1994, 1996–98; Hockey Hall of Fame, 1999

Critics may argue whether Wayne Gretzky was the greatest player of all time—and a convincing argument can be made against him—but if nothing else, he was the most recognized player in the history of the game.

His nickname, The Great One, helped considerably, as did his numbers. A one-dimensional player, Gretzky nevertheless achieved remarkable records: most points, most goals, most assists, most OT assists, most 100-point seasons, most playoff goals, assists, and points, most playoff game-winning goals, most all-star game goals, and most all-star points are just a few of the 61 records held by The Great One.

Wayne "The Great One" Gretzky with the Kings

Many observers said Gretzky's view of the ice was of radar quality, and that he never had to bother about defense, since his line in Edmonton, which included Jari Kurri and Dave Semenko, were always on attack. Although he also played for the Los Angeles Kings, St. Louis Blues, and the New York Rangers, the only team with which he won the Stanley Cup was the Oilers (four).

As a 16-year-old boy, Gretzky was denied wearing his idol's number (Gordie Howe, 9), so he doubled it and wore the number 99. Not only would he double his idol's jersey number, but eventually he would virtually double his idol's career point total.

In 1978, Gretzky joined the WHA's Indianapolis Racers. The Racers folded after just eight games, and the young Gretzky's services were sold to the rival Edmonton Oilers. He would finish the 1978–79 season with 110 points and was named the WHA's rookie of the year. When the NHL absorbed the Oilers and three other franchises, Gretzky got the opportunity to live one of his dreams— to play in the NHL.

Both Wayne Gretzky and the Edmonton Oilers made their NHL debuts on October 10, 1979, at Chicago Stadium versus the Blackhawks. Gretzky got his first NHL point when he assisted on defenseman Kevin Lowe's goal in the first period. Four nights later, he scored his first goal on a power play against

Vancouver Canucks goalie Glen Hanlon in the third period; and away went Wayne.

Number 99 would become the most dominant player the sport had ever seen, and it could be argued that he was the most dominant in all of sports, as he is statistically the most significant player in the history of North American team sports. His quick thinking, pure scoring touch, lightning quick passes, and uncanny ability to zero in on a target, would raise the performance bar for all future players and alter the sport forever. With Gretzky at the wheel and passengers on board with names like Kevin Lowe, Jari Kurri, Mark Messier, Glenn Anderson, Paul Coffey, and Grant Fuhr tending the nets, the Oilers were always in the fast lane, setting virtually every team scoring record that currently stands.

Smart, savvy coach Glen Sather knew he had a rare gem in his pocket in Gretzky, and dubbed him their squad's captain. In his first full NHL season, he finished with 137 points (51–86–137) and won the first of eight consecutive Hart Trophies, as the NHL's Most Valuable Player. He was ineligible for the Calder Trophy, as the league didn't identify former WHA players as rookies, and lost out on the Art Ross Trophy to Marcel Dionne, as they were tied in points, but Dionne had more goals.

The following season, 1980–81, was the first of seven consecutive Art Ross Trophies, and Gretzky set a new season assist record by eclipsing Bobby Orr's record when he notched 109. The records continued to fall the next year, when he obliterated Phil Esposito's 76 goals (called unbreakable by many) by blistering the nets for an unimaginable 92 goals, a record that may stand for eternity. In just the 39th game of the season that year, The Great One netted his 50th goal, in a five-goal performance. Gretzky finished with 212 points, his first of four 200-point seasons; to date, he is the only player to have ever done so *once*.

The first taste of the Stanley Cup finals was not sweet for The Great One, as the dynastic New York Islanders quickly—in a four-game sweep—grounded his high-flying Oilers. Using their loss as a learning experience, the Oilers returned to the finals for a rematch in 1984, and they disposed of the Islanders in five games and began their own dynasty.

Gretzky had his first encounter with the holy grail of hockey, a feeling he would experience four times in the next five years. Along the way he set various records and achievements, including winning the Canada Cup with Team Canada in 1984 and 1987. Gretzky was a machine, setting record after record, scoring goals and winning awards, trophies, honors, and the hearts of many, for off the ice Gretzky was as modest and unassuming as he was bold and assertive on. His style was unique and he made much of his living behind the net. Making goalies crazy, he made countless perfect passes from behind the cage. In his prime, he was the most consistent and constant threat and impenetrable force ever seen in the NHL.

In 1988, the Oilers won their fourth Stanley Cup and Gretzky won his second Conn Smythe Trophy. King Gretzky married his queen that summer, actress Janet Jones, and just days afterward Gretzky truly became a king, a Los Angeles King, in perhaps one of the most stunning deals in NHL history. Gretzky was sent to LA with Marty McSorley and Mike Krushelnyski for Jimmy Carson, Martin Gelinas, cash, and Los Angeles's first round picks in 1989, 1991, and 1993. Shock, dismay, bewilderment, disbelief, and utter disappointment echoed through the cold air of Canada in the following days, weeks, and years as Wayne Gretzky took off for the United States and never looked back.

More Hart and Art Ross Trophies piled up for The Great One while in LA, and in 1993 the Kings not only reached the Cup finals for the first time in franchise history, but Gretzky and his Kings paved the way for future successes in warm climates unfamiliar to hockey (Dallas, Phoenix, San Jose, Anaheim, Tampa, Florida, Carolina, and Nashville). That season

in the 1993 Campbell Conference finals, Gretzky played in what he himself would later call his, "finest game ever." Behind a Gretzky hat trick, the Kings eliminated a worthy opponent in feisty Doug Gilmour and his Toronto Maple Leafs. But Patrick Roy, John LeClair, and the Montreal Canadiens spanked the Kings, out of gas and energy from the grueling three previous rounds, four games to one. Gretzky was still great with 40 points in 24 games after missing most of that season with a serious back injury. He would never again get this close to the Stanley Cup.

Feeling right at home with LA, Gretzky became the NHL's all-time leading scorer on October 15, 1989, in Edmonton, passing Gordie Howe with point number 1,851. On March 23, 1994, The Great One became The Greatest One when he scored goal number 802, to eclipse idol Howe as the all-time leading goal scorer. Mr. Hockey would later say of Gretzky's accomplishments, "The fact that the record was broken by someone who is such a great person, takes away any sense of loss I might have."

Late in 1996, the Kings were crumbling and Gretzky was sent to St. Louis to play with good friend Brett Hull. He appeared in only 18 regular season games and after a disappointing playoffs, the Blues decided against offering The Great One a new contract. Gretzky, that summer, eventually signed a three-year deal with the New York Rangers, reuniting with his old Edmonton pals, Mark Messier and Esa Tikkanen.

Gretzky had an immediate impact with a 15-game scoring streak in his first month and tied the club's single season record for assists (72) by a center. A year later, Messier left New York and Gretzky behind him for big money the Vancouver Canucks threw at him. Gretzky was now on a mediocre team heading downward in the respectability department. He remained the leading scorer as the Rangers missed the playoffs his last two seasons.

In 1998, at the age of 37, Gretzky realized another dream when he represented his country at the Winter Olympics in Nagano, Japan. After a disappointing Olympics and not being able to play up to his own lofty standards in 1999, Gretzky announced his retirement. Although he could still score, and many players would have killed to have the skills of an aging number 99, Gretzky could not play at such a diminished level. His final two games, in Ottawa and New York, were emotionally difficult.

After 20 seasons, 1,487 games played, 2,857 points, 1,963 assists, 894 goals, 57 awards, and four Stanley Cups, the ride was over. Gretzky played his final game on April 18, 1999, capping a lifetime of thrills and achievements. Upon retirement, Wayne Gretzky held or shared 61 NHL records (40 for regular season, 15 for Stanley Cup playoffs, and six for All-Star games).

When Gretzky retired, the league bestowed on him the ultimate honor by retiring his number league-wide, and he was immediately enshrined in the NHL Hall of Fame. At the start of the 1999–2000 season, the Edmonton Oilers raised his number 99 to the rafters, and that summer, he became the minority owner of the Phoenix Coyotes to help save the franchise from moving.

In 2002, he assembled perhaps one of the greatest collections of star power and talent, one that may have even given his Oilers a run for their money, when he was general manager for Team Canada at the Winter Olympics. With names like Lemieux, Kariya, Sakic, Brodeur, Blake, Yzerman, Lindros, and Iginla, The Great One's magic was apparent again as Canada's son orchestrated their first gold medal for ice hockey in 50 years.

Late in the twentieth century, when ESPN picked their 100 greatest athletes, Gretzky was tabbed number five, behind Michael Jordan, Babe Ruth, Muhammad Ali, and Jim Brown. When ESPN later aired several of these sport immortals' biographies, only two luminaries went completely without a single word of criticism, Wayne Gretzky and Secretariat—the great triple crown–winning horse—which says a great deal about The Great One!

The Great One, Wayne Gretzky, Number 99 in your program books, was numerically the greatest player ever to put on a pair of skates.

BILL GUERIN

BORN: Worcester, Massachusetts, November 9, 1970
POSITION: Right Wing, New Jersey Devils, 1991–98; Edmonton Oilers, 1998–2000; Boston Bruins, 2000–02, Dallas Stars, 2002–
AWARDS/HONORS: Olympics, 1992, 1998, 2002; NHL All-Star Game, 2001

Shortly after he had spearheaded the New Jersey Devils' Stanley Cup conquest in 1995, Bill Guerin was feted in his hometown of Worcester, Massachusetts. One of the speakers noted that the key goal scored by Guerin was reminiscent of the legendary Maurice "The Rocket" Richard, considered the Babe Ruth of hockey.

The comparison was made again after Guerin was traded from the Edmonton Oilers to the Boston Bruins in 2001. At first, Boston writers were skeptical, but in time they came to recognize the explosiveness of Guerin's shot and his ability to lift the team because of his leadership qualities.

A product of the New Jersey Devils' farm system, Guerin originally made his mark in the American Hockey League with Utica after playing for two years with Boston College. A top prospect, Guerin was New Jersey's first pick, fifth overall, in the 1989 Entry Draft and traded to Edmonton in 1998 with Valeri Zelepukin for Bryan Muir and Jason Arnott, who would then become one of New Jersey's leading men.

The six-feet-two, 210-pound Guerin was a force on the ice, proving a solid goal scorer and huge asset for each of his teams. He was named Most Valuable Player at the 2001 NHL All-Star game, where he had three goals and two assists. He also participated in three Olympic runs and was key to getting the Stanley Cup for the Devils in 1995.

After teaming with Doug Weight in Edmonton for three seasons, Bill arrived in Boston in October 2001 in a deal for Anson Carter. Although Guerin was not designated the Bruins' captain—the team never assigned one—he led the Bostonians on and off the ice.

Along with Joe Thornton, Sergei Samsonov, and Glen Murray, Bill paced the 2001–02 Bruins to an Eastern Conference title. He ended the season with 41 goals and 25 assists in 78 games.

After the 2001–02 season, Guerin became a free agent and signed a lucrative long-term deal with the Dallas Stars.

ALDO GUIDOLIN

BORN: Forks of Credit, Ontario, June 6, 1932
POSITION: Defenseman/Forward, New York Rangers, 1952–56; Coach, Colorado Rockies, 1978–79

First cousin of Armand "Bep" Guidolin, Aldo was an underrated defenseman-forward with the Rangers during the mid 1950s. However, he later became a successful coach in Baltimore and Omaha. His best minor-league days were spent with Baltimore, Cleveland, and, briefly, with Springfield of the American League. At Springfield, Aldo became a close observer of boss Eddie Shore's bizarre coaching techniques. "He harped on three points," said Guidolin. "He wanted the hands two feet apart on the stick, the feet eleven inches apart on the ice, and he wanted you to skate in a sort of sitting position. You had to do it exactly right, or you were in big trouble."

Guidolin discovered this one morning during a practice. He had just completed what he considered a perfect pass that resulted in a goal while skating at top speed. Then he heard the whistle and saw Shore motion to him. "Mister Guidolin," he said, "do you know what you did wrong?"

"The pass was perfect," said Guidolin. "I was in the sitting position. My two hands were on the stick. What more do you want?"

"Mister Guidolin," Shore said, "your legs were two inches too far apart!"

Guidolin coached in the American League (Baltimore), as well as the NHL with the Colorado Rockies in 1978–79. He later did NHL scouting while operating a real estate practice in Guelph, Ontario.

BEP GUIDOLIN

BORN: Thorold, Ontario, December 9, 1925
POSITION: Forward, Boston Bruins, 1942–47; Detroit Red Wings, 1947–48; Chicago Blackhawks, 1948–52; Coach, Boston Bruins, 1973–74; Kansas City Scouts, 1974–76

Through most of his adult life in hockey, Armand "Bep" Guidolin's chief claim to fame was that he had been the youngest player (16) ever to perform in the NHL. But in the fall of 1971, the Boston Bruins brought all of their top farmhands to Boston and created the Braves, a new AHL team, installing Bep Guidolin as coach.

No team in the AHL was better conditioned, better disciplined, or more spirited. Bep's Braves won the Eastern Division title their first year in the AHL, leading the race from wire to wire. Midway through their second season, Bep got the call to replace Tom Johnson as coach of the parent Bruins. Observers immediately noted that the Bruins practices became much more exhausting, characterized by relentless drills and rink-length wind sprints. And their games became more conservative. "Other teams have been capitalizing on our mistakes," Bep complained. "We're going to start concentrating on little things again, like making at least two good passes in our own end."

Suddenly the Bruins, who had picked up just 12 points in the final 15 games of Johnson's regime, began to flex their muscles again.

But then in the 1973–74 season, Guidolin feuded with Derek Sanderson and Phil Esposito and coached the first established NHL team (Boston) to ever lose to an expansion club in the Stanley Cup finals. As a result, he was fired by the Bruins and hired to coach the new Kansas City Scouts, one of the two baby expansion clubs of 1974–75.

Bep could not inspire the dismal Scouts, and by the time the franchise moved from Kansas City to Colorado, Guidolin was behind the bench of the American Hockey League's Philadelphia Firebirds before fading out of the hockey scene.

VIC HADFIELD

BORN: Oakville, Ontario, October 4, 1940
POSITION: Left Wing, New York Rangers, 1961–74; Pittsburgh Penguins, 1974–77
AWARDS/HONORS: NHL Second Team All-Star, 1972; Team Canada, 1972; NHL All-Star Game, 1965, 1972

A New York Ranger for 13 seasons before being traded to the Pittsburgh Penguins for defenseman Nick Beverley, Vic Hadfield was the portsider on the Broadway Blueshirts' Goal-a-Game (GAG) Line, with center Jean Ratelle and right wing Rod Gilbert.

Normally a plodding digger with a reputation as a tough guy, Vic scored 50 goals in 1971–72, a New York Ranger record until Adam Graves scored 52 goals in 1994.

Named captain of the Broadway sextet in 1971, Hadfield was later beset by a series of nagging injuries that limited his potential as an enforcer as well as his ability to blast the puck past opposing netminders. In 1974, Vic and his reported $100,000 salary were shipped to Pittsburgh, where knee problems forced him to retire in 1977. Hadfield returned to the Rangers as a scout for the 1978–79 season. He later went into private business, remaining an active member of the Rangers alumni association. During their annual gathering in September 2001, Hadfield was honored by his alumni chums at a golf tournament near New York City.

GEORGE HAINSWORTH

BORN: Toronto, Ontario, June 26, 1895
DIED: October 9, 1950
POSITION: Goaltender, Montreal Canadiens, 1926–33, 1937; Toronto Maple Leafs, 1933–36
AWARDS/HONORS: Vezina Trophy, 1927–29; NHL All-Star Game, 1934; Hockey Hall of Fame, 1961

Montreal Canadiens goalie George Hainsworth was an English Canadian who measured only five feet six, short compared to his tall, distinguished French predecessor, Georges Vezina. Furthermore, at age 33, Hainsworth seemed to be approaching the end, rather than the beginning, of his major-league career.

His debut was something less than impressive. He was beaten, 4–1, in the season opener at Boston and returned to Montreal where Ottawa outscored Les Canadiens, 2–1. This was followed by a 2–1 loss to the Maroons, thus confirming the suspicions of Canadien fans that Hainsworth was an unworthy successor to Vezina.

However, Hainsworth played every one of the 44 games on the Canadiens' schedule, and finished the season with a goals-against average of 1.52, bettered only by Clint Benedict of the Maroons, who registered a 1.51 mark.

Little by little, the Canadiens' fans began warming up to Hainsworth. He won the Vezina Trophy first in 1926–27, again in the 1927–28 season, with a remarkable 1.09 goals-against average, and managed to improve on that in 1928–29, this time allowing only 43 goals in 44 games for a 0.98 mark.

On the night of January 24, 1929, the Toronto Maple Leafs were visiting the Forum. As the Canadiens were peppering Hainsworth in the pregame warm-up, a practice shot caught the goaltender unawares and smashed into his nose, knocking him unconscious. A bloody mess, Hainsworth was carried into the dressing room and a call went over the Forum loudspeaker for the Canadiens' spare goalie. He couldn't be located.

The team physician worked over Hainsworth's broken nose, but the blow was so severe that within a matter of minutes the swelling had completely shut one eye. "Bandage me up," Hainsworth insisted, "I want to get out there."

Neither the doctor nor the Canadiens had much choice. Ten minutes later, George skated out to his position for the opening face-off. The goal-hungry Maple Leafs immediately swarmed to the attack and bombarded Hainsworth with every variety of shot at their command.

Veteran reporters could hardly remember the fans sitting down throughout the game as Hainsworth portrayed a hockey version of Horatio at the bridge, and soon George himself was yelling and screaming along with his fans. "His face," wrote a critic, "one-sided and bulging, feverish and red from excitement and injury, loomed livid and macabre above the forest of sticks and whirling forms crowding close about him. This was his night of nights!"

The Maple Leafs managed to jam one shot behind him, but the inspired Canadiens scored a goal, too. The game ended in a 1–1 tie. From that point on, Hainsworth was a Forum hero and played seven full seasons, until he was 40 years old.

Hainsworth improved with age. In 1928–29, he recorded 22 shutouts in 44 games and continued to excel for the Canadiens until the 1932–33 campaign. The entire Montreal team, from Morenz to Hainsworth, was in a slump that year. It hit its lowest point on February 21, 1933, when Les Canadiens visited Boston and were demolished, 10–0. His boss, Leo Dandurand, was furious with Hainsworth, who had given up several "easy" goals and made up his mind to trade him at the earliest

opportunity. One afternoon he picked up the telephone and called Conn Smythe, manager of the Maple Leafs. Within a few minutes it had been agreed that Smythe would trade the Toronto goalie Lorne Chabot for Hainsworth.

Chabot played only one season for Les Canadiens and registered a 2.15 goals-against average, whereas Hainsworth's mark was a less impressive 2.48. But Hainsworth lasted three full seasons in Toronto, during which the Leafs twice led the league, before returning briefly to Montreal in 1937, where he played several games before retiring.

GLENN HALL

BORN: Humboldt, Saskatchewan, October 3, 1931
POSITION: Goaltender, Detroit Red Wings, 1952–57; Chicago Blackhawks, 1957–67; St. Louis Blues, 1967–71
AWARDS/HONORS: Calder Memorial Trophy, 1956; Vezina Trophy, 1963, 1967 (shared with Denis DeJordy), 1969 (shared with Jacques Plante); Conn Smythe Trophy, 1968; NHL First Team All-Star, 1957–58, 1960, 1963–64, 1966, 1969; NHL Second Team All-Star, 1956, 1961–62, 1967; NHL All-Star Game, 1955–58, 1960–65, 1967–69; Hockey Hall of Fame, 1975

Among the more poignant examples of Detroit Red Wings mismanagement, the case of Glenn Hall ranks at the top.

A goaltender extraordinaire, Hall would one day earn the title "Mister Goalie," a title bestowed upon no other NHL puck-stopper—ever.

Unfortunately for Motown fans, by the time Hall became Mister Goalie, he was playing somewhere else. Chicago, of all places.

It began with Red Wings general manager Jack Adams in the early 1940s. Jolly Jawn, as he was known, was obsessed with developing high-quality netminders on his developmental teams. In fact, goalies grew so well and so fast on Detroit's farms, that Adams had a surplus.

Johnny Mowers won a Stanley Cup for Adams in 1942–43, but he soon was crowded out of the crease by another Red Wings up-and-comer, Harry Lumley. When Lumley took Detroit to another Cup in 1949–50, he seemed set in goal for at least a decade.

But the goalie crop continued to flourish. Adams's scouts raved about Terry Sawchuk, a prodigy starring at Indianapolis. There was only one thing to do, trade Lumley and promote Sawchuk, which is precisely what the general manager did.

With Sawchuk between the pipes, Detroit won Stanley Cups in 1952, 1954, and 1955. Like Lumley before him, Sawchuk appeared to have a mortgage on the goaltending job, but Adams couldn't help himself. Once again a goaltending ace-in-the-making was on the farm.

Glenn Hall was so good that Adams invited him to play two games during the 1954–55 season despite the presence of Sawchuk. Hall allowed only one goal in the pair of matches, hinting he might be even better than the great Sawchuk.

Adams got the message and, following the 1955 Stanley Cup triumph, dealt Sawchuk to Boston. Glenn Hall was *the* Red Wings goaltender for the start of the 1955–56 season. He wasted no time making his mark, skating off

with the Calder Trophy as the league's rookie of the year.

After Hall completed two campaigns in Detroit, Adams did it again: Hall was traded to Chicago, where he captured the Vezina Trophy in 1963 and 1967 (shared with Denis DeJordy). In 1961, Hall led the Blackhawks to their first Stanley Cup since 1938, performing spectacularly as Chicago eliminated, ironically, the Red Wings in the final round.

Glenn appeared in an amazing 502 consecutive contests, yet was so fearful of his hazardous occupation, he would get violently ill before games.

With the coming of expansion, Hall was drafted by the St. Louis Blues, with whom he won his third Vezina in 1969 (shared with Jacques Plante), and the Conn Smythe Trophy in 1968. Hall also was an 11-time All-Star; his seven First Team berths a record for NHL goaltenders. Hall retired with a shining 2.51 goals-against average to go with 84 shutouts in 906 career contests, and was named to the Hockey Hall of Fame in June 1975. Glenn spent his retirement on his farm, although he remained active as a goaltending consultant through the end of the twentieth century.

JOE HALL

BORN: Stratfordshire, England, 1882
DIED: April 5, 1919
POSITION: Defenseman, Quebec (ECAHA), 1906; Montreal Canadiens and Shamrocks (ECAHA), 1908; Montreal Wanderers (ECAHA), 1909; Montreal Shamrocks (NHA), 1910; Quebec Bulldogs (NHA), 1911–17; Montreal Canadiens, 1917–19
AWARDS/HONORS: Hockey Hall of Fame, 1961

Glenn "Mister Goalie" Hall, the Iron Man as a Blackhawk

"Bad" Joe Hall was born in England but learned his hockey in western Canada. He first achieved distinction—or notoriety—playing for Houghton, Michigan, in the bloodthirsty International Pro League in 1905 and 1906. Close friends of Hall's insisted he was the victim of overzealous typewriters and really wasn't a bad fellow after all.

"He wasn't mean," said friend and teammate Joe Malone, "despite what a lot of people said about him. He certainly liked to deal out a heavy check and he was always ready to take it as well as dish it out. That in itself was remarkable when you consider that Joe weighed in at only a hundred fifty pounds. As far as I'm concerned he should have been known as 'Plain' Joe Hall and not 'Bad' Joe Hall. That always was a bum rap."

Whatever the case, Hall and Malone ignited the Canadiens to a successful first half of the 1917–18 season and by midpoint the Flying Frenchmen—by now dotted with English-speaking players—were in first place. Then, on January 2, 1918, fire reduced the Montreal Arena to rubble. Both Les Canadiens and the Wanderers lost all their equipment and the arena damage was put at $150,000.

With the fall of the Montreal Arena, Les Canadiens lost their momentum until they adjusted to playing in the Jubilee Rink for the 1918–19 season. They then regained their winning ways and defeated Ottawa for the right to go west and challenge Seattle for the Cup.

The series opened on March 19. Seattle bombed The Habs, 7–0, and appeared destined to sweep the series. But with Newsy Lalonde in command of his game, the visitors rebounded neatly to capture the second match, 4–2, and the teams settled down for what appeared to be a thrilling series. Seattle captured the third game, 7–2, setting the stage for what NHL historian Charles L. Coleman has described as "the greatest match ever played on the Pacific Coast."

Neither team scored in regulation time. One hour and 40 minutes of sudden-death overtime were played before the game was called a draw. When the teams met again four nights later, the score was 3–3 going into overtime, but this time the Canadiens prevailed after 15:57 of extra play on a goal by Odie Cleghorn. "Bad" Joe Hall, who in earlier games had battled vehemently with Seattle's Cully Wilson, appeared to lose his zest, finally left the ice, and made his way to the dressing room. Unknown to onlookers, it was to be the last time Joe was ever to step on a rink.

Hall was rushed to the hospital, stricken with the flu bug that was causing an epidemic throughout North America. Immediately after the game, several other Canadiens, including Lalonde and manager George Kennedy, were bedded with influenza, but none as badly as Joe Hall.

With the series tied at two apiece, an attempt was made to finish the playoff for the Stanley Cup. Kennedy requested permission to "borrow" players from Victoria to finish the series, but the hosts declined the bid and the playoff was canceled without a winner.

Six days after he had stumbled off the ice, Joe Hall died of influenza in a Seattle hospital. His friend and admirer, Joe Malone, was the most seriously affected by the news because he believed that Hall never had the opportunity to erase the bad name he had acquired. "There were plenty of huge, rough characters on the ice in Joe's time," said Malone, "and he was able to stay in there with them for more than 18 years. His death was a tragic and shocking climax to one of the most surprising of all Stanley Cup series."

It would be the only year in the entire history of the Stanley Cup—amateur or professional—that the coveted trophy would not be awarded. The flu that killed Hall would kill nearly 20 million people before the epidemic ended.

ROMAN HAMRLIK

BORN: Gottwaldov, Czechoslovakia, April 12, 1974
POSITION: Defenseman, Tampa Bay Lightning, 1992–97; Edmonton Oilers, 1997–2000; New York Islanders, 2000–
AWARDS/HONORS: NHL All-Star Game, 1996, 1999

Among European players who have come to the NHL, one of the most highly touted was Roman Hamrlik, a defenseman.

The Czech backliner was selected first overall by the Tampa Bay Lightning in the 1992 Entry Draft.

He then was expected to lift an expansion team to a competitive level, but it was too much of a burden for him. Hamrlik was immediately criticized by management and eventually traded, despite the fact that he had 65 points as a 22-year-old in his fourth season, 1995–96. Tampa Bay made the postseason for the first time in their existence as an NHL franchise.

Roman was dealt to the Edmonton Oilers the following season. Among the top-scoring defensemen in any season, Hamrlik had 8 goals and 37 assists in 80 games during the 1999–2000 campaign for Edmonton.

The Oilers traded Hamrlik to the New York Islanders in exchange for Eric Brewer, Josh Green, and a second-round draft pick at the 2000 Entry Draft (Brad Winchester).

With Hamrlik as a cornerstone defenseman, the Islanders rebuilt rapidly. Frequently playing through pain, Hamrlik helped the Islanders reach the postseason in 2001–02 with 11 goals and 26 assists.

TERRY HARPER

BORN: Regina, Saskatchewan, January 27, 1940
POSITION: Defenseman, Montreal Canadiens, 1962–72; Los Angeles Kings, 1972–75; Detroit Red Wings, 1975–79; St. Louis Blues, 1979–80; Colorado Rockies, 1980–81
AWARDS/HONORS: NHL All-Star Game, 1965, 1967, 1973, 1975

When Terry Harper first came up to the NHL, he was one of the few "hit men" on the artistic Montreal Canadiens. Les Habitants boasted a bevy of stickhandling virtuosos who could transform a game of shinny into an art form, but they also understood the need for a couple of not-so-subtle bodyguards to help protect the valuable merchandise.

Harper and forward John Ferguson became the awkward, but effective, heavies in the glittering Canadien troupe of players. Terry understood his role, and accepted it, and came to be known as the league's leading bleeder.

Over Terry's nine seasons as a regular Montreal blueliner, the Habs copped five Stanley Cups and failed but once to make the playoffs. Then, in August 1972, Harper was traded to the Los Angeles Kings.

After a brief period of adjustment, Harper settled into his new surroundings nicely. When he teamed with ex-Blackhawk Gilles Marotte, the duo formed one of the best "expansion" defensive pairings in the league, until Marotte went to New York in 1973. Harper was named captain after one season with LA, and improved the defense and team immensely before being traded to Detroit in June 1975.

One of the most underrated, hard-trying players of his era, Harper concluded his career with the Colorado Rockies in 1981.

BILLY HARRIS

BORN: Toronto, Ontario, January 29, 1952
POSITION: Right Wing, New York Islanders, 1972–80; Los Angeles Kings, 1980–81, 1984; Toronto Maple Leafs, 1981–84

When the time came for the baby New York Islanders to make the National Hockey League's number one junior draft pick in June 1972, they chose 20-year-old Billy Harris.

Harris, six feet two and 195 pounds, like Yvan Cournoyer of the Canadiens, was a left-handed shooting right wing. Unlike Cournoyer, Harris played Junior A hockey with the Toronto Marlboros of the Ontario Hockey Association. In his final season with the Marlies, he led the league in scoring with 57 goals and 72 assists for 129 points.

Harris's NHL contract was awesome for its time, considering he had not played a single game of pro hockey. It involved an estimated $300,000 for a three-year deal, with the last year renegotiable after two seasons.

Although he scored a healthy 28 goals, Harris's rookie season could best be described as miserable. He was expected to carry the full load for the fledgling club, but lacked the maturity to handle the expectations, publicity, and general punishment a touted rookie gets from opponents. After his freshman year, Harris settled into his duties with respectability, largely because defensive phenom Denis Potvin had arrived to fill the vacuum as team leader and resident superstar.

Harris was traded to the Los Angeles Kings at the 1980 trade deadline, along with defenseman Dave Lewis, for Butch Goring. While Goring was a catalyst for four consecutive Islander Stanley Cup wins, Harris settled in for a modest career that ultimately concluded with Toronto in 1984.

TED HARRIS

BORN: Winnipeg, Manitoba, July 18, 1936
POSITION: Defenseman, Montreal Canadiens, 1963–70; Minnesota North Stars, 1970–73; Detroit Red Wings, 1973–74; St. Louis Blues, 1974; Philadelphia Flyers, 1974–75; Coach, Minnesota North Stars, 1975–77
AWARDS/HONORS: NHL Second Team All-Star, 1969; NHL All-Star Game, 1965, 1967, 1969, 1971–72

Ted Harris was a throwback defenseman to the days when crunching body checks were more the vogue than in contemporary hockey. He served a long minor-league apprenticeship, beginning with Philadelphia in the old Eastern League, then Springfield in 1956–59, where Hall of Famer Eddie Shore taught him how to skate effectively and body-check with authority.

Harris reached the NHL in 1963–64 and spent six full seasons with the Canadiens before being acquired by the Minnesota North Stars in 1970. Harris had long been considered one of the NHL's three most effective fistfighters, coequal with John Ferguson and Orland Kurtenbach. Harris and Kurtenbach staged two classic one-on-one bouts in which each took a decision. Harris reached the Philadelphia Flyers in 1974–75 after briefly touching base in Detroit and St. Louis.

Harris announced his retirement as a player in the dressing room of the 1974–75 Stanley Cup champion Philadelphia Flyers. Shortly thereafter he was named coach of the Minnesota North Stars, but was fired 19 games into his third season when the team went 5–12–2.

BOB HARTLEY

BORN: Hawkesbury, Ontario, September 7, 1960
POSITION: Coach, Colorado Avalanche, 1998–

The American Hockey League has delivered many head coaches who went on to acclaim in the National Hockey League, but few so successful so fast as Bob Hartley.

Hired as bench boss of the Colorado Avalanche in 1998, Hartley had success as a Calder Cup–winning coach with the 1996–97 Hershey Bears.

Alternately severe, pensive, and amusing behind the bench, Hartley voraciously digested coaching information and then disseminated it to his skaters. Less than a legend, he knew—like virtually any coach, especially Larry Robinson—that the distance between champ and chump can be measured by three periods of a Game Seven.

After his first two seasons, 1998–99 and 1999–2000, in which Colorado lost in the Conference finals, Hartley was in grave danger of losing his job, and was not exactly revered by a Denver media that would just as soon knife him as it would slice a tender Rocky Mountain steak.

That view, however, changed dramatically after the Avalanche disposed of the New Jersey Devils in seven games to capture the 2001 Stanley Cup.

"I live for the playoffs," said Hartley. "The playoffs bring the best out of everyone. I know that as a coaching staff, the practices and preparation have turned on the playoff switch for about two weeks. We're demanding; we're focusing on the little details."

With a cadre of stars such as Joe Sakic, Patrick Roy, Adam Foote, and Peter Forsberg leading a never-ending crop of quality young players like Chris Drury and Alex Tanguay, Bob found ways to keep his group an unsinkable one, even in times of extreme adversity.

Stunned by Forsberg's unexpected health problems that prevented him from playing in the 2001 postseason and subsequent 2001–02 campaign, Hartley nevertheless got the Avalanche on track. In some ways, it was the challenge of his four-year coaching career. Defeating the Devils for the Cup, Hartley's team was commended for its composure after falling behind three games to two.

"I'm the leader of this team and I have to make sure that we have great composure and we do everything for a reason," said Hartley. "The playoff season is the time of year where what you did yesterday doesn't count anymore."

Not surprisingly, the 2001–02 season began hesitatingly for the defending champs. The long road through the finals took a severe mental and physical toll on the winning club. But, by December, the Avalanche had moved into high gear, indicating they were ready to take a good run at the Cup even without Forsberg, who in fact made a triumphant return against Los Angeles in the first round. The Kings would take the Avs to a seventh game for the second year in a row, only to fall, as they had in 2001. Hartley and his Avs would then best San Jose in the second round, to face off against an old rival, the Detroit Red Wings, in the Western Conference finals.

But Hartley and his Avs were not meant to repeat, as the Motor City squad vanquished Colorado in yet another seven-game thriller.

CRAIG HARTSBURG

BORN: Stratford, Ontario, June 29, 1959
POSITION: Defenseman, Minnesota North Stars, 1979–89; Coach, Chicago Blackhawks, 1994–98; Anaheim Mighty Ducks, 1998–2000
AWARDS/HONORS: NHL All-Star Game, 1980, 1982–83

A stalwart for the Minnesota North Stars through his entire playing career, Craig Hartsburg was a defenseman who could put up points with some of the best forwards in the NHL. During the 1981–82 season, he totaled 77 points on 17 goals and 60 assists. The previous spring, he helped his Cinderella North Stars to the Stanley Cup finals, averaging almost a point-per-game with 15 points in 19 games.

Hartsburg broke into pro hockey in the last year of the World Hockey Association, signing as an underage free agent by the Birmingham Bulls in June 1978. Craig, also made an imprint on the coaching front, albeit with less success. He began as the Blackhawks' bench boss in 1995–96, and posted 40 wins and a first-round sweep over Calgary. However, Hartsburg's Hawks would decline in his two following seasons, missing the postseason in 1997–98.

The Mighty Ducks of Anaheim came calling, and Hartsburg was back behind an NHL bench the following autumn, guiding the Paul Kariya–Teemu Selanne–led sextet to a first-round playoff berth in 1998–99. However, Hartsburg could not shepherd the Ducks into further success in his next two seasons, and was fired in December 2000. He resurfaced in the summer of 2002 as Ken Hitchcock's assistant on the Philadelphia Flyers.

DOUG HARVEY

BORN: Montreal, Quebec, December 19, 1924
DIED: December 26, 1989
POSITION: Defenseman, Montreal Canadiens, 1947–61; New York Rangers, 1961–64; Detroit Red Wings, 1966–67; St. Louis Blues, 1968–69; Coach, New York Rangers, 1961–62
AWARDS/HONORS: James Norris Memorial Trophy, 1955–58, 1960–62; NHL First Team All-Star, 1952–58, 1960–62; NHL Second Team All-Star, 1959; NHL All-Star Game, 1951–62, 1969; Hockey Hall of Fame, 1973

Defenseman Douglas Harvey was so laconic in style, so calmly sure of himself, that he executed plays of extreme complexity with consummate ease. Lacking the flamboyance of Eddie Shore or other Hall of Fame defensemen, Harvey was slow to receive the acclaim he deserved. "Often, Harvey's cool was mistaken for disinterest," said author Josh Greenfeld. "Actually it was the result of an always calculating concentration." But by 1955–56 Harvey's excellence had become apparent. "Doug Harvey was the greatest defenseman who ever played hockey, bar none," said Toe Blake. "Usually a defenseman specializes in one thing and builds a reputation on that, but Doug could do everything well."

Harvey was a superb rusher but lacked the blazing shot later characterized by Boston's Bobby Orr. "Harvey," wrote Greenfeld, "could inaugurate a play from farther back and carry it farther than any other defenseman."

Harvey was a consummate craftsman, perhaps unmatched among defensemen for a union of style, wisdom, and strength. He won the Norris Trophy seven times as the best defenseman in the game; he was selected an All-Star 11 times.

Toe Blake coached Harvey in Montreal in the late 1950s, during one dominant span from 1955 to 1960 when the Canadiens won the Stanley Cup for five successive seasons. Harvey was distinguished then as the hub of

Doug Harvey, Montreal defensive ace

Montreal's smothering power play, associated with Boom-Boom Geoffrion, Jean Beliveau, Rocket Richard, and Richard Winston "Dickie" Moore.

"No player put my heart in my mouth as often as Doug," Blake said. "But I learned to swallow in silence. His style was casual, but it worked. He made few mistakes, and, ninety-nine percent of the time correctly anticipated the play or pass."

Blake added the definitive estimate of the most imposing NHL defenseman since the immortal Eddie Shore: "Doug played defense in a rocking chair."

Harvey began playing professionally in 1947, after rejecting an offer from the Boston Braves to play baseball. He had played two summers in the Border Baseball League at Ottawa, once leading all batsmen with an average of .351. Before that, in World War II, he spent 16 months as a gunner on a Canadian merchant ship in the North Atlantic.

When Harvey hit the far slope of his career, and kept playing, hockey's rigid group-think suggested there was something not quite respectable in a player refusing to admit he had been caught by age. His persistence, purists insisted, made a mockery of The Game.

Harvey became a nomad in 1964, when the NHL governors made him a free agent in return for his long service. Such gestures are rare because many sportsmen discard nothing as long as they suspect there is some wheat left in the husk.

He coached the New York Rangers to brief success for one season, sufficiently gifted at leadership to guide them into an uncommon appearance in the Stanley Cup playoffs. Critics wondered why he abandoned the executive end of the pastime for service among the yeomanry. "Aw, what the hell," he said. "When I was a coach, I couldn't be one of the boys. This way, if I want a beer with 'em, I get a beer."

It appeared that Harvey's NHL career had ended after his 1963-64 campaign with the Rangers, but he returned to the majors in

1966-67 with the Red Wings. Again, he seemed to be through, but in 1968, the St. Louis Blues inserted Doug into their lineup for the playoffs against Philadelphia and he helped the Blues oust the favored Flyers. He played the entire 1968-69 season for St. Louis and quite capably.

Harvey's playing career ended at this point, but he remained a factor in hockey, was inducted into the Hall of Fame in 1973, and, when the WHA was organized, was named an assistant manager of the Houston Aeros. Harvey's most significant move was advising the Aeros to sign Gordie Howe's sons, Mark and Marty, who would later become WHA and NHL stars.

Harvey had barely turned 65 when he died in his native Montreal, after a long illness.

DOMINIK HASEK

BORN: Pardubice, Czechoslovakia, January 29, 1965

POSITION: Goaltender, Chicago Blackhawks, 1990-92; Buffalo Sabres, 1992-2001; Detroit Red Wings, 2001-02

AWARDS/HONORS: William M. Jennings Trophy (shared with Grant Fuhr), 1994; Hart Memorial Trophy, 1997-98; Lester B. Pearson Award, 1997-98; Vezina Trophy, 1994-95, 1997-98; NHL All-Rookie Team, 1992; NHL First Team All-Star, 1994-95, 1997-99; NHL All-Star Game, 1996-1999, 2001-02

Glenn Hall, Terry Sawchuk, Jacques Plante, Vladislav Tretiak.

These are a few of the greatest goaltenders of all time.

When he finished his NHL career in 2002, Dominik Hasek would rank alongside them as one of the best puckstoppers the world had ever known.

Dominik Hasek

While growing up in Czechoslovakia, Hasek did not have a goaltending coach, instead relying on his own ingenuity and cleverness to improvise a truly unique, wild style.

Hasek climbed the ranks of the Czechoslovakian junior hockey system and was drafted by the Chicago Blackhawks in the tenth round in 1983, but turned down the chance to play in the National Hockey League, electing to stay in his native country, where he was the top national team goaltender from 1986 to 1990. Hasek finally came stateside as a 25-year-old in 1990, but the Blackhawks had perennial All-Star Eddie Belfour between the pipes.

Mike Keenan, then coach of the Blackhawks, was unsure how Hasek's style would work in the NHL and sent Hasek to the Indianapolis Ice of the IHL, where he unhappily remained for two seasons until he asked Keenan for his release, to return and play in his homeland.

Keenan refused, and in August of 1992, Hasek was dealt in a then-insignificant trade from Chicago to Buffalo for goaltender Stephane Beauregard and a draft pick that would become Eric Dazé, in one of the most lopsided deals in the history of the ice game.

In Buffalo, Dominik initially was relegated to a backup role behind the legendary, but aging Grant Fuhr. When Hasek did play, his unusual goaltending antics made Buffalo coaches nervous. Sabres management was unimpressed and made the goalie available during the Expansion Draft, protecting Fuhr and Tom Draper. Anaheim and Florida passed.

During the 1993–94 season, Fuhr injured his knee and Hasek was thrust into a starting role and quickly began to show the world a new type of goaltending. Soon, NHL highlight reels became filled with unbelievable Hasek stops, shocking opponents, fans, and teammates alike.

In the first round of the playoffs that season, Buffalo faced the New Jersey Devils. Dominik Hasek outdueled Martin Brodeur in Game Six, when Dave Hannan finally ended the scoreless marathon more than five minutes into the fourth overtime at 1:52 A.M. In total, Hasek made 70 saves, including 39 in overtime.

At the conclusion of the 1993–94 season, Hasek was named a First Team All-Star, awarded his first Vezina and Jennings trophies, and became the first goaltender since Bernie Parent 20 years earlier to register a goals-against average below 2.00.

In years to come, Hasek, with arms and legs flying around NHL goal creases, continued to puzzle NHL shooters, earning him the nickname "The Dominator" for his ability to determine the outcome of games virtually by himself.

Hasek captured another Vezina trophy in 1995 and in 1997 he became the first goaltender in 35 years to win the Hart Trophy, along with the Lester Pearson Award and another Vezina. In 1998, he equaled the accomplishment with another triple crown, winning all three awards yet again, in addition to the 1998 gold medal for Team Czech Republic at the Nagano Olympic Games.

Among several remarkable traits were Hasek's willingness to intentionally stop the puck with his helmet, as well as his trademark ability to miraculously recover position when a goal seemed inevitable. While other goaltenders were prone and virtually motionless when lying on the ice or when losing the goalstick, it was in those situations Hasek was at his best.

During the 1998–99 season, Hasek posted a career-best goals-against average of 1.87 and led Buffalo to the Stanley Cup finals. Dallas, the Western Conference champions, were unsure if they could solve the Dominator. "When he's in the net, his pads seem to cover post-to-post better than any goalie I've seen," Brett Hull said during the series, shaking his head. "He just doesn't give you anything to shoot at."

The series culminated in Game Six with another multi-overtime marathon game that saw some of Hasek's usual heroics. Hull, however, would have the last laugh, as it was his controversial goal that defeated Hasek and the Sabres in the third overtime.

Hasek stunned the hockey world a few weeks later when he announced that the 1999–2000 season would be his last. In the first month of what would have been his farewell year, Hasek seriously injured his groin, forcing him to miss half the season and reconsider his retirement decision. Astoundingly, by season's end, Hasek had won another Vezina.

After the accolades and the individual awards, the one thing missing from the Dominator's resume was a Stanley Cup ring. In the summer of 2001, Hasek asked Buffalo general manager Darcy Regier to trade him to a team that had the tools to win hockey's ultimate prize. Regier complied, and Hasek was sent to the Detroit Red Wings for winger Slava Kozlov, a first-round draft pick, and future considerations.

When he left Buffalo, Hasek held Sabres records in virtually all goaltending categories and had joined Gilbert Perreault and Pat LaFontaine as the greatest players in the history of the franchise.

Hasek's arrival in Detroit reinvigorated his career and made the Dominator reevaluate and rethink his retirement timeline, especially with the additions of Luc Robitaille and Brett Hull to the Motor City sextet. The Wings dominated 2001–02, attaining their 100th point a full month before any other team did, a formidable mark of a championship-caliber team. Hasek, who had looked less than his most dominating self for much of the regular season, began to flash his best again, as Detroit recovered to defeat Vancouver in six. The Wings went on to best St. Louis in five, by which time Dom was definitely back in fine fettle. Hasek and his Red Wings then met their old nemesis, the Avalanche, in the Western Conference finals, defeating the Stanley Cup defenders in seven. Then, in a five-game series, Hasek and Detroit defeated the Carolina Hurricanes. Dom had his ring and promptly retired.

DERIAN HATCHER

BORN: Sterling Heights, Michigan, June 4, 1972
POSITION: Defenseman, Minnesota North Stars, 1991–93, Dallas Stars, 1993–
AWARDS/HONORS: NHL All-Star Game, 1997

Among contemporary defensemen, there were few more intimidating than this product of the Detroit-area hockey systems.

Standing six feet five and weighing in at 230 pounds, Derian Hatcher played a bruising brand of defense from the moment of his National Hockey League debut in 1991–92 with the Minnesota North Stars. When the club left Bloomington, Minnesota, for its new digs in Dallas (1993–94), Hatcher found his niche and soon became a leader of a Stars club that went on to win the Stanley Cup in 1998–99.

The younger brother of NHL defenseman Kevin Hatcher—who played a much milder brand of defense—Derian had two career years as a point-getter, totaling 31 in 1993–94 and again in 1997–98. By the 2000–01 season, Hatcher finished tenth in the NHL among defensemen and led the Stars in hits (250). He also ranked tenth in the NHL and second on the Stars' in average ice time (25:52) and in blocked shots (114). Hatcher, who once broke Jeremy Roenick's jaw with one of his heavy hits, also represented his native United States at the 1998 Olympics at Nagano.

In 2001–02, the Stars sagged around Hatcher. They missed the playoffs as the team aged and coach Ken Hitchcock was fired and former Conn Smythe Trophy winner Joe Nieuwendyk was traded away. Nevertheless, Hatcher remained one of the better NHL defenders.

DALE HAWERCHUK

BORN: Toronto, Ontario, April 4, 1963
POSITION: Center, Winnipeg Jets, 1981–90;
Buffalo Sabres, 1990–95; St. Louis Blues,
1995–96; Philadelphia Flyers, 1996–97
AWARDS/HONORS: Canadian Major Junior
Player of the Year, 1981; Calder Memorial Trophy,
1982; NHL Second Team All-Star, 1985; NHL All-
Star Game, 1982, 1985–86, 1988, 1997;
Hockey Hall of Fame, 2001

It never helps to be called The Next Gretzky, and it certainly was no asset to Dale Hawerchuk when he was drafted by the Winnipeg Jets in 1981.

Since there has been only one "next Gretzky"—the incomparable Mario Lemieux—it is hardly surprising that Hawerchuk always seemed to come up somewhere short of marvelous.

Still, no Winnipeg fan could complain about Dale's production. He consistently ranked among the NHL's top ten scorers during the 1980s, and virtually carried the Jets franchise after winning the Calder Trophy as Rookie of the Year for 1982 at age 19. His 103-point effort was third-best all-time for first-year players.

Drafted behind American-born Bobby Carpenter, and playing in the shadow of contemporaries Gretzky, Lemieux, and Steve Yzerman, Hawerchuk quietly rattled off 13 straight seasons in which he averaged more than a point-per-game, something even more rare in the current NHL.

Skating ability is what allowed Hawerchuk to perform in the fast lane. He possessed excellent lateral movement and a tremendous stride that enabled him to get to any spot on the ice quickly.

Learning how to win was something "Ducky" did well. "He lived up to the expectations right from his first year," said former Jets scout Tom Savage. "He more or less carried the load year after year after year. But in the East, you didn't hear much about any players

in Winnipeg. The rest of the country had to be convinced."

The Winnipeg captain, who flourished under Mike Keenan in Junior B hockey in Oshawa, surprised no one who watched him acquire accolade after accolade during his teen years. But Dale, shy to the media, put forth a workman's approach to help Winnipeg succeed.

His point production soared only three seasons after arriving in the NHL. In 1984–85, he recorded a career-high 130 points, including 53 goals. He would crack the 100-point mark six times, fueled by transforming his style of play from that of a player who would not go into the corners, to a bumping and grinding all-around player.

"That's what I thought I had to do for us to win," Dale explained. "As you get older, you realize that it's not necessary to get two or three points in a game. You learn to win instead of just putting numbers up."

Hawerchuk had all the qualifications of a superstar, although he never skated for a NHL championship team. Although he led his team to the playoffs in all but one of his seasons in Winnipeg, the second round was as far the Jets got.

In 1990, the Buffalo Sabres acquired Hawerchuk in a deal that eventually landed the Jets another future star forward in Keith Tkachuk. Meanwhile, Dale thrived once again in Buffalo playing with a high-octane offense that included Dave Andreychuk, Pat LaFontaine, and Alexander Mogilny.

After five solid years in Buffalo, and a brief stop in St. Louis, he concluded his brilliant career with the Philadelphia Flyers in 1996–97. Led by Eric Lindros, the Flyers would get Hawerchuk to his only Stanley Cup finals series, only to lose in four straight at the hands of the Detroit Red Wings.

Happily, the Hockey Hall of Fame came calling in 2001, and the Toronto-born Hawerchuk was enshrined for his notable accomplishments in the NHL, as well as for key roles on the 1987 and 1991 Canada Cup teams.

RED HAY

BORN: Saskatoon, Saskatchewan, December 8, 1935
POSITION: Center, Chicago Blackhawks, 1959–67
AWARDS/HONORS: Calder Memorial Trophy, 1960; NHL All-Star Game, 1960–61

Insightful and creative, Bill "Red" Hay was one of the earlier university graduates to skate successfully in the big time. He broke in with the Blackhawks in 1959–60 and remained with Chicago until his premature retirement in 1966–67 at the age of 32. A center, Hay contributed mightily to the Blackhawks' last Stanley Cup triumph in 1961 and was one of the most effective skaters in Chicago's ice renaissance. His teammate, Stan Mikita, said it best about Bill: "The trick in making us a winner," said Mikita, "was getting the team working—this is where a leader comes in, and Billy Hay was just such a leader." Hay teamed with Bobby Hull and the late Murray Balfour on what was dubbed "the Million-Dollar Line."

His distinguished career ended in 1967 with Chicago, after which he became a successful businessman and an official of the Hockey Hall of Fame.

DANY HEATLEY

BORN: Freibourg, Germany, January 21, 1981
POSITION: Right Wing, Atlanta Thrashers, 2001–
AWARDS/HONORS: Calder Memorial Trophy, 2002

The ratio of top number one draft picks making an emphatically positive impact on the NHL in their freshman year is relatively low. But in the 2000–01 season, the son of a former major-leaguer, Murray Heatley, inspired headlines in Atlanta in his very first week on NHL ice.

A star for two years at the University of Wisconsin, Heatley stayed away from pro hockey to remain at the university level while Atlanta fans impatiently awaited his arrival.

When Dany finally made his debut in October 2001, the reviews were all raves. Powerful, insightful, speedy, and tenacious, Heatley showed he had all the moves and that Thrashers general manager Don Waddell made the right move in drafting him.

It didn't hurt Heatley to have another top draft pick as his line mate, the Russian ace, Ilya Kovalchuk. As a duet, they made beautiful music together on the ice, while amassing goals and assists on their way to the All-Rookie Team. Later Heatley would edge his buddy for the Calder Trophy.

Born in Germany and raised in Calgary, this six-feet-three, 205-pound forward was selected by Atlanta in the first round, second overall, of the 2000 Entry Draft. In a two-year collegiate career at the University of Wisconsin, Heatley finished with 113 points (52 goals, 61 assists) and 106 penalty minutes in 77 games. A finalist for the 2001 Hobey Baker award, Heatley was named a First Team NCAA All-American in 2000–01. While helping Wisconsin to the Western Collegiate Hockey Association regular season championship in 1999–2000, he was also the WCHA's Rookie of the Year.

Heatley was only the second U.S. college player considered to be the top-rated prospect heading into draft day; only goalie Rick DiPietro was chosen higher. Often compared to the likes of John LeClair and Keith Tkachuk, Heatley led a younger, new breed of power forwards into the NHL, finishing his rookie stint as Atlanta's leading scorer with 26 goals and 41 assists.

ANDY HEBENTON

BORN: Winnipeg, Manitoba, October 3, 1929
POSITION: Right Wing, New York Rangers, 1955–63; Boston Bruins, 1963–64
AWARDS/HONORS: Lady Byng Memorial Trophy, 1957; NHL All-Star Game, 1960

One of the most durable players of all time, right-winger Andy Hebenton played nine consecutive seasons—70 games each—in the NHL without missing a single game. His total was 630 matches, then a record, without having been sidelined because of injury or incompetence. In 1956-57, Andy won the Lady Byng Trophy while playing for the Rangers, a club for whom he quietly excelled from 1955-56 through 1962-63. He was drafted by the Bruins and played in Boston for one season before being dropped to the Western League, where he played superior hockey for several years thereafter.

Hebenton's finest hour as a scorer occurred in a 1957 Stanley Cup playoff in New York's Madison Square Garden, when he scored a sudden-death goal at 13:38 against Montreal's Jacques Plante after eluding defenseman Bob Turner. It was the first overtime playoff game in Madison Square Garden since 1940, and the Rangers won, 4–3, although they ultimately lost the series.

Hebenton retired in 1964.

ANDERS HEDBERG

BORN: Ornkoldsvik, Sweden, February 25, 1951
POSITION: Right Wing, Winnipeg Jets (WHA), 1974–78; New York Rangers, 1978–85; Assistant General Manager, New York Rangers, 1985–86; Toronto Maple Leafs, 1997–99
AWARDS/HONORS: Bill Masterton Memorial Trophy, 1985; Rookie of the Year (WHA), 1975; Second Team All-Star (WHA), 1974; First Team All-Star (WHA), 1975–78; NHL Challenge Cup All-Star, 1979; NHL All-Star Game, 1985

After an outstanding WHA career, Anders Hedberg brought his tremendous skating speed and scoring power to Broadway when he and Swedish pal Ulf Nilsson signed with the New York Rangers in 1978.

The amiable Swede quickly became popular with his new teammates and fans, electrifying the Ranger faithful with dazzling stickhandling displays. After scoring over 100 points in each of four seasons with the WHA's Winnipeg Jets, Anders led the Rangers with 79 points in his inaugural season.

It was feared by many NHL viewers that the Swedes would not survive the violence of North American hockey, but "when somebody tried to run us and got a penalty," said Hedberg, "we'd get even by scoring goals. That is the best revenge."

Completing his career in 1985 with 397 career NHL points, the keen Hedberg eventually found himself as the first European in NHL management when he was made an assistant general manager with the Rangers in 1985-86. He became the director of scouting for the Toronto Maple Leafs in 1991, and eventually assistant general manager and director of player development, through 1999. In 2002, Hedberg was introduced as director of player personnel for the Ottawa Senators.

PAUL HENDERSON

BORN: Kincardine, Ontario, January 28, 1943
POSITION: Left Wing, Detroit Red Wings, 1962–68; Toronto Maple Leafs, 1968–74; Toronto Toros (WHA), 1974–76; Birmingham Bulls (WHA), 1976–78
AWARDS/HONORS: Team Canada (NHL), 1972; Team Canada (WHA), 1974

Nothing will ever dim the memory of Paul Henderson's breathtaking heroics in the classic 1972 series between Team Canada and the artful icemen of the Soviet Union.

Team Canada, or Team NHL, was rudely awakened to the harsh realities of world-class hockey by the fifth game of the series when the USSR held a seemingly insurmountable 3-1-1 edge. This meant Team Canada would have to win all of the three remaining games in order to eke out a victory—a shocking turn of events, since all but a few so-called shinny experts had proclaimed that anything less than an eight-game Canadian sweep would be tantamount to a national disgrace.

Then came Henderson, already a high-scoring portsider in the NHL for a decade, with Detroit and then Toronto. Like the fairy-tale knight in shining armor, the quick left-winger proceeded to rescue his mates from the very jaws of defeat. Incredibly, in each of the three remaining games, Henderson personally dashed Soviet hopes for victory with dramatic tie-breaking goals. The final game saw Henderson rap his own rebound past a fallen Soviet netminder with only 34 seconds remaining to win the series for Canada.

CAMILLE HENRY

BORN: Quebec City, Quebec, January 31, 1933
DIED: September 12, 1997
POSITION: Left Wing, New York Rangers, 1953–64, 1967–68; Chicago Blackhawks, 1964–65; St. Louis Blues, 1968–70; Coach, New York Raiders/Golden Blades/New Jersey Knights (WHA), 1972–74
AWARDS/HONORS: Calder Memorial Trophy, 1954; Lady Byng Memorial Trophy, 1958; NHL Second Team All-Star, 1958; NHL All-Star Game, 1958, 1963–64

When the majestic, six-feet-two, 192-pound Jean Beliveau graduated from the Quebec (Junior) Citadelles, the man picked to fill his skates was scrawny Camille "The Eel" Henry, a five-feet-nine, 150-pound weakling with an extraordinary puck sense and so beloved a disposition, Camille actually was able to succeed in following Beliveau's impressive act with the Citadelles. What Beliveau had in size, Henry had in brains. There never was a craftier forward who could thread a needle with a puck and stick if need be.

Camille Henry, property of the Broadway Blueshirts, was an instant hit in the NHL. However, the Rangers employed Henry mostly in power-play situations during his freshman year. The Eel not only scored 24 goals, but also won the Calder Trophy as Rookie of the Year. Perhaps more amazing was the night Camille scored four goals in one game against Detroit goalie Terry Sawchuk, then believed the best in the game.

"That four-goal night won the Calder Trophy for me as a Rookie of the Year. It also knocked Sawchuk out of all the honors [Vezina Trophy and First Team All-Star] he practically had in his pocket," recalled Henry.

In 1965, Henry, one of the most popular of all Rangers, was dealt to Chicago, but returned for the 1968 season before ending his playing career with the St. Louis Blues. When the now defunct WHA was organized, Henry coached the allergic-to-work New York entry, the Raiders. However, when the club left New York, Camille mercifully lost his job.

SUGAR JIM HENRY

BORN: Winnipeg, Manitoba, October 23, 1920
POSITION: Goaltender; New York Rangers, 1941–42, 1945–48; Chicago Blackhawks, 1948–49; Boston Bruins, 1951–55
AWARDS/HONORS: NHL Second Team All-Star, 1952; NHL All-Star Game, 1952

When goaltender Davey Kerr retired in 1941 after helping the Rangers to the Stanley Cup in 1940, manager Frank Boucher replaced him with Samuel James "Sugar Jim" Henry, who had starred for the Regina (Saskatchewan) Rangers, a senior team. Henry was an instant hit, and proved it by orchestrating the New Yorkers to first place. His 2.98 goals-against average in the 1941–42 season suggested Vezina trophies to come, but Henry immediately enlisted in the Canadian Armed Forces and didn't return until 1945–46, by which time he was a bit rusty. In addition, the Rangers now had Chuck Rayner (formerly with the Americans) in the nets. Henry and Chuck split the Rangers' goaltending until Sugar Jim was dealt to Chicago in 1948–49. He played well for a lousy team, but still better for the Bruins from 1951–52 until he left the NHL at the end of the 1954–55 season.

WALLY HERGESHEIMER

BORN: Winnipeg, Manitoba, January 8, 1927
POSITION: Right Wing, New York Rangers, 1951–56, 1958–59; Chicago Blackhawks, 1956–57

During the New York Rangers' darkest days in the early 1950s, the most consistent bright light was smallish right-winger Wally Hergesheimer, who broke into the NHL with several handicaps. He was a relatively slow skater; he had lost two fingers on his right hand as a result of a punch press accident; and he lacked a particularly hard shot. But Wally had a surplus of good humor and guts. Dubbed a "garbage collector" because of his knack of scoring goals from rebounds near the crease, "Hergie," as he was known, led the Rangers in scoring during 1952–53.

Hergie and fellow Winnipegger Nick Mickoski were the only Rangers to live in Brooklyn. The two then-bachelors had an apartment in Brooklyn Heights overlooking Lower New York Bay and the Statue of Liberty. Still, the posh Brooklyn Heights pad was not enough to keep Wally in The Apple, as he finished his career with the Chicago Blackhawks.

Wally Hergesheimer, Rangers right wing

FOSTER HEWITT

BORN: Toronto, Ontario, November 21, 1902
DIED: April 21, 1985
AWARDS/HONORS: Hockey Hall of Fame, 1965

In 1922, Foster Hewitt, the son of W. A. Hewitt, sports editor of the *Toronto Daily Star,* went to work for his father's paper. He soon switched from the news beat to the *Star*'s new radio desk, and on March 22, 1923, radio editor Basil Lake assigned young Foster to broadcast a Senior League hockey match between Toronto's Parkdale Club and Kitchener. When Foster tried to shunt the job to a regular sports staffer, his boss held firm and prophetically replied, "Some thirty or forty years from now you may be proud to say: 'I was the first person in all the world ever to broadcast a hockey game.'"

How right Lake was. Foster Hewitt entered the hockey scene in a unique manner, and was to popularize the game more than any single person in the world. He began his career at the age of 18, and despite the most adverse conditions—his glass-enclosed booth fogged up, making it almost impossible to distinguish the players—public reaction was overwhelmingly positive. Radio station CFCA made hockey broadcasts a staple, along with other sporting events, all covered by Hewitt. But best of all, Hewitt began to report NHL games from the rafters of Mutual Street Arena. In no time at all, Foster developed a play-by-play style that has never been duplicated.

His inimitably high-pitched voice entranced his listeners. It would reach a crescendo at the precisely correct time. Hewitt wasted few words, using such expressions as "It's a scramble," to describe frenzy in front of the net. Nothing in Foster's repertoire matched his description of a goal. The quick ascent began with the words "He shoots!" Inevitably a pause would follow. If the shot missed by an inch or two, Hewitt might bellow "Ohhh!" matching the sentiment of the audience. But if the puck went in, "He scores!" would leap over the loudspeaker in such a manner that the listener could feel the red light go on. Hewitt's voice announcing a goal inevitably sent a tingle through the body of even the most insensitive fans and thrilled everyone who ever heard him. More than that, "He shoots! He scores!" soon became a trademark throughout Toronto, creating an unprecedented interest in hockey in an already hockey-crazed metropolis.

BRYAN HEXTALL

BORN: Grenfell, Saskatchewan, July 31, 1913
DIED: July 25, 1984
POSITION: Center, New York Rangers, 1936–48
AWARDS/HONORS: Art Ross Trophy, 1942; NHL First Team All-Star, 1940–42; NHL Second Team All-Star, 1943; Hockey Hall of Fame, 1969

A hard-nosed native of Saskatchewan, Bryan Hextall twice led the NHL in goal-scoring and once in total points (56 in 1942). He had a terrific burst of speed, was appropriately tough, and could stickhandle with the best of them. Like the Cooks-Boucher line, the

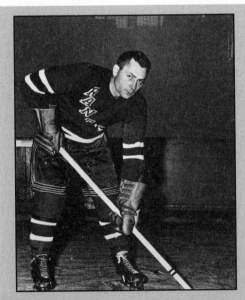

Bryan Hextall Sr., hero of the Rangers' 1940 Stanley Cup win

Hextall-Watson-Patrick unit dazzled the enemy with their stickwork until the outbreak of World War II depleted their ranks.

Bryan scored the fateful overtime goal in 1940 against the Toronto Maple Leafs that would give the Rangers their last Stanley Cup until 1994.

He played last in 1948–49, in the American Hockey League, but spawned a legacy with son Bryan Jr. and grandson Ron becoming NHL players.

RON HEXTALL

BORN: Brandon, Manitoba, May 3, 1964
POSITION: Goaltender, Philadelphia Flyers, 1986–92; Quebec Nordiques, 1992–93; New York Islanders, 1993–94; Philadelphia Flyers, 1994–98
AWARDS/HONORS: Vezina Trophy, 1987; Conn Smythe Trophy, 1987; NHL All-Rookie Team, 1987; NHL First Team All-Star, 1987; NHL All-Star Game, 1988

Ron Hextall will be remembered for his extraordinary puckhandling ability as well as his truculence between the goal pipes. Prior to a landmark injury that forever altered his performance, Ron had been at the very top of the National Hockey League list of puckstoppers.

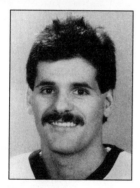

Ron Hextall

Another aspect of his game that also was underplayed in terms of its historic significance was his ability to act as a "third defenseman." Hextall not only advanced the art of goaltender participation in the action, he often became directly involved in play behind the net and along the boards.

Ron turned pro with Kalamazoo of the International League and then moved on to Hershey in the American League. Hextall was invited to the Flyers' training camp in September 1986. He played 66 games as an NHL rookie, posting a 3.00 goals-against average as well as 37 wins, 21 losses, and 6 ties.

After a gallant defeat in the 1987 Stanley Cup finals, in which he clashed with Chris Chelios on numerous occasions, Hextall won the Conn Smythe, a rarity, considering that the trophy usually is given to a player on the winning team.

After seven high-profile years and 130 wins in Philadelphia, the Flyers decided Ron was expendable. As part of the complicated deal that brought Eric Lindros to Broad Street, Hextall was moved to Quebec on June 20, 1992. He then went on to play one year with the Islanders in 1994, where he endured a first-round playoff sweep at the hands of the rival Rangers.

He finished his career where he began, in Philly, with 83 wins in 154 games from 1995 through 1998 before retiring to become a Flyers' scout. Ron is a member of the illustrious Hextall hockey family—son of Bryan Jr. and grandson of Hall of Famer Bryan Sr.

MEL HILL

BORN: Glenboro, Manitoba, February 15, 1914
DIED: April 11, 1996
POSITION: Forward, Boston Bruins, 1937–41; Brooklyn Americans, 1941–42; Toronto Maple Leafs, 1942–46

The 1939 Stanley Cup finals best-of-seven series opened at Madison Square Garden on March 21, and after three periods, Boston and New York had battled to a 1–1 tie. Now the teams pushed into the perilous waters of sudden-death overtime, and again there was no score. A second sudden-death also produced no goals, the players bone weary from skating.

By now, the Rangers' strategy had become apparent to Bruins manager Art Ross. The home club was determined to stifle Bill Cowley's scoring with some blanket checking while keeping an eye on Roy Conacher as well. New York's hope was to force the Bruin attackers into an errant pass, snare the puck, and capitalize.

A few seconds before the third overtime, Ross summoned Cowley to his side. "We've got to fool them," he told his superb center. "They're watching Conacher so carefully it would be better to feed Mel Hill."

There is no record of Cowley's response, but the chances are he was stunned. "Feed Hill?" This seemed a joke. Compared with Conacher, Mel Hill was a feeble shooter who had managed only ten goals over the entire season. Surely, Ross couldn't be serious. But the manager was never more concerned about a play in his life. By the time the teams took the ice Cowley realized Hill was going to get that puck if Ross had anything to say about it.

It took nearly an entire overtime period before Cowley could convert Ross's advice into action. Late in the third sudden-death, the Bruin center crossed into Ranger territory and lured Murray Patrick toward him. Patrick was a big, hulking skater, and the long game had slowed him down considerably. He didn't quite get to Cowley in time and the Bruin eluded him, skated into the corner and made a perfect pass to Hill, who was camped in front of goalie Dave Kerr. Hill swung and Kerr missed, and at 1:10 A.M., the Bruins had won the game.

The Bruins went on to win the series, four games to three, and thereafter number 18 on the Bruins was known as "Sudden Death" Hill throughout the NHL.

KEN HITCHCOCK

BORN: Edmondton, Alberta, December 17, 1951
POSITION: Coach, Dallas Stars, 1996–2002; Philadelphia Flyers, 2002–

Had he not been a professional coach, Ken Hitchcock would have been a professor of Civil War history. Even as a full-time hockey man, Hitchcock spent innumerable hours studying such battlefields as Antietam and Gettysburg as an avocation.

In the coaching realm, Hitchcock began his career in low-level amateur ranks before moving on to Kamloops, British Columbia, and one of the Western Hockey League's most powerful franchises. From 1984 through 1990, the likeable Hitchcock established his credentials as a winner, but also became a curious celebrity because of his girth.

Weighing over 300 pounds, Hitchcock eventually dieted himself down to a more reasonable level and was hired in 1990 by the Philadelphia Flyers as an assistant coach. The experience earned him his first pro head coaching assignment for the 1993–94 season with Kalamazoo in the International League.

On January 8, 1996, Ken was named head coach of the Dallas Stars and led the franchise to heights never before known, either in Minnesota, as the North Stars, or in Texas. An insightful disciplinarian, Hitchcock orchestrated a Stanley Cup victory in 1998–99 over the Buffalo Sabres and took his club to the finals the following year before losing in six games to the New Jersey Devils.

By the start of the 2001–02 campaign, he had a career regular season record of 254–143–54–2, but was also feeling the pressure of declining production. After the Stars floundered through the first half of the season, ownership decided to make a change. Hitchcock was fired and replaced by assistant coach Rick Wilson.

It was a temporary setback for Ken. In May 2002, he was hired as head coach of the Flyers.

"Hitch was the only coach we interviewed," said owner Ed Snider, "and the only one we wanted."

Toronto Sun columnist Mike Ulmer described Ken as follows: "Hitchcock is as open and enchanting to outsiders as he is demanding to those inside his tent."

LIONEL HITCHMAN

BORN: Toronto, Ontario, 1903
DIED: January 12, 1969
POSITION: Defenseman, Ottawa Senators, 1922–25; Boston Bruins, 1925–34

Along with Eddie Shore, Lionel Hitchman gave the Boston Bruins one of the most fearsome defense combinations in National Hockey League history. The Toronto-born backliner broke into the majors with Ottawa in 1922–23, but was traded to Boston in 1924–25. He remained a Bruin until his retirement after the 1933–34 season. Defense-oriented to a fault, Hitchman scored more than ten points only once in his NHL career—11 points in 1925–26—but more than compensated for that deficiency with his superb backline hitting, stickchecking, and playmaking.

CHARLIE HODGE

BORN: Lachine, Quebec, July 28, 1933
POSITION: Goaltender, Montreal Canadiens, 1954–67; Oakland Seals, 1967–70; Vancouver Canucks, 1970–72
AWARDS/HONORS: Vezina Trophy, 1964, 1966 (shared with Lorne Worsley); NHL Second Team All-Star, 1964–65; NHL All-Star Game, 1964–65, 1967

At one point in his National Hockey League career, Charlie Hodge was so popular a Montreal Canadiens goalie that enthused citizens named a street after him in the Canadian metropolis. Until 1963–64, Hodge had been the Canadiens' second fiddle to crack goalie Jacques Plante. Hodge became a regular in 1963–64, turning a commendable 2.26 goals-against average, which won him the Vezina Trophy. Charlie won the Vezina again, teaming with Lorne "Gump" Worsley, in 1965–66. When Oakland joined the NHL in 1967–68, Hodge was drafted by the expansion franchise, and played his last season with Vancouver in 1972 before switching to the scouting field.

KEN HODGE

BORN: Birmingham, England, June 25, 1944
POSITION: Right Wing, Chicago Blackhawks, 1964–67; Boston Bruins, 1967–76; New York Rangers, 1976–78
AWARDS/HONORS: NHL First Team All-Star, 1971, 1974; NHL All-Star Game, 1971, 1973–74

Ken Hodge gained prominence as Phil Esposito's right-hand man, notching more than 400 assists while the two played together. With the Bruins, Hodge, the right-winger, and Wayne Cashman, the portsider, would work the corners with one thing in mind: Feed the puck to Espo, who usually could be found parked near the goal crease.

If, as many observers claim, hockey games are won in the corners, Hodge was one of the most valuable Bruins. Ken had 800 career points in just 881 games, including a 50-goal campaign in 1973–74.

Hodge followed Espo to the New York Rangers in a 1976 trade for injury-prone Rick Middleton. Middleton went on to stardom with Boston, while Hodge went sour in the Big Apple. It was considered one of the worst trades in hockey history. Hodge retired, but son Ken Hodge Jr. played briefly for Boston with 30 goals in 1990–91.

BENOIT HOGUE

BORN: Repentigny, Quebec, October 28, 1966
POSITION: Center/Left Wing, Buffalo Sabres, 1987–91; New York Islanders, 1991–95; Toronto Maple Leafs, 1995–96; Dallas Stars, 1996–98, 1999, 2001; Tampa Bay Lightning/Phoenix Coyotes, 2000; Boston Bruins, 2001–02; Washington Capitals, 2002

If ever there was a player who defines resiliency, it was Benoit Hogue.

The slight French-Canadian center began his career in Buffalo, but achieved stardom after being traded to the New York Islanders early in the 1991–92 season. It was a huge deal. Hogue was dealt along with Pierre Turgeon, Dave McLlwain, and Uwe Krupp to Long Island for Pat LaFontaine, Randy Wood, and Randy Hillier.

Hogue immediately paid dividends, scoring 30 goals his first season on the Island, with 45 assists. A year later, he hit the 75-point mark again, this time with 33 goals and 42 assists.

Hogue played a key part in the Islanders' 1992–93 playoff surge, scoring 6 goals and 6 assists in 18 games. Benoit eventually moved on to Toronto, Dallas, Tampa Bay, and Phoenix, during which time he endured personal family tragedy which braked his career, but did not break it. By 2001–02, Hogue was on the move again, starting with Dallas, then Boston, and finishing the season with nine games for the Washington Capitals.

Not many players can say they competed for 15 years on a solid level, but Hogue was one of them.

BOBBY HOLIK

BORN: Jihlava, Czechoslovakia, January 1, 1971
POSITION: Center, Hartford Whalers, 1990–92; New Jersey Devils, 1992–2002; New York Rangers, 2002–
AWARDS/HONORS: NHL All-Star Game, 1998–99

Bobby Holik was the Devils' big bruising center for nearly a decade. When he was signed as a free agent by the New York rangers in the summer of 2002, Holik had earned a reputation as a player who struck fear in the hearts of opposing players and changed their style of play.

Arriving in a 1992 trade for goaltender Sean Burke, Bobby averaged over 100 penalty minutes from 1997–98 through 1999–2000, and normally scored upward of 20 goals while doing so. He was the most dominant checking center in the Eastern Conference, and continually led the Devils through the postseason with his aggressive style of play.

Forthcoming in the press and abrasive on the ice, Holik evolved from his role as center of the Devils' Crash Line—which included Randy McKay and Mike Peluso—to the perfect number two man, and in 1997–98, scored a career-best 29 goals and 36 assists. Holik tallied 16 points in the 2001 playoffs, including the series-clinching goal in the 2001 Eastern Conference finals, and always performed well in the Devils' Stanley Cup playoff runs.

When he attained free-agent status, Holik became one of the most sought-after players until the Rangers signed him to a lucrative, long-term contract.

A native of Czechoslovakia, Holik eventually obtained U.S. citizenship and became a keen student of American history.

KEN HOLLAND

BORN: Vernon, British Columbia, November 10, 1955
POSITION: Goaltender, Hartford Whalers, 1980–81; Detroit Red Wings, 1983–84; General Manager, Detroit Red Wings, 1997–

The trail to the general manager's office of an NHL team takes many strange turns, depending on the manager in question.

Lou Lamoriello of the New Jersey Devils launched his career at Providence College. David Poile of the Nashville Predators learned from his father, Bud, a former NHLer who later was general manager of the Philadelphia Flyers.

As for Ken Holland, the road to the top began in Vernon, British Columbia, in a most curious way.

Holland was goalie for the Vernon Lakers, but his true passion was collecting souvenirs. He coveted the jersey of the Medicine Hat Tigers. Since his Lakers was the farm team of Medicine Hat, Ken arranged to go to the Tigers' training camp, not so much to make the varsity, but rather to get that jersey he wanted so badly!

Holland's goaltending made such an impression, that not only did he get the jersey, he got the job, and a professional goaltender's career was off and running. Ken played two years for Medicine Hat and eventually was the Toronto Maple Leafs' 13th pick (188th overall) in the 1975 draft.

Holland bounced around the minors, but reached the NHL for a few cups of coffee, debuting with Hartford's Whalers in 1980–81. He played one game for The Whale and later three for Detroit, in 1983–84. When it was obvious he would never be another Bill Smith or Grant Fuhr, Holland began looking for a day job.

Then-Red Wings general manager Jimmy Devellano was on the lookout for a Western Canada scout. Holland took to birddogging and immediately impressed with his insights and loyalty. When Neil Smith left the Wings to become general manager of the Rangers, Jimmy D needed a chief scout. He didn't have a second thought; Holland was the man.

"He already showed he wasn't afraid to get his hands dirty," said Devellano. "And he always had been smart. Once Bryan Murray and Doug MacLean left Detroit, I brought Kenny over as assistant general manager. When I decided to move on, I recommended to Mr. (Mike) Ilitch (Red Wings owner) that Kenny be made our general manager." The date was July 18, 1997.

Holland's ability to assess talent was already proven, as he had recommended the club draft such players as Martin Lapointe, Chris Osgood, Darren McCarty, and Slava Kozlov, and he was on staff when Detroit signed Sergei Fedorov and Nicklas Lidstrom.

In Holland's rookie year as general manager, Detroit won its second straight Stanley Cup. A year later, with Holland at the helm, the Wings acquired—within a 24-hour period—Chris Chelios, Ulf Samuelsson, Wendel Clark, and Bill Ranford.

One of his most arresting summers took place in 2001, when he obtained Frederick Olausson, Dominik Hasek, Luc Robitaille, and Brett Hull. The result of all his moves was another Stanley Cup for Detroit in 2002.

"To see where I came from and now realize where I am," noted Holland, "I sometimes have to pinch myself."

FLASH HOLLETT

BORN: North Sydney, Nova Scotia, April 13, 1912
DIED: April 20, 1999
POSITION: Defenseman/Left Wing, Toronto Maple Leafs, 1933, 1934–36; Ottawa Senators, 1934; Boston Bruins, 1935–44; Detroit Red Wings, 1944–46
AWARDS/HONORS: NHL Second Team All-Star, 1943; NHL First Team All-Star, 1945

He started his NHL career with Toronto, then played the lion's share of it with the Boston Bruins. But it was as a Detroit Red Wing, late in his career, that William "Flash" Hollett etched his name in NHL history books.

Hollett showed up at the Toronto Maple Leafs' Kingston, Ontario, training camp in 1933, looking for a spot on the Toronto defense. He impressed everyone with one destructive body check that sent King Clancy to the ice. "If they don't sign you to this team," Clancy told the kid later in the dressing room, "look me up, and I'll see that you're placed somewhere in the NHL."

Flash was sent to Buffalo in the minors, only to be recalled after the Shore-Bailey affair, when Red Horner was suspended. Upon Horner's return, Hollett was traded to Ottawa, but he returned to the Maple Leafs the next season (1934–35). He scored 10 goals and 16 assists for 26 points, best among NHL defensemen.

But Hollett was sold to the minor-league Boston Cubs shortly thereafter and from there, he worked his way up to the NHL Bruins. Finally, during the 1938–39 season, Hollett became a full-fledged star. He scored 10 goals—remarkable for a defenseman during those low-scoring years—and 17 assists. On the Bruins' excursion to the Stanley Cup, he added a goal and three assists in a dozen playoff games.

In 1943–44, the Bruins began slipping and on January 5, 1944, Boston coach and manager Art Ross dealt Hollett to Detroit for defenseman Pat Egan. It was one of Ross's worst moves, as the Bruins missed the playoffs while Detroit finished second.

At first Hollett was crushed by the deal. "Boston was like home to me," he declared.

Nevertheless, he reported to the Red Wings, and in 1944–45, Flash showed why Ross had erred. Hollett tallied 20 goals and 21 assists for 41 points during the regular season, followed by 3 goals and 4 assists in 14 playoff games, leading to the Cup finals (where, ironically, they were beaten by Toronto). The numbers were nothing short of remarkable for a defenseman of that era.

A year later Flash suffered pleurisy, plus groin and knee injuries. The medical problems hurt his game and caused Red Wings general manager Jack Adams to trade Hollett to the New York Rangers. Flash refused to report.

"When I got traded," said Hollett, "I was pretty mad. When I didn't go to the Rangers, they suspended me. There were a lot of factors involved. I had a young family and the prospect of apartment living in Manhattan didn't appeal to me or my wife.

"But from a hockey standpoint, I should have gone. Frank Boucher was running the Rangers and he was a great fellow; plus the Rangers played my kind of game. I could have fit in with them because I was a playmaker and they were a passing team."

Sadly, Flash Hollett never played big-league hockey again. He eventually drifted to senior-level hockey in Ontario, playing for the Kitchener Dutchmen and the Toronto Marlboros. He ended his playing career in 1950 and retired to the Toronto area. Hollett died in 1999.

PAUL HOLMGREN

BORN: St. Paul, Minnesota, December 2, 1955
POSITION: Right Wing, Minnesota Fighting Saints (WHA), 1975–76; Philadelphia Flyers, 1976–84; Minnesota North Stars, 1984–85; Coach, Hartford Whalers, 1992–94; General Manager, Hartford Whalers, 1993–94; Assistant General Manager, Philadelphia Flyers, 1999–
AWARDS/HONORS: NHL All-Star Game, 1981

After a modest stint in the WHA, Paul Holmgren came into the NHL breathing fire. The American-born winger out of the University of Minnesota kept the myth of the "Broad Street Bullies" alive, accumulating 201 penalty minutes in his inaugural season with the Flyers (1976–77).

Holmgren was a mean man when the action flew his way, but could also score his share of goals, as evidenced by his career-high 30 goals in 1979–80.

Paul, who had a serious eye injury early in his Flyer career, was suspended and fined during the 1979 season for chopping down New York Ranger defenseman Carol Vadnais with his stick and for kicking Boston Bruin Terry O'Reilly.

Holmgren was traded to the Minnesota North Stars in 1984, then retired in 1985, later to join the coaching ranks with alma mater Philadelphia in 1988. The rebuilding team missed the playoffs from 1989–90 through 1991–92 after making the Conference finals in Holmgren's first year.

The following four seasons were spent as head coach of the Hartford Whalers, and included a stint as general manager in 1993–94. After Paul Maurice replaced him in November 1995, Paul returned to Philly where he eventually became director of pro scouting as well as assistant general manager to Bob Clarke.

RED HORNER

BORN: Lynden, Ontario, May 29, 1909
POSITION: Defenseman, Toronto Maple Leafs, 1928–40
AWARDS/HONORS: NHL All-Star Game, 1934, 1937; Hockey Hall of Fame, 1965

George Reginald "Red" Horner, who was signed by Conn Smythe in the fall of 1928, took his basic training in hockey on the Toronto playgrounds, although he was born on his father's farm near Lynden, Ontario.

Just before Christmas, 1928, Horner played for the Toronto Marlboros on a Friday night and for his Broker's League team on the following Saturday afternoon. Conn Smythe was at the Saturday game, and he walked into the dressing room after the game. "Red," Smythe declared, "I was wondering whether you'd be in shape to play still another game tonight—for the Toronto Maple Leafs."

Slightly stunned by the invitation, Horner just barely mumbled something about a great thrill. Smythe replied that he personally would drive Red to the game. That night Horner made his debut as a Maple Leaf at the Mutual Street Arena.

Toronto was playing the Pittsburgh Pirates, and young Horner was starting on defense for the Maple Leafs. The game was less than a minute old when Frank Frederickson, the marvelous Icelandic-Canadian forward, moved the puck into the Toronto zone. Frederickson dropped his head one way and lurched the other way, leaving Horner immobilized like a statue. The shot went wide, and the puck skittered back to Pittsburgh territory, where Frederickson recaptured it and launched another attack.

Once again Frederickson tested the rookie Horner. By then Red had sized up his foe, and he dispatched Frederickson to the ice with an emphatic body check. The referee blew his whistle, and Red was sent to the penalty box with his first two-minute infraction. In his career, he would eventually serve 1,254 minutes' worth of penalties—a record unbroken for many years. Of course, the kid wasn't too sure that Smythe approved, but it didn't take long to find out for sure.

"Penalties," said Smythe, "what do they matter? We just write them off as mistakes. No man ever became a millionaire who didn't make mistakes. Besides, penalties show that we have a fighting team."

Horner made a different kind of mistake in his second NHL game, on Christmas night against the Montreal Maroons. He moved the puck out of his zone and detected what he believed was an opening between Nels Stewart and Jimmy Ward, of Montreal. Red skated for daylight. But the old veterans closed the vise on Homer, and in so doing one of the Maroons rapped Red smartly on the hand with his stick. Red skated to the sidelines with a broken hand and was through for the rest of the season.

Nevertheless, Red already had persuaded Smythe that he was in the NHL to stay, and as usual, the boss was right. Horner soon became so feared a blueliner that columnist Ted Reeve, of the *Toronto Telegram,* authored the following parody:

> *Our Reginald Horner*
> *Leaped from his corner*
> *Full of ambition and fight;*
> *He broke up the clash with a furious dash*
> *While the stockholders shrieked with delight!*

On the night of December 12, 1933, Horner was on the ice at Boston Garden when Eddie Shore of the Bruins knocked Ace Bailey of the Maple Leafs unconscious—and nearly killed Bailey—with a behind-the-back charge. Shore's seeming callousness infuriated Horner, who then hit Shore with a punch on the jaw. It was a right uppercut that stiffened the big defense star like an axed steer and got a suspension for Horner.

Horner maintained such robust play through the 1930s. In a playoff game against

Chicago in April 1938, Red rapped Chicago forward Doc Romnes across the face with his stick. This time Red's attack was in vain. Chicago went on to win the Stanley Cup. Red continued playing through the 1939–40 season, after which he finally retired. Red was accepted into the Hockey Hall of Fame in 1965.

TIM HORTON

BORN: Cochrane, Ontario, January 12, 1930
DIED: February 21, 1974
POSITION: Defenseman, Toronto Maple Leafs, 1949–70; New York Rangers, 1970–71; Pittsburgh Penguins, 1971–72; Buffalo Sabres, 1972–74
AWARDS/HONORS: NHL First Team All-Star, 1964, 1968; NHL Second Team All-Star, 1954, 1963, 1967; Hockey Hall of Fame, 1977

On February 20, 1974, the Buffalo Sabres visited Toronto for a game with the Leafs. Prior to the opening face-off, Buffalo trailed Toronto by seven points; a big but not insurmountable gap. A Sabres' win would narrow the margin enough to make the home-stretch interesting and Buffalo coach Joe Crozier planned accordingly. His plan was to start five bruising skaters and disrupt the Maple Leafs with aggressiveness, then beat the supposedly disorganized enemy. The plan looked good on paper but, alas, it failed in practice. Buffalo's big men hit the Leafs, to be sure, but they were handed two early penalties that Toronto immediately converted into power-play goals.

After the game, Sabres manager Punch Imlach and veteran defenseman Tim Horton took a stroll up Church Street in Toronto, near Maple Leaf Gardens. Tim had a badly bruised jaw and was depressed about the loss. The perennial optimist, Imlach tried to cheer his old pal. "You played only two periods," said Imlach, "and one shift in the third, yet you were picked as a star of the game. If all the guys had played so well, we'd have won going away."

Horton forced a smile. "Well, Punch, there's always tomorrow."

But for Tim Horton there would be no tomorrow. En route to Buffalo in his sports car, Tim died instantly when he lost control of his automobile, crashing on the Queen Elizabeth Way.

The beloved 44-year-old defenseman never had a chance, according to police who discovered the wreck. By early morning, news of Horton's tragedy had circulated through the hockey world and resulted in grieving from coast to coast and league to league.

"There were defensemen you had to fear more because they were vicious and would slam you into the boards from behind," said Bobby Hull of the Winnipeg Jets. "But you respected Horton because he didn't need that kind of intimidation. He used his tremendous skill and talent to keep you in check."

Horton had played most of his 22 NHL seasons with the Maple Leafs alongside veteran Allan Stanley. "Tim was an All-Star on the ice," said former Leafs captain George Armstrong, "and a superstar off it."

Tim Horton's, a Canadian food chain specializing in doughnuts, had been partly-owned by Horton and its placards can be seen stretching around the Leafs end-boards—right where Tim Horton made some of his best hits.

MARIAN HOSSA

BORN: Stara Lubovna, Czechoslovakia, January 12, 1979
POSITION: Right/Left Wing, Ottawa Senators, 1997–
AWARDS/HONORS: NHL All-Rookie Team, 1999; NHL All-Star Game, 2001

As the flow of European players to the National Hockey League increased in the late 1990s, scouts focused more than ever on former Iron Curtain countries, particularly the former Czechoslovakia. The Ottawa Senators found a gem in Czech-born Marian Hossa, the right wing whom they selected in the 1997 First Round Entry Draft 12th overall.

Ottawa's first choice that year, Hossa didn't begin to show his value until the turn of the century when he became one of the Senators' most productive young forwards. During the 1999–2000 season, Marian tied for team leader in goal-scoring, reaching career highs in goals (29), assists (27), and points (56). He also served as an Iron Man during the playoffs, appearing in all games versus Toronto, although he didn't record any points.

The 2000–01 season was another good one for Hossa. He reached career highs in goals (32), assists (43), and points (75) again. He also reached the 30-goal plateau for the first time in his NHL career. Seven of those goals were game winners. Hossa set franchise records with most assists in one game (5) and most shorthanded goals in a game (2). The six-feet-one, 199-pound Hossa proved to be a wise investment for the talent-rich Ottawa franchise.

He maintained his pace in 2001–02, tallying 31 goals and 35 assists for 66 points.

RÉJEAN HOULE

BORN: Rouyn, Quebec, October 25, 1949
POSITION: Right Wing, Montreal Canadiens, 1969–73, 1976–83; Quebec Nordiques (WHA), 1973–76; Vice President/General Manager, Montreal Canadiens, 1995–2000

When the Montreal Canadiens defeated the Chicago Blackhawks to capture the Stanley Cup in 1971 and 1973, a young French-Canadian named Réjean Houle was one of the most exuberant and effective Habitant forwards. His job of shadowing superscorer Bobby Hull during the 1971 round is considered a Stanley Cup classic.

Following the 1973 triumph, Houle jumped to the WHA's Quebec Nordiques, but returned to the Canadiens in 1976—in the midst of their four Stanley Cup run—to close out the decade before retiring in 1983 with 408 career points.

In 1995, Réjean became general manager of the Canadiens after a long public relations tenure with parent company Molson Breweries. The move drew skepticism from all angles. Two months after his hiring, the Habs were forced to trade superstar goalie Patrick Roy after his public dispute with rookie coach Mario Tremblay embarrassed the organization. Ultimately, Habs fans would demand Houle's head after Roy won the 1996 Stanley Cup with the Colorado Avalanche.

Many fruitless deals, including the 1996 exchange of productive Pierre Turgeon and two-way stud Craig Conroy to St. Louis for an aging Shayne Corson, followed. The Canadiens found themselves floundering out of the playoffs for two straight seasons (1998–99 and 1999–2000) under Houle, until his dismissal in November 2000.

PHIL HOUSLEY

BORN: St. Paul, Minnesota, March 9, 1964
POSITION: Defenseman, Buffalo Sabres 1982–90; Winnipeg Jets, 1990–93; St. Louis Blues, 1993–94; Calgary Flames, 1994–96, 1998–2001; New Jersey Devils, 1996; Washington Capitals, 1996–98; Chicago Blackhawks, 2001–
AWARDS/HONORS: NHL All-Rookie Team, 1983; NHL Second Team All-Star, 1992; NHL All-Star Game, 1984, 1989, 1990–93, 2000

Most hockey observers consider Phil Housley one of the most gifted Minnesota products ever. Born and raised in St. Paul, Housley played both Junior and high school hockey before turning pro. After a brief stint with St. Paul of the United States Junior League in 1980–81, Phil put up stellar numbers for South St. Paul High School the following season. Playing in only 22 games, he scored 31 goals and amassed 65 points for the Packers.

Smooth-skating and deceptive, Housley was the Buffalo Sabres' first choice (sixth overall), in the 1982 NHL Entry Draft. Before joining the Sabres, he played for Team USA in both the 1982 World Junior and World Cup tournaments.

In 1982–83, Housley stepped into the Sabres' lineup and although a defenseman, he immediately added scoring punch to the Buffalo backline. During eight seasons with the Sabres, Housley scored 178 goals and accumulated 558 points while playing 608 games. His outstanding play earned him seven All-Star appearances and the honor of being named to the 1983 NHL All-Rookie team.

In June 1990, Housley was traded to the Winnipeg Jets as part of a multiplayer deal. In 1991–92 and 1992–93, Phil enjoyed his two most productive seasons as a pro, amassing 86 and 97 points, respectively.

After the Jets traded him to St. Louis in September 1993, the crafty blueliner added visits with the Flames, Devils, and Capitals. In the summer of 2001, Housley signed as a free agent with the Chicago Blackhawks, who, under fiery coach Brian Sutter, reemerged as a force in the NHL, largely due to Housley's resilience as an offensive cog.

GARRY HOWATT

BORN: Grand Center, Alberta, September 26, 1952
POSITION: Left Wing, New York Islanders, 1972–81; Hartford Whalers, 1981–82; New Jersey Devils, 1982–84

Garry was known more for pugilistic prowess than goal-scoring skill, but this did not prevent the smallish (five-feet-nine and 170 pounds) Islander fireplug from delighting spectators at the Nassau Coliseum. In fact, Islander fans screamed in delight when Howatt and an opponent went into the corners with sticks held high.

In his first full season with the Islanders, in

1973–74, Howatt scored only 6 goals and 17 points. But he also set a record of sorts: most penalty minutes without a misconduct, 204, as he fought his way through the National Hockey League schedule.

Howatt played for the Hartford Whalers in 1981–82 and finished his career in New Jersey in 1984. He remained active with the Islanders' alumni team, staying in mint condition into the new century.

GORDIE HOWE

BORN: Floral, Saskatchewan, March 31, 1928
POSITION: Right Wing, Detroit Red Wings, 1946–71; Houston Aeros (WHA), 1973–77; New England Whalers (WHA), 1977–79; Hartford Whalers, 1979–80; Detroit Vipers, 1997–98; President, Houston Aeros, 1975–77
AWARDS/HONORS: Hart Memorial Trophy, 1952, 1953, 1957–58, 1960, 1963; Art Ross Trophy, 1951–54, 1957, 1963; Lester Patrick Trophy, 1967; Gary L. Davidson Trophy, 1974; NHL First Team All-Star, 1951–54, 1957–58, 1960, 1966, 1968–70; NHL Second Team All-Star, 1949–50, 1956, 1959, 1961–62, 1964–65, 1967; WHA First Team All-Star, 1974–75; Team Canada (WHA), 1974; NHL All-Star Game, 1948–65, 1967–71, 1980; Hockey Hall of Fame, 1972

It was a measure of Gordie Howe's dominant position in hockey that when he finally retired from the NHL—for the first time—prior to the 1971–72 season, he had played in 1,687 regular season games, scored 786 goals, 1,023 assists, 1,809 points, and received 1,643 minutes in penalties—each item a league record.

Gordie Howe

Between the years of 1946 and 1957, Howe won the Hart Trophy as the most valuable player six times and the Art Ross Trophy as leading scorer six times. His artistry, versatility, and durability, and the fact that he successfully spanned three distinct hockey eras, marked him as unique in sports and at the apex of hockey achievements.

"He was not only the greatest hockey player I've ever seen," said former teammate and Hall of Famer Bill Gadsby, "but also the greatest athlete."

Howe was born on the outskirts of Saskatoon in Canada's wheat belt. He was the fourth of the nine children of Catherine and Albert Howe. After an unsuccessful try at farming, Albert Howe moved the family to town, where he got a job in a garage. It was in Saskatoon that Gordie learned to play hockey. In the winter, temperatures in Saskatoon would drop to 50 below zero. Ten below was balmy.

"As a kid," Gordie remembered, "the only equipment I had was skates and a stick. I took magazines and mail-order catalogues, stuck 'em in my socks, and had shin pads. I tied 'em together with rubber bands made from inner tubes. We played with tennis balls instead of a puck. The ball would get so hard from the cold we'd have to get new ones all the time. A woman next door used to warm them up in an oven for us."

Gordie quit school and got a job with a construction company that was building sidewalks. It was tough work lugging 85-pound cement bags, but it firmed his muscles. Construction work, though, was just a fill-in between hockey seasons.

"I guess he always knew he'd become a hockey player," Howe's mother once said. "He used to practice at night by the hour under the city lamp on the streets. I put papers on the kitchen floor so he wouldn't have to take his skates off while he ate."

Gordie carried his diffidence right into the dressing room when he attended a Rangers training camp in Winnipeg as a 15-year-old. He was especially embarrassed because he had no idea how to adjust the complicated equipment the pros wore.

"I just dropped the gear on the floor in front of me and watched the others," he said. "I found out pretty early that the best way to learn was to keep my mouth shut and my eyes open."

He was a homesick teenager. Finally, when his roommate left for home, Gordie sulked for two days and then he, too, departed. The next year he was invited to the Detroit camp at Windsor, Ontario. He was signed to a contract by Jack Adams and assigned to the Wings' junior farm team in Galt, Ontario. Because of a Canadian Amateur Hockey Association ruling, he was unable to play for a year. Instead he worked out with the team and played exhibitions.

The Wings wanted him to enroll in the Galt high school. When Gordie saw all the kids clustered in front of the building, he turned around, walked down a railroad track, and applied for a job with Galt Metal Industries as a spot welder.

The next year found him playing with Omaha, and in 1946 he joined the Red Wings. In his first three years he scored 7, 16, and 12 goals. His genius finally surfaced during the playoffs of 1949, when he was high scorer with 8 goals and 11 points.

"I still wasn't so sure I was a star," he said. "When I went home to Saskatoon that summer, I started playing baseball again. One day, a kid came up for my autograph, and while I signed it, he said, 'Mr. Howe, what do you do in the winter?'"

The goals began to come in bunches, and Howe mesmerized both enemy and teammate alike. His stickhandling was so uncanny, Captain Sid Abel felt moved to reprimand young Gordie. "I don't mind this great stickhandling of yours," said Abel, "but why stickhandle around the same player three times?"

Howe was the perfect athlete. Taken to a golf course, he outdrove Chick Harbert, then PGA champion. When Gordie told former Cleveland Indians manager Lou Boudreau that he could hit big-league pitching, Boudreau invited him out to the park. The Indians manager fetched one of his best pitchers and told him to throw good and hard at Howe. Gordie proceeded to line the third pitch into the left field bleachers.

As a hockey player, Howe reached the top in 1950–51, when he led the NHL in scoring with 86 points (43 goals, 43 assists); in 1951–52 with 86 points (47 goals, 39 assists); in 1952–53 with a then-record 95 points (49 goals, 46 assists); and in 1953–54 with 81 points (33 goals, 48 assists). No other player had ever led the league more than two years in a row. Gordie again was at the top of the scoring list in 1956–57 (44 goals, 45 assists), and continued to dominate the game through the late '50s and early '60s.

Howe remained a major factor in the NHL until his retirement. Then, to everyone's amazement, he surfaced again, this time in 1973 in the World Hockey Association.

Miracles occur in big-league hockey about once a half-century. In 1973–74, there were several: Gordie Howe returned to the ice at age 45, and sons Marty and Mark signed to skate alongside Pop with the Houston Aeros. Then the three Howes led Houston to the AVCO World Cup and the WHA title. Gordie next starred for Team Canada in 1974 against the young Russians, before orchestrating a second AVCO Cup win in 1975. The Gordie of 1973–75 was not the Howe who won six NHL Hart Trophies. He was a stride slower, but a stride wiser. His shot had less whammo and injuries inspired him to put a bit of a curve in his formerly flat stick. But when he skated at a foe, he was the same Gordie Howe who once pulverized NHL "heavyweight champion" Lou (Rangers) Fontinato and anybody else who dared challenge him.

Gordie made his debut with the kids on September 25, 1973, playing in a WHA spectacular at Madison Square Garden. Less than a minute after he stepped on the ice, he scored a goal. He received a standing bravo, but the decibel count didn't fool Gordie. His muscles were rusty and his timing off. It was this way during the early weeks of the season. Once, during a practice, he crashed headfirst into the boards and looked like a corpse. But he rebounded, and with each week gained more speed and more points. When the season had ended, the Aeros were champs of the WHA's Western Division, and Gordie had scored 31 goals and 69 assists for 100 points, third best in the WHA.

When Houston bowed out of the WHA, Gordie and family moved north to the New England Whalers for the 1977–78 campaign. The Whalers were admitted to the NHL in 1979, and with Gordie really beginning to show the strain, he called it quits (a second time) in 1980. His NHL totals were an astounding 801 goals and 1,049 assists over 26 seasons as an NHL gladiator, which stood long and proud, until broken by Wayne Gretzky in the 1990s.

Howe's legacy remained visible to many new hockey audiences partly thanks to Gretzky's accomplishments, and "Mr. Hockey" still remained the NHL's all-time leader in games played with 1,767 entering the millennium—not even counting the WHA years. A brief stunt in which he played one shift with the IHL Detroit Vipers in 1997–98, in order to set a record for most decades of playing professional hockey (six), may have been farce; still, it reminded the hockey world of Howe's unparalleled athleticism and longevity.

In terms of comprehensive abilities, Howe is still considered, by many critics, to be the greatest hockey player of all time.

MARK HOWE

BORN: Detroit, Michigan, May 28, 1955
POSITION: Left Wing/Defenseman, Houston Aeros (WHA), 1973–77; New England Whalers (WHA), 1977–79; Hartford Whalers, 1979–82; Philadelphia Flyers, 1982–92; Detroit Red Wings, 1992–95
AWARDS/HONORS: Rookie of the Year (WHA), 1974; First Team All-Star (WHA), 1979; NHL Second Team All-Star, 1974, 1977; NHL First Team All-Star, 1983, 1986–87; NHL Plus/Minus Leader, 1986; NHL All-Star Game, 1981, 1983, 1986, 1988

Regarded at first as one of the most gifted defensemen in North America, Mark Howe was the second—and youngest—of Gordie Howe's sons to play major-league hockey. On occasion, he also played forward. Mark first tasted stardom as a member of the 1972 American Olympic Team. Like older brother Marty, Mark was a vital member of the Toronto Marlboros team in the Ontario Hockey Association's Junior A League in 1972–73. Although only 18 years old at the time, Mark was drafted by the Houston Aeros (WHA) for the 1973–74 season along with Marty. Mark played left wing on a line with father Gordie and Jim Sherrit and scored 38 goals and 41 assists for 79 points in 76 games. He was named WHA Rookie of the Year and finished second in Aeros' playoff scoring as Houston won the 1974 AVCO World Cup, emblematic of WHA playoff supremacy. He was similarly effective in the 1974–75 campaign; being high playoff scorer with 22 points, as the Aeros copped the AVCO again in 1975. His dad once said to Mark that he'd try to set the puck up for him to help him score more. "That's okay, Dad," Mark replied, "I'll get my chances. You worry about yours."

Most analysts agree Mark was a born hockey player, like his famous pop. "Hockey is all I ever wanted to do," said Mark. "I used to sweep the stands at Detroit Friday night and skate with the Red Wings during Saturday practices. I knew every number, name, and star in the league."

Mark joined Dad and brother Marty again with the New England Whalers (later Hartford Whalers) in 1977–78.

Mark, who had now switched roles and was more-than-ably playing defense, was responsible for a major NHL equipment change as a result of a near-fatal injury to the defenseman. While playing for Hartford, he tripped and slipped legs first into the net, which then had a bayonet-like steel shaft in its center. The metal impaled Howe near the bowel area resulting in emergency surgery and threatening his life.

Afterward, the league mandated changes in the net's structure, eliminating the center piece. After Mark recovered, he went on to play superbly until concluding his playing career with the Red Wings in 1994–95 with 742 career points.

He began scouting for the Red Wings, and continued as a bird dog through the 2001–02 season.

MARTY HOWE

BORN: Detroit, Michigan, February 18, 1954
POSITION: Defenseman, Houston Aeros (WHA), 1973–77; New England Whalers (WHA), 1977–79; Hartford Whalers, 1979–82, 1983–85; Boston Bruins, 1982–83
AWARDS/HONORS: Team Canada (WHA), 1974

Like brother Mark, Marty Howe matured into a bright professional prospect early in the 1970s playing for the Toronto Marlboros of the Ontario Hockey Association Junior A League. However, as bright a professional prospect as Mark when the Houston Aeros were scouting the Howes for the 1973–74 season, "We didn't pick Marty until the fourteenth round," said Aeros coach Bill Dineen. "We were really dumb." Yet Marty played hard,

capable defense in his rookie WHA season, 1973–74, and was good enough to be selected, along with Mark and Gordie, for Team Canada (WHA-style), 1974.

As an aggressive skater, Marty suggested his father's style more than Mark. "Dad taught us never to immediately rush at somebody who takes a shot at us," said Marty. "Hit 'em when they don't see you coming." Marty was also witty like Dad. "Dad got a little more money than we did for signing with Houston," said Marty, "but we came out ahead because he had to buy a house in Houston."

Dad obviously didn't mind, especially because his sons helped him win the WHA's most valuable player award in 1974. "I was MVP," said Gordie, "simply for raising two very good hockey players. It was the most joyous year of my life."

Marty experienced a less distinguished career than his brother Mark. He departed the NHL in 1985, but never completely left The Game, bouncing around as an assistant coach and minor-league mentor through the turn of the century.

SYD HOWE

BORN: Ottawa, Ontario, September 18, 1911
DIED: May 20, 1976
POSITION: Forward, Ottawa Senators, 1929–30, 1932–34; Philadelphia Quakers, 1930–31; St. Louis Eagles, 1934–35; Detroit Red Wings, 1935–46
AWARDS/HONORS: NHL Second Team All-Star, 1945; Hockey Hall of Fame, 1965

The other Howe who starred for the Detroit Red Wings, Syd Howe preceded superman Gordie in the Motor City by more than a decade. Like Gordie, Syd Howe was a Red Wings superscorer. He was also a major factor in Detroit's Stanley Cup championships in 1936 and 1937. Syd broke into the NHL with Ottawa in 1929–30. In the following season, he skated for the hapless Philadelphia

Quakers, followed by two more years with
Ottawa. In 1934–35, he skated first for St.
Louis and then the Red Wings, for whom he
played for the remainder of his NHL career,
which ended after the 1945–46 campaign.
Curiously, Gordie Howe made his Red Wings
debut as a rookie the following season, and
from that point on Syd Howe's lustre dimmed
as Gordie's brightened. By the way, they were
not related.

HARRY HOWELL

BORN: Hamilton, Ontario, December 28, 1932
POSITION: Defenseman, New York Rangers,
1952–69; Oakland Seals, 1969–70; Los Angeles
Kings, 1970–73; New York Raiders/Golden
Blades/Jersey Knights/San Diego Mariners
(WHA), 1973–74; Player/Coach, San Diego
Mariners, 1974–75; General Manager, Cleveland
Barons, 1977–78; Coach, Minnesota North Stars,
1978
AWARDS/HONORS: James Norris Memorial
Trophy, 1967; NHL First Team All-Star, 1967; NHL
All-Star Game, 1954, 1963–65, 1967–68, 1970;
Hockey Hall of Fame, 1979

Blueliner par excellence, Harry Howell spent
22 years in the NHL; 17 of those years
were spent with the New York Rangers, for
whom Howell played more than 1,000 games,
a team record.

The defenseman began his career with the
Guelph (Ontario) Biltmores in the Ontario
Junior Hockey Association in 1949 and was
called up to the Rangers in 1952. From that
time on, Howell established himself as one of
the game's best defensive defensemen with his
subtle—some deprecatingly called it dainty—
style of play. Although Howell actually managed to accumulate 101 minutes of penalty
time one year, his play was so habitually void
of vengefulness that the Madison Square
Garden fans took to calling him names such
as "Harriet" and "Sonja." But Howell was
named to the NHL All-Star squad in 1967, and

was the last player to win the Norris Trophy
(1966–67) as the league's best defenseman
before Bobby Orr took sole possession of that
award for eight consecutive years.

After leaving the Rangers in 1969, Howell
played two years with the Oakland Seals and
three with the Los Angeles Kings before jumping to the San Diego Mariners of the WHA.
In 1977, Harry became general manager of
the Cleveland Barons, and when they merged
with the North Stars in 1978, he was named
coach of the team. But coaching wasn't for
Harry, and when his health began to suffer
shortly after the start of the 1978–79 season,
he resigned to become a scout with the North
Stars and, more recently, with the Rangers.

Howell was voted to the Hockey Hall of Fame
in 1979 and continued scouting through the
2001–02 season.

KELLY HRUDEY

BORN: Edmonton, Alberta, January 13, 1961
POSITION: Goaltender, New York Islanders,
1984–89; Los Angeles Kings, 1989–95; San Jose
Sharks, 1996–98

When all-time goaltending performances
are recalled, the effort delivered on April
18, 1987, by Kelly Hrudey stands near the top.

His 73-save masterpiece enabled the
New York Islanders to score a 3–2 victory over
the Washington Capitals in Game Seven of
the Patrick Division semifinals after 68:47
of overtime.

"One of the things we never seem to do in
this business is give credit to the other team,"
said then-Capitals general manager David
Poile, "and Kelly Hrudey beat us."

If that was Hrudey's finest hour (or hours!),
it was not his only noteworthy performance.
As a member of the Los Angeles Kings in
1992–93, he guided the club to the Stanley Cup
finals before losing to Montreal in five games.

Successor to Hall of Famer Billy Smith as
the Isles' number one goaltender, the affable

Hrudey took over after the four–Stanley Cup dynasty went into decline. Nevertheless, he was a capable, often outstanding, puckstopper.

As the Isles began to rebuild again, Hrudey was dealt to the Kings during the Wayne Gretzky era, and electrified LA fans with his quick reflexes and trademark bandannas. Kelly stands second on the Kings' all-time wins list with 145, and twice won the team MVP during his LA tenure.

Although he didn't don the goalie pads until age 12, Hrudey amassed 271 wins and a goals-against average of 3.43 over his career, which included a stop in San Jose.

Upon retiring, Hrudey provided stellar commentary for CBC's famed *Hockey Night in Canada*. By 2002, he was regarded as one of the best analysts in North America.

BOBBY HULL

BORN: Point Anne, Ontario, January 3, 1939
POSITION: Left Wing, Chicago Blackhawks, 1957–72; Winnipeg Jets, 1979; Hartford Whalers, 1980; Coach, Winnipeg Jets (WHA), 1972–78
AWARDS/HONORS: Hart Memorial Trophy, 1965–66; Art Ross Trophy, 1960, 1962, 1966; Lady Byng Memorial Trophy, 1966; Lester Patrick Trophy, 1969; Howe Trophy, 1973, 1975; NHL First Team All-Star, 1960, 1962, 1964–69, 1972; NHL Second Team All-Star, 1963, 1971; WHA First Team All-Star, 1974–75; WHA Second Team All-Star, 1976, 1978; Team Canada (WHA), 1974; NHL All-Star Game, 1960–65, 1967–72; Hockey Hall of Fame, 1983

When Bobby Hull executed his sensational leap from the National Hockey League's Chicago Blackhawks to the Winnipeg Jets of the World Hockey Association in the summer of 1972, several hasty predictions were made. Some experts were confident that the Golden Jet would score more than 100 goals against WHA goaltenders. Others ventured that Bobby would certainly guarantee first

place and the Avco World Cup for Winnipeg. Then, there were those who believed that Hull's presence would guarantee nothing but standing room crowds at the Winnipeg Arena.

Hardly any of these events took place. For two straight years, Hull missed the WHA scoring title, never nearing the 100-goal mark. True, the Jets finished first their rookie season, but they were far off the mark in the 1973–74 season and attendance was conspicuously disappointing, despite the fact that Hull's defection from the National Hockey League had been the major reason for the WHA's ability to become the game's second major hockey league overnight.

The Golden Jet had led the NHL in goal-scoring seven times and three times had been points leader. He was named to the All-Star team in 12 out of 15 seasons and had won just about every available award, including the Lady Byng Trophy for good sportsmanship combined with ability. He also led Chicago to the Stanley Cup in 1961, the last time the Blackhawks won the championship. At the age of 34, when he put on the Winnipeg Jets uniform for the first time, Bobby Hull had done

Bobby "The Golden Jet" Hull

just about everything that had been asked of him; but now he was facing the biggest challenge of his life.

His first challenge, however, would be maintaining his mental stability. In its desperate attempt to kill the WHA, the NHL attempted to bar Hull from playing by using every legal method at its command. A court injunction sidelined him for the first month of the campaign until, finally, that restriction was lifted. Once again the red lights began flashing as soon as Bobby hit the ice. "I got awfully run down from all the litigation," Bobby admitted. "I lost more than ten pounds, down from 194 to 180, and since I don't carry any fat, that loss was all in muscle and red meat. I felt just plain unhealthy."

But he never stopped smiling and he never stopped providing the new league with that positive image it needed so badly at the start. Bobby took an instant pride in the new league, but he was the first to admit he left the Chicago Blackhawks for reasons other than building the WHA.

"If I told you that the big contract had nothing to do with my signing with Winnipeg," Hull smiled, "I'd be telling you a lie. It made the future secure for my family. That was the most important thing. Then there were some things that disenchanted me in the NHL, and the way the Hawks handled their attempts to sign me. They just didn't think I'd consider jumping."

Hull moved his wife, Joanne, and their five children into a 14-room, $185,000 home in the Winnipeg suburb of Tuxedo. Natives of the Manitoba metropolis appropriately greeted him as a national hero and Bobby repaid them by taking the Jets to the top of the WHA's Western Division. The Jet scored 51 goals and 52 assists in 63 games to finish in a three-way tie for fourth place in the WHA scoring list with Tom Webster of New England and Winnipeg's Norm Beaudin. However, Webster played in 77 games and Beaudin in 78. Bobby's point total was amazing, considering that he frequently was skating at less than top speed.

"I never had many injuries until I joined the WHA," he explained, "but every part of me seemed to hurt after I started skating for the Jets—my elbow, my shoulder, and my knee. It was part of the complete changeover in the schedule. For fifteen years in the NHL, we had three games a week with two days off after each game. In the first year of the WHA, we had doubleheader and back-to-back games, which meant that my little injuries never got a chance to heal."

Still, he was able to take Winnipeg to the 1973 finals of the WHA playoff, before New England defeated the Jets four games to one.

During the 1977–78 season, incensed at the way WHA officials were allowing intimidators to go after his Swedish linemates, Ulf Nilsson and Anders Hedberg, Bobby staged a one-man, one-game strike in protest against violence in hockey. By the time the 1978–79 campaign rolled around, Bobby was still not convinced anything was being done by the league to curb violence. He had also run into serious family problems that were affecting his play. So a tired and discouraged Bobby Hull decided it was time to get away from it all, and he retired. Many hockey people, however, felt that with the NHL expansion to WHA cities, it was possible that Bobby would change his mind and return. When the WHA breathed its last breath in 1979, Hull wished to come back to the NHL with his former Chicago Blackhawk mates, but he was claimed in the draft by John Ferguson's Winnipeg Jets, forcing the Hawks to deal for the right to sign the one-time NHL star.

By the time the WHA had merged with the National Hockey League, Hull had become deified for his courage in sticking with the new league, which in turn, helped lift salaries all across the board. Unfortunately, Hull's career ended on a sad note. He played only nine games for the Whalers in 1979–80, scoring twice and adding five assists. While he did help the hockey club annex its first playoff berth in its first NHL season, Hull never was the same as a player and retired.

He remained in the limelight as a frequent guest at hockey dinners, and was the focus of media attention when son Brett became an NHL star in the 1990s, as well as when Luc Robitaille broke Bobby's mark of 610 goals by a left-winger in 2001–02.

BRETT HULL

BORN: Belleville, Ontario, August 9, 1964
POSITION: Right Wing, Calgary Flames, 1986–88; St. Louis Blues, 1988–98; Dallas Stars, 1998–2001; Detroit Red Wings, 2001–; Team U.S.A., 1991 Canada Cup; Team U.S.A., 1996 World Cup; Team U.S.A., 1998 and 2002 Olympics
AWARDS/HONORS: Hart Memorial Trophy, 1991; Lady Byng Memorial Trophy, 1990; NHL First Team All-Star, 1990–92; NHL All-Star Game, 1989–94, 1996–97, 2001

Growing up the son of legendary great Bobby Hull was not the easiest thing a child can do. Following in the footsteps of a hockey immortal can take its toll on even the strong of heart. But Brett Hull not only followed his father's path to success, he ultimately surpassed him.

A sixth-round draft pick of the Calgary Flames in 1984, Hull played college hockey at Minnesota-Duluth, and, in 1986, made his professional debut with the Flames in Game Three of the 1986 Stanley Cup finals against the eventual champion Montreal Canadiens. Having clanked a shot off the post in that game, Hull eventually scored his first NHL goal six months later, on November 13, 1986, against the Hartford Whalers, playing on a line with Gary Roberts and Joe Nieuwendyk.

On March 7, 1988, the Flames dealt Hull and Steve Bozek to the St. Louis Blues for goaltender Rick Wamsley and defenseman Rob Ramage. In St. Louis, under the tutelage of coach Brian Sutter, Hull began to score goals with such regularity and consistency that the rest of the league began to notice the pudgy towheaded kid. When the Blues acquired center Adam Oates before the 1989 season, Sutter immediately paired the playmaking center with the natural scorer.

It was a match made in heaven as the two stars began to put up amazing numbers. Hull, who had scored 41 goals his first full season with the Blues, tallied an amazing 72 the first year that Oates joined him on a line.

But it was during the 1990–91 season that Hull began to chase down a record many thought no one would come close to, let alone break. The record was Wayne Gretzky's 92 goals in a season, and Hull and Oates were on a mission to eclipse the mark.

Hull chased Gretzky's record with a vengeance. He scored his 50th goal of that season in only his 49th game; he scored a goal against every team in the league, and put the puck in the net in 56 of the team's 78 contests. Finishing the season with an incredible 86 goals, Hull did not break Gretzky's record, but did legitimize himself as one of the best snipers in the game.

In 1991–92, he lit the lamp another 70 times, giving him a mind-boggling 228 goals in three seasons.

Ironically, it was Hull's explosive temperament that made the decision by the Blues management not to re-sign the superstar an easy one. In the summer of 1998, Brett Hull began to solicit offers from other teams as an unrestricted free agent.

The sentimental choice for Hull was to go to Chicago, where his father had enjoyed all of his NHL success. But one day before Independence Day, 1998, Brett Hull signed with the Dallas Stars, thinking the club had a good chance of winning the Stanley Cup. Hull, who had never won a team trophy, wanted to fill that void, and the Stars knew Hull would be the final piece to their puzzle.

The team got off to a fast start in 1998, and after Hull clashed with defense-first coach Ken Hitchcock, the team and Hull began to gel, as he played on the number one line with center Mike Modano and left wing Jere Lehtinen.

As the season ended, Hull was second on the team in scoring (32 goals, 58 points) and Dallas again won the President's Trophy as best team in the regular season. Brett knew this year's playoffs would be much different than in years past.

Hull started out slowly, registering just one assist as the Stars defeated the Edmonton Oilers in four straight in the first round of the 1999 playoffs. But his more defensive style of play had begun to show during the regular season and continued in the postseason. Hull had finally learned to be an all-around player under Hitchcock and his defense-first orientation.

After the Stars subsequently defeated the Blues and the Colorado Avalanche, the Buffalo Sabres, led by all-world goaltender Dominik Hasek, were their final roadblock on the road to the Stanley Cup championship.

Hull, playing in his first Stanley Cup final, nursed a sore groin all series long. But by Game Six, after five periods of play, Brett Hull stepped onto the ice to make history. Hull skated directly to the front of Hasek, while linemate Mike Modano fought for the puck along the boards in the Sabres end. Suddenly, the puck squirted in front of Hull. Barely able to stand, Brett feverishly whacked the puck into the net.

That season, according to NHL rules, a player could not score if he or anyone else on his team was in the crease before the puck entered it. Hull's skate was clearly in the goal crease before he released his shot, and Buffalo coach Lindy Ruff demanded a second look from the officials. But his pleas went unanswered, and the Stars were declared 1999 Stanley Cup champions.

For Hull, the goal couldn't have been more golden. The most prolific goal scorer of the 1990s, Hull sat in the joyous Dallas locker room, taking turns laughing, shouting, and crying. After more than 13 years in the league, he had finally vindicated himself.

With over 600 career goals and a Stanley Cup ring, Hull next decided to sign as a free agent with the Detroit Red Wings in the summer of 2001, joining fellow 600-goal scorers Steve Yzerman and Luc Robitaille, as well as former archrival, Dominik Hasek.

The Red Wings, attaining 100 points a full month before the 2001–02 season ended, easily took the President's Trophy and began a trek toward Lord Stanley's silverware by defeating a surprisingly difficult round one foe, the Vancouver Canucks.

Of course, they did so, in part because somebody woke up Brett Hull and he responded by scoring twice in the sixth and decisive game against the Canucks. Hull's value increased as he paced the Red Wings to their Stanley Cup victory over Carolina in the finals. There was a time when you couldn't win a Stanley Cup with Brett. Times have changed.

DENNIS HULL

BORN: Point Anne, Ontario, November 19, 1944
POSITION: Left Wing, Chicago Blackhawks, 1964–77; Detroit Red Wings, 1977–78
AWARDS/HONORS: Team Canada, 1972; NHL Second Team All-Star, 1973; NHL All-Star Game, 1969, 1971–74

Dennis Hull, a powerfully built left-winger, didn't come into his own as a recognized NHL star until his more-famous brother, Bobby, opted for the World Hockey Association in 1972. Both siblings had been accounting for much of the Chicago Blackhawk offense since 1966, when Dennis established himself as a Hawk regular, joining the already legendary "Golden Jet."

It was a pretty difficult act to follow for the youngster. The elder Hull had already blasted his way to two 50-goal seasons, led the league in scoring three times, and twice won the Hart Trophy as the league's most valuable player. At that point in time, Bobby Hull was the most electrifying player in The Game. No one could have been expected to live up to the Golden One's larger-than-life dimensions—not even his own sibling.

Naturally, comparisons between the two brothers were endless, with Dennis always coming up short. The younger Hull was a more than competent winger and on any other team, said the experts, might have been the number one star of the show. But teamed with Bobby, he just blended in with the supporting cast of characters. A tiny minority of hockey pundits dared point out that Dennis's intimidating shot was just a mite harder than Bobby's.

Once, during a Blackhawk practice session at cavernous Chicago Stadium, Dennis put the screws to a wrist shot that sailed into the second level and splintered one of the seats to kindling wood.

In 1972, when brother Bobby signed with the WHA Winnipeg Jets, Dennis seemed to break out of an unseen shell, responding with his best point production ever, and joining the NHL All-Star team for the first time in his career. But Chicago fans still never took Dennis to their hearts and were continually "getting on him." In 1977, he was traded to the Detroit Red Wings, played one season, then retired.

Dennis eventually moved into the area of after-dinner speaking with a humorous touch. He usually twitted his older brother Bobby, often with the Golden Jet present, and was considered one of the funniest performers on the NHL rubber-chicken circuit.

DALE HUNTER

BORN: Petrolia, Ontario, July 31, 1960
POSITION: Center, Quebec Nordiques, 1980–87; Washington Capitals, 1987–99; Colorado Avalanche, 1999
AWARDS/HONORS: NHL All-Star Game, 1997

In some ways, Dale Hunter was one of the most versatile hard guys to come down the NHL pike since Stan Mikita. He hit, he disturbed, he played defense, *and* he could score.

During the 1993 playoffs between the Washington Capitals and New York Islanders, Hunter scored a pair of goals—including the winner—in Game One, then followed with a hat trick in Game Two. Not many players known more for bashing than scoring could make that statement.

Sometimes Hunter overstepped the lines of propriety. In the third period of the sixth and final game of the Islanders-Capitals series, Dale pursued New York's Pierre Turgeon well after his opponent had scored a series-clinching goal and peeled off to his exuberant teammates at Nassau Coliseum. Hunter rammed the unsuspecting Turgeon from behind, separating the Islander player's shoulder and causing him to miss most of the Patrick Division final against Pittsburgh. NHL commissioner Gary Bettman's response was a 21-game suspension for Hunter during the 1993–94 season.

At five-feet-ten and 198 pounds, Hunter was less than an imposing figure—except to opponents who happened to have run into Dale's stick, a not-infrequent occurrence. There simply was no more determined in-your-face foe anywhere in hockey, but also one who continually surprised with his offense.

Gentlemanly and soft-spoken away from the ice, the native of Petrolia, Ontario, blunted all barbs with a grin and the conviction that he was playing hockey the most practical way he knew how and that's all there was to it.

For more than a dozen years, Dale Hunter was one of the most consistent, and irascible, of professionals; a Peck's Bad Boy of the pond. He played with the Capitals until 1999, when he signed with Colorado. Dale then retired after 19 years in the NHL. He recorded 1,407 regular season games and 186 playoff games, and was an All-Star in 1997.

AL IAFRATE

BORN: Dearborn, Michigan, March 21, 1966
POSITION: Defenseman, Toronto Maple Leafs, 1984–91; Washington Capitals, 1991–94; Boston Bruins, 1994; San Jose Sharks, 1996–98
AWARDS/HONORS: NHL Second Team All-Star, 1993; NHL All-Star Game, 1988, 1990, 1993–94

A series of knee injuries derailed the career of one of the most gifted defensemen of the late twentieth century. Notorious for his mighty shot which exceeded 100 miles per hour, as well as his punishing body checks, Al Iafrate was a multi-talented defenseman who managed to play through 14 NHL seasons, before the knee problems ended his career.

Al "Planet" Iafrate as a Washington defenseman

Iafrate joined the professional hockey scene in the 1984–85 season, and was the Toronto Maple Leafs' first pick, fourth overall, in the 1984 Entry Draft. He was an intimidating defenseman, standing at six feet three, 235 pounds. After being named to the Second All-Star Team in 1993, Iafrate was named to the U.S. National Team and the U.S. Olympic Team in the same year.

A great offensive defenseman who hit the 20-goal plateau three times (1987–88, 1989–90, 1992–93), Iafrate played for the Leafs for seven seasons before being traded to the Washington Capitals in the 1990–91 season. He was a force in the Caps lineup until dealt to the Boston Bruins for Joe Juneau in the 1993–94 season. But knee problems debilitated him for the entire 1994–95 and 1995–96 campaigns. Thought to be finished, Iafrate then attempted a comeback in 1996–97 with the San Jose Sharks, where he played very little for two years before retirement in 1998.

JAROME IGINLA

BORN: Edmonton, Alberta, July 1, 1977
POSITION: Right Wing, Calgary Flames, 1995–
AWARDS/HONORS: Art Ross Trophy, 2002; Maurice Richard Trophy, 2002; Lester B. Pearson Award, 2002; NHL All-Rookie Team, 1997; NHL All-Star Game, 2002

When the Calgary Flames dealt popular performer Joe Nieuwendyk to the Dallas Stars in 1995, the player they received, Jarome Iginla, would steadily pay tremendous dividends in subsequent seasons.

Iginla was a scoring machine in the minor leagues, his most astounding total being the 63 goals and 73 assists for Kamloops in the WHL before being called up to the NHL in 1995–96. Later in that season, Jarome would score his first NHL goal in a Flames' playoff game.

Iginla remained with the Flames, and rightfully so. He scored 50 points during his rookie season of 1996–97 and was the Calder Trophy runner-up.

During 2000–01, Iginla led the Flames in goals and points, but nothing compares to what he did during the 2001–02 season. An unexpected superstar, Iginla led the NHL in goals (52) and points (96), as his MVP-caliber performance helped Calgary off to an excellent start. His game, in which he did everything well, trumped expectation, and vaulted the Edmonton native of African descent into superstardom.

A compact powerful skater at six feet one, the affable Iginla merited a berth on the 2002 Canadian Olympic Team and scored two goals in the gold medal–winning game. Unfortunately, Jarome alone was not capable of propelling his Flames into the 2002 postseason.

In fact, with restricted free agency looming, there was some question as to whether Calgary would be able to afford Iginla's talented services. But shortly before the start of training camp in September 2002, Iginla signed a new lucrative contract with Calgary.

PUNCH IMLACH

BORN: Toronto, Ontario, March 15, 1918
DIED: December 1, 1987
POSITION: Coach, Toronto Maple Leafs, 1958–69; Buffalo Sabres, 1970–71; General Manager, Toronto Maple Leafs, 1958–69; Buffalo Sabres, 1970–79
AWARDS/HONORS: Hockey Hall of Fame, 1984

One of the most successful and cantankerous characters in major-league hockey history was George "Punch" Imlach. Imlach's tough-as-nails approach to the game won him four Stanley Cups with the powerhouse Leaf teams of the 1960s. Only two other NHL coaches, Toe Blake (Montreal) and Hap Day (Toronto), have ever accounted for more silverware than that.

Visually impressive, Imlach always wore a fedora while coaching behind the bench, and was renowned for his no-nonsense approach to both friend and foe.

During the 1958–59 season, he engineered the single greatest homestretch drive in NHL history. With only two weeks left in the regular season, Imlach's Maple Leafs were seven points behind the New York Rangers, who were coached by his archrival Phil Watson.

Starting with a win over the Blueshirts at Madison Square Garden, the Leafs began a relentless surge that brought them to the final night of the campaign still trailing the Rangers by a point.

After Montreal defeated the Rangers, 3–1, in New York, Imlach coaxed his Leafs to a 6–4 triumph over the Detroit Red Wings at Olympia Stadium, putting Toronto into the playoffs for the first time since 1955–56.

Imlach never hesitated to gamble, nor to innovate. He took an aging defenseman, Red Kelly, who had never played forward, and turned him into a center, whereupon the redhead became pivot on a line with Frank Mahovlich and Bob Nevin. Kelly soon became one of the league's best centers.

Punch took another aging defenseman, Allan Stanley, and turned him into a future Hall of Famer. He also worked with youngsters such as Carl Brewer, Bobby Baun, Dave Keon, and Bob Pulford, each of whom became a Toronto star.

But Imlach had a dark side as well. His Spartan tactics angered players. He constantly mispronounced Mahovlich, calling him "Mahalovich," which angered the ace, who left the team with a nervous breakdown. Brewer, also infuriated by Imlach, walked out on the team to attend university.

Some critics said the Leafs won because the players hated Punch so much, that they wanted to win in spite of him. Whatever the case, four Stanley Cups in six years was a testament to Imlach's genius.

Before his days as coach of the Leafs, Punch spent 11 years with the minor-league Quebec Aces as a player, coach, general manager, and, eventually, part owner. Then Mach joined the Boston Bruin organization as manager/coach of the AHL's Springfield Indians for one year, until he took over the coaching duties for the Leafs.

Imlach was named coach and general manager of the Buffalo Sabres in 1970 and built the team into a powerhouse in two seasons, but was forced to step aside from the coaching duties following a massive heart attack during the 1971–72 season.

In 1978, with his team very much in trouble on the ice, Imlach got into a nasty and unnecessary brouhaha with a reporter. It all added up to the Sabres' owners deciding Punch had to go, so he was fired.

Punch's old pal, Maple Leafs owner Harold Ballard, was having troubles of his own at the end of the 1978–79 season and hired Imlach to manage his club starting in 1980. Imlach's tour of duty in Toronto was less successful the second time around. Punch had lost his touch and soon was gone from the Leafs' high command, and with his departure Toronto lost one of its most memorable hockey characters.

EARL INGARFIELD

BORN: Lethbridge, Alberta, October 25, 1934
POSITION: Center, New York Rangers, 1958–67; Pittsburgh Penguins, 1967–69; California Seals, 1969–71; Coach, New York Islanders, 1973

While the New York Rangers floundered throughout the early 1960s, there wasn't much for their few loyal fans to cheer about. However, one player who made things a bit easier for the Blueshirts and their faithful followers was a center-iceman named Earl Thompson Ingarfield.

Ingarfield was not considered a star by most standards, but rather a journeyman hockey player who did his job well, but was virtually unnoticed. His five-feet-eleven, 185-pound frame did not stand out, nor did his graceful, long-stride skating motion. He was an ordinary, unpublicized player who seldom engaged in fisticuffs or ever scored anywhere near 50 goals in a single season. Still, with a booming slap shot, he managed to score 179 goals and 405 points in a career spanning 12 seasons—not bad in the pre-Expansion days.

Three successful years, one with Saskatoon and two with Winnipeg, earned Earl a trial with the New York Rangers in 1958. He saw little action for the first two years and then in

1960, mild-mannered Ingarfield made the team permanently and scored 13 goals in 66 games. The following season, he enjoyed his best season as a pro, scoring 26 goals and 57 points and playing the entire 70-game schedule.

Ingarfield's best nights were those when he centered for Andy Bathgate and Dean Prentice, especially in 1961–62, when the Rangers went up against Toronto in the Stanley Cup semifinals. Earl had been injured early in the series, at a point when it appeared that the New Yorkers would upset Toronto. The Rangers desperately needed Ingarfield's productive stick and, as a result, the *New York Journal-American* ran a six-column headline that immortalized the likeable center: RUSTY RANGERS NEED SHOT OF EARL.

Ingarfield returned to spark the Rangers to playoff wins in Games Three and Four.

When his playing days were over, Ingarfield turned to front office work with the expansionist New York Islanders. He briefly—and successfully—coached the Islanders in the latter part of their first season, 1972–73. However, he refused an offer to return, preferring amateur coaching in his native Alberta.

He later became one of the Islanders' primary Western Canada scouts, holding that position for many years.

MICKEY ION

BORN: Paris, Ontario, February 25, 1886
DIED: October 26, 1944
POSITION: Referee, NHL, 1926–43
AWARDS/HONORS: Hockey Hall of Fame, 1961

Mickey Ion was one of the NHL's foremost officials from the mid '20s into the '40s. One night when Ion was refereeing a game in Seattle, he took exception to a front-row fan armed with a large megaphone. Whenever Ion skated by, the fan would assail his ears with an assortment of curses. "Ion finally stopped the game," Lester Patrick recalled, "and demanded that the megaphone or the fan be removed. Ion won the battle this time, but the next time he appeared in Seattle the fans really gave it to him. There were six thousand fans at the game and it seemed all six thousand of them had brought megaphones."

The moment the megaphones blared, Patrick noticed that Ion had stopped play. He wanted all the megaphones confiscated and removed from the stands. Lester walked down to rinkside and beckoned the referee to the boards.

"For Heaven's sake, Mickey," said Patrick, "you can't get all six thousand megaphones."

"If I don't get the megaphones," said Ion, "the game will end here and now!"

Patrick had no choice but to back his referee, whose decision was made known to the crowd. They were compelled to give up their megaphones. As Lester fondly recalled, the crowd did give Ion the megaphones, although obviously not the way he wanted them. "They threw them at him," said Patrick. "When all the noise had ended, Mickey was standing at center ice, knee-deep in megaphones."

ARTURS IRBE

BORN: Riga, Latvia, February 2, 1967
POSITION: Goaltender, San Jose Sharks, 1991–96; Dallas Stars, 1996–97; Vancouver Canucks, 1997–98; Carolina Hurricanes, 1998–
AWARDS/HONORS: NHL All-Star, 1994, 1999

When the Carolina Hurricanes played the Stanley Cup champion New Jersey Devils in the opening round of the 2001 playoffs, one player emerged as the hero for the underdogs. That was the Hurricanes' tiny goaltender, Arturs Irbe.

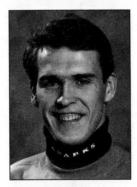

Arturs Irbe as a Shark

A native of Latvia, Irbe proved a master of angled goaltending with supersharp reflexes. He was able to help Carolina win two games against New Jersey and once again demonstrated that there's room in major-league hockey for goaltenders under six feet.

Drafted in 1989 to Minnesota from the Soviet League, Irbe was first acquired by the San Jose Sharks, where he tended goal for five years. He was critical in lifting up a faltering club, leading the Sharks to the playoffs in his second season there. During this stay, he played in the NHL All-Star game and was nominated for the King Clancy Award.

Irbe then jumped to Dallas for a season, and Vancouver for the following season, then landed in Carolina, where he seemed to be most comfortable and most respected. Besides being an iron goaltender leading the franchise in most games played, he also had the most shutouts, wins, and consecutive games.

Short in stature, but solid in goal, Irbe excelled. His quick reflexes and ability to stop a puck at any angle made him an NHL commodity. Unfortunately, he was driven out of round one of the 2002 Stanley Cup playoffs in two games, before his backup, Kevin Weekes, took over for the exhausted Irbe.

After Carolina eliminated New Jersey in round one, Irbe returned to the nets and spearheaded the Hurricanes' magical ride to the Stanley Cup finals.

Even in defeat, Irbe was considered a major star of the 2002 finals.

DICK IRVIN

BORN: Limestone Ridge, Ontario, July 19, 1892
DIED: May 1957
POSITION: Forward, Chicago Blackhawks, 1926–29; Coach, Chicago Blackhawks, 1930–31, 1955–56; Toronto Maple Leafs, 1931–40; Montreal Canadiens, 1940–55
AWARDS/HONORS: Hockey Hall of Fame, 1958

Dick Irvin learned the value of hard work as a youngster, when employed in the neighborhood butcher shop. He earned enough from that job to buy a pair of ice skates (before that he played in neighborhood games in an old pair of overshoes), and gradually worked his way up the hockey ladder to the majors, eventually to become one of the most successful players and then coaches with Toronto, Montreal, and Chicago.

A full-fledged NHL star with the Blackhawks, Dick Irvin's career was curtailed when he suffered a fractured skull from being checked by Red Dutton of the Montreal Maroons. It was then that he turned to coaching, first with the Blackhawks and then with the Maple Leafs. Toronto's young crew was well suited to Dick's accent-on-speed philosophy. "As long as they play this game on skates," Irvin would say, "you have to be able to skate to win. Personally, I'll take a young pair of legs over an old head anytime."

Irvin's mind was fertile and quick. Opponents knew he would go to extreme lengths to make a point for his team. A typical example was an incident during a game against the Rangers on the night of February 18, 1932, at Maple Leaf Gardens. Charlie Conacher and Red Horner of Toronto dressed for the match, but they were unable to play because of injuries. Nevertheless, they remained in uniform and stayed on the bench.

As it turned out, Conacher and Horner acted wisely. Both skaters had accumulated two major penalties in the season, and, according to NHL rules of the day, a third major would result in an automatic one-game suspension. The 1931–32 rulebook also called for a major penalty to any player who took the ice while his team already was at full strength.

Midway in the game Irvin sent Conacher and then Horner on the ice, although the Maple Leafs were already at full strength. Both were given major penalties and suspended for one game, which was perfectly all right with Irvin since injuries would have prevented them from playing in their next game anyway. In that way Dick did away with the suspension, and his Leafs edged the Rangers 5–3.

Irvin's most productive years were in the '40s and early '50s, coaching the Montreal Canadiens, paced by Maurice "Rocket" Richard. His last coaching stint was in 1955–56 with Chicago. He died in 1957.

Irvin's son, Dick Jr., became a legend in his own right, as a Canadian broadcaster.

TOMMY IVAN

BORN: Toronto, Ontario, January 31, 1911
DIED: June 24, 1999
POSITION: Coach, Detroit Red Wings, 1947–54; Coach, Chicago Blackhawks, 1956–58, General Manager, Chicago Blackhawks, 1954–77
AWARDS/HONORS: Hockey Hall of Fame, 1974

When a severe facial injury ended Tommy Ivan's playing career in junior hockey, his love for The Game kept him around as a referee and then as coach of a junior team in Brantford, Ontario.

After serving as a gunnery instructor in the Canadian army during World War II, Ivan began his pro career

Tommy "Dapper" Ivan

as a scout in the Detroit Red Wings organization. In 1945–46, he coached the Omaha Knights of the now-defunct United States Hockey League, and the following year he was promoted to the Indianapolis Capitols of the American Hockey League.

In 1947–48, Ivan made his National Hockey League debut as a coach with the Detroit Red Wings, when Jack Adams relinquished the position to become the Wings' general manager. There, his teams won six straight NHL championships and three Stanley Cups (1949–50, 1951–52, and 1953–54) in six years.

While with the Red Wings, Ivan coached in four All-Star games, leading the All-Stars to successive wins over Toronto in 1948 and 1949 with identical 3–1 scores. He then piloted the Wings the next year to a 7–1 win over the All-Stars, and, finally, coached the First Team All-Stars to a 1–1 tie with the Second Team.

In 1954–55, Ivan left the winning Detroit team and took the general manager's job with the Chicago Blackhawks, where he would build a Windy City squad containing such luminaries as Stan Mikita and Bobby Hull.

From 1959 on, the Blackhawks, with Ivan again solely as general manager, qualified for the playoffs every year but one, and won the Stanley Cup for the first time in 23 years in 1960–61. In 1966–67, the Hawks captured their first division title in their 40-year history. They added another one three years later, then won three straight division championships when they moved over to the West Division in 1970–71.

Building an excellent farm system, Ivan was given credit for transforming the floundering and financially troubled Blackhawks into one of the most powerful organizations in the NHL. However, Ivan received much criticism for a trade he initiated in 1967, in which he sent Phil Esposito, Ken Hodge, and Fred Stanfield to the Boston Bruins in exchange for Gilles Marotte, Pit Martin, and minor-league goalie Jack Norris.

Retiring in 1977, Tommy remained with the team as assistant to the president, devoting time to amateur hockey in the United States. Ever loyal to the Hawks, Ivan continued to be a fixture on the Chicago general staff virtually until his death in 1999.

BUSHER JACKSON

BORN: Toronto, Ontario, January 17, 1911
DIED: June 25, 1966
POSITION: Left Wing, Toronto Maple Leafs, 1929–39; New York Americans, 1940–41; Boston Bruins, 1942–44
AWARDS/HONORS: Art Ross Trophy, 1932; NHL First Team All-Star, 1932, 1934–35, 1937; NHL Second Team All-Star, 1933; Hockey Hall of Fame, 1971

Harvey "Busher" Jackson was the most tragic figure on Toronto's Kid Line of Charlie Conacher, Joe Primeau, and Jackson. Unlike his linemates who acquired fortune after their retirement in the late 1930s, Jackson encountered hard times throughout his life. He was even given trouble by the Hall of Fame committee which hesitated for years to nominate him allegedly because of his drinking problems.

A product of Frank Selke's Toronto Junior Marlboros, Jackson turned pro in 1929–30 with the Maple Leafs. According to Selke, Jackson was the "classiest" player he had ever seen. "He could pivot on a dime, stickhandle through an entire team without giving up the puck, and shoot like a bullet from either forehand or backhand. His backhand was the best I ever saw."

Following his starry years in Toronto, Jackson continued playing first with the New York Americans and finally with the Boston Bruins. By 1944, his skills had eroded, forcing his retirement.

JAROMIR JAGR

BORN: Kladno, Czechoslovakia, February 15, 1972
POSITION: Right Wing, Pittsburgh Penguins, 1990–2001; Washington Capitals, 2001–
AWARDS/HONORS: Art Ross Trophy, 1995, 1998–2000; Lester B. Pearson Award, 1999–2000; Hart Memorial Trophy, 1999; NHL All-Rookie Team, 1991; NHL First Team All-Star, 1995–96, 1998–2000; NHL Second Team All-Star, 1997; NHL All-Star Game, 1992–93, 1996, 1998–2000, 2002

The promise was enormous and for many years it was fulfilled: Jaromir Jagr was considered by some to be the greatest hockey player in the world.

When Wayne Gretzky retired in 2000, Jagr was handed a symbolic torch by The Great One, who considered Jagr his

Jaromir Jagr as a Penguin

legitimate heir apparent. Certainly Jagr underlined the point in a scoring sense. He won the Art Ross Trophy as the NHL's leading scorer five times, starting in the 1994–95 season—the first European to do so. He also was winner of the Lester B. Pearson Award two years in a row (1999 and 2000), the Hart Trophy (1999), and was an All-Star in 1992, 1993, 1996, 1998, 1999, 2000, and 2002. He was named to the Czechoslovakian team in the 2002 Winter Olympics.

As a young member of the Pittsburgh Penguins, the Czech-born ace teamed with

Mario Lemieux to win a pair of Stanley Cups for the club in 1991 and 1992. But despite these triumphs, Jagr never matched Gretzky's appeal in the area of public relations. While Wayne invariably was a poster boy for big-league hockey, Jagr became notorious for his evasiveness and lack of media cooperation.

By the 2000–2001 season, Jagr seemed to have lost the *joie de vivre* that symbolized his earlier demeanor. When the Penguins—rearmed with Lemieux, who had come out of retirement—met the New Jersey Devils in the playoffs, Jagr's play ranged from below-average to mediocre.

Jagr became the hockey equivalent of the fat-cat athlete who predominated in other sports. By the summer of 2001, Jagr was too expensive for the Pens, and in the biggest deal of the year, was traded to the Washington Capitals. He left with Pittsburgh teammate Frantisek Kucera, for Kris Beech, Ross Lupaschuk, Michal Sivek, and future considerations. It was a trade that gained a lot of hype, but turned out a disappointment for the Caps.

What made Jagr terrific was his solid goal-scoring, coupled with his finesse and endurance on the ice. His first decade in the NHL was highly successful and he became a household name for hockey greats. But before and following the trade to Washington, Jagr's talents became muffled. Despite Jagr's presence, the Caps missed the 2001–02 playoffs. To help him in 2002–03, Washington signed Jaromir's former line mate Robert Lang.

CRAIG JANNEY

BORN: Hartford, Connecticut, September 26, 1967
POSITION: Center, Boston Bruins, 1988–92; St. Louis Blues, 1992–95; San Jose Sharks, 1995–96; Winnipeg Jets, 1996; Phoenix Coyotes, 1996–98; Tampa Bay Lightning, 1998–99; New York Islanders, 1999

In the 1988 Stanley Cup playoffs between the Boston Bruins and New Jersey Devils, it appeared the Devils would score a major upset, until Craig Janney delivered pivotal offense for the Bruins, helping to eliminate the underdog Devs.

After two years in NCAA hockey with Boston College (1985–87), Janney moved on to the Bigs of the same city, acquired by the Bruins in round one, 13th overall in the 1986 Entry Draft.

Although consistently productive, Janney also consistently produced *less* than several coaches would challenge Craig to do, throughout his career. A less-than-friendly relationship with the Fourth Estate didn't help Janney win friends and influence managers either. Still, the six-feet-one, 200-pound centerman played five years in Boston before moving to St. Louis during the 1991–92 season, where he recorded some of his best numbers.

In his first full season with the Blues, Janney reached 106 points in the regular season, an additional 11 in the playoffs. But this was followed by a steady decline in productivity as he bounced from San Jose to Winnipeg, to Tampa Bay, and finally the New York Islanders, from which he retired in 1999, leaving a 12-season pro career behind.

DOUG JARVIS

BORN: Peterborough, Ontario, March 24, 1955
POSITION: Center, Montreal Canadiens, 1975–82; Washington Capitals, 1982–85; Hartford Whalers, 1985–88; Assistant Coach, Minnesota North Stars, 1988–93; Dallas Stars, 1993–
AWARDS/HONORS: Frank J. Selke Trophy, 1984; Bill Masterton Memorial Trophy, 1987

The powerhouse Montreal Canadien teams of the late 1970s featured so many dynamic performers that a quiet, defensive specialist such as Doug Jarvis tended to be overlooked— except by his peers.

Doug Jarvis as a Capital

"If you underestimated him at all," said former NHL ace Peter McNab, "he'd kill you."

Jarvis was a key face-off man and excelled in corner skirmishes with much larger opponents, with 403 career points to show for a career that was beyond rock solid. Doug became hockey's modern Iron Man, setting a virtually unbreakable NHL record in 1987, after appearing in 962 consecutive games.

Jarvis played for the Canadiens through the 1981–82 season before moving on to the Washington Capitals. He was traded to the Hartford Whalers for Jorgen Petterson in 1985 and served as a player/assistant coach for the Whalers' Binghamton farm team until moving to coaching permanently. In 1988, he was hired as an assistant coach with the Minnesota North Stars, who later relocated to Dallas, and held the post into the millennium.

BILL JENNINGS

BORN: New York City, New York, December 16, 1920
DIED: August 17, 1981

William "Bill" Jennings emerged from total obscurity in the early 1960s as one of the most powerful National Hockey League bosses, as president of the New York Rangers.

An attorney for the New York firm of Simpson, Thatcher, and Bartlett, Jennings was leader of the NHL "Young Turks," a group of newer league governors who favored expansion. Jennings spearheaded the leap from six to 12 NHL teams in 1967 and became one of hockey's most influential leaders. He also was one of its most volatile. Following an especially rough game between the Rangers and Boston Bruins, Jennings demanded that a "bounty" be placed on the head of then Bruins' defenseman Ted Green. He later was reprimanded for the outburst by NHL president Clarence Campbell. Jennings was responsible for the creation of the Lester Patrick Trophy, awarded annually to the person who contributes to the growth of hockey in the United States, which he himself was awarded in 1971.

Jennings was also elected to the Hockey Hall of Fame in 1975. He was later honored with the creation of the William M. Jennings Trophy, which is awarded annually to the goaltender(s) having played a minimum of 25 games for the team with the fewest goals scored against it. He died on August 17, 1981.

CALLE JOHANSSON

BORN: Göteborg, Sweden, February 14, 1967
POSITION: Defenseman, Buffalo Sabres, 1987–89; Washington Capitals, 1989–
AWARDS/HONORS: NHL All-Rookie Team, 1988

Calle Johansson was one of two European players chosen in the first round in the 1985 Entry Draft, a far cry from today's talent-rich drafts filled with players from all over the world. He was picked 14th overall by Buffalo.

Johansson was a solid, all-around defenseman, and with an above-average shot he turned out to be the fifth player born and trained in Europe to play in 1,000 NHL games.

A 1989 trade with the Washington Capitals turned out to be a great fit for Johansson; he went on a five-game point streak to begin the Washington phase of his NHL career, becoming an indispensable member of the Capital blueline corps for years. The durable Johansson never played fewer than 65 games in any of his full seasons in Washington—until 2001-02—and played a steady, dependable brand of hockey for almost a dozen years in DC. Outside of Scott Stevens and Rod Langway, Johansson was probably the best two-way defenseman ever to wear a Capitals sweater.

He was a key cog in the Capitals' drive to the Stanley Cup finals in the 1998 playoffs with a career-high 15 goals in the regular season. The most tenured Capital in 2001-02, Calle suffered a torn rotator cuff in November, and following season-ending surgery, watched helplessly as the Caps missed the playoffs without him. He had already passed Stevens on the team's all-time lists for points (457) and assists (349) by defensemen, and was second on the all-time Caps games played list with 890.

BOB JOHNSON

BORN: Farmington, Michigan, November 12, 1948
DIED: November 26, 1991
POSITION: Coach, Calgary Flames, 1982-87; Pittsburgh Penguins, 1990-91

No American hockey figure had more impact on the game than Bob Johnson, alias Badger Bob, a name originally coined at the University of Wisconsin that carried over into Johnson's NHL coaching with Calgary and Pittsburgh.

Johnson's theme, "This is a great day for hockey," became a byword for stickhandlers worldwide.

Ebullient, insightful, and intense, Johnson established a keen rivalry with another American hockey icon, Herb Brooks, who coached at the University of Minnesota before turning to the big time.

In 15 seasons at the University of Wisconsin, Johnson finished every season but one with an over .500 record, while leading the Badgers to three National Championships in 1973, 1977, and 1981. He was named NCAA Coach of the Year at the conclusion of the 1977 season. He missed the 1975–76 season at Wisconsin, coaching the U.S. Hockey team.

In 1982, Johnson moved to the NHL with Calgary and served as head coach for five seasons, leading the Flames to their first Campbell Conference championship in 1986 and a berth in the Stanley Cup finals, before bowing to the legendary Montreal Canadiens.

After leaving Calgary, he spent three years as executive director of USA Hockey, in Colorado, where he supervised a period of unprecedented growth for amateur hockey efforts throughout the United States.

In the 1990–91 season, Johnson's first as coach of the Pittsburgh Penguins, he guided his team to heights they had previously only dreamed of in their 24-year history. The Pens captured the Patrick Division title, the Wales

Conference championship, and the coveted Stanley Cup. Johnson was only the second American-born coach to win the Cup, when his Penguins beat the Minnesota North Stars four games to two. He had a wealth of talent to work with, names like Mario Lemieux, Ron Francis, Tom Barrasso, Larry Murphy, Mark Recchi, Bryan Trottier, and a young budding prospect named Jaromir Jagr; and Johnson was the maestro who orchestrated them to the franchise's first of back-to-back Stanley Cup championships.

Late in the summer of 1991, Johnson was diagnosed with brain tumors, and had emergency surgery that night. Scotty Bowman, an advisor in the organization, was named interim coach. On November 26, 1991, Badger Bob had no more fight left in him. He passed away at his home in Colorado Springs, Colorado, much too early at the age of 60. In 1992, Badger Bob Johnson was inducted into the Penguins Hall of Fame as well as the NHL Hall of Fame.

CHING JOHNSON

BORN: Winnipeg, Manitoba, December 7, 1897
DIED: June 16, 1919
POSITION: Defenseman, New York Rangers, 1926–37; New York Americans, 1937–38
AWARDS/HONORS: NHL First Team All-Star, 1932, 1933; NHL Second Team All-Star, 1931, 1934; Hockey Hall of Fame, 1958

There have been few more colorful personalities in sport than Ivan Wilfred "Ching" Johnson, a bald defenseman who skated for the New York Rangers from their original NHL season, 1926–27, through the 1936–37 campaign. He ended his career a year later, skating for the New York Americans. Johnson was nicknamed "Ching" because he wore a wide grin on his face whenever he body-checked an enemy to the ice—which was often—and when he smiled his eyes gave him an Oriental look; therefore an expression used

in that era, Chink or Ching as in Ching-a-ling. Johnson became an instant hit on Broadway, along with his large defensive sidekick, Taffy Abel. Ching was a buddy of center Frank Boucher, who once described the Johnson style:

"Ching loved to deliver a good hoist early in a game because he knew his victim would probably retaliate, and Ching loved body contact. I remember once against the Maroons, Ching caught Hooley Smith with a terrific check right at the start of the game. Hooley's stick flew from his hands and disappeared above the rink lights. He was lifted clean off the ice, and seemed to stay suspended five or six feet above the surface for seconds before finally crashing down on his back. No one could accuse Hooley of lacking guts. From then on, whenever he got the puck, he drove straight for Ching, trying to outmatch him, but every time Ching flattened poor Hooley. Afterwards, grinning in the shower, Ching said he couldn't remember a game he'd enjoyed more."

Johnson lost his original partner after three seasons when Abel was traded to the Chicago Blackhawks. But manager Lester Patrick obtained blocky French-Canadian Leo Bourgault, who became an outstanding defensemate for Ching. Of the three, only Johnson is in hockey's Hall of Fame.

TOM JOHNSON

BORN: Baldur, Manitoba, February 18, 1928
POSITION: Defenseman, Montreal Canadiens, 1947–63; Boston Bruins, 1963–65; Coach, Boston Bruins, 1970–73
AWARDS/HONORS: James Norris Memorial Trophy, 1959; NHL First Team All-Star, 1959; NHL Second Team All-Star, 1956; Hockey Hall of Fame, 1970

When defenseman Tom Johnson was inducted into the Hockey Hall of Fame in June 1970, veteran Hall of Famer Eddie Shore reportedly was so upset that he demanded to buy back his own acceptance. Actually Johnson was an unobtrusive, effective defenseman who skated for six Stanley Cup winners with the Montreal Canadiens in 15 NHL years. Throughout his career, Johnson was overshadowed by the more capable Doug Harvey. Notorious as a dangerous man with his stick, Johnson was lowly regarded as a fighter and once was indicted, along with several players, by the Rangers' Andy Bathgate in an article in *True* magazine as a "spearer."

After his playing career, Johnson became an administrator with the Boston Bruins, coaching the Hub sextet in 1970–71 and 1971–72. "People said," Johnson once remarked, "that I showed no emotion on my face, although that's not quite true. I showed plenty when we won the Stanley Cup at Boston in 1972." A year later Johnson was replaced as coach—he reputedly was too relaxed with the players—by Armand "Bep" Guidolin and given a front office position which he held through the end of the twentieth century.

EDDIE JOHNSTON

BORN: Montreal, Quebec, November 24, 1935
POSITION: Goaltender, Boston Bruins, 1962–73; Toronto Maple Leafs, 1973–74; St. Louis Blues, 1974–78; Chicago Blackhawks, 1978; Coach, Chicago Blackhawks, 1979–80; Pittsburgh Penguins, 1980–83, 1993–97; General Manager, Pittsburgh Penguins, 1983–88; Hartford Whalers, 1989–92; Assistant General Manager, Pittsburgh Penguins, 1997–
AWARDS/HONORS: Team Canada, 1972

Eddie Johnston spent the first 11 years of his major-league career with the Boston Bruins, guiding them to two Stanley Cups.

E.J., who was always a popular player with the fans and his teammates, didn't adopt the ever-present goalie mask until late in his career, but it was for good reason. Johnston

suffered the most serious injury of his career during a 1967 pregame warm-up. The peerless Bobby Orr was bearing down on Eddie when suddenly, the bare-faced netminder averted his gaze for a deadly split second. In that instant, Orr snapped off a wicked shot that caught Eddie on the side of his head and knocked him unconscious.

"It knocked me down," Eddie recalled later. "I was in a hospital in Detroit for three days and then they flew me to Massachusetts General in Boston. My weight went from 194 to 155 in that first week. There was a blood clot at the back of my head. They kept taking me to the operating room in case the clot had moved and they had to drill a hole. They never had to, though. When I got back playing I put on a mask, you better believe it."

Very interested in a coaching career, E.J. remained with the Blackhawks' organization after he hung up the pads. He was assigned to coach their AHL entry in New Brunswick, where he had a fine freshman season. After a short but successful career in the minor leagues, Johnston was named to replace Bob Pulford as the mastermind behind the Chicago Blackhawk bench in 1979.

Eddie Johnston (left), Bruins goalie chatting with Bobby Orr

He became Penguins general manager shortly afterward, and held a vast array of posts with the Pens over the years, including scouting, while becoming their all-time winningest coach, garnering two division titles and drafting Mario Lemieux in 1984. Eddie also served as Hartford Whalers general manager from 1989 to 1992 before returning to Steel City, where he held an assistant general manager's post through 2001–02 and often would assist the Penguins coaching staff.

AUREL JOLIAT

BORN: Ottawa, Ontario, August 29, 1901
DIED: June 2, 1986
POSITION: Left Wing, Montreal Canadiens, 1922–38
AWARDS/HONORS: Hart Memorial Trophy, 1934; NHL First Team All-Star, 1931; NHL Second Team All-Star, 1931, 1934–35; Hockey Hall of Fame, 1945

Aurel Joliat was a native of Ontario, having grown up in the New Edinburgh district of Ottawa. He learned his hockey on the frozen Rideau River along with Bill and Frank Boucher, who also were to achieve enormous fame in the NHL. In time, Joliat graduated to a fast league in western Canada and arrived in a Canadiens uniform when manager Leo Dandurand decided to unload the aging Newsy Lalonde.

Aurel weighed 135 pounds at his heaviest and was five feet six, but his size never bothered him. It apparently motivated him to compensate with a vast repertoire of stickhandling maneuvers and pirouettes. "He transported the world of ballet to the hockey arena," said one admirer. To which Aurel replied, "A fellow needs finesse when he weighs only 135 pounds!"

Joliat teamed up with Howie Morenz in the 1923–24 season. The pair jelled perfectly right from the start, although Aurel was to prove

that season that he could excel with or without Morenz at his side. The Canadiens had gone up against Calgary in the playoffs and Morenz's shoulder was broken after he was hit successively by Red Dutton and Herb Gardiner. That's when Aurel took over. He intercepted an enemy pass in the third period and circled his own net to gain momentum.

"I traveled through the entire Calgary team," said Joliat, "and faked a shot to the far corner of the net. But even as I let it go I sensed I was covered on the play. So I kept going, rounded the net, and backhanded a shot into the open corner. I tumbled head over heels after that one. We went on to win the Cup and I consider it the best goal I ever scored."

Joliat was a constant source of annoyance to his larger opponents. Once, after Aurel had thoroughly confounded Toronto's Babe Dye with a series of fakes, the distressed Dye skated over to Dandurand at the Canadiens' bench and said: "I'm tired of chasing that shadow of yours, that Frenchman, Joliat. Move him over to center, Leo, hold a mirror to each side of him—you'll have the fastest line in hockey."

Aurel Joliat, an early Montreal hero

KENNY JONSSON

BORN: Angelholm, Sweden, October 6, 1974
POSITION: Defense, Toronto Maple Leafs, 1994–96; New York Islanders, 1996–
AWARDS: NHL All-Star Rookie Team, 1995

Highly regarded when he broke in with the Toronto Maple Leafs in the 1994–95 season, Kenny Jonsson became an even better player when he was dealt to the Islanders on March 13, 1996.

Despite playing for a mediocre Islanders team, of which he was briefly captain, Jonsson remained one of the club's premiere players. And as the Islanders grew stronger in 2001–02, so did Ken.

A member of the gold medal–winning Swedish Olympic team in Lillehammer in 1994, Jonsson was traded to the Islanders along with Sean Haggerty, Darby Hendrickson, and Toronto's 1997 first-round draft pick for Wendel Clark, Mathieu Schneider, and D. J. Smith. The Islanders claimed that the Swedish defenseman had all the makings of a Norris Trophy winner, as Kenny led a "Fab Four" of young stud backliners that the Islanders wanted to build around, including Bryan McCabe, Bryan Berard, and Scott Lachance. Within two and a half seasons, all were traded, except Jonsson.

After suffering through constant trade rumors, myriad teammates that came and went, injuries and concussions, as well as having been one of the only bright spots on a mismanaged team, Jonsson persevered as one of the cleanest, smartest defenseman in the National Hockey League. Even though Kenny was named captain for the league-worst Butch Goring–coached club in 2000–01, he relinquished the responsibility after struggling with his own game. Frequent concussions also became a problem for Jonsson, although he constantly rebounded in mint condition.

With new owners Charles Wang and Sanjay Kumar bringing stability and leadership to the franchise in the form of Michael Peca, Chris Osgood, and Alexei Yashin, Kenny's game was revitalized in 2001–02. His ability to make quick, safe decisions in his own end to smooth down dangerous situations, as well as play the point on the power play, were more appreciated in the limelight of the Islanders' resurgence, of which he was a crucial element along with fellow tenured veterans Steve Webb and Claude Lapointe.

The six-feet-three Jonsson was paired with Adrian Aucoin as the Isles' top duo on the blueline with both logging between 30 and 40 minutes per game. With 32 points in 76 games and a plus-15 rating, Kenny enjoyed his best season since 1997–98, when he played a full season and had 14 goals and 26 assists for 40 points.

CURTIS JOSEPH

BORN: Keswick, Ontario, April 29, 1967
POSITION: Goaltender, St. Louis Blues, 1989–95; Edmonton Oilers, 1995–98; Toronto Maple Leafs, 1998–2002; Detroit Red Wings, 2002–
AWARDS/HONORS: King Clancy Memorial Trophy, 2000; NHL All-Star Game, 1994, 2000

Curtis Joseph was one of the most dominating goaltenders in the NHL, anchoring the Maple Leafs' success in the late 1990s, while posting low goals-against averages of close to 2.50 while playing for an offensive-minded team.

He also piled up over 30 wins five times in his career, and did so for three straight seasons beginning with 1998–99. By 2001–02, "Cujo" also had 44 career shutouts, with 12 coming during the playoffs, including back-to-back shutouts of the Ottawa Senators in the first round of the 2000–01 playoffs. Joseph also served as a goalie on Canada's 2002 Olympic team.

Playing deep in the net and relying on lightning reflexes, Joseph had been the guiding force for the Toronto Maple Leafs after they picked up the free agent in 1998 after his heroic tenure in Edmonton, where his timely saves helped Edmonton upset the league-best Dallas Stars in the first round of the 1997–98 Stanley Cup playoffs. He originally evolved as the St. Louis Blues' main netminder, beginning in 1989–90, and posted a 36-win season in 1993–94 before Edmonton acquired him, along with Mike Grier, for two first-round draft choices.

Upon coming to the Leafs in 1998, Joseph displaced former star Felix Potvin as the number one stopper, and allowed the Leafs to flourish into the new century. In the 2001–02 season, Cujo and the Leafs survived two seven-game series in the postseason, battering their way past the Islanders and the Senators before losing to the Cinderella team of 2002, the Carolina Hurricanes. Following the 2001–02 season, Joseph became a free agent and signed a long-term contract with the Detroit Red Wings.

ED JOVANOVSKI

BORN: Windsor, Ontario, June 26, 1976
POSITION: Defenseman, Florida Panthers, 1995–99; Vancouver Canucks, 1999–
AWARDS/HONORS: NHL All-Rookie Team, 1996; NHL All-Star Game, 2001–02

In an era when outstanding defensemen such as Raymond Bourque, Brian Leetch, and Scott Stevens were at the top of their games, another potential blueline star entered the majors.

Ed Jovanovski appeared to have all the credentials for greatness as a teenager, and that's why the Florida Panthers drafted him in the first round, first overall.

He was mean, he could carry the puck, and he was equally adept in his own zone as well as on the attack. His career sputtered at first but finally bloomed after he was traded to Vancouver.

The six-feet-one, 210-pound defenseman didn't start playing hockey until the age of 11, and started his career for three years with Windsor. When he went to the Panthers, he was named to the NHL All-Rookie Team in 1995–96, and the following season he tied third among Panthers defensemen in scoring.

When he was dealt to Vancouver in 1998 as part of the Pavel Bure deal, he set career highs in points (27) and assists (22), which rose in the following years, to win him the assistant captain spot in October 2000.

He also notched an assist in his first NHL All-Star game in 2000 and was named to the Canadian team in the 2002 Winter Olympics. Though he didn't have the highest numbers in the league, he was an exceptional defenseman whose growing confidence and savage physical play resulted in nearly doubling his point total in 2000–01 with 47.

Ed helped lead the Canucks to a stellar second half during the 2001–02 season, in which they made the playoffs in the last week of the schedule after a horrendous start.

ALEX KALETA

BORN: Canmore, Alberta, November 29, 1919
DIED: July 9, 1987
POSITION: Left Wing, Chicago Blackhawks, 1941–48; New York Rangers, 1948–51

A flamboyant skater who could have inspired the line "much ado about nothing," Alex Kaleta launched his big-league career with the Blackhawks in 1941–42. After a stint in the Canadian Armed Forces, Kaleta returned to the NHL in 1945–46 with Chicago, where he remained until 1948–49 when he was traded to the Rangers.

Blueshirts public relations honcho Stan Saplin immediately dubbed Kaleta "Killer"— mainly because he was exactly the opposite; in fact, Alex would harm neither beast, man, nor enemy hockey player. But New York fans immediately took him to their collective hearts, despite his peaceful nature, joyfully shouting KILLER! KILLER! each time Kaleta took to the ice. Alex's last NHL season was 1950–51, with the Rangers.

BINGO KAMPMAN

BORN: Kitchener, Ontario, March 12, 1914
DIED: December 22, 1987
POSITION: Defenseman, Toronto Maple Leafs, 1937–42

Not many NHL defensemen were better nicknamed than Rudolph Kampman, who played for the Toronto Maple Leafs from 1937–38 through 1941–42, when the Leafs captured the Stanley Cup. When Kampman bodychecked an opponent, a "bingo" resounded off the rafters; and for good reason. Kampman was built along the generous dimensions of a Clydesdale stallion and offered various ways of demonstrating his Herculean powers. Off the ice, one of his favorite routines was lifting a heavy table by clenching its top in his teeth.

PAUL KARIYA

BORN: Vancouver, British Columbia, October 16, 1974
POSITION: Left Wing, Anaheim Mighty Ducks, 1994–
AWARDS/HONORS: Lady Byng Memorial Trophy, 1996–97; NHL All-Rookie Team, 1995; NHL First Team All-Star, 1996–97, 1999; NHL Second Team All-Star, 2000; NHL All-Star Game, 1996–97, 1999–2000

When the National Hockey League sought a marquee successor to Wayne Gretzky, they hoped to find a gifted skater with exceptional playmaking abilities, who embodied Gretzky's clean play and who was also at home with the media.

The obvious choice was Paul Kariya. From the very beginning, the native of British Columbia epitomized the Lady Byng Trophy style of play that had been Gretzky's trademark.

Unfortunately, the lithe stickhandler never reached the Gretzky level, but his total play was good enough to put the Anaheim Mighty Ducks franchise on the map and turn it into an instant success at the box office.

Kariya already was a household name in hockey circles before he graduated to the NHL. He played college hockey from 1992–94 at the University of Maine, which he attended on a hockey scholarship, along with two brothers. During that time, he became the first freshman ever to win the Hobey Baker Award and set countless records on the team, which won the NCAA championship in 1992–93. He also led Team Canada in scoring at the 1994 Olympics in Lillehammer, which ended in a heartstopping shoot-out session that saw Paul, Canada's last shooter, get stonewalled by Swedish goalie Tommy Salo as Canada settled for the silver medal.

Undoubtedly, if the 1993 NHL Entry Draft had to be redone, the Ottawa Senators—or any team, for that matter—would have taken the electrifying Kariya with the first pick, which was used on disappointing Alexandre Daigle. Ultimately, Kariya's career points would exceed, by far, those of any other first-rounder in that stellar draft year, which included Jason Allison, Saku Koivu, Chris Pronger, Adam Deadmarsh, and Jason Arnott, to name a few.

Breaking into the NHL in 1994–95, Paul scored a team-high 39 points in 47 games, and was a finalist for the Calder Trophy. His second season yielded 108 points, a Lady Byng Trophy, a First Team All-Star selection, and an inseparable linemate in Teemu Selanne, who arrived in a February 1996 trade. The dynamic duo formed a partnership on the Ducks' top line that would carry the team, in every sense, through the rest of the 1990s.

Kariya, at age 21, was named captain of the franchise in 1996–97, and led the Ducks to their only playoff-round victory, a seven-game triumph over the Phoenix Coyotes. But a lingering concussion, resulting from a Gary Suter cross-check, limited Kariya to 22 games in the subsequent season, leaving linemate Selanne, and precious little else, to return to a playoff berth. Kariya returned for an 82-game, 101-point masterpiece in 1998–99, but the Mighty Ducks were swept in four by Detroit to open the postseason.

Possessing unfathomable speed, Gretzky-like stickhandling skills, and a backhand shot practiced and executed to a rare accuracy, Kariya had the misfortune of thriving in a franchise too bereft of talent to complement his abilities and win meaningfully. Other than Selanne, whose trade to San Jose in 2000 deflated Kariya and the team, the Disney-backed Ducks did not draft, nor spend, nor trade well enough to build a supportive team around Kariya.

Perennially averaging over a point-per-game, the young veteran found team success on the gold medal–winning Team Canada at the 2002 Olympics at Salt Lake. With a goal in the medal–winning game, while playing on a dream line with Mario Lemieux and Joe Sakic, Kariya salvaged an otherwise dismal year with Anaheim, which finished last again. The franchise may have gotten a boost, however, when coach Bryan Murray was promoted to general manager in May 2002.

ALEXEI KASATONOV

BORN: Leningrad, USSR, October 14, 1959
POSITION: Defenseman, SKA Leningrad, 1976–78; Soviet World Junior Team, 1977–79; Central Red Army, 1978–90, 1994, 1996–97; Soviet National Team, 1979–89; New Jersey Devils, 1990–93; Anaheim Mighty Ducks, 1993–94; St. Louis Blues, 1994; Boston Bruins, 1994–96
AWARDS/HONORS: Best Defenseman WJC-A, 1979; USSR All-Star, 1981–88; WEC-A All-Star, 1982–83, 1985–86, 1991; Best Defenseman WEC-A, 1983; NHL All-Star Game, 1994

The New Jersey Devils broke the Iron Curtain barrier by signing Soviet star-defenseman Slava Fetisov in 1989. Another Russian blueline star, Alexei Kasatonov, followed right behind, signing with New Jersey later in the 1989 season.

Although Kasatonov and Fetisov had been teammates in Russia, they suffered a philosophical split when Kasatonov came to the Devils and neither spoke to the other off the ice throughout their years with the Devils. On the ice, however, they worked well together. The taller Kasatonov played a heady, two-way game and never was intimidated by the NHL scene.

In 1990–91, Kasatonov had his NHL career-high 41 points for the Devils, which reflected his typical output while playing for CSKA Moscow.

He remained a Devil until the Mighty Ducks of Anaheim selected him in the 1993 expansion draft; he was later shipped to St. Louis at the trade deadline that year. In 1994, he joined the Boston Bruins before returning to play in Moscow in the 1996–97 season.

DARIUS KASPARAITIS

BORN: Elektrenai, USSR, October 16, 1972
POSITION: Left Defenseman, New York Islanders, 1992–96; Pittsburgh Penguins, 1996–2002; Colorado Avalanche, 2002; New York Rangers, 2002–

If ever there was a throwback defenseman to the bodychecking backliners of the '30s and '40s, the blocking Lithuanian was that man. Darius Kasparaitis was a first-round pick of the New York Islanders in 1992, and made an immediate impact on the National Hockey League with his exuberance as well as his bodychecking ability.

Only five feet eleven, 205 pounds, Kasparaitis mastered the open-ice check as well as any player in the last half century. As an Islanders rookie, he took special delight in lining up the enemy's top scorers, such as Mario Lemieux, Eric Lindros, and Mark Messier, for his patented hits.

Opposition critics sometimes claimed Darius's hits were somewhat to the left of legal. But Kasper remained undaunted and in the process became the most popular player on the Cinderella Islanders team of 1992–93. Despite language limitations, Kasparaitis was also a hit in the locker room, both for his hits on the ice and his lust for life.

During Game Six of the 1992–93 playoffs against the high-flying Penguins, the score was tied 4–4 late in the second period. After getting cross-checked to the ice by Lemieux, Kasparaitis threw a right cross to Mario's chin and "Le Magnifique" crumpled to the ice as though shot. When Lemieux grabbed Darius's stick, the defenseman punched him again.

A few moments later, as Lemieux approached him from behind, Kasparaitis threw a wild elbow that missed. Finally, he ran Lemieux behind the net and drew a roughing penalty. The Islanders won the game 7–5 and went on to the Conference championships, which they lost.

Darius played with the Isles for five years before getting traded to Pittsburgh, to team with former enemy Lemieux. By the 2000–01 season, he would be ranked third among Penguins defensemen in points and lead the team in hits and blocked shots. His hard-hitting defensive plays may have been controversial, but they truly did pay off, and once in a while, Darius would score a goal—none of which were bigger than the Game Seven overtime blast that beat Dominik Hasek and the Buffalo Sabres in round two of the 2001 Stanley Cup playoffs.

With the Penguins battered and financially strapped in 2001–02, Kasper, the subject of yearlong trade rumors, was finally traded to the Colorado Avalanche in March 2002 in time for the Avs' futile drive to repeat as Cup champions. Following the 2001–02 season, Darius became a free agent. He then signed a lucrative contract with the New York Rangers.

DUKE KEATS

BORN: Montreal, Quebec, March 1, 1895
DIED: January 16, 1971
POSITION: Center, Toronto Arenas (NHAO), 1916–17; Edmonton Eskimos (WCHL), 1922–26; Boston Bruins, 1926–27; Detroit Cougars, 1927–28; Chicago Blackhawks, 1929
AWARDS/HONORS: Hockey Hall of Fame, 1958

Quick-witted Duke Keats was one of hockey's first bonafide superstars, yet he will always be recalled as the fellow who almost played for two teams at once! At the mere age of 16, Keats came to Toronto to play for the Arenas. He also enlisted in the 228th Sportmen's Battalion, which iced a team in the NHA in 1916–17.

"Instead of playing for the Battalion," recalled Babe Donnelly, ex-defenseman, "Keats decided it would be more profitable to skate for the Arenas. After all, they were paying him a salary; the Battalion boys were playing for nothing."

Keats was thrown into the guardhouse for his sins, but the Battalion released him on the night of a game, since the Toronto newspapers had printed Duke's whereabouts. The Battalion, fearing a rabid reaction from the fans who expected to see their star, gave him "endless latrine duty" instead, according to Donnelly.

While with the Toronto team, Keats centered for the Denneny brothers, Corbett and Cy, and Frank Patrick recalled seeing him make "thirty perfect passes to his wingmates one night."

After the 228th Battalion returned from World War I, Duke joined Edmonton of the WCHL, captaining the Eskimo team for five seasons and leading them in scoring. After guiding the Eskimos to a league championship in 1923, Keats finished his playing days in three seasons, joining Boston, Chicago, and Detroit for one campaign each.

Gordon "Duke" Keats, an early NHL star

BUTCH KEELING

BORN: Owen Sound, Ontario, August 10, 1905
DIED: Unknown
POSITION: Left Wing, Toronto Maple Leafs, 1926–28; New York Rangers, 1928–38; Referee (NHL), 1947–50

There have been few sturdier forwards in the NHL than Melville Sidney "Butch" Keeling. Although his NHL career began in 1926–27 with the Toronto Maple Leafs, Butch spent only two years there. In 1928–29, he was dealt to the Rangers, where he played continuously through the 1937–38 season. Butch later became an NHL referee and remained one of the most likeable men in hockey.

Despite his many exploits on ice for the Rangers, Keeling is most affectionately remembered for an incident that took place on the club's Pullman car in the early 1930s, following a game in Ottawa. The Rangers won the game, 9–1, and were to return to the Pullman that was parked on a siding at Ottawa terminal.

Keeling and his teammates realized that manager-coach Lester Patrick had expected them back on the Pullman shortly after the match, but the Rangers stumbled in after a party which lasted until 3 A.M. Their leader, Frank Boucher, warned them to avoid waking Patrick at all costs, or they would face fines for their tardiness.

However, the well-juiced Keeling, in his haste to find a urinal, stumbled into Patrick's compartment wearing only an undershirt that barely reached his navel. "Butch put his finger to his lips," Lester recalled, "and said, 'Shhh, don't wake Lester!'"

Keeling was always revered on Broadway for assisting on Bill Cook's sudden-death goal in 1933 that won the Rangers their second Stanley Cup.

MIKE KEENAN

BORN: Toronto, Ontario, October 21, 1949
POSITION: Coach, Philadelphia Flyers, 1984–88; Chicago Blackhawks, 1988–92; Coach/General Manager, Chicago Blackhawks, 1990–92; Coach, New York Rangers, 1993–94; Coach/General Manager, St. Louis Blues, 1994–97; Coach, Vancouver Canucks, 1997–98; General Manager, Vancouver Canucks, 1998–99; Coach, Boston Bruins, 2000–01; Coach/Assistant General Manager, Florida Panthers, 2001–
AWARDS/HONORS: Jack Adams Award, 1985

The always-controversial Mike Keenan took command of a 1993–94 New York Ranger club that had dismally finished out of a playoff berth the year before, and hadn't won a Stanley Cup in 54 years. With an intensity rarely matched in New York coaching circles, Iron Mike guided his Rangers to first place and kept them there throughout the season en route to a magical drought-ending Stanley Cup victory.

Mike Keenan

Keenan experienced the Stanley Cup finals early on as a rookie coach with the President's Trophy–winning Philadelphia Flyers in 1984–85, riding the heroics of fellow first-timer, goaltender Ron Hextall. He was fired after losing the 1987 Stanley Cup finals to Edmonton, in the seventh game.

Mike was soon tapped by Chicago, however. In the Windy City, Keenan resumed his winning ways, guiding the Hawks to the Conference finals in 1989 and 1990, and quenching a thirst for power by assuming the team's general manager duties before visiting the Cup finals—again unsuccessfully—in 1992. His disciplinarian's reputation and fear-inducing motivational tactics had become legendary in his short tenures, and may have helped wear out his welcome with the Blackhawks despite his excellent record.

"It's either you're winning or you're losing," said Mike, "it's not whether you won or lost. If you're winning, that means you're teaching and there is a learning curve being developed. Sometimes you learn valuable lessons in losses. You have to be able to accept the loss in light of the fact you may have learned a big deal."

But the championship-famined New York Rangers, with the likes of the battle-tested Mark Messier up front and steady Brian Leetch on the blueline and Mike Richter in the net, emerged as the perfect nest of potential accomplishment—and control—for the mercurial Keenan.

"I like to be the favorite. I enjoy the pressure," proclaimed Keenan in response to the *Hockey News*'s prediction of a Ranger Cup victory. "I'm at my best under pressure."

In March 1994, with the Rangers in sight of the President's Trophy and cruising under his command, coach Keenan demanded that his general manager Neil Smith trade for size. Smith obliged by dealing Mike Gartner and Tony Amonte and obtaining bigger, better checkers, Brian Noonan, Stephane Matteau, and Craig MacTavish.

The Rangers steamrolled through the Islanders in four and Washington in five before winning a grueling Conference final against the Devils in double overtime of Game Seven on Matteau's wraparound goal.

New York was expected to rout mediocre Vancouver in the Cup finals. Leading three games to one, Keenan's Rangers lost the possible clinching Game Five at the Garden and Game Six in Vancouver.

Despite an early lead, New York almost blew Game Seven. A bad penalty call against Vancouver and a hit goal post in the third period enabled the Rangers to escape with a one-goal win. Manhattan went berserk as their hockey club ended its 54-year drought.

But no sooner had the champagne lost its fizz than the bad blood began flowing. Claiming the Rangers were late with a bonus check, Keenan declared himself a free agent and added he was exploring other opportunities. After declining a Detroit Red Wings offer, Keenan met with the St. Louis high command and accepted their offer to be general manager and coach for six years, at $2 million a year.

After the Rangers filed suit against Keenan, deals were made to assuage both parties, fines were levied against the participants, and conspiracy theories abounded concerning the resolution to the power struggle between Iron Mike and Neil Smith. St. Louis, however, was only too happy to receive Keenan, as they hungered for long-overdue playoff success as much as the Rangers did.

Keenan mentored the Blues to their third-best record in club history the following year, while predictably ruffling the wings of "The Golden" Brett Hull, the Blues captain, and later on, Wayne Gretzky, who was dramatically dealt to St. Louis at the trade deadline before his free-agent year. He also irked fans by trading crowd favorite Brendan Shanahan for Chris Pronger. By 1997–98, Keenan was leading yet another team, the Vancouver Canucks. There, he promptly alienated fans by shipping long-time captain Trevor Linden, for Todd Bertuzzi and Bryan McCabe. His team faltered again, despite the presence of old ally Mark Messier, who had left the Rangers in the summer of 1997, opting to lead the Keenan-powered Canucks. Keenan was axed again, since the team hadn't managed to win in the playoffs.

After a few stints as an on-line columnist for the *Sporting News,* Iron Mike was hired by the Boston Bruins in the early stages of the 2000–01 season to take over from Pat Burns, but they failed to re-sign him after the B's skidded, missing the playoffs in the second to last game of the season.

But once again, a faltering team looked to the steely Keenan for resurgence in the fall of 2001, as the Florida Panthers hired Keenan as coach. By 2002–03, Keenan was firmly in charge of the team along with general manager Rick Dudley.

RED KELLY

BORN: Simcoe, Ontario, July 9, 1927
POSITION: Defenseman, Detroit Red Wings, 1947–59; Toronto Maple Leafs, 1959–67; Coach, Los Angeles Kings, 1967–69; Pittsburgh Penguins, 1970–73; Toronto Maple Leafs, 1973–77
AWARDS/HONORS: James Norris Memorial Trophy, 1954; Lady Byng Memorial Trophy, 1951, 1953–54, 1961; NHL First Team All-Star, 1951–55, 1957; NHL Second Team All-Star, 1950, 1956; NHL All-Star Game, 1950–58, 1960–63; Hockey Hall of Fame, 1969

Leonard Patrick "Red" Kelly was perhaps the most deceptively versatile player ever to don the red-and-white Detroit Red Wings jersey.

So mild-mannered that he never uttered a curse word, Kelly nevertheless was one of the National Hockey League's most feared fighters.

Leonard "Red" Kelly as a Red Wing

Likewise, he was a nonpareil defenseman, yet could carry the puck on attack better than most of the foremost forwards. Half his career was spent as an All-Star backline; the other half as a commanding center. An NHL hockey player just doesn't come more versatile than that.

One also could make a solid case that the Redhead was the finest Detroit blueliner of the pre-Expansion era and perhaps the best of them all. In a sense, Kelly also was a revolutionary.

Through the first half-century of hockey history, defensemen were expected to defend and defend only. Goaltenders were paid to stop the puck while forwards had a target of their own: Score goals. Few defensemen ever broke the tradition. One who did was Eddie Shore, the immortal Boston Bruin backliner who developed the end-to-end rush during the late '20s and '30s.

Like Shore before him, Kelly was as proficient at rushing the puck as he was at protecting his own end. Kelly was the first modern backliner to carry the rubber deep into the enemy zone. Kelly was every bit as smooth a rushing defenseman as Orr and better as a defensive defenseman. What better proof than the fact that Red skated for eight championship squads and four Stanley Cup winners in Detroit, won the Lady Byng Trophy for competence combined with gentlemanly play four times, and was a First Team All-Star six times.

In 1959, after more than 12 seasons and four Stanley Cups as a Red Wing, Kelly was dealt to the Toronto Maple Leafs by the Detroit high command, who estimated that Red was washed up. The Leafs, on the other hand, were being rejuvenated by general manager George "Punch" Imlach. Punch didn't think Kelly was through, by a long shot.

The night of February 10, 1960, proved to be a milestone in Red's life and in the life of the Maple Leafs. He donned the royal-blue-and-white Toronto jersey and was presented with the same number 4 he had worn in Detroit.

Imlach, the innovator, was not certain precisely how he would exploit Kelly's talents, but he knew for sure that he would at least experiment with him at center, although Red had been a defenseman all his life. The Leafs' opponents that night were the Montreal Canadiens, already winners of four straight Stanley Cups and, perhaps, the greatest team of all time.

"I want you to go up against [Jean] Beliveau," said Imlach. The tall, majestic Beliveau was merely the best center in the league. Kelly skated to center ice, lined up opposite Beliveau and waited for the referee to drop the puck for

the opening face-off. "I was as nervous as a rookie," said Kelly. "I won the draw and sent the puck straight into the Montreal zone. The Canadiens' goalie, Jacques Plante, darted out to intercept the puck before I got there. I came right down like a shot and somehow got tangled up and went head over heels—into the net!"

Although the Leafs lost the game, 4–2, Imlach knew his instincts had been accurate: Red would be more valuable to him as a center than as a defenseman. Never has the game known a more brilliant brainstorm. The next question was, with whom should Kelly play?

Imlach had a huge, brooding young left wing named Frank "The Big M" Mahovlich, who could skate like a zephyr and fired the puck with the fury of a howitzer. But The Big M's power had not yet been harnessed, no doubt for want of a competent center. The Leafs also possessed Bob Nevin, an unobtrusive right wing but one who excelled at all of a forward's basic skills. Imlach decided to unite Kelly with Mahovlich and Nevin.

From that point on, the Maple Leafs' troubles were over. With Kelly ladling the passes to The Big M and Nevin, the Maple Leafs won four Stanley Cups in the seven and a half years Red performed in Toronto.

Even more astonishing is the fact that Kelly was able to maintain his standard of playing excellence in Toronto while serving a term as a member of Canada's Parliament!

Kelly finally retired as a player after the Maple Leafs' stunning 1967 Cup win and accepted the coaching post for the fledgling Los Angeles Kings. After two seasons with LA, the redhead moved on to serve as coach and general manager of the Pittsburgh Penguins.

In 1973, John McLellan was forced out as coach of the Maple Leafs and Kelly stepped in, leading the young team into a playoff berth.

Crusty Leaf owner Harold Ballard complained at length, and often in public, that Kelly was too nice a guy, and Roger Neilson replaced Red behind the bench in 1977.

Low-key throughout his hockey and political careers, Kelly remained the most underrated superstar to come down the pike, yet his dossier cannot be disputed. He was the balance wheel of champions as a defenseman in Detroit, and as a center, the most decisive factor in creating a dynasty in Toronto more than a decade later.

No other NHL hockey player can make that statement, which is why Red Kelly lives in the annals of the Detroit Red Wings and Toronto Maple Leafs.

TED KENNEDY

BORN: Humberstone, Ontario, December 12, 1925
POSITION: Center, Toronto Maple Leafs, 1942–56
AWARDS/HONORS: Hart Memorial Trophy, 1955; NHL Second Team All-Star, 1950–51, 1954; NHL All-Star Game, 1947–51, 1954; Hockey Hall of Fame, 1966

One of the most tenacious forecheckers in modern hockey, Ted "Teeder" Kennedy became captain of the Toronto Maple Leafs in 1948 upon the retirement of Syl Apps. Kennedy centered the second Toronto Kid Line (the first featured Charlie Conacher, Joe

Ted "Teeder" Kennedy as Toronto captain

Primeau, and Harvey Jackson in the early 1930s), with Howie Meeker and Vic Lynn. Kennedy not only made the most of limited abilities (he was a notoriously poor skater), but had tremendous leadership qualities and, as captain, led the Leafs to Stanley Cup wins in 1949 and 1951.

As a face-off man, he was peerless. "Kennedy," Philadelphia Flyers coach Fred Shero once said, "seldom lost an important face-off and was never beaten. I remember one night when I was playing for the Rangers. We had the Leafs, 2–1, with less than a minute to play and the face-off was in our zone. Edgar Laprade, our center, said: 'I don't want to face that Kennedy in this spot, you take him.' I did, Kennedy won the face-off, and hit the goal post. I turned to Edgar and said: 'Like I told you, it was a cinch. I knew Kennedy would hit the post.'" Few opponents ever were so sure, or so successful against Teeder Kennedy.

DAVE KEON

BORN: Noranda, Quebec, March 22, 1940
POSITION: Center, Toronto Maple Leafs, 1960–75; Minnesota Fighting Saints (WHA), 1975–76, 1976–77; Indianapolis Roadrunners (WHA), 1976; New England Whalers (WHA), 1977–79; Hartford Whalers, 1979–82
AWARDS/HONORS: Calder Memorial Trophy, 1961; Lady Byng Memorial Trophy, 1962–63; Conn Smythe Trophy, 1967; NHL Second Team All-Star, 1962, 1971; NHL All-Star Game, 1962–64, 1967–71, 1973; Hockey Hall of Fame, 1986

Dave Keon, the hardworking leprechaun, joined the Toronto sextet in 1960 directly from the St. Michael's College junior club. The rookie scored 20 goals in his maiden campaign, no small accomplishment in pre-Expansion days, and was awarded the Calder Trophy as the NHL's rookie of the year.

Combining diligent, two-way hockey with gentlemanly play, Keon twice won the Lady Byng Trophy and in 1967 was named the recipient of the Conn Smythe Trophy as the most valuable performer in the Cup playoffs.

Keon was lured to the WHA in 1975, first playing with the Minnesota Fighting Saints, then the Indianapolis Roadrunners, and finally settling down with the New England Whalers, where he twice won the league's "Most Gentlemanly Player" award.

Keon retired after the 1982 season with Hartford. Although he was one of the most popular Toronto players of all time with his 365 goals—second only to Darryl Sittler on the all-time Leafs goal-scoring list—Keon became estranged from the Leafs organization because of a dispute with the high command. It was not until the late 1990s that Keon was seen again at hockey functions in the Toronto area. Meanwhile, his son David Jr. had become an NHL employee, and by the 2001–02 season was working as manager of public relations for the league.

DAVEY KERR

BORN: Toronto, Ontario, January 11, 1910
DIED: May 12, 1978
POSITION: Goaltender, Montreal Maroons, 1930–31, 1932–34; New York Americans, 1931–32; New York Rangers, 1934–41
AWARDS/HONORS: Vezina Trophy, 1940; NHL First Team All-Star, 1940; NHL Second Team All-Star, 1938

Davey Kerr gained fame when he joined the Rangers in 1934 and became one of the NHL's finest goaltenders until his retirement after the 1940–41 season.

Kerr won the Vezina Trophy in 1940 when the Rangers won the Stanley Cup for the third time in franchise history. Agile as a ballet dancer, Kerr could do a split with one skate firmly anchored against one goal post and the other skate stretching right across the goalmouth to the other post.

One of Davey's favorite practice maneuvers was to lay his stick across the goalmouth in front of the goal line. Then, he'd prop his left skate against the right post, thus spread-eagling his body across much of the net. This would leave his two hands free to catch the puck, and his stick to deflect pucks along the ice. Kerr then would dare his teammates to beat him. According to center Frank Boucher, they never did. Boucher, who later coached the Rangers, studied the goalie's style carefully, both on and off the ice, and once offered this analysis of the NHL ace:

"Kerr was gifted with an excellent right hand that picked off shots like Bill Terry playing first base for the Giants. He was deliberate and methodical in everything he did. Davey retired long before his time, when he was at his peak and only thirty years old. In a commanding way, Davey was able to shout at his defensemen, giving them guidance without offending them, and getting them to do the job he wanted done in front of him, talking continually when the puck was in our end. I don't ever remember Dave accusing a defense player for a mistake when a goal was scored against him. He always assumed the blame."

TIM KERR

BORN: Windsor, Ontario, January 5, 1960
POSITION: Center, Philadelphia Flyers, 1980–91; New York Rangers, 1991–92; Hartford Whalers, 1992–93
AWARDS/HONORS: Bill Masterton Memorial Trophy, 1989; NHL Second Team All-Star, 1987; NHL All-Star Game, 1984–86

In many ways, the resemblance between Hall of Famer Jean Beliveau—one of the legendary Montreal Canadiens aces—and Tim Kerr was striking. Beliveau was physically huge at the time he performed in the National Hockey League but less than physically intimidating in terms of aggressive play. Ditto for the six-feet-three, 230-pound Flyer. Kerr could, and would, get angry from time to time, but those occasions were the exception rather than the rule. And the rest of the NHL was pleased about that state of affairs.

As it happened, the rest of the NHL was in big trouble because of Kerr's scoring proclivities. In 1983–84 and 1984–85, Kerr nabbed a remarkable 54 goals, but could he do it again? Tim continued his prolific ways by setting off the opponent's red light 58 times in 1985–86, then duplicated that total the next season.

Kerr starred for Flyers clubs that reached the Stanley Cup finals in 1985 and 1987, scoring 14 points in 1985, and 13 points in 1987. In 1988–89, when he won the Masterton Trophy, Kerr garnered 25 points in 19 playoff games, yet never brought the Stanley Cup to the City of Brotherly Love.

Kerr's production began slipping in 1990–91 and he was claimed by San Jose, then dealt to the Rangers. He played 32 games for New York, scoring only seven goals and eleven assists. He managed only one goal in eight playoff games. The Rangers traded him to Hartford in July 1992 for future considerations. He collected six assists in 22 games for the Whalers but not a single goal. Tim retired after that season.

NIKOLAI KHABIBULIN

BORN: Sverdlovsk, USSR, January 13, 1973
POSITION: Goaltender, Winnipeg Jets, 1994–96; Phoenix Coyotes, 1996–99; Tampa Bay Lightning, 2001–
AWARDS/HONORS: NHL All-Star Game, 1998–99

Nikolai Khabibulin was one of the great young goaltenders in the NHL at the end of the twentieth century and into the new millennium.

Prone to delivering eye-popping saves at key moments, the nimble Nikolai was dubbed "The Bulin Wall" for his sparkling puckstopping for the Winnipeg Jets, which became the Phoenix Coyotes and, more recently, the Tampa Bay Lightning.

After emerging as Winnipeg's premier netminder in 1995–96, Khabibulin recorded three straight phenomenal seasons of 30 or more wins (1996–97 through 1998–99), including 19 shutouts in that same span.

Unfortunately, in 1999, at the peak of his career, Khabibulin and the Coyotes had a contract dispute and the goalie refused to play for the team for almost two seasons. He opted instead to play for Long Beach of the IHL for a season, posting the lowest GAA in the league as Phoenix desperately tried to trade him. He was replaced on the Coyotes by Sean Burke, whom many believed to be an improvement.

Finally, in March 2001, Khabibulin was traded to the Tampa Bay Lightning, playing just two games before the season finished. He regained his previous form in 2001–02, solidifying the goalmouth for the rebuilding Lightning with acrobatic saves, earning him a berth on the World Team at the 2002 NHL All-Star game, as well as an impressive stint as lead goaltender for the Russian Olympic team at the 2002 Winter Games at Salt Lake City.

JOE KLUKAY

BORN: Sault Ste. Marie, Ontario, November 6, 1922
POSITION: Forward, Toronto Maple Leafs, 1946–52, 1954–56; Boston Bruins, 1952–54

Joe Klukay and his Toronto Maple Leafs partner, Nick Metz, were known as the two best penalty killers in pre-expansion NHL history. Klukay became a Leaf in 1946–47 and by no coincidence the Leafs won the Stanley Cup that year, the year after that, and the year after that! Klukay, who frequently worked with Max Bentley on the best third line in NHL annals, played on another Stanley Cup winner in 1951. In 1952–53, he was traded to the Bruins and played capably for them until the middle of the 1954–55 campaign, when he was returned to Toronto. Nicknamed the Duke of Paducah, he completed his NHL career a season later.

JOE KOCUR

BORN: Calgary, Alberta, December 21, 1964
POSITION: Right Wing, Detroit Red Wings, 1984–91, 1996–99; New York Rangers, 1991–96; Vancouver Canucks, 1996

Rarely in NHL annals has there been a more effective enforcer than Joey Kocur, especially when he played for the Detroit Red Wings and New York Rangers.

To say that Kocur had a checkered past would be roughly equivalent to suggesting that Al Capone had an occasional brush with the law. As a Red Wing, Kocur's notoriety stemmed directly from his fists. Along with the equally turbulent Bob Probert, Kocur gave the Red Wings a mean-spirited one-two punch on the forward wall; his right cross and uppercut became the scourge of the league.

Although the Rangers did finally win a Cup in 1994 while Kocur was with them, it was definitely no thanks to Joey and his 17 playoff penalty minutes! This led to his trade in 1996 to Vancouver, where he stayed for seven games before being traded back to Detroit in the 1996–97 season.

Kocur played with Detroit for two more seasons and retired in 1998 after the Wings' back-to-back Stanley Cups. His best days were in the Wings red and white, when he collected 377 penalty minutes as a rookie, and scored 16 goals and 20 assists in 1989–90. Upon entering his final season, Kocur was ranked 14th among all-time penalty-minute leaders, and eventually was hired as the Wings' video coordinator after retirement. During the summer of 2002, Kocur was promoted to the role of assistant coach under newly appointed head coach, Dave Lewis.

The Red Wings high command believed that Kocur had a bright future as a coaching aide.

SAKU KOIVU

BORN: Turku, Finland, November 23, 1974
POSITION: Center, Montreal Canadiens, 1995–
AWARDS/HONORS: Bill Masterton Memorial Trophy, 2002; NHL All-Star, 1998

One of the most touching episodes in NHL history developed before the 2001–02 season, which the Montreal Canadiens' Saku Koivu spent recovering from cancer of the abdomen.

The ace forward first knew he was in trouble on a flight from Amsterdam to Montreal, during which he was alternately vomiting with a bloated stomach and suffering back pain. The 26-year-old was admitted to Montreal General Hospital, where he was diagnosed with Burkitt's lymphoma. But on opening night of the 2001–02 season in front of a crowd of 21,273 at the Molson Centre, Koivu donned a Canadiens jersey and received a seven-minute standing ovation.

Almost the entire 2001–02 season was spent in therapy, including eight chemotherapy cycles. His weight dropped from 181 pounds to 165. But by late March, Koivu was actually participating in full contact practices and getting back to a near-normal life.

"Every day I am pushing myself more and more," said Koivu at the time. "It becomes more realistic to think of a comeback. It will be the biggest day of my life when I come back, and if it's this year, that'll be great. But I won't push or risk anything. There's no pressure on myself to come back."

Saku Koivu meant a tremendous amount to Montreal fans. He was the Canadiens' first-round draft pick (21st overall) in the 1993 draft and evolved into the Habs' undisputed leader and captain through years of rebuilding and dealing of key players. He also served Finland on their 1998 Olympic bronze-medal winner in Nagano.

Diminutive but fearless, Koivu was often injured. It was, however, exactly that trait that endeared him to teammates and fans. Koivu's career high was only 57, and Montreal did not make the playoffs for much of his early tenure, but his skills, and heart, were world-class.

Amazingly, Koivu would return for the post-season, his presence lending inspiration, heart, and some much-needed points, as eighth-seeded Montreal knocked number one seed Boston out in the first round. Unfortunately, Koivu & Co. encountered a determined Carolina club in round two, and lost to the Canes in six.

OLAF KOLZIG

BORN: Johannesburg, South Africa, April 9, 1970
POSITION: Goaltender; Washington Capitals, 1989–
AWARDS/HONORS: Vezina Trophy, 2000; NHL First Team All-Star, 2000; NHL All-Star Game, 1998, 2000

When Bryan Murray coached the Washington Capitals from 1982 to 1989, his perennial lament about his club's playoff failures invariably included mention of mediocre goaltending. Washington never seemed to have an ace between the pipes; and then Olaf Kolzig came along. Signed by the team in 1989 (selected in the first round), he stayed with the Caps until becoming a regular in 1996.

The South African–born goalie grew up in Germany and played for the Germans in several championships, including the 1998 Olympics in Nagano.

Kolzig held the Capitals' career records in wins (151), games played (344), and shutouts (21) by the end of the 2000–01 season. He had led a previously unsteady club to the playoffs five times, including a 1998 Stanley Cup finals appearance, and radically changed the outlook of the team.

Kolzig earned the Vezina Trophy and an All-Star nod in 2000 after 41 wins, 5 shutouts,

and a 2.24 goals-against average. Big, quick, and agile enough to cover the entire net while playing the angles, "Olie the Goalie" could not backstop the Capitals into the playoffs after the team, which now included Jaromir Jagr, slumped their way out of the playoff picture in 2001–02.

VLADIMIR KONSTANTINOV

BORN: Murmansk, Russia, March 19, 1967
POSITION: Defenseman, Detroit Red Wings, 1991–97
AWARDS/HONORS: Alka-Seltzer Plus Award, 1996; NHL All-Rookie Team, 1992; NHL Second Team All-Star, 1996

If ever there was a heart-and-soul on the modern Red Wings—or a last line of defense on their 1997 Stanley Cup championship team—it was Vladimir Konstantinov. Vladdie, or "The Vladinator" as his teammates called him, joined the Wings with little fanfare in 1991, but quickly established himself as a tremendous physical force on the blueline. Even though only five feet eleven and 190 pounds, he was, pound for pound, one of the toughest players in the NHL.

The Red Wings' 12th pick (221st overall) in the 1989 NHL Entry Draft, Vlad made an immediate impact. In his freshman year, he registered 34 points and 172 penalty minutes, helping the Wings to a 22-point improvement over 1990–91. Konstantinov frustrated opponents with relentless drive, passion, and competitive fire, although some sometimes labeled his tactics "dirty" and "cheap." Whether praised or reviled for the way he got the job done, Vlad was respected.

In the Wings' 1996–97 championship season, Konstantinov finished with a plus-38 rating while collecting a career-high 38 points before the Red Wings embarked on their Stanley Cup voyage. He was runner-up to New York Ranger Brian Leetch in voting for the Norris Trophy as the best defenseman in hockey.

Konstantinov became a major contributor to a Detroit franchise that began to dominate in the mid 1990s. But that star's bright glimmer would tragically flicker away on the evening of Friday, June 13, 1997. Six days after the Red Wings had won their first Stanley Cup in 42 years, Konstantinov, fellow Russian teammate Slava Fetisov, and team masseur Sergei Mnatsakanov were involved in an auto crash that, save for Fetisov, inflicted massive and near-fatal head injuries. Vlad survived, but was confined to a wheelchair, thus ending his NHL career.

Detroit began 1997–98 determined to win their second straight Cup—for Konstantinov and Mnatsakanov. Wearing patches on their right shoulders with their mates' initials and the word "believe" in English and Russian, Detroit dittoed in another four-game sweep, this time over the Washington Capitals.

During the postgame presentation, Konstantinov, who had watched from a private box in the Caps' MCI Center, was wheeled onto the ice wearing his number 16 Red Wings jersey. After NHL commissioner Gary Bettman presented the silver chalice to Detroit center Steve Yzerman, the captain skated over to Vladdie, placing the cherished trophy on his lap. Teammates formed a circle around him, then whisked their inspiration around the rink in a victory lap.

Konstantinov feebly raised two fingers in recognition of Detroit's second straight Stanley Cup victory, then sat in the joyous locker room that evening, sipping champagne and holding a cigar, his gleaming smile assuring everyone that he comprehended exactly what was happening. When Detroit won another Stanley Cup in 2002, Konstantinov was there to celebrate again.

ILYA KOVALCHUK

BORN: Tver, Russia, April 15, 1983
POSITION: Left Wing, Atlanta Thrashers, 2001–

It isn't often that an 18-year-old playing for a desperately inept team can make such a positive and immediate impact as Ilya Kovalchuk did in 2001–02.

Drafted first overall by Thrashers general manager Don Waddell, Kovalchuk dazzled opponents with his footwork as well as his devastatingly accurate shot. Teaming with another rookie, Dany Heatley, Kovalchuk gave the Thrashers a smidgen of respectability in an otherwise woeful year, in which they finished last overall in the NHL.

After he became the first Russian player to be taken first overall in NHL Entry Draft history, Kovalchuk made his NHL debut on October 4, 2001, at Buffalo, scored his first NHL goal two nights later in Boston, and notched his first multiple-point, multiple-assist NHL game in New York City on November 18, 2001.

A rookie-of-the-year caliber performance was truncated when Kovalchuk suffered a dislocation of the right sternoclavicular joint during the second period of a game with the New York Islanders in March 2002. He collided with Islanders forward Shawn Bates, fell awkwardly into the boards, and ended a beautiful season.

In 65 games played, the dynamic and crafty Kovalchuk finished with 29 goals and 22 assists, totaling 51 points, with four of those goals being game winners. However, it wasn't enough to win the Rookie-of-the-Year prize, which went to Heatley. Ilya wore the number 17 in honor of the late Soviet hockey star Valeri Kharlamov, who performed for the Soviet Union in the 1972 Summit series.

ALEXEI KOVALEV

BORN: Togliatti, Russia, February 24, 1973
POSITION: Right Wing, New York Rangers, 1992–98; Pittsburgh Penguins, 1998–
AWARDS/HONORS: NHL All-Star Game, 2001

The first Soviet player ever drafted in the first round of the NHL Entry Draft, Alexei Kovalev was touted as the Second Coming for the New York Rangers. Kovalev's speed and stickhandling ability were supposed to launch the Rangers straight to the top of the NHL hierarchy. In fact, Kovalev helped propel the Rangers to their 1994 Stanley Cup championship with 23 goals and 33 assists in 76 games that season. His goal in Game Six of the Rangers-Devils series in 1994 sparked a Rangers rally and comeback to beat New Jersey.

However, after the Rangers won the Cup, they began to decline, and in 1998, finished the season with only 25 wins, their least in a full season since their 1965–66 campaign. Many fans pointed at Kovalev's underachieving 53 points, and as insults like "You shoot like Kovalev" rained down from the Madison Square Garden rafters. It was clear that Kovalev had to go.

In November 1998, Alexei was traded to the Penguins as the main component in a deal that sent Petr Nedved to New York. In Pittsburgh, with a clean slate, Kovalev excelled. The winger scored 46 points in only 63 games, after coming over to Pittsburgh that year. In 2000–01, Kovalev scored 44 goals and 95 points, clearly finding his niche on the high-powered Pittsburgh team, emerging as one of the most prolific scorers in the NHL.

Alexei spent the start of 2001–02 injured, and couldn't help lift the decimated Penguins into the playoffs upon his return.

JARI KURRI

BORN: Helsinki, Finland, May 18, 1960
POSITION: Right Wing, Edmonton Oilers, 1980–90; Los Angeles Kings, 1991–96; New York Rangers, 1996; Anaheim Mighty Ducks, 1996–97; Colorado Avalanche, 1997–98
AWARDS/HONORS: Lady Byng Memorial Trophy, 1985; NHL First Team All-Star, 1985, 1987; NHL Second Team All-Star, 1984, 1986, 1989; NHL All-Star Game, 1983, 1985–86, 1988–90, 1993, 1998; Hockey Hall of Fame, 2001

How valuable was Jari Kurri to the teams on which he played? Was he in the right place at the right time, or a sure-fire Hall of Famer?

It takes more than being in the right place at the right time to have a 17-season career in the NHL. However, the most spectacular sea-

Jari Kurri as a King

sons of Kurri's distinguished career came while playing wing for Wayne Gretzky on the go-go Oilers teams of the 1980s. It was Kurri's fate to be constantly overshadowed by his friend and linemate, and Kurri's skills were often dismissed by fans who couldn't see past The Great One. His own coach, and later general manager, Glen Sather said, "A fire hydrant could get forty goals playing with Wayne." Yet Gretzky himself said the two were "almost telepathic" on the ice, and believed Kurri should be a shoe-in for the Hall. Jari finally made it in 2001.

Kurri was no fire hydrant, although he was certainly lucky to be drafted by the Oilers, a tremendously fast, skilled team on which his talents could be utilized fully. And while playing with Gretzky certainly brought out the best in Kurri, Gretzky had *his* best years with

Kurri on right wing. Additionally, Kurri had two seasons of more than 90 points for the Oilers after Gretzky had been traded to the LA Kings, and was a key performer in the Oilers' fifth Cup win in 1990. There seems little doubt there was more to Jari Kurri's career than a role as Gretzky's favorite winger.

In Kurri's draft year, 1980, European players were still somewhat rare in the NHL; Finnish players were rarer still. The Oilers stole Kurri in the fourth round, 69th overall, because most teams simply weren't paying attention. There was a common misconception among NHL teams that Finland's top young players were bound to the national team, but Edmonton's scouting staff wasn't fooled. Kurri's play in exhibition games against Edmonton caught their eye, and by Christmas, 1980, Kurri had joined the Oilers and was ensconced on Gretzky's right side.

Playing on a team with so many young stars (not just Gretzky, but Mark Messier, Paul Coffey, Kevin Lowe, Grant Fuhr, et alia) helped Kurri in more ways than one. It enabled him to be his best on the ice, but it also shielded him from excessive public scrutiny until he was comfortable with both North America and with English.

Kurri had a spectacular career with the Oilers, scoring over 30 goals in every one of his ten seasons in Edmonton. He also had two 50-goal seasons, one 60-goal season, and one 70-goal season. His point totals reached over 100 in six out of the ten seasons. These were fantastic numbers, even for the goal-happy 1980s. Also first-rate: He led the Oilers in goals in three out of their five Cup victories, and tied for the highest goals in a fourth. He collected ten goals, including a key, record-tying seventh career playoff hat trick, to help the post-Gretzky Oilers to their fifth and last Cup in 1990.

While it is true that any player could look good playing with Gretzky, Kurri had a few unique attributes that made the most of their collective talents. Gretzky was the greatest passer in NHL history, but Kurri was one of the best ever at shooting off the pass without stopping the puck (the one-timer). Kurri was able to take what Gretzky gave him and turn it into something special. Even his excellent defensive skills could be an offensive plus, since the Oilers employed Kurri and Gretzky on the penalty kill, and they set new records for shorthanded goals.

Kurri's defensive skills were often overshadowed by his marvelous offensive numbers. But, in fact, his last years were spent primarily as a defensive forward, which extended his career several years.

Between his years as an Oiler and his retirement in 1998, Kurri skated on both coasts of North America, as well as in Europe. He spent the 1990–91 season playing in Italy after a contract dispute with the Oilers, who traded his rights to the LA Kings in 1991. There, he was reunited with Gretzky and helped the Kings to the Cup finals in 1993. His defensive skills sustained him through stops with the New York Rangers, Anaheim Mighty Ducks, and Colorado Avalanche.

Jari was a First Team All-Star twice, a Second Team All-Star three times, and retired as the greatest European scorer in NHL history.

However, if it's ever said that Kurri would never have been what he was without Gretzky, this is what should be said in reply: Of the 1,669 points Gretzky scored in Edmonton, Kurri was involved in 630 of them, which is no doubt why Wayne said, when his old linemate was eligible for selection to the Hall of Fame, "If Jari Kurri doesn't make the Hall of Fame, they ought to board the thing up."

LEO LABINE

BORN: Haileybury, Ontario, July 22, 1931
POSITION: Right Wing, Boston Bruins, 1951–60; Detroit Red Wings, 1961–62

Opponents never could make up their minds whether Leo Labine was more to be feared as a scorer or a bodychecker. A member of the Boston Bruins from 1951–52 through 1960, Labine terrorized the enemy while patrolling right wing on a line with Real Chevrefils and whoever else the Bruins could find as the third man. Labine was traded to Detroit in 1960–61 and finished his career in the Red Wings uniform a season later, but he is really remembered as a Bruin.

In 1956–57, when he scored 18 goals and 29 assists for 47 points in 67 games, Leo's boss, Lynn Patrick, compared Labine with the great Jean Beliveau. Actually, Leo was more a needler than a scorer. During a playoff match with Montreal, Labine nearly killed Maurice Richard with a vicious body check, yet he could also be terribly amusing. Once, when the Bruins were playing an exhibition game against the Rangers at New Haven, Leo decided that he would use the early September fog on the ice as a smokescreen. After the play shifted from the New York to the Boston end, Labine hid behind the Rangers' net. Soon, he began laughing. Rangers goalie Lorne Worsley turned around, saw Leo, and called to referee Red Storey who, himself laughing, ordered the linesman to blow an offside. By this time everyone in the rink, including Worsley, was laughing at Leo's jape. However, when Labine was on his game he was a major threat and fan favorite in Boston.

ELMER LACH

BORN: Nokomis, Saskatchewan, January 22, 1918
POSITION: Center, Montreal Canadiens, 1940–54
AWARDS/HONORS: Hart Memorial Trophy, 1945; Art Ross Trophy, 1945, 1948; NHL First Team All-Star, 1945, 1948, 1952; NHL Second Team All-Star, 1944, 1946; Hockey Hall of Fame, 1966

Elmer Lach, the center on the Montreal Canadiens' fabled Punch Line, broke in with the Habs in 1940–41, promptly helping the Frenchmen squeeze into the Stanley Cup playoffs.

The following season, the infamous Lach injury jinx that was to earn him the handle of "Elmer the Unlucky" began to surface. In the opening game of the 1941–42 season, Lach crashed into the boards, breaking his arm in two places. He was sidelined for the entire season, but it was only the first in a long line of painful injuries for the pivot.

After his year of convalescence, Lach was elevated to first-line status, where the aggressive forward took a regular shift, skated on the power play, and killed penalties as well.

In 1943–44, the legendary Rocket Richard joined the Habs' forward line, and along with Lach and Toe Blake completed the Punch Line. With that kind of firepower behind them, the Canadiens steamrolled to their first Stanley Cup in 13 years.

In all, Lach labored for 13 seasons wearing the *bleu, blanc, et rouge,* a stretch that saw the Frenchmen win three Stanley Cups and finish first in the league four consecutive times. Lach finished his career in 1954, having scored 215 goals and 623 points, and adding an endless number of stitches for the Canadiens.

PIERRE LACROIX

BORN: Montreal, Quebec, August 3, 1948
POSITION: General Manager, Quebec
Nordiques, 1994–95; Colorado Avalanche, 1995–

Pierre Lacroix was appointed the fourth general manager of the then-Quebec Nordiques franchise on May 29, 1994, after 21 years as a respected player agent. This arrival opened a period of unparalleled success for the team, which would soon become the Colorado Avalanche. The franchise would win division titles and make six appearances in the Western Conference finals in seven years, win two President's Trophy titles (1996–97 and 2000–01), and, most importantly, two Stanley Cup championships in 1996 and 2001.

Lacroix took a team that had missed the playoffs six of the seven previous years and transformed it into a contender, acquiring Sylvain Lefebvre, Wendel Clark, and Uwe Krupp to add experience to a young and talented team. Lacroix also showed he was not afraid to pull the trigger on big deals, bringing in Claude Lemieux, Sandis Ozolinsh, Patrick Roy, and Mike Keane. The benefits of these deals quickly came to fruition as the Avs won the cup in 1995–96.

Lacroix continued his successful trading ways, as he lured the lifetime Bruin backliner Ray Bourque to Colorado with Dave Andreychuk, for Brian Rolston, Martin Grenier, Sami Pahlsson, and Martin Samuelsson in 2000. But Lacroix wasn't finished: He next acquired premier defenseman Rob Blake and Steve Reinprecht from Los Angeles for Adam Deadmarsh, Aaron Miller, David Steckel, and Jared Aulin. The result: Stanley Cup number two in 2001.

Lacroix proved—as did Brian Burke and Michael Barnett—that a player agent could make the transition to general manager.

GUY LAFLEUR

BORN: Thurso, Quebec, September 20, 1951
POSITION: Right Wing/Center, Montreal Canadiens, 1971–85; New York Rangers, 1988–89; Quebec Nordiques, 1989–91
AWARDS/HONORS: Art Ross Trophy, 1976–78; Hart Memorial Trophy, 1977–78; Conn Smythe Trophy, 1977; Lester B. Pearson Award, 1976–78; NHL First Team All-Star, 1975–80; NHL All-Star Game, 1975–78, 1980, 1991; NHL Challenge Cup All-Star, 1979; Hockey Hall of Fame, 1988

Until the 1974–75 campaign, when he was among the league leaders in scoring, Guy Lafleur hadn't really caught fire in the NHL. Playing both right wing and center, "point" on the power plays, and killing penalties, Guy was far from the French-Canadian star of the Habs, much less the entire league.

Guy Lafleur as a Ranger

But in 1974, Guy began to earn his *tricouleurs*. No one doubted his skating ability, shooting, or stickhandling, but he was far from aggressive. Once he adapted to the harder hitting of the NHL, Lafleur became a full-fledged Canadiens star, the dream of any Quebecois boy.

Lafleur won every scoring trophy awarded to NHL forwards between 1975 and 1978. His awesome totals for those three seasons were 225 goals, 512 points, and a playoff performance in 1977's Stanley Cup games that produced 26 points in 14 games. Against the Boston Bruins in Cup finals, Lafleur scored or set up the last nine goals tallied by the Canadiens, making him an easy choice for Most Valuable Player of that series.

Lafleur's hot goal-scoring streaks left a string of goaltenders prone throughout the NHL, as Guy followed in the able footsteps of Montreal superstars such as Maurice Richard, Jean Beliveau, and Howie Morenz.

Like Richard, Lafleur not only was a hero, but a tempestuous figure in Montreal sports. After clashes with Canadiens management, and former teammates Serge Savard and Jacques Lemaire, Lafleur was hastened into retirement and left Montreal. But he would continue to grab headlines with the New York Rangers and Quebec Nordiques after a four-year sabbatical from the NHL.

His tenure with the Rangers turned him into a Broadway hero despite his advanced age. When he tallied 45 points in 67 games, chants of "GUYEEEEEEEEE!" cascaded down from the Madison Square Garden faithful. Guy had two abbreviated seasons for the Quebec Nordiques (1989–90 through 1990–91) before he finally retired, this time for good. Enshrined in the Hall of Fame in 1988, Lafleur became Montreal's all-time leading point-getter with 1,246, and his number 10 was one of only seven in team history to have been retired, joining those of Jacques Plante, Doug Harvey, Jean Beliveau, Howie Morenz, Henri Richard, and Maurice "The Rocket" Richard.

PAT LaFONTAINE

BORN: St. Louis, Missouri, February 22, 1965
POSITION: Center, New York Islanders, 1983–91; Buffalo Sabres, 1991–97; New York Rangers, 1997–98
AWARDS/HONORS: Dodge Performer of the Year Award, 1990; Bill Masterton Memorial Trophy, 1995; NHL Second Team All-Star, 1993; NHL All-Star Game, 1988–91, 1993

There have been few smaller, classier players who have graced the NHL than center Pat LaFontaine, who starred for the 1984 United States Olympic team.

"Patty was one of the greatest American contributors to the U.S. hockey scene," said Lou Vairo, coach of the 1984 American Olympic team. "He played with skill, speed, savvy, and cleanliness. Few players could make that statement."

Following the 1984 Olympics, LaFontaine graduated to the Islanders and became an instant star in the NHL.

The center's impact was immediately felt in the 1984 Stanley Cup finals against Edmonton and soon, he was the darling of the Nassau Coliseum.

Lafontaine's greatest career moment was in Game Seven of 1987 Patrick Division quarter-finals against the Washington Capitals. The overtime game, which lasted seven periods, was sealed on a LaFontaine slap shot at two in the morning.

However, in the 1988 opening round against the New Jersey Devils, LaFontaine was constantly assaulted by his bigger foes and received little protection from his teammates.

His Isles career was sullied by a contract dispute with owner John Pickett, and Pat was traded to Buffalo along with Randy Hillier, Randy Wood, and Dean Melanson for Pierre Turgeon, Uwe Krupp, Benoit Hogue, and Dave McLlwain. In Buffalo, LaFontaine continued his sensational playmaking to form a lethal scoring combo between Alexander Mogilny and Dave Andreychuk. However, LaFontaine would fall victim to a concussion when he was viciously cross-checked by Francois Leroux in a 1996–97 regular season game against Pittsburgh. The hit knocked LaFontaine unconscious and finished him for the rest of the season. Pat sat out the rest of the 1996–97 campaign in hopes of a 100 percent recovery, so he could be cleared to play by concussion specialist Dr. Jim Kelley.

The comeback would happen, with Pat in a New York Rangers jersey, as he was traded to the Blueshirts just days before the start of the 1997–98 season. That year, LaFontaine averaged almost a point a game (62 points in 67 games) before a hideous accident during a game in which he collided with his own teammate Mike Keane. It resulted in another concussion and spelled the end of an otherwise brilliant career.

LaFontaine was second only to Joe Mullen in all-time goals scored by an American-born player, with 468.

Also a member of the 1996 World Cup–winning United States team, LaFontaine authored an inspirational book entitled *Companions in Courage,* and was frequently seen at Ranger and Islander games beginning in 2000–01, after the Pat LaFontaine Trophy, named in his honor, was created, with each of the two rival teams donating funds to various charities based on the winner of the season series.

NEWSY LALONDE

BORN: Cornwall, Ontario, October 31, 1887
DIED: November 21, 1970
POSITION: Defenseman/Forward, Montreal Canadiens, 1910–22; Coach, New York Americans, 1926–27; Montreal Canadiens, 1932–34
AWARDS/HONORS: Art Ross Trophy, 1919, 1921; Hockey Hall of Fame, 1950

Edouard "Newsy" Lalonde was one of the toughest, most controversial figures to skate in pro hockey. He was a member of the original Montreal Canadiens team and a legend in his time.

Lalonde, nicknamed "Newsy" during a brief stint working in a newsprint plant, broke into pro hockey with Sault Ste. Marie when he was only 18. In his first game against Pittsburgh he discovered that the defensemen had a habit of backhanding the puck into the air when they wanted to clear the puck from their zone.

"Once I figured that out," Newsy revealed, "I made a point of getting in front of them and then, suddenly, swerving around so that I actually had my back to the defensemen."

Lalonde soon proved there was a method to his madness. The next time a Pittsburgh player attempted to clear the puck, Lalonde executed his pirouette. The puck struck him in the back and slipped through his baggy hockey pants to the ice directly behind him. He then deftly spun around, captured the puck, and skimmed it into the net. Newsy executed this maneuver twice in the same game, and Sault Ste. Marie came out on top, 3–1. "After that," he said, "I was in pro hockey for good."

With Newsy leading the team in scoring, with 16 goals in 16 games, Les Canadiens finished second in their second season. Newsy earned a reputation as one of the roughest players in the game. His clashes with "Bad" Joe Hall, who later became a teammate on the Habs, were studies in jungle brutality, but Newsy didn't reserve his venom for Hall.

On December 22, 1912, the Canadiens played their hometown rivals, the Wanderers, in an exhibition game to unveil the new Toronto hockey rink. Midway into the game Lalonde dispatched Odie Cleghorn of the Wanderers into the boards with such force that Odie's teammate and brother, Sprague, charged across the rink and smashed Newsy across the forehead with his stick. The blow just barely missed Lalonde's eye and it required twelve stitches to close the gaping wound. The episode didn't go unnoticed officially and a constable served a summons on Cleghorn. Sprague turned up in a Toronto court and was fined $50 for his efforts, and an additional fine of $50 was slapped on him by NHA president Emmett Quinn. Cleghorn was also suspended for four weeks, but such was the *laissez faire* atmosphere of pro hockey at the time that Sprague absented himself from only one game and then returned to the Wanderers' lineup with impunity.

Following his playing career, which ended in 1922, Lalonde turned to coaching, first with the New York Americans and then the Canadiens.

LOU LAMORIELLO

BORN: Providence, Rhode Island, October 21, 1942
POSITION: President/General Manager, New Jersey Devils, 1987–
AWARDS/HONORS: Lester Patrick Trophy, 1992; New Jersey Sports Hall of Fame, 2002

Until the 1987 arrival of Lou Lamoriello in New Jersey, the Devils had failed to make the playoffs from the beginning of their move to East Rutherford in 1982.

Coincidental with Lamoriello's coming, the Devils reached the postseason and marched all the way to the third round of the 1987–88 playoffs, missing the playoffs only once (1996) through 2002.

The former athletic director and hockey coach of Providence college sharply changed the Devs' image from much-ridiculed team to one of respect. By the 1993–94 season, the team climbed from the level of competitive to that of championship contender, and a year later, in June 1995, New Jersey defeated the Detroit Red Wings for their first of two Stanley Cups.

Lamoriello's disciplined and progressive style of management served as an A-1 model for all of professional sports, with his smart trades, signings, and numerous draft selections constructing a consistently solid, fiscally prudent, and deep team. He harvested his numerous draft picks at the team farm club in Albany, and maximized their value by steadily weaving them into the big club, or dealing them at the right time for vital performers such as Bobby Holik, Neal Broten, Bernie Nicholls, Claude Lemieux, Doug Gilmour, Alexander Mogilny, and Vladimir Malakhov. His selection of defense-oriented coaches over the years—namely Jacques Lemaire, Robbie Ftorek, Larry Robinson, Kevin Constantine, and Pat Burns—reflected his careful, no-nonsense approach to building a winner.

Lou shrewdly maximized his leverage in the legal issues of player movement, resulting in key draft picks and cornerstones in Scott Stevens and Randy McKay, who would fortify New Jersey's size and strength for years. Undrafted signees Brian Rafalski and John Madden, who helped New Jersey win the 2000 Stanley Cup, were other coups in Lamoriello's arsenal of strong moves. The overall result was six 100-point seasons and four Eastern Conference/Atlantic Division titles in addition to the two Cups by 2001.

An unpredictable trader and acute businessman, Lamoriello oversaw all business and hockey operations top-to-bottom in the New Jersey organization, and picked his moments perfectly. He shocked everyone when he fired coach Robbie Ftorek near the very end of a 103-point 1999–2000 season, replacing him with assistant Larry Robinson, who inspired the slumping team through their season's end and improbable playoff comebacks to the Stanley Cup. After a return visit to the finals in 2000–01, Lamoriello then fired Robinson midway through the following year—in favor of Constantine—only to rehire Robinson as an assistant weeks later when the Devils' under-achieving play improved. But his injury-ridden team was eliminated in the first round by the Carolina Hurricanes. He then replaced Constantine with Burns.

In addition to his success with the Devils, the prestigious Hockey East Association, cofounded by Lamoriello, produced many NHL players and executives under his administration as the association's first commissioner. The Providence native also won the Lester Patrick Trophy in 1992 for his service to United States hockey, and was instrumental in bringing Soviet players into the NHL. In 2001–02, he was named CEO of the NBA New Jersey Nets, whereupon his savvy and leadership produced the team's best season and a trip to the NBA finals.

MYLES LANE

BORN: Melrose, Massachusetts, October 2, 1905
DIED: 1987
POSITION: Defenseman, New York Rangers, 1928–29; Boston Bruins, 1929–30, 1933–34

Among the graduates of the National Hockey League, some of whom have traveled from the ice to the Canadian Parliament, New York State Supreme Court judge Myles J. Lane ranks as one of the most distinguished. He began wearing the black robes on January 1, 1969. Before that he was a member of the New York State Commission of Investigation, a team of top-level gang-busters that he joined after working as a United States attorney. Lane was also the first American ever to play on a Stanley Cup team, the Bruins of 1929.

Hockey had helped Lane become a lawyer. He worked his way through law school by playing the game, first for the Rangers, then for the Bruins, then by managing the Boston Cubs, a Bruin farm team.

Lane was a competent player, if not a star, and, as one of the first Americans in the big league, he had tremendous curiosity value at the box office. This was not always to his advantage, though. In a locker room interview after his first Ranger game, a sportswriter misquoted Lane as saying that this game is a cinch compared to college hockey. When the Rangers arrived in Montreal the following Saturday night, the newswriters were exhorting the populace to come out and see the wise guy and the arena was packed. The Montreal Maroons were out to get the American college boy who scoffed at the Canadian professionals.

Lane's first rush down ice ended with a bone-crushing body check and a charging penalty for his overanxious opponent. His next rush ended the same way and so did the third. Emotions were running high and the game grew rougher. Lane escaped unhurt, but by the time the game was over there were two major casualties—

Taffy Abel needed twelve stitches in his foot and the great Ching Johnson broke his leg, an injury from which he never fully recovered.

Lane thought of Johnson as his big brother and mentor, but as for the greatest player he ever saw, Lane gave the award to Eddie Shore of the Bruins. He was not alone in his admiration. When Lane was with the Rangers, the New York club tried to set up a deal with the Bruins that would involve trading Myles Lane for Eddie Shore. The Boston reply was quick and to the point: "You're so many Myles from Shore, you need a life preserver!" Within his first year in the league, though, Lane was sold to Boston, where he became Shore's teammate. There he performed ably until an automobile accident forced him to hang up his skates and turn to managing the Boston Cubs.

PETE LANGELLE

BORN: Winnipeg, Manitoba, November 4, 1917
POSITION: Forward, Toronto Maple Leafs, 1938–42

Although Pete Langelle played only three full seasons with the Toronto Maple Leafs, he achieved a permanent niche in hockey history as the forward who scored the winning goal in the 1942 Stanley Cup final between Detroit and Toronto. In that series, the Red Wings took a 3–0 lead in games before the Maple Leafs tied the series at three games apiece. With the score tied, 1–1, in the seventh and final game at Maple Leaf Gardens on April 18, 1942, Langelle beat goalie Johnny Mowers, banging home a rebound from a shot by linemate Johnny McCreedy. It turned out to be Langelle's finest hour and final game. He soon left for the Canadian armed forces and never played big-league hockey again.

Nevertheless, the Langelle-McCreedy scoring play remains enshrined in the memories of Toronto fans. After all, no other NHL team ever rebounded from a 0–3 deficit in games to win the finals and the Stanley Cup.

AL LANGLOIS

BORN: Magog, Quebec, November 6, 1934
POSITION: Defenseman, Montreal Canadiens, 1957–61; New York Rangers, 1961–64; Detroit Red Wings, 1964–65; Boston Bruins, 1965–66

It was Al Langlois's grand good fortune to play defense alongside Doug Harvey for three seasons (1958–59, 1959–60, 1960–61) with the Montreal Canadiens and then again with Harvey on the New York Rangers for another two and a half seasons. As Harvey's play deteriorated, so did Langlois's, and "Junior," as the latter was nicknamed, was finally traded to Detroit in 1963–64, and on to Boston for the 1965–66 season, where he ended his NHL career. A mediocre-to-solid defenseman, Langlois excelled when he had someone beside him; which helps explain why he skated for three Stanley Cup winners at Montreal—of course, playing alongside the inimitable Harvey.

ROD LANGWAY

BORN: Maag, Formosa (Taiwan), May 3, 1957
POSITION: Defenseman, Montreal Canadiens, 1978–82, Washington Capitals, 1982–93
AWARDS/HONORS: James Norris Memorial Trophy, 1983–84; NHL First Team All-Star, 1983–84; NHL Second Team All-Star, 1985; NHL All-Star Game, 1981–86; Hockey Hall of Fame, 2002

Few hockey players have earned the title "majestic" and perhaps only one Hall of Famer, Jean Beliveau, comes immediately to mind when the term is mentioned. Even fewer players can legitimately be called "franchise-savers" in the true sense of the word.

Rod Langway, Capitals captain

But when one talks about Rod Langway, it is not stretching the point to suggest that what we have here is a "majestic franchise-saver," or, as they said when he played in Washington, "a class act."

Throughout his early years, Langway demonstrated leadership potential. He began his pro career with the Birmingham Bulls of the defunct World Hockey Association. He moved to the NHL in 1978–79 with the Canadiens, and they won the Stanley Cup that same season.

When the towering defenseman joined the Washington Capitals in 1982, the club had never made the Stanley Cup playoffs. But with Langway leading the way, the Caps enjoyed postseason action in every season of his tenure. He was not only the chief shaper-upper, the leader-with-words-and-deeds, but a commanding figure like few others in big-league professional hockey.

On top of that, at one point, Langway was the best defenseman in the NHL. Despite the fact that he was known as a defensive defenseman, Langway was able to outdo Paul Coffey and Ray Bourque for the Norris Trophy in 1983 and 1984.

But the Langway years were not without hardship. His Caps teams were tagged with the "choke" label, and captain Langway had already lived through his share of controversy, including a money-oriented trade that took him from Montreal to Washington.

The most remarkable aspect of Langway's career was his transformation from a relatively obscure backliner with the Montreal Canadiens (1978–82) to a franchise-maker with the Capitals. Then-Canadiens general manager Irving Grundman sent Rod, Doug Jarvis, Craig Laughlin, and Brian Engblom to the Caps for Rick Green and Ryan Walter. The deal eventually cost Grundman his job, partially because Langway blossomed into a superstar for the Caps.

When Rod came to Washington, he emerged as the most visible player on the franchise and a respected member of the Capital district sports community.

Despite the accolades, Langway had one major cross to bear during his Caps career, and that was Washington's failure to make any noticeable dent at playoff time. Even after the Caps waived the greybeard in 1993, the ex-captain trudged around the minors until 1998, extracting the remaining steam he had in his search for further victory.

Nevertheless, any man who can save a franchise almost single-handedly merits mention, and no one deserved it more than Langway.

His numbers were not eye-popping, but, as fellow ex-defenseman Mike Milbury put it, "If I had to pick [between contemporaries Langway, Coffey, and Bourque], I'd rather have Langway because he had a better approach to the game. He was more of a team player with a lot more character. And that's the thing you want most of all on a hockey team."

JACQUES LAPERRIERE

BORN: Rouyn, Quebec, November 22, 1941
POSITION: Defenseman, Montreal Canadiens, 1962–75
AWARDS/HONORS: Calder Memorial Trophy, 1964; James Norris Memorial Trophy, 1966; NHL First Team All-Star, 1965–66; NHL Second Team All-Star, 1964, 1970; Hockey Hall of Fame, 1987

When All-Star defenseman Doug Harvey was traded by the Montreal Canadiens to the New York Rangers in 1961, the Montreal brass scoured their farm system for a good, young replacement.

In time they found beanstalk Jacques Laperriere, who

Jacques Laperriere clears the puck for the Canadiens

honed his skills to sharpness with Montreal Junior Canadiens. Laperriere played six games with the Canadiens in 1962–63 and became a regular the following season. He easily won the National Hockey League Rookie of the Year award and emerged as one of the best of contemporary defensemen. His size (six feet two, 190 pounds) enabled him to use the poke check to great advantage. Jacques played a hard but clean game and remained a Montreal ace through the 1972–73 season, when he was hospitalized with a leg injury. Although he played part of the 1973–74 season, the leg still bothered Laperriere so badly that he failed to start the 1974–75 campaign and retired in July 1975 to become coach of the Montreal Juniors, an amateur team.

Jacques would become a sage to a host of NHL benches through the years as an assistant with the Habs, the Boston Bruins, and, in 2001–02, the New York Islanders.

CLAUDE LAPOINTE

BORN: Lachine, Quebec, October 11, 1968
POSITION: Center/Left Wing, Quebec Nordiques, 1990–95; Colorado Avalanche, 1995; Calgary Flames, 1995–96; New York Islanders, 1996–

One of the better, but less-heralded defensive forwards of the late 1990s and early 2000s, Claude Lapointe diligently toiled for nonplayoff teams with the New York Islanders until 2001–02, when he helped the Isles into the postseason for the first time since 1992–93.

Playing in an age where professional athletes were drawn more toward large salaries than loyalties, Lapointe continued to skate against the grain. During the down years on Long Island, Lapointe faced free agency, with an opportunity to leave and join a wealthier and more successful hockey operation.

But, Lapointe obviously felt a bond to his lame Islanders organization. Wanting to restore a winning tradition to the once-dominant

Isles, Claude took less money to stay with a team he felt could regain a place of prominence on the NHL map.

A fan-favorite for fearless hustle and face-off prowess, Claude had a career-best 37 points in 1998–99, and remained a durable penalty killer, leader, and occasional goal scorer for Long Island. Originally Quebec Nordique property, Claude moved with the team to Colorado in 1995–96, but was dealt to Calgary. He landed on Long Island in 1996 as a free agent.

Lapointe's dedication paid off when the assistant captain helped lead a revamped team, including Alexei Yashin and Michael Peca, into the postseason in April 2002 after the Islanders' brilliant 96-point comeback year.

GUY LAPOINTE

BORN: Montreal, Quebec, March 18, 1948
POSITION: Defenseman, Montreal Canadiens, 1968–82; St. Louis Blues, 1982–83; Boston Bruins, 1983–84
AWARDS/HONORS: Team Canada, 1972; NHL First Team All-Star, 1973; NHL Second Team All-Star, 1975–77; NHL Challenge Cup All-Star, 1979; Hockey Hall of Fame, 1993

In the spring of 1973, Guy Lapointe, the Montreal Canadiens' agile defenseman, was named to the NHL's First All-Star Team, and not coincidentally the Canadiens won their 18th Stanley Cup championship.

Combining bruising body checks with nimble puck-carrying, Guy quarterbacked the Canadiens' attack. In a typical attack, Guy would circle the net, driving his legs like pistons en route to the enemy goal. The opposing team was confounded by Lapointe's versatile activities, particularly his hard shot from the point or his radar-sharp passes that bore the Canadiens' "head-man-the-puck" trademark.

Until the 1972–73 season, Lapointe was known as a defenseman with modest offensive abilities. He scored 15 and 11 goals in the 1970–71 and 1971–72 seasons, respectively,

before bursting out with 19 goals in 1972–73. It was then that coach Scotty Bowman decided to place Guy on the potent Montreal power play. The result: The Canadiens improved their scoring on man-advantage situation after Guy began sharpshooting from the blue line. The Canadiens, searching for a bouncer since the retirement of John Ferguson following the 1970 season, happily discovered that Guy also reveled in physical play.

Guy won a spot on the Canadiens during the last, hectic, unfortunate days of the 1969–70 season, after skating for the Canadiens' Montreal Voyageurs' farm club. On the season's final night, Montreal was eliminated from a playoff berth and the Forum was shrouded in gloom. It was the first time that the proud Habitants had failed to make the playoffs in 30 years!

Although the team was down, Lapointe was on the way up, and nobody could stop him. On the ice, the Canadiens looked like a brand-new team as Lapointe orchestrated both defense and offense as the Habs skated to the 1971 Stanley Cup championship. Lapointe's 107 penalty minutes correctly suggested that the Canadiens boasted a stickhandler who wasn't afraid to battle, yet was prudent enough not to fight at the drop of a puck. A fractured cheekbone ruined the 1971–72 season for Lapointe. Even after it had healed, Guy appeared hesitant and hardly the musketeer of old. But by 1972–73, his health was A-1 again and so were the Canadiens. The point was demonstrated most vividly in the third game of the Stanley Cup quarterfinal series with the pesky Buffalo Sabres.

Trailing 2-0, the Frenchmen appeared grounded after one period of action. Guy tongue-lashed his teammates during the intermission. The Canadiens responded to Lapointe's bilingual blast and went from a collection of Clark Kents to Supermen. They disposed of Buffalo, then Philadelphia, and Chicago en route to their 18th Stanley Cup triumph. Lapointe thus followed a long and distinguished tradition set by All-Star Montreal defensemen Doug Harvey, Tom Johnson, Butch Bouchard, and Jacques Laperriere. None of those, however, combined the strongest elements of offense with defense in the manner of Guy Lapointe. It was no surprise that Lapointe surpassed his personal points record in 1974–75 with 28 goals and 47 assists, nor that the Canadiens were the NHL powerhouse of the regular season.

Lapointe was a cornerstone of one of the all-time best defense corps, including Larry Robinson, Serge Savard, and Rod Langway. His final NHL season was 1983–84, but he remained active in hockey as an assistant coach and scout for the Calgary Flames from 1991–99 before becoming the director of amateur scouting for the Minnesota Wild in 2000.

EDGAR LAPRADE

BORN: Mine Center, Ontario, October 10, 1919
POSITION: Center, New York Rangers, 1945–55
AWARDS/HONORS: Calder Memorial Trophy, 1946; Lady Byng Memorial Trophy, 1950; NHL All-Star Game, 1947–50; Hockey Hall of Fame, 1993

Edgar Laprade played ten seasons for the Rangers, beginning with 1945–46, when he won the Calder Trophy as the National Hockey League's top rookie. A smooth skater and expert stickhandler, Laprade betrayed one shortcoming—a terribly weak shot. He frequently would find himself in scoring position only to shoot ineffectively, either weakly or wide of the mark. Yet, Laprade's playmaking emerged as one of the jewels of a relatively lackluster New York team. "I've always felt that he missed the general acclaim he deserved," said Rangers manager Frank Boucher, "because it was his misfortune never to be cast with a winner." Laprade starred for the Rangers in their vain try for the Stanley Cup in 1950, scoring 3 goals and 5 assists in 12 Stanley Cup games. He retired following the 1954–55

season, and returned to Thunder Bay, Ontario, where he became a sporting goods dealer and village alderman.

IGOR LARIONOV

BORN: Voskresensk, Russia, December 3, 1960
POSITION: Center, Vancouver Canucks, 1989–92; San Jose Sharks, 1993–95; Detroit Red Wings, 1995–2000; Florida Panthers, 2000; Detroit Red Wings, 2000–
AWARDS/HONORS: NHL All-Star Game, 1998

His teammates called him "The Professor," not only for his bespectacled look, but more importantly, for his wizardry with the puck. With his five-feet-eleven, 170-pound frame, Igor Larionov looked more like a college professor than a hockey player. But the lessons he taught on the ice throughout his career certainly proved otherwise.

Larionov was born in Voskresensk, a grimy industrial town of 80,000 about an hour away from Moscow, and honed his skills as a 17-year-old with Khimik, a local team.

In 1981, he began his tenure with the Central Red Army team, where he soon centered one of the greatest forward lines in history, the infamous KLM line, flanked by wingers Vladimir Krutov and Sergei Makarov.

The world had never seen a triumvirate like this before. Appearing to keep the puck on a string between them, the trio became instant heroes in their homeland, and drew rave reviews from players, coaches, and scouts alike across the globe.

Larionov earned Soviet Player of the Year honors in 1987–88 and was named to five All-Star teams with the Central Red Army squad. Additionally, he captured gold medals at the 1984 and 1988 Winter Olympics and a gold medal at the 1983 World Championships.

But Larionov never wanted to play his entire career with the Red Army team. He originally wanted to just fulfill his mandatory two-year term in the Army and return home to rejoin Khimik. But Red Army coach Viktor Tikhonov did not allow the anchor of his most gifted line to leave, forcing Larionov to stay against his will. He ended up playing eight seasons under Tikhonov, collecting 165 goals and 361 points in 334 league games.

The names of the most gifted Soviet hockey players had begun showing up in the annual NHL Entry Draft. But teams would draft these untouchable Soviet players in the late, late rounds, knowing that as long as the Soviet Union existed, Russian players would not be allowed west of the Iron Curtain. Larionov, in fact, was drafted by Vancouver in 1985—214th in the draft, the Canucks' 11th pick.

In 1989, the Iron Curtain began to rust and crack, as gifted players like Sergei Fedorov and Alexander Mogilny defected to North America. But Larionov did not want to defect, instead waging a self-imposed war with Soviet authorities in order to secure his freedom from their iron fist.

Finally, after years of negotiating, the Soviet hockey regime relented, and Larionov was able to go to Vancouver to play with the Canucks, making his NHL debut on October 5, 1989, against the Edmonton Oilers.

Though he was thousands of miles from Moscow, Larionov played as if still in the Soviet Union. His dazzling puck movement and ability to complete passes blindly immediately endeared him to the Vancouver faithful, not to mention hockey fans across the country, who were amazed at the Russian's grace and finesse.

When Larionov was dubbed "the Russian Wayne Gretzky," the comparisons between the two playmakers immediately began. Like Gretzky, Larionov was not the fleetest of foot. But he captivated those in and around the game with his ability to thread passes through a maze of sticks and skates to a waiting teammate.

Larionov played three seasons with the Canucks, registering 51 goals and 92 assists

in 210 games. But in 1991, he decided to play for a team in Switzerland after the Russian government demanded compensation from Vancouver for signing what they considered their "property."

Rather than have the Canucks make transfer payments to a government he now despised, Larionov regretfully bolted. The Canucks consequently put him on waivers, and the San Jose Sharks ultimately selected him on October 4, 1992.

But before putting on a Sharks uniform, he played one season in Switzerland (1992–93). Then it was off to the Bay area for 1993–94, where he reunited with former Red Army linemate Sergei Makarov.

Although many considered the 32-year-old to be a fading offensive player, Larionov collected 56 points in 60 games with the Sharks that season. He was also an integral part of that team's most defining moment: the shocking first-round playoff upset over prohibitive favorite Detroit.

Larionov led the Sharks in scoring (18 points in 14 games) during that emotional 1994 playoff season, and played one more season with San Jose before he was traded to Detroit on October 24, 1995, in exchange for Red Wing forward Ray Sheppard.

The acquisition allowed the Wings' Hall of Fame coach Scotty Bowman to organize one of the most exciting units on the ice. He soon put together a five-man, all-Russian unit, which consisted of forwards Larionov, Sergei Fedorov, and Vyacheslav Kozlov and defensemen Slava Fetisov and Vladimir Konstantinov—"The Russian Five."

The quintet soon began to skate and weave just as Tikhonov had taught them in the Soviet Union. It was a daring but highly successful experiment, and in 1997 secured Detroit's first Stanley Cup championship since 1955.

In the summer of 1997, Larionov, Fetisov, and Kozlov brought the world's most famous trophy to their homeland. The trio spent five days in Russia sharing the Cup with masses of fans and posing for pictures on Red Square. Larionov and Kozlov also made an emotional trip back to their hometown of Voskresensk, lugging the Cup to the Khimik hockey school, where they had perfected their craft as youngsters.

Larionov finished the 1997 playoffs fourth on the team in scoring, with 4 goals and 12 points in 20 games. The following season, Larionov won his second Stanley Cup championship with Detroit, defying age with his remarkable skills as the 1998–99 season began.

By the 2000–01 season, Larionov was with the Florida Panthers, with management's hope he could help Pavel Bure, the Russian "Rocket." By the end of the 2001 season, however, he was back in Detroit as the oldest player in the NHL. Despite the fact that he came to Detroit at the end of his illustrious career and didn't play five complete seasons with the Red Wings, Larionov was ranked in the Top 50 All-Time leading scorers in Detroit history, with 282 points, and collected his 500th career NHL point in 2000. By 2001–02, Igor accepted a lesser role. Nevertheless, he catapulted Detroit to another Stanley Cup with a pivotal sudden-death goal against North Carolina in the finals.

PETER LAVIOLETTE

BORN: Norwood, Massachusetts, December 7, 1964
POSITION: Defenseman, New York Rangers, 1988–89; Assistant Coach, Boston Bruins, 2000–01; Coach, New York Islanders, 2001–

Sparkling as a minor-league coach for the Providence Bruins, Peter Laviolette appeared to be heir-apparent for the parent Boston Bruins' head coaching job for the 2001–02 season, after Mike Keenan was fired in summer of 2001.

When the Bruins bypassed Laviolette in favor of Rob Ftorek, the Norwood, Massachusetts, native instead was signed by Mike Milbury as

head coach of the Nassau skaters. Laviolette made an instant impact on a club which had become a near-perennial no-show in the postseason.

Under Laviolette's orchestration, the Islanders started the 2001–02 campaign with one of the best starts in their history (11–1–1) and remained a playoff contender until the night of April 6, when they beat the Washington Capitals, clinching their first playoff birth since 1994. A calm and organized players' coach, Peter was lauded for his installation of a confident and disciplined attitude with the rebuilt Islanders.

A career minor-league defenseman, who toiled briefly for the New York Rangers, Laviolette fulfilled all the notices that had preceded him, as someone who could turn a team around quickly; i.e., an AHL Calder Cup win in 1998–99 with the longtime championship-starved Providence franchise.

HAL LAYCOE

BORN: Sutherland, Saskatchewan, June 23, 1922
DIED: April 29, 1997
POSITION: Defenseman, New York Rangers, 1945–47; Montreal Canadiens, 1947–51; Boston Bruins, 1951–56; Coach, Los Angeles Kings, 1969; Vancover Canucks, 1970–72

One of the few bespectacled defensemen in National Hockey League history, Hal Laycoe arrived in the majors via the New York Rangers' farm system, originally starring for the Eastern League's New York Rovers. He made his NHL debut playing 17 games in 1945–46 with the Rangers and became a regular in the following season.

Laycoe was more a thinker than a hitter and was dealt to Montreal prior to the 1947–48 season. After three and a half seasons with the Canadiens, Laycoe was dealt to the Boston Bruins in 1950–51, and finished his career in Boston following the 1955–56 season.

Although Laycoe was not considered an especially belligerent type, he is regarded as the catalyst for what became the biggest riot in hockey, the March 1955 eruption in Montreal after which Maurice "Rocket" Richard was suspended for the remainder of the 1954–55 season and the playoffs. It was Laycoe who originally struck Richard in a Bruin-Canadien game, and inspired the Rocket to retaliate. When linesman Cliff Thompson intervened, Richard hit Thompson. It was that blow that led to Richard's suspension, but it was Laycoe who originally hit Richard. Laycoe briefly coached Los Angeles and Vancouver of the NHL—but not too well.

VINCENT LECAVALIER

BORN: Île Bizard, Quebec, April 21, 1980
POSITION: Center, Tampa Bay Lightning, 1998–

Few young hockey players were placed in a pressure cooker so soon in their careers as Vincent Lecavalier.

Selected first overall in the 1998 Entry Draft, the tall, gangly French-Canadian was immediately dubbed "The Michael Jordan of Hockey" by his impetuous club owner Art Williams. The premature superstar nomination was based on an excellent amateur career, but did not allow for the fact that Lecavalier would be playing for an inept Tampa Bay Lightning team that he would have to carry.

Compounding his troubles was the fact that the team named him captain at age 20, although he was far too immature for this demanding role.

Affable and articulate, Lecavalier did his best to adjust to the demands until the 2001–02 season, when a falling-out with management inspired the club to trade him. A deal actually was made but cancelled at the 11th hour by ownership. Lecavalier finished the season disappointingly, and the Lightning once again missed the playoffs, as they had since Vince joined the team.

Swift and rangy, Lecavalier had the ability to both finesse and play physically, which made him a complete package with enormous potential. By the end of an excellent sophomore season in 1999–2000, Lecavalier more than doubled his rookie output with a team-leading 67 points and was anointed captain—the youngest in NHL history. But the responsibility weighed him down the following year, and a leg injury allowed him to play only 68 games and score just 51 points. Junior linemate Brad Richards joined the team as a rookie and picked up the scoring slack, but some wondered if the young Francophone would ever carry the team on his back.

A contract holdout to start 2001–02 led to turmoil between Lecavalier and coach John Tortorella, and the stripping of Vince's captaincy. Worse, the Quebec native only had 20 goals and 17 assists in 76 games, a frightening setback for a supposed franchise player.

JOHN LeCLAIR

BORN: St. Albans, Vermont, July 5, 1969
POSITION: Left Wing, Montreal Canadiens, 1991–95; Philadelphia Flyers, 1995–
AWARDS/HONORS: Bud Light Plus/Minus Award, 1997, 1999; NHL First Team All-Star, 1995, 1998; NHL Second Team All-Star, 1996–97, 1999; NHL All-Star Game, 1996–2000

Every so often a team is fortunate enough to make a trade that proves to be a high-octane catalyst; a deal that galvanizes a club from the realm of so-so to superior. For the Flyers just such a deal was made on February 9, 1995, when general manager Bob Clarke exchanged top scorer Mark Recchi for Montreal Canadiens John LeClair, Eric Desjardins, and Gilbert Dionne.

From the moment the six-feet-three, 225-pound left wing donned the black, orange, and white of the Flyers he became a literal goal machine. In his very first game for Philadelphia against the New Jersey Devils at The Meadowlands, the massive forward scored his 50th career goal and gave every indication that he had found his niche, which he could never do in Montreal. In his first 37 games with the Flyers, LeClair scored 25 goals and tallied 24 assists.

John and big Eric Lindros worked together like perfectly meshed gears, and with Mikael Renberg on right wing, formed the "Legion of Doom" line. LeClair was named an NHL All-Star in the 1994–95 season and finished ninth in league scoring. The next season, he became the seventh Flyer ever to enter the prestigious 50-goal club, scoring 51.

Unquestionably, John LeClair closed the decade of the 1990s as one of the most productive Flyers ever to grace Broad Street. He became only the second Philadelphia forward in history to record three consecutive 50-goal seasons (1995-96 through 1997-98) and managed to limit his penalty minutes in the process.

A two-time United States Olympian, LeClair's string of 40-plus goal seasons ended at five in 2000-01 when a chronic back injury limited him to 16 games and 7 goals. Before the trading of exiled linemate Eric Lindros in summer 2001, LeClair re-upped his contract with Philadelphia, but struggled mightily as the Atlantic Division–champion Flyers were eliminated in the first round by the Ottawa Senators. By the autumn of 2002, LeClair seemed free of injury and poised to regain his scoring form.

Clearly, the acquisition of the Vermonter ranked among the finest deals ever made by Bob Clarke and one of the best things to happen to Philadelphia hockey.

ALBERT LEDUC

BORN: Valleyfield, Quebec, July 31, 1901
DIED: Date unknown
POSITION: Defenseman, Montreal Canadiens, 1925-33, 1934-35; New York Rangers, 1933-34; Ottawa Senators, 1934

Defensemen such as Albert "Battleship" Leduc infused the Canadiens with the kind of pizzazz that earned them the label of hockey's most colorful pre–World War II team. Except for a brief exile in 1933-34, when he played for both the New York Rangers and the Ottawa Senators, Leduc skated exclusively for the Flying Frenchmen from 1925 through his NHL finale in 1934-35. Leduc frequently was overshadowed by his defense partners, Sylvio Mantha and Herb Gardiner. But Leduc, according to former Canadiens managing director Frank Selke Sr., was "a typical Habitant." As Selke described Leduc, "Battleship had a highly excitable temperament. On the ice he made all of his moves at top speed. He could score on his long end-to-end rushes but, more than all else, he handed out a body check which, in his day, was the most important attribute of any defenseman."

BRIAN LEETCH

BORN: Corpus Christi, Texas, March 3, 1968
POSITION: Defenseman, New York Rangers, 1988–
AWARDS/HONORS: Calder Memorial Trophy, 1989; James Norris Memorial Trophy, 1992, 1997; Conn Smythe Trophy, 1994; NHL All-Rookie Team, 1989; NHL First Team All-Star, 1992, 1997; NHL Second Team All-Star, 1991, 1994, 1996; NHL All-Star Game, 1990-92, 1994, 1996-98, 2001-02

Brian Leetch was the New York Rangers' best defenseman for well over a decade.

The two-time Norris Trophy winner was the linchpin of the Blueshirt lineup following his arrival after the 1988 Olympics.

Smooth, clean, and calm in both zones, Leetch metamorphosed into a perennial All-Star, frequently appearing at the top of scoring races among defensemen along with contemporaries Ray Bourque, Paul Coffey, and Larry Murphy.

Brian Leetch, Rangers defenseman

His first full season, 1988–89, saw Leetch storm the NHL with 23 goals and 48 assists from the Broadway backline, as well as Rookie of the Year honors. He markedly improved in his own zone as the Rangers built their franchise around the dynamic Leetch, young goaltender Mike Richter, and, in 1991–92, the game's premier leader, Mark Messier, whose arrival that year lifted Leetch to a career-high 102-point season and a Norris Trophy.

A broken ankle would hinder Brian's progress during the next season, but he would prove durable afterward, having only one abbreviated season (a 50-game 1999–2000) through the end of the century.

During the Rangers' magical postseason of 1993–94, Leetch led all players with 11 goals and 23 assists in 23 postseason matches en route to a Conn Smythe win and a Stanley Cup.

The 1996–97 campaign featured the addition of Wayne Gretzky, an appearance in the Eastern Conference finals, and a second Norris Trophy for the Corpus Christi native. Messier abruptly departed to Vancouver that summer, and Leetch assumed the captaincy. But Brian never appeared comfortable in the role, often overcompensating in myriad situations for his underachieving team, and his shift from a plus-31 rating the season before to a minus-36 proved it. But when Messier returned in 2000–01, Leetch was rejuvenated and turned in a vintage 79-point performance.

The greatest American-born defenseman ever, Leetch scored 205 goals and 655 assists over 939 career games, all as a Ranger, with 89 points in 82 playoff games coming into 2001–02. As the Rangers tried again and again to surround him with veteran players who would bring the team back to its 1994 form, Leetch's Rangers missed the postseason for five straight seasons through 2001–02, despite his expert play.

HUGH LEHMAN

BORN: Pembroke, Ontario, October 27, 1885
DIED: April 8, 1961
POSITION: Goaltender, Vancouver Millionaires (PCHA), 1915–26; Chicago Blackhawks, 1926–28
AWARDS/HONORS: Hockey Hall of Fame, 1958

Hugh Lehman, a Hall of Fame goaltender, broke into hockey in 1909 with Berlin (now Kitchener) of the OPHL. After shuttling around between Berlin, Galt, and New Westminster, Hugh settled down with Vancouver of the PCHA, where he minded their nets for the next 12 seasons.

Lehman was on eight championship squads over his 20-year pro career, but only one Cup winner—the 1915 Millionaires. Hugh moved east in 1927, spending the last two seasons of his career with the Chicago Blackhawks of the NHL.

JACQUES LEMAIRE

BORN: La Salle, Quebec, September 7, 1945
POSITION: Center, Montreal Canadiens, 1967–79; Coach, Montreal Canadiens, 1983–85; New Jersey Devils, 1993–98; Minnesota Wild, 2000–
AWARDS/HONORS: Jack Adams Award, 1994; NHL All-Star Game, 1970, 1973

Speedy Jacques Lemaire ranks among the most underappreciated stars of Montreal's dynastic Canadiens, despite scoring 44 goals in the 1972–73 season. Jacques was known for his potent slap shot, which he was not afraid to use, whether from within

Jacques Lemaire

60 feet or six feet. It was Jacques's 80-footer, which sailed by Chicago goalie Tony Esposito, that tied the seventh game of the 1970–71 Stanley Cup finals, eventually leading to the Habs' 16th Stanley Cup. Lemaire picked up 9 goals and 10 assists in that playoff.

Lemaire was hot again in 1977–78, tallying 36 goals and 61 assists for 97 points in the regular season.

It was a measure of his value to the four-Stanley Cup Montreal dynasty that following his retirement after the 1978–79 season, the Canadiens' Cup reign ended.

Jacques then pursued a coaching career at the bottom of the ladder, starting in Switzerland, then moving to the Quebec Major Junior League and finally to the National Hockey League with the Habs from 1983 to 1985, with whom he won an Adams Division championship before moving to their front office.

But it would be as bench-boss of the New Jersey Devils that Jacques would achieve his greatest success. Purveyor of "The Trap," a stingy defensive neutral zone strategy, Lemaire did more with a lot less, and infuriated opponents with his clever systematic style. The wizard guided the Devils to a Stanley Cup in 1995, but had the misfortune of missing the playoffs the following year, and he resigned in 1998.

"Jacques Hockey" returned to the NHL, this time with the expansion Minnesota Wild, in 2000, where he recorded a 25-win, 39-loss, 13-tie inaugural season, sensational by modern NHL standards. Lemaire's talent-deprived team emerged as a competitive unit in the West through the 2001–02 season.

CLAUDE LEMIEUX

BORN: Buckingham, Quebec, July 16, 1965
POSITION: Right Wing, Montreal Canadiens, 1983–90; New Jersey Devils, 1990–95, 1999–2000; Colorado Avalanche, 1995–99; Phoenix Coyotes, 2000–
AWARDS/HONORS: Conn Smythe Trophy, 1995

Claude Lemieux has been called many things; most of them even favorable. In 1993, the *Hockey News Yearbook* tabbed him an "overachiever," adding, "he may be pound for pound, the hardest guy to play against in the league."

That statement held up two years later during the 1995 Stanley Cup playoffs as the French-Canadian right-winger, who speaks impeccable English, scored big goal after big goal, leading his New Jersey Devils to the championship finals against the Detroit Red Wings. The Devils got that far because Lemieux put them there. With the New Jersey–Philadelphia East Conference finals tied at two games apiece, Lemieux won Game Five, 3–2, with a heavy blast from the right point at 19:15 of the third period.

By the end of the fourth game of the Stanley Cup finals against the Detroit Red

Wings, the Devils had won their first Stanley Cup and Claude Lemieux had won the Conn Smythe Trophy as the playoffs' MVP.

"I am not the type of player who drives himself crazy thinking about the game," Lemieux said. "I am a reaction-type person. When I go to the rink in the morning, I am not the type of guy who could go out on a business lunch the day of a game."

In 1995, Lemieux was traded to Colorado, where he played for five years. He was then added again to the Jersey roster for the 2000 Cup run, but went to the Phoenix Coyotes as a free agent in December of 2000.

Upon his arrival in Phoenix, Claude had won four Stanley Cup championships with three teams: Montreal, 1986; New Jersey, 1995 and 2000; and Colorado, 1996. He also ranked third in the league as a "clutch" player, having scored 19 playoff game-winning goals, behind only Brett Hull and The Great One, Wayne Gretzky (who just happened to be a co-owner of the Phoenix Coyotes).

Lemieux once said that his only wish was to win another Stanley Cup, since he had only won a measly four.

Disliked by many foes for his needling and other annoying traits, Lemieux, nevertheless, was respected for his clutch play and competitive zeal. However, by the 2002–03 season, he appeared to have lost his touch.

MARIO LEMIEUX

BORN: Montreal, Quebec, October 5, 1965
POSITION: Center, Pittsburgh Penguins, 1984-97; 2000-
AWARDS/HONORS: Calder Memorial Trophy, 1985; Lester B. Pearson Award, 1986, 1988, 1993, 1996; Dodge Performer of the Year Award, 1988-89; Art Ross Trophy, 1988-89, 1992-93, 1996-97; Hart Memorial Trophy, 1988, 1993, 1996; Dodge Ram Tough Award, 1989; Conn Smythe Trophy, 1991-92; ProSet/NHL Player of the Year Award, 1992; Alka-Seltzer Plus Award, 1993; Bill Masterton Memorial Trophy, 1993; Lester Patrick Trophy, 2000; NHL All-Rookie Team, 1985; NHL First Team All-Star, 1988-89, 1993, 1996-97; NHL Second Team All-Star, 1986-87, 1992, 2001; NHL All-Star Game, 1985-86, 1988-90, 1992, 1996-97, 2001; Hockey Hall of Fame, 1997

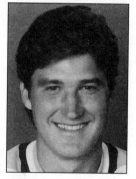

Mario Lemieux, Penguins captain

Mario Lemieux was probably the most talented scorer ever to play in the NHL, Wayne Gretzky and Gordie Howe notwithstanding. By the time of his first retirement at the young age of 31, he had a collection of scoring titles, MVP awards, and Stanley Cups to his name. Oh, yes, he also played through excruciating back pain, survived cancer, and he saved hockey in Pittsburgh—twice.

Yet there were some who felt that he could have been more, should have done more. It took years, two Stanley Cups, and a dramatic return from cancer before Lemieux was accorded the respect for his total game. Earlier many refused to give him credit despite outstanding play.

Like some superstars, Lemieux was a legend before he ever made it to the NHL. Up to 5,000 fans would show up to watch him play in youth hockey games at the tender age of six. When Lemieux was 12, Scotty Bowman was calling him the greatest prospect he'd ever seen.

By Lemieux's draft year, 1984, there were even rumors that teams would throw games to finish last and have the privilege of drafting him. As the season wore down, two teams, the New Jersey Devils and the Pittsburgh Penguins, were bad enough to have a chance at Lemieux. New Jersey was the weaker team, but they actually tried to win games down the stretch.

No one can say with certainty what Pittsburgh was trying to do, but what happened was obvious. Pittsburgh benched regulars down the stretch, played untried rookies and lost enough games to win the Lemieux sweepstakes. When teams approached him to deal the number one pick in the 1984 draft, Penguins general manager Eddie Johnston announced what it would take: "Up front, $1 million in a suitcase," he said. "Plus $200,000 a year for the rest of my life."

Johnston was probably asking for too little. The Penguins would not have stayed in Pittsburgh if they had not drafted Lemieux. As then-Oiler coach Glen Sather put it, "Without Lemieux, they pack up the team and move to another city." Paul Steigerwald, then the marketing director for the Penguins, described the pre-Lemieux scene in Pittsburgh: "You'd walk into the arena and there would be 3,800 people in the place and most of them were booing. Some of them had bags on their heads. The team would take the ice and they'd yell obscenities. Hockey in Pittsburgh had reached the bottom, the absolute pits of professional sports." Lemieux gave the fans hope, and a reason to show up at games.

Once Mario hit the NHL in 1984, fans could see the wondrous skills that had inspired all the fuss. Lemieux was endowed by nature with a six-feet-four, 225-pound frame, soft hands, a huge reach, speed, vision, creativity, an accu-

rate, disguised shot, and excellent passing skills. It's no wonder that in one game against New Jersey on New Year's Eve, 1988, Lemieux scored a goal in every way possible: at even strength, on a power play, shorthanded, on a penalty shot, and into the empty net.

The years from 1984 to 1988 were really about three things for Lemieux: improving the team in Pittsburgh, winning his first scoring title, and solidifying his reputation during the 1987 Canada Cup final against the Soviet Union. By the end of the 1987–88 season, the Penguins actually had a winning record, and Lemieux had his scoring title and the Hart Trophy as league MVP. However, many critics dismissed Lemieux, contending that because the Penguins hadn't won a Cup yet, he must be all about statistics, and he wasn't a winner. They called him a floater. These critics were ignoring the fact that no player, not Gretzky, not Howe, not Orr, could have won with the team Pittsburgh had surrounding Lemieux.

During the 1987 Canada Cup tournament, Lemieux had the chance to show the hockey world what he could do when he was surrounded by the best the NHL had to offer. He silenced his critics; the 1987 Canada Cup firmly established Lemieux as a superstar and a big game player as he set a Canada Cup scoring record with 11 goals while playing on a line with Wayne Gretzky and winning the title.

The seasons between 1989 and 1992 were filled with emotional joy and the beginnings of chronic physical pain for Lemieux. He reinforced his superstar reputation with a 46-game point scoring streak in 1989–90, but he was playing in constant pain as he coped with a herniated disc. Off-season back surgery led to a spinal infection that kept him out until January 1991. His health problems would continue throughout the rest of his career, and it was a rare event for him to play without back pain, or worse.

Lemieux returned in 1991 and led the Penguins to the Stanley Cup with a dominating 44-point performance in 23 playoff games. Pittsburgh was finally able to surround Lemieux with a high-quality supporting cast, which included forwards Ron Francis, Jaromir Jagr, Kevin Stevens, Mark Recchi, defensemen Paul Coffey, Larry Murphy, Ulf Samuelsson, and goalie Tom Barrasso. It was a deep, profoundly talented group that allowed Mario to shine. He won the Conn Smythe Trophy as the MVP of the playoffs despite back pain so severe he was unable to bend over and tie his own skate laces.

The Penguins won the Cup again in 1992, with Lemieux earning the playoff MVP trophy once again; but what happened in the 1992–93 season finally silenced anyone who still doubted Lemieux's dedication to the game. In January 1993, he was diagnosed with Hodgkin's disease, a form of cancer that had invaded his lymph nodes. He underwent two months of radiation treatment and then returned to turn in what was the most amazing single-season performance ever seen in the NHL.

The day of his return, March 2, 1993, in Philadelphia, Lemieux played the same day as his final radiation treatment, and received a 90-second standing ovation from the Flyers fans. Lemieux responded with a goal and an assist, and then went on a scoring spree that saw him finish the season with 160 points in only 60 games. He won the scoring title and the league MVP award, and his 2.67 points per game were the third best in league history.

An intensely private man, and often solitary figure, the last years of Lemieux's career were spent deciding whether he wanted to play. Continual back pain and anemia from the radiation treatments caused him to sit out the 1994–95 season. He came back for two more seasons, and retired in 1997 after two more scoring titles and one more MVP trophy. He felt that his physical condition, and the hooking and restraining fouls that were being let go, made it impossible for him play up to his own standards. And he did what no other NHL star of his talent has done; he walked away the best player in the game. The NHL Hall of Fame waived the traditional 3-year waiting period and enshrined Lemieux immediately in 1997.

By the 1998–99 season, the Penguins' financial woes had become acute. The team's deferred contracts were coming due and the revenues were not there to cover the costs. Declining attendance, coupled with an out-of-date arena that had few revenue-generating amenities, had cut into the cash flow and the Penguins were facing bankruptcy. If the team were sold it seemed likely that it would be moved.

Lemieux was actually one the Penguins' main creditors, as he was still owed millions in deferred salary. He not only wanted his money, but felt strongly that the team belonged in Pittsburgh. Mario recruited a group of partners and came up with the money to purchase the Penguins. Before the start of the 1999–2000 season, he stood in front of a judge and presented the plan to buy the club and save it from both bankruptcy and the moving vans. The plan was accepted; the team remained in Pittsburgh.

In 2000, however, everything changed. Mario became tired of sitting in the owner's box, and feeling better than he had in years, decided to make an unprecedented return to the game of hockey. In doing so, he became only the third player, after Gordie Howe and Guy Lafleur, already inducted into the Hall of Fame to play in an NHL game.

In the final half of the 2000–01 season, Lemieux scored 35 goals and had 41 assists, easily making him the second-half MVP of the season as the Penguins made a surprising run to the Eastern Conference finals against New Jersey before losing to the Devils.

The following season, however, would not be as fortuitous. Hip and back problems would keep Lemieux out of action for much of the season, though he did play in the 2002 Olympic Games at Salt Lake for gold medal–winning Team Canada, which exasperated the fans of the injury-riddled Penguins. Having traded Jaromir Jagr over the summer, the 2001–02 Penguins did not make the playoffs, with Mario vowing to be at 100 percent for the next campaign, or else he'd fire himself!

PIT LEPINE

BORN: St. Anne de Bellevue, Quebec, July 30, 1901
DIED: August 2, 1955
POSITION: Center, Montreal Canadiens, 1925–38

Pit Lepine epitomized the French-Canadian hockey player who gave his all for Les Canadiens, the sporting symbol of French Canada. Every National Hockey League game that the center Lepine played from his rookie year, 1925–26, through his retirement after the 1937–38 season, he played for Montreal's Canadiens.

If Lepine had a problem it was the fact that he was chronically overshadowed by the Canadiens' superstar of the late '20s and early '30s, Howie Morenz. "Lepine brought to the game a polish seldom seen before," said former Canadiens managing director Frank Selke Sr. "On any other team Pit would have been a blazing meteor, but he was doomed to play all of his hockey in the shadow of the truculent Morenz who, at that time, was the fiercest competitor in hockey."

TONY LESWICK

BORN: Humboldt, Saskatchewan, March 17, 1923
DIED: July 1, 2001
POSITION: Left Wing, New York Rangers, 1945–51; Detroit Red Wings, 1951–55, 1957–58; Chicago Blackhawks, 1955–56
AWARDS/HONORS: NHL Second Team All-Star, 1950; NHL All-Star Game, 1955

Tony Leswick came to Detroit in one of Jack Adams's least-discussed but most important deals the Red Wings' general manager ever executed. It happened in 1951 and would directly result in a Red Wings' Stanley Cup triumph.

But before Leswick became a Red Wing, he already had established himself as one of New York's most popular stickhandlers.

In 1946, it was clear to Frank Boucher, who had taken over the helm of the Rangers, that new blood was needed to replace the prewar heroes, who had lost their spark and their style. One of the first of the "finds" was a small, bulldog-type forward named Tony Leswick. Within two years, "Tough Tony," as he was known on Broadway, became the team's leading scorer.

The turnabout for the Rangers from chronic losers to consistent winners didn't happen overnight, but Leswick went a long way to pumping fighting blood into the postwar team. He not only led them in scoring during the 1946–47 campaign, but was just as useful as the supreme needler of the opposition and "shadow" of its leading scorers, until traded to Detroit in 1951–52.

More than anyone else, the fabulous "Rocket" Richard of the Montreal Canadiens had the life annoyed out of him by Leswick. Once, at the Montreal Forum, Leswick needled the Rocket, and Richard swung his stick at Leswick. The referee sent Richard to the penalty box with a two-minute minor. Leswick didn't stop there and pestered the Rocket

Tony Leswick as a Ranger

throughout the match. With just a minute remaining, Richard blew up again, and again the referee sent him to the penalty box.

At game's end, Richard bolted from the penalty box and charged Leswick, whereupon the two of them brawled for several minutes while teammates and officials attempted to separate the pair. The Richard-Leswick feud continued for several years.

Of course Richard wasn't Leswick's only target. Once, in a playoff game against the Detroit Red Wings, he was given a two-minute penalty, followed closely by a two-minute penalty to teammate Nick Mickoski. The time-keeper, whose duty it was to wave inmates back onto the ice when their penalty time had expired, became Leswick's target.

"Tony chattered and argued about the time he was to return to the ice," said Rangers publicist Stan Saplin, "and so confused the time-keeper that he was allowed back in the game long before his penalty time was up."

Leswick also could score. During an era of low scoring, "Mighty Mouse" recorded 27- and 24-goal seasons, which put him in the high echelon of attackers.

After starring on the minor-league level during the World War II years, Leswick made his major-league debut during the 1945–46 season with the Rangers.

"Tony was a combative little bugger," said Boucher, general manager of the Broadway Blueshirts. "He played a lot bigger than his size."

In the 1949–50 playoffs, Leswick was a key Ranger as the Blueshirts upset Rocket Richard's Montreal Canadiens in the opening round. Tony also was an offensive force when New York extended the eventual Stanley Cup champion Detroit Red Wings to seven games—and double-overtime in the finale—before losing on a screened shot.

The playoff also was a scouting opportunity for Jack Adams, who liked what he had seen of Leswick. Adams made a mental note to keep tabs on the winger and on June 8, 1951, the scouting report paid off for Detroit. In one of the best unheralded deals in franchise history, Adams shipped forward Gaye Stewart to New York for Leswick.

A onetime Calder Trophy winner, Stewart was a complete bust with the Rangers, playing barely two seasons in New York, while Leswick proved to be a timely performer with the Wings.

In Game Seven of the 1953–54 Stanley Cup finals, with the score tied, 1–1, after regulation time, the Wings looked to top scorers such as Gordie Howe and Ted Lindsay for the big goal. But at the four-minute mark of the first extra session, coach Tommy Ivan dispatched a checking unit featuring Leswick and Glen Skov to the ice.

As they completed their turn, Skov dished the puck to Leswick, who shot a soft drive—almost like a baseball Texas Leaguer—at Canadiens goalie Gerry McNeil. It should have been an easy shot for the Montreal netminder to handle, but for the fact that All-Star defenseman Doug Harvey was fronting for McNeil.

Ironically, Harvey was a top-ranking baseball player in the off-season and was attempting a baseball play on the rink as Leswick's shot approached the goal. Harvey reached up either to glove the puck or deflect it harmlessly into the corner. For some strange reason, the rubber richocheted off the index finger of Harvey's glove and flew over the defenseman and the crouched McNeil.

Tony Leswick's most meaningful shot sailed into the Montreal net at exactly 4:29 of the overtime and won another Stanley Cup for the Red Wings.

A year later, Tough Tony again played on a Detroit Cup winner, although his contribution was only one goal, and not the championship shot, as it had been a year earlier.

Manager Adams apparently believed that Leswick had had it after the 1955 championship year. On May 28, 1955, Tony was traded with Skov, Johnny Wilson, and Benny Woit to Chicago for Jerry Toppazzini, John McCormack, Dave Creighton, and Gord Hollingworth. However, Adams relented and reacquired

Leswick on September 1, 1956, from Chicago for cash alone.

Tony's last NHL season was 1957–58, when he scored 1 goal and 2 assists in 22 games. He finished his pro career in the minors with the Edmonton Flyers, concluding in 1959–60 with the Western League's Vancouver Canucks.

Never a Hall of Famer, nonetheless Tony Leswick would always be remembered for his hustle—and the 1954 blooper that turned into a Cup winner.

RICK LEY

BORN: Orillia, Ontario, November 2, 1948
POSITION: Defenseman, Toronto Maple Leafs, 1968–72; New England Whalers (WHA), 1972–79; Hartford Whalers, 1979–81; Coach, Hartford Whalers, 1989–91; Vancouver Canucks, 1994–96
AWARDS/HONORS: Team Canada (WHA) 1974; First Team All-Star (WHA), 1979; Second Team All-Star (WHA), 1978; Outstanding Defenseman (WHA), 1979

Originally a member of the Toronto Maple Leafs "Kiddie Korps" on defense, along with Jim Dorey and Brad Selwood, Rick Ley joined the WHA's New England Whalers in 1972.

Only five feet nine, Ley was built like a fireplug and was impossible to get around when on the ice and fired up. Although he didn't appear to be, Ley was a thinking defenseman and seldom made dumb moves. Better defensively than offensively, Ley was chosen for the 1974 Team Canada–Russia series in which he unfortunately distinguished himself by gratuitously thrashing Russian forward ace Valery Kharlamov seconds after the game ended in a loss for Team Canada. He later apologized, but the Canadians lost the series, anyway.

He was named the Whalers' captain in 1975, and was one of three players in Hartford history, joining John McKenzie and Gordie Howe, to have his jersey retired. After retiring

in 1981, Ley coached the Whalers for two seasons (1989–91) before serving the Vancouver Canucks organization for seven years as scout, coach, assistant coach, and minor-league affiliate head coach. By the end of the century, Rick brought his leadership to the Toronto Maple Leaf bench as an assistant to coach–general manager Pat Quinn, whom Ley worked under in Vancouver. When Quinn took ill during the 2002 playoffs Ley took over as temporary head coach, receiving rave reviews for his efforts.

NICKLAS LIDSTROM

BORN: Vasteras, Sweden, April 28, 1970
POSITION: Defense, Detroit Red Wings, 1991–
AWARDS/HONORS: James Norris Memorial Trophy, 2001–02; Conn Smythe Trophy, 2002; NHL All-Rookie Team, 1992; NHL First Team All-Star, 1998–2001; NHL All-Star Game, 1996, 1998–2002

"I'd hate to think how ordinary we would be without him," said Detroit's Steve Yzerman during the summer of 1999. The "him" to whom the Red Wing captain was referring was not Sergei Fedorov nor Brendan Shanahan. It was defenseman Nicklas Lidstrom.

Nicklas Lidstrom broke into the NHL as a shy rookie in the fall of 1991. After being selected by Detroit in the third round (53rd overall) of the 1989 draft, Lidstrom played in the Swedish Elite League for three seasons before debuting in a Red Wing uniform.

He registered his first two points of his career on October 5, 1991, against Toronto, en route to tying Reed Larson's franchise record for most points by a rookie defenseman (60). That year, he also tied Marcel Dionne's club mark for most assists by a rookie (49), was named to the NHL All-Rookie team, and finished second to Pavel Bure in the Calder Trophy voting for rookie of the year.

Not bad for a kid whose boyhood idol was perhaps the best Swedish defenseman to ever lace up a pair of skates, Borje Salming.

With his lean physique, Lidstrom played more of a mental game than a physical one. He positioned himself perfectly on nearly every play, keeping the opposition away from scoring chances. Offensively, Lidstrom skated effortlessly out of his zone, passing the puck at the precise moment with pinpoint accuracy. His intelligence helped him seemingly trick and outmaneuver his opponents.

However unassuming Lidstrom's style of play, it helped the Detroit organization win back-to-back Stanley Cups in 1997 and 1998.

After a spectacular rookie year, Lidstrom struggled during his sophomore season. He slumped to 7 goals and 41 points in 1992–93, his lowest goal and point total in his career, through 2001–02.

Part of the problem that year was adjusting to his new defensive partner, future Hall of Famer Paul Coffey. The smooth-skating Coffey relieved some of Lidstrom's offensive load while lending his knowledge and expertise of the game to the young defenseman.

Bouncing back, Lidstrom played in the All-Star game for the first time during the 1995–96 season. That year, he posted then-career highs in goals (17) and points (67). It was also during that season he developed his powerful one-time shot.

Perhaps Lidstrom's most amazing feat throughout his career has been his lack of time spent in the penalty box. He has never accumulated over 30 minutes in penalties in one season. In fact, in 1999, he was the runner-up for the Lady Byng Trophy, given to the most sportsmanlike player in the league.

Lidstrom finished the 1998 postseason by setting a Detroit record for most points (19) and most assists (13) by a defenseman, as the Red Wings won their second consecutive Stanley Cup championship.

But as his career began to prosper and Hall of Fame greatness began to beckon, Nicklas Lidstrom was ready to throw it all away. Late in the 1998–99 season, Lidstrom began to ponder returning to his native Sweden.

Not because he was sick of playing hockey for the Detroit Red Wings. Not because he thought he had accomplished everything there was to the game. But simply because he wanted his family, and in particular his two young sons, to grow up in Sweden.

As his contract expired in the summer of 1999, Lidstrom's threats of leaving became very real. But Lidstrom still was unsure what was best.

Finally, in June 1999, Lidstrom instructed his agent Don Meehan to begin negotiations with general manager Ken Holland and the Wings, and the two sides agreed on a three-year contract worth close to $22 million.

With the new contract under his belt, Nicklas went on to enjoy his best season of his career in 1999–2000. He recorded career highs in goals (20), assists (53), and points (73).

As Lidstrom's career began to turn the page, the recognition of his accomplishments increased, and in 2000–01, Lidstrom was finally awarded the Norris Trophy. The following season, Detroit loaded their roster with more future Hall of Famers in Dominik Hasek, Luc Robitaille, and Brett Hull, and promptly wrapped up the President's Trophy one month before season's end, with the Stanley Cup in their sights, and eventually annexed the Stanley Cup.

PELLE LINDBERGH

BORN: Stockholm, Sweden, May 24, 1959
DIED: November 10, 1985
POSITION: Goaltender, Philadelphia Flyers, 1981–85
AWARDS/HONORS: Vezina Trophy, 1985; NHL All-Rookie Team, 1983; NHL First Team All-Star, 1985

Pelle Lindbergh was a young goaltender primed to star in the National Hockey League. During the 1984–85 season, Lindbergh was named to the NHL's First All-Star Team, won the Vezina Trophy, and most importantly, brought the Flyers to the Stanley Cup finals.

It took the young Swede a season to adjust to the NHL, but he soon acclimated himself to the North American brand of hockey. He posted 40 wins during his marquee 1985–86 season.

At the age of 26, Pelle was at the top of his game, and one of the league's best backstops, when he was killed instantly in a high-speed car crash on November 10, 1986. The shocking and untimely tragedy left the Flyers devastated. It would be several seasons before the huge void left by Lindbergh's death would be filled, with the flowering of Ron Hextall in the Philadelphia net.

TREVOR LINDEN

BORN: Medicine Hat, Alberta, April 11, 1970
POSITION: Center/Right Wing, Vancouver Canucks, 1988–98, 2001–; New York Islanders, 1998–99; Montreal Canadiens, 1999–2000; Washington Capitals, 2000–01
AWARDS/HONORS: King Clancy Memorial Trophy, 1997; NHL All-Rookie Team, 1989; NHL All-Star Game, 1991–92

From his rookie season, 1988–89, with Vancouver, Trevor Linden displayed a calm and confidence rarely seen among young hockey players. He finished second in voting for the Calder Trophy and was named Rookie of the Year by the *Hockey News*. In time, the center–right wing developed a majesty about his presence.

The overall package was nothing but success as he led the Canucks to the Stanley Cup finals in 1994. Ultimately, Vancouver lost in seven games to the New York Rangers, but Linden clearly had established himself as one of the foremost players in the league.

His reputation was further enhanced when he was named president of the National Hockey League Players' Association, although that association caused some concern among ownership.

Injuries during the 1996–97 and 1997–98 seasons limited Linden's production and

soured him with the team brass. His unusually low 9 goals in 49 games sparked a trade to the New York Islanders, where he stayed for two years and played for Team Canada in the 1998 Winter Olympics.

The six-feet-four, 220-pound center became captain of the Islanders, but his efforts brought no success to a weak, transitional team, and he was dealt to Montreal in less than two years, and traded to the Washington Capitals during the 2000–01 season.

Trevor played only 18 games in Washington, six of those in the 2001 Stanley Cup playoffs, before being traded back to the Canucks in the off-season. Clearly, Vancouver fans welcomed him back with open arms. During his rookie season with the Canucks, Linden had become the first rookie to be named team MVP, led the team in power play goals (10), even-strength points (40), shooting percentage (16.1 percent), tied for first on the team in goals (30), and was second in points (59). The Iron Man had returned to his rightful home, helping the Canucks gain a playoff berth with a dynamic homestretch drive.

ERIC LINDROS

BORN: London, Ontario, February 28, 1973
POSITION: Center, Philadelphia Flyers, 1992–2000; New York Rangers, 2001–
AWARDS/HONORS: Hart Memorial Trophy, 1995; Lester B. Pearson Award, 1995; NHL All-Rookie Team, 1993; NHL First Team All-Star, 1995; NHL Second Team All-Star, 1996; NHL All-Star Game, 1994, 1996–2000

No player ever created a bigger stir in the hockey world before joining the NHL than Eric Lindros. The most publicized player in Canadian Junior hockey history, Lindros was frequently compared to the league greats of the time, Mario Lemieux, Mark Messier, and Wayne Gretzky.

After refusing to sign with the Quebec Nordiques when they drafted him in 1991,

Lindros was soon traded to the Flyers in a 1992 blockbuster deal. Philadelphia, who immediately signed Lindros to a six-year contract, gave up goalie Ron Hextall, defensemen Steve Duchesne and Kerry Huffman, centers Mike Ricci and Peter Forsberg, left wing Chris Simon, top draft picks in 1993 and 1994, and $15 million in exchange for the rookie who had yet to play in an NHL game.

During his rookie season, Eric starred, centering a line with Mark Recchi and Brent Fedyk. However, he soon found that his hulking size was matched by other NHLers and due to injuries suffered from on-ice hits, Lindros missed 23 games during his first year.

While he frequently missed games during his early years, he was still able to put up big numbers, scoring 41 goals in his rookie year and 45 in his sophomore year. But it would take three seasons before he could lead his team back into the playoffs.

During the lockout-shortened 1994–95 season, Eric teamed up with John LeClair and Mikael Renberg to form the Legion of Doom line and catapulted the Flyers into the playoffs. In only 46 games that year, Eric netted 70 points, leading his team into the Conference finals before they were eliminated. In 1995–96, Lindros scored 47 goals and 115 points, but could not take his team past the second round. With the Flyers in the Stanley Cup finals, 1997 seemed to be a promising year, but they could not make it past a solid Red Wing team. Cup-hungry critics were becoming restless, and many placed blame on Lindros.

Soon, concussions began to affect Lindros's career. He frequently had to miss games, and after a hard hit from Devils defenseman Scott Stevens during Game Seven of the 2000 Eastern Conference finals, it was questionable whether Lindros would play again. He had missed the entire 2000–01 season recovering from previous concussions.

After a bitter feud with Philadelphia general manager Bobby Clarke, Lindros demanded to be traded, and during the summer of 2001, was moved to the Rangers for winger Jan Hlavac, defenseman Kim Johnsson, prospect Pavel Brendl, and a draft pick.

It was an incredible risk for the Rangers, but proved a worthy move when Eric and linemates Mike York and Theo Fleury propelled the Rangers to first place early in the 2001–02 season. Lindros suffered another "mild" concussion in December 2001, and returned a shell of his mean, hard-nosed self, although he would lead the team with goals (37) and points (73) in only 72 games. Despite the presence of boyhood idol, Mark Messier, Lindros became the Rangers' new symbol; as he went, so did the team. Unfortunately, Lindros and his Blueshirts did not go into the postseason for the fifth straight year. However, Lindros's game improved with the arrival of Pavel Bure in a late-season trade. The primary concern as the 2002–03 season began was whether Eric would remain healthy.

TED LINDSAY

BORN: Renfrew, Ontario, July 29, 1925
POSITION: Left Wing, Detroit Red Wings, 1944-57, 1964-65; Chicago Blackhawks, 1957-60; General Manager, Detroit Red Wings, 1977-80
AWARDS/HONORS: Art Ross Trophy, 1950; NHL First Team All-Star, 1950-54, 1956-57; NHL Second Team All-Star, 1949; Hockey Hall of Fame, 1966

One of the most determined and fearsome skaters in National Hockey League history, "Terrible Ted" Lindsay is best remembered as the left-winger on the Detroit Red Wings' "Production Line" with center Sid Abel and right-winger Gordie Howe. The son of Bert Lindsay, himself a splendid player and later the inventor of the collapsible hockey net, Ted skated in the NHL 17 years, most of the time with the Red Wings. Lindsay was not especially big (five feet eight, 163 pounds), but he was regarded as totally tough.

"By my definition," said Lindsay, "there's one helluva lot more to being a tough guy than getting into a few phony fights where no real punches are tossed. To me, being tough includes wanting to win so badly that you give it all you've got every shift, going into corners without phoning ahead to see who's there, backing up your mates if they are in trouble, and stepping into guys, even if they're bigger than you." Which just about defined Ted Lindsay's career on ice!

One of Lindsay's most devastating bouts involved the Bruins' Wild Bill Ezinicki. The fight, at Olympia Stadium in Detroit, took place on January 25, 1951. When it was over Ezinicki had lost a tooth, had acquired two black eyes, a broken nose, and 19 stitches. Lindsay needed only five stitches above his eye, but was treated for badly scarred and swollen knuckles on his right hand. It was episodes such as that which caused Lindsay to become the all-time NHL penalty leader at the time with 1,808 minutes in 17 seasons with Detroit and later Chicago. Ironically, today, the all-time penalty-minute leader list starts with a minimum of 2,000 penalty minutes!

But Lindsay could score, too, and finished his career with 379 career goals, was named All-Star left wing nine times, and also made "trouble" in areas outside the rink itself.

Lindsay was a leader in the formation of an NHL players' union in the mid 1950s. When Red Wings manager Jack Adams discovered Lindsay's role with the proposed union, he had the left-winger traded to the Chicago Blackhawks prior to the 1957–58 season. "The concept we had for the players' association," said Lindsay, "was not the creation of one household for all the players in the NHL. What we were aiming for was to benefit the game of hockey, not just the players."

Lindsay finished his NHL career back with the Wings in 1964–65, but remained in the hockey limelight. He was hired as color commentator for the NBC-TV network *Game of the Week* in 1972 and never hesitated to speak out on controversial issues. Lindsay was especially critical of the NHL Players' Association and its then-director, Alan Eagleson. "The Players' Association," said Lindsay, "has encouraged familiarity among the players. They're one big happy family now. The coaches have no way of pushing players. They can't send them to the minors; they can't fine them because the Players' Association will raise hell." Lindsay's colorful comments lessened only slightly when he was named manager of the ailing Detroit Red Wings in 1977, where he was well known for old-fashioned, traditional ideas about training and dedication.

His tenure as Red Wings general manager failed after three seasons, yet Ted Lindsay remained a popular figure in the Detroit hockey community into the new century.

Ted Lindsay, Red Wings captain

CARL LISCOMBE

BORN: Perth, Ontario, May 17, 1915
POSITION: Left Wing, Detroit Red Wings, 1937–46

Before Gordie Howe became a household word in Detroit, skaters such as Carl Liscombe were the Motor City hockey heroes. A left wing from Perth, Ontario, Liscombe came to Detroit from the Hamilton, Ontario,

Tigers and became a regular in the 1937–38 season. In the 1943 Stanley Cup round, Carl was the leading goal scorer with 6 and point maker with 14 as the Red Wings won the Stanley Cup. Until 1951, Liscombe held the NHL record for fastest three goals—in 1:04—and he scored 3 goals and 4 assists against the Rangers in the 1942–43 season, for what was then a new league record. He remained with Detroit through the 1945–46 season. A year later, Carl was terrorizing American League goaltenders. In 1947–48, playing for Providence, Liscombe led the league in scoring with 50 goals and 68 assists for 118 points in 68 games. The following season, Carl scored 55 goals in 68 games for Providence, but never returned to the bigs.

He later moved to the Detroit area where Liscombe became active in the Red Wings' Alumni Association. In the year 2002, at the age of 87, Liscombe was believed to be the oldest living ex-NHL player in the United States.

EDDIE LITZENBERGER

BORN: Neudorf, Saskatchewan, July 15, 1932
POSITION: Center, Montreal Canadiens, 1952–55; Chicago Blackhawks, 1955–61; Detroit Red Wings, 1961–62; Toronto Maple Leafs, 1962–64
AWARDS/HONORS: Calder Memorial Trophy, 1955; NHL Second Team All-Star, 1957

A tall, awkward-looking forward, Ed Litzenberger seemed destined for a long career with the Montreal Canadiens when he reached the NHL to stay in 1954–55. But the Blackhawks' franchise was close to folding at the time and the league governors agreed to help Chicago whenever possible. The Canadiens therefore donated Litzenberger to the Blackhawks and Ed became a star in the Windy City. In 1961, he helped the Hawks to a Stanley Cup championship. After being dealt to the Maple Leafs in 1962, Ed became a key contributor as the Leafs enjoyed three straight Cup victories—1962, 1963, and 1964. He left the majors after the 1964 win.

CLAUDE LOISELLE

BORN: Ottawa, Ontario, May 29, 1963
POSITION: Center, Detroit Red Wings, 1982–86; New Jersey Devils, 1986–89; Quebec Nordiques, 1989–91; Toronto Maple Leafs, 1991–92; New York Islanders, 1992–94

It isn't often that a penalty killer can turn a season around, and help give his team a playoff berth. But Claude Loiselle did just that. During the 1987–88 campaign, the New Jersey Devils were shooting for their first playoff berth. New Jersey trailed the Pittsburgh Penguins and New York Rangers late in the season, when they visited the Washington Capitals at Cap Centre on March 20. Loiselle—and his sidekick penalty killer, rookie Doug Brown—took over after the Devils came from behind to tie the score. Brown, and then Loiselle, each scored shorthanded goals less than a minute apart, an amazing feat under any circumstances, enabling the Devils to win, 4–2. It marked the beginning of a wild unbeaten streak that would clinch New Jersey's first playoff berth.

The defensive specialist finished with a career-high 17 goals, including that huge shorthanded score against Washington, not to mention 6 goals in 10 games.

Claude's career ended on Long Island when he suffered a torn ACL in 1994, after a productive run that saw him help the Isles to unexpected success in 1993. Afterward, Loiselle obtained a law degree and became the associate director of Hockey Operations for the National Hockey League.

His intelligence and wit made him one of the most popular NHL officials.

SAM LoPRESTI

BORN: Eveleth, Minnesota, January 30, 1917
DIED: December 11, 1984
POSITION: Goaltender, Chicago Blackhawks, 1940–42

Sam LoPresti was the Chicago Blackhawks' goalie in 1940–41 and 1941–42. More than that, he was in the nets on March 4, 1941, the night that more shots were fired at an NHL goalie than ever before—or since. It happened at Boston Garden and the total was 83 shots, of which 80 were saves. The Bruins won the game, 3–2, but LoPresti won the acclaim, for life.

"The Bruins didn't get the winning goal until near the end of the game," LoPresti, who later became an Eveleth tavern owner, recalled. "Eddie Wiseman got it on a rebound. But we couldn't do anything right from the opening face-off, just couldn't get the puck out of our zone. They were shooting from every angle and I didn't see half the shots. They were bouncing off my pads, my chest protector, my arms, my shoulders. I didn't even know where they were coming from. At the other end, Boston's goalie Frankie Brimsek only had to make 18 saves all night. In between periods, they had to clean off only one end of the ice—my end. I lost between eight and ten pounds that night." After his second big-league season, Sam joined the United States Navy, on the theory that it was safer to face Nazi U-boats in the North Atlantic than vulcanized rubber in the Boston Garden.

A member of the U.S. Naval Armed Guard, LoPresti was on a freighter in the Atlantic torpedoed by a Nazi U-boat. After weeks adrift in the ocean, he was rescued and returned home a war hero. But he never played big-league hockey again.

KEVIN LOWE

BORN: Lachute, Quebec, April 15, 1959
POSITION: Defense, Edmonton Oilers, 1979–92; New York Rangers, 1992–96; Edmonton Oilers, 1996–98; Assistant Coach/Coach, Edmonton Oilers, 1999–2000; General Manager, Edmonton Oilers, 2000–
AWARDS/HONORS: Bud Man of the Year Award, 1990; King Clancy Memorial Trophy, 1990; NHL All-Star Game, 1984–85, 1988, 1989–90, 1993

A quintessential defensive defenseman of the 1980s and early 1990s, Kevin Lowe carried a special burden while playing for the Edmonton Oilers.

The team, coached by Glen Sather, specialized in high-tempo firewagon hockey, disdaining defense. It was Lowe's

Kevin Lowe as an Oiler

job not only to bring up the rear, but to protect it. The first draft pick by the Oilers in 1979 (first round, 21st overall), Kevin displayed consummate ability and class for five Stanley Cup-winning teams north of the border before being traded to the New York Rangers in 1992.

During his tenure with the Oilers during their Stanley Cup-winning era, Lowe had a positive double-digit plus/minus rating for eight of nine seasons, topping out at plus-46 in 1981–82. Although somewhat slower than in his prime after arriving on Broadway, Lowe continued to excel and became a major component of Mike Keenan's Stanley Cup-winning team of 1993–94.

Kevin never scored more than 46 points in a season on an offense-oriented team, but steadily guided the Oilers' backline for 15 years, the last two of which closed out his career in 1997–98 after his Ranger stint.

A debilitating ear infection that affected his balance proved to be Lowe's undoing as a player. After a long and, ultimately, successful recuperation, Lowe returned to hockey, this time as coach. In his one season as coach, Lowe led the team to the playoffs, only eight points behind the division-winning Colorado Avalanche. In 2000, he became general manager of the Oilers and despite a low budget, Lowe was able to ice a competitive team and was instantly acknowledged as one of the best young executives in the NHL.

Lowe quickly made a name for himself, pulling off huge deals such as sending Roman Hamrlik to the New York Islanders for Eric Brewer, Josh Green, and a second-round draft choice, as well as obtaining Anson Carter from the Bruins for Bill Guerin. He was also able to sign Tommy Salo and Ryan Smyth to long-term deals.

While never scoring many goals, Kevin Lowe had his share of assists and played excellent defense. He was a cornerstone on the six championship teams for which he played.

DON LUCE

BORN: London, Ontario, October 2, 1948
POSITION: Center, New York Rangers, 1969–70; Detroit Red Wings, 1970–71; Buffalo Sabres, 1971–81; Los Angeles Kings, 1981; Toronto Maple Leafs, 1981–82
AWARDS/HONORS: Bill Masterton Memorial Trophy, 1975

A study in clean living—he neither drank nor smoked—Don Luce reached the high point in his NHL career on May 21, 1975, when the Buffalo Sabres center received the annual Bill Masterton Trophy.

A former New York Ranger and Detroit Red Wing, Luce turned into a star when he improved his checking and scoring in Buffalo. In 1974–75, he had his best season with 33

goals and 76 points, helping the Sabres reach the Stanley Cup finals. He also won the Sabres' Unsung Hero and Most Improved Player awards, the Charlie Barton Silver Stick, given to the "player who most exemplifies love of the game," and Buffalo's Most Valuable Player Award.

Years after his retirement in 1982, Luce continued his long tenure in Buffalo as the Sabres' director of Player Personnel following a brief scouting role with the team in the mid 1980s, which helped result in the defection of Alexander Mogilny to the Sabres in 1989.

HARRY LUMLEY

BORN: Owen Sound, Ontario, November 11, 1926
DIED: September 13, 1998
POSITION: Goaltender, Detroit Red Wings, 1943–44, 1945–50; New York Rangers, 1944; Chicago Blackhawks, 1950–52; Toronto Maple Leafs, 1952–56; Boston Bruins, 1957–60
AWARDS/HONORS: Vezina Trophy, 1954; NHL First Team All-Star, 1954–55; NHL All-Star Game, 1951, 1954–55; Hockey Hall of Fame, 1980

Harry Lumley, an outstanding goalkeeper who labored for 16 years in professional hockey as one of the stingiest netminders around, had an inauspicious NHL debut in a two-game trial with the Detroit Red Wings, allowing 13 pucks to elude his flailing limbs.

Looking back on that embarrassing goal splurge, one can forgive Lumley if he was a bit awed by it all, since the netminder was only 17 years old at the time. This was the 1943–44 season and World War II had decimated the ranks of the NHL, necessitating Lumley's adolescent awakening to the harsh realities of big-league shinny.

Harry matured, though, into one of the NHL's most proficient puckstoppers. He remained with the Wings for six more seasons, guiding them into the playoffs each year and sipping Stanley Cup champagne in 1949–50, his last campaign with the Wings.

At the end of that season, the Red Wings came up with another whiskerless wonder in the 20-year-old Terry Sawchuk, and Lumley was dispatched to a hapless Chicago Blackhawk team where he spent two frustrating seasons. In 1952, Harry hit the road once more, this time to his home province of Ontario and the blue and white of the Toronto Maple Leafs. It was in Toronto that Lumley enjoyed his best years as a pro, leading the NHL in shutouts for two consecutive seasons and copping the Vezina Trophy in 1953–54 with an amazing 1.85 goals-against average in 69 games.

Nearing the end of his career, Lumley had a three-year stint with the Boston Bruins and then played in the minor leagues until his retirement in 1960–61.

When Harry Lumley broke into the National Hockey League in 1943, the 17-year-old was nicknamed "Apple Cheeks" and won the hearts of all but those who fired the puck at him or rooted against the goaltending prodigy. This crimson complexion often took on an even deeper hue when the big fellow took arms against enemy skaters—which was often.

Lumley eventually returned to his home-town of Owen Sound, Ontario, where he had a share in an auto dealership and owned an interest in the Orangeville Raceway, Ltd., a harness track. He remained active at the race-way, working 52 weeks a year. Harry continued playing goal with old-timer teams until 1977, when a close friend suffered a heart attack. "That," said Lumley, "was when I decided to hang up the pads."

PENTTI LUND

BORN: Helsinki, Finland, December 1925
POSITION: Left Wing, New York Rangers, 1948–51; Boston Bruins, 1951–53
AWARDS/HONORS: Calder Memorial Trophy, 1949

Pentti Lund briefly attained stardom in the 1950 Stanley Cup playoffs, playing left wing for the New York Rangers. Lund played opposite the immortal Maurice "Rocket" Richard, the Montreal Canadiens' high-powered scorer, in the semifinal round. While Richard's stick was muzzled, Lund stunned the Canadiens with an outburst of goals that led the Rangers to a four-games-to-one victory in the series. The Rangers reached the seventh game of the Cup finals against Detroit before losing. In 12 Cup games, Lund scored 6 goals and 5 assists. However, his play sagged in 1950–51, and the Rangers traded him to Boston a year later. He completed his NHL career in 1952–53, scoring only 8 goals in 54 regular season games and neither a goal nor an assist in two playoff matches. He later turned to journalism and became sports editor of the *Thunder Bay Times*.

VIC LYNN

BORN: Saskatoon, Saskatchewan, January 26, 1925
POSITION: Defenseman/Forward, Detroit Red Wings, 1943–44; Montreal Canadiens, 1945–46; Toronto Maple Leafs, 1946–50; Boston Bruins, 1950–52; Chicago Blackhawks, 1952–54

Rabbit McVeigh, a star with the old New York Americans, noticed a burly left-winger skating for Buffalo in the American League named Vic Lynn and advised Toronto Maple Leafs manager Conn Smythe to sign the energetic skater. Lynn had received brief trials with Detroit (1943–44) and the Canadiens (1945–46), but failed on both counts. Smythe, however, took McVeigh's advice and signed Lynn for the 1946–47 season, put him on a line with center Ted "Teeder" Kennedy and Howie Meeker, and the Maple Leafs' second Kid Line was born.

Lynn was not an especially prolific scorer, but he was big and rough and he hit hard. He complemented his linemates perfectly and the trio gave Toronto the spark to win three consecutive Stanley Cup championships (1947, 1948, 1949). Following the 1949–50 season, Lynn was traded to Boston. In 1952–53, he was acquired by the Chicago Blackhawks and completed his NHL career in the Windy City in 1953–54.

TOM LYSIAK

BORN: High Prairie, Alberta, April 22, 1953
POSITION: Center, Atlanta Flames, 1973–79; Chicago Blackhawks, 1979–86
AWARDS/HONORS: NHL All-Star Game, 1975–77

Tom Lysiak was one of the most highly rated youngsters to come along in the NHL in a long time. He was the second pick in the 1973 amateur draft behind that year's Calder Trophy winner, Denis Potvin of the New York Islanders.

Although scoring only 19 goals in his rookie season, Lysiak assisted on 45 tallies, and was instrumental in the Flames' surge to the playoffs in only their second season.

Lysiak continued to score goals for Atlanta, but lost favor with management, and was traded to the Chicago Blackhawks late in the 1978–79 season. He continued to score goals, including a 32-goal campaign in 1981–82, but couldn't do much for a weak Chicago team.

He retired in 1986 after a rapid decline in numbers, which couldn't detract from his career 843 points in 919 games.

AL MacINNIS

BORN: Inverness, Nova Scotia, July 11, 1963
POSITION: Defenseman, Calgary Flames, 1981–94; St. Louis Blues, 1994–
AWARDS/HONORS: Conn Smythe Trophy, 1989; James Norris Memorial Trophy, 1999; NHL First Team All-Star, 1990–91, 1999; NHL Second Team All-Star, 1987, 1989, 1994; NHL All-Star Game, 1985, 1988, 1990–92, 1994, 1996–2000

Over the years, there were many spectacular offensive defensemen, Bobby Orr, Denis Potvin, and Paul Coffey, to name a few.

But there never was anyone who possessed so terrifying a shot as Al MacInnis.

With shots clocked at speeds of more than 102 miles per hour, MacInnis not only delivered velocity with his drives, but also had what goaltenders refer to as a "heavy" shot; meaning that the puck felt more like a lead weight than vulcanized rubber.

But the tall defenseman—six feet two, 209 pounds—had more than a dynamic drive from the blue line. He mastered both ends of the rink and when timely body checks or poke checks were needed, he would deliver.

The Nova Scotia native began his professional career with Calgary in 1981, scoring his first goal on October 23, 1982. The following season, he paced all team defensemen with 45 points despite playing only 51 games, and in 1984–85, he led Flames defensemen with 52. Calgary then defeated the Canadiens in six games to win its first Stanley Cup. MacInnis won the Conn Smythe Trophy as playoff MVP, as his 24 assists and 31 points led all league scorers.

In 1989–90, MacInnis set team records for goals by a defenseman (28) and shots on goal

(304), and on November 8, 1990, he passed Guy Chouinard (336) to become the team's all-time assist leader. He was only the fourth defenseman in league history to score 100 points.

Though MacInnis repeatedly held records for defensemen during his stay with Calgary, on July 4, 1994, Al was traded with a fourth-round draft pick to the St. Louis Blues, for Phil Housley and a pair of second-round draft picks. "Chopper," as he's called in the locker room, continued to shine.

By 1998–99, his seventh 20-goal season, Al led all league defensemen with 20 goals, 62 points, 11 power-play goals, and 314 shots. He averaged 29:07 minutes per game, recorded 128 blocked shots, and was the only defenseman on the St. Louis Blues to score a short-handed goal. After 18 seasons, MacInnis finally captured the Norris Trophy for his outstanding performance.

Paired with fellow Norris-winner Chris Pronger on the blueline, MacInnis helped the St. Louis power play in the late 1990s and his presence led to the club's emergence as a Western power, recording a franchise-best 51 wins and 114 points in 1999–2000.

Al MacInnis came a long way from his early days loading lobster trucks in the Canadian Maritimes. He ranked fifth in most career points by a defenseman entering the 2001–02 season.

JACK MacINTYRE

BORN: Brussels, Ontario, September 8, 1930
POSITION: Left Wing, Boston Bruins, 1949–53; Chicago Black-hawks, 1953–57; Detroit Red Wings, 1958–60

Jack MacIntyre holds the NHL record for having his name misspelled for the longest period of time before correction. He became a Bruin in 1949–50 and despite seasons of just-average play, he starred for Boston in the 1953 Stanley Cup semifinal round. It was then, three years after he had entered the NHL, that the misspelling was corrected. Until then, writers spelled Jack's name McIntyre. However, with the Detroit-Boston series tied at one game apiece, Jack came through with a goal in the 12th minute of sudden-death overtime to give Boston a lead—and what proved to be the turning point in Boston's favor—in the series. In the postgame news conference, Jack called for time-out and informed the press they had better spell his name correctly. "It's MacIntyre," he insisted. "Capital m, small a, small c; not McIntyre like you've been writing!"

Jack was traded to Chicago in the following season and then to Detroit in 1957–58, where he finished his NHL career in 1959–60. To his dismay, writers kept spelling his name McIntyre, big goals or not.

FLEMING MACKELL

BORN: Montreal, Quebec, April 30, 1929
POSITION: Forward, Toronto Maple Leafs, 1947–52; Boston Bruins, 1952–60

One of the speediest skaters ever to grace the National Hockey League, Fleming Mackell immediately attained notoriety as one of the few players to have lost all of his teeth before turning pro with the Toronto Maple Leafs in 1947–48. Mackell played for two Maple Leafs Stanley Cup champions (1949 and 1951) before being traded to the Boston Bruins for defenseman Jim Morrison during the 1951–52 season.

In 1957–58, Mackell reached a personal point high with 20 goals and 40 assists for 60 points in 70 NHL games and followed that by totaling 5 goals and 14 assists for 19 points in only 12 Stanley Cup playoff games. Mackell's halcyon days were spent in Boston, where he became one of Beantown's favorite athletes and concluded his NHL career in the 1959–60 season.

JOHN MacLEAN

BORN: Oshawa, Ontario, November 20, 1964
POSITION: Right Wing, New Jersey Devils, 1983–97; San Jose Sharks, 1997–98; New York Rangers, 1998–2001; Dallas Stars, 2001–02
AWARDS/HONORS: NHL All-Star, 1989, 1991

Among the New Jersey Devils heroes after the franchise was transferred from Denver to East Rutherford in 1983, John MacLean stands among the most revered. He holds the record for the most points in Devils history (701) and played with the team for 14 years.

His claim to fame centers on goals he scored on the final night of the 1987–88 season, which catapulted the Devils into the playoffs for the first time in the club's history.

Skating against the Blackhawks at Chicago Stadium, the Devils needed a win to beat out the Rangers for the final playoff berth. At 2:21 in the overtime period, MacLean shot a rebound past goalie Darren Pang to give New Jersey a 3–2 victory.

A consistent goal scorer and a workmanlike force on the ice, MacLean was a faithful Devil until the 1997–98 season, when he was traded to San Jose. He played 51 games for the Sharks, recording a disappointing 13 goals, and was traded the next season to the New York Rangers. As a Ranger, MacLean's numbers faltered, and the team missed the playoffs for his three-year stay. The Rangers traded MacLean to the Dallas Stars in 2001, who then signed the 38-year-old winger to a minor-league contract in 2002. By the spring of 2002, MacLean was back in the NHL with Dallas.

He retired after the 2001–02 season and returned to New Jersey where he became active in the Devils Alumni Association. MacLean also helped during some team practices.

RICK MacLEISH

BORN: Lindsay, Ontario, January 3, 1950
POSITION: Center, Philadelphia Flyers, 1970–81; Hartford Whalers, 1981; Pittsburgh Penguins, 1981–83; Philadelphia Flyers, 1983; Detroit Red Wings, 1984
AWARDS/HONORS: NHL All-Star Game, 1976–77, 1980

Mention the name Rick MacLeish to any Philadelphia hockey fan who happened to be in The Spectrum on the night when *it* finally happened, and he or she will immediately mention *the* goal. The date was May 19, 1974. The Flyers were facing the Boston Bruins. It was the sixth game of the Stanley Cup finals and, somehow, Philadelphia was leading the series, three games to two. Until that point in time, no expansion team had ever won a Stanley Cup. Few, if any, experts anticipated that Fred Shero's skaters could defeat a club that already had won championships in 1970 and 1972. The Big, Bad Bruins already had proven to be one of the most formidable teams in history. Paced by high-scoring Hall of Famers Phil Esposito and Bobby Orr, the Bostonians were favored to easily win again in 1974.

But they did not bargain for the amazing MacLeish. Heading into Game Six, he had collected a playoff-leading dozen goals, three more than Esposito. Fortunately for the Flyers, he was not finished with his work. With the score deadlocked at zero, and almost 15 minutes gone in the first period, MacLeish took a pass from defenseman Andre "Moose" Dupont and fired it past Bruins goaltender Gilles Gilbert.

Somehow—almost magically—the Flyers weathered the endless Bruins' assaults and when the final green light signaled the game's end, Bernie Parent owned a shutout and MacLeish's "Shot Heard 'Round Broad Street" proved to be the Stanley Cup winner. As a neat postscript to the triumph, Rick also led all 1974 playoff scorers with 22 points.

In true Flyers tradition, MacLeish also occasionally revealed a tough side. Once, in junior hockey, he fought with Bob "Hound" Kelly, a notorious pugilist. The two became teammates on Broad Street when MacLeish joined the club in 1971. A solid five feet eleven, 185 pounds, MacLeish claimed to have gone undefeated in the Central League. Beyond his fighting ability, MacLeish displayed a willingness to play hurt. Early one season, he suffered an ankle injury in a game against the Pittsburgh Penguins. It was painful but he insisted on playing through the hurt the next night against the Chicago Blackhawks. MacLeish scored three goals that night and the Flyers beat Chicago, 5–3. It was the portent of even bigger things to come in a career that has surprisingly been overlooked by many hockey historians.

In 1990, Rick MacLeish was elected to the Flyers Hall of Fame. Surely, the voters must have had that big, *big* goal against the Boston Bruins in 1974 on their collective minds. After all, it did produce the first Stanley Cup championship for Philadelphia.

CRAIG MacTAVISH

BORN: London, Ontario, August 15, 1958
POSITION: Center, Boston Bruins, 1979–84; Edmonton Oilers, 1985–94; New York Rangers, 1994; Philadelphia Flyers, 1994–96; St. Louis Blues, 1996–97; Coach, Edmonton Oilers, 2000–
AWARDS/HONORS: NHL All-Star Game, 1996

As tough a customer as ever came down the pike, Craig MacTavish spent 18 seasons in the NHL as a gritty two-way forward who became popular with every team for which he played.

The last helmetless player to grace NHL ice, "MacT" skated for the Boston Bruins, New York Rangers, Philadelphia Flyers, and St. Louis Blues, but made his most lasting marks in Edmonton, both as a player and head coach.

Craig was part of the Oilers dynasty of the 1980s as a checking centerman on the team's 1987, 1988, and 1990 Stanley Cup winners. He then captained the 1993–94 and 1994–95 teams, and eventually returned as an assistant, then head coach in 2000, as previous mentor Kevin Lowe stepped up to the general manager's desk.

MacTavish's tenacious style suited the Boston Bruins, who drafted him in 1978 out of Lowell University, and he made his NHL debut in 1979–80. Five seasons later, MacTavish signed on with Edmonton and proceeded to become one of their all-time leaders in games played (sixth with 701) and points (11th with 331).

One of four players dealt to the New York Rangers at the March 1994 trade deadline, MacTavish, in the playoff stretch drive, helped New York capture their first Stanley Cup since 1940. After retiring as a member of the St. Louis Blues, he returned to the Rangers as an assistant coach in 1997 before signing on as the Oilers' head coach in 2000.

In Craig's first year as head coach in Edmonton, the Oilers managed 39 wins and finished second in the Northwest Division, only to lose in round one of the playoffs to the Dallas Stars for the third straight year. With the departure of Doug Weight for the 2001–02 season, MacTavish's team missed the playoffs in the last week of the season, after a spring-time slump allowed Vancouver and Phoenix to pass Edmonton. Nevertheless, he was regarded as one of the NHL's brightest young coaches.

KEITH MAGNUSON

BORN: Saskatoon, Saskatechwan, April 27, 1947
POSITION: Defenseman, Chicago Blackhawks, 1969–80
AWARDS/HONORS: NHL All-Star Game, 1971–72

Keith Magnuson often looked like an enraged carrot on the Chicago Blackhawks defense, courtesy of his bright red hair, his height (six feet), and his anger. The fiery Magnuson had a thing about psyching himself up for games so that he always seemed to be in a fit of pique.

Magnuson came to Chicago by way of Denver University. Perhaps because he had to overcome the college-boy image and his slight physique, he took boxing lessons to toughen his fighting technique, if not his defensive style. He made his mark in the NHL the first couple of years by going after anyone in sight and usually losing! Keith calmed down considerably after taking on the responsibility of captaining the Blackhawks, and his defensive play improved, though he tended to check wildly and ineffectively at times. On two such occasions, Magnuson blocked shots with his jaw, rendering the tenacious defenseman useless for much of 1977–78. The injury jinx continued to haunt Magnuson in 1979, when he appeared in only 26 games.

His career ended in the 1979–80 season, but he remained active with the Chicago Blackhawks Alumni Association for many years.

FRANK MAHOVLICH

BORN: Timmins, Ontario, January 10, 1938
POSITION: Left Wing, Toronto Maple Leafs,
1956–68; Detroit Red Wings, 1968–71;
Montreal Canadiens, 1971–74; Toronto Toros/
Birmingham Bulls (WHA), 1974–78
AWARDS/HONORS: Calder Memorial Trophy,
1958; NHL First Team All-Star, 1961, 1963,
1973; NHL Second Team All-Star, 1962, 1964–66,
1969–70; NHL All-Star Game, 1959–65,
1967–74; Hockey Hall of Fame, 1981

A superstar whose career was star-crossed, that is the most accurate way to describe the hockey life of Frank Mahovlich, alias The Big M.

Perhaps the most misunderstood man in professional hockey, Mahovlich, the one-time skating behemoth of the NHL, weathered two nervous breakdowns in his successful quest for superstardom. The Big M reached high and low points in his career with the Toronto Maple Leafs before being freed to join, first, the Detroit Red Wings, then the Montreal Canadiens.

Son of a Croatian immigrant, Frank was scouted as a teenager by the Maple Leafs and several other NHL clubs. As a young, dashing left-winger with the Maple Leafs, Frank played

Frank "The Big M" Mahovlich in action for Montreal

under tyrannical general manager–coach Punch Imlach, and achieved stardom during the 1960–61 campaign, when he nearly reached a goal-a-game pace. Notching 48 goals, he almost matched Maurice "Rocket" Richard's record 50-goal plateau. For Mahovlich, it was too much, too soon.

The demanding fans expected the huge, gifted skater to surpass his 48 goals the following year. But the pressure cooker atmosphere in the NHL did not suit Frank's psyche. The more he pressed for goals the more he worried.

Skating on a line with veteran center Red Kelly and workmanlike right wing Bob Nevin, the diffident Mahovlich was the most exciting shooter of his day, but was assailed by newsmen in the manner of Roger Maris at the time that the New York Yankees outfielder was challenging Babe Ruth's 60-home-run record.

Unlike Maris, Mahovlich never did break the record, although he ultimately did well by himself and his assorted teams. He won the Calder Trophy as rookie of the year in 1958 and was a First Team All-Star left wing in 1961, 1963, and 1973. He made the Second Team in 1962, 1964, 1965, 1966, 1969, and 1970. Frank played on no fewer than five Stanley Cup champions, four with the Maple Leafs and one with the Montreal Canadiens.

Statistics suggest that Mahovlich luxuriated through a lengthy career sprinkled with laughs and coated with dollars. In fact, Mahovlich was plagued with trauma and tribulation from 1960–61, as the Mahovlich-Imlach relationship plummeted and Frank's scoring diminished. A stubborn martinet, Imlach always held to the hope he could mold Mahovlich into his kind of player. The arithmetic said otherwise. Frank's goal-scoring dropped from the high of 48 to an abysmal 18 in 1967.

"It reached a point," said Mahovlich, "where I felt I was beating my head against a wall. If I had to play in Toronto one more year I would've probably retired, although I like hockey and wouldn't want to leave it."

By then, Imlach was ready to consider any reasonable trade offer for Mahovlich. He finally received one from Detroit. On March 3, 1968, one of hockey's biggest deals was consummated by the Red Wings and Maple Leafs.

Mahovlich was dealt to Detroit with Peter Stemkowski, Garry Unger, and the rights to Carl Brewer for Paul Henderson, Norm Ullman, Floyd Smith, and Doug Barrie.

Mahovlich obliged with 49 goals, the most he had scored in twelve NHL seasons, and the most goals for a Red Wings player since Gordie Howe had scored the same in 1952–53. Frank was also voted the number one star in the 1969 All-Star game in Montreal.

Skating with Howe and Alex "Fats" Delvecchio, Mahovlich was a new man. With 118 goals, the line broke the 105 record set in 1943–44 by the famed Montreal Punch Line of Maurice Richard, Toe Blake, and Elmer Lach. The line's 264 points smashed the 223-point mark set in 1956–57 by Detroit's Production Line of Howe, Ted Lindsay, and Norm Ullman. In 1969–70, Frank scored 38 goals and 32 assists for 70 points and was a prime catalyst in pushing the Red Wings into a playoff berth for the first time in four years.

Still, there was a gray cloud hanging over Mahovlich's future in Detroit. His brother Peter, an enormously gifted center, had fallen into disfavor with the Red Wings' front office and was traded to Montreal. In addition, the Red Wings now had a new coach, Ned Harkness, who had new ideas.

Harkness failed as coach, but was elevated to management, while Frank played as if skating in mud. Trade was inevitable, and on January 13, 1971, Mahovlich was dealt to the Canadiens in exchange for Mickey Redmond, Guy Charron, and Bill Collins.

For the fourth time in his big-league career Frank was being asked to make a major comeback. He produced better than ever.

Canadiens' fans immediately took Frank to their collective hearts and he responded by helping Montreal win the 1971 Stanley Cup as he broke the playoff goal-scoring record with 14 red lights. Manager Sam Pollock acknowledged Frank's leadership qualities by naming him an alternate captain. Mahovlich was touched. "It's the first time I've ever been chosen for anything," he said. "The Canadiens management showed that they respected me. It's a nice feeling."

In 1971–72, his first full year in Montreal, he scored 96 points in 76 games and followed that with 93 points in 78 contests during 1972–73. Once again he was a tower of power as Montreal marched to the Prince of Wales Trophy and the Stanley Cup in 1973.

It was a remarkable accomplishment for a misunderstood athlete who had thrice been written off. Nothing emphasized the value of Frank Mahovlich more than his ability, which enabled him to surpass the 500-goal mark and finish the 1972–73 campaign with an all-time goal total of 502.

In his final NHL season, Mahovlich scored 31 goals and 49 assists to lift his all-time NHL totals to 1,182 games played, 533 goals, 570 assists, 1,103 points, and 1,052 penalty minutes. He jumped from the Canadiens to the WHA's Toronto Toros during the off-season and was named team captain. In his first WHA game, Mahovlich scored a hat trick and went on to a respectable 82-point season. Mahovlich followed the Toros when they moved South to Birmingham, Alabama, ending his playing career with the Bulls in 1978 to devote time to his travel agency in Toronto.

He was inducted into the Hockey Hall of Fame in 1981. As a stamp of accomplishment, Frank's longtime rival, Bobby Hull, described Mahovlich as the "Greatest Left-Winger of all time."

The Big M was later named as honorary senator by the Canadian government.

PETE MAHOVLICH

BORN: Timmins, Ontario, October 10, 1946
POSITION: Center/Left Wing, Detroit Red Wings, 1965–69, 1979–81; Montreal Canadiens, 1969–77; Pittsburgh Penguins, 1977–79
AWARDS/HONORS: Team Canada, 1972; NHL All-Star Game, 1971, 1976

Peter Mahovlich was the kind of younger brother anyone would like to have. At six feet four, 210 pounds, Pete was the youthful sibling of hockey great Frank Mahovlich, one of the game's outstanding left-wingers.

Pete didn't feel his size was always an asset. "When I had a bad game, it was really bad," Little M stated. "Because of my size, I stuck out more."

The Canadiens obtained him in 1969 from Detroit, where he was seldom used. A year later, Les Habitants dealt for brother Frank, and the two helped Montreal to a pair of Stanley Cups.

Peter was a fine penalty killer and backchecker, but his offensive prowess was unknown until he joined Montreal. He tallied 127 goals in his first four seasons with the Habs. Although he was instrumental in the development of his star linemate, Guy Lafleur, Mahovlich and the Canadiens fell afoul of one another and Pete was sent to Pittsburgh, where he struggled to regain his earlier form. Peter's finest hour came during the 1972 Team Canada-Soviet series. In a marvelous individual effort, Mahovlich stickhandled into scoring position and fired home a huge goal.

His NHL career ended with the Detroit Red Wings in 1981, but Pete remained prominent in the hockey world, fighting off serious illness to remain active. When the Atlanta Thrashers became an expansion franchise in 1999, Mahovlich was hired as a scout.

VLADIMIR MALAKHOV

BORN: Ekaterinburg, USSR, August 30, 1968
POSITION: Defenseman, New York Islanders, 1992–95; Montreal Canadiens, 1995–2000; New Jersey Devils, 2000; New York Rangers, 2000–
AWARDS/HONORS: NHL All-Rookie Team, 1993

He had all the ingredients of the perfect defenseman: strength, speed, savvy, and a blazing shot. On top of that, Vladimir Malakhov came to the Islanders after several years of top-level hockey in the Soviet Union.

His rookie year, 1992–93, was a huge plus, as he teamed up with another European rookie, Darius Kasparaitis, to pace the Islanders to a playoff berth and a Cinderella march through the third round. Malakhov's numbers suggested a future All-Star: 14 goals, 38 assists, and 52 points, followed by 3 goals, 6 assists, and 9 points in 17 playoff games. However, Malakhov's ability—or inability—to withstand pain immediately raised questions about his durability. Although desperately needed in the final game of the Islanders-Montreal series, Malakhov begged off, as the Islanders went down to defeat.

Vlad had one more successful season on the Island before being traded to the Montreal Canadiens with Pierre Turgeon for Kirk Muller, Mathieu Schneider, and Craig Darby. Malakhov played competently for the Canadiens, but never reached the stardom predicted of him. Then things became nasty between the taciturn Russian and the Habs, as Malakhov was allegedly spotted skiing while out with an injured knee.

Traded to the New Jersey Devils for Sheldon Souray, Josh DeWolf, and a draft pick late in the 1999–2000 season, Malakhov stayed injury-free long enough to help the Devils to their second Stanley Cup. But in the summer of 2000, Vlad decided to try the free-agent waters and was signed by the New York Rangers.

An early season injury negated 2000–01 for him, but Malakhov returned with the Rangers in 2001–02 and became the team's best backliner, playing 81 games and tallying 6 goals and 22 assists and managing a plus-10 rating on a team that couldn't make the playoffs. It was Vlad's best season since his rookie year.

JOE MALONE

BORN: Quebec City, Quebec, February 28, 1890
DIED: May 15, 1969
POSITION: Forward, Quebec Bulldogs, 1909–17, 1919–20; Montreal Canadiens, 1917–19, 1920–21, 1922–24; Hamilton Tigers, 1921–22
AWARDS/HONORS: Art Ross Trophy, 1918, 1920; Hockey Hall of Fame, 1950

Many respected observers regard Joe Malone as the greatest all-around scorer of the early NHL years. "He might have been the most prolific scorer of all time if they had played more games in those days," said Frank J. Selke, the former Canadiens managing director who remembered Malone as a young professional. "It was amazing the way Joe used to get himself in position to score. In that respect his style was similar to Gordie Howe's. Joe was no Howie Morenz as far as speed was concerned. But he was a clean player like Dave Keon and Frank Boucher. On the other hand, though, Joe never took a backwards step from anybody."

Malone's career long preceded television and mass media attention. He retired in 1922 before any American teams entered the NHL, therefore few U.S. hockey fans knew of his on-ice exploits. However, in Canada he is widely regarded as the most dangerous scorer of the early NHL years.

SYLVIO MANTHA

BORN: Montreal, Quebec, April 14, 1902
DIED: August 1974
POSITION: Defenseman, Montreal Canadiens, 1923–36; Boston Bruins, 1936–37
AWARDS/HONORS: NHL Second Team All-Star, 1931–32; Hockey Hall of Fame, 1960

When the Montreal Canadiens were called to training camp for the 1924–25 NHL season, one of the new faces in the lineup was Sylvio Mantha. Mantha played defense and, as such, was obscured by the more exciting young forwards in camp, especially Howie Morenz. Like Morenz, Mantha was to play a vital part in the Canadiens' future success. He played on Montreal's Stanley Cup winners in 1930 and 1931 and remained with the Habs until 1936, when he was traded to Boston, where he finished his career in 1936–37. He was inducted into the Hockey Hall of Fame in 1960.

MUSH MARCH

BORN: Silton, Saskatchewan, October 18, 1908
DIED: January 9, 2002
POSITION: Right Wing, Chicago Blackhawks, 1928–45
AWARDS/HONORS: NHL All-Star Game, 1937

The Chicago Blackhawks' successes in their early National Hockey League years can be credited in large part to Harold "Mush" March, who played exclusively for the Hawks from the 1928–29 season to his concluding year in the majors, 1944–45. March was at his best in the 1930s, working on a line with Tommy Cook at center and Paul Thompson on the other wing. On April 10, 1934, March scored the Stanley Cup–winning goal against Red Wings goalie Wilf Cude in double overtime to give the Windy City its first NHL championship. Not surprisingly, March also was in on the Hawks' second Stanley Cup championship in April 1938, scoring a key goal in the fifth and final game of the series against the Toronto Maple Leafs. Although March never played on another Chicago Cup winner, he sparked the Hawks in the 1941 playoffs with two goals and three assists.

It has been said that one of big league hockey's funniest sights was March, a smallish skater, hiding behind huge Taffy Abel, a Chicago defenseman, as Abel carried the puck into enemy territory. With March obscured, Abel would then drop his teammate the puck and allow Mush to shoot it between his opened legs.

His nickname "Mush" derived from the Dick Tracy comic strip character Mush Mouth.

March, one of Chicago's most popular hockey players, died in January 2002, inspiring huge obituary stories in the Windy City newspapers.

JOHN MARIUCCI

BORN: Eveleth, Minnesota, May 8, 1916
DIED: March 23, 1987
POSITION: Defenseman, Chicago Blackhawks, 1940–42, 1946–48
AWARDS/HONORS: Lester Patrick Trophy, 1977

One of the toughest hombres ever to glide over a big-league hockey rink, Johnny Mariucci was a fearsome football player as well. After playing end for Bernie Bierman's super Minnesota Gopher teams of the late 1930s, Mariucci made his NHL debut with Chicago in the 1940–41 season. As one newsman put it, it was a sports parlay without precedent.

"Maroosh," as he was known, turned to hockey from a promising National Football League career because of money. The most a good blocking lineman could make in pro football in 1940 was $150 per game or $1,500 per season. The Blackhawks signed him for $3,000.

"Besides," said Mariucci, "I preferred to play

hockey. Football is nothing but hard work. Hockey is fun." Mariucci enlisted in the United States Coast Guard during World War II and played defense for the Cutters' sextet. Following the war, he played three more seasons in Chicago. John's fistic ability was remembered by those who chronicled his 15-minute fight with Detroit's Black Jack Stewart, both in and out of the penalty box. He retired in 1948 and entered the coaching realm, including a stint for the University of Minnesota, where a rink was named after him. He later became assistant general manager of the Minnesota North Stars.

DON MARSHALL

BORN: Montreal, Quebec, March 23, 1932
POSITION: Center/Left Wing; Montreal Canadiens, 1951–52, 1954–63; New York Rangers, 1963–70; Buffalo Sabres, 1970–71; Toronto Maple Leafs, 1971–72
AWARDS/HONORS: NHL Second Team All-Star, 1967; NHL All-Star Game, 1956–61, 1968

One of the classiest centers ever to grace the National Hockey League during its six-team era of the late '50s and early '60s, Don Marshall had the misfortune to play on one of the greatest teams of all time.

When the Montreal Canadiens won an unprecedented five Stanley Cups from 1956 through 1960, their primary centers were Jean Beliveau, Ralph Backstrom, Henri Richard, and Phil Goyette. Don Marshall, also a member of the team, had difficulty gaining a regular berth because of the surplus of talent, but when he did play, he played well.

A smooth skater who could find an opening behind a goaltender, as well as feather a neat pass, Marshall came into his own in 1963 after he was traded to the New York Rangers. He became more popular in New York than he ever was in Montreal, putting together career years in 1965–66 with 26 goals and 28 assists, and in 1967–68 with 49 points. All the while, he took very few penalties; he had 127 for his entire career.

Don spent seven years on Broadway, including three years of playoff hockey. Marshall's admirable career resurged again with a 49-point mark for the Buffalo Sabres in 1970–71, and concluded in Toronto after 1971–72.

PIT MARTIN

BORN: Noranda, Quebec, December 9, 1943
POSITION: Center, Detroit Red Wings, 1961–62, 1963–65; Boston Bruins, 1965–67; Chicago Blackhawks, 1967–77; Vancouver Canucks, 1977–79
AWARDS/HONORS: Bill Masterton Memorial Trophy, 1970; NHL All-Star Game, 1971–74

Based on his teenage exploits, Hubert "Pit" Martin was expected to be a major-league superstar. Unfortunately, he never reached that level, although he was a competent NHLer.

Martin stayed in the bigs for quite a while, always doing a superior job at center. He began with Detroit in 1961, but couldn't secure a slot with the Wings. After several seasons of scooting back and forth between Detroit and Pittsburgh of the AHL, he was traded to Boston for Parker MacDonald in 1965. He stayed with the Bruins for only a season and a half.

In 1967, Martin was traded by Boston with Gilles Marotte and goalie Jack Norris for Phil Esposito, Ken Hodge, and Fred Stanfield, in one of the most one-sided deals in hockey history. Of course, it favored Boston! Esposito went on to break practically every scoring record there was, with Hodge not far behind, and naturally everyone thought Chicago got robbed. That might have been, but Martin was a competent centerman. He also flew his own plane, which could not be said of Esposito. After nearly a decade centering Chicago's high-scoring MPH Line (Martin, Jim Pappin, and Bobby or Dennis Hull), Martin was traded to

the Vancouver Canucks, where his scoring totals dropped considerably.

Pit retired after 1978–79 with 809 career points in 1,101 NHL games.

BILL MASTERTON

BORN: Winnipeg, Manitoba, August 16, 1938
DIED: January 15, 1968
POSITION: Forward, Minnesota North Stars, 1967–68
AWARDS/HONORS: An award to "the National Hockey League player who best exemplifies the qualities of perseverance, sportsmanship, and dedication to hockey" is given annually (starting in 1968) by the National Hockey League Writers' Association in his honor.

Masterton was not a hockey star in the Bobby Hull–Gordie Howe sense of the word. In fact, he'd never played regularly in the National Hockey League until the 1967–68 season. In 1962–63, he scored 82 points for the Cleveland Barons of the American League, but decided to quit pro hockey when none of the NHL teams drafted him. He went to Denver University and obtained a master's degree in finance. After graduation, he accepted a job with the Honeywell Company in Minneapolis. For all intents and purposes, his pro hockey career was over.

But when the NHL expanded to 12 teams, the Minnesota North Stars expressed an interest in Masterton. Although Bill was satisfied with his new job, he couldn't resist the temptation of trying out with an NHL team. He reported to the North Stars' training camp and impressed general manager–coach Wren Blair enough to win a berth on the team. The 29-year-old center had finally realized his lifetime ambition.

On January 13, 1968, the North Stars played the Oakland Seals at the Metropolitan Sports Center in Bloomington, Minnesota. In the first period of the game, Masterton led a North Star rush into Oakland territory. The

Seals' defensemen, Larry Cahan and Ron Harris, braced for the attack just inside their blue line. According to Blair, Masterton was checked by the two players after passing the puck in the Oakland zone.

Together, Cahan and Harris totalled more than 400 pounds. Their combined check was described by observers as hard but clean. A split second after Masterton was hit, the North Stars' center flipped backward, hitting his head on the ice. "It was a momentary check," said Blair, "and they [Cahan and Harris] skated right on after the puck. Masterton hit [the ice] so hard that I'm sure he was unconscious before he fell. I've never seen anybody go down that way. We heard him crash to the ice from the bench."

NHL president Clarence Campbell was not at the game, but received a report from referee Wally Harris, who did not impose a penalty when Masterton fell to the ice. "I got it second-hand from the referee," said Campbell, "the same as everybody else. There was no suggestion of anything but a routine accident. His feet went out from under him and he landed on the back of his head. He had dumped the puck into the attacking zone and was chasing it."

Bill Masterton never regained consciousness. He was removed to a Minneapolis hospital where a team of five doctors was prevented from performing surgery by the seriousness of the injury. For 30 hours, they managed to keep Masterton alive by use of a respirator, but the massive internal brain injury was too severe. Early on the morning of January 15, Bill Masterton died. He was the first NHL player to die as a result of injuries suffered in league play in what was then the 52-year history of the league and, as nearly as could be ascertained, the first professional player to be killed since Owen McCourt in 1907, ten years before the NHL was formed.

Dr. John Coe, the medical examiner said: "The actual injury was not as marked as we expected but occurred in a very critical area [the pons] within the brain. So it is not difficult to account for death. It has not been determined whether the massive hemorrhaging which occurred was of primary or secondary nature . . . there was no preexisting injury or disease which was a factor in death."

Following the tragedy, league governors, in cooperation with the National Hockey League Writers' Association, created a Bill Masterton Memorial Trophy to go to a player who demonstrates the qualities exemplified by the late North Stars center.

The first winner of the Masterton Trophy was Claude Provost of the Montreal Canadiens.

STEPHANE MATTEAU

BORN: Rouyn-Noranda, Quebec, September 2, 1969
POSITION: Left Wing, Calgary Flames, 1990–91; Chicago Blackhawks, 1991–94; New York Rangers, 1994–95; St. Louis Blues, 1995–97; San Jose Sharks, 1997–2002; Florida Panthers, 2002–

MATTEAU . . . MATTEAU . . . MATTEAU!!!"

The voice belonged to Rangers' broadcaster Howie Rose and the sound could still be heard in the minds of every Ranger fan.

The date was May 27, 1994. The time was the second sudden-death overtime period between the New Jersey Devils and the New York Rangers.

Matteau, then a young Ranger forward, had captured the puck behind the visitors' net. Before goalie Martin Brodeur could fix his radar on the Ranger, Matteau wheeled to his left, came out in front to Brodeur's left and stuffed the puck into the opening between the goalpost and Brodeur's left pad.

When the red light flashed, it signaled one of the most dramatic scores in professional hockey history and enabled the Rangers to reach the Stanley Cup finals, where they defeated Vancouver and won their first Stanley Cup since 1940.

Never a first-line star, Matteau nonetheless created a career as a solid, workmanlike player who moved to St. Louis the following season, and was traded from the Blues to the San Jose Sharks in 1997-98. Stephane was named assistant captain for the Sharks in 1998. By the end of the 2000-01 season, Matteau had been in the playoffs for all 11 seasons he had been in the National Hockey League, having won one Stanley Cup. However, before the 2002-03 season, he was acquired by the Florida Panthers. Thus Stephane was reunited with Mike Keenan, who coached him in 1994 as a Ranger. Before his memorable stint with the Rangers, he battled on the bench for Chicago and Calgary, who drafted the six-feet-four, 220-pound Quebec native in the 1987 NHL Entry Draft (second round, 25th overall).

PAUL MAURICE

BORN: Sault Ste. Marie, Ontario, January 30, 1967
POSITION: Coach, Hartford Whalers/Carolina Hurricanes, 1995–

No coach in the history of the NHL has been "fired" by the media as many times as Paul Maurice. He survived those "firings" because his bosses Peter Karmanos and Jim Rutherford believed that Maurice was a good one behind the bench.

Which he was.

Originally hired as head coach at the age of 28, Maurice was the youngest mentor in the league and remained so through the 2001-02 season.

Maurice began his big-league coaching career in Hartford with the Whalers and moved with the team to Greensboro, North Carolina, when Karmanos decided to find a new audience.

Despite the franchise's failure to gain a playoff berth for the first three seasons of Maurice's stewardship, Rutherford and Karmanos had faith that he would eventually produce a winner. It finally happened in the 2000-01 season, when the Hurricanes gained a playoff berth on the final weekend of the season.

Although Carolina was ousted in six games by the defending champion New Jersey Devils, Maurice was hailed for guiding Carolina from a 0-3 deficit to a 2-3 tally, before his club was ousted in Game Six. A year later Maurice led his team to a six-game playoff victory over New Jersey as prelude to an improbable march to the Stanley Cup finals.

A one-time professional prospect, Maurice had to abort his playing career when he lost the sight in one eye during his junior hockey days. Maurice began coaching the Detroit Red Wings junior team at the age of 19 and never looked back.

BRYAN McCABE

BORN: St. Catharines, Ontario, June 8, 1975
POSITION: Defenseman, New York Islanders, 1995-98; Vancouver Canucks, 1997-99; Chicago Blackhawks, 1999-2000; Toronto Maple Leafs, 2000–

Among the many mistakes committed by Islanders management in the late 1990s, one of the worst was the decision to take a young defenseman and turn him into the team captain.

Bryan McCabe had been a favorite of general manager Mike Milbury, but at age 22, he was not prepared to lead a team already in a state of disarray.

McCabe undertook the challenge, but was busy learning how to play defense and could not be expected to earn the respect of teammates while still learning on the job. The result was a disaster for McCabe, as well as the team. In time, the young defenseman was dealt to the Vancouver Canucks (1998), with fellow young stud Todd Bertuzzi, for Trevor Linden.

McCabe gained maturity in Vancouver, and by the time he landed in Toronto (via Chicago) in 2000, he had become an effective regular defenseman who combined a measure of toughness with offensive skills. His shot from the point was one of the most effective among NHL defensemen, and his overall game was rejuvenated with the high-flying Maple Leafs after five seasons on losing, non-postseason teams. Bryan's 29 points were a new career high, and his first playoff series yielded 2 goals and 3 assists in 11 games.

His leadership skills fortified, McCabe was awarded the assistant captain's role by Leafs coach Pat Quinn in 2001–02, and teamed with Tomas Kaberle for a deadly power play combination on the point.

JACK McCARTAN

BORN: St. Paul, Minnesota, August 5, 1935
POSITION: Goaltender, New York Rangers, 1959–61; Minnesota Fighting Saints (WHA), 1972–75

Talk about a hero twice in a row and then a forgotten man thereafter, Jack McCartan was that hockey player. McCartan's heroics began with a 1960 Olympic gold medal, followed by an NHL contract.

Jack McCartan played parts of two NHL seasons, replacing New York Rangers Al Rollins after McCartan had starred for the American entry in the 1960 Olympics. As a big-leaguer, McCartan failed miserably after an impressive early start. The Rangers demoted him to the minors after he played seven and one-third games in 1960–61 for a 4.91 goals-against average. In time, McCartan became a WHA goalie for the now-defunct Minnesota Fighting Saints and then an assistant coach for the same team. Still, he is best remembered for guiding the United States Olympic team to one of the biggest upsets in international sports, defeating heavily favored Canada, Russia, and finally Czechoslovakia.

Following that gold medal triumph, McCartan was signed by the Rangers and faced the Detroit Red Wings at Madison Square Garden in his big-league debut. In the first period, he stopped Hall of Famer Gordie Howe on a breakaway, and went on to win the game. He finished the season as a local hero, but the following year, he couldn't handle NHL shooters. He was able to remain in the NHL as a scout for many years.

FRANK McCOOL

BORN: Calgary, Alberta, October 27, 1918
DIED: Date unknown
POSITION: Goaltender, Toronto Maple Leafs, 1944–46
AWARDS/HONORS: Calder Memorial Trophy, 1945

Not many goalies could claim three straight shutouts in their first three games of the Stanley Cup finals but Frank McCool could.

His saga opened as the 1944–45 season began. Toronto scouts, needing a netminder for the big club, raced all over Canada in search of a goaltender. The ultimate choice was McCool, a tall, skinny Albertan who appeared eminently suited for the job of librarian or bank clerk, but not goaltender. Not only was McCool nervous but he was assailed by a chronic case of ulcers. "Every game was a life-and-death struggle for Frank," Canadian author Ed Fitkin remembered. "He sipped milk in the dressing room between periods to calm his fluttering stomach. There were times when he took sick during a game—but one thing about him, he'd never quit." Nevertheless, it was believed that Toronto's Achilles' heel would be goaltending. "Ulcers" McCool had finished the season with a mediocre 3.22 goals-against average, although he did win the Calder Trophy as Rookie of the Year.

More importantly, McCool backstopped Toronto to the Stanley Cup in 1944–45, defeating Detroit in seven games following his three opening shutouts. After World War II, he retired to become the sports editor of the *Calgary Albertan*.

DALE McCOURT

BORN: Falconbridge, Ontario, January 26, 1957
POSITION: Center, Detroit Red Wings, 1977–81; Buffalo Sabres, 1981–83; Toronto Maple Leafs, 1983–84

When the 1978–79 NHL season began, Dale McCourt was listed as a member of the Los Angeles Kings in its official yearbook, yet McCourt had never left the Detroit Red Wings. Dale decided he did not like being the "player named later" in the Rogie Vachon deal, he was not impressed with the Southern California climate, he was very happy to be a Red Wing, and he would go to court to stay with his chosen team. The granting of a temporary restraining order against the center's shift from Detroit to LA, as compensation for the Wings' signing of free-agent goalie Vachon, overshadowed young McCourt's scoring exploits and gave him a place in hockey history. He finished his career playing for Ambri Piotta in Switzerland until 1991.

In the end, McCourt was more remembered for his legal exploits than his on-ice performance.

BRAD McCRIMMON

BORN: Dodsland, Saskatchewan, March 29, 1959
POSITION: Defenseman, Boston Bruins, 1979–82; Philadelphia Flyers, 1982–87; Calgary Flames, 1987–90; Detroit Red Wings, 1990–93; Hartford Whalers, 1993–96; Phoenix Coyotes, 1996–97
AWARDS/HONORS: NHL All-Star Game, 1988

If ever there was a player who earned the title "the defenseman's defenseman," this compact, hard-hitting backliner was the man. Completely without ostentation, Brad McCrimmon patrolled his area behind the blue line with vigor and smarts over a period of 18 years.

Although he hit hard, his play was normally clean, and fighting was not necessarily part of his repertoire, although he would deliver in that department when called upon. His offensive game peaked in 1985–86, when he had 56 points, including 43 assists and a whopping plus-83, for the Mike Keenan–coached Philadelphia Flyers, who had dealt goaltender Pete Peeters straight-up for Brad in 1982.

A member of the 1990 Stanley Cup champion Calgary Flames, McCrimmon lent his presence to various NHL backlines at the end of his career, finishing with 403 points, 1,416 penalty minutes, and, oddly, 8 shorthanded goals. He retired in 1997 to pursue coaching and scouting posts with the New York Islanders and Calgary Flames.

BUCKO McDONALD

BORN: Fergus, Ontario, October 31, 1911
DIED: July 21, 1991
POSITION: Defenseman, Detroit Red Wings, 1934–39; Toronto Maple Leafs, 1939–43; New York Rangers, 1944–45
AWARDS/HONORS: NHL Second Team All-Star, 1942

Among hard-rock, bodychecking defensemen, Wilfred McDonald was among the sturdiest. Hence the nickname, Bucko. Actually, he launched his athletic career as an exceptionally fine lacrosse player who had a go with the 1932 professional indoor "box" lacrosse league. When the loop folded after only one year of operation, McDonald was beside himself. In a desperate move, he went to Frank Selke, an aide to Conn Smythe, boss of the Toronto Maple Leafs, to inquire about a career in pro hockey.

"Can you skate?" asked Selke, trying to sound sympathetic.

"Oh," replied Bucko, trying his best to sound confident. "I can skate a little."

Selke advised Bucko to practice his skating, which he did faithfully for the next three years. After a stint with the minor-league Buffalo club, McDonald caught on with the 1935 Detroit Red Wings. The awkward McDonald became an instant favorite with the Olympia Stadium fans and led the Wings to two successive Stanley Cups.

McDonald played five steady years with Detroit before being dealt to the Maple Leafs on December 19, 1938, for Bill Thoms and $10,000. He became a star in Toronto, but Detroit is where the defenseman began to make a name for himself. After scoring 1 goal and 2 assists in his 15-game rookie year, 1934–35, McDonald would score 4 goals and 6 assists for a total of 10 points in 47 games played in his sophomore year in 1935–36. That same year, McDonald scored 3 goals in 7 playoff games. For his career in Detroit, McDonald

tallied 11 goals and 20 assists for 31 total points in 170 games.

His playmaking skills would improve once he became a Maple Leaf. He reached double figures in assists three different times, including the 1941–42 season, during which McDonald recorded 19 assists in only 48 games. That was the same year he made the NHL All-Star team, clearly his best season. The irony is that McDonald was benched after Toronto lost the first three games of the 1942 finals to Detroit and Toronto won the next four in a row—and the Cup.

He remained with Toronto until 1944, when Selke, of all people, traded him to the New York Rangers, where he closed out his career in 1945.

LANNY McDONALD

BORN: Hanna, Alberta, February 16, 1953
POSITION: Right Wing, Toronto Maple Leafs, 1973–79; Colorado Rockies, 1979–81; Calgary Flames, 1981–89
AWARDS/HONORS: Bill Masterton Memorial Trophy, 1983; NHL Second Team All-Star, 1977, 1983–84; NHL Challenge Cup All-Star, 1979; NHL All-Star Game, 1977–78, 1983–84; Hockey Hall of Fame, 1992

Lanny McDonald was tagged for superstardom when he joined the Toronto Maple Leafs as its first selection in the 1973 Amateur Draft following a brilliant junior hockey career.

Despite a disappointing, injury-plagued rookie campaign, the strapping Alberta farm boy began living up to his advance press clippings in 1976 with 37 goals and 93 points. Two years later, McDonald moved into second place in Toronto goal-scoring history with 47 tallies, and shocked the heavily-favored New York Islanders with a Game Seven overtime goal that propelled the Leafs to the 1978 Conference finals.

Opponents feared McDonald's blazing wrist shot above his many other skills, and his three straight 40-goal seasons—from 1976–77 to 1978–79—proved it.

But ornery general manager-coach Punch Imlach feuded with his players over his tyrannical ways and traded Lanny to the Colorado Rockies in 1979, along with future NHL bench boss Joel Quenneville, for Wilf Paiement and Pat Hickey. The Leafs went into a decade-long decline, while Colorado was on the verge of relocating to New Jersey. Lanny scored 60 goals in 120 games for the Rockies.

A 1981–82 midseason trade brought the veteran McDonald to the Calgary Flames, and almost instantly, the thickly-moustached Lanny became a local favorite. He scored a franchise-record 66 goals at age 30 the following season and won the Masterton Trophy. Lanny's presence in Calgary helped establish professionalism in a rising club that, by 1989, included the fiery Terry Crisp behind the bench and Doug Gilmour, Al MacInnis, Gary Suter, and Joe Nieuwendyk on the ice.

Constantly rivaling the dominant province darlings, the dynastic Edmonton Oilers, Lanny's Flames made the Cup finals in 1986 after a brutal series in Edmonton that was won on Oiler defenseman Steve Smith's gift goal in his own net. But the Flames would not win the Cup until 1989, when captain McDonald scored a key go-ahead goal, which would be his last, in Game Six of the finals to secure the first Cup win for the Flames.

McDonald finished his career immediately afterward with 500 goals and 506 assists to his credit, as well as a ticket to the Hall of Fame in 1992. The only Flame to have his sweater number retired, McDonald served the organization as an executive through the end of the century.

JIMMY McFADDEN

BORN: Belfast, Northern Ireland, April 15, 1920
POSITION: Center, Detroit Red Wings, 1947–51; Chicago Blackhawks, 1951–54
AWARDS/HONORS: Calder Memorial Trophy, 1948; NHL All-Star Game, 1950

Jimmy McFadden was the first—and last—native of Belfast, Northern Ireland, to win the Calder Trophy (1947–48) as the NHL rookie of the year. Since McFadden was 27 years old at the time of the honor, it was considered terribly unique and McFadden was hailed as a senior wunderkind.

A chunky, little (five feet seven, 178 pounds) guy, McFadden had played some of his best hockey for the Ottawa Senators in the Quebec Senior League. Although he never quite duplicated the excellence of his rookie year (60 games, 24 goals, 24 assists, for 48 points), McFadden played capably for Detroit, helping them win the Stanley Cup in 1950. He was traded to Chicago in 1951–52 and starred for the Blackhawks' surprise playoff team in 1952–53, which nearly upset the favored Canadiens in the Stanley Cup semifinals. Jimmy rounded out his big-league career in 1953–54 with Chicago.

FRANK McGEE

BORN: 1880s
DIED: September 16, 1916
POSITION: Center/Rover, Ottawa Silver Seven (CAHL, FAHL, and ECAHA), 1903–06
AWARDS/HONORS: Scoring Leader, 1905 (prior to NHL's Art Ross Trophy); Hockey Hall of Fame, 1945

There are those who still insist that Frank McGee, star of the legendary Silver Seven, was the greatest player of the pre-NHL era. It's a pretty good argument. A center and rover (rover was the seventh position), McGee was a fast skater who could stickhandle and shoot with the very best of them. Testimony to McGee's greatness is the fact that the Silver Sevens copped three consecutive Stanley Cups during Frank's brief career while staving off a host of challengers for the mug.

McGee scored better than three goals per game in the 23 regular season contests he appeared in, but even more incredible are his Stanley Cup statistics. In 22 Cup games, Frank scored 63 goals, including an amazing 14-goal game against Dawson City in 1905! An equally dazzling footnote to these astronomical numbers is the fact that Frank had lost an eye prior to his playing days with Ottawa!

But just as his handicap didn't prevent Frank's hockey heroics, neither did it deter him from military service when World War I broke out in Europe. McGee enlisted with the Canadian armed forces for overseas action and was killed in France in 1916. Deservedly, he is a member of the Hockey Hall of Fame

RANDY McKAY

BORN: Montreal, Quebec, January 25, 1967
POSITION: Right Wing, Detroit Red Wings, 1988–91; New Jersey Devils, 1991–2002; Dallas Stars, 2002; Montreal Canadiens, 2002–

When Devils' favorite Troy Crowder was plucked by the Detroit Red Wings during the summer of 1991, New Jersey hockey fans mourned the loss of their enforcer. However, the Devils received Dave Barr and Randy McKay as compensation.

To the delight of Devils devotees, McKay not only emerged as an effective enforcer, but also displayed a scoring talent that far exceeded Crowder's. While Troy quietly faded into obscurity, McKay emerged as the archetypal slugger-checker who could also put points on the board.

"My work in the corners and my forechecking are the strong points of my game," said McKay. "I have to get in there crashing and banging to get the puck loose. I like to go to the net. That's where I've scored most of my goals. A lot are scored within three feet of the net. I'll go in deep and work for the puck and go after rebounds. That's what I have to keep doing."

The six-feet-two, 210-pound Montreal native was Detroit's sixth choice in the 1985 Entry Draft. Before hitting the bigs, McKay played for four years with Michigan Tech, and while with Detroit he played for their farm team in Adirondack.

When he was traded to New Jersey, McKay instantly became a force and mainstay for 11 years. He won his first Stanley Cup with the team in 1995, scoring huge goals, including an overtime tally in Game Four of the Eastern Conference quarterfinals against Boston and the series clincher versus the Philadelphia Flyers two rounds later.

Along with Bobby Holik, McKay evolved from Crash Line banger to a two-way dependable winger over the years and despite numerous injuries, including a fractured hand in the first game of the 2001 Stanley Cup finals that caused him to miss the rest of the series, McKay's hard-hitting style and ability to put the puck in the net made him well-liked in the Meadowlands.

With the aging Devils in turmoil during the 2001–02 season, McKay was traded, along with Jason Arnott, to the Dallas Stars for Joe Nieuwendyk, Jamie Langenbrunner, and a first-round pick. The change invigorated the veteran McKay, as he scored three goals in his first two games with the team, which could not make the playoffs. He then became an unrestricted free agent and signed with Montreal in July 2002.

DON McKENNEY

BORN: Smith Falls, Ontario, April 30, 1934
POSITION: Center/Left Wing, Boston Bruins, 1954–62; New York Rangers, 1962–64; Toronto Maple Leafs, 1964–65; Detroit Red Wings, 1965–66; St. Louis Blues, 1967–68
AWARDS/HONORS: Lady Byng Memorial Trophy, 1960

In the late '50s and early '60s, Don McKenney was regarded as an "untouchable" forward on the Boston Bruins. A center who also could play left wing, Don was a mild-mannered skater who graduated to the pros after skating for the Barrie (Ontario) Flyers. His efficiency as a Bruin deteriorated in 1962, and he was traded to the New York Rangers. In February 1964, McKenney was involved in one of hockey's most important trades, going to Toronto with Andy Bathgate for Bill Collins, Rod Seiling, Arnie Brown, Dick Duff, and Bob Nevin.

McKenney played superbly in the 1964 Stanley Cup playoffs, scoring 4 goals and 8 assists for 12 points as Toronto won the Cup. However, he was dealt to Detroit for the 1965–66 season and ended his NHL career in 1967–68 with the St. Louis Blues. More recently, he has operated hockey schools in the Boston area.

JOHNNY McKENZIE

BORN: High River, Alberta, December 12, 1937
POSITION: Right Wing, Chicago Blackhawks, 1958–59, 1963–65; Detroit Red Wings, 1959–61; New York Rangers/Boston Bruins, 1965–66; Boston Bruins, 1966–72; Player/Coach, Philadelphia/Vancouver Blazers/Calgary Cowboys (WHA), 1972–75; Cincinnati Stingers, 1975; Minnesota Fighting Saints, 1976–77; New England Whalers, 1977–79
AWARDS/HONORS: All-Star (WHA, Second Team), 1970; NHL All-Star Game, 1970, 1972

In 1970, John McKenzie was voted the Most Popular Player on the Bruins, a long way from his doldrum days in Buffalo (American Hockey League) in 1963. "That's where I got the 'Pie' nickname," said McKenzie. "A guy named Gerry Melnyk gave it to me. He was on Buffalo too, and I guess he figured my round face looked like a pie so I've been Pie ever since."

One of the peskiest, most effective skaters ever to skate in the NHL, Johnny McKenzie quit the Boston Bruins and jumped to the Philadelphia Blazers of the World Hockey Association in 1972 as player-coach. The move was slightly disastrous. McKenzie argued with his aide, Phil Watson, through most of the season and the Blazers floundered. A year later, the team and McKenzie moved to Vancouver, where they continued as the Blazers and continued to stay near the depths of the league standings.

A true journeyman, McKenzie shifted from team to team within the WHA until he landed with New England in 1976. The 18-year veteran of both leagues was a 27-goal scorer during the 1978 season, the tenth time he had passed the 20-goal plateau. McKenzie was still a regular with New England during his final season, 1978–79, when the Whalers announced plans to join Pie's native league, the NHL.

MAX McNAB

BORN: Watson, Saskatchewan, June 21, 1924
POSITION: Center, Detroit Red Wings,
1947–50; President, Central Hockey League,
1974–75; General Manager, Washington
Capitals, 1976–81; New Jersey Devils,
1983–1987

Max McNab, frequently called the nicest guy in hockey (and not without validity) never quite made it in the big time the way the Detroit Red Wings had hoped in the late 1940s. A product of the Saskatoon Elks' senior club, Max was groomed as the heir apparent to center Sid Abel, who was the aging pivot on the Ted Lindsay–Gordie Howe Production Line.

McNab led the United States League in goal-scoring in 1947–48 with Omaha, ringing up 44 goals in 44 games. That same season he was given a 12-game trial with the Red Wings and scored 2 goals and 2 assists. A year later, he played 51 NHL games in Detroit, this time scoring 10 goals and 13 assists. But McNab's major-league career was shortened by a series of injuries in the early 1950s and he never fulfilled his promise as a player.

After his playing days ended, he became one of the game's foremost executives, helping San Diego become a hot hockey city. In 1974, Max was named president of the Central League. McNab returned to the big leagues on December 30, 1975, when he was selected as general manager of the expansion Washington Capitals, giving Max a new area of untried hockey fans to conquer.

Under McNab's stewardship, the futile Capitals failed to make the playoffs in their early years, and he was replaced in 1982 by David Poile.

He was then hired as general manager of the New Jersey Devils, and once again, his club failed to gain a playoff berth. During the 1987–88 season, he was replaced by Lou Lamoriello, but remained in an advisory capacity before retiring to Las Vegas with his wife June. His son Peter enjoyed a long big-league career before becoming a broadcaster. Another son, David, was assistant general manager of the Mighty Ducks of Anaheim.

PETER McNAB

BORN: Vancouver, British Columbia, May 8,
1952
POSITION: Center, Buffalo Sabres, 1973–76;
Boston Bruins, 1976–84; Vancouver Canucks,
1984–85; New Jersey Devils, 1985–87
AWARDS/HONORS: NHL All-Star Game, 1977

Some would say that Peter McNab was too modest in denying that he belonged in the Hockey Hall of Fame. Starting with a 38-goal year in 1976–77, he then proceeded to follow that with 41 goals, 35, and then 40. Granted, he never reached 40 goals again, but in 1980–81 he came up with 37 and a career points high of 83.

Born in Vancouver, where his father Max once guided the minor-league Vancouver Canucks, Peter learned his hockey in balmy San Diego, when Max was running the pro team in Southern California. Ironically, McNab won a baseball scholarship to Denver University, but made the varsity hockey team, playing well enough to attract NHL scouts. He was signed by Buffalo and then alternated between the Sabres and Cincinnati in the American League in 1973–74. He latched onto a permanent big-league job the following year.

But it wasn't until he was dealt to Boston that McNab flowered into a major player. Fortuitously, he arrived in Beantown at the apex of Don "Grapes" Cherry's stewardship as coach, while some of the most gifted big-leaguers—such as Jean Ratelle, Brad Park, John Bucyk, and Terry O'Reilly—were skating for the black, gold, and white.

The McNab wrist drive was as effective in the playoffs as it was during the regular season.

In 1977–78, Peter tallied 8 goals and 11 assists for 19 points in 15 playoff games. In the 1980 playoffs, he scored 8 goals in 10 games. Over a period of five winters, he had banged home 191 goals, which was a 38.2 clip.

On February 3, 1984, Peter was dealt to the Vancouver Canucks for Jim Nill and he played one full season in Vancouver (1984–85) before turning free agent once more. When released by the Canucks, Peter was signed by—of all people!—Max McNab, who had become general manager of the New Jersey Devils.

McNab concluded his NHL career with the 1986–87 season, retired from the ice, and moved up to the broadcast booth, where he became the Devils' television analyst for SportsChannel, and more recently the Colorado Avalanche expert with Fox Sports.

GERRY McNEIL

BORN: Quebec City, Quebec, April 17, 1926
POSITION: Goaltender, Montreal Canadiens, 1947–48, 1949–50, 1956–57
AWARDS/HONORS: NHL All-Star Game, 1951–53

Gerry McNeil played goal for the Montreal Canadiens in the early 1950s, filling the void between Bill Durnan's retirement and the later emergence of the spectacular Jacques Plante, each a Hall of Famer, although McNeil was not.

McNeil was victimized by a couple of memorable sudden-death goals. In Game Five of the Montreal-Toronto Stanley Cup finals, Bill Barilko beat McNeil over the shoulder for the Leafs' Cup winner. Three years later, McNeil blew another.

The playoffs of 1954 found the youngster Plante between the Hab pipes as McNeil was coming off a painful midseason injury. Jake the Snake was erratic in the Cup finals, however, and after the Detroit Red Wings had downed the Habs in three of the first four games, McNeil took over.

Gerry was fantastic in goal as Montreal pulled even at three games apiece; and then battled the Wings to sudden-death overtime in the seventh and final game. Tony Leswick, a Montreal nemesis all series long, broke into his offensive zone with Montreal's All-Star defenseman Doug Harvey the only object between goaltender McNeil and him. Leswick fired a lazy long shot that McNeil had lined up until suddenly, Harvey stuck out his glove in an attempt to deflect the puck out of harm's way.

Deflect it he did—right over McNeil's shoulder and into the cords to end the series and Montreal's hopes for the Cup. Needless to say, McNeil had nightmares about that shot all summer long. Finally deciding it wasn't worth the aggravation, McNeil retired from hockey for one season, but he briefly returned to the Canadiens in 1956–57.

GEORGE McPHEE

BORN: Guelph, Ontario, July 2, 1958
POSITION: Left Wing, New York Rangers, 1982–87; New Jersey Devils, 1988–89; General Manager, Washington Capitals, 1997–
AWARDS/HONORS: Hobey Baker Memorial Award, 1982

Pound for pound one of the best fighters in NHL history, George McPhee came to the NHL after being a four-year letter winner at Bowling Green from 1978–82, while he earned a business degree. McPhee became one of college hockey's most decorated players, and was the second recipient of the Hobey Baker Award as college hockey's top player.

McPhee broke into the NHL with the New York Rangers in 1982–83 and remained with the Blueshirts until the 1987–88 season, when he became a New Jersey Devil. He scored 3 goals in 5 games before a serious groin injury sidelined him. He played one more game for the Devils in 1988–89, but never recovered sufficiently to resume his career.

After retiring, McPhee obtained degrees in both law and business. He was then named the fifth general manager in the Washington Capitals' history on June 7, 1997. As vice president and general manager of the Capitals, McPhee totally rebuilt the franchise and renewed interest in the Capitals organization through a trip to the Stanley Cup finals in 1998 and back-to-back Southeast Division titles in 1999–2000 and 2000–01.

Considered one of the brightest of the new breed of NHL executives, McPhee orchestrated the publicity campaign of the Capitals until, by 2002, the franchise had achieved unprecedented popularity in the nation's capital.

MARTY McSORLEY

BORN: Hamilton, Ontario, May 18, 1963
POSITION: Defenseman, Pittsburgh Penguins, 1983–85; Edmonton Oilers, 1985–88; Los Angeles Kings, 1988–93; Pittsburgh Penguins, 1993–94; Los Angeles Kings, 1994–96; New York Rangers, 1996; San Jose Sharks, 1996–98; Edmonton Oilers, 1998–99; Boston Bruins, 1999–2000; Head Coach, Springfield (AHL), 2002–
AWARDS/HONORS: Alka-Seltzer Plus Award (shared with Theoren Fleury), 1991

If ever there was a hockey player who could be regarded as a "personal bodyguard," it was Marty McSorley. And the man he guarded was Wayne Gretzky, the most prolific scorer of the modern hockey era.

McSorley was signed as a free agent by the Penguins in 1982 and played 72 games for Pittsburgh as an NHL rookie in the 1983–84 season.

While his style was crude, there was an exuberance about him that should have signaled the Pittsburgh high command that they had a winner. But the Pens traded him to Edmonton in September 1985, where he would play on the 1987 and 1988 Oilers Stanley Cup winners and demonstrate that he was more than a tough guy. During the 1987

Cup run, he had 4 goals and 3 assists in 21 playoff games.

When Edmonton traded Wayne Gretzky to Los Angeles in June 1989, Gretzky insisted that McSorley be included in the deal. It was a fortuitous move for the Kings. McSorley, who had alternated between forward and defense, was moved permanently to the back line. His play improved during the year and by 1990–91 he had become one of the most reliable members of the Kings' blueline brigade.

He remained supremely intense and as truculent as he had been during his rookie days and blossomed into one of the league's most eloquent and amusing personalities.

But most of all, McSorley was known for his toughness, particularly when he played for the Edmonton Oilers, when players such as Wayne Gretzky and Mark Messier were starring for the team.

"If you are a goal scorer like Mark Messier, you may be able to fight," said McSorley, "but you don't want him to fight more than once a game because it's not good for the hockey club. That's where the tough guy has to step in and be the guy that goes out and does that role and lets Mark Messier play hockey."

He was also the centerpiece of one of hockey's most notorious blunders, in Game Two of the 1993 Stanley Cup finals on June 3, 1993. The Kings had won the opening game 4–1 and were leading 2–1 late in the game. It appeared that the Kings might get a stranglehold on the series. However, McSorley was caught with an illegal stick. With McSorley in the penalty box, the Montreal Canadiens scored and then went on to win the game in overtime, 3–2. The Canadiens then won the next three straight games and the Stanley Cup.

More infamously, McSorley's career in the NHL ended after he chopped his stick over forward Donald Brashear's head during a game on February 21, 2000, against the Vancouver Canucks. McSorley, then with the Boston Bruins, was found guilty of assault with a weapon and was sentenced to 18 months of probation. The NHL suspended McSorley for 23 games. He never played major-league hockey again but returned as head coach at Springfield of the AHL for the 2002–03 season.

TOM McVIE

BORN: Trail, British Columbia, October 6, 1935
POSITION: Coach, Washington Capitals, 1975–78; Winnipeg Jets, 1979–81; New Jersey Devils, 1983–84, 1990–92

Job security long eluded former Boston Bruins assistant coach Tom McVie, but his survival instincts were second to none in the NHL. The gravel-voiced McVie was a head coach for 22 years before becoming top aide to the Bruins' Brian Sutter in 1992–93. "Tommy has forgotten more hockey than any of us will ever know," said Sutter.

Respect did not come easy to McVie, partly because he had been aligned with so many weak teams, and partly because of his vocal personality. But Tom took pride in a record that includes stints with two of the worst teams in NHL history, the Washington Capitals and the Winnipeg Jets, and resented the lack of reverence accorded somebody of his experience.

He was not surprised, though. McVie was nothing if not realistic. "Somebody once told me," he said, "that if you really want to be a good coach, get some good players. Now that's what I call good advice.

"I like to hang out with the ordinary guys. You won't find me staying around an Adam Oates or a Ray Bourque. The second- and third-stringers are the ones who I should be with. They know I'll be at the rink when they get there and won't leave till they go home."

How good a head coach Tommy actually was is a moot point. His head coaching days left a mark of 126 wins, 263 losses, and 73 ties, including a woeful 1980–81 season in Winnipeg where his team was victorious just once in the first 28 games, before two different successors relieved him that same year.

Under McVie, New Jersey pushed the eventual Stanley Cup champion Pittsburgh Penguins to the seven-game limit in 1991. A year later, he lost a seven-game series to the rival Rangers before being fired. After Herb Brooks replaced him in New Jersey, McVie then moved to Boston, where he found himself in an assistant's role for old adversary Brian Sutter, before moving into the scouting department.

HOWIE MEEKER

BORN: Kitchener, Ontario, November 4, 1924
POSITION: Right Wing, Toronto Maple Leafs, 1946–54; Coach, Toronto Maple Leafs, 1956–57
AWARDS/HONORS: Calder Memorial Trophy, 1947; NHL All-Star Game, 1947, 1948, 1949

When Maple Leafs boss Conn Smythe returned to Toronto after serving in Europe during World War II and began rebuilding his hockey club, he emphasized a policy of hard-nosed play. "Nobody," said Smythe, "pops anybody on this club without getting popped back. I'm not interested in hockey players who don't play to win. You can take penalties, but you gotta play to win." Then, Smythe went about the business of finding youngsters who fulfilled his requirements.

One of those kids was Howie Meeker, a fighter of the Smythe mold. During World War II, a grenade blew up in Meeker's face, and doctors said he'd never play hockey again. But there he was, a rookie on the 1946–47 Leafs. Meeker was fast and tough, and he loved to fight with Gordie Howe of Detroit and Tony Leswick of the Rangers.

Meeker was part of the famed second-generation Kid Line, along with Vic Lynn and Teeder Kennedy. Lynn was not an especially heavy scorer, but he was big and rough and he hit hard. Kennedy couldn't skate very well, but he seemed to have the puck all the time. As a unit they meshed perfectly, reaching their collective peak in the 1947–48 season.

Complemented by two other strong lines, the Kid Line steered the Leafs to another Stanley Cup win in 1948 and still another in 1949. Toronto missed in 1950, but in 1951 the Leafs reached the Cup finals against Montreal's Canadiens. With Toronto leading the series three games to one, and the fifth game in sudden-death overtime, Meeker helped create the Cup-winning goal by mate Bill Barilko. Howie outsped several pursuing Montreal players early in the overtime, captured the puck, and set up teammate Harry Watson who, in turn, got the puck to Barilko, who shot the rubber over goalie Gerry McNeil.

The quality of Meeker's play ebbed after that grand moment, and he retired after playing only five games for the Leafs in 1953–54. Meeker was named coach of the Leafs in 1956–57 (they finished out of the playoffs) and by season's end gave way to Billy Reay. However, Meeker had been promoted to manager and remained in that position until Stafford Smythe became chairman of the new Maple Leafs hockey committee, when Smythe promptly fired Meeker.

In the 1970s, Meeker became a household name in Canada when he joined *Hockey Night in Canada* as a lead analyst. He also authored several books on hockey.

BARRY MELROSE

BORN: Kelvington, Saskatchewan, July 15, 1956
POSITION: Defenseman, Winnipeg Jets, 1979–80; Toronto Maple Leafs, 1981–83; Detroit Red Wings, 1983–84, 1985–86; Coach, Los Angeles Kings, 1992–95

Like many hockey television personalities such as Don Cherry and Darren Pang, Barry Melrose did better behind the mike than on the ice. His NHL career spanned 300 games, during which he was more a journeyman banger than anything else.

Following his playing career, Melrose moved into the coaching and administrative end. With a penchant for developing players, he won a Calder Cup as coach of the Adirondack Red Wings in 1991–92, and became the Los Angeles Kings' mentor the following season. Armed with Luc Robitaille, Kelly Hrudey, Rob Blake, Wayne Gretzky, and a host of ex-Edmonton Oilers, rookie coach Melrose guided the team to the Stanley Cup finals, where they were swept by the Canadiens in their quest for the 1993 Stanley Cup after an illegal stick blunder by McSorley late in the opening game cost Los Angeles the match and irreversibly disturbed the club's momentum.

Two seasons later, the team faltered and Melrose was sacked. Almost immediately afterward, Barry was hired as a hockey analyst for ESPN and cohosted *NHL 2Nite*, the show that endeared him to United States hockey fans and eclipsed his coaching accomplishments.

MARK MESSIER

BORN: Edmonton, Alberta, January 18, 1961
POSITION: Center/Left Wing, Edmonton Oilers, 1979–91; New York Rangers, 1991–97, 2000–; Vancouver Canucks 1997–2000
AWARDS/HONORS: Conn Smythe Trophy, 1984; Lester B. Pearson Award, 1990, 1992; Hart Memorial Trophy, 1990, 1992; NHL First Team All-Star, 1982–83, 1990, 1992; NHL Second Team All-Star, 1984; NHL All-Star Game, 1982–1984, 1986, 1988–1992, 1994, 1996–1998, 2000

Without question, Mark Messier emerged as the ultimate power forward of the 20-year period beginning in 1981 and ending just after the turn of the new century. There are many who will claim that Messier was a better all-around player than his former Edmonton Oilers teammate, Wayne Gretzky.

"Numbers don't tell you everything you have to know about hockey players," said Lou Vairo, author of an in-depth hockey manual and assistant coach of the 2002 U.S. Olympic team. "There are intangibles that can be seen and felt but can't be calculated with a computer."

Mark Messier as an Oiler

The intangibles, combined with his lifetime stats, give Messier an edge over Gretzky. Energy, toughness, checking ability, fighting ability, and desire were the intangibles.

It is significant that Gretzky never played on a Stanley Cup winner after he and Messier split, when The Great One was traded to Los Angeles. On the other hand, Messier became the first player in league history to serve as captain on two Stanley Cup teams—in 1990 with the Edmonton Oilers (without Gretzky) and in 1994 with the New York Rangers, also minus Gretzky.

Former Montreal Canadiens coach Jacques Demers said it best about Messier: "When Mark gets going, it's impossible to stop that man."

A second-round pick in the 1979 Entry Draft, Messier broke into the NHL the following season with 33 points in 75 games. Under the tutelage of Oilers leader Glen Sather, Messier, together with youngsters Gretzky, Kevin Lowe, Paul Coffey, and Grant Fuhr, learned to win by failing in the playoffs. His numbers increased rapidly, but the Oilers could not get by the second round of the playoffs, and when they did reach the 1983 playoffs, they were swept by the New York Islanders in four straight games.

Finally, in 1984, Edmonton won the first of its four Cups in five years as Messier won the Conn Smythe with a 26-point performance in 19 matches.

After Gretzky was dealt in 1988, Messier carried the Oilers to the Cup in 1990 with a

Hart Trophy nod as league Most Valuable Player. Before he was dealt to the Rangers in 1991 for Bernie Nicholls, Steven Rice, and Louie DeBrusk, Messier captured a top slot in every offensive category in Edmonton team history, including games played (second with 851), goals (fourth with 392), assists (second with 642), and points (third with 1,034).

New York became a haven for the superstar, its glamorous stage and media blitz a perfect setting for greatness to emerge. After two years of failure, the Blueshirts went on a mission in 1994. Under coach Mike Keenan, Mark helped linemate Adam Graves net 52 goals as the Rangers won the President's Trophy and iced a Keenan-designed veteran team that knew no failure in the playoffs, thanks to the media-dubbed "Messiah."

The six-feet-one, 210-pound center was a courageous leader for the Cup-starved New Yorkers, publicly announcing that his Rangers would win the crucial Game Six of the 1994 Eastern Conference finals against the New Jersey Devils. He netted a hat trick to back it all up. When the Rangers defeated the Vancouver Canucks in the finals, Messier's mission was completed. He carried the Rangers to their first Stanley Cup since 1940.

After old friend Gretzky joined him on Broadway in 1996–97, Messier again led his Rangers to a strong playoff, only to be felled by the Philadelphia Flyers in the Eastern Conference finals. Feuding with general manager Neil Smith, Messier exercised his unrestricted free agency and bolted to, ironically, the Canucks, where he became captain of a team that would not make the playoffs once during his tenure despite the presence of Pavel Bure.

He returned to the Rangers in the year 2000 and reassumed his captaincy from Brian Leetch, who had struggled mightily with the role in Messier's absence.

At age 40 in the 2000-01 season, he still persevered, notching 67 points in his Broadway return, providing guidance to the club. He appeared in all games of the season, one of only four Rangers to do so, which marked the second time in his career that he was an iron man. But in 2001–02, the Rangers stumbled out of the playoff picture again when both Messier and newly-acquired superstar Eric Lindros were saddled with injuries, in Messier's case a bad shoulder that limited his movement.

Messier had all the charismatic makings of a solid hockey player, as was summed up by Rangers general manager and Edmonton's former boss Glen Sather: "Mark seems to have that unbeatable spirit. He reminds me of a galloping thoroughbred in the wind. He gets that look in his eye; it's a look that I've only seen once before in a great hockey player, and that was Maurice Richard. But Mark has it even more. At critical times in the playoffs he'll give everyone that look in the dressing room and away we go!"

Messier's injuries sidelined him at the end of the 2001-02 season, but he returned for another season as a player in 2002-03.

DON METZ

BORN: Wilcox, Saskatchewan, January 10, 1916
DIED: Date unknown
POSITION: Forward, Toronto Maple Leafs, 1939–49

A product of the Wilcox, Saskatchewan, wheat fields, Don Metz played occasionally for the Toronto Maple Leafs from 1939–40 through the 1948–49 season, but is best remembered for two episodes that contributed to two Stanley Cup victories. In 1942, with the Leafs trailing the Red Wings three games to none in the Cup finals, Metz replaced high-scoring Gordie Drillon. Don popped in 4 goals and 3 assists—every one of them vital—and orchestrated the Toronto Cup championship. In the 1947 Cup semifinals with Montreal, Don bowled over the Canadiens' crack center Elmer Lach, sidelining

him for the series. Montreal coach Dick Irvin insisted that if it was, in fact, a deliberate attempt to injure, God would see to it that the Leafs lost. Toronto, with Don contributing an important 2 goals and 3 assists, won the Stanley Cup.

His older brother, Nick, teamed with Don through most of the latter's career with Toronto.

NICK METZ

BORN: Wilcox, Saskatchewan, February 16, 1914
DIED: Date unknown
POSITION: Forward, Toronto Maple Leafs, 1934–48

Older than brother Don by two years, Nick Metz, along with teammate Joe Klukay, developed the best penalty-killing combination the NHL had ever seen. Nick became a Leaf in 1934–35 and remained with the Toronto club through the 1947–48 campaign when the Leafs finished first and won the Stanley Cup. He was regarded as one of the most versatile forwards of all time and many critics believed that he retired prematurely.

Nick Metz, nevertheless, proved his worth having skated on Stanley Cup winners in 1941–42, 1946–47, and 1947–48.

RICK MIDDLETON

BORN: Toronto, Ontario, December 4, 1953
POSITION: Right Wing, New York Rangers, 1974–76; Boston Bruins, 1976–88
AWARDS/HONORS: Lady Byng Memorial Trophy, 1982; NHL Second Team All-Star, 1982; NHL All-Star Game, 1981–82, 1984

It is a measure of the esteem in which Rick Middleton was held by hockey sages that he was recommended as a candidate for the Hall of Fame.

Middleton didn't make it, but he permanently endeared himself to New Englanders with a brand of artistry that helped provide balance to a roster sprinkled with tough guys, characters, and the irrepressible coach, Don "Grapes" Cherry.

Originally a New York Ranger, Middleton arrived in Boston for the 1976–77 season precisely when Cherry was reaching his apex on Causeway Street.

After a so-so (20-22-42) opening season with the Bruins, Middleton blossomed under Grapes's coaching and soon was being called "Nifty" around Boston Garden.

One day somebody asked why he was nicknamed "Nifty." Bruins forward Keith Crowder had an immediate answer: "Just watch him."

"I've seen them all," said ex-mate Brad Park, "and Nifty was the best one-on-one player in hockey at the time. You could take anyone in the league, give Nifty the puck and ninety percent of the time he'd turn the other guy inside out."

When John Ferguson was Rangers general manager, he dealt Middleton to Boston for Ken Hodge, insisting he was forced into the deal by Blueshirts' star and ex-Bruin Phil Esposito, who was languishing on Broadway and wanted Hodge, his former linemate, to skate with him again. In retrospect, Ferguson called it the worst deal he ever made. Hodge faded quickly, and Middleton spent a decade in Boston, topping 100 points twice (103 in 1980-81 and 105 in 1983-84) although his primary mentor, Cherry, had since been fired.

Middleton never earned a Stanley Cup ring, but his 988 career points were as impressive as anyone's. He closed out his career in Beantown in 1987-88 after his production dropped way down, but he never lost the respect of management, fans, teammates, and coaches.

"I have to hand it to Middleton," said Cherry. "When he came over from New York, he had a reputation as a free spirit. From the way people were talking you would have thought he had committed everything short of murder. But for me, he did everything I asked of him."

Middleton went on to coach the United States Men's Sled Hockey Team at the 2002 Paralympics at Salt Lake and remained a hero to Boston hockey fans.

STAN MIKITA

BORN: Sokolce, Czechoslovakia, May 20, 1940
POSITION: Center, Chicago Blackhawks, 1958-80
AWARDS/HONORS: Hart Memorial Trophy, 1967-68; Art Ross Trophy, 1964-65, 1967-68; Lady Byng Memorial Trophy, 1967-68; Lester Patrick Trophy, 1976; Team Canada, 1972; NHL First Team All-Star, 1962-64, 1966-68; NHL Second Team All-Star, 1965, 1970; NHL All-Star Game, 1964, 1967-69, 1971-75; Hockey Hall of Fame, 1983

If any single player can be described as the guts of a hockey team, Stan Mikita, the shifty Chicago center, was precisely that man. More than any National Hockey League club, the Hawks were decimated by World Hockey Association raids. First, Bobby Hull, the Golden Jet, jumped to Winnipeg. Then, in 1973, the Hawks lost first-string defenseman Pat Stapleton and reliable center Ralph Backstrom to the Chicago Cougars. They were quality players that a team could ill afford to lose, unless it possessed a very strong backbone. Which is where Mikita came in. His combined excellence as a leader and an artistic scorer enabled coach Billy Reay's team to weather the storm.

He was a member of Chicago's last (1960-61) Stanley Cup–winning team.

Chicago finished first in the West Division in 1972-73, following Hull's exit, and Stan scored 27 goals and 56 assists for 83 points. His guidance for the younger players enabled the Hawks to reach the Stanley Cup finals before the Canadiens eliminated them in six games. The Hawks had more trouble in 1973-74 with Stapleton and Backstrom gone and the Philadelphia Flyers coming on strong.

Chicago, nonetheless, finished a strong second while Mikita led the team in scoring with 30 goals and 50 assists for 80 points.

Early in his career, Mikita was one of the feistiest players in the NHL. Nicknamed "Le Petit Diable" (The Little Devil) by fans in Montreal, the five-feet-nine, 165-pound Mikita was always getting into fights. During the 1964–65 season, Mikita spent 154 minutes in the penalty box. However, Mikita soon changed his ways. After Mikita's daughter saw a game of his on television and repeatedly saw him being escorted to the penalty box, she asked why he was always in there while everyone else was playing. Mikita responded by altering his style of play. By the 1966–67 season, the reformed Mikita won the MVP, scoring title, and to the surprise of many, the Lady Byng Trophy. He again won all three awards the next year.

To purists, Mikita was the total hockey player. Coach Billy Reay once said that Stan had Rocket Richard's accuracy as a shooter, Gordie Howe's defensive mastery, Bobby Hull's speed and shot, and Jean Beliveau's stickhandling ability. "Mikita," added Reay, "does more with everything he's got than any player I've seen."

In February 1974, Chicagoans displayed their appreciation for Mikita by throwing a "night" in his honor at Chicago Stadium. At first Stan was reluctant to participate, but told the promoters he would agree to the fete on one condition: He didn't need or want any gifts such as the cars that were donated to previous aces. He appreciated the thought behind the ceremony, but he wanted the money channeled into a scholarship fund at Elmhurst College in Illinois. "Then," said Mikita, "I'll have the satisfaction of knowing some kids will get educations that otherwise would be out of reach."

If hockey doctorates were awarded, the Czechoslovakia-born Mikita would be first in line, judging from his cerebral play. "He automatically made the right play," said Chicago's general manager Tommy Ivan, "and was already thinking about where the next one would develop, and headed in that direction."

In 1979, Mikita entered his 20th season with Chicago, seeing limited playing time because of injuries. Mikita remained a Blackhawk despite lucrative offers from the WHA that lured Hull, Stapleton, and Backstrom from the Hawks. He retired at the end of the season, having only played 17 games.

"Unless a man believes in himself, makes a total commitment to his career, and puts everything he has into it," Mikita concluded, "he will never be successful in anything he undertakes."

The 11th all-time leading scorer entering the twenty-first century, Mikita was a permanent Chicago resident and active member of the Blackhawks alumni after his career ended, and was immortalized by a cameo appearance as himself in the 1992 comedic film *Wayne's World,* starring Michael Meyers.

Stan Mikita celebrating his 200th goal as a Blackhawk

MIKE MILBURY

BORN: Brighton, Massachusetts, June 17, 1952

POSITION: Defenseman, Boston Bruins, 1975–87; Coach, Boston Bruins, 1989–91; New York Islanders, 1995–96, 1997–98; General Manager, New York Islanders, 1996–

As a defenseman for the Bruins, Mike Milbury was like an old, reliable automobile that won't win any beauty contests but will take you where you want to go. There never was anything fancy about him, not as a National Hockey League rookie in 1975–76 and not in 1986–87, his last season in the bigs. But over a dozen seasons, this much could be said without equivocation: He got the job done.

Sometimes he did it with undue force and other times with an overdose of emotion. Rarely did he execute his job as a backliner with exquisite grace or grandeur. A Bobby Orr he was not, and yet when Milbury was out of the Bruins' lineup, the team invariably was the worse for it.

When you think about it, the mere fact that Mike played a single game as a Bruin is something of a minor miracle. Hockey hardly was uppermost on his mind when he attended Walpole High. The recruiters at Colgate wanted him for the football team. In time, though, hockey took over from football, and he was scouted by the Bruins and wound up playing in the American Hockey League for Rochester. After a few glitches here and there, he made the big team. He was an American playing a Canadian game at a time when it still was unusual to find Uncle Sam's skaters in the NHL.

Milbury blossomed into a dependable, throwback defenseman, although his awkward style occasionally evoked derision. Ironically, his coach in Boston was the ultimate Canadian chauvinist, Don Cherry, who, somehow, took a liking to the local boy. His relationship with Cherry was priceless. The chemistry between the two was as good as it gets. The Cherry years were a delight for Milbury, who went to the Stanley Cup finals, won plenty of games, and, in 1977, was on a team that came close to actually beating Montreal for the title.

Milbury remained one of the top four Bruins defensemen through the mid 1980s. His teams never missed the playoffs and always had a winning record. As NHL players go, Milbury certainly would be rated an intellectual. He was a voracious reader and uninhibited about revealing his thoughts.

As Milbury's career wound down, his boss, Harry Sinden, began suggesting that Mike might have a postplaying career as an executive. The 1986–87 season was Milbury's last in the bigs, and one of his most depressing. But Mike always displayed a high degree of resilience.

In time, he would become Bruins coach and a member of the high command. He left Sinden's organization in 1994 to become a television analyst at ESPN. When the New York Islanders offered him a coaching job, he moved to Long Island and eventually was named general manager. Despite several tumultuous—and losing—seasons, he miraculously held the job through the 2001–02 season, after the cash-strapped team endured numerous changes in coaches, players, and ownership.

With the team missing the playoffs for seven straight years, Milbury became the subject of the fans' ire, which featured a "MIKE MUST GO!" chant at the Nassau Coliseum, when the undermanned Islanders would find themselves out of the playoff picture by December. None of the trades or player signings, nor coaches that Milbury produced improved the team, and their crop of high draft picks were years away or rushed into NHL service before they were ready.

But when Charles Wang and Sanjay Kumar bought the team in 1999, Milbury was retained, as the new owners looked to Milbury to lead an NHL-caliber team with a clean slate.

Armed with funds, "Mad Mike," as Milbury would dub himself to the media, pulled off a slew of trades at the 2000 and 2001 Entry Drafts. They netted key components Roman Hamrlik and Mark Parrish (2000), along with Alexei Yashin and Michael Peca (2001), resulting in the Islanders' resurgence in the 2001–02 season.

Milbury took a risk by hiring rookie coach Peter Laviolette to guide the team, and his gamble paid off. The team went 11–1–1 to start the season, and their inspired play filled the Nassau Coliseum for 21 regular season sell-outs. They finally made the playoffs for the first time since 1994. The often-outspoken Milbury, once vilified, was now working at NHL standards, and, thanks to Wang and Kumar, made admirable moves to right the ship and buoy the Islanders' dramatic turnaround.

His efforts paid off as the Islanders extended favored Toronto to seven games before bowing in the opening playoff round.

KELLY MILLER

BORN: Lansing, Michigan, March 3, 1963
POSITION: Left Wing, New York Rangers, 1985–87; Washington Capitals, 1987–99

One of the best American-born players of the 1990s, Kelly Miller made his reputation as a dauntless penalty killer and defensive forward who also had a deft scoring touch.

Originally a member of the New York Rangers, Miller was dealt to Washington on January 1, 1987, along with Mike Ridley and Bob Crawford for Bob Carpenter and a draft pick, in one of the most one-sided deals ever made. Miller went on to become a Capitals mainstay for over a decade, appearing in a franchise record 940 games through the 1998–99 season.

For the Caps, he teamed with Ridley on penalty kills. He became one of Washington's first hockey poster boys, and also was active in the NHL Players' Association.

A native of Lansing, Michigan, and graduate of Michigan State, Kelly was one of three Miller brothers to earn a niche in the NHL and collegiate hockey. Kevin was a Ranger standout in 1990–91 before performing for Detroit, Washington, St. Louis, San Jose, Pittsburgh, and Chicago.

Youngest of the trio, Kip was the 1990 Hobey Baker Award winner, and became a deft stickhandler who also bounced around the AHL and NHL, excelling for the Pittsburgh Penguins in 1998–99 and New York Islanders in 2001–02. Coincidentally, or not, brother Kelly entered the coaching realm as an assistant with those same Islanders that same year.

MIKE MODANO

BORN: Livonia, Michigan, June 7, 1970
POSITION: Center, Minnesota North Stars, 1989–93; Dallas Stars, 1993–
AWARDS/HONORS: NHL All-Rookie Team, 1990; NHL Second Team All-Star, 2000; NHL All-Star Game, 1993, 1998–2000, 2002

As a boy growing up in a suburb of Detroit, Mike Modano was an energetic youngster. In fact, Modano was so hyperactive that his parents registered him for pee-wee hockey at the age of nine so he could "get rid of some of that steam that seemed to bottle up inside him,"

Mike Modano

said his mother, Karen. And with that, one of the most graceful skaters to play the game began his journey toward stardom.

Tall and lean, Modano chose to play junior hockey in Canada rather than opting for college in the States. Playing for the Western Hockey League Prince Albert Raiders, Modano became the premium player available in the 1988 NHL Entry Draft, and the Minnesota North Stars snagged the handsome teenager with the first overall pick.

Modano's rookie year with the North Stars in 1989–90 bordered on spectacular. He scored 29 times as a freshman, registering 75 points in the process. Modano was the runner-up for the Calder Trophy as Rookie of the Year, and his future was filled with promise.

The following year, the North Stars gave the NHL a postseason to remember. Heading into the playoffs, the North Stars were 12 games under .500, posting a 27–39–14 record. Their first-round opponents, the Chicago Blackhawks, were a league best 49–23–8. Modano, Bobby Smith, Brian Bellows, and the rest of the North Stars rained on Chicago's parade, defeating the Hawks four games to two.

The North Stars defeated the St. Louis Blues and defending Cup champions Edmonton Oilers in the ensuing rounds. Reaching the Stanley Cup finals for the second time in franchise history, the North Stars were primed to face their next opponent, the Pittsburgh Penguins.

The North Stars won the first game of the series, but in the end the Penguins prevailed, defeating Minnesota in six games. It was during these playoffs that the hockey world saw Mike Modano at his finest. He was unstoppable at times, especially on the power play, where he would routinely pick the puck up behind his own net to embark on a furious end-to-end rush. He registered 20 points during that playoff run, and many observers began to wonder if the kid from Livonia could become one of the best offensive players in the history of the league.

Although Modano continued his scoring prowess, the North Stars were ousted in the first round of the 1991–92 playoffs, and didn't even qualify for the postseason the following year. Then, citing huge financial losses, North Stars owner Norm Green moved his club from the extreme cold of Minnesota to the extreme heat of Dallas, Texas, in 1993. And it was

there, in Dallas, where Mike Modano's career changed dramatically.

In 1998–99, he centered Brett Hull and Jere Lehtinen. Modano began to play with more determination and grit, and the Stars finished the year as the best team in the league, posting a 51–19–12 record. Modano finished the year leading the Stars in goals (34) and points (81), played on both the power-play and penalty-killing units, and always lined up to take important face-offs late in games. Heading into the postseason, Dallas was a juggernaut that was not to be denied, not even in the playoffs.

After defeating the Colorado Avalanche in a tough seven-game Western Conference finals series, Modano and the Stars were heading to the Stanley Cup finals for the third time in franchise history, this time to face the Buffalo Sabres. The upstart Sabres were underdogs, but gave the Stars everything that they could handle early on in the series. The teams went at each other ferociously, splitting the first four games and setting up a pivotal Game Five to be played on June 17, 1999, at Reunion Arena in Dallas.

The Stars and Modano answered the bell, as they took the crucial Game Five by a score of 2–0. Modano did not score a goal in the contest, but did the dirty work along with the pretty work to propel the Stars to victory.

The Stars won Game Six and captured their first Stanley Cup championship. In the victorious Stars locker room afterward, Modano disclosed that he had played the whole series with a broken wrist. But it wasn't enough to deter this warrior from claiming the ultimate prize.

His Stars would lose the Cup in a return visit in 2000 against the New Jersey Devils, and even miss the postseason dance altogether in 2001–02, after coach Ken Hitchcock was fired. Still, Modano, who scored 900 points in 868 games coming into that disappointing season, remained one of the only bright spots for the Stars with a 40-goal season and a berth on the 2002 silver medal–winning USA team at the Salt Lake Olympic Winter Games.

ALEX MOGILNY

BORN: Khabarovsk, USSR, February 18, 1969
POSITION: Right Wing, Buffalo Sabres, 1989–95; Vancouver Canucks, 1995–2000; New Jersey Devils, 2000–01; Toronto Maple Leafs, 2001–
AWARDS/HONORS: NHL Second All-Star Team, 1993, 1996; NHL All-Star Game, 1992–94, 1996

While scouting at the World Junior Championships in Anchorage, Alaska, in 1989, Buffalo Sabres director of player personnel Don Luce met with a young Russian fifth-round draft pick who was in Alaska with his Soviet junior team. A few months later, Luce received a long-distance call

Alexander Mogilny as a Sabre

from Stockholm. It was Alexander Mogilny, asking for assistance to come to America and to Buffalo. Literally that same evening, Luce and Sabres general manager Gerry Meehan boarded a plane to Sweden, and returned a few days later with a player who would change the Sabres franchise—and the NHL—forever.

While some older, aging Soviet players were being granted permission to leave for the NHL, young Russian talent was still guarded almost as closely as the secrets of the Cold War. Mogilny's defection surprised many and introduced the world to an exciting, swift player who would serve as the model for young Russian talent for years to come.

"There were very few Russians playing in the NHL in 1988," recalled his agent, Dan Meehan, "and that was the only reason why Mogilny was drafted so late. Had he been from North America, he certainly would have been a first-rounder, maybe even the top overall pick.

The entire hockey world knew he was the next Soviet star."

Wearing number 89 in recognition of the year he arrived in America, Mogilny scored his first goal on his first NHL shift. Mogilny would later score 76 goals in 77 games during the 1992–93 season, playing alongside superstar center Pat LaFontaine. With magical chemistry, both established team records in numerous categories and led the Sabres to a first-round playoff victory for the first time in almost a decade. In the fall of 1993, however, LaFontaine was forced to undergo knee surgery and was out of the lineup for almost two years. The duo would never again be reunited.

During the summer of 1995, Mogilny was traded from Buffalo to the Vancouver Canucks. Alex scored 55 goals in his first campaign in British Columbia, but injuries began to slow the Russian and Mogilny's games played—and goals—began to decrease. Mogilny's career was rejuvenated in 2000, when a late season trade sent him to the New Jersey Devils, where he would regain form, score 43 goals, and help the Devils to a Stanley Cup before signing with Toronto as a free agent in the summer of 2001. There, Mogilny would become a major presence in Toronto's postseason drive.

DOUG MOHNS

BORN: Capreol, Ontario, December 13, 1933
POSITION: Defenseman, Boston Bruins, 1953–64; Chicago Blackhawks, 1964–71; Minnesota North Stars, 1971–74; Washington Capitals, 1974–

Apart from being the only NHL player nicknamed "Diesel" (he used to skate fast), Doug Mohns achieved latter-day fame as one of the first NHL players to wear a toupee. "It makes me look younger," Mohns said. "I wish it made me feel younger."

The first time Mohns wore the rug, Stan Mikita of the Blackhawks introduced him to Al Eagleson, executive director of the NHL

Players' Association, with the explanation: "This is one of our new men." The Eagle was expressing his pleasure before he realized he was being taken.

"I went to the Blackhawks in exchange for Reggie Fleming and Ab McDonald, after eleven seasons in Boston," Mohns recalled. "I've outlasted those two guys and I've outlasted all the guys who were with me on the old Barrie Memorial Cup teams."

He began his NHL career with the Bruins in 1953, before some of his 1974–75 Washington Capitals teammates were born. Among his credentials are being only the second defenseman to score 20 goals in an NHL season (although some of the goals were scored while he was at left wing), in 1959-60; a lifetime total of some 250 goals and 450 assists; and a streak of 21 consecutive NHL seasons before joining Washington in 1974.

ALFIE MOORE

BORN: Toronto, Ontario, December 1, 1905
DIED: Date unknown
POSITION: Goaltender, New York Americans, 1936–37, 1938–39; Chicago Blackhawks, 1938; Detroit Red Wings, 1939–40

In April 1938, the Chicago Blackhawks, coached by the American-born Bill Stewart, who doubled as a major-league baseball umpire in the off-season, encountered the Toronto Maple Leafs in a best-of-five-games round for the Stanley Cup.

The Blackhawks were given no more chance of winning the Stanley Cup than a walrus has of crossing the Sahara Desert. Toronto had finished in first place with 57 points. Chicago was a woefully weak third in the American division with 37 points—20 fewer than the Maple Leafs. Besides, Chicago had "those American players," considered singularly inept for the NHL by their Canadian counterparts; and the upstart Stewart wasn't considered any bargain either! With two strikes already against

them, the Blackhawks appeared to take a third whiff when it was learned that their regular goalie, Mike Karakas, had suffered a broken toe in his final game against the Americans. Karakas didn't realize the extent of the damage until he tried to lace on his skates for the Toronto game. He couldn't make it, and the Hawks suddenly became desperate for a goalie.

A minor-league goalkeeper who had had a brief stint with the New York Americans, Moore, according to NHL legend, was quaffing some liquid refreshment in a local tavern a few hours before game time. Whether this was true or not turned out to be irrelevant to Moore's performance in the Chicago nets. If anything, Smythe had erred in causing a rumpus over Stewart's original request for Davey Kerr. Once the Chicago coach told his players about Smythe's lack of hospitality, the Blackhawks stormed out of their dressing room determined to support Alfie Moore and exact revenge against Smythe. Only Gordie Drillon seemed capable of stopping them. He scored for Toronto early in the game, but then the Blackhawks' defense of Bill McKenzie and ex-Leaf Alex Levinsky threw up a wall in front of their net, and the Chicago attack took over. Johnny Gottselig scored twice, and Paul Thompson got the third Blackhawks goal; Alfie Moore had done the impossible, stopping Toronto at Maple Leaf Gardens.

Stewart could hardly contain his joy, and he immediately announced that Alfie would start in the second game, April 7, 1938, also at Maple Leaf Gardens. But this time Smythe objected to Moore, and NHL president Frank Calder ruled that the Blackhawks would have to employ their minor-league goaltender, Paul Goodman. Goodman had never played an NHL game before, and when he played the second game, he lacked Alfie's poise. The Maple Leafs won the second game, 5–1.

But Alfie's single game was enough to provide a catalyst for the Blackhawks, who went on to win the Stanley Cup. As for Moore, he surfaced briefly during the 1938–39 season, playing two games for the New York Americans. He allowed 14 goals for a 7.00 goals-against average. His swan song in the NHL was with Detroit in 1939–40, when he played a single game and allowed three goals.

DICKIE MOORE

BORN: Montreal, Quebec, January 6, 1931
POSITION: Left Wing, Montreal Canadiens, 1951–63; Toronto Maple Leafs, 1964–65; St. Louis Blues, 1967–68
AWARDS/HONORS: Art Ross Trophy, 1958–59; NHL First Team All-Star, 1958–59; NHL Second Team All-Star, 1961; NHL All-Star Game, 1953, 1956–60; Hockey Hall of Fame, 1974

When the Montreal Canadiens were building one of the best hockey clubs of all time during the early 1950s, Richard Winston "Dickie" Moore was among the most gifted young players signed by the Montreal brass. Brash to a fault, Moore was at first believed to be uncontrollable, but the combination of tough coach Dick Irvin, later the equally tough Toe Blake, and Maurice Richard and Doug Harvey settled Dickie into a calmer, more manageable position. The results were sensational. Along with Boom-Boom Geoffrion, Jean Beliveau, and Claude Provost, Moore became one of the most significant Canadiens. So significant that out-of-town newspapermen soon took notice of his talents.

"We like Moore," said Jim Vipond in his Toronto *Globe and Mail* column. "He's a chippy operator who mixes with the toughest and still knows how to stickhandle and skate his way to the opposition net. He's not unmindful of Milt Schmidt as he leans far forward in gaining top speed. These Montreal kids are making the customers forget Maurice Richard."

Well, not quite. Dickie was placed on a line with young Henri Richard at center and Maurice Richard on right wing and it became one of the best the NHL has known. Dickie won the scoring championship in 1958 and

1959. He was lionized for playing the second half of the 1958–59 season while wearing a cast to protect a broken hand, yet he still managed to capture the scoring title.

Moore remained with the Canadiens until the 1962–63 season, when he temporarily retired. However, Toronto Maple Leafs' manager-coach Punch Imlach coaxed Moore out of retirement for the 1964–65 campaign. Injuries forced him to "quit" again, but only temporarily. In 1967–68, he was signed by the then brand-new St. Louis Blues. He played in only 27 regular-season games alongside his old-time Canadiens crony, Doug Harvey, and helped steer the Blues into the playoffs. Moore was absolutely stupendous in the playoffs, old legs and all. He scored 7 goals and 7 assists in 18 games and was as important as any St. Louis player in the Blues' march to the Stanley Cup finals, and this in their first season. Moore retired once and for all after the 1967–68 season. In June 1974, Dickie Moore was inducted into the Hockey Hall of Fame.

He retired in his native Montreal and became enormously successful as a businessman specializing in industrial rentals.

HOWIE MORENZ

BORN: Brampton, Ontario, September 21, 1902
DIED: March 8, 1937
POSITION: Forward, Montreal Canadiens, 1923–34, 1936–37; Chicago Blackhawks, 1934–35; New York Rangers, 1935–36
AWARDS/HONORS: Hart Memorial Trophy, 1931–32; NHL Scoring Leader, 1928, 1931; NHL First Team All-Star, 1928, 1931–32; NHL Second Team All-Star, 1933; NHL All-Star Game, 1934; Hockey Hall of Fame, 1945

Howie Morenz was the first genuine superstar forward of the National Hockey League.

Son of a railroad man, Morenz was a little fellow who was often beaten by older boys with whom he played hockey in the neighborhood games. He'd return home so badly cut and bruised, he'd consider quitting the game; but his love for hockey was so passionate he'd inevitably return to the rink. Soon he was the star of the nearby Stratford team that journeyed to Montreal for a playoff game. Canadiens' owner Leo Dandurand was in the stands on the night Morenz dipsy-doodled around the hometown defensemen from the start to the finish of the game. Leo conferred with aide, Cecil Hart, and both agreed it would be prudent to sign Morenz before the Maroons, Hamilton, Ottawa, or Toronto beat them to it.

Raw speed was Howie's forte as he gained a varsity center ice berth on Les Canadiens. Within weeks he was dubbed "the Stratford Streak," "the Mitchell Meteor," and assorted other appellations that almost but never quite described his presence on the ice. "The kid's *too fast*," said one observer. "He'll burn himself out."

Morenz was a superstar by his second year. He finished second in scoring to Cecil "Babe" Dye of Toronto and was doing things with the puck that astonished even such skeptics as Conn Smythe, founder of the Leafs and the dean of hockey in Toronto.

Many respected hockey observers claim Morenz was single-handedly responsible for the successful expansion of the NHL into the United States in the 1920s. New York promoter Tex Rickard became a hockey fan the moment he spied Morenz in action. Not long afterward Rickard introduced the Rangers to New York.

"There isn't a team in the league that has not in some way been affected by some aspect of Montreal hockey," wrote Peter Gzowski, "even if the link is as tenuous as the Detroit Red Wings' crest, which is based on the old Montreal Athletic Association's winged wheel."

But Gzowski was quick to point out that Morenz was the leader of "the most exciting team in hockey from the mid-1920s to the mid-1930s." He added, "While most fans remember Morenz mainly for his blistering speed and his headlong rushes on goal, he also provided one

of the most remarkable examples of the passionate dedication to the game—to winning—that has been another characteristic of Canadien teams. Many people say, of course, that Morenz's fierce involvement in hockey, and in the Canadiens, led to his untimely death, although Morenz's dedication is not unique in the annals of the Montreal team."

It was easy enough for Montreal players and writers to wax ecstatic about Morenz and it was not uncommon for opponents to do likewise. But when the opponent happened to be Eddie Shore, the fiercest defenseman in the game, then Morenz knew he had arrived!

"He's the hardest player in the league to stop," Shore admitted. "Howie comes at you with such speed that it's almost impossible to block him with a body check. When he hits you he usually comes off a lot better than the defenseman. Another thing that bothers us is his shift. He has a knack of swerving at the last minute that can completely fool you. Everybody likes Howie. He's one player who doesn't deserve any rough treatment."

Howie's scoring abilities began eroding in 1933–34, when he finished 48th on the NHL scoring list. Even worse, Morenz was booed several times by his formerly loyal Forum supporters. He was 33 years old at the time and appeared to be at the end of the line. Just prior to the 1934–35 season, Howie was traded to the Chicago Blackhawks. Morenz scored only eight goals for the Hawks and, a season later, he was dealt to the New York Rangers, but was a shadow of his former self and New York's Lester Patrick was happy to return him to the Canadiens for the 1936–37 season.

Wearing the *bleu, blanc, et rouge* once more proved to be a tonic for Morenz. True, he had lost his old getaway power, but he was reunited with his old buddies, Johnny Gagnon and Aurel Joliat, and every so often he'd bring the Forum crowd to its feet with one of the exquisite Morenz rushes.

He was doing just that on the night of January 28, 1937, at the Forum when a

Chicago defenseman caught him with a body check, sending Morenz hurtling feet first into the endboards. It wasn't a normal spill and Howie had lost all control as he skidded toward the boards. When his skate rammed into the wood, a snap could be heard around the rink and Morenz crumpled in excruciating pain.

Howie was rushed to the hospital with a badly broken leg, and there was some doubt that he would recover in time to return for another season of play. Once in the hospital, the 36-year-old Morenz began brooding about his fate. Instead of recuperating, he suffered a nervous breakdown, then developed heart trouble.

Early on March 8, 1937, Morenz was given a complete checkup. It appeared he was rallying; a deceptive analysis. A few hours later, Howie Morenz was dead.

The funeral service for Morenz was held at center ice of the Forum where thousands filed silently past his bier. Andy O'Brien, of *Weekend Magazine*, was there at the time and recalled the scene as thousands of hockey fans lined up outside the rink that Morenz had made famous:

"Outside," said O'Brien, "the crowd was so great, we of the press had to enter through the boiler room on Closse Street. As I walked below the north end, profound silence left an impression of emptiness, but at the promenade I stopped in breathless awe. The rink was jammed to the rafters with fans standing motionless with heads bared."

The NHL paid an official league tribute to Morenz on November 7, 1937, by sanctioning an All-Star game at the Forum. In it, the Canadiens and Maroons combined forces to challenge a select squad of NHL stars, including Frank Boucher, Charlie Conacher, Eddie Shore, et alia. The All-Stars won 6–5, before some 8,683 fans who contributed $11,447 to a fund for the Morenz family. Howie's uniform was presented to his son, Howie Morenz Jr.

KEN MORROW

BORN: Flint, Michigan, October 17, 1956
POSITION: Defenseman, New York Islanders, 1979–89
AWARDS/HONORS: Lester Patrick Trophy, 1996

Rare is the player who can claim to have won an Olympic gold medal and a Stanley Cup championship in the same year, or can be acknowledged on a team that won four consecutive Cups.

A graduate of Bowling Green University, defenseman Ken Morrow starred for the 1980

Ken Morrow, the most underrated Islanders defenseman

U.S. Olympic team that upset the powerful Soviet Union squad at Lake Placid. He was promptly signed by the New York Islanders, and stepped right into the NHL lineup immediately

Montreal's first major hero, Howie Morenz

after the Games. He played on a Stanley Cup winner that same year.

As a traditional defensive defenseman, Ken's goals were unlikely, but timely. Teamed alongside Hall of Famer Denis Potvin, Morrow developed an uncanny knack of scoring game-winning overtime goals. In round one of the 1980 playoffs, he scored from the point to beat the Los Angeles Kings, 4–3, in Game Three, en route to the Isles' first Cup. The next season, he tallied the winner again in Game Four of the quarterfinals against the Edmonton Oilers to put the Isles up three games to one.

After his empty net goal in Game Four of the 1983 Stanley Cup finals clinched the fourth, and last, Cup for Al Arbour's sextet, Ken delivered the ultimate overtime gem in the 1984 Patrick Division semifinals against the hated rival New York Rangers. His memorable screen shot from the right boards beat Glen Hanlon and fittingly concluded the classic playoff series.

Morrow patrolled the Long Island blue line for ten years, until the dissipation of the Islanders dynasty. His steadiness was recognized by Islanders brass, and, after coaching stints in the IHL and behind the bench as Arbour's assistant, he was appointed to the Islanders scouting staff, where he continued to serve as director of pro scouting through 2001–02.

GUS MORTSON

BORN: New Liskeard, Ontario, January 24, 1925
POSITION: Defenseman, Toronto Maple Leafs, 1946–52; Chicago Blackhawks, 1952–58; Detroit Red Wings, 1958–59
AWARDS/HONORS: NHL First Team All-Star, 1950; NHL All-Star Game, 1947, 1948, 1950–54, 1956

In the autumn of 1946, Toronto manager Conn Smythe took one of pro hockey's biggest gambles. He dropped many of his veterans and imported a bunch of raw kids, including a pair of defensemen, Jim Thomson

and Gus Mortson. The pair was teamed together and named "the Gold Dust Twins."

Mortson was a splendid skater and fearless checker. Immediately, the Gold Dust Twins hit it off perfectly and the Leafs began the first year of a three-consecutive-year Stanley Cup reign. Fans in foreign rinks were infuriated by Mortson's robust style. A Detroit fan hurled a chair at him one night, but Mortson was nonchalant. The Leafs won four Stanley Cups with Gus on the back line. He was traded to Chicago in 1952–53 and was a significant asset as the Blackhawks won a playoff berth. His last NHL season was 1958–59 with the Detroit Red Wings.

KENNY MOSDELL

BORN: Montreal, Quebec, July 13, 1922
DIED: Date unknown
POSITION: Center, Brooklyn Americans, 1941–42; Montreal Canadiens, 1944–56, 1957–58; Chicago Blackhawks, 1956–57
AWARDS/HONORS: NHL First Team All-Star, 1954; NHL Second Team All-Star, 1955; NHL All-Star Game, 1951–55

Maurice "Rocket" Richard once said that the most underrated center he ever played with was Ken Mosdell. A tall, speedy forward, Mosdell broke into the NHL with the Brooklyn Americans in 1941–42. After two years in the Canadian armed forces, Ken joined the Canadiens in 1944–45 and remained with them through 1955–56. He spent the 1956–57 season with Chicago and finished his lengthy career in 1957–58 with Montreal.

BILL MOSIENKO

BORN: Manitoba, November 2, 1921
DIED: July 9, 1994
POSITION: Right Wing, Chicago Blackhawks, 1941–55
AWARDS/HONORS: Lady Byng Memorial Trophy, 1945; NHL Second Team All-Star, 1945–46; NHL All-Star Game, 1947, 1949–50, 1952–53; Hockey Hall of Fame, 1965

Bill Mosienko was an integral part of one of Chicago's best units with Max and Doug Bentley. A speedy winger, William "Bill" Mosienko carved his niche in the Hall of Fame on March 23, 1952, when he scored three goals in 21 seconds against the Rangers at Madison Square Garden. "Like they say," Mosienko observed, "I caught lightning in a beer bottle."

Actually, Mosienko's lightning moves were evident before and after that memorable game. He came to the Blackhawks at training camp for the 1940–41 season, a 19-year-old who appeared too fragile for the NHL. At first, Mosienko was farmed to Providence and then Kansas City, but eventually he was returned to Chicago where he was put on a line with the Bentleys. Dubbed the Pony Line because of the small, coltish moves of the skaters, the unit ultimately became one of the most exciting in Chicago's history.

Mosienko remained a Blackhawk from 1941–42 until his retirement following the 1954–55 season. He never played on a Stanley Cup winner nor a first-place team, but he scored a creditable 258 goals, 282 assists, for 540 points in 711 NHL games. And it is likely his 21-second hat trick will remain a record never to be equaled in the NHL.

JOHN MUCKLER

BORN: Midland, Ontario, April 3, 1934
POSITION: Coach, Minnesota North Stars, 1968–69; Edmonton Oilers, 1989–91; Buffalo Sabres, 1991–95; New York Rangers, 1997–2000; General Manager, Buffalo Sabres, 1993–97; General Manager, Ottawa Senators, 2002–

Few careers have been as long and as varied as John Muckler's. A career minor-league defenseman, Muckler first attracted attention while playing for the Long Island Ducks in the early 1960s. He would eventually become the team's coach, thus beginning a career which would take him to the National Hockey League as a coach and general manager.

His first big-league stint behind the bench was in 1968–69 with the Minnesota North Stars, before various coaching and general manager stints in the minor leagues. He returned two decades later and worked the Edmonton Oilers' bench, minus the traded Wayne Gretzky, in 1989–90, the last time the team won the Stanley Cup.

He remained with Edmonton for one more season before moving on to Buffalo, where he also became the Sabres' general manager.

After four seasons with the Sabres, in which Muckler struggled to keep a small-market team competitive while having several run-ins with his aggressive, overachieving coach, Ted Nolan, he moved to New York, where he became the Ranger head coach during the 1997–98 season. He coached 25 games after succeeding Colin Campbell and took over for a full season in 1998–99.

His clash with the general manager Neil Smith caused dissension in the Blueshirts high command. The disagreements peaked when prized draft pick in the 1998 Entry Draft, Manny Malhotra, was described by Muckler as no better than a third-line forward. In the long run, Muckler was proven right. The disappointing Malhotra was traded to Dallas late in the 2001–02 season, but this was well after both Smith and Muckler were fired. Muckler surfaced again in the summer of 2002 when he was named general manager of the Ottawa Senators.

BRIAN MULLEN

BORN: New York, New York, March 16, 1962
POSITION: Right Wing, Winnipeg Jets, 1982–87; New York Rangers, 1987–91; San Jose Sharks, 1991–92; New York Islanders, 1992–93
AWARDS/HONORS: Lester Patrick Trophy, 1995; NHL All-Star Game, 1989

From the sidewalks of Manhattan to the big time of the NHL is a story that had to be scripted by Hollywood until the Mullen brothers came along. Although less talented than older brother Joe, Brian nonetheless made an impact playing with the Jets, Sharks, Rangers, and Islanders.

In the 1993 Patrick Division semifinals, the Islanders were at their best against the Washington Capitals, and so was Brian Mullen. With the Islanders trailing the series 1–0, Mullen scored possibly the biggest goal of his career in the second overtime of Game Two. With the addition of Mullen's all-around good play, the Isles defeated the Caps in six games.

After Brian's NHL career was cut short by a rare heart disorder, his motivation to lead wasn't hindered at all. In a career move perhaps no less significant than his NHL playing days, Mullen became one of the league's prime motivators, working with grassroots children's hockey organizations all over the country. In September 2002, Mullen was hired as the Rangers radio analyst by the Madison Square Garden Network.

JOE MULLEN

BORN: New York, New York, February 26, 1957
POSITION: Right Wing, St. Louis Blues, 1980–86; Calgary Flames, 1986–90; Pittsburgh Penguins, 1990–95, 1996–97; Boston Bruins, 1995–96
AWARDS/HONORS: Lady Byng Memorial Trophy, 1987, 1989; Lester Patrick Trophy, 1995; NHL First Team All-Star, 1989; NHL Plus/Minus Leader, 1989; NHL All-Star Game, 1989–90, 1994; Hockey Hall of Fame, 2000

Joe Mullen, New York's own hero

Raised in Manhattan's Hell's Kitchen neighborhood on the island's West Side, Joey Mullen and his younger brother, Brian, also a former NHLer, grew up playing street and roller hockey. During the 1970s, Joey, Brian, and their brother Kenny, played in the Fort Hamilton Roller Hockey League, which at the time was considered the highest caliber circuit of its kind in the country.

After playing for years in the New York Major Junior Hockey League, including his MVP season of 1974–75, Joey attended Boston College, where he became a standout goal scorer, earning ECAC All-Star honors in both his junior and senior years. As a junior, Joey helped lead the Eagles to the 1978 NCAA championship game against Boston University. One of his more memorable performances came earlier that season against RPI in the first game of the ECAC Tournament, when he scored the tying goal and then the winning goal in overtime.

When his college days were over, Mullen was one of a handful of players highly coveted by Herb Brooks for the 1980 Olympic Team.

Knowing that his dad was ill, Joey opted for the pros to get a sizable paycheck in order to help his dad. In August 1979, he signed with the St. Louis Blues.

The Blues sent him to their CHL Salt Lake City affiliate for the season before calling him up to the big club for postseason action. For his 40-goal performance at Salt Lake that season, Mullen was voted the recipient of the Ken McKenzie Trophy as the CHL's top rookie and was thrown into playoff action with the Blues for one game. He followed that performance with a league-leading 117-point season in 1980–81, which made him the clear choice for the Tommy Ivan Trophy as the CHL's MVP.

In 1982–83, a long and prolific NHL career got under way for the tough little right-winger. Through four and one half seasons in St. Louis, Mullen averaged better than one point per game. In February 1986, the Blues sent him to Calgary as part of a six-player blockbuster deal. It was with the Flames that he enjoyed his most productive years.

His best season ever was 1988–89, when, while helping the Flames to the first Stanley Cup triumph in franchise history, Mullen led the league in plus-minus, won the Lady Byng Trophy, was named to the NHL First All-Star Team, and led all playoff goal scorers with 12.

In June 1990, the Flames surprisingly dealt him to Pittsburgh for a second-round choice (Nicolas Perreault) in the 1990 Entry Draft.

The move to Western Pennsylvania worked out well for the New York City native, who saw his name inscribed on Lord Stanley's Cup after each of the next two seasons.

On February 7, 1995, Joey made hockey history by becoming the first American-born player to score 1,000 points in an NHL career with an assist in a 7–3 victory over Florida—his 935th career game.

Later in 1995, Joey, his brother Brian, and amateur hockey executive Bob Flemming were each awarded the 1995 Lester Patrick Award for outstanding contributions to U.S. hockey.

In September 1995, Mullen signed as a free agent with the Boston Bruins. After an injury-riddled year in Beantown, Joe returned to Pittsburgh the following season to become the first American-born NHLer to score 500 goals. He retired at season's end and became an assistant coach with the team in 2001–02.

With 502 goals and 1,063 points, Mullen stood alone as the most prolific American-born goal scorer and point producer in NHL history as well as a Hall of Famer in 2000.

KIRK MULLER

BORN: Kingston, Ontario, February 8, 1966
POSITION: Left Wing, New Jersey Devils, 1984–91; Montreal Canadiens, 1991–95; New York Islanders, 1995–96; Toronto Maple Leafs, 1996–97; Florida Panthers, 1997–99; Dallas Stars, 1999–
AWARDS/HONORS: NHL All-Star, 1985–86, 1988, 1990, 1992–93

The 1984 NHL Entry Draft yielded some of the most dynamic players hockey has ever seen—Patrick Roy, Luc Robitaille, and Brett Hull, to name a few. Mario Lemieux was selected first overall by the Pittsburgh Penguins.

The New Jersey Devils, at the time looking for their voice in the Metro hockey scene, had the number two pick and forged ahead with tireless talent Kirk Muller. Making the club the following fall, the left-winger rapidly emerged as the epitome of the work ethic that became the young club's trademark.

He was an instant asset as a relentless penalty killer, formidable physical force, and exemplary leader. His point total (54) was impressive as a rookie and grew steadily for the next three seasons, as he assumed the Devils' captaincy in 1987. Three 70-plus-point seasons ensued as the Devils ascended into the NHL elite.

But by 1991, it seemed their perennial All-Star was conspicuously absent—not from the hard work department, but from the scoresheet in his playoff performances. General manager Lou Lamoriello, who had just acquired Scott Stevens, dealt Muller and goalie Roland Melanson to the Montreal Canadiens for Stephane Richer and Tom Chorske.

As a result, the gritty Canadiens, with Muller leading them, came out of nowhere to beat the Los Angeles Kings in the 1992–93 Stanley Cup finals, just one season after acquiring Captain Kirk. His 17 points in 20 playoff games proved he was a big-time player worthy of his high selection in the draft as second to Lemieux.

Just two seasons later, Muller's leadership was coveted by New York Islanders general manager Don Maloney, whose floundering team needed a jolt of veteran blood. When French-Canadian scoring ace Pierre Turgeon was offered, Montreal jumped at the deal. But Muller balked at joining the struggling Isles and did not report immediately.

By the next season, his glaring disinterest prompted new Islander general manager Mike Mibury to deal Muller yet again, this time to Toronto.

For the next few seasons, Muller would assume a more defensive identity, with additional stops in Florida and and in Dallas, where the former All-Star anchored the Stars' "Grumpy Old Men" checking line.

While he still ranked atop many Devils all-time records, Muller's gumption kept him in The Game. In 2000–01, his overtime goal against Edmonton in Game Five of the Western Conference quarterfinals proved that lunchpailers like Muller can pay off in the clutch. It was his fourth career playoff overtime goal, good for third on the all-time list.

Eighteen years after his NHL baptism, Muller still packed a punch on the ice. He continued with Dallas through the 2001–02 season.

MURRAY MURDOCH

BORN: Lucknow, Ontario, May 19, 1904
DIED: May 17, 2001
POSITION: Left Wing, New York Rangers, 1926–37
AWARDS/HONORS: Lester Patrick Trophy, 1974

One of the earliest NHL iron men, Murray Murdoch broke into the majors in 1926–27 with the Rangers and remained with the big club until his retirement at the conclusion of the 1936–37 season. During that span, Murdoch compeleted 11 seasons without missing a game. He played a total of 508 consecutive games and played in every one of the Rangers' 55 Stanley Cup playoff games during that span.

Among Murdoch's claims to fame was the fact that he was one of the first college players to become an NHL star. He tells the story of his rookie Ranger camp as follows:

"I was one of the first players he [Conn Smythe] contacted. I was just out of the University of Manitoba and had gotten married in Winnipeg when I received a wire from Smythe in Duluth, where he had signed Abel and Johnson. The wire said: MEET ME HERE IN DULUTH STOP ALL EXPENSES PAID.

"I wired back: IF YOU WANT TO SEE ME COME TO WINNIPEG.

Murray Murdoch of the Rangers, the NHL's first Iron Man

"Well, he came to Winnipeg, we talked, and he offered me a $1,500 signing bonus and a $5,000 salary. I remember sitting in the lobby of the Fort Garry Hotel, thinking it over, and I was just about to say no when Conn leaned over a coffee table and slowly counted out $1,500 in $100 bills. That clinched it. For a young guy just married and with a summer job selling insurance, that looked like an awful lot of money.

"Lester never dealt that way. He just made his proposition, and you knew his word was his bond.

"Lester took over from Conn quietly, without any fuss, and after a couple of days he called a team meeting. 'Gentlemen,' he said, 'when we start playing in the National Hockey League you're going to win some games and you're going to lose some. I just want to stress this: If you lose more than you win, you won't be around.'"

Murdoch retired at age 33 to become head hockey coach at Yale University, where he became something of a collegiate legend. Following his retirement from Yale, Murray continued to appear regularly at Yale and Rangers alumni events and was the oldest living Stanley Cup winner at the time of his death on May 21, 2001.

Although Murdoch's numbers (192 goals) don't look impressive by today's standards, he was a speedy, defense-minded player, a member of the original Rangers, and one of the reasons the New Yorkers won Stanley Cup championships in 1928 and 1933.

LARRY MURPHY

BORN: Scarborough, Ontario, March 8, 1961
POSITION: Defenseman, Los Angeles Kings, 1980–83; Washington Capitals, 1983–89; Minnesota North Stars, 1989–90; Pittsburgh Penguins, 1990–95; Toronto Maple Leafs, 1995–97; Detroit Red Wings, 1997–2001
AWARDS/HONORS: NHL Second All-Star Team, 1987, 1993, 1995; NHL All-Star Game, 1994, 1996, 1999

In an era of such dazzling defensemen as Brian Leetch, Paul Coffey, and Raymond Bourque, Larry Murphy often was overlooked when it came to Norris Trophy nominations.

Yet his value could be calculated by his number of games played and the success of the teams on which he played. Murphy was a member of the Stanley Cup champion Detroit Red Wings in 1997 and 1998, as he had been earlier with the Pittsburgh Penguins in 1991 and 1992. He concluded his career in 2000–01 a full 20 years after he entered the NHL as a rookie.

After a promising three years with the Los Angeles Kings, Murphy was dealt to the Washington Capitals, where he was the linchpin of an enviably high-scoring defensive unit that also featured Rod Langway and Kevin Hatcher. Larry had an outstanding tenure with the Caps, with an 81-point breakout in 1986–87.

After being dealt with Mike Gartner to the Minnesota North Stars for Dino Ciccarelli and Bob Rouse in 1989, Murphy only played one full season with Minnesota. But it was his trade to the Pittsburgh Penguins in December 1990 that put the spotlight on his offensive abilities. Complementing players such as Mario Lemieux, Ron Francis, and Ulf Samuelsson, Murphy helped power the Pens to back-to-back Stanley Cup championships during the 1990–91 and 1991–92 seasons. He remained the Penguins' all-time leader in career playoff points as a defenseman through 2001–02 with 72, while recording 301 points in 336 games as a Penguin.

Larry was dealt yet again, this time to Toronto, in 1996, where he spent parts of two seasons with the Maple Leafs. Murphy put up fair numbers, but could not please Toronto fans before he was moved to the Detroit Red Wings at the NHL's March trade deadline in 1997.

The Wings went on to win back-to-back Stanley Cup championships (1997 and 1998) with the veteran defender helping out on the offensive side as well. It was the Wings' first championship in over 40 years.

Durable and deceptively dynamic, Murphy played 21 seasons, barely missing a game; he was second only to Gordie Howe in all-time games played, with 1,615 entering the 2001–02 season.

BRYAN MURRAY

BORN: Shawville, Quebec, December 5, 1942
POSITION: Coach, Washington Capitals, 1981–90; Detroit Red Wings, 1990–93; Florida Panthers, 1997–98; Anaheim Mighty Ducks, 2001–; General Manager, Detroit Red Wings, 1990–94; Florida Panthers, 1994–2001; Coach, Anaheim Mighty Ducks, 2001–02; General Manager, Anaheim Mighty Ducks, 2002–
AWARDS/HONORS: Jack Adams Award, 1984

Any coaching career that lasts from 1981 to 2002—with some general managing thrown in—can't be all bad. Which is the story of Bryan Murray's big-league career: not bad at all. A product of the Shawville, Quebec, outdoor hockey rinks, Murray enjoyed a career as

Bryan Murray as Capitals coach

schoolteacher before taking a run at professional hockey. His big break came when he was

named head coach of the Washington Capitals and remained with them for nine years.

Murray was released by Washington in 1990, resuming his career in Detroit that fall, this time as general manager. In Murray's first ten full seasons coaching in the NHL, his team never missed the second season.

As general manager in HockeyTown, Murray helped mold future superstars like Sergei Fedorov, Vladimir Konstantinov, and Nicklas Lidstrom. His presence was felt further as general manager of the Florida Panthers (1994–2001), a team Murray built from scratch. The Panthers went to the Stanley Cup finals in 1996, only their third year in existence.

A Murray trademark throughout his career was his petulance with referees. Hardly a game went by without him venting his spleen against the striped ones.

One of his most challenging jobs occurred when he was named coach of the woefully-weak Mighty Ducks of Anaheim for the 2001–02 season. Despite a paucity of talent on the team, Murray managed to keep them competitive and showed that there was plenty of good coaching in him at the age of 59. Following the season, he relinquished coaching to become general manager of the Mighty Ducks.

EVGENI NABOKOV

BORN: Kamenogorsk, Kazakhstan, July 25, 1975
POSITION: Goaltender, San Jose Sharks, 1999–
AWARDS/HONORS: Calder Memorial Trophy, 2001; NHL All-Rookie Team, 2001

Ever since Vyacheslav Tretiak captured the attention of hockey people during Team Canada-Soviet series in 1972, attention has been trained on Russian goaltenders as potential North American big-leaguers. By the 2001–02 season, the Russian Nikolai Khabibulin had become acknowledged as one of the best—if not *the* best—goalie in the National Hockey League.

Another, who initially received less attention but also proved effective, was San Jose Sharks goalie Evgeni Nabokov.

Evgeni made his debut with San Jose in 1999–2000, after two years of minor-league hockey in the American League. Nabokov really turned heads in his first full season (2000–01) by capturing the Calder Trophy as the "player selected as the most proficient in his first year of competition in the National Hockey League," totaling 565 points and 50 of 62 first-place votes. He also finished fourth in voting for the Vezina Trophy as the "goalkeeper adjudged to be the best at his position."

Nabokov didn't have time to suffer sophomore slump in 2001–02 as he backstopped a resurgent Sharks team into the playoffs. Only four other goalies played more than Evgeni's 70 games, and still he managed the fifth-best save percentage, .920.

LOU NANNE

BORN: Sault Ste. Marie, Ontario, June 2, 1941
POSITION: Defenseman/Right Wing, Minnesota North Stars, 1968–78; General Manager, Minnesota North Stars, 1978–88

When the Minnesota North Stars' popular defenseman, Lou Nanne, moved into the position of general manager, it could not have been under more strained circumstances. Minnesota had been faltering for years, and then the North Stars were combined with the equally terrible Cleveland Barons in

Lou Nanne as general manager of the Minnesota North Stars

the 1978 dispersal draft. Once the new unit began playing under Nanne and coach Glen Sonmor, however, the Minnesotans had a fine 1979 season, challenging Toronto and Buffalo for second place in the Adams Division.

As a youngster in Sault Ste. Marie, Nanne starred on a team that included the brothers Esposito. Before joining Minnesota, Nanne captained the 1968 U.S. Olympic squad. As an NHLer, Nanne was one of the more versatile North Stars, alternately playing defense and right wing. He was voted North Star Defenseman of the Year and Most Popular Player before retiring to the front office.

One of Minnesota's most popular hockey personalities, Lou continued as a front-office type until his removal in 1988. He remained in the hockey scene in several capacities through the end of the 1990s, surfacing as a consultant to coaching legend Herb Brooks in 2002.

MARKUS NASLUND

BORN: Ornskoldsvik, Sweden, July 30, 1973
POSITION: Right Wing, Pittsburgh Penguins, 1993–96; Vancouver Canucks, 1996–
AWARDS/HONORS: NHL All-Star Game, 1999, 2001–02

The Vancouver Canucks have boasted many impressive leaders over the years, including Trevor Linden, Richard Brodeur, and Stan Smyl. But for a Scandinavian to follow in their skate-ruts was quite an accomplishment.

Markus Naslund seemed to creep up on the rest of the hockey world. Not that the big, mobile Swede didn't play well at the start, but it wasn't until his 36-goal 1998–99 season that he began to compel attention.

Acquired from Pittsburgh in 1996 for brief NHLer Alex Stojanov, Naslund elevated his game and leadership skills while stewarded by ex-Canucks captain Mark Messier, whose departure in 2000 allowed for Naslund's ascent to his first 40-goal season in 2000–01 (41 goals and 34 assists for 75 points).

He burst to center stage in 2001–02, when his Vancouver Canucks staged an arresting homestretch drive that moved them from non-playoff oblivion to a 94-point second-place finish in the Northwest Division.

Naslund's contributions as both captain and point-getter were significant, with his 40 goals and 50 assists atop the team.

In the playoffs, Naslund's Canucks fought valiantly against the powerful Detroit Red Wings, winning the first two games, but they eventually lost their lead and dropped the series in six.

MATS NASLUND

BORN: Timra, Sweden, October 31, 1959
POSITION: Left Wing, Montreal Canadiens, 1982–90; Boston Bruins, 1994–95
AWARDS/HONORS: Lady Byng Memorial Trophy, 1988; NHL All-Rookie Team, 1983; NHL Second Team All-Star, 1986; NHL All-Star Game, 1984, 1986, 1988

Swedish native Mats Naslund played for his home country for five seasons before being drafted by the Montreal Canadiens (second choice, 37th overall) in the 1979 Entry Draft. His rookie season, 1982–83, brought 26 goals and 45 assists for 71 points in 74 games.

A clever stickhandler and reliable playmaker, Mats's numbers grew through his next seven seasons with the Habs, hitting a career-high 43 goals and 67 assists for 110 points in 80 games during the 1985–86 regular season, plus an additional 8 goals and 11 assists for 19 points in 20 playoff games. The Canadiens went to the playoffs all eight seasons that Naslund was with them, and he won the Lady Byng Trophy in 1988.

After an unusually low production year during the 1989–90 season, Naslund left the NHL for four seasons, returning to play in Sweden. He attempted a comeback with the Boston Bruins in 1994, but after one less-than-impressive season, left the NHL for good.

HARRY NEALE

BORN: Sarnia, Ontario, March 9, 1937
POSITION: Coach, Vancouver Canucks, 1978–85; Detroit Red Wings, 1985–86

Typical of the coach who made it to the top without any big-league playing experience, Harry Neale skated for the Galt, Ontario, Allan Cup (Canadian senior championship) team in 1961. He began his coaching career with Ohio State University and remained there for four seasons before moving on to the

Hamilton Red Wings of the Ontario Hockey Association's Junior A League. In 1972–73, he moved up to the World Hockey Association as assistant to Minnesota Fighting Saints coach Glen Sonmor.

Before the season ended, Neale was head coach of the Fighting Saints. He later moved on to the New England Whalers, before making his National Hockey League debut with the Vancouver Canucks in the 1978–79 season. Although the Canucks' record was unimpressive, Neale steered Vancouver into a playoff berth and a victory over the Philadelphia Flyers in the first game of the Stanley Cup opening playoff round, before the Flyers ultimately eliminated Vancouver.

His most successful season as a coach was in 1981–82, when the Canucks went 30–33–17 and reached a Cinderella Stanley Cup finals berth against the New York Islanders. But health problems forced Neale to take a backseat to assistant Roger Neilson, who kept his job in the playoffs even after Harry got better, so that chemistry could keep rolling.

Harry tried one more year of coaching, this time in Detroit, 1985–86, then had the smarts to give it up. Witty and insightful, Neale gravitated to the airwaves, where he emerged as one of the foremost analysts on Canadian television.

VACLAV NEDOMANSKY

BORN: Czechoslovakia, 1944
POSITION: Center, Toronto Toros (WHA), 1974–76; Birmingham Bulls (WHA), 1976–77; Detroit Red Wings, 1978–82; New York Rangers, 1982, 1983; St. Louis Blues, 1982, 1983
AWARDS/HONORS: Most Gentlemanly Player (WHA), 1976

Until 1974, there was but one successful Czechoslovakian player in professional hockey: Stan Mikita of the Chicago Blackhawks.

Then, in the mid 1970s, two more Czechs would suddenly show up, at first in the new World Hockey Association. Vaclav Nedomansky

and Richard Farda were enjoying summer vacations with their families in Switzerland when they jumped leagues, moving from the established Czechoslovakian National Team to the three-year-old WHA.

Of the two, Nedomansky was the prize. Formerly captain of the Czech team, big Ned was one of the top WHA scorers. Voted the WHA's Most Gentlemanly Player in 1976, Nedomansky continued his consistent scoring in his first full season with the NHL after joining the Red Wings in 1978. Nedomansky led Detroit with 38 goals and 73 points while tying an NHL record by tallying two consecutive hat tricks.

However his major-league career didn't last long, concluding with the New York Rangers in 1983. He remained in North America where his son, Vaclav, played pro hockey, but not at his dad's level. Later, the elder Nedomansky became the European scout for the Los Angeles Kings.

PETR NEDVED

BORN: Liberec, Czechoslovakia, December 9, 1971
POSITION: Center, Vancouver Canucks, 1990–93; St. Louis Blues, 1994; New York Rangers, 1994–95, 1998–; Pittsburgh Penguins, 1995–1998

After defecting from Czechoslovakia to Canada while his teammates were traveling home from a hockey tournament, Petr Nedved was determined to make it as a star in the NHL.

Nedved was drafted with the second overall pick in the first round by Vancouver, and in his third season, showed why he had been drafted so highly, as he scored 38 goals. Nedved and Vancouver parted ways after the 1992–93 season. After taking NHL time off to play for the Canadian Olympic and National teams, Nedved signed with St. Louis in March 1994, scoring 20 points in 19 games.

Petr was traded to the Rangers by St. Louis in July of that year, but performed spottily. By August 1995, he was traded again, this time to Pittsburgh, where he continued to have success. Over the course of two seasons with the Penguins, Nedved scored 78 goals and 92 assists for a respectable 170 points.

Nedved was later traded back to New York, where he seemed to at last find a niche with the Blueshirts, regaining his scoring touch. Nedved scored 32 goals, which led the Rangers for that season, and assisted on 46 more in 2000–01, when he was a member of the powerful "Czech Line," featuring Nedved, Radek Dvorak, and Jan Hlavac.

In 2001–02, the speedy center struggled mightily to find his role on a renovated Ranger team that was missing Jan Hlavac and employing Eric Lindros as the go-to number one center. A disappointing non-playoff season had many thinking about Nedved's future on Broadway.

CAM NEELY

BORN: Comox, British Columbia, June 6, 1965
POSITION: Right Wing, Vancouver Canucks, 1983–86; Boston Bruins, 1986–96
AWARDS/HONORS: Bill Masterton Memorial Trophy, 1994; NHL Second Team All-Star, 1988, 1990–91, 1994; NHL All-Star Game, 1988–91, 1996

What were the Canucks thinking? This was a question asked thousands of times since D-Day, June 6, 1986, when Vancouver traded Cam Neely to Boston—along with the Canucks' first-round pick (Glen Wesley)—for Barry Pederson.

While Pederson performed adequately for Vancouver for four seasons, Neely became the distilled essence of Boston's lunchpail ethic for a decade, while scoring 50 goals or more twice and redefining the term "power forward."

The hockey brains in Vancouver had given up on Neely, but the moment Cam put on a

Boston uniform, he suddenly blossomed. By the 1989–90 campaign, Neely had established himself as a genuine power forward. His 55 goals and 37 assists spoke volumes about his value.

In fact, had Neely not suffered a crippling knee injury (due to a dubious check by defenseman Ulf Samuelsson), one wonders what heights Cam might have reached as a Boston hockey hero. It wasn't simply a matter of scoring or playmaking or bodychecking; it was a matter of guts. Neely had them in spades; he once took a slap shot to the forehead for 16 stitches, then returned the next period and got in a fight with Montreal's Shayne Corson.

Typically, Neely minimized his gutsy behavior. His game was a Bruins legacy dating back to Eddie Shore, Milt Schmidt, Wayne Cashman, and others who gave the Big, Bad Bruins a good name in Beantown.

In his 44th game of the season, on March 7, 1994, Neely scored twice and lifted his season total to 50 goals. Thus, the bruising right-winger had completed the third-fastest 50-goal season in NHL history.

Unfortunately, the injury jinx continued to plague him. His right pinky tip was torn off by a slash in a game against the New Jersey Devils on March 13, 1994, and less than a week later, in another game with New Jersey, a Ken Daneyko check caused a tear to the medial collateral ligament in Cam's right knee.

Neely was awarded the Masterton Trophy that spring and would gamely try to maintain his own high standards for two more seasons, only to yield to the inexorable effect of the injuries in 1996.

After a brief fling with an idea for a comeback in 1998–99, Neely continued to make appearances at Bruins games, as well as in the feature film *Dumb and Dumber,* and tirelessly devoted himself to his Cam Neely Fund, a charitable organization.

ROGER NEILSON

BORN: Toronto, Ontario, June 16, 1934
POSITION: Coach, Toronto Maple Leafs, 1977–79; Buffalo Sabres, 1980–81; Vancouver Canucks, 1981–84; Los Angeles Kings, 1984; New York Rangers, 1989–93; Florida Panthers, 1993–95; Philadelphia Flyers, 1998–2000; Ottawa Senators, 2002; Hall of Fame, 2002

Named coach of the Toronto Maple Leafs in June 1977, Roger Neilson previously had established a reputation as the brilliant but eccentric coach of the Peterborough Petes in the Ontario Hockey Association Junior A League. One of Neilson's most

Roger Neilson

bizarre ploys was executed in Peterborough when he was having a few problems teaching some of his more offensive-minded players how to forecheck. Roger brought his dog, Jacques, to practice and used him to illustrate his point. Neilson stood behind the net and positioned Jacques in front. No matter how many times Neilson started to move, the dog stayed put, showing the players that even a dog had the patience to wait until his opponent made the first move. "I don't think they liked the reference," said Neilson, "but they got the message."

After 25 years of coaching in the minors, Neilson got his chance in the National Hockey League in 1977–78. Although the Leafs had an adequate, but not superlative, regular season record, they scored a major upset in the Stanley Cup playoffs by ousting the favored New York Islanders in seven games. Neilson was expected to still do better in 1978–79, but the Leafs were a major disappointment. Neilson was "fired" by owner Harold Ballard

late in the season, but when players protested, Neilson was rehired just days later. However, after Toronto was defeated in four straight games by Montreal in the quaterfinals, Neilson joined Scotty Bowman in Buffalo under the innovative "multi-coach" system (1980–81).

Roger spent the next three seasons in Vancouver, with one Stanley Cup appearance in the 1982 playoffs in place of an ill Harry Neale, until halfway into the 1983–84 campaign. Thereafter, Neilson, known for his colorfully blinding ties, spent brief time as the Los Angeles Kings' coach, then disappeared from the NHL as a head coach for almost five full seasons. He was hired to coach the Rangers in 1989–90.

A Jack Adams Award nominee for his President's Trophy-winning Rangers in the 1991–92 season, Roger next joined the Philadelphia Flyers as the organization's 12th head coach at the end of 1997–98. He would hold that position until February 2000, when he was diagnosed with a form of cancer, multiple myeloma. Forced to undergo debilitating chemotherapy, Neilson handed over the head-coaching reins to assistant Craig Ramsay while receiving treatment, but didn't get them back when he returned during the playoffs.

Battling his health problems head-on, Roger entered his first season with the Ottawa Senators, the tenth NHL team to employ him, in August 2000 as an assistant coach to Jacques Martin. The positive Neilson was graciously allowed by the Senators' organization to assume head-coaching duties for two games in order to reach the 1,000 games-coached plateau in April 2002. Neilson was inducted into the Hockey Hall of Fame in 2002.

BERNIE NICHOLLS

BORN: Haliburton, Ontario, June 24, 1961
POSITION: Center, Los Angeles Kings, 1981–90; New York Rangers, 1990–91; Edmonton Oilers, 1991–93; New Jersey Devils, 1993–94; Chicago Blackhawks, 1994–96; San Jose Sharks, 1996–99
AWARDS/HONORS: NHL All-Star Game, 1984, 1986, 1990

Considering his ratio of points scored per games played, Bernie Nicholls belongs in the Hockey Hall of Fame.

During a period of 1,127 games over 18 seasons, he scored 1,209 points, numbers few could match. Thin and wiry, Nicholls could be dubbed the poor man's Wayne Gretzky, and in Los Angeles in 1988–89, he had a season even Gretzky would envy. He scored 70 goals to go with 80 assists.

Deceptively lighthearted, Nicholls was dead serious on the ice. His playmaking skills were evident not only to the Kings, but the New York Rangers, Edmonton Oilers, New Jersey Devils, Chicago Blackhawks, and San Jose Sharks.

Nicholls began skating when he was three. Drafted by the Kings in 1980 as their sixth choice, 73rd overall in the fourth round, Bernie made his first National Hockey League appearance in 1981–82. He played 22 games with the Kings, netting 14 goals and 18 assists for 32 points, after playing 55 games with their American Hockey League farm team.

In the beginning, Bernie was only interested in being a goal scorer and didn't focus on the defensive aspect of the game. But eventually, he became a complete player at both ends of the ice.

In his second full year with the Kings, 1983–84, he piled on 95 points in 78 games; a year later he got 100 points in eighty games. In 1988–89, with Wayne Gretzky's arrival in Los Angeles, Bernie reached the 70-goal plateau, but was traded to the New York Rangers in the middle of the next season for Tomas Sandstrom and Tony Granato. His first two years with New York involved playoff games, though they were knocked out of the playoffs both times by Washington.

When Rangers general manager Neil Smith saw that Edmonton's ice general, Mark Messier, was available, he included Nicholls in a landmark deal in 1991–92, as Nicholls moved off Broadway and into Edmonton. Bernie helped the Oilers reach the Conference finals with 19 points in 16 playoff matches.

But Nicholls's pivot skills were acquired by New Jersey the following season. Bernie's return East pitted him against his former Ranger team in a classic 1994 Western Conference final that went to a double-overtime Ranger win in Game Seven as Stephane Matteau ended a parade of near-series-clinching-goals by members of both teams, including Nicholls.

Off the ice, Bernie was now suffering, as his infant son lost an agonizing battle with spinal meningitis. But Bernie persevered and signed on with the Chicago Blackhawks in 1994–95 for two years before moving to San Jose, where he retired in 1999.

Despite the lack of a Stanley Cup championship on his resume, Nicholls's mark of 1,207 points was definitely on the top-40 all-time scorer list.

SCOTT NIEDERMAYER

BORN: Edmonton, Alberta, August 31, 1973
POSITION: Defenseman, New Jersey Devils, 1991–
AWARDS/HONORS: NHL All-Rookie Team, 1993; NHL Second Team All-Star, 1998; NHL All-Star Game, 1998

The formula for offensive defensemen was established in the post–World War II years, first by Red Kelly of the Detroit Red Wings and later Bobby Orr of the Boston Bruins. In time, it was further refined by Denis Potvin of the New York Islanders and Brian Leetch of the New York Rangers.

More recently, Scott Niedermayer of the New Jersey Devils has added a few other touches to the role of defense-as-offense. He has been less flamboyant than Leetch and more defense-oriented than Orr. But none of the above were able to match Niedermayer when it came to the art of pokechecking.

Scott's ability to relieve opponents of the puck with a deft slice of his stick was without equal in the NHL. Because Niedermayer did it unobtrusively, this important aspect of his game often went unnoticed.

But there is no doubting his accomplishments. He played on Stanley Cup winners in 1995 and 2000, often employing what some would consider a cat and mouse type game; one minute he's down in the defensive zone clearing the puck, the next you're chasing him into your own zone and trying to get the puck from him.

Niedermayer was drafted by the New Jersey Devils in the first round (third overall) in 1991, becoming the youngest Devil ever at the age of 18 years, 1 month, and 15 days. He matured smoothly with each passing year, honing his defensive zone skills under coaching wizard Jacques Lemaire. In the 1997–98 season, he exceeded expectations with 14 goals and 43 assists in 81 games as a defenseman.

Although he had the physical ability to be a dominant force as a defenseman, being paired with the likes of Scott Stevens and Kenny Daneyko allowed him to skate fluidly as an offensive-minded defender, sometimes jumping into rushes commandingly. That characteristic helped the Devils capture the Stanley Cup in the 1994–95 and 1999–2000 seasons, as Niedermayer was a member of both teams. In the 1994–95 championship season, he led all defensemen in points during the regular season as well as in the playoffs and his well-documented end-to-end game-tying goal at Joe Louis Arena in Game Two of the Stanley Cup finals was a lyrically typical example of Scott's abilities.

Playoff time was not always as fortuitous for Scott, as he was blindsided by the notorious

Tie Domi with a vicious elbow in the first round of the 2001 playoffs against the Maple Leafs. The Devils reached the finals, but Niedermayer was, by that time, useless from the dirty hit.

He recovered to play well in the 2001–02 season although the Devils lost in the first playoff round to the Carolina Hurricanes.

JOE NIEUWENDYK

BORN: Oshawa, Ontario, September 10, 1966
POSITION: Center, Calgary Flames, 1986–95; Dallas Stars, 1995–2002, New Jersey Devils, 2002–
AWARDS/HONORS: Calder Memorial Trophy, 1988; Conn Smythe Trophy, 1999; NHL All-Star, 1988–90, 1994

Tall and lanky, Joe Nieuwendyk burst upon the NHL scene like few rookies have ever done. In his first game in the National Hockey League, March 10, 1987, versus the Washington Capitals, Joe scored the first goal of his career.

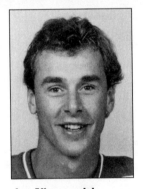
Joe Nieuwendyk

It was to be the beginning of an incredible journey for Nieuwendyk, one that took him from the depths of injury and contract disputes to the heights of winning the Conn Smythe Trophy as the Most Valuable Player in the 1999 Stanley Cup playoffs, with Dallas.

After completing his freshman year at Cornell University, Joe was drafted by the Calgary Flames in the second round of the 1985 draft. A Hobey Baker finalist as one of the top players in the collegiate ranks, Nieuwendyk had all the goods to be a star.

The Calgary Flames upper brass was salivating for Nieuwendyk when he finally suited up with the club in the spring of 1987. The Flames were one of the NHL's elite teams at the time, having just competed in the Stanley Cup finals the previous year against the eventual champion Montreal Canadiens. Being strong up the middle with the playmaking of Doug Gilmour at center, Al MacInnis anchoring the defense, and Mike Vernon manning the nets, the Flames looked upon Joe to complete the puzzle, and help them to win a Stanley Cup.

Joe certainly did not disappoint. In his rookie year of 1987–88, he scored 51 goals, which at that time was only the second time in NHL history that a rookie had scored 50-plus goals (Mike Bossy, 1977–78, 53). He earned NHL Rookie of the Year honors, and was everything that the Flames had expected him to be, and more.

In 1988–89, he followed his sensational rookie year with another 51-goal season. More importantly, he helped lead the Calgary Flames to their first Stanley Cup victory. At 22 years of age, Nieuwendyk had reached the pinnacle of his sport. He would nail down two more consecutive 45-goal seasons to close out the decade.

After the Stanley Cup–winning year, the Flames began to fall on harder times, as the club began a remarkable string of either first-round playoff exits or nonqualifying campaigns. One by one they left—Gilmour, MacInnis, Vernon. It was Joe's turn in 1995, when, after a contract dispute, the Flames traded their all-time leading scorer to the Dallas Stars for Corey Millen and future leading scorer Jarome Iginla.

Making an immediate impact with his new Dallas club, Nieuwendyk seemed comfortable being the center on the number two line. The Stars soon began to improve under head coach Ken Hitchcock, who promoted a well-disciplined defensive game, remaining near or at the top of the Western Conference. But a controversial hit by Bryan Marchment of the San Jose Sharks in Game One of the 1998 Western Conference quarterfinals knocked

Nieuwendyk out of the playoffs, and the Stars fell two rounds later.

The Stars, looking to rebound after their disappointing exit in the playoffs, began the 1998–99 season a more determined and committed club. Over the summer, the Stars signed perennial All-Star Brett Hull, and it was clear that just as Nieuwendyk was Calgary's last piece to the puzzle in the late 1980s, the Stars looked at Hull as being their final component.

The Stars defeated the Edmonton Oilers, St. Louis Blues, and Colorado Avalanche to win the Western Conference. In the Stanley Cup finals against the younger Buffalo Sabres, the Stars' seasoned veterans outlasted the quicker Sabres, and the Stars won their first Stanley Cup. And although the Stars had won the Cup in controversial style, thanks to a Hull goal some say should not have counted, the story of that playoff year was Nieuwendyk.

He tied a record with six game-winning goals during that playoff year, two in overtime. Utilizing his deceptive and deadly off-wing wrist shot, Joe tickled the twine 11 times overall during that magical run, and fittingly won the Conn Smythe Trophy.

When the Stars faltered in the 2000 finals with the New Jersey Devils, followed by a second-round exit the following year, Nieuwendyk was slowed by constant injuries to his big frame that limited his production.

Amid a year of trade rumors, Joe was dealt to the Devils in March 2001, along with Jamie Langenbrunner, for Jason Arnott, Randy McKay, and a first-round pick. Expected to bring maturity and an all-around game to the struggling team, Joe was felled by a stomach virus that limited his action in the opening round of that spring's playoff series against the Carolina Hurricanes, which the Devils lost in six games. Meanwhile, his ex-Dallas mates didn't make the postseason dance at all.

DUTCH NIGHBOR

BORN: Pembroke, Ontario, January 26, 1893
DIED: April 13, 1966
POSITION: Center, Toronto Arenas (NHA), 1913; Vancouver Millionaires (PCHA), 1914–15; Ottawa Senators, 1916–30; Toronto Maple Leafs, 1930
AWARDS/HONORS: Hart Memorial Trophy, 1924; Lady Byng Memorial Trophy, 1925–26; Hockey Hall of Fame, 1945

Whenever old-timers got together to reminisce about the great two-way players of all time, Hall of Famer Frank Nighbor's name invariably popped up. Never a rough or dirty player, Dutch was a model of controlled, artistic hockey whether playing offense or backchecking on defense.

Frank started his career with Toronto of the NHA and then spent two seasons with Vancouver of the PCHA, helping the Millionaires to the Stanley Cup in 1915.

But Dutch Nighbor was best remembered for his long and distinguished career with the Ottawa Senators. Nighbor spent 13 years with the Senators, playing on four Stanley Cup winners and helping to earn his team the nickname of "the Super Six."

Frank was the very first recipient of the Hart Trophy, awarded annually to the league's most valuable player. He also was a two-time winner of the Lady Byng Trophy for combining sportsmanship and playing excellence.

ULF NILSSON

BORN: Nynashamn, Sweden, May 11, 1950
POSITION: Center, Winnipeg Jets, 1974–78; New York Rangers, 1978–1983
AWARDS/HONORS: WHA Playoff MVP, 1976; First Team All-Star (WHA), 1976, 1978; Second Team All-Star (WHA), 1977; NHL Challenge Cup All-Star, 1979

A scoring phenom in the WHA, center Ulf Nilsson joined the Rangers with a flourish. After averaging 121 points per season in the WHA, Nilsson led the Rangers and was among the NHL leaders in scoring midway through the 1978–79 season. Unfortunately, Ulf came away from a corner collision with New York Islander Denis Potvin with a broken leg and torn ligaments, sidelining him for the remainder of the year. Despite his absence, the outgoing, personable Swede was voted the annual Players' Player Award by his new teammates.

Nilsson never was the same player after the Potvin incident, exiting big-league hockey in 1983. In a rather ironic way, Nilsson was still remembered by Madison Square Garden fans. Every year, alluding to the check that wasted his hockey life, Garden fans derided Potvin regularly with unpleasant chants.

OWEN NOLAN

BORN: Belfast, Ireland, February 12, 1972
POSITION: Right Wing, Quebec Nordiques/Colorado Avalanche, 1990–96; San Jose Sharks, 1996–
AWARDS/HONORS: NHL All-Star Game, 1992, 1996–97, 2000, 2002

Owen Nolan was a force to be reckoned with on the San Jose Sharks. The North Irish winger emerged as a very involved player in all facets of the game upon his entry into the NHL in 1990. Nolan could score, fight, and excel—and his stats proved it.

Nolan began his career with the Nordiques, and in only his second season of play, he totaled 42 goals to go with 31 assists; not bad for a sophomore. However, even more impressive is the fact that he had enough ice time to score all of his 42 goals that year, as he spent a whopping 183 minutes in the penalty box, an average of 2.44 minutes per game. This pattern of scoring and toughness continued throughout his career, as he has scored over 30 goals in six of his NHL seasons and has spent over 100 minutes in the penalty box in eight. When his Nordiques moved to Colorado and became the Avalanche, Nolan was dealt in the first month of the season straight-up for premium offensive defenseman Sandis Ozolinsh.

Most of Nolan's offense came on the power play; he was continually among the league leaders in power-play goals, scoring over ten in seven of his seasons. A wicked shooter, Owen, during a breakaway at the 1997 NHL All-Star game in his hometown San Jose, once playfully pointed to the spot in the net where he would score his third goal of the game.

More impressive than over 300 goals and more than 600 points is the fact that Nolan has done it by the age of 30 while maintaining a tremendous competitive fire. In true old-school fashion, he once completed a game against the Dallas Stars after receiving 35 stitches to his face and forehead. As captain of the Sharks, Nolan nobly led his team through its ascendance into the NHL's elite.

TED NOLAN

BORN: Sault Ste. Marie, Ontario, April 7, 1958
POSITION: Center, Detroit Red Wings, 1981–82, 1983–84; Pittsburgh Penguins, 1985–86; Coach, Buffalo Sabres, 1995–97
AWARDS/HONORS: Jack Adams Award, 1997

In an age when NHL talent comes from different cultures and all parts of the world, Ted Nolan paved the way for First Nation Canadians in major-league hockey. Nolan came off the reservation to play junior hockey in Sault Ste. Marie, Ontario, one Central Hockey League season, and two more in the American Hockey League before making the NHL with Detroit in 1980–81. He played a total of 78 games with Detroit and Pittsburgh and soon after joined the coaching ranks in the Canadian junior hockey system.

Nolan coached the Soo Greyhounds for six seasons in the OHL. During that span, the club made three Memorial Cup appearances, winning the title in 1992–93. Nolan was hired as an assistant coach with the Hartford Whalers in 1994–95, and when Buffalo general manager–coach John Muckler elected to step down as coach and concentrate on his role as general manager, Buffalo management called upon Nolan as his successor.

Buffalo missed the playoffs in Nolan's first season, but won the Northeast Division title in his second year, 1996–97, and won a first-round series—only Buffalo's second series win since 1983.

Nolan had the ability to get the most out of his players, commanding discipline, respect, accountability, and consistent effort. This approach made him very popular in Buffalo, with players and fans. Despite success behind the bench, Nolan publicly feuded with John Muckler and star goalie Dominik Hasek. Although Nolan won the Jack Adams Trophy for Coach of the Year in 1997, Buffalo only offered the coach a take-it-or-leave-it one-year contract offer, which he declined.

Apparently spurned by other NHL clubs, Nolan was passed over for a succession of other NHL coaching jobs, into the new millennium. Still concerned with the plight of his people, however, Nolan, while living on the Garden River Reservation in northern Ontario, organized and coached a team of indigenous players to play in international tournaments, serving as inspiration to young Native American athletes. His name continually emerged as an NHL coaching prospect through 2002, but Nolan never got the nod.

BRUCE NORRIS

Under the leadership of James Norris Sr., hockey not only survived, but thrived in Detroit during the 1930s. Big Jim, the wheat magnate, passed his love of hockey on to his sons, James Jr., who eventually became president of the Blackhawks, and Bruce, who took over the Red Wings as well as Olympia Stadium in Detroit. In time, Bruce Norris became one of the most powerful NHL governors. However, his numerous business interests frequently diverted his attention from the Red Wings and, as a result, the Detroit club began melting down toward the bottom of the standings.

Mismanagement on all levels resulted in the decline and fall of the Red Wings. Compounding Norris's woes was a serious auto accident that hospitalized him in the fall of 1974 in Florida.

Once one of the most influential NHL power brokers, Norris fell on hard times by the 1980s, and sold the Red Wings to Mike Ilitch in 1982, two years before his death.

JAMES NORRIS SR.

A wealthy grain broker from St. Catharines, Ontario, James once played for the Montreal Victorias. He began his hockey dynasty by purchasing the Chicago Shamrocks of the AHA in 1930.

He popped up in Detroit three years later, where he bought the Detroit Olympia arena and the Detroit NHL franchise, whereupon he promptly changed their name from the Falcons to the Red Wings.

Norris's most important hire was Jack Adams, who doubled as manager and coach. Within two years of Norris's acquisition of the team, Adams delivered a Stanley Cup (1935–36) and another a year later.

Norris, a member of the Hall of Fame, became one of the most powerful NHL owners. It once prompted *New York Daily Mirror* columnist Dan Parker to refer to the NHL as the Norris House League. However, without the financial and moral support provided by Norris in critical financial times, it is questionable whether the NHL would have survived fiscal crises during the early 1950s. In the end, Norris must be viewed as a heroic figure in building the league and maintaining its stability.

The James Norris Memorial Trophy, awarded annually to the best defenseman in the league, was first presented to the league in 1953 by the four children of James Norris Sr., in his honor.

JAMES D. NORRIS

James D. Norris was co-owner of the Detroit Red Wings with his father, James. Then, in 1946, he and partner Arthur Wirtz became owners of the Chicago Blackhawks. Like his father, James Norris Sr., the younger Jim emerged as a prominent NHL power broker and a key figure in the rise of the Blackhawks as an NHL marquee franchise. Norris was rewarded for his efforts when he was inducted into the Hall of Fame.

WILLIAM M. NORTHEY

It was William Northey who prevailed upon Sir Montague Allan to present his silver cup as the new emblem of amateur hockey supremacy, when the Stanley Cup became the professional award.

For years the managing director of the Montreal Forum, Northey supervised construction of that venerable arena, and for his years of supporting the development of hockey, he was elected a member of the Hall of Fame.

BOBBY NYSTROM

BORN: Stockholm, Sweden, October 10, 1952
POSITION: Right Wing, New York Islanders, 1972–86

Bob Nystrom was considered one of the hardest-working players in the NHL. When he realized his skating ability did not match his desire, Bobby trained with a power skating coach to improve his play and became one of several Islander 30-goal scorers in club history. Swedish born and Canadian raised, Nystrom was known as one of the tougher forwards to play in the big leagues, but he could actually score, with 235 career goals to his credit.

In time, Nystrom became an Islander icon for several reasons, including a talent for scoring clutch playoff goals. By the twenty-first century, his four career playoff overtime goals were still tied for third all-time, behind only Maurice Richard and Glenn Anderson. The most memorable Nystrom vignette encompassed the seventh minute of overtime in Game Six of the 1980 Stanley Cup finals. Skating on a line with center Lorne Henning and left-winger John Tonelli, Nystrom crisscrossed with Tonelli into the Philadelphia Flyers' zone and then took a cross-ice feed

that he deflected past goalie Pete Peeters at 7:11, thus giving the Islanders their first Stanley Cup.

Nystrom's never-say-die attitude came to epitomize Islanders hockey. He was a key member of all four Stanley Cup–championship teams, but his career was shortened after he was accidentally hit in the eye with a hockey stick during practice.

Respected by hockey fans everywhere, Bobby remained on Long Island as the Isles' director of Corporate Relations, appearing at virtually every Islander Alumni event conceivable more than 20 years after his historic goal gave birth to a dynasty.

Nystrom's son, Eric, emerged as a star at the University of Michigan in 2002 and was drafted by the Calgary Flames at the 2002 Entry Draft in round one.

Bob Nystrom after scoring the Cup-winning goal in 1980

ADAM OATES

BORN: Weston, Ontario, August 27, 1962
POSITION: Center, Detroit Red Wings, 1985–89;
St. Louis Blues, 1989–92; Boston Bruins, 1992–97;
Washington Capitals, 1997–2002; Philadelphia
Flyers, 2002; Anaheim Mighty Ducks, 2002–
AWARDS/HONORS: NHL Second Team All-
Star, 1991; NHL All-Star Game, 1991–94, 1997

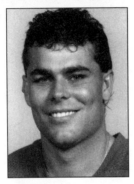

Adam Oates

Once upon a time there was a radio program called "Mister Keene, Tracer of Lost Persons." Each week, the hero would find people who, for whatever reason, had disappeared. Had Mister Keene been around for the past 15 years, he certainly would have "discovered" Adam Oates several times.

Not that it was Oates's fault that he was constantly overlooked by smart hockey people who should have known better. Yet it happened over and over and over again.

The oversights began during the early 1980s, when Adam left his native Weston, Ontario, for the prestigious Rensselaer Polytechnic Institute in Troy, New York. As the kingpin of RPI's offense in 1984–85, Oates tallied 31 goals and 60 assists for 91 points, but it was as if it all happened somewhere in the South Sea Islands.

Oates was overlooked by everyone, until the Detroit Red Wings signed him as a free agent on June 28, 1985, one of the best free-agent signings in NHL history.

Over four seasons, culminating in 1988–89, Oates got progressively better and seemed destined for a long career in Motor City. But in a bizarre misjudgment, the Wings dispatched Oates, along with Paul MacLean, to St. Louis for Bernie Federko and Tony McKegney; both were on the last legs of their careers.

Oates was even better with the Blues. Centering for Brett Hull, he surpassed the 100-point mark for two straight seasons (1989–90 and 1990–91) and appeared to be a fixture in the Mound City for years. But St. Louis management seemed enthralled with a pair of disappointing Bruins, Craig Janney and Stephane Quintal.

Harry Sinden was delighted to make the exchange that brought Oates to Boston on February 7, 1992, and Sinden soon looked like a genius again. Previously Janney had been the center, doling sweet passes to Cam Neely, but Oates was even better. The Oates-Neely duet made beautiful music together, and Adam's passes soon put him right behind Mario Lemieux (1.36) and Wayne Gretzky (1.33) in terms of assists-per-game average. Adam checked in at 1.08 and was, by 1993–94, rated one of the NHL's ultimate playmakers.

Oates had to adjust to the smaller Boston Garden ice surface after playing on traditional rinks in Detroit and St. Louis. He also got to register more points as a Bruin than ever before. In 1992–93, he scored a career-high 45 goals and similarly, a career-high 97 assists for 142 points. Oates also became one of the league's best at winning face-offs.

Washington acquired Oates in a 1997 blockbuster that landed the Bruins Jason Allison, and immediately paired Adam with sniper Peter Bondra. Eventually, Oates captained the team, and helped lead them to the Stanley Cup finals in 1998, where the Cinderella Capitals were defeated by Detroit.

After leading the league in assists in 2000–01 with 69, Oates feuded with management, and his captaincy was stripped. After the Caps' major acquisition of superstar Jaromir Jagr, Oates found himself moving again, this time to the talent-laden Philadelphia Flyers for top netminding prospect Maxime Ouellet and three draft picks at the 2002 trading deadline.

The Flyers welcomed the creative Oates to Philadelphia, expecting a high contribution to their 2002 Stanley Cup drive. But an overall anemic Flyers offense sputtered in an opening round loss to the Ottawa Senators and led to the firing of coach Bill Barber.

A free agent after the 2001–02 season, Oates was signed by the Anaheim Mighty Ducks to center for Paul Kariya.

MIKE O'CONNELL

BORN: Chicago, Illinois, November 25, 1955
POSITION: Defenseman, Chicago Blackhawks, 1977–80; Boston Bruins, 1980–86; Detroit Red Wings, 1986–90; General Manager, Boston Bruins, 2000–
AWARDS/HONORS: NHL All-Star Game, 1984

Mike O'Connell had over 20 years of professional hockey experience before being promoted to vice president and general manager of the Boston Bruins organization in 2000, succeeding his mentor Harry Sinden.

Originally a hard-hitting defenseman, O'Connell played six seasons with the Boston Bruins, beginning in 1980 after being acquired from the Chicago Blackhawks. During his playing days in Boston, O'Connell recorded three consecutive 50-plus point seasons (1982–85) and represented the Bruins in the 1984 All-Star game in New Jersey. Mike played his last NHL years in Detroit before retiring after the 1989–90 season.

Once behind the desk in Boston, O'Connell focused on making Boston bigger and quicker, and his deal for fleet power forward Bill Guerin to open his tenure helped accomplish this, but the Mike Keenan–coached Bruins would fall short of a playoff berth.

In just his second season as team general manager and fourth as vice president, O'Connell's Boston club finished with the best record in the Eastern Conference in the 2001–02 campaign, after a successful summer free-agent shopping spree that brought in key forwards Martin Lapointe, Rob Zamuner, and defenseman Sean O'Donnell to supplement Guerin and Joe Thornton. Although beaten by an upstart Montreal Canadiens team in the first round of the postseason dance, O'Connell's handpicked coach, Robbie Ftorek, was nominated for coach of the year shortly afterward.

BUDDY O'CONNOR

BORN: Montreal, Quebec, June 21, 1916
DIED: August 24, 1977
POSITION: Center, Montreal Canadiens, 1941–47; New York Rangers, 1947–51
AWARDS/HONORS: Hart Memorial Trophy, 1948; Lady Byng Memorial Trophy, 1948; NHL Second Team All-Star, 1948

Buddy O'Connor, a tiny, wisplike centerman, broke into pro hockey with the 1941–42 Montreal Canadiens, pivoting a unit of mighty mites known as the Razzle-Dazzle Line. This fulfilled a boyhood ambition of

Buddy O'Connor as a Ranger

Buddy's that began on the frozen ponds near his suburban Montreal home.

But it was easy for the diminutive forward to get lost in the shuffle of the Canadien's awesome firepower. So after six successful but anonymous seasons with the Habitants, Buddy was peddled to the New York Rangers in 1947 for the paltry sum of $6,500.

O'Connor was welcomed to New York with open arms, and it was there that he truly began to find himself. He finished out the 1947–48 campaign in grand style, missing out on the NHL scoring crown by only a single point, but he copped both the Hart Trophy, as the league's most valuable player, and the Lady Byng Trophy for sportsmanship.

An automobile accident forced Buddy to miss much of the following season, which Ranger manager Frank Boucher pointed to as the only reason the Rangers failed to make the playoffs.

Buddy played two more seasons with the Rangers before retiring at the end of the 1950–51 campaign.

BERT OLMSTEAD

BORN: Scepter, Saskatchewan, September 4, 1926
POSITION: Left Wing, Chicago Blackhawks, 1948–51; Montreal Canadiens, 1951–58; Toronto Maple Leafs, 1958–62
AWARDS/HONORS: NHL Second Team All-Star, 1953, 1956; NHL All-Star Game, 1953, 1956–57, 1959; Hockey Hall of Fame, 1985

Known around the NHL as "Dirty Bertie," Montreal's Bert Olmstead gained the reputation as one of the best left-wingers in the sport. Rarely would he get involved in fist-fights, although he started many of them by provoking his opponent.

Olmstead's most famous bouts were with Lou Fontinato of the Rangers. "Dirty Bertie" had moved to Toronto by 1959, when the two assailed each other following a high stick by

the Maple Leaf. Fontinato blackened Olmstead's eye with one punch.

As the pair attempted to leave the penalty box following their banishments, Olmstead jumped in front of Fontinato in an effort to get on ice first. Lou simply opened the door to the box, knocking Bertie down, then proceeded to beat up on his rival.

"If he didn't block the door," Louie said, "nothing would have happened."

The battle continued later in the season before a sellout crowd in Madison Square Garden. Fontinato skated from the face-off circle toward Olmstead and hurled himself, nearly parallel to the ice, at Bertie. "I don't know how Olmstead got up," related Camille Henry, who was on the ice at the time and nearly served as an unwary roadblock to Fontinato, the Flying Ranger. "Louie broke his stick on Olmstead's face, put his knee in his ribs, and threw him into the glass. It was the dirtiest check I've ever seen." Furthermore, no penalty was called.

Olmstead survived and starred for the Toronto Maple Leafs Stanley Cup–winning team in 1961–62. His gritty play along the boards helped win him a nomination to the Hall of Fame.

JEFF O'NEILL

BORN: Richmond Hill, Ontario, February 23, 1976
POSITION: Center, Hartford Whalers, 1995–97; Carolina Hurricanes, 1997–

The Raleigh media knew Jeff O'Neill had taken on the trappings of a superstar during the 2000–01 playoffs, when he made it clear he was not doing day-of-game interviews.

Unfortunately, O'Neill had not quite achieved that status on the ice, although he had performed just a notch below that level, with 41 goals in 82 regular season games. However, Jeff's failure to deliver in the playoffs against New Jersey left critics wondering about his ability in key situations.

O'Neill answered that question a year later, helping Carolina to first place in the Southeast Division with 31 goals and 33 assists, then sparking them to playoff victories as they bested New Jersey, Montreal, and Toronto, respectively.

O'Neill was the Hartford Whalers' fifth overall pick in the first round of the 1994 NHL Entry Draft. The Whalers remained very patient with their draft pick, but it was not until the team relocated to Carolina that their patience began to pay off. In his sixth season in the league (2000–01), O'Neill potted the aforementioned 41 goals.

By the time the Canes faced off in the 2002 Stanley Cup finals against the Detroit Red Wings, Jeff O'Neill was a proven offensive force and seasoned postseason performer with a long future to come.

WILLIE O'REE

BORN: Fredericton, New Brunswick, October 15, 1935
POSITION: Right Wing, Boston Bruins, 1957–58, 1960–61

The first black player to skate in the NHL, Willie O'Ree was hardly the Jackie Robinson of hockey in terms of ability. A successful minor-league player, O'Ree finally broke the color line during the 1957–58 season. He played two games for the Boston Bruins without scoring a goal.

The Bruins gave O'Ree another chance in 1960–61. This time, he scored 4 goals and 10 assists in 43 games and was dispatched to the minors. Some critics believed that O'Ree deserved another shot at the majors but he never returned to the NHL as a player. Nevertheless, Willie became a star of West Coast minor-league hockey, playing for teams in Los Angeles and San Diego, where he was one of the area's most popular sports figures.

Following his playing career O'Ree returned to his native New Brunswick, where he taught hockey to children. Following Gary Bettman's appointment as NHL commissioner in 1993, O'Ree achieved new prominence. The NHL created a Diversity Task Force promoting hockey in inner city areas and O'Ree became an NHL spokesman, promoting tournaments and encouraging youngsters throughout North America.

O'Ree later revealed he had suffered a serious eye injury during his junior hockey days and effectively had sight in only one eye thereafter, which made his resume even more impressive.

TERRY O'REILLY

BORN: Niagara Falls, Ontario, June 7, 1951
POSITION: Right Wing, Boston Bruins, 1971–85
AWARDS/HONORS: NHL All-Star Game, 1975, 1978

Of all the players Harry Sinden brought to the National Hockey League, none was more Sinden's type of player than Terry O'Reilly.

"The most important thing to any player," Sinden once said, "is his teammates. It's not important how he feels about the coach, the

Terry O'Reilly, the Bruins' Tazmanian Devil

fans, or the press. What matters is how he feels about his teammates and how they feel about him."

No Bruin ever felt more keenly about his teammates than the right-winger from Niagara Falls, Ontario. O'Reilly, all six feet one, 199 pounds of him, was the quintessential Bruin. After playing junior hockey for the Oshawa (Ontario) Generals, O'Reilly was drafted by Boston in the second round of the 1971 Entry Draft, 14th overall.

The early O'Reilly was more prominent for his fists than his shots. He was not the NHL's best fighter, but he was certainly one of the most energetic jabbers the game has ever known. As a result, the Boston Garden's Gallery Gods eagerly awaited his next bout—whenever it would occur.

The harder O'Reilly tried, the bigger his numbers grew. By 1975-76, he had cleared the 20-goal plateau (23-27-50) for the first time and by 1977-78 had reached 90 points (29-61). He was not the very soul of smoothness but nobody seemed to care.

He was soon named "Taz," as in Tasmanian Devil, which was about as appropriate a hockey nickname as ever was coined. In 1977-78, O'Reilly became only the second player in NHL history to lead his team in both scoring and penalty minutes (211) and nobody but opponents complained about the latter.

If there was a negative to O'Reilly, it was his awkward skating, which suggested a lumberjack snowshoeing the Canadian tundra. But he compensated well by mastering the art of manipulating the puck with his skates.

Not surprisingly, O'Reilly became a frequent winner of the "Most Popular Bruin" award from Boston Garden's Gallery Gods and played his entire career for the same franchise, even coaching the B's to the Stanley Cup finals in 1988 as a rookie coach eradicating a 45-year playoff-curse of losing to the Montreal Canadiens.

"Whenever someone asked what I did for a living," said O'Reilly, "I'd say I played for the Bruins. Just saying it would send a chill down my spine."

During the summer of 2002, O'Reilly was named an assistant coach of the New York Rangers. Nevertheless the Bruins honored him with a "night" at the start of the 2002–03 season.

BOBBY ORR

BORN: Parry Sound, Ontario, March 20, 1948
POSITION: Defenseman, Boston Bruins, 1966–76; Chicago Blackhawks, 1976–79
AWARDS/HONORS: Hart Memorial Trophy, 1970–72; Calder Memorial Trophy, 1967; James Norris Memorial Trophy, 1968–75; Art Ross Trophy, 1970, 1975; Conn Smythe Trophy, 1970, 1972; Lester B. Pearson Award, 1975; Lester Patrick Trophy, 1979; NHL First Team All-Star, 1968–75; NHL Second Team All-Star, 1967; NHL All-Star Game, 1968–73, 1975; Team Canada, 1972; Canada Cup All-Star, 1976; Canada Cup MVP, 1976

It has been said that Bobby Orr was the most accomplished contemporary offensive defenseman and, perhaps, the best of all time. Although he was not a forward for the Boston Bruins, Orr led the National Hockey League in scoring twice (1970, 1975). He won the Hart Trophy as the NHL's most valuable player three years in a row (1970, 1971, 1972) and won the James Norris (best defenseman) Trophy a record eight years in a row, from 1968 through 1975. He won the Calder (rookie) Trophy and was a First Team All-Star defenseman from 1968 to 1975.

Some historians insist that Bruins defenseman Eddie Shore, Canadiens center Howie Morenz, Red Wings right wing Gordie Howe, and Blackhawks left wing Bobby Hull were better players than Orr. But only Hull and Howe were contemporaries of Orr and many experts give the nod to Orr.

"Howe could do everything but not at top speed," said Bruins managing director Harry Sinden. "Hull went to top speed but couldn't do everything. Orr could do everything, and at top speed."

Some even argue that Orr was better than Wayne Gretzky, Mark Messier, or Mario Lemieux. One fact is indisputable: Before Orr became a Bruin, the Boston franchise was buried at the bottom of the NHL. When he arrived, he helped turn it into a contending and eventually a Stanley Cup champion team. This was hardly surprising, considering that major-league scouts had touted him as a thoroughly unique skater and stickhandler before he reached high school age in his native Parry Sound, a summer fishing resort town some three hours north of Toronto.

Orr was discovered by hockey professionals as a 12-year-old playing in a midget hockey game in the Ontario town of Gananoque. At that time, a professional team could gain control of a 12-year-old simply by putting his name on a protected list.

Several Bruins officials were sitting in on the game at Gananoque, scouting two other players, but whenever they looked up, towheaded Bobby had control of the puck. The Bruins immediately drafted plans to keep young Orr within their system, and when he was 14 he was signed to play for the Oshawa (Ontario) Generals of the strong Ontario Hockey Association's Junior A League. Although Orr was skating against older and stronger players, he was an almost immediate hit. By the time he was 16, his picture had appeared on the cover of *Maclean's,* the national magazine of Canada. It was already clear that Bobby Orr was the most remarkable young player to come along since Gordie Howe.

At the time, the Bruins were in last place. In order to soothe their disappointed fans, Boston officials began promoting Bobby. When he comes up, they said, the Bruins will be great again. He finally arrived at the Boston training camp in the autumn of 1966, barely 17. "I was scared stiff," said Bobby. "I didn't know whether I could play in the NHL. And I was alone."

There was only one threat to Bobby's prospect of becoming the greatest hockey player ever. A seemingly insignificant knee injury became aggravated, and after two NHL seasons he underwent two operations. "It was the cartilage the first time," said Orr. "Then I think I came back a little too soon and the two

bone surfaces rubbed together and the knee went all hairy on me. I don't think there's too much you can do to prevent it. I think everyone will say the same thing. If you get hit, there's nothing you can do."

The second operation was completed before the 1968–69 season, and there was serious concern in Boston that Orr might never be fit to skate normally again. When he arrived in training camp, the knee bothered him so much that he was ordered off the ice. In time, however, he returned, and with each week the knee grew stronger and stronger. It was so strong in the 1969–70 season that Orr was able to play the entire 76-game schedule, as well as the lengthy playoffs, without missing a game.

From time to time, thoughtful hockey writers attempted to put Orr in perspective by comparing him with immortals from other sports. The easiest analogy was Babe Ruth, but Robert Markus, the *Chicago Tribune* columnist, argued that Orr wasn't a home-run hitter in the Ruthian tradition, but more like Joe DiMaggio. "Orr," said Markus, "was a stylish, graceful athlete who did everything extremely well, much in the manner of DiMaggio."

Some observers insist that for all Orr's superhuman efforts he received special treatment from referees throughout the league. Chicago Blackhawks coach Billy Reay, for one, said at one time that officials gave Orr too much credit for his "Academy Award performances," frequently taking dives to inspire referees to whistle penalties against the opposition.

Although Orr continued to dominate the NHL scene through the 1974–75 season because of his offensive contributions, his defensive weaknesses became more pronounced. Despite Orr and high-scoring teammate, Phil Esposito, the Bruins were unable to overtake the Buffalo Sabres in the regular season race for first in the NHL Adams Division. In the playoffs, a weaker Chicago Blackhawks club wiped out the Bruins in the opening round. Orr's disenchantment with Bruins management eventually led to a rupture in the relationship. On June 24, 1976, he was signed as a free agent by the Chicago Blackhawks. Bad knees curtailed his play and he retired after playing six games in 1978–79.

Orr himself admitted that his much-operated-upon knees had braked his skating ability. He finally said a teary-eyed good-bye to the NHL as a player, becoming an assistant to NHL president John Ziegler. Orr's retirement represented the end of an era, when the "wonder kid" from Parry Sound reigned as the dominant athlete in big-league hockey.

Orr's onetime agent, Alan Eagleson, became Bobby's enemy after the defenseman's retirement. Eagleson was eventually jailed, an event that confirmed Orr's later view of his erstwhile pal.

Bobby returned to Boston and maintained a low profile for years, emerging more prominently in the 1990s, when he became a hockey player agent, eventually heading his own firm. Sadly, his damaged knees continued to haunt him and more surgery was required in 2002 to alleviate pain.

However, Orr remained the most popular athlete in Boston history and, arguably, the most popular figure in all of New England sports.

Bobby Orr checking out his stick with trainer John "Frosty" Forristal

CHRIS OSGOOD

BORN: Peace River, Alberta, November 26, 1972
POSITION: Goaltender, Detroit Red Wings, 1993–2001; New York Islanders, 2001–
AWARDS/HONORS: William M. Jennings Trophy (shared with Mike Vernon), 1996; NHL Second Team All-Star, 1996; NHL All-Star Game, 1996–98

For his entire Red Wings career, Chris Osgood was almost always fighting for respect as a top-drawer goaltender. At times, he was brilliant and at other times he would be the target of coach Scott Bowman's ire.

Small in stature, Osgood loomed large in the nets as the Red Wings began its climb to the top in the mid 1990s.

A third-round draft pick in the 1991 NHL Entry Draft, Osgood was picked by Wings scouting director Ken Holland in the hope of reversing a string of suspect goaltending that Detroit suffered in the late 1980s and early 1990s.

Displaying the maturity of a veteran throughout the 1993–94 season, Osgood accumulated a 23–8–5 freshman record and was named rookie of the month in February 1994. More impressive, the diminutive Osgood blanked San Jose in Game One of the Western Conference quarterfinals, the first Detroit rookie to record a shutout in a playoff game since the great Terry Sawchuk in 1951. But his bad clearing attempt that led to the Sharks' winning goal late in Game Seven spawned doubts about "Ozzy."

Coach Scotty Bowman flip-flopped his two goaltenders. Mike Vernon led the Wings to the Stanley Cup final in 1995, where they eventually lost to the New Jersey Devils, while Osgood took over the reins the following season, leading the Wings to the Western Conference finals before being ousted by Colorado.

Osgood was named to the All-Star team in the 1995–96 season, after tying for the NHL's best goals-against average (2.17), and leading the league in victories (39). He also rattled off a 21-game unbeaten streak (19-0-2)—a new club record—that included a 13-game winning streak, which broke Terry Sawchuk's club record of nine.

During the 1996–97 season, Bowman utilized Osgood for the majority of the season, yet named Vernon his starting goaltender for the playoffs, putting a dagger through Osgood's confidence. But as the veteran Vernon led the Wings to their first Stanley Cup victory since 1955 and was dubbed the Conn Smythe Trophy winner as MVP of the playoffs, young Osgood watched and learned, knowing full well that someday he would be called upon.

General manager Ken Holland decided next season that Osgood was the team's future, and furthermore, the future was now. Holland shopped Vernon to San Jose in the summer of 1997.

Suddenly Osgood became a major focal point on the Wings. Few predicted the quiet netminder could lead the Wings to a second straight Stanley Cup victory, especially because he had done virtually nothing in postseason play to redeem himself since that fateful error in 1994. There were whispers that Osgood's regular season success was a by-product of the overall team prosperity enjoyed by the Red Wings in the mid to late 1990s.

After Detroit eliminated Phoenix, St. Louis, and Dallas, the Stanley Cup final series against Washington was mere formality, as the Wings captured their second straight championship by sweeping the Capitals behind Osgood's spectacular 30-save performance in Game Four.

Osgood started all 22 Red Wing postseason games in the spring of 1998, posting a 16–6 record along with a 2.15 goals-against average and .917 save percentage. Along the way, he outdueled future Hall of Fame netminders Grant Fuhr and Ed Belfour to capture his second Stanley Cup ring.

Ozzy did not win another Stanley Cup but played adequately for Detroit through the 2000–01 season, posting a 25–19–4 record, 2.67 goals-against average, and a meager .903 save percentage. Osgood could not carry his team out of the first round of the playoffs, losing to Los Angeles in six games. When Dominik Hasek was acquired over the summer, the Red Wings could not afford both goalies and couldn't trade Osgood; thus, the former Stanley Cup winner was exposed in the Waiver Draft just before the start of the 2001–02 season.

With the good fortune of picking first, the New York Islanders, with rookie Rick DiPietro and much-traveled Garth Snow in net, selected Osgood, a no-brainer for a franchise needing a kick-start. Chris helped the Isles get off to a 11-1-1 start and keyed the confidence of the young team, who, under rookie coach Peter Laviolette, made the playoffs for the first time since 1994. Despite a gallant performance by Osgood, the Isles lost a seven-games series to Toronto in the opening round.

ZIGGY PALFFY

BORN: Skalica, Czechoslovakia, May 5, 1972
POSITION: Right Wing, New York Islanders, 1993–99; Los Angeles Kings, 1999–
AWARDS/HONORS: NHL All-Star Game 1998, 2001–02

It didn't take long for Zigmund Palffy to find himself on center stage in the National Hockey League.

In the final week of the 1993–94 season, the Czech-born skater was inserted into the Islanders lineup for a game against the Florida Panthers at Miami Arena. Awarded a penalty shot, the freshman skated down on Panthers goalie John Vanbiesbrouck, who beat him cleanly. Undaunted, the young right wing shrugged off the setback and proceeded to become one of the most popular Islanders of the late 1990s.

His ability to stickhandle laterally and swiftly made him difficult to check, and that creativity led to three straight 40-plus goal seasons (1995–96 to 1997–98). But the right-winger did not have a legitimate center on his line with whom to mesh. Nevertheless, the oft-smiling sniper emerged as the most feared shooter on a New York team short on both talent and victories.

His 331 points in as many games as an Islander wasn't enough to stop general manager Mike Milbury from dealing the team's only star to the Los Angeles Kings for a package of prospects during an ownership-mandated salary purge in 1999.

Palffy excelled in LA, teaming with talented center Josef Stumpel, and, later, Jason Allison, for a potent scoring line to help fill the brand-new Staples Center. He finally tasted playoff competition, where his Kings upset the Detroit Red Wings in seven games during the first round of the 2001 Stanley Cup playoffs.

LA surged in the second half of 2001–02, drawing the defending Cup champion Colorado Avalanche in the Western Conference quarterfinals. Palffy led all NHL forwards in scoring with nine points during the first round as the Kings came back from a three-games-to-one deficit to force a seventh game, which was won by the Avs, 4–0.

By any standard, Ziggy Palffy, at 5 feet 10 and 183 pounds, had become a premier forward in the NHL by the age of 30.

BERNIE PARENT

BORN: Montreal, Quebec, April 3, 1945
POSITION: Goaltender, Boston Bruins, 1965–67; Philadelphia Flyers, 1967–71, 1973–79; Toronto Maple Leafs, 1971–72; Philadelphia Blazers (WHA), 1972–73
AWARDS/HONORS: Vezina Trophy, 1974 (shared with Chicago's Tony Esposito), 1975; Conn Smythe Trophy, 1974–75; NHL Second Team All-Star, 1969; NHL First Team All-Star, 1974–75; Second Team All-Star (WHA), 1973; Hockey Hall of Fame, 1984

He crouched slightly at the waist. His trapper's mitt hung off his left hand, ready to snare the flying chunk of black rubber flak. Behind the white perforated mask, his eyes were riveted to the puck. Rarely did they ever lose sight of it, even at speeds of up to 100 miles per hour.

The human rubber radar machine was none other than Bernie Parent of the Philadelphia Flyers, who climbed to the top rung as one of the best goaltenders in the National Hockey League. Thanks to the French-Canadian from Montreal, the Flyers finished first in the West Division in 1974, first in the Lester Patrick Division in 1975, and then marched triumphantly to the Stanley Cup both years.

Playing 73 of 78 regular season games in 1973–74, more than any other NHL goalie, Parent produced a dazzling 1.89 goals-against average, the best in the league. Unfortunately for Bernie, the Vezina Trophy is a team award and both the Flyers and Chicago Blackhawks finished with identical 2.10 goals-against averages (Bobby Taylor played seven games for Philadelphia and compiled a 4.26 average). Consequently, there was a Vezina tie.

Parent made up for that in the 1974 playoffs. While Chicago's Tony Esposito and his Blackhawks were bombed out of the semifinals by Boston, Bernie was virtually flawless in the Flyers' goal.

In the sixth and final game of the last round against Boston, Parent shut out the high-scoring Bruins, 1–0, and won the Conn Smythe Trophy as the most valuable player in the playoffs. It was a remarkable comeback, considering that a year earlier Parent had been playing for the World Hockey Association's Philadelphia Blazers and quit that club during the playoffs because of contract problems. The Blazers eventually moved to Vancouver while Bernie returned to the NHL and the Flyers, for whom he had played previously. Only this time he had a new coach in Fred Shero and fans who weren't exactly sure, at first, about welcoming him back.

The decisive moment occurred opening night in October 1973, against the Toronto Maple Leafs at Philadelphia's Spectrum. Parent had also played for Toronto and openly criticized the city. Now the Maple Leafs were out for revenge. However, they didn't accomplish much. Nothing, in fact. The Flyers scored twice and Parent shut out the Leafs.

Bernie's biggest smile was reserved for that moment on May 19, 1974, when the final buzzer sounded at the Spectrum and the Flyers had beaten Boston four games to two for the Cup, a feat duplicated in 1975 against the Buffalo Sabres.

Bernie continued his phenomenal goaltending until a damaged disc in his neck forced him to sit out most of the 1975–76 season. The following year, a fully recovered Parent returned to the Philadelphia nets and in 61 games recorded a respectable 2.71 goals-against average. In 1978, Parent proved his recovery was complete by posting a 2.22 average in 49 games.

Tragedy struck the unlucky goalie again when, in the middle of the 1978–79 season, Parent was accidentally struck in the right eye by a New York Ranger stick in a bizarre incident in front of the net. The stick actually found its way through the tiny opening in Parent's mask.

Bernie, who knew immediately that he was in trouble, was rushed to the hospital, where he spent the next ten days with both eyes bandaged. With injury to the retina and a dislocation of the lens, observers feared Parent's days as a netminder were over because of sight impairment. At the conclusion of the 1978–79 season, the popular goalie announced his retirement.

His credentials were more impressive than those of any goalie to have worn the Flyers' orange and black. Bernie had a lifetime goals-against average of 2.42 and an overall record of 232-141-103, including an amazing 50 shutouts.

Parent's playoff numbers were equally impressive: His 35-28 record was supported by a 2.38 goals-against average and six shutouts.

In 1982, Bernie became the Flyers' goaltending coach, a position he held until 1994. Parent was a classic, from style to performance, and was inducted into the Hockey Hall of Fame in 1984.

BRAD PARK

BORN: Toronto, Ontario, July 6, 1948
POSITION: Defenseman, New York Rangers, 1968–75; Boston Bruins, 1975–83; Detroit Red Wings, 1983–85; Coach, Detroit Red Wings, 1985–86
AWARDS/HONORS: Bill Masterton Memorial Trophy, 1984; Team Canada, 1972; NHL First Team All-Star, 1970, 1972, 1974, 1976, 1978; NHL Second Team All-Star, 1971, 1973; NHL All-Star Game, 1970–78; Hockey Hall of Fame, 1988

Brad Park played the game precisely the way it was meant to be played: hard but clean and with smarts. He perfected the "submarine body check," thrusting his hip into onrushing opponents and catapulting them upside down to the ice.

Brad Park

The check, rare in contemporary hockey, was a throwback to the days when the game was slower and defensemen had more time to plan such devastating, yet clean maneuvers. Park's submarine checks were not feared more than his fists. When suitably provoked, he retaliated with a barrage of lefts and rights that usually guaranteed him no less than a draw and often a victory over his enemies.

Park made it to the NHL in 1968 with the New York Rangers. During the 1971–72 season, when the Boston Bruins were intimidating most of the Rangers, it was Park who, virtually single-handedly, took on the bruising Bruins, whipping Ted Green and Johnny McKenzie.

The Park versus Boston war lasted through the 1972 Ranger-Bruin Stanley Cup final. Whenever possible, such heavyweights as Wayne Cashman, Ken Hodge, and Carol Vadnais singled Brad out for punishment. He took it well and dished it out, too, once even fighting Bobby Orr to a draw at center ice.

But Brad couldn't do it alone, and the Bruins overwhelmed him and the Rangers to take the 1972 Cup in six games. Only seconds after the final buzzer sounded, the man leading the Rangers' handshaking parade to the Bruins was none other than the skater Boston hated the most, Brad Park.

During the 1973–74 season, Park led all Rangers in scoring, but they finished third in the NHL's East Division and were wiped out of the Stanley Cup semifinal round after a brutal series with the Philadelphia Flyers. Philadelphia's Mean Machine singled out Park for considerable punishment. Leading the Flyers' assault was the aggressive Dave Schultz, who dealt Brad several lumps—not all of them legal. Park fought back nobly but, when the series had ended, he stuck by his philosophy that hockey can be played tough but clean.

"I thought about it a couple of times and I made a decision. I decided that if I have to maim somebody to win the Stanley Cup, I don't want to win it!"

In the summer of 1974, Park was named captain of the Rangers, and his troubles began. Park heard boos from the once friendly Madison Square Garden crowd as his play deteriorated. Then came "The Trade."

On November 7, 1975, the Ranger captain was shuffled off to Beantown, along with teammates Jean Ratelle and Joe Zanussi, in exchange for hockey's most prolific scorer, Phil Esposito, and Carol Vadnais. After seven years of battling and bad-mouthing the Bruins while wearing a New York uniform, Park found himself a member of his once-hated rivals.

Hate never became adoration so quickly as in the case of Park and the city of Boston. The All-Star defenseman, after two sub-par years, was immediately asked to fill the shoes of one Bobby Orr, and he did just that. Despite recurring knee problems, Park returned to earlier form, concentrating more on his defensive game. With Park's leadership, Boston went to the Cup finals in 1977 and 1978, although the treasured championship continued to elude Park.

He never did play for a Stanley Cup winner, even after being dealt to the Detroit Red Wings. His career hit a wall after a brief and disastrous coaching stint with the Wings (1985–86). He returned to New England, where he was involved with an assortment of hockey jobs. Park came full circle in 2001–02, when he was named a scout for his alma mater, the Rangers.

CRAIG PATRICK

BORN: Detroit, Michigan, May 20, 1946
POSITION: Right Wing, California Golden Seals, 1971–74; St. Louis Blues, 1974–75; Kansas City Scouts, 1975–76; Washington Capitals, 1976–79; Assistant Coach, 1980 U.S. Olympic Team; Assistant General Manager, 1980 U.S. Olympic Team; Coach, New York Rangers, 1980–81, 1984–85; Pittsburgh Penguins, 1989–90; 1996–97; General Manager, New York Rangers, 1981–86; Pittsburgh Penguins, 1989–; United States Canada Cup Team, 2001; U.S. Olympic Team, 2002
AWARDS/HONORS: Lester Patrick Trophy, 2000; Hockey Hall of Fame, 2001

Few hockey people have accomplished more with less fuss and fanfare than Craig Patrick. Grandson of legendary player-coach-manager Lester "the Silver Fox" Patrick, Craig originally attracted attention as a junior player in Montreal before signing with the California Golden Seals. His father, Lynn, had been a star forward with the New York Rangers when they won the Stanley Cup in 1940, but Craig never achieved that level of ability as a player, although he also skated for the St. Louis Blues, the Kansas City Scouts, and the Washington Capitals.

Following his playing career, Patrick was assistant coach and assistant general manager of the gold medal 1980 "Miracle On Ice" United States Hockey Team, general manager of the 1991 United States Team at the Canada Cup, and general manager of the silver medal 2002 United States Olympic Hockey Team.

He became general manager of the New York Rangers in 1981 and led them to the playoffs in each of his five seasons. However, his foremost accomplishments were in Pittsburgh, where he led the Penguins to two Stanley Cups, five Division trophies, one President's Trophy, and 11 straight playoff berths in his first 11 full seasons on the job.

Patrick engineered key deals in the Penguins' Stanley Cup runs in 1991 and 1992, with the crown jewel of his deals landing gritty performers Ron Francis and Ulf Samuelsson from Hartford for John Cullen and Zarley Zalapski in time for the stretch drive in March 1991.

Once Mario Lemieux took over ownership of the Penguins in 2000–01, he retained Patrick as general manager. Craig obliged, and the Penguins again made the playoffs. But in 2001–02, injuries crippled his club and Pittsburgh finished out of the running.

FRANK PATRICK

BORN: Ottawa, Ontario, December 21, 1885
DIED: June 29, 1960
POSITION: Defenseman, Montreal Victorias (CAHL), 1904; Westmount (CAHL), 1905; Montreal Victorias (ECAHA), 1908; Renfrew Millionaires (NHA), 1910; Vancouver Millionaires (PCHA), 1912–18; Vancouver Millionaires (WCHL), 1925; Coach, Boston Bruins, 1934–36
AWARDS/HONORS: Hockey Hall of Fame, 1958

Less publicized than his brother, Lester "the Silver Fox" Patrick, Frank was nonetheless as influential in his way. There are 22 pieces of legislation in the NHL rulebook that Frank proposed, including the origination of the blue line.

Frank Patrick was an excellent defenseman, starring first with McGill University and later for the Renfrew Millionaires with Lester.

The Patricks moved west to Nelson, British Columbia, where they began their own league and built arenas for all the teams; how's that for starting from the ground up? They were so successful that they bagged the Stanley Cup in 1915, but they later sold their players to the newly formed NHL.

A Hall of Famer, Frank Patrick later coached the Boston Bruins, managed the Montreal Canadiens, and once was the NHL's supervisor of officials. He died in 1960.

JAMES PATRICK

BORN: Winnipeg, Manitoba, June 14, 1963
POSITION: Defenseman, New York Rangers, 1984–93; Hartford Whalers, 1993–94; Calgary Flames, 1994–98; Buffalo Sabres, 1998–

Considered a prodigy when signed by the Rangers late in the 1983–84 season, James Patrick made an impact the moment he joined the Broadway Blueshirts. The tall, rangy defenseman never became a superstar, but lasted almost two decades playing at a consistently solid level.

For nine seasons Patrick served the Rangers as a defenseman who could play at both ends of the ice. Among the most reliable offensive defensemen in the NHL and always near the top in scoring for blueliners, Patrick registered a minus rating only twice in his Gotham tenure.

Patrick was traded twice during the 1993–94 season, first from New York to Hartford, then later to Calgary, where he would play for four seasons before signing with Buffalo as a free agent in 1998. Patrick tutored a defense-minded team that advanced to the Stanley Cup finals in 1999. Unfortunately, Patrick's overtime shot deflected off the crossbar and out of play during Game Six, which ended with a controversial Cup-winning goal by the Dallas Stars' Brett Hull.

Having played over 1,000 games in the NHL, with considerable consistency, skill, and class, Patrick re-upped with Buffalo for the 2002–03 season.

LESTER PATRICK

BORN: Drummondville, Quebec, December 30, 1883
DIED: June 1, 1960
POSITION: Rover/Defenseman/Goaltender, Westmount (CAHL), 1905; Montreal Wanderers (ECAHA), 1906–07; Renfrew Millionaires (NHA), 1910; Victoria Aristocrats (PCHA), 1912–16, 1919–26; Spokane (PCHA), 1917; Seattle Metropolitans (PCHA), 1918; New York Rangers, 1927–28; Coach, New York Rangers, 1926–39
AWARDS/HONORS: All-Star Coach, 1931–36, 1938; Hockey Hall of Fame, 1945; Trophy for outstanding service to hockey in United States named in his honor in 1966; Division of NHL named in his honor, 1974

No single individual contributed more to the improvement of professional hockey on every level—playing, coaching, managing, and operating—than Lester Patrick. Dubbed "the Silver Fox" because of his shock of gray hair and his uncanny foxiness in dealing with opponents, Lester was born in Drummondville, Quebec. He and his brother Frank moved to Montreal when Lester was ten years old, and it was there that the Silver Fox mastered the game.

Lester Patrick as Rangers manager

Lester could play any position, from goalie to defenseman to rover. The latter position was an integral part of the seven-man game of hockey. A rover could play forward or defense, and Lester did both with equal agility.

When Canadian millionaire Martin J. O'Brien decided to place a National Hockey Association team in Renfrew, Ontario, O'Brien offered the Patricks $3,000 apiece to skate for the new club and they accepted.

Even then, while playing professionally and making a good living, Lester concentrated on the administrative end of the game. His ambition was to operate his own team and his own league, while continuing to play. His dream was realized in 1911 when his father, Joseph Patrick, a millionaire lumberman, retired. With their father's financial support, Lester and Frank organized the Pacific Coast Hockey League.

Their base of operation was Victoria, British Columbia, the most British of all of Canada's cities. Lester had his cake and ate it, too. He not only helped run the PCHL but also played for Victoria, and later Spokane and Seattle before returning to play, coach, and manage in Victoria again, while also operating the league and overseeing its growth. Thus, Lester was at once player, developer, and entrepreneur through the start of the Roaring Twenties. His earliest successes, however, were in Victoria, where he and Frank built Canada's first artificial ice rink, followed by another rink in Vancouver and franchises in Seattle, Spokane, Portland, Victoria, and Vancouver. By 1914, an East-West playoff for the Stanley Cup had begun, and the Patricks had reached the pinnacle in big-league hockey.

In 1924, at the age of 42, Lester coached and managed the Victoria Cougars to a Stanley Cup triumph over the Montreal Canadiens, three games to one. In the same year, NHL franchises were awarded to the Montreal Maroons and the Boston Bruins, and a year later to the Pittsburgh Pirates and New York Americans. Patrick realized he couldn't match the salaries the big-time eastern moguls were offering players. He knew that the time of the Pacific Coast League had ended, so he sold his entire roster to the new owners in the East and planned to retire and move to California.

Then Conn Smythe was fired as Rangers manager and Lester was called. He took the first available train east, and the new era in hockey for New York City had begun.

Patrick labored for 13 seasons behind the Ranger bench, dominating the annual balloting for coach of the year. In fact, from the time that honor was first started in 1930, Patrick was named to the prestigious post seven of the first eight years.

Patrick's finest hour as a coach came during the 1928 Stanley Cup playoffs, when the Rangers were facing the powerhouse Montreal Maroons in the final round. The Montrealers were highly favored in the series and to make matters worse, Madison Square Garden was unavailable to the Blueshirts because of the annual New York appearance of the circus. All the games of the best-of-five series were to be played in the unfriendly Montreal Forum.

The Maroons won the first game, 2–0, and all of Montreal was expecting a workmanlike, three-game Maroon sweep. Undaunted, the Rangers skated out to meet the Maroons in the second game. Early in the second period, with no score on the board, Nels Stewart, a dangerous Maroon forward, broke into the clear and unleashed a whizzing shot that caught the Ranger netminder, Lome Chabot, squarely in the left eye.

With Chabot out of the game, surely now the Rangers were sunk. The gloating Maroons refused the Blueshirts the services of a major-league netminder watching the game from the stands. In typical Patrick fashion, the 44-year-old Silver Fox stepped forward and strapped on the pads.

With the Rangers backchecking like fiends to protect their aging leader, Patrick preserved a 1–1 tie as the game went into sudden-death overtime. After seven nail-biting minutes of the extra frame, Ranger defenseman Ching Johnson whipped a pass to Frank Boucher, who put the puck past the Maroon goalie to win the game and tie the series at one game apiece.

Patrick's heroics in goal became an instant legend as the inspired Rangers rallied to win the Stanley Cup.

With his goaltending days behind him, Patrick continued behind the Ranger bench until 1939, when he was succeeded by Frank Boucher. Patrick remained very much a part of hockey, staying on as general manager of the Rangers until 1946. He died in 1960.

LYNN PATRICK

BORN: Victoria, British Columbia, February 3, 1912
DIED: January 26, 1980
POSITION: Forward, New York Rangers, 1934–46; Coach, New York Rangers, 1949–50; Boston Bruins, 1950–54; Coach/General Manager, Boston Bruins, 1955–65; St. Louis Blues, 1966–67; Executive Vice President, St. Louis Blues, 1967–77
AWARDS/HONORS: NHL First Team All-Star, 1942; NHL Second Team All-Star, 1943; Hockey Hall of Fame, 1980; Lester Patrick Trophy, 1989

No hockey player ever faced more pressure in his major-league debut than Lynn Patrick, the eldest son of hockey patriarch Lester Patrick, manager of the New York Rangers. Lester had managed the Blueshirts ever since the team's inception, but never faced a more difficult decision than during training camp in the fall of 1934, when Lynn seemed ready for the big NHL. Lester sensed that his 22-year-old son was good enough to play left wing, but he was anxious about charges of nepotism. Before making his decision, Lester consulted with two of the Rangers' older players, Bill Cook and Frank Boucher.

"We'd watched Lynn," Boucher recalled, "and told Lester his son had a lot to learn but we believed he'd eventually help us."

Lynn's start was modest, 9 goals and 13 assists in 48 games during his rookie year, but he showed noticeable improvement every season thereafter. In the 1937–38 season, Lynn

played left wing on a line with center Phil Watson and Bryan Hextall, comprising what was to be one of the best lines in NHL history. During the 1941–42 season, Lynn was named First Team All-Star left-winger and helped the Rangers win the Stanley Cup in 1940.

His last big season was 1942–43, before a stint in the armed forces. He returned to the Rangers in 1945–46, but lacked his earlier speed and finally decided to retire. Like his brother Muzz, Lynn turned to coaching and in 1949–50 he directed the Rangers to the Stanley Cup finals, losing to the Red Wings in the second sudden-death overtime period of the seventh game.

A season later, Lynn "jumped" to the Bruins where he continued his success behind the bench. In time, he became Bruins manager and eventually moved to the administrative chambers of the St. Louis Blues in 1967. He began by coaching and managing the Blues before turning over the coaching reins to Scotty Bowman. Thus, Patrick helped launch the most successful run in NHL coaching history.

MUZZ PATRICK

BORN: Victoria, British Columbia, June 28, 1916
DIED: July 23, 1998
POSITION: Defenseman, New York Rangers, 1937–46; Coach, New York Rangers, 1954–55; General Manager, New York Rangers, 1955–64

One of the two hockey-playing sons of former Rangers manager Lester Patrick, "Muzz" was an exceptional athlete who at one time was a six-day bike racer, basketball star, and a heavyweight boxer of repute, not to mention being the first NHL player to enlist in the armed forces at the dawn of World War II. Like his older brother, Lynn, Muzz was under heavy pressure when his father promoted him to the NHL club late in the 1937–38 season. He was 22 years old and huge, but clumsier on skates than Lynn.

Muzz was paired with Art Coulter and the two gave the Rangers one of the game's toughest backline corps. Patrick soon refined his style and also acted as the team's policeman. His classic bout on ice was against Boston Bruins' badman Eddie Shore. It happened when Shore had picked on Rangers center Phil Watson one night at Madison Square Garden. Muzz came to the rescue and wasted Shore with a flurry of punches.

After World War II, Muzz turned to managing hockey clubs in the minors as well as coaching. He returned to New York as coach in 1954–55 and then became Rangers manager in 1955–56, succeeding Frank Boucher. He remained manager until October 1964, when he was pushed "upstairs" at the Garden to make way for Emile Francis, Muzz's former assistant.

MARTY PAVELICH

BORN: Sault Ste. Marie, Ontario, November 6, 1927
POSITION: Left Wing, Detroit Red Wings, 1947–57
AWARDS/HONORS: NHL All-Star Game, 1950, 1952, 1954–55

When the Detroit Red Wings juggernaut ran over the opposition during the early 1950s, Ted Lindsay and Gordie Howe captured most of the headlines among the forwards. But just as vital was defensive forward Marty Pavelich. Wings manager Jack Adams knew it all the time. "Pavelich," said Adams, "was one of the four key men around whom we built our hockey club."

Marty, also known as "Blackie," came to Detroit via the Red Wings' junior affiliate in Galt, Ontario. He played 41 games during the 1947–48 NHL season and remained a Red Wing regular through his final year, 1956–57. During that period, Pavelich played on four Stanley Cup winners. "His scoring records never stood out," said Adams, "but he always had the toughest jobs—checking the great

scoring right wings such as Maurice Richard. We practically had to put handcuffs on him to keep him off the ice."

Following his playing career, Pavelich became a successful businessman and a member of the Hockey Hall of Fame Selection Committee.

MICHAEL PECA

BORN: Toronto, Ontario, March 26, 1974
POSITION: Center, Vancouver Canucks 1994–95; Buffalo Sabres, 1995–2001; New York Islanders, 2001–
AWARDS/HONORS: Franke J. Selke Trophy, 1997, 2002

When the Buffalo Sabres traded Alexander Mogilny to Vancouver in 1995, the package of no-name players they received in return included Michael Peca, Mike Wilson, and a 1995 first-round pick (Jay McKee).

At the time, Peca was no more than a name listed in player transactions. That he became a star is a tribute to the center's perseverance and grim determination.

Within a year of his arrival in Buffalo, the Sabres realized that the perpetual motion performer was an exceptional talent with courage above and beyond the call of duty.

His wide range of assets covered the art of backchecking, as well as scoring, and for several years Peca proved the perspicacity of John Muckler, the Buffalo general manager who acquired him.

Muckler dealt for hungry, inexpensive players, and Peca fit the bill, as Vancouver jumped at the chance to pair Mogilny with chum Pavel Bure. Peca wound up as Buffalo's number two center behind the great Pat LaFontaine.

Mike's second season in Buffalo bore fruit for the Sabres. Shockingly, the gritty young Sabres won the Northeast Division title behind Dominic Hasek's sparkling play in goal. Peca emerged quickly as a leader, dominating defensively on the ice, and netted 20 goals, eight of them shorthanded, to lead the league.

In the ensuing playoffs, with LaFontaine injured, Peca stepped up his game, terrorizing fellow centers Alexei Yashin (Ottawa) and Eric Lindros (Philadelphia). The Selke Trophy, for the NHL's top defensive forward, was Mike's for 1997. He was appropriately named team captain after the concussed LaFontaine was traded to the Rangers in the summer.

By the 1998–99 playoffs, Mike had emerged as the game's best two-way player. With a personal best of 56 regular season points, Peca blossomed in the playoffs as Buffalo reached the finals. Alas, spirits were dampened when Brett Hull's overtime tally in Game Six of the Cup finals sent the Dallas Stars home as the victors.

Peca became a restricted free agent after 1999–2000, but couldn't come to terms with Buffalo general manager Darcy Regier and sat out the entire 2000–01 season, hoping to be traded.

That wish was realized in a grandiose off-season of prosperity for the New York Islanders, as general manager Mike Milbury dealt promising center Tim Connolly and left wing Taylor Pyatt to Buffalo for Peca at the 2001 Entry Draft.

Mike was thrilled at the challenge of helping to restore the once-proud franchise. The Islander organization saw the fearless on-ice leader they craved and the perfect complement to old foe Alexei Yashin, acquired one day earlier. This one-two punch appeared poised to lead the Islanders out of the doldrums, with Peca, as he had done so valiantly in Buffalo, brandishing the captain's "C" on his sweater.

Leading the 96-point Isles to a rebirth with their first playoff since 1994, Peca led the NHL in shorthanded points and established new career highs in goals and points. A borderline-low hip check delivered by Darcy Tucker in Game Five of the Isles' ugly first-round battle with the Toronto Maple Leafs wrecked Peca's anterior cruciate ligament, and his season was finished as the Isles bowed in seven games. Faced with surgery and a lengthy rehabilitation, Peca found small consolation in winning the Selke Trophy for a second time.

PETE PEETERS

BORN: Edmonton, Alberta, August 17, 1957
POSITION: Goaltender, Philadelphia Flyers, 1978–82; Boston Bruins, 1982–85; Washington Capitals, 1985–89; Philadelphia Flyers, 1989–91
AWARDS/HONORS: Vezina Trophy, 1983; NHL First All-Star Team, 1983; NHL All-Star Game, 1980–81, 1983–84

Pete Peeters always will be remembered as the Philadelphia Flyers goalie who gave up a Stanley Cup–winning score. At the peak of his career, in the spring of 1980, after four seasons with the Flyers, Peeters was beaten by Bob Nystrom of the New York Islanders at 7:11 of overtime in Game Six of the finals. A photo of the goal still can be seen in bars and restaurants throughout Long Island.

The photograph was taken on the afternoon of May 24, 1980, at Nassau Coliseum. Two players were shown. One of them was Nystrom of the Islanders and the other was Peeters.

Nystrom had just taken a pass from John Tonelli and deflected the puck off his stick and over the sliding pads of Peeters. The goal won the first Stanley Cup for the Islanders and sent the Flyers packing. But not Peeters. He finished the Stanley Cup round with eight wins against five losses and established a record unbeaten streak of 27 games, the second longest in NHL history by any goalie until that point. (He would later break that mark.)

Peeters's goaltending style was clean and efficient, developed with the Medicine Hat Tigers of the Western (Junior) League and refined with both the Milwaukee Admirals in the International League and Maine Mariners of the American League, whom he helped win a Calder Cup.

Following his noteworthy 1979–80 season, Peeters's next year was a disappointment, as he won just 22, lost 12, and tied 5. This, in addition to a 1982 playoff loss in the first round to the underdog New York Rangers, led to Peeters

being traded to the Boston Bruins for defenseman Brad McCrimmon. For Peeters, the deal
proved a blessing, and in his first season he
went from 3.71 to 2.36 goals-against average
and had eight shutouts.

In 1983, Peeters won the Vezina Trophy,
but the next season he was slipping again.
By 1985–86, his record was 19–26–4 (3.47)
and Peeters was traded to the Washington
Capitals, where his career ranged from
mediocre to excellent. A 1988–89 playoff loss
led Peeters back to Broad Street, where he
ended his pro career in 1991. Peeters later
became goaltending coach of teams such as
the Edmonton Oilers.

GIL PERREAULT

BORN: Victoriaville, Quebec, November 13,
1950
POSITION: Center, Buffalo Sabres, 1970–87
AWARDS/HONORS: Calder Memorial Trophy,
1971; Lady Byng Memorial Trophy, 1973; Team
Canada, 1972; NHL Second Team All-Star,
1976–77; NHL All-Star Game, 1971, 1977–78,
1980, 1984; NHL Challenge Cup All-Star, 1979;
Canada Cup All-Star Team, 1981; Hockey Hall of
Fame, 1990

Hockey is far more than just a sport in the
French-speaking province of Quebec,
Canada. It is more like a religion. Stars such as
Maurice "the Rocket" Richard, Jean Beliveau,
and Bernie "Boom-Boom" Geoffrion have been
worshiped as folk heroes. When Gil Perreault
joined the Buffalo Sabres, it was thought that
the lyrical skater would find a spot on the
distinguished list.

Obviously, it would not be easy for the
six-feet, 195-pound Perreault. One must be
more than merely a point-getter to join such
ranks. Nobody knew that better than Beliveau
himself. "Among French Canadians," said
Beliveau, "there is a lot of pride in our hockey
playing. That has been our game. Now many
eyes are turning to Perreault. There's no doubt

that he can become a great leader and everybody in our province will be proud."

In only four NHL seasons, Perreault won
both the Calder and Lady Byng Trophies and
almost immediately took over as leader of
Buffalo's hockey club. He became an example
of what scoring finesse was all about. "He's
always tempting you to go for the puck," said
Boston superman Bobby Orr. "His head and
shoulders will be going one way and his legs
are going the other way and the puck is doing
something else."

In that sense, Perreault most resembled
Beliveau when Jean was having his finest years
with the Montreal Canadiens. "Like Beliveau,"
said Rangers general manager Emile Francis,
"Gil has all the moves and great range. There's
no way to stop him if he's coming at you
one-on-one."

Perreault's finest season was 1975–76, when
the classy forward scored 44 goals and 113
points, his first of two consecutive Second
Team All-Star selections. When the Sabres
made it to the finals against the Philadelphia
Flyers, Buffalo seemed on the verge of becoming a hockey power. Instead, Gil and his
teammates slacked off each year in playoff
competition, falling to the Pittsburgh Penguins
in the opening round of the 1979 Stanley
Cup games. Gil, however, continued to be the
Sabres' leading scorer.

**Gilbert Perreault (left) with Buffalo coach
George "Punch" Imlach**

His career faded into the 1986–87 season, after which he hung up his skates. A bitter split with Buffalo management left the hero in a state of exile from his one and only NHL club. Eventually, the rift was repaired, and Gil returned to the Sabres alumni in good standing, playing in charity games from time to time.

PIERRE PILOTE

BORN: Kenogami, Quebec, December 11, 1931
POSITION: Defenseman, Chicago Blackhawks, 1955–68; Toronto Maple Leafs, 1968–69
AWARDS/HONORS: NHL Second Team All-Star, 1960–62; James Norris Memorial Trophy, 1963–65; NHL First Team All-Star, 1963–67; Hockey Hall of Fame, 1975

One of the least-heralded of outstanding Chicago players of the 1961 Stanley Cup-winning Blackhawks, Pierre Pilote was a small but tough defenseman.

When the Blackhawks began their ascent from the depths, in the '50s, to respectability in the '60s, Pierre Pilote was in a large part responsible, although teammates Bobby Hull, Stan Mikita, and Glenn Hall received most of the credit.

Pilote was effective defensively and offensively; he could hit and hurt and he could skate well and score. Before retiring after the 1968–69 season, Pilote amassed 80 goals and 418 assists for 498 points in 890 games.

Pierre's credentials include First All-Star Team (five times), Second All-Star Team (three times), Norris Trophy (three), as well as the captaincy of the Blackhawks when they won the Stanley Cup. It was Chicago's last Cup triumph.

During Pilote's later years friction developed between the captain and outspoken stars such as Mikita. As captain, Pierre frequently had to deal with management and was unfairly labeled by some as "a company man." In June 1975, he was elected to the Hall of Fame.

JACQUES PLANTE

BORN: Shawinigan Falls, Quebec, January 17, 1929
DIED: February 26, 1986
POSITION: Goaltender, Montreal Canadiens, 1952–63; New York Rangers, 1963–65; St. Louis Blues, 1968–70; Toronto Maple Leafs, 1970–73; Boston Bruins, 1973; Edmonton Oilers (WHA), 1974–75; Coach, Quebec Nordiques (WHA), 1973–74
AWARDS/HONORS: Hart Memorial Trophy, 1962; Vezina Trophy, 1956–60, 1962, 1969 (shared with Glenn Hall); NHL First Team All-Star, 1956, 1959, 1962; NHL Second Team All-Star, 1957–58, 1960, 1971; NHL All-Star Game, 1956–60, 1962, 1969–70; Hockey Hall of Fame, 1978

The most remarkable of the modern goaltenders, Jacques Plante pioneered the use of a goalie mask after a near-fatal injury at Madison Square Garden on November 1, 1959. Plante was struck in the face by a hard backhand shot fired from the stick of the Rangers' Andy Bathgate. Jacques, who had been experimenting with the mask in practice scrimmages, donned the protector and reappeared on the ice after his wounds were dressed. From then

Jacques Plante as a Ranger, talking to New York reporters

on, with only one exception, he always wore the mask, and soon more and more goalies began using the device.

Nicknamed "Jake the Snake," Plante broke into the NHL with the Canadiens in 1952–53 and starred for Montreal in a critical semifinal playoff round with Chicago in which the Canadiens triumphed. He soon was hailed as a superb goalie and an innovative one at that. A superior skater, Plante frequently would wander from his net to field pucks and relay them to teammates. He starred for the Canadiens until 1963 when he was dealt to the Rangers. In 1968–69, he was traded to St. Louis, where he starred with Glenn Hall. He was a Maple Leaf for two seasons (1970–71 and 1971–72) and two-thirds, being traded to Boston late in the 1972–73 season.

Plante was extremely gifted, but also troublesome in many ways. He was an excellent tutor and helped refine the style of Flyers goalie Bernie Parent when he and Parent played for the Maple Leafs. On the other hand, Plante was notorious as a clubhouse lawyer. This is believed to be the reason he was dealt by Montreal, New York, and St. Louis. He also suffered from asthma and occasionally would change hotels because of severe breathing problems.

Following a weak playoff performance for Boston in April 1973, Plante signed as general manager–coach of the WHA's Quebec Nordiques. He held that position during the 1973–74 season and saw his team finish out of the playoffs. At the age of 45, Jacques returned to active play with the Edmonton Oilers in 1974–75 and appeared to have lost little of the ability that classified him as one of the best goaltenders in hockey history. After 31 games with the Oilers, Plante ended his active playing career and returned to the NHL as a goaltending coach for the Philadelphia Flyers. Jacques later made his home in Europe. He died in 1986, at the age of 57.

LARRY PLEAU

BORN: Lynn, Massachusetts, January 29, 1947
POSITION: Center, U.S. Olympic Team, 1968; Montreal Canadiens, 1969–72; Hartford Whalers (WHA), 1972–79; Coach, Hartford Whalers, 1980–83; 1987–89; General Manager, Hartford Whalers, 1981–83; General Manager of Player Development/Vice President of Player Personnel, New York Rangers, 1989–97; Senior Vice President and General Manager, St. Louis Blues, 1997–

At a time when NHL players were almost always exclusively bred in Canada, Larry Pleau caught the attention of scouts while playing amateur hockey in New England.

Pleau was scouted by the Montreal Canadiens and signed to a contract by the Habs in 1969. That in itself was startling, since the Canadiens generally shunned American-born players. Pleau made his Montreal debut in 1970 and played adequately at the forward position, although he never put up big numbers.

When the World Hockey Association opened for business in October, 1972, Pleau signed with the New England Whalers and remained with the WHA for the remainder of his playing career, until the 1978–79 season.

Part of the Whalers organization for 17 years, Pleau was elevated to general manager after the team merged into the NHL (1979–80) and drafted Hartford stars Ray Ferraro, Ron Francis, Kevin Dineen, and Ulf Samuelsson.

In 1989, Pleau began a developmental role with the New York Rangers organization and helped draft Doug Weight, Sergei Zubov, and Alexei Kovalev, further cementing Larry as an NHL highbrow.

In 1997, Pleau was named general manager of the St. Louis Blues and was directly responsible for reestablishing the organization as a force to be reckoned with in the league, with deft moves for Keith Tkachuk, Dallas Drake, and Doug Weight. Larry was also named associate general manager of the 2002 United States silver medal–winning Olympic team.

BUD POILE

BORN: Fort William, Ontario, February 10, 1924

POSITION: Right Wing, Toronto Maple Leafs, 1942–44, 1945–47; Chicago Blackhawks, 1947–49; Detroit Red Wings, 1949; New York Rangers, 1949–50; Boston Bruins, 1950; General Manager, Philadelphia Flyers, 1967–69; Vancouver Canucks, 1970–74; Vice President, WHA, 1974–77; President, Central Hockey League, 1976–84; President, International Hockey League, 1988–89

AWARDS/HONORS: NHL All-Star Game, 1947–48; NHL Second Team All-Star, 1948; Lester Patrick Trophy, 1989; Hockey Hall of Fame, 1990

Feared by National Hockey League goaltenders because of his hard shot, Norman Robert "Bud" Poile was one of three players from Fort William, Ontario, to make it big with the Toronto Maple Leafs in the mid 1940s. Along with Gus Bodnar and Gaye Stewart, Poile led "the Flying Fort" line in Toronto's march to the Stanley Cup in 1947. However, in the middle of the following season, Poile and his linemates were dealt to the Chicago Blackhawks, along with defenseman Ernie Dickens and Bob Goldham, for Max Bentley and Cy Thomas. Within a year, Poile was dispatched to the Detroit Red Wings, and in 1949–50 moved to the New York Rangers and, finally, the Boston Bruins. His NHL playing career ended in Boston in 1950.

Poile turned to managing and coaching in the minors with considerable success. In 16 years, Bud's teams missed making the playoffs only twice. When the Philadelphia Flyers were admitted to the NHL in 1967, Poile was named general manager of the new club and remained in that position until he was replaced by Keith Allen in December 1969. Poile soon became manager of the Vancouver Canucks, but relinquished the position in 1974 and moved to the World Hockey Association, where he was named vice president and director of Hockey Operations. The hockey executive then brought his know-how to the Central Hockey League in 1977, when he began his duties as president.

Bud remained a part of the hockey world as a member of the Hockey Hall of Fame Selection Committee. Meanwhile, his son, David, became a hockey power player in his own right as general manager with the Washington Capitals and Nashville Predators. When David won the Lester Patrick Trophy (for service to The Game in the United States), Bud was in the audience proudly applauding his son.

DAVID POILE

BORN: Toronto, Ontario, February 14, 1949

POSITION: Assistant General Manager, Atlanta Flames, 1976–81; Vice President/General Manager, Washington Capitals, 1982–97; Executive Vice President of Hockey Operations/General Manager, Nashville Predators, 1997–

AWARDS/HONORS: Lester Patrick Trophy, 2001

If ever there was a successful chip off the old block in the executive realm, it was David Poile, following in the footsteps of his father, Norman "Bud" Poile. The latter had played in the NHL and later was the first general manager of the Philadelphia Flyers, before assuming various roles with an assortment of other hockey organizations.

David broke in with the Atlanta Flames' high command and gradually moved up the ladder. He became general manager of the Washington Capitals in 1982 and proceeded to make one of the best deals in the club's history, obtaining Rod Langway from the Montreal Canadiens just 11 days after taking office.

Before young Poile's arrival in Washington, the Caps had never been to the playoffs. Under his 15 years' tutelage, they made 14 postseason appearances, winning their first Patrick Division title in 1989 and in 1990, the Wales Conference finals.

With a sharp eye for talent, Poile acquired many key Capitals players through the draft (Peter Bondra, Steve Konowalchuk, Sergei Gonchar, Olaf Kolzig, and Jason Allison), as well as through free agency and trades (Bill Ranford, Adam Oates, Rick Tocchet, Dale Hunter, Don Beaupre).

The Caps' record under Poile was 594-454-124, and as a member of the General Managers Committee he was a driving force behind the NHL's adoption of an instant replay rule for the 1991–92 season. His leadership, along with growing prominence in the NHL, led to his being named the 1991–92 *Inside Hockey* Man of the Year.

In the summer of 1997, Poile moved on to build another team, the expansion Nashville Predators. Named executive vice president of hockey operations and general manager, Poile stockpiled the Predators with 15 of the top 76 selections (David Legwand, Scott Hartnell) and made good trades (Kimmo Timmonen, Cliff Ronning) through the 1999–2002 seasons.

In 2001, David Poile, along with commissioner Gary Bettman and legendary coach Scotty Bowman, was the recipient of the Lester Patrick Trophy for contributions to hockey in the United States. David and his father, Bud (1989), are one of six father-son combinations to have won the Lester Patrick award.

SAM POLLOCK

BORN: Montreal, Quebec, December 15, 1925
POSITION: General Manager, Montreal Canadiens, 1964–78

Succeeding Frank Selke Sr. as Canadiens' manager in 1964 was 38-year-old Sam Pollock, who had been director of the Canadiens' farm system since 1958 and thus became the youngest club manager in the NHL. Pollock's credentials were quite sound. He had devoted 19 of his years to hockey management, 17 of them as a full-time employee of the Forum. He was instrumental in developing the Junior Canadiens and led them to the Memorial Cup, emblematic of national supremacy, in 1950. Later, Pollock took a more active role in the actual manipulating of players on the NHL Canadiens and helped negotiate the famed Lorne Worsley–Jacques Plante deal, sending Plante to the Rangers for Worsley.

Pollock knew what he wanted, and he was going to run Les Canadiens his way. Thus, having Selke around would soon prove to be an embarrassment and an irrelevancy until the elder statesman finally moved gracefully into the background. Pollock then peddled off enough fringe talent to enable Les Canadiens to retain the nucleus of a future winner and they entered the 1967–68 season as strong as possible.

In a matter of four years, Pollock had completely overshadowed his predecessor, and was hailed as the most successful manager in modern hockey. Actually, Selke was the brainier boss and better builder, while Pollock mainly inherited the system and techniques of Selke's genius.

The Canadiens underwent an ownership change in the late 1970s and although Pollock's club had just won four straight Stanley Cups, Sam was replaced by Irving Grundman, unknown in hockey circles.

Pollock remained active on several fronts, but never returned as an NHL leader.

DENIS POTVIN

BORN: Ottawa, Ontario, October 29, 1953
POSITION: Defenseman, New York Islanders, 1973–88
AWARDS/HONORS: Calder Memorial Trophy, 1974; Norris Trophy, 1976, 1978–79; NHL First Team All-Star, 1975–76, 1978–79, 1981; NHL Second Team All-Star, 1977, 1984; NHL Challenge Cup All-Star, 1979; NHL All-Star Game, 1974–78, 1981, 1983–84, 1988; Hockey Hall of Fame, 1991

Along with Bobby Orr, Larry Robinson, Red Kelly, and Serge Savard, Denis Potvin ranked among the foremost defensemen of the modern era.

He could play offense with the best of them. His bodychecking was scary to opponents, and his knowledge of the game nonpareil. If not for the fact that his coach, Al Arbour, demanded that Potvin concentrate as much on defense as he did on attack, Denis's point totals would have reached record-breaking levels.

"Potvin was the foundation of our Stanley Cup–winning teams," said Bill Torrey, the general manager who drafted him in 1973.

Potvin's early press notices heralded him as another Bobby Orr. "I'm not Bobby Orr and I know it," he said while en route to his Calder Trophy–winning 1974 season. "You can't compare us anyway because our styles are different. I can't skate as well as Bobby, but I feel there are a couple of other things I do better—like hitting. That's a big part of my game. I just hope I can accomplish some of the things Bobby has done."

As Orr's career came to a close, Potvin began compiling the impressive accomplishments for which he had hoped. A perennial All-Star following his rookie season, Denis was voted the NHL's best defenseman in 1976, 1978, and 1979, when he was awarded the Norris Trophy. Older brother Jean also was an Islanders defenseman.

Potvin's defensive abilities were overshadowed by his scoring feats. After falling just a few points short for three consecutive years, the Islander blueliner finally eclipsed the 100-point mark in 1979, becoming the second defenseman in NHL history to reach the plateau at that time. Potvin was also only the second defenseman to score over 30 goals in a season, a feat he accomplished three times.

In the view of some critics, Potvin was the most complete defenseman of the post-Expansion era, and a primary leader—as captain—of Islander teams that won four Stanley Cups from 1980 through 1983.

Following the 1987–88 season, Potvin finally retired. Though he was eventually passed on the all-time defenseman's scoring list by the longer careers of Ray Bourque, Paul Coffey, Larry Murphy, Phil Housley, and Al MacInnis, Denis briefly passed Orr for the all-time lead with an eye-popping 310 goals and 742 assists over 16 seasons. Denis and Mike Bossy were the first Islanders to be inducted into the Hockey Hall of Fame in 1991. He stayed on the hockey scene in various capacities, eventually becoming a television analyst.

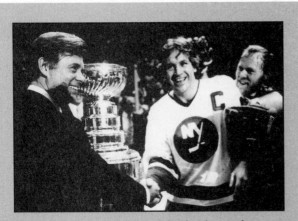

Denis Potvin (center), the Islanders' captain, shakes the hand of NHL president John Zeigler with Butch Goring in the background

FELIX POTVIN

BORN: Anjou, Quebec, June 23, 1971
POSITION: Goaltender, Toronto Maple Leafs, 1991–99; New York Islanders, 1999; Vancouver Canucks, 1999–2001; Los Angeles Kings, 2001–
AWARDS/HONORS: NHL All-Rookie Team, 1993; NHL All-Star Game, 1994, 1996

There have been occasions when goaltenders enjoyed too much success too soon.

Jim Carey is one example and Blaine Lacher another, not to mention Mike Moffet, Jack Gelineau, and other goalies who came and went faster than you can say Georges Vezina.

One might legitimately wonder whether Felix Potvin suffered from the too-much-too-soon affliction.

This much is certain: Felix became an overnight sensation in Toronto; so good, in fact, that he displaced future Hall of Famer Grant Fuhr from the number one goaltending slot on the Maple Leafs.

An even more astonishing aspect of the Potvin saga was the rapidity of his rise. He was a second-round selection, 31st overall, in the 1990 Entry Draft after being virtually overlooked by most NHL clubs.

Potvin demonstrated his verve with kick saves, glove saves, butterflies, and a brand of confidence that was transmitted throughout the lineup. In a powerful show of force, the Leafs defeated the Detroit Red Wings and St. Louis Blues to sweep the Conference playoffs. Then they extended the Wayne Gretzky–led Los Angeles Kings to seven games before The Great One, himself, deposited the winner behind The Cat.

By the end of the 1995–96 season, The Cat was numbered among the NHL elite goaltenders. More importantly, he seemed immune to pressure.

By the start of the 1996–97 season, Potvin had a lucrative new contract and 104 regular season wins, tied for fifth on the Leafs' all-time list. His 25 playoff victories put him third on the Toronto chart. The Cat entered the 1997–98 season with a new boss, Ken Dryden, a Hall of Fame goaltender and president of Maple Leaf Gardens. Dryden's Argus eye for netminding was focused on Potvin, and Dryden was less impressed with what he saw than others. Felix was traded to the New York Islanders, for Bryan Berard, where he stayed for a year, and then Vancouver, whereupon he was traded in midseason to Los Angeles.

After failing miserably to catch a regular stint with the Vancouver Canucks in 2000–01, it may have seemed as though he was a legend fading. Incredibly, Felix went on a rebirthing stretch drive later that year in Los Angeles and seized the spot as the Kings' top goalie with a 13–5–5 record and miniscule 1.96 goals-against average. The Kings would upset the Detroit Red Wings in the first round of that spring's postseason pair-offs, but lost to the eventual Cup-champion Colorado Avalanche in seven games, and then repeated the pattern against the Avs in the 2002 playoffs.

DAVE POULIN

BORN: Timmins, Ontario, December 17, 1958
POSITION: Center, Philadelphia Flyers, 1982–90; Boston Bruins, 1990–93; Washington Capitals, 1993–95
AWARDS/HONORS: Frank J. Selke Trophy, 1987; NHL All-Star Game, 1986 and 1988; King Clancy Memorial Trophy, 1993

Dave Poulin arrived on Broad Street in 1982, when Bobby Clarke was winding down his illustrious career, and enjoyed one of those rare metamorposes from unknown to star in a rather short time.

Poulin had no thoughts about playing in the NHL but rather wanted to concentrate on a college education. NHL scouts were not especially interested in him because he was considered too small at the time. He graduated from Notre Dame with a business degree after playing four years of college hockey. Clearly, he was getting the ice bug, so he jetted to Sweden and played for Vaxco H.C., coached by Ted Sator, who would figure prominently in Dave's future.

As soon as Sator took over as Flyers coach, he invited Poulin to training camp, and in no time at all, Dave made the same kind of impression he continued to make throughout his playing career. Never a three-digit scorer, Poulin played both ends of the ice. In 1984–85, he finished with a plus-43 in the plus/minus ratings and two years later was plus-47.

The Poulin years in Philadelphia never produced a Stanley Cup but there were a couple of trips to the finals. Midway through the 1989–90 season, he was traded to Boston for Ken Linseman. During the 1990 playoffs, as a Bruin, he played in 18 postseason games and went 8-5-13. He remained a Bruin until the conclusion of the 1992–93 season and signed as a free agent with Washington on August 3, 1993. It was a disappointing conclusion to a distinguished NHL life. Dave managed only 29 games with the Capitals and put only 9 points, including 4 goals, on the board. After that he called it a career.

Rather appropriately, Poulin went from the NHL back to the collegiate ranks and eventually emerged as head coach of Notre Dame, where he was regarded as one of the best collegiate coaches in North America.

EDDIE POWERS

BORN: Toronto, Ontario, August 24, 1917
POSITION: Referee, NHL, 1956–63

One of the most respected and forceful referees the National Hockey League has known, Eddie Powers officiated in the majors from 1956 to 1963, when he quit, following a long history of conflict with his bosses, the owners. Powers objected to interference from referee-in-chief Carl Voss, who would relay messages from NHL president Clarence Campbell. "A referee would call a game in a certain way in the first period," complained Powers, "and then the next thing that would happen is he'd get a visit in the dressing room and be told he's calling it too close. Another time he'd let everything go and be told he's not calling it close enough." Because of his forthright position, Powers was unofficially blackballed by several major-league officials. He returned to private life in Toronto, respected by those who recalled his courage and ability, but ignored by the league that he helped so much by his presence.

BABE PRATT

BORN: Stony Mountain, Manitoba, January 7, 1916
DIED: December 16, 1998
POSITION: Defenseman, New York Rangers, 1935–42; Toronto Maple Leafs, 1942–46; Boston Bruins, 1946–47
AWARDS/HONORS: Hart Memorial Trophy, 1944; NHL First Team All-Star, 1944; NHL Second Team All-Star, 1945; Hockey Hall of Fame, 1966

The ideal successor to New York Rangers defensive legend Ching Johnson, when the blueline workhorse reached the end of his career, Babe Pratt had a lovable disposition when he wasn't flattening the foe. He replaced Ching during the 1937 playoffs against Toronto and made headlines by scoring

Walter "Babe" Pratt as a Toronto defenseman

the winning goal in the deciding game. Babe remained a Ranger for seven years, starring on the 1940 Cup winners and for the 1942 winners of the Prince of Wales Trophy. The next year he was dealt to Toronto, where he continued to excel, scoring the Cup-winning goal for Toronto in Game Seven of the 1945 Stanley Cup finals against Detroit.

Pratt was always good for a laugh, whether on the giving or receiving end of a joke. When Babe reported to training camp in September 1940, he was full of ginger, and he didn't slow down as the Rangers embarked on their usual exhibition tour. One night he checked into the team's Pullman car at 3 A.M., only to discover that Lester Patrick was waiting. "Babe," said Patrick, "I'm fining you $1,000. But if you don't take another drink for the rest of the campaign, I'll refund your money at the end of the season."

Pratt went on the wagon and the Rangers went on a long, long losing streak. Patrick was worried and, one day, suggested to Babe that maybe a drink wouldn't hurt after all. "No, no," said Pratt, "my word is my bond." Word of the Patrick-Pratt meeting leaked to the players. They figured that if Babe didn't get off the wagon the club would really be in trouble. They told Pratt they would chip in and raise $1,000 if only he would have an occasional drink or two. But Pratt was adamant. The Rangers wound up in fourth place and were knocked out of the playoffs by Detroit. "There's a moral to that story," Pratt said years later, "but I've been trying for thirty years and still haven't been able to figure it out."

The Babe and Lester didn't always get along, especially when money was the subject. According to Pratt, Patrick wasn't tight with money, "He was adjacent to it!" Lester finally traded Babe to Toronto in 1942, and to Pratt's astonishment he was paid more by the Leafs than Lester ever paid him. As a result, he began to play even better. When Lester found out about Pratt's good fortune, he asked Babe about it. "Lester," Pratt explained, "now I'm being paid enough to eat. I'm finally getting the wrinkles out of my belly!"

In time, he became a spokesman for the NHL's Vancouver Canucks and a popular after-dinner speaker. Pratt once asked for

questions from the audience after addressing a banquet.

"How many goals a season would Cyclone Taylor score in today's watered-down NHL?" somebody asked.

"Seven or eight," Pratt replied.

"How can you say that?" the man cried. "Taylor was one of the greatest players who ever lived."

"Certainly," Pratt said, "but you must remember the man is ninety years old."

DEAN PRENTICE

BORN: Schumacher, Ontario, October 5, 1932
POSITION: Left Wing, New York Rangers, 1952–62; Boston Bruins, 1962–66; Detroit Red Wings, 1966–69; Pittsburgh Penguins, 1969–71; Minnesota North Stars, 1971–74
AWARDS/HONORS: NHL Second Team All-Star, 1960; NHL All-Star Game, 1957, 1961, 1963, 1970

One of the most underrated skaters in modern National Hockey League history, Dean Prentice broke in with the Rangers in 1952–53 and skated for five NHL teams until his retirement after the 1973–74 season. Dean's best years were spent in New York in the late 1950s, working left wing on a line with center Larry Popein, later Earl Ingarfield, and right-winger Andy Bathgate. Prior to the 1962–63 season, Prentice was dealt to the Boston Bruins and remained in Beantown through the 1965–66 campaign. He skated for the Detroit Red Wings for the next four seasons and split his final years between the Pittsburgh Penguins and the Minnesota North Stars. Prentice, who never spent a minute in the minors as a player, became coach of the American League New Haven Nighthawks in 1974–75. Under his baton, the Nighthawks finished last in the North Division. An active member of the Federation of Christian Athletes, Prentice spent considerable time addressing church groups.

He was suggested to the Hockey Hall of Fame for membership, but inevitably missed winning nomination by a few votes. That's the definition of underrated! In New York, he was remembered as a clean, hard, very good left wing.

JOE PRIMEAU

BORN: Lindsay, Ontario, January 29, 1906
DIED: May 14, 1989
POSITION: Center, Toronto Maple Leafs, 1928–36
AWARDS/HONORS: Lady Byng Memorial Trophy, 1932; NHL Second Team All-Star, 1934; Hockey Hall of Fame, 1963

Few opponents ever got the better of Montreal immortal Howie Morenz when Howie was in his prime. Joe Primeau, the crack Toronto center, did just that one night when Les Canadiens and the Maple Leafs were locked in a Christmas Eve match. The teams were tied, 1–1, after regulation time and nobody scored in overtime.

Joe "Gentleman Joe" Primeau, who coached Memorial Cup, Allan Cup, and Stanley Cup champions

When the siren sounded to end the game, both clubs headed for the dressing room until they were halted by the referee. Apparently the timekeeper had erred by ten seconds and the referee ordered the players back to the ice to play out the remaining unused time.

This act of recall nettled Morenz, who was anxious to get home to his family. Before the referee dropped the puck, Howie urged Primeau not to touch it after it hit the ice; that way the ten seconds would be squandered and everybody could quit for the night. Primeau understood Howie's point, but had no intentions of complying. Once the puck hit the ice the Leaf center slapped it to the left side, where his winger, Busher Jackson, gathered it in and roared toward the Montreal goal. His shot fooled goalie George Hainsworth and Toronto won the game, 2–1.

This necessitated another face-off and now Morenz was furious. He glared at Primeau as they went through the ritual of the last face-off and then told him in no uncertain terms that he would get even, which he did less than a week later when the teams clashed again. Nobody could touch Howie for the three periods of regulation time, but he, in turn, couldn't get the puck past the Leaf goalie.

At last, the teams went into overtime and Morenz took possession of the puck immediately after the opening face-off. Bobbing and weaving through the Leaf defense, Howie worked his way right up to the goalmouth before depositing the puck where it belonged. Primeau, who was known as "Gentleman Joe," recalled that Morenz never said a word to him after scoring. "He had promised to get his revenge," said Primeau, "and he did. There was nothing more to say." Primeau remained the ace center on Toronto's Kid Line with Busher Jackson and Charlie Conacher.

Known for his artistry and clean play, Primeau was one of Toronto's all-time favorite players. He later coached teams to Canada's Memorial Cup championship as well as the Allan Cup, and, in 1951, the Stanley Cup while behind the Leafs' bench. It marked a remarkable triple parlay.

KEITH PRIMEAU

BORN: Toronto, Ontario, November 24, 1971
POSITION: Center, Detroit Red Wings, 1990–96; Hartford Whalers, 1996–97; Carolina Hurricanes, 1997–99; Philadelphia Flyers, 1999–
AWARDS/HONORS: NHL All-Star Game, 1999

In the 1995 Stanley Cup finals, the Detroit Red Wings were favored to defeat the New Jersey Devils rather easily. Instead, the underdogs swept the favorites in four straight games. Analysts immediately declared that the Red Wings' demise was directly linked to the fact that Detroit's star forward Keith Primeau was sidelined throughout with an injury.

Primeau was then regarded as one of the more promising young power forwards and eventually would fulfill most of those predictions, although his career would be marked with controversy.

Despite the Red Wings' hopes, Primeau did not fulfill their expectations and was traded to Hartford for the 1996–97 season, then moved with the team to Carolina. After two seasons, Keith engaged in a long contract battle with management, solved only when the Hurricanes dealt Primeau to the Flyers.

Philadelphia would prove to be a good fit. In the 1999–2000 season, Primeau entered his first Stanley Cup playoffs with the Flyers, recording an assist in his first game versus Buffalo (April 13, 2002) and a goal five days later at Buffalo. Keith also scored the game-winning goal in the five-overtime Game Four of the Eastern Conference semifinals at Pittsburgh (May 4, 2000).

The next season, 2000–01, Keith won the Yanick Dupre Class Guy Memorial Award as the Flyer who best illustrates character, dignity, and respect for the sport both on and off the ice. During this season, Primeau led the Flyers in goals (34), power-play goals (11), and in shooting percentage (20.6 percent, 34 goals on 165 shots), which was second in the entire NHL.

With Jeremy Roenick and Jiri Dopita on board in 2001–02, the Flyers were loaded for a Stanley Cup run. But Primeau had considerable trouble scoring, although his defensive game shone. The team hobbled into the playoffs and came out the losers of their first-round series against the Ottawa Senators. Primeau publicly aired the team's problems concerning coach Bill Barber's methods following elimination, and the 2001 Jack Adams Award–winning coach was fired two days later.

BOB PROBERT

BORN: Windsor, Ontario, June 5, 1965
POSITION: Left Wing, Detroit Red Wings, 1985–94; Chicago Blackhawks, 1995–
AWARDS/HONORS: NHL All-Star Game, 1988

Mention Bob Probert to the average hockey fan and the name conjures up the image of brawling and assorted other forms of intimidation that go with the violent side of hockey.

For good reason: From 1985–86 to 1994–95, Probert ranked as the heavyweight champion of the NHL.

His IQ—as in Intimidation Quotient—ranked among the NHL's highest. But any opposition goaltender from that era will confirm that Probert also was a major offensive threat. This he proved in 1987–88, when he tallied 29 goals and 33 assists to go along with 398 penalty minutes—all career highs. Probert was also capable of those numbers when it mattered most, in the playoffs. That same year, Probert scored 21 points (8 goals, 13 assists) in 16 playoff games, along with 51 penalty minutes. Pretty impressive for an NHL bad boy.

No matter how adequate the number of goals and assists, the number of punches Probert threw over the years, particularly as a Red Wing, remained his most impressive stats. And if Probert was remembered for any of his legendary fights, it would be those with long-time nemesis Tie Domi.

Probert's bouts were innumerable until his Detroit career ended in 1994. He signed as a free agent with Chicago. Although he had lost some speed, Probert remained an effective enforcer with the Hawks through the 2001–02 season.

CHRIS PRONGER

BORN: Dryden, Ontario, October 10, 1974
POSITION: Defenseman, Hartford Whalers, 1993–95; St. Louis Blues, 1995–
AWARDS/HONORS: James Norris Memorial Trophy, 2000; Hart Memorial Trophy, 2000; Bud Ice Plus/Minus Award, 1998; NHL All-Rookie Team, 1994; NHL First Team All-Star, 2000; NHL Second Team All-Star, 1998; NHL All-Star Game, 1999–2002

When Chris Pronger originally was drafted (first round, second overall) in 1993 by then Hartford Whalers general manager Brian Burke, the tall defenseman was projected as a superstar in the mold of Hall of Famer Larry Robinson.

Instead, Pronger's immaturity disenchanted the Whalers management. After two seasons in Hartford, Chris was dealt to the St. Louis Blues for Brendan Shanahan on July 27, 1995.

The move proved a blessing to both Pronger and the Blues. Teamed with the veteran Al MacInnis, Pronger matured as a player and a person and began using his six-feet, five inches and 220 pounds to total advantage. MacInnis served as an inspiration to Pronger, who as a youth once had a poster of MacInnis in his bedroom.

Pronger continued to improve and was named captain of the Blues in 1997, as he finished first in the NHL in plus/minus (plus-47). He played for Team Canada in the 1998 Winter Olympics. He did it again four years later at Salt Lake City, helping Canada earn its first gold medal in over 40 years.

The 1999–2000 season proved to be especially fruitful for Pronger, whose average ice time per game was 29.26 minutes. We won the Norris Trophy and the Hart Trophy in the same season. Pronger also led the NHL in plus/minus with a plus-52. He finished third on the Blues in points (62) and first in assists (48), establishing career highs in each.

Pronger was an all-star in 1999, 2000, 2001, and 2002. By the 2001–02 season, he ranked ninth in the NHL in points by a defenseman (226), and led his St. Louis team to a five-game, first-round victory over the Blackhawks in the 2001–02 playoffs. But Pronger was injured in round two and St. Louis was swiftly eliminated by Detroit thereafter.

JEAN PRONOVOST

BORN: Shawinigan Falls, Quebec, December 18, 1945
POSITION: Right Wing, Pittsburgh Penguins, 1968–78; Atlanta Flames, 1978–80; Washington Capitals, 1980–82
AWARDS/HONORS: NHL All-Star Game, 1975–78

Jean Pronovost was first or second in almost every offensive category for the Pittsburgh Penguins when the Pens' 1978 housecleaning saw him swept off to Atlanta.

The usually soft-spoken Pronovost left Pittsburgh after an outburst in which he accused the Penguins of "a country club atmosphere." He maintained that he "started with Pittsburgh and this team was a loser and it's still a loser."

Brother of one-time Detroit Red Wings all-star defenseman Marcel Pronovost, Jean's assets were speed and a shot potent enough to net him 52 goals in the 1975–76 season for the Pens. This was not a fluke. In other seasons with the Pens, he scored 43, and reached the 40-goal mark twice more.

After more than a decade, he concluded his NHL career in 1981–82 with the Washington Capitals and then did a short stint in the minors.

MARCEL PRONOVOST

BORN: Shawinigan Falls, Quebec, June 15, 1930
POSITION: Defenseman, Detroit Red Wings, 1950–65; Toronto Maple Leafs, 1965–70
AWARDS/HONORS: NHL First Team All-Star, 1960–61; NHL Second Team All-Star, 1958–59; NHL All-Star Game, 1950, 1954–55, 1957–59, 1963, 1965, 1968; Hockey Hall of Fame, 1978

Of all modern hockey players, Marcel Pronovost had the best claim to an unofficial trophy for the most injured man in hockey.

Episodes of Marcel's derring-do were legend around NHL rinks. He broke into big-league hockey with Detroit in the Stanley Cup play-offs of 1950 and was around to play a few games for the Toronto Maple Leafs in the 1969–70 season. In between, he collected hundreds of stitches and innumerable broken bones. Once, in a game against the Chicago Black Hawks, Marcel sped across the blue line as two husky Chicago defensemen dug their skates into the ice, awaiting his arrival. They dared Pronovost to pass.

"I decided there was only one move," said Marcel. "Bust through the middle." Even the most ironfisted hockey players shudder at the thought of crashing a defense, but Pronovost wasn't thinking about getting hurt. He never did. He eyed the two-foot space between the Hawks, boldly pushed the puck ahead, and leaped at the opening.

Too late. The crouched defensemen slammed the gate, hurling Pronovost headfirst over their shoulders. In that split second of imminent danger—when even the strongest of men would have shut their eyes—Marcel looked down and saw the puck below him. He swiped at it, missed, and had to settle for a three-point landing on his left eyebrow, nose, and cheek.

A few minutes later the doctor was applying ice packs to Pronovost's forehead as he lay on the dressing room table. Marcel's skull looked as if it had been the loser in a bout with a bulldozer. His nose was broken and listed heavily toward starboard. His eyebrow required 25 stitches. "And my cheekbones," Marcel recalled in his deep tone, "felt as if they were pulverized." He was right; they were cracked like little pieces of china.

"What hurt most," says Pronovost, whose face became as craggy as an alpine peak, "was that I had to miss the next two games. As for the injuries, I didn't think twice about them." Marcel always regarded his misfortunes casually. "To me," he says, "accidents are as common as lacing on skates. One of the prizes of my collection of injuries is a break of the fourth dorsal vertebra." In 1959, after Pronovost had broken his beak for the 13th time, he examined it with the air of a true connoisseur and said, "Frankly, I was disappointed. After a few towels were put on I could see out of both eyes. The first time I broke my nose in a hockey game, my eyes were swollen shut for three days."

He played for two decades, always underrated, but one of the most versatile defensemen of all time. Marcel retired in 1969–70, then began a coaching career that brought him to the NHL in 1977 with the Buffalo Sabres. He was the Red Wings' assistant coach for part of 1979–80 through 1980–81. In the late 1980s, he was hired to scout for the New Jersey Devils and remained in that post through the 2001–02 season.

CLAUDE PROVOST

BORN: Montreal, Quebec, September 17, 1933
DIED: April 17, 1984
POSITION: Right Wing, Montreal Canadiens, 1955–69
AWARDS/HONORS: Bill Masterton Memorial Trophy, 1968; NHL First Team All-Star, 1965; NHL All-Star Game, 1956–65, 1967

One of two "lantern-jawed" skaters in big-league hockey, the other being Jack Evans, Claude Provost skated for years in the shadows of more famous Montreal Canadiens while doing key legwork as a checker and penalty killer. In many ways, Provost was as vital to the Montreal machine during his career as were Maurice Richard and Jean Beliveau. Provost shadowed aces such as Bobby Hull, but did it with a gentility and efficiency that bespoke the ultimate in fair play. A genial sort, he culminated his career by winning the Masterton Trophy for good sportsmanship in 1968. During his 1,005 games, he scored 254 goals, 335 assists, and 589 points while accumulating only 469 minutes in penalties. His other unique quality was his legs-wide-apart skating style which led one observer to note that, "When Provost skates, he looks like a drunken sailor walking the deck during a hurricane."

BOB PULFORD

BORN: Newton Robinson, Ontario, March 31, 1936
POSITION: Center, Toronto Maple Leafs, 1956–70; Los Angeles Kings, 1971–72; Coach, Los Angeles Kings, 1972–77; Chicago Blackhawks, 1977–79; General Manager, Chicago Blackhawks, 1977–97, 1999
AWARDS/HONORS: Jack Adams Award, 1975; NHL All-Star Game, 1960, 1962–64, 1968; Hockey Hall of Fame, 1991

Bob Pulford, a classy, two-way centerman, labored for 16 seasons in the National Hockey League with the Toronto Maple Leafs and later the Los Angeles Kings.

Never a flamboyant player in the "superstar" category, Pulford quietly and efficiently got the job done, taking a regular shift, skating on the power play, and killing penalties.

He was a pivotal figure on coach Punch Imlach's Maple Leaf team that won three consecutive Stanley Cups from 1961–62 through 1963–64, and again in 1966–67. He was on the Leafs' all-time top ten list of goals, assists, points, and games. He was traded to the Los Angeles Kings in 1970, playing three seasons in Tinseltown.

Pulford graduated into the management ranks after his active playing career ended in 1972, by retiring as the Kings' captain and stepping right into their coaching post. After Bob molded the Beverly Hills squad into one of the finest defensive units in the league and made them serious contenders, Pulford took over as general manager–coach of the Chicago Blackhawks in 1977, and won the Smythe Division, but gave up coaching duties two years later to devote himself to managing.

The first NHL Players' Association president, Bob later would move to the management side for good. He was appointed Blackhawks senior vice president by owner Bill Wirtz in 1990.

His 20 productive seasons as the Blackhawks general manager were an enviable run considering the number of teams that occupied the league by 2000; his Hawks made the playoffs every season. Pulford stepped down as general manager in 1997 and turned the franchise over to Bob Murray, then Mike Smith in 2000. He was elected to the Hockey Hall of Fame in 1991.

HARVEY PULFORD

BORN: Toronto, Ontario, 1875
DIED: October 31, 1940
POSITION: Defenseman, Ottawa Silver Seven (AHA, CAHL, ECAHA), 1894–1908
AWARDS/HONORS: Hockey Hall of Fame, 1945

Harvey Pulford, a Hall of Famer who labored for Ottawa's ice men for his entire 14-year career, was considered a masterful defensive defenseman.

Although only faded, yellowing newspaper accounts of the day remain to determine what style of player Pulford was, his career statistics illustrate that he was a pure defender who left the scoring chores to the forwards and rarely ventured past his opponent's blue line.

Not surprisingly, it took Harvey seven full seasons before registering his first big-league goal. His lack of scoring punch didn't seem to bother his Ottawa squad though, because Pulford was a regular through most of his career, captaining the great turn-of-the-century Silver Seven teams to three consecutive Stanley Cups.

In the twilight of Pulford's career, he was paired on defense with a brash youngster named Fred "Cyclone" Taylor. Taylor earned his nickname via his whirlwind, rink-length rushes—the exact opposite of his linemate's conservative play. A dramatic illustration of the two contrasting defensive philosophies came in Taylor's rookie campaign when he scored eight goals, equaling Pulford's entire career output!

JEAN PUSIE

BORN: Montreal, Quebec, October 15, 1910
DIED: April 21, 1956
POSITION: Defenseman, Montreal Canadiens, 1931–32, 1935–36; New York Rangers, 1933–34; Boston Bruins, 1934–35

A husky French-Canadian defenseman with an immense ego and a low-comedy accent, Pusie made his debut in the autumn of 1930 at the Montreal Canadiens' training camp. Coach Cecil Hart was startled when the 20-year-old rookie entered his office, introduced himself, vigorously pumped his hand, and declared: "Meestair 'art. Pewsee weel be zee greatess. Heet's 'ockey playairs like me dat weel make dis game pop-u-lair."

Hart admired the youngster's office exuberance, but he detected two serious flaws in his playing technique. Fusie's heavy shot worked only when he had ample time to lower his head for a protracted windup, and when Jean Baptiste skated, his eyes remained dangerously and blindly glued to the puck.

Hart was unimpressed; thus Pusie was depressed when he joined the London (Ontario) Tecumsehs of the International League, but confident that he would yet be an NHL star. "I weel show dem," he assured coach Clem Loughlin. "Dey make beeg mistake."

In his first home game, Pusie was fed a lead pass and broke into the clear. This was a perfect opportunity for Jean Baptiste to fire his unusual shot. He wound up in the classic style and hit the puck so hard it yanked the goalie's mitt from his hand. Both puck and glove sailed into the net.

Before the goalie could move, Pusie dived into the cage, retrieved the glove and presented it to the goaltender with a low bow. He held his opponent's bare hand up to the crowd, carefully counted the fingers and said: "Dey are all dere. You are luck-Y." He replaced the glove and patted the goalie on the back.

Pusie went on to ever greater shenanigans, but never cracked the majors, gaining trials with the New York Rangers, Boston Bruins, and the Canadiens, but failing to produce more than startled laughter at his crazed antics.

The rather sad end of Jean Baptiste Pusie was symbolized one night as he played for St. Louis in the American Association. Pusie found himself stranded on the blue line, the lone defenseman confronted by a four-man rush. He looked pleadingly at the crowd, gazed at the onrushing skaters, and executed a play which had never been seen in hockey before.

"He dropped his stick," recalled Jack Riley, an executive with the Pittsburgh Penguins, "lifted his hands in surrender, and fell to his knees. When the skaters had almost reached him, he buried his face in his gloves." The opponents skated easily past the ostrichlike form of Pusie and scored.

Pusie retired from hockey in 1942 and died of a heart attack in Montreal on April 23, 1956.

BILL QUACKENBUSH

BORN: Toronto, Ontario, March 2, 1922
POSITION: Defenseman, Detroit Red Wings, 1942–49; Boston Bruins, 1949–56
AWARDS/HONORS: Lady Byng Memorial Trophy, 1949; NHL First Team All-Star, 1948–49, 1951; NHL Second Team All-Star, 1947, 1953; NHL All-Star Game, 1947–54; Hockey Hall of Fame, 1976

Arguably the stupidest trade ever made for the most inane reason resulted in the Detroit Red Wings losing a Hall of Fame defenseman in the prime of his career.

The defenseman was Hubert George "Bill" Quackenbush and the reason he was traded was because he won the Lady Byng Trophy for good sportsmanship and high quality play.

Macho-minded Red Wings general manager Jack Adams considered the Lady Byng award a badge of dishonor and supposedly said, "Any player who wins the Lady Byng doesn't belong on my club."

Apparently Adams meant it, because he promptly dispatched Quackenbush to Boston, along with Pete Horeck, for Pete Babando, Clare Martin, Lloyd Durham, and Jim Peters.

Quackenbush never won another Lady Byng Trophy but spent the second half of his career with Boston playing as splendidly as he had the first half with Detroit.

Although he made his debut during the 1942–43 National Hockey League season, it wasn't until 1943–44 that Bill established himself as a regular in the Motor City.

Although the temptation to join the brawlers always was quite apparent, Quackenbush resisted the lure and played a pure defense. In so doing, he made a greater impact on the game than some of his more violent teammates.

More than anything, Quackenbush was an extraordinary practitioner of his art. He was named to the National Hockey League's First All-Star Team in 1948, 1949, and 1951 during an era when the NHL was oozing with top-notch backliners. Bill made the Second Team in 1947 and 1953.

It is a measure of the influence of Quackenbush that some hockey writers have over the years suggested that the NHL name a trophy in his honor to be given to the league's best defensive defenseman.

Along with winning the Lady Byng Trophy in 1949—quite an accomplishment for a defenseman—he once went a span of 137 games (over three different seasons) without taking a penalty.

Quackenbush played on the Red Wings' 1943 Stanley Cup–winning team and played on two first-place teams. When the Red Wings finished first at the conclusion of the 1948–49 season there was no hint Bill would be traded, but Adams stunned the hockey world by dealing Bill to the Boston Bruins.

At the conclusion of the 1955–56 season, Quakenbush hung up his skates for good, opting to return to school, attending

Bill Quackenbush as a Red Wing

Northeastern University in Massachusetts at night while working as a manufacturer's agent during the day. He also raised three sons after retiring from the NHL, while at the same time earning an associate's degree in engineering. Missing the game, he talked Northeastern coach Herb Gallagher into giving him an assistant coach's role with the varsity hockey squad.

In the mid 1960s, Princeton University was looking for a quality coach for their men's ice hockey team. Quackenbush applied and was accepted. He coached the team for six years, lending them his vast knowledge and great understanding of the game. When the team began losing, Quackenbush stepped down as coach, but soon was back coaching the women's hockey team, as well as the varsity golf team.

There have been better defensemen than Quackenbush but none were classier, on or off the ice, lending credibility to the line that nice guys can survive in the war games on ice.

JOEL QUENNEVILLE

BORN: Windsor, Ontario, September 15, 1958
POSITION: Defenseman, Toronto Maple Leafs, 1978–80; Colorado Rockies, 1980–82; New Jersey Devils, 1982–83; Hartford Whalers, 1983–90; Washington Capitals, 1990–91; Coach, St. Louis Blues, 1997–
AWARDS/HONORS: Jack Adams Award, 2000

The best National Hockey League coaches are often those who had modest big-league careers rather than those who achieved superstardom.

An example would be Joel Quenneville, an average defenseman when skating for Toronto, Colorado, New Jersey, Hartford, and Washington. His best season would come with the Rockies during 1980–81, when he recorded 10 goals and 24 assists for 34 points. In 803 games played, Quenneville totaled 54 goals and 136 assists for 190 points.

After his final NHL season with Washington in 1990–91, Quenneville became a player-coach

with the AHL St. John's Maple Leafs, and ascended to a key assistant coach role with the Colorado Avalanche for three seasons, culminating in their 1996 Stanley Cup victory.

His future as a head coach was apparent even then and Quenneville got his first break with St. Louis.

Joel delivered admirably with a 1997–98 campaign that secured a 45–29–8 record for the Blues, third best in club history. By his sixth season, 2001–02, the astute Quenneville already had coached the most games in Blues' history with 368, and won the Jack Adams Award in 2000. He would also pass Scotty Bowman for second place on the Blues all-time win list when he got his 111th win against Toronto on November 17, 2000.

Coach "Q" had another superior season in 2000–01, in which the Blues finished with 103 points and battled into the Western Conference finals against Colorado, which ended with the Avalanche winning in five.

Known as a player's coach, Quenneville found himself with a star-studded lineup in 2001–02 as Doug Weight joined a Blues team that already included Keith Tkachuk, Pavol Demitra, Al MacInnis, and Chris Pronger, but the Blues struggled to maintain their chemistry and a playoff position, eventually being eliminated by Detroit in the second round.

PAT QUINN

BORN: Hamilton, Ontario, January 29, 1943
POSITION: Defenseman, Toronto Maple Leafs, 1968–70; Vancouver Canucks, 1970–72; Atlanta Flames, 1972–77; Coach, Philadelphia Flyers, 1978–82; Los Angeles Kings, 1984–87; Coach/General Manager, Vancouver Canucks, 1990–96; Toronto Maple Leafs, 1998–
AWARDS/HONORS: Jack Adams Award, 1980, 1992

Pat Quinn began his NHL life with Toronto, and continued on to Vancouver, Atlanta, Philadelphia, and Los Angeles before coming full circle with Toronto as coach–general manager in 1997.

As a player, Pat was the policeman, "the Irish Enforcer" for each city in which he played. Quinn once ignited a 1969 playoff brawl with practically the entire Boston Bruins' club after smashing Bobby Orr into the boards.

Pat Quinn as Flyers coach

In 1972, Quinn was obtained by the Atlanta Flames and his improvement as a backliner became obvious. During 1973–74, Pat collected a total of 32 points, indicating his growing confidence as a puck carrier and playmaker, rather than a simple mayhem producer.

Pat Quinn retired from the pro ranks at the conclusion of the 1976–77 season and joined the Philadelphia Flyers' organization as a coach in their minor-league system.

During the 1978–79 season, Quinn was brought up from the AHL Maine Mariners to rescue the parent Flyers from a midyear slump threatening to dump the once-powerful squad into the cellar of the Patrick Division. Quinn, with his defensive background and excellent hockey instinct, provided the impetus to raise the Flyers to a second-place finish ahead of the Rangers and Flames, cohabitants of the tough Patrick Division. The following year, the Flyers had the best record in the league with 48 wins, 12 losses, and 20 ties, and set an NHL record with a 35-game undefeated streak, only to lose the Stanley Cup finals to the New York Islanders in six games. Quinn nevertheless won his first Jack Adams Award. By 1982, Quinn and the Flyers had parted ways.

Quinn had less success in pre–Wayne Gretzky Los Angeles. From 1984 to 1987, the Kings made the playoffs just once (1984–85), and were eliminated in three straight. Quinn had by now earned a law degree from Widener University, with an eye on managing a club.

Still vocal and intimidating behind the bench, Quinn next stewarded the Vancouver Canucks beginning in 1990, and posted three consecutive 40-win seasons for a franchise that had endured a losing tradition. Pat earned his second Jack Adams Award in 1992. Armed with Kirk McLean in goal and Trevor Linden and Pavel Bure up front, Quinn's team reached the seventh game of the Stanley Cup finals against the New York Rangers in 1994, and came within a hit goalpost of winning it all. Exit Quinn once again.

Undeterred, the wily Quinn resurfaced as head coach of his alma mater, the Toronto Maple Leafs, in 1998, and ultimately added general manager to his title the following summer. Fostering a gritty, but free-flowing style, Pat's 1999–2000 club set Leaf club records for points in a season with 100, and brought a division title to the Mecca of hockey for the first time in nearly 40 years.

Losing in two successive playoffs to the big, battle-tested New Jersey Devils in 2000 and 2001, Quinn maintained a playoff-type roster with captain Mats Sundin and physical forwards Gary Roberts, Shayne Corson, and Darcy Tucker, bruising a recharged Islander team in the 2002 Eastern Conference quarter-finals. His Leafs advanced through the first two playoff rounds before being eliminated by the Carolina Hurricanes. As coach of Team Canada at the 2002 Winter Olympics at Salt Lake, Quinn bristled at media attention, and steered his squad to a gold medal victory over the United States.

He continued coaching and managing the Maple Leafs although a health problem briefly sidelined him during the 2002 playoffs.

DON RALEIGH

BORN: Kenora, Ontario, June 27, 1926
DIED: Date unknown
POSITION: Center, New York Rangers, 1943–44, 1947–56
AWARDS/HONORS: NHL All-Star Game, 1951, 1954

The 1950 Stanley Cup finals had been a particularly grueling series for center Don Raleigh. Nicknamed "Bones" by his teammates for his conspicuous lack of flesh, Raleigh was "mod" 20 years before his time. He lived alone on the remote New York borough of Staten Island, wrote poetry, grew a moustache, and always gave the impression that one more turn on the ice would be his last.

But Raleigh was on the ice as the clock passed the eight-minute mark of the first sudden death in the fourth game of the finals, in which the Rangers trailed Detroit two games to one. He took a pass from bulky linemate Ed Slowinski and, as he was falling, swiped the puck past goalie Harry Lumley. The Rangers had tied the series at two apiece.

Now the Red Wings were reeling. They fell behind, 1–0, in the fifth game and appeared to be doomed to a Chuck Rayner shutout when Ted Lindsay tied the score with less than two minutes remaining in the third period. Once again it was time for sudden death—and Bones Raleigh.

Raleigh wasted little time in his second dramatic sudden-death effort. Only a minute and a half had elapsed when he took a pass from Slowinski and beat Lumley with a ten-foot drive. But it was all to no avail, as the Rangers lost the finals in the seventh game.

ROB RAMAGE

BORN: Byron, Ontario, January 11, 1959
POSITION: Defenseman, Colorado Rockies, 1979–82; St. Louis Blues, 1982–88; Calgary Flames, 1988–89; Toronto Maple Leafs, 1989–91; Minnesota North Stars, 1991–92; Tampa Bay Lightning, 1992–93; Montreal Canadiens, 1993; Philadelphia Flyers, 1993–94
AWARDS/HONORS: NHL All-Star Game 1981, 1984, 1986, 1988

Like Barry Beck, once his teammate in Colorado, defenseman Rob Ramage never lived up to his superstar expectations, although he enjoyed a long and successful career with eight big-league NHL teams.

A rugged performer and leader, Ramage was a favorite in St. Louis, where he played six seasons, 1982 to 1988, as their most versatile defenseman, with a 10-goal, 56-assist career season in 1985–86.

Upon being traded to the Calgary Flames in 1988, as part of a deal for a young Brett Hull, Ramage led a vaunted defense that won Calgary the Stanley Cup in 1989.

The only man to be named captain of the Maple Leafs before ever suiting up for them, Rob headed the Leafs for two years (1989–90, 1990–91), but became an NHL journeyman right after being acquired by Minnesota in the 1991 Expansion Draft.

After stops in Tampa Bay, Montreal (where he was a spare part of their 1993 Cup winner), and Philadelphia, Ramage ended his hockey-playing career in 1994 and moved into broadcasting.

MIKE RAMSEY

BORN: Minneapolis, Minnesota, December 3, 1960
POSITION: Defenseman, Buffalo Sabres, 1980–93; Pittsburgh Penguins, 1993–94; Detroit Red Wings, 1994–97
AWARDS/HONORS: NHL All-Star Game, 1982–83, 1985–86

United States colleges produced a number of top defensemen, among them Brian Leetch and Chris Chelios. Less spectacular, Mike Ramsey belonged to that group, having starred for the University of Minnesota before launching a long career with the Buffalo Sabres. In 1979, he was drafted 11th overall by Buffalo. Mike then played for the 1980 U.S. Olympic team, which won the gold medal at Lake Placid.

Ramsey certainly lived up to the billing of first American ever selected in the first round. He played 14 seasons with the Sabres as a force on the Buffalo defense. He was named to the All-Star team in 1982, 1983, 1985, and 1986.

Late in March 1993, the Sabres dealt him to the Pittsburgh Penguins for left wing Bob Errey. Ramsey then signed with the Detroit Red Wings as a free agent in 1994 and was a vital cog for the Wings' defense machine. Following his playing career, Ramsey became an NHL assistant coach.

BILL RANFORD

BORN: Brandon, Manitoba, December 14, 1966
POSITION: Goaltender, Boston Bruins, 1985–87, 1995–97; Edmonton Oilers, 1987–95, 1999–2000; Washington Capitals, 1997–98; Tampa Bay Lightning, 1998–99; Detroit Red Wings, 1999
AWARDS/HONORS: Conn Smythe Trophy, 1990; NHL All-Star Game, 1991; Canada Cup All-Star Team, 1991

The Boston Bruins' 52nd selection overall in the 1985 Entry Draft, Bill Ranford spent little time in Beantown.

Ranford was traded to Edmonton for another goalie, Andy Moog, during the 1987–88 season and their paths would cross again in a few years. With the Oilers, Ranford faced certain relegation to number two spot behind Grant Fuhr, but it also gave him the chance to apprentice with the best. In the 1989–90 season, Fuhr was in and out of the lineup with sickness and injury problems and Ranford wound up playing most of that year, and playing phenomenally enough to win the starting job come playoff time.

Ranford played in every game that playoff run, led the team to the Stanley Cup victory over Moog and his Boston Bruins, and was named winner of the Conn Smythe Trophy. In 22 games, the 23-year-old Ranford was 16–6 with one shutout and a 2.53 goals-against average. Younger than Fuhr by a few years, his play also meant that general manager Glen Sather could wheel and deal to make his team better because he had two number one goaltenders.

Ranford was now among the elite goaltenders of the NHL. He was named Canada's starter for the 1991 Canada Cup, and not only did he lead the team to victory, he was named the outstanding player of the tournament.

Bill was traded back to Boston midway through the 1995–96 season, and a series of trades and new teams that hurt his consistency began. Unable to find a groove in Washington,

Tampa Bay, and Detroit, Ranford signed in the summer of 1999 with the Oilers again as a free agent, but posted a dismal 3.59 goals-against average and retired.

JEAN RATELLE

BORN: Lac Ste. Jean, Quebec, October 3, 1940
POSITION: Center, New York Rangers, 1960–75; Boston Bruins, 1975–81
AWARDS/HONORS: Lady Byng Memorial Trophy, 1972, 1976; Bill Masterton Memorial Trophy, 1971; Lester B. Pearson Award, 1972; NHL Second Team All-Star, 1972; NHL All-Star Game, 1970–73, 1980; Hockey Hall of Fame, 1985

Jean Ratelle could feel streams of pain coursing through his long lean body. The gifted young New York Rangers center felt the shock waves near the end of the 1965–66 season.

Jean Ratelle as a Bruin

The end of a bright career loomed for the French-Canadian ace. He was taken to a doctor who diagnosed chronic lower spinal deterioration and prescribed delicate spinal fusion surgery. It was a tricky operation, involving bone grafts. Chances of complete recovery for a hockey player were not bright.

The spinal fusion operation was followed by a black cloud of fear. Jean was plagued with doubts as he journeyed to Kitchener, Ontario, for the Ranger training camp in September 1966. Could he make a comeback?

Ratelle played only 41 games and scored a disillusioning six goals. Some believed that the trouble was in the coaching. When Francis fired Red Sullivan and took over the coaching duties in 1966–67, he immediately inserted Ratelle on

a line with Vic Hadfield and Jean's boyhood chum, Rod Gilbert. The gears meshed neatly and the Rangers made the playoffs for the first time in five years. The Ratelle-Hadfield-Gilbert trio—later to be nicknamed the GAG (for goal-a-game) Line—emerged as the Rangers' most consistent unit. Ratelle scored 28 goals and finally seemed ready to fulfill his promise.

Employing a crisp wrist shot, Jean embarked on a string of three consecutive 32-goal seasons. Midway through the 1971–72 season, Ratelle was the NHL's leading scorer, outpointing even the fabulous Phil Esposito of the Boston Bruins.

With the Rangers in first place, and Ratelle's line setting all kinds of scoring marks, Ranger fans were flying high. One of the loudest and longest ovations was heard on February 27, 1972, when Jean became the first Ranger in history to score 100 points in a single season. Ratelle briefly and modestly acknowledged the cascading applause and, looking embarrassed, skated back to the bench.

Less than a week later, disaster struck. Shooting against the California Golden Seals, defenseman Dale Rolfe fired the puck at a maze of players in front of the net. The shot careened goalward and struck Ratelle on the right ankle. Jean's ankle was fractured. He was disabled for the rest of the regular season.

He had accumulated 109 points. With 15 games left, he had scored 46 goals. Fifty was clearly in sight, but it was not to be. His value was underscored as the Rangers faltered without number 19 in the lineup. They fell to second place and barely finished ahead of the onrushing Canadiens.

Ratelle briefly returned for the Stanley Cup finals against Boston, but clearly was not the same Ratelle. As a result, the Rangers were outclassed by the powerful Bruins in six games. Nevertheless, Ratelle led his club in scoring, and finished third in the league, behind Esposito and Orr. For his efforts, and for his sportsmanship on the ice, Jean was awarded the Lady Byng Trophy.

On November 7, 1975, Jean Ratelle was involved in what many considered a landmark trade in hockey history. Along with Brad Park and Joe Zanussi, Jean was sent packing to the Boston Bruins in exchange for Phil Esposito and Carol Vadnais. Originally, the deal was labeled a steal for the Rangers, and Ratelle, whom management considered "over the hill," was regarded as a "throw-in" part of the package, Park and Esposito being the prime components.

However, it didn't take long for Gentleman Jean to prove his critics wrong. At the end of the 1975–76 season, Ratelle was at the top of the Bruins' scoring list with 90 points; the Bruins' face-lift was far more successful than that of the Rangers.

The following year, Ratelle again proved the Bruins had gotten the better of the deal, when once more he led the team in scoring with 94 points on 33 goals and 61 assists, quite an achievement for an "over the hill" hockey player.

He completed his playing career in 1981 and became a longtime scout for the Bruins, retiring early in the twenty-first century.

CHUCK RAYNER

BORN: Sutherland, Saskatchewan, August 11, 1920
POSITION: Goaltender, New York/Brooklyn Americans, 1940–42; New York Rangers, 1945–53
AWARDS/HONORS: Hart Memorial Trophy, 1950; NHL Second Team All-Star, 1949–51; NHL All-Star Game 1949–51; Hockey Hall of Fame, 1973

A classic example of a superb goaltender yoked to a mediocre hockey club was the New York Rangers' Charlie Rayner. "Bonnie Prince Charlie," a bushy-browed, acrobatic netminder, broke into the professional ice wars with the New York (then Brooklyn) Americans before donning the red, white, and blue Ranger sweater in 1945. For a time, Rayner shared the Rangers goaltending duties with his close friend Jim Henry, inaugurating what later became the standard two-goalie system.

Laboring for a Rangers team that never finished higher than fourth place, Charlie almost single-handedly guided the Rangers to the final round of the 1950 playoffs, only to see his Blueshirts fall to the mighty Detroit Red Wings in the final game—a heart-stopping, double overtime affair.

"Goaltending," the beleaguered Rayner had once said, "is like walking down a dark alley and never knowing when someone is going to chop you down."

Chuck was picked for the 1950 Hart Trophy as the NHL's most valuable player. It was only the first time since 1929 that the honor was bestowed upon a backstop. A courageous netminder who constantly played with a painful assortment of injuries that would have kept lesser men on the sidelines, Rayner was in such agony near the end of his career that he literally had to be lifted off the ice by teammate Leo Reise Jr. and propped up against the goal cage after making a save.

In addition to his illustrious netminding career, Rayner was the only goaltender in big-league hockey to dash the length of the ice and score a goal against an opposing goalie. It happened during World War II when Charlie

Chuck "Bonnie Prince Charlie" Rayner as a Ranger

was minding the nets for an All-Star Royal Canadian Army team. A wild scramble for a loose puck saw all five opposing skaters charge behind Charlie's net. Somehow, the lozenge squirted out in front of Chuck's crease with nothing but wide open spaces between Rayner and the opposing netminder.

With a ten-stride lead on his opponents, Charlie cradled the puck on his oversized goalie's lumber and set off toward the enemy net. While all ten skaters stopped and stared in amazement, Rayner barreled into the offensive zone and nudged the puck past his shocked opposite number.

Injuries ended Rayner's career in 1953, whereupon he went into coaching. Charlie and his wife, Ina, later retired to Vancouver, but he regularly attended Rangers Alumni Association reunions in New York.

KEN REARDON

BORN: Winnipeg, Manitoba, April 1, 1921
POSITION: Defenseman, Montreal Canadiens, 1940–42, 1945–50
AWARDS/HONORS: NHL First Team All-Star, 1947, 1950; NHL Second Team All-Star, 1946, 1948–49; NHL All-Star Game, 1947–49; Hockey Hall of Fame, 1966

Kenny Reardon, a tough defenseman for the powerhouse clubs of the 1940s Montreal Canadiens, was not exactly the type of skater one associates with the flamboyant Flying Frenchmen. A lumbering, straight-ahead blueliner, Reardon's punishing body checks and deft stickwork more than earned him his keep on the star-studded Habitant roster.

One of the quickest men in hockey with his fists, Reardon is credited with starting one of the bloodiest brawls in modern hockey history, even though Kenny himself missed much of the fun and games.

On March 16, 1947, the Canadiens were playing the New York Rangers in Madison Square Garden. As Kenny lugged the rubber disc out of his defensive zone, New York's Bryan Hextall loomed in wait at the blue line. Hex delivered a crunching check on the Canadiens rearguard and sent him caroming into the razor-sharp stick blade of the Rangers' Cal Gardner.

With his upper lip resembling raw chopped liver, Reardon was escorted to the tunnel leading to the trainer's room when all hell broke loose. A slightly inebriated Ranger fan lunged at Reardon as the bloodied warrior passed the first row of seats, causing the startled Hab to swing his stick in self-defense. Immediately, Reardon was pounced on by several burly Garden cops. This hubbub caused the entire Ranger bench to stand up for an innocent look-see.

Back at the Canadien bench, the Habs thought the entire Ranger reserve corps was beating up on their wounded comrade. In an instant, the Montreal bench emptied and streaked across the rink to Reardon's aid. Pairing off with every Ranger they could, the outraged Montrealers chopped away for 20 solid minutes before order was restored.

And Reardon? Throughout the mayhem, Kenny was in the trainer's room, having his shredded lip repaired.

Reardon never forgave Gardner—and vice versa—so the blood feud continued for years. Once, Reardon authored an article in *Sport Magazine* threatening Gardner. At that point NHL president Clarence Campbell intervened, ordering Reardon to post a bond insuring that he wouldn't harm Gardner. Reardon obliged and the feud was put to rest.

MARK RECCHI

BORN: Kamloops, British Columbia, February 1, 1968
POSITION: Right Wing, Pittsburgh Penguins, 1988-92; Philadelphia Flyers, 1992-95; Montreal Canadiens, 1995-99; Philadelphia Flyers, 1999-
AWARDS/HONORS: NHL Second All-Star Team, 1992; NHL All-Star Game, 1991, 1993, 1994, 1997-2000

In Mark Recchi's first go with the Flyers, he did not wear their colors for very long. But in that relatively brief stint the pint-sized right wing won the hearts of Philadelphians because of his tenacity, and tendency to be in the right place at the right time when a big goal was required.

He surprised no one.

Before his arrival in The City of Brotherly Love, Recchi not only surpassed the 100-point level as a Pittsburgh Penguin (40-73-113) but also played a major role in the Pens' first Stanley Cup championship in 1991. En route to the silverware, Recchi registered 10 goals and 24 assists for 34 points in 24 playoff games.

Mark was on target for another three-digit point season when the Penguins announced that Recchi was the centerpiece of a three-team deal.

Recchi didn't miss a beat. He continued to average more than a point per game and quickly endeared himself to the Spectrum crowd. His first full season on Broad Street was 1992-93, and with 123 points (53-70), he broke Bobby Clarke's team record of 119 points. Recchi skated alongside Eric Lindros at center and Brent Fedyk on the left side. They were called The Crazy 8's and, for a time, comprised the NHL's most explosive trio. In 1993-94, Recchi totaled 40 goals and 67 assists for 107 points, his third season over the century mark. But Philadelphia missed the playoffs yet again and demands for change led to the trading of Mark to the Montreal Canadiens for John LeClair, Gilbert Dionne, and Eric Desjardins.

But after playing four seasons with the Canadiens, it was back to Broad Street for Mark in 1999, where he seemed to belong.

Recchi's 63 assists led the NHL in 1999-2000, but the Flyers could not get past the New Jersey Devils after a three-games-to-one lead in the Conference finals was blown. The Flyers bowed in the first round the following two seasons.

LARRY REGAN

BORN: North Bay, Ontario, August 9, 1930
POSITION: Center, Boston Bruins, 1956-59; Toronto Maple Leafs, 1959-61; Coach/Manager, Los Angeles Kings, 1967-74
AWARDS/HONORS: Calder Memorial Trophy, 1957

As stickhandlers and playmakers go, slick would be the best description of Larry Regan. Regan was among the better members of the breed during the late 1950s, spent first with Boston and then Toronto. His most significant contribution occurred on March 22, 1959, when he scored two critical goals against the Red Wings as the Leafs beat the Rangers for a playoff berth on the final night of the season. Just as important, Regan set up Dick Duff for what proved to be the fifth goal of the match; and the winner in a 6-4 decision. Prior to the decisive play, Regan told Duff: "Dick, you're goin' to get the winner. I'm goin' to give it to you. Just be there." Regan won the face-off and eventually delivered a needlepoint pass to Duff who shot the puck past goalie Terry Sawchuk. No player was ever more responsible for a successful homestretch drive than Regan was for the Maple Leafs in 1958-59.

After his playing days had ended, Regan turned to front office work. He coached and managed the Los Angeles Kings rather unsuccessfully. In 1974, he moved to Montreal, where he became a coach on the junior level, quitting in May 1975. He later headed an NHL Alumni group, helping retired big-leaguers.

LEO REISE JR.

BORN: Stoney Creek, Ontario, June 7, 1922
POSITION: Defenseman, Chicago Blackhawks, 1945–46; Detroit Red Wings, 1946–52; New York Rangers, 1952–54
AWARDS/HONORS: NHL Second Team All-Star, 1950–51; NHL All-Star Game, 1950–53

There are not many chips off the old block who are as identical in style and ability as Leo Reise Sr. and Leo Jr. The younger Reise also was a defenseman, and a much-feared one at that. Although Leo Jr. broke in with the Chicago Blackhawks in 1945–46, he was dealt to Detroit the next year and played his best hockey for the Red Wings through the 1951–52 season. His most memorable play was a sudden-death goal in the seventh game of the bitter 1950 Stanley Cup semifinal against Toronto. He also scored a sudden-death goal for Detroit earlier in the series. Single-handedly, Reise won two of the four games. In 1952–53, he became a New York Ranger and, like his dad, finished his big-league tenure on Broadway (1953–54). Although Gordie Howe, Ted Lindsay, and Red Kelly received much of the attention, it was Leo Reise Jr. who did much of the unheralded spadework for the champion Red Wing teams in 1950 and 1951, when they won the Prince of Wales Trophy.

CHICO RESCH

BORN: Moose Jaw, Saskatchewan, July 10, 1948
POSITION: Goaltender, New York Islanders, 1974–82; Colorado Rockies/New Jersey Devils, 1982–86; Philadelphia Flyers, 1986–87
AWARDS/HONORS: Bill Masterton Memorial Trophy, 1982; NHL Second Team All-Star, 1976, 1979; NHL All-Star Game, 1976–77, 1984

Glenn "Chico" Resch was a sportswriter's dream. The talented, outgoing New York Islander goalie was never at a loss for words and usually bubbled with enthusiasm.

His on-ice exploits were just as noteworthy: Resch delighted fans by kissing his goal-posts after recording a shutout against the Pittsburgh Penguins in the 1975 Stanley Cup playoff quarterfinal series. Resch was no stranger to shutouts, setting an Islanders career record of 19 in 1979. Not once since Resch began his NHL career in 1975, when he was runner-up for Rookie of the Year honors, did his goals-against average exceed 3.00 with the Isles. In his sophomore season, Resch posted a miserly 2.07 average with a club record of seven shutouts.

Chico became the most popular Islander and played for the club's first Stanley Cup–winning team in 1979–80. However, general manager Bill Torrey also had another top goalie, Bill Smith, and decided in 1980–81 to deal Smith to the Colorado Rockies.

Glenn moved to Colorado, which soon relocated to New Jersey. Resch emerged as an early Devils star and fan favorite. Glenn moved to Philadelphia, where he finished his playing career with a respectable 231 wins under his belt.

Chico spent time as a coach and scout for the Minnesota North Stars (1990–91) and Ottawa Senators (1992–96), but gravitated toward broadcasting and returned to the New Jersey Devils to provide color commentary on telecasts for Fox Sports New York and Madison Square Garden Network.

HENRI RICHARD

BORN: Montreal, Quebec, February 29, 1936
POSITION: Center, Montreal Canadiens, 1955–75
AWARDS/HONORS: Bill Masterton Memorial Trophy, 1974; NHL First Team All-Star, 1958; NHL Second Team All-Star, 1959, 1961, 1963; NHL All-Star Game, 1956–61, 1963, 1965, 1967, 1974; Hockey Hall of Fame, 1979

A superstar in his own right, Henri Richard nevertheless had to take a backseat to his older brother Maurice, the fabled Rocket. And this although Henri played on a record 11 Stanley Cup–winning teams.

Henri and Maurice Richard began drifting apart as the kid brother came into his own around the NHL. If the Rocket was the home-run hitter, the Pocket was more the base stealer and opposite-field hitter on the Montreal Canadiens.

The "Pocket" Rocket was an essential cog in Frank Selke's rebuilding plan during the 1955–56 season, and he later was an asset to Sam Pollock, in Sam's first years in Montreal. Les Canadiens finished first in 1965–66, breezed past Toronto in the first round of the playoffs with four straight wins, and appeared capable of disposing of the Detroit Red Wings at will in the Cup finals, especially since the series opened with two games at the Forum. But Detroit's hot goalie Roger Crozier was sizzling, and the Red Wings upset Les Canadiens in the first two games. They became favorites as the series shifted to Olympia Stadium. But coach Toe Blake rallied his crew and Montreal didn't lose again. The Cup-winning goal was scored by the Pocket Rocket in sudden-death overtime as he slid feet-first toward the net.

Within five seasons of big-league hockey Henri had helped win five Stanley Cups; he made the All-Star team; led the league in assists; he finished second in scoring; and he was called the fastest skater of all time. "The Pocket," said Blake, "became a better all-around

player than Rocket was. But it's asking an awful lot of any man to be the scorer that Rocket was. He was the greatest scorer under pressure that I've ever seen."

When Maurice retired after the 1959–60 season, Henri continued to excel. Meanwhile, comparisons continued. Some critics defined their differences in another but equally cogent way: "Henri is mechanically better than Rocket was. But he doesn't have the killer instinct to be the great scorer that Rocket was."

Henri himself once elaborated on that theme. "My brother's biggest thrills came when he scored many goals. I am most satisfied when I play in a close game and do not have any goals scored against me. Sometimes people have asked me whether it helped or hurt having Maurice as an older brother.

"Sometimes it was not easy, because many people expected me to be as spectacular as Maurice. But I believe it helped me more than it hurt me. Don't forget, Maurice was a great scorer, and he could get goals that many other players could not get. That helped my passing because I knew that he would always be near the net waiting for a shot. But Maurice never gave me any advice. I never asked him for it and he never offered it. Except for a few fundamentals, it is hard to teach anyone how to play hockey. It is a game that you must learn yourself." Henri retired at the end of the 1974–75 season.

Were there any doubts about Henri's greatness, they were erased when he was elected to the Hall of Fame, alongside his older brother. Together, they were a study in contrasting excellence on the ice.

JACQUES RICHARD

BORN: Quebec City, Quebec, October 7, 1952
POSITION: Left Wing, Atlanta Flames, 1972–75; Buffalo Sabres, 1975–79; Quebec Nordiques, 1980–83

It was difficult for anyone in hockey to carry the Richard name other than Maurice or Henri, each a Hall of Famer. When Jacques Richard—no relation—appeared, he automatically was closely watched. The best way to tell how a young player is reacting to life in the NHL is by the way he speaks. French Canadian–born Jacques Richard rarely spoke to anyone in his rookie season, a disappointing campaign that resulted in but 13 goals and 18 assists. But Atlanta Flames top pick Jacques was absolutely effervescent in his sophomore year, much of his flowing verbiage attributable to center Tom Lysiak, who helped Jacques to 27 goals. Richard was the second man chosen in the 1972 amateur grab bag, mainly because of his 227 goals as an amateur with the Quebec Remparts. At the time he was the junior hockey sensation of Canada.

After three unproductive seasons in Atlanta, Richard was traded to the Buffalo Sabres for veteran defenseman Larry Carriere. Though he was so highly regarded during his junior career, he was a major disappointment in the NHL and spent much of his time on the bench or in the minor leagues.

Quebec signed Richard in February 1980, after everyone had given up on him, and the next season, he repaid them, finally breaking out with 103 points in 1980–81. However, he played only two more years, and had little success in either.

MAURICE RICHARD

BORN: Montreal, Quebec, August 4, 1921
DIED: August 27, 2000
POSITION: Right Wing, Montreal Canadiens, 1942–60
AWARDS/HONORS: Hart Memorial Trophy, 1947; NHL First Team All-Star, 1945–50, 1955–56; NHL Second Team All-Star, 1944, 1951–54, 1957; NHL All-Star Game, 1947–59; Hockey Hall of Fame, 1961

Maurice Richard, without a doubt, was the Babe Ruth of hockey. That would be one of many ways to describe The Rocket. "Maurice Richard," summed up Peter Gzowski, a prize-winning writer for a Canadian magazine, "was the most exciting athlete I have ever seen. So much has been written about Richard that for me to offer a flood of new praise would be roughly equivalent to a Ph.D. candidate announcing he is going to prove Hamlet is an interesting play."

Richard was *the* greatest at scoring exciting goals. In the beginning, though, the elder son of Onesime Lucien Richard preferred baseball to hockey.

The Babe Ruth of hockey—Maurice "The Rocket" Richard

Some of his neighborhood chums suspected that Maurice would make a better boxer than either a baseball or hockey player. In his teens, Richard entered the Golden Gloves tournament in Montreal, and, according to one report, handled himself quite well. It was a portent of things to come on the ice.

In summer, he would play ball in the fast Provincial League, and in winter, he'd play hockey for the Paquette Club of Montreal's Intermediate Hockey League. Four men who were to play a significant role in Richard's future entered his life at this time.

His manager was sports commentator Paul Stuart, who immediately detected the spark of a supercompetitor in Richard and began touting him to coaches around the city. Georges Norchet, the trainer, would soon become Richard's father-in-law. It was while Richard skated for the Paquette Club that Aurel Joliat, the former Canadiens' ace, and Arthur Therrien recommended Maurice as a candidate for the Verdun Maple Leafs, one of Montreal's most distinguished junior teams.

As a 19-year-old, he was promoted to the Montreal Canadiens of the crack Quebec Senior Hockey League, although there was some doubt whether he could handle the severe bodychecking and assorted illegalities of minor-league hockey. The suspicions were almost immediately confirmed in his first game with the Senior sextet when he crashed heavily into the boards and broke his left ankle. Maurice was finished for the season.

He returned to the Senior Canadiens for the next season, and after about 20 games, he was careening down the ice in one of his characteristic headlong dashes, when he tripped and slid headfirst into the steel upright of the goal cage. He was able to thrust his arm in front of his face before striking the net, but was carried off the ice with a broken left arm.

Word soon filtered up and down the hockey grapevine that Richard was too brittle to get anywhere in the pros. Scouts turned their attention to more substantial types.

Richard's recovery came about sooner than it had the first time he was injured and returned to the lineup at playoff time. His response was six goals in a four-game series and an invitation from Dick Irvin to attend the Canadiens' autumn training camp.

Irvin inserted Richard on a line with the veteran Tony Demers and young center Elmer Lach. The line clicked immediately and Demers scored two goals as the Canadiens won their opening game from Boston, 3–2. The result was especially appealing to one of the game's linesmen—Aurel Joliat.

On November 8, 1942, Richard played his third NHL game. Montreal's opponents in the Forum that night were the Rangers who had beaten them on the previous night in New York. This time Les Canadiens were the winners by a score of 10–4. The highlight of the game was a pulsating end-to-end rush by Richard, who made his way through the Ranger defense like a pinball bouncing its way past the obstacles to the goal. Richard's shot beat goalie Steve Buzinski, and even so critical an analyst as Newsy Lalonde raved about the rookie.

After 15 games, Richard had played commendably, if not always spectacularly. His record was 5 goals and 6 assists for 11 points, and the Canadiens, as a team, appeared refreshed by his vitality. Then, in the 16th game, it happened again. The Canadiens were skating against the Bruins when Jack Crawford, a big but clean defenseman, collided with Richard and sent Maurice sprawling to the ice in pain. He had suffered a clean break just above his right ankle and was finished once again for the season.

But Richard came back again. "Not only will he be a star," Irvin predicted at the start of the 1943–44 season, "but he'll be the biggest star in hockey!"

Upon Richard's return, Dick Irvin decided that Toe Blake would be worthy of an experiment on the unit, and in no time the line was made—for keeps. The trio, soon named the Punch Line, finished one-two-three (Lach,

Blake, Richard) in scoring on the team with Richard collecting 32 goals and 22 assists for 54 points in 46 games.

Les Canadiens iced virtually the same team they had when they won the Stanley Cup in April, with only a few exceptions. The Punch Line remained intact and launched the season with the same syncopated attack that had stirred the fans in 1943–44. Richard seemed particularly bolstered by a full season under his belt without serious injury and he broke from the post like an overzealous thorough-bred. His scoring was so prolific that opposing coaches began mapping specific strategies to stop Maurice alone. These stratagems took on many variations over the years. One of the favorites was simply to goad Maurice into a fight, not exactly difficult since the brooding French Canadian still couldn't speak English and was self-conscious about his language barrier.

Maurice cruised along at a goal-a-game pace, surpassing Joe Malone's goal-scoring record, for which he received a standing ova-tion at the Forum. The pressing question was whether or not Richard would reach the hitherto unattainable plateau of 50 goals.

He had scored number 49 by March 15 with only two games remaining on the schedule. In the next-to-last game, against the Blackhawks on Forum ice, Les Canadiens triumphed, but somehow Maurice was thoroughly blanked. That left only one more match, the final game of the season at Boston Garden. This time Richard came through in a 4–2 win over the Bruins and he finished the season with 50 goals in 50 games.

Richard's heroic achievements had already become too numerous for most fans to remember. Some rooters preferred to recall the goals he scored. Others remembered the fights, and still others pointed to the obscure episodes that made Maurice so unique. Others noted that the Rocket captained Montreal to an unprecedented five straight Stanley Cups from 1956 through 1960 when he returned.

Late in the 1954–55 season, Richard struck linesman Cliff Thompson in a Boston Garden brawl. The Rocket was about to win his first point-scoring title, but NHL President Clarence Campbell suspended Richard for the remainder of the season and the playoffs. Prior to the Habs' next home game against Detroit, a riot exploded outside The Forum and inside as well when Campbell appeared. The game was forfeited to Detroit and Richard went on radio and television to calm the fans. The Rocket lost his scoring title to teammate Bernie Geoffrion and Montreal lost the playoff finals to Detroit.

In 1999, the Montreal organization pre-sented the Maurice "Rocket" Richard Trophy as a gift to the NHL. It was to be awarded to the league's leading goal scorer after each sea-son. Finnish-born winger Teemu Selanne was the first recipient.

Richard successfully battled illness for many years until his death from cancer in August 2000. Modest to a fault, he was revered throughout French Canada, and this intense idolatry was never more evident than after he died. The Rocket's state funeral, a sprawling street procession held in Montreal and broad-cast all over Canada, was considered one of the largest for any sports figure in North America.

STEPHANE RICHER

BORN: Ripon, Quebec, June 7, 1966
POSITION: Right Wing, Montreal Canadiens, 1984–91; New Jersey Devils, 1991–96, 2002–; Tampa Bay Lightning, 1997–2000; St. Louis Blues, 2000; Pittsburgh Penguins, 2001

Stephane Richer promised so very much as a scorer. A smooth skater with a powerful stride, Richer, and his low, hard shot, tormented goaltenders for 16 seasons.

A member of three Stanley Cup–winning teams, Richer's career was revived in 1995 when he was picked up by New Jersey. As point-man on the power play, as well as hard-shooting winger, Richer scored pivotal goals for the Devils in the 1995 playoffs against Boston (two game-winners), Pittsburgh, Philadelphia, and Detroit.

Richer broke the 50-goal barrier twice as one of the Canadiens' francophone superstars, first in 1987–88 (50), then in 1989–90 with 51. Acquired by the Devils for popular captain Kirk Muller in 1991, Richer consistently hit the back of the net for New Jersey, never scoring less than 20 goals in a season. His 39 points led the team in the lockout-shortened 1994–95 season. However, Stephane would only score 32 points in 73 games the following year as the Cup champions desperately missed both his scoring and the playoffs.

An ineffective return to Montreal in 1996–97 and stops in Tampa Bay and St. Louis thereafter seemed to signal Richer's demise on the ice, with his numbers sharply on the decline after the 1995 Stanley Cup win. He participated in the Washington Capitals' 2000–01 training camp, but quit abruptly, feeling he had lost a step.

But Pittsburgh Penguins owner/player Mario Lemieux invited Richer to training camp in September 2001 and Richer found himself in the NHL again, skating on the top line with Lemieux and rookie Kris Beech. When the Penguins faltered later in the season, Richer was traded to the Devils, to continue his reawakening on familiar ground, as well as to provide scoring depth. When the 2002 playoffs began Richer was sidelined with a foot injury. He returned briefly, but was unable to help the Devils, who lost a six-game set to Carolina.

MIKE RICHTER

BORN: Abington, Pennsylvania, September 22, 1966
POSITION: Goaltender, New York Rangers, 1988–
AWARDS/HONORS: NHL All-Star Game, 1992, 1994, 2000; NHL All-Star Game MVP, 1994; World Cup MVP, 1996

Lorne Chabot, Charlie Rayner, Lorne Worsley, and Ed Giacomin: The Rangers have boasted many starry goaltenders. But the all-time leader in wins by a Rangers goaltender was Mike Richter, the glue of the team once he succeeded John Vanbiesbrouck.

It was Richter's performance that made the difference in the Rangers' Stanley Cup season of 1993–94. He had a league-leading 42 wins in the regular season to go along with 16 playoff wins, a whopping four playoff shutouts, including two on back-to-back days against the rival New York Islanders, and a series-saving stop on Pavel Bure's penalty shot in the final round against the Vancouver Canucks.

One of the best American-born goaltenders to strap on the pads, Richter became a mainstay on the international circuit, representing the United States as the starting goaltender at the 1996 World Cup, in which he won a gold medal and the Most Valuable Player. He also played on the 1988 and 2002 Olympic teams.

Richter was enjoying a spectacular season in 1999–2000, but in the All-Star Game's Skills Competition, Richter tore his left knee, and for the final portion of the season, was a shell of himself. As a result, the Rangers missed the playoffs for the third straight year. In the 2000–01 season, Richter also tore his right anterior cruciate ligament, finishing his campaign early again. Fully recovered from both injuries, Richter carried the 2001–02 Rangers on his back through the first few months of the season, as the team fought for first place and searched for chemistry.

Unfortunately, the Rangers stumbled, and then, in a late-season game at Madison Square Garden, Richter was struck on the ear by a long slap shot that actually cracked his skull. The Rangers, suddenly without their ace and relying on 18-year-old Dan Blackburn, were beaten, and their playoff hopes again went down with Richter. An unrestricted free agent in July 2002, Richter signed a two-year contract with the Rangers.

JACK RILEY

BORN: Boston, Massachusetts, June 15, 1920
POSITION: General Manager/Coach, 1960 U.S. Olympic Team
AWARDS/HONORS: Hockey Hall of Fame, 1979

Although the 1980 gold medal–winning U.S. Olympic team coached by Herb Brooks commanded more attention, it was Uncle Sam's stunning 1960 Olympic victory at Squaw Valley that put American hockey on the map.

Like Brooks two decades later, Jack Riley was a miracle maker. Taking a team of unknowns, Riley molded a championship sextet around the brilliant goaltending of Jack McCartan. Riley also helped avert catastrophe when his players threatened to miss the competition because of a couple late additions to the team, including Bill and Bob Cleary. Bill demanded that both brothers make the team or he wouldn't play. (Interestingly, the addition of the Cleary brothers meant that a young player named Herb Brooks was cut from the final roster.)

Riley made a name in coaching at West Point. Entering the 1960 Games, Jack had logged 10 years behind Army's bench, where he had grown accustomed to coaching on a larger ice surface. At West Point, Riley engineered several upsets, but the most stunning was Team U.S.A.'s victory over the Soviet Union.

Two of Riley's players on that U.S. team, Bill Cleary and John Mayasich, are enshrined in the United States Hockey Hall of Fame; Jack himself was inducted in 1979.

DOUG RISEBROUGH

BORN: Guelph, Ontario, January 29, 1954
POSITION: Center, Montreal Canadiens, 1974–82; Calgary Flames, 1982–87; Coach, Calgary Flames, 1990–91; General Manager, Calgary Flames, 1991–95; Minnesota Wild, 2000–

Doug Risebrough moved directly from junior hockey to a regular spot on the powerhouse Montreal Canadiens in 1974. Obscured by the prolific scorers on Montreal's squad, Risebrough made his presence felt as a checker and enforcer. In 1977, the young center led the Habs

Doug Risebrough as a Montreal Canadien

with 132 penalty minutes, almost 20 percent of the club's season total.

Risebrough was an asset to the Canadiens no matter how they decided to play the game, and won four Cups with the storied franchise, from 1976 through 1979.

He later brought his rugged style to the Calgary Flames, where he captained the team for four seasons, which included a Stanley Cup finals appearance in 1986 against his Montreal ex-mates. The Flames would win the Cup in 1989 with Risebrough behind the bench as an assistant coach. After a brief stint as head coach the following season—the result of Terry Crisp's dismissal—Doug evolved into the general manager's role and drew Calgary fans' ire when popular Doug Gilmour was sent to Toronto in a ten-player deal that yielded little return. While the Flames' marquee players bolted the small-market team, Risebrough was fired in 1995.

Doug resurfaced in 2000 as the executive vice president and general manager of the expansion Minnesota Wild. A competitive outfit, the Wild were bolstered by youngster Marian Gaborik and goaltender Manny Fernandez as Risebrough flavored the club with Montreal luminaries. His choice of Jacques Lemaire as coach and Guy Lapointe as scouting director were considered superb, proven by the Wild's two successful seasons as an expansion team.

GORDON ROBERTS

BORN: September 5, 1891
DIED: September 2, 1966
POSITION: Left Wing, Ottawa Senators (NHA), 1910; Montreal Wanderers (NHA), 1911–16; Vancouver Millionaires (PCHA), 1917, 1920; Seattle Metropolitans (PCHA), 1918
AWARDS/HONORS: Hockey Hall of Fame, 1971

Gordon Roberts ranks as one of the greatest left wingers of the pre-NHL era. Although he never skated on a Cup winner over his entire ten-year career, he scored better than a goal per game and was one of the most feared shooters of his day.

All of these heroics came, by the way, while Roberts was studying and/or practicing medicine. After playing one year for Ottawa, Roberts joined the Wanderer squad in order to be nearer to McGill University where he was a medical student. He played with the Wanderers for six seasons until his graduation from McGill. Roberts moved to the West Coast to begin his practice in 1917, and while he was in the neighborhood, he signed with the Vancouver Millionaires of the PCHA.

Between house calls, Roberts found time to establish an all-time PCHA scoring record, lighting the lamp 43 times in 23 games. Dr. Roberts's medical obligations brought him to Seattle in 1918 where he played for the Mets and led them into the playoffs, only to see them fall to Vancouver. Roberts sat out the 1919 season, but returned to Vancouver in 1920 to have one last go at it before retiring.

LARRY ROBINSON

BORN: Winchester, Ontario, June 2, 1951
POSITION: Defenseman, Montreal Canadiens, 1972–89; Los Angeles Kings, 1989–92; Coach, Los Angeles Kings, 1995–98; New Jersey Devils, 2000–02
AWARDS/HONORS: James Norris Memorial Trophy, 1977, 1980; Conn Smythe Trophy, 1978; NHL First Team All-Star, 1977, 1979–80; NHL Second Team All-Star, 1978, 1981, 1986; NHL Challenge Cup All-Star, 1979; NHL All-Star Game, 1974, 1976–78, 1980, 1982, 1986, 1988–89, 1992; Hockey Hall of Fame, 1995

One of hockey's greatest defensemen of all time, Larry Robinson later became one of the most controversial head coaches.

After starring for the Montreal Canadiens on numerous Stanley Cup–winning teams in the 1970s and a 1986 revisit, he finished his career

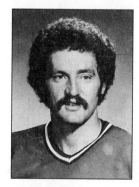

Larry Robinson on defense for Montreal

with the Los Angeles Kings, and ended up as coach of the California sextet for four seasons, attaining one playoff berth.

After that stint ended in failure, Robinson would again take on head coaching with the New Jersey Devils, winning a Stanley Cup (2000) in New Jersey, a remarkable feat on its own.

Sportsmanship was always a part of Robinson's game, and he was always one of the most respected figures in the NHL. An affable, soft-spoken giant, the six-feet-four Robinson was a talented, rugged, defenseman who came into his own as the Habs' cornerstone defenseman during the 1974–75 season, with a 61-point outburst and a victorious bout with notorious Philadelphia Flyers' tough guy,

Dave Schultz. Robinson won the Norris Trophy as the league's best defenseman with 85 points in 1977 and was voted the playoff star a year later, receiving the Conn Smythe Trophy for his efforts. Robinson and his teammates were Stanley Cup winners each of those years.

The Habs' all-time leader in playoff games played, playoff assists—and second only to Henri Richard with 1,202 games played in the *bleu, blanc, et rouge*—Robinson finished his playing career in 1992 in the midst of the Wayne Gretzky era in Los Angeles. He began coaching as an assistant to old teammate Jacques Lemaire on the 1995 Stanley Cup–champion New Jersey Devils before his LA assignment, where he was unable to bring his underachievers to the playoffs on a consistent basis.

Returning to his familiar assistant's role with the Devils in 1999, under Robbie Ftorek, Larry was plunged into the role of life-preserver when Ftorek lost the pulse of his first-place team in March 2000, and was fired with eight games left in the regular season. The Devils would finish with 103 points, as Robinson's more diplomatic hand steered the team into the playoffs, and—after overcoming a three-games-to-one deficit in the Conference finals against Philadelphia—on to the franchise's second Stanley Cup. Robinson's team almost repeated as champions the following spring. After a 111-point Eastern Conference title, the Devils lost the Cup finals in seven games to the Colorado Avalanche, despite nursing a three games-to-two lead.

When 2001–02 began, the Devils—minus departed goal scorer Alexander Mogilny—struggled to score and maintain a level of consistency. Thus, just nine months after he brought the New Jerseyans to their second straight Cup final, Robinson was dismissed in favor of Kevin Constantine. But in a bizarre twist, Robinson was asked back behind the bench as a replacement for ill assistant John Cunniff, and accepted the role. Larry concentrated on the Devs' blueline corps and watched as Constantine's hard-nosed approach lifted the team out of mediocrity and into the 2002 playoffs.

But the Carolina Hurricanes whacked the Devils in six games, and the future of Robinson, and his eight Stanley Cup rings, was uncertain once the season ended.

In June 2002, Larry received the prestigious Canadian Society of New York Hockey Award.

LUC ROBITAILLE

BORN: Montreal, Quebec, February 17, 1966
POSITION: Left Wing, Los Angeles Kings, 1986–94, 1997–2001; Pittsburgh Penguins, 1995; New York Rangers, 1995–97; Detroit Red Wings, 2001–
AWARDS/HONORS: Canadian Major Junior Player of the Year, 1986; Calder Memorial Trophy, 1987; NHL All-Rookie Team, 1987; NHL First Team All-Star, 1988–91, 1993; NHL Second Team All-Star, 1987, 1992, 2001; NHL All-Star Game, 1988–93, 1999, 2001

There are few cases of players drafted so late who accomplished as much over a career as Luc Robitaille.

Considered slow and unskilled by a legion of scouts, the French-Canadian from Montreal was plucked 171st in the talent-laden 1984 annual Entry Draft by the Los Angeles Kings. No one could have dreamt that he was a Hall of Famer in the making.

That year, the top five selections were Mario Lemieux, Kirk Muller, Ed Olczyk, Al Iafrate, and Petr Svoboda, followed later by Patrick Roy, Brett Hull, Gary Roberts, Shayne Corson, and Gary Suter. Nobody gave Robitaille a tumble until the ninth round, which is as low as it gets.

Luc gained a regular National Hockey League berth in the 1986–87 season, after piling up 340 points over his last two Junior seasons, and proceeded to make an imprint as one of the most consistent and accurate goal scorers of the 1990s and into the new century.

Luc was an instant hit in glitzy Los Angeles, scoring in his NHL debut on his first shift, first shot, leading into a 45-goal, 84-point season. Robitaille earned the Calder Trophy as the NHL's top rookie, as well as the everlasting adoration of Californians. The landmark trade for Wayne Gretzky in 1988 only amplified the Kings and with the Los Angeles hockey market in full bloom, Luc's career thrived.

He proceeded to score 40-plus goals in each of his first eight NHL seasons—the third longest streak in league history, only behind goal-scoring wizard Mike Bossy (9) and The Great One (12) himself. He also cracked the 100-point mark four times before the age of 30, and became a fixture on the NHL First- and Second-Team All-Stars. Eventually, no player—other than the great Marcel Dionne— scored more goals as a member of the Kings than Robitaille.

In LA's magical season of 1992–93, Luc's 63 goals and 125 points set NHL single-season records for left-wingers. The Kings electrified the Great Western Forum with an incredible playoff charge led by coach Barry Melrose and stormed into the Stanley Cup finals. Despite the cast of Robitaille, Gretzky, Marty McSorley, Jari Kurri, and Rob Blake, Los Angeles lost in five games to the gritty Montreal Canadiens, with the turning point of the series coming on a controversial "illegal stick" penalty called on McSorley. The Kings spiraled out of the playoffs the following season, and, despite contributing 86 points to the club, Luc was a casualty.

Upon being dealt to the Pittsburgh Penguins for Rick Tocchet in 1994, Luc ran into a string of unproductive seasons. Late in the summer of 1995, when the New York Rangers offered Petr Nedved and Sergei Zubov to the Pens for Robitaille and Ulf Samuelsson, Pittsburgh jumped at the deal, with the idea of infusing youth into the former champion team. Neither Steel Town, nor Broadway, unfortunately, proved a good fit for Robitaille, as injuries and inconsistency plagued his game, notwithstanding some excellent playoff performances.

The lack of a physical element on the New York squad prompted Luc's movement again, back to Tinsel Town, with the Rangers receiving banger Kevin Stevens in return. Luc battled back with two straight 74-point seasons from 1998–2000, then delivered an 88-point season in 2000–01 as a 35-year-old.

Excitement returned to Robitaille's LA stomping grounds in 2001, with the new Staples Center echoing the Great Western Forum's chants of "Luuuuuuuc!!!! Luuuuuuuuc!!!" Luc led his Kings in a six-game upset of heavily-favored Detroit after being down 2–0 in round one of the Stanley Cup playoffs, and they nearly repeated the feat against Colorado, the eventual champs.

Though Luc scored key goals during that improbable playoff drive, his status as an unrestricted free agent led him to sign with the Detroit Red Wings. His quest for a Stanley Cup finally was realized after marching to a 116-point season and eclipsing Bobby Hull's all-time NHL mark of 610 goals as a left-winger. Robitaille finally got to sip the champagne after Detroit beat Carolina in a five-game finale.

JEREMY ROENICK

BORN: Boston, Massachusetts, January 17, 1970
POSITION: Center, Chicago Blackhawks, 1988–96; Phoenix Coyotes, 1996–2001; Philadelphia Flyers, 2001–
AWARDS/HONORS: NHL All-Star Game, 1991–94, 1999–2000, 2002

While most major-league hockey players tend to eschew the flamboyant style of their pro-basketball counterparts, Jeremy Roenick was an exception. The New Englander combined intense, high-quality performance with a *joie de vivre* that placed him in a unique category among his contemporaries. This was translated into television commercial work and even a spot in a soap opera series.

Drafted by Chicago in the first round, eighth overall, of the 1988 NHL Entry Draft, the six-feet, 205-pound center immediately started setting records. His 1989–90 rookie season netted him the Rookie of the Year honors from NHL players and the *Sporting News,* with 66 points in 78 games. He completed his freshman stint by setting a Blackhawks playoff record of 18 points by a rookie.

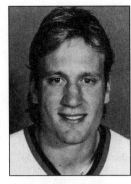

Jeremy Roenick as a Blackhawk

In his next year with Chicago, the Boston native was named the Blackhawks-Gatorade Player of the Year and earned a spot on the All-Star team. The 1991-92 and 1992-93 seasons brought consecutive over-50 goal records, and by 1993-94, Roenick was leading the club in goals, assists, points, power-play goals, and plus/minus rating. Disputes with management finally led him to be traded to the Phoenix Coyotes in 1996.

In his first year at Phoenix, Roenick ranked second on the team in points, assists, and power-play goals, was third in goals, and first for game-winning goals, before suffering a third-degree ligament tear in his knee during the playoffs. Jeremy healed over the off-season, however, and came back stronger in the next few years.

Phoenix fans were dismayed when Roenick was signed by the Flyers on July 2, 2001. The local news even had a tribute to him, lamenting that they would miss his inspired play and leadership on and off the ice. Roenick moved on to join former teammate Rick Tocchet, instantly becoming a fan favorite as his skills and talent contributed weightily to a resurgent Broadstreet Bullies squad in 2001-02, that, unfortunately, sputtered in the playoffs.

AL ROLLINS

BORN: Vanguard, Saskatchewan, October 9, 1926
DIED: July 27, 1996
POSITION: Goaltender, Toronto Maple Leafs, 1949–52; Chicago Blackhawks, 1952–57; New York Rangers, 1959–60
AWARDS/HONORS: Hart Memorial Trophy, 1954; Vezina Trophy, 1951; NHL All-Star Game, 1954

A case could be made for Al Rollins as the most underrated superb goalie in NHL history. As understudy for Toronto's legendary Turk Broda in 1949-50, Rollins consistently came up with the good game, but was always overshadowed by his more colorful partner. In 1950-51, Rollins played 40 games for the Leafs, gaining the Vezina Trophy. Rollins's goals-against average was an impeccable 1.75. Better still was his playoff work—only six goals allowed in four games for a 1.50 average. Needless to say, the Leafs won the Stanley Cup that year. Rollins played one more season in Toronto and again was superb, ending up with a 2.20 average. However, he slipped during the playoffs and was traded to Chicago before the 1952-53 campaign.

The Blackhawks had been a consistent nonplayoff club until Rollins came along. He made miracles for the patchwork Chicago sextet and helped them into the playoffs. In turn, he won the Hart Trophy as the NHL's most valuable player. Rollins performed gallantly in the playoffs against the powerful Canadiens as Chicago took a three-games-to-two lead. But Montreal rebounded to win the semifinal round. In 1959-60, Rollins was acquired by the Rangers and he finished his major-league career in New York, where he played excellent hockey, but was again overshadowed this time by 1960 Olympic hero Jack McCartan.

After retiring from the NHL, he remained in hockey for many years as a coach and manager on the minor-league level.

DOC ELWYN ROMNES

BORN: White Bear, Minnesota, January 1, 1909
DIED: Date unknown
POSITION: Center, Chicago Blackhawks, 1930–38; Toronto Maple Leafs, 1938–39; New York Americans, 1939–40
AWARDS/HONORS: Lady Byng Memorial Trophy, 1936

One of the classiest American-born players to skate in the National Hockey League, Doc Romnes was an offensive star for the Chicago Blackhawks in two (1934, 1938) of Chicago's three Stanley Cup triumphs. Lionel Conacher, Canada's athlete of the half-century, called Romnes one of the best centers he ever skated with. Doc scored the winning goal in the 1938 semifinal series against the New York Americans, and scored a pivotal goal in the finals against the Toronto Maple Leafs. He originally broke in with the Blackhawks in 1930–31 and played in the Windy City until 1938–39, when he was traded to the Toronto Maple Leafs. He concluded his big-league career in 1939–40 with the New York Americans.

ART ROSS

BORN: Naughton, Ontario, January 13, 1886
DIED: August 5, 1964
POSITION: Defenseman, Westmount (CAHL), 1905; Brandon (MHL), 1907; Kenora Thistles (MHL), 1907; Montreal Wanderers (ECAHA), 1908–09; Haileybury (NHA), 1910; Montreal Wanderers (NHA), 1911–14, 1917; Ottawa Senators (NHA), 1915–16; Montreal Wanderers, 1917–18; General Manager, Boston Bruins, 1924–55
AWARDS/HONORS: Art Ross puck, net, and trophy (begun 1947) in his name; Hockey Hall of Fame, 1945; Lester Patrick Trophy, 1984

The official NHL puck, "the Art Ross puck" and the official goal net, "the Art Ross net," were not named after the former Boston Bruins' manager for nothing. One of the more creative minds in hockey, Ross redesigned the rubber puck, which formerly had sharp edges that caused painful cuts. He had the edges beveled, and improved the game. Pre-Ross nets were simple devices with sloping flat rear sections that frequently allowed pucks to bounce out of the twine as fast as they went in. Ross's improvement became today's net with a double half-moon interior built to retain pucks shot into the webbing.

But Ross did considerably more than that. His major accomplishment was building the Boston Bruins into a dynasty in the late 1920s and constantly rebuilding the Bruins so that they remained the class of the NHL for most of Art's life. He developed such aces as Eddie Shore, Frankie Brimsek, the Kraut Line, Bill Cowley, and Dit Clapper. He also was a cantankerous sort who frequently feuded with his managerial colleagues, especially Conn Smythe of the Maple Leafs.

The feud started when Smythe bought the Toronto franchise in the late 1920s and was on the lookout for talent. Ross recommended a player named Jimmy "Sailor" Herberts. Smythe bit, paid $18,000 for Herberts, and then learned that he had purchased a dud.

According to Smythe, Ross's chief goal in life was making a fool of Smythe. "Once," said Smythe, "Ross stationed two longshoremen near our bench in Boston Garden and their instructions were to goad me into a fight. Ross wanted to have me put in jail."

Sure enough, the longshoremen pushed and shoved Smythe as he was heading for the dressing room after the game. Smythe snarled at them and then noticed Ross in the background, apparently ready to charge at Smythe. "My assistant, a little guy named Frank Selke, saw Ross coming and dove at him with a flying block that knocked Ross down," Smythe recalled. "We got out of there fast, but not before I yelled at the longshoremen, 'When your boss gets up tell him I can't waste my time with anybody that a man as small as Selke can lick.'" All Smythe had done was pour gasoline on the flames of his feud with Ross.

During a Bruins slump, Smythe bought four columns of space in all of the Boston newspapers. Addressed to the fans, the ad read: "If you're tired of what you've been looking at, come out tonight and see a decent team, the Toronto Maple Leafs, play hockey."

Livid, Ross demanded that league president Frank Calder fine Smythe $3,000 for conduct detrimental to the NHL. He snapped that Smythe was nothing more than "the big wind from Lake Ontario."

When the Leafs returned to Boston, Conn rented a tuxedo and pranced haughtily around Boston Garden, tipping his hat and waving to the Bruins' fans as if he was the city's official greeter. A bouquet of roses were dispatched to Ross as added insult.

Smythe always respected Ross's hockey ability and following World War II, they patched up their feud, allegedly based on Ross's sons' participation in the armed forces. "His two sons served overseas," Smythe explained, "and had excellent records. I figured anybody who could rear two boys like that must be all right!"

PATRICK ROY

BORN: Quebec City, Quebec, October 5, 1965
POSITION: Goaltender, Montreal Canadiens, 1984–95; Colorado Avalanche, 1995–
AWARDS/HONORS: Conn Smythe Trophy, 1986, 1993, 2001; William M. Jennings Trophy, 1987–89 (shared with Brian Hayward), 1992; Trico Goaltending Award, 1989–90; Vezina Trophy, 1989–90, 1992; NHL All-Rookie Team, 1986; NHL Second Team All-Star, 1988, 1991; NHL First Team All-Star, 1989–90, 1992; NHL All-Star Game, 1988, 1990–94, 1997–98, 2001–02

Patrick Roy with the Canadiens

One of the greatest goaltenders of all time? Some critics believe Patrick Roy deserves that accolade. Others consider him vastly overrated. Certainly there is evidence that Roy was the best goalie of the decade 1986–96. There were three Stanley Cups (with two Conn Smythe Trophies), three Vezina Trophies (best goaltender), and two all-time win records (regular season and playoffs). There was also the fateful game in December 1995, when his Canadiens career came to an end, leading to his trade to the Colorado Avalanche.

Roy perfected the butterfly style of goaltending and inspired a generation of French-Canadien goaltenders to follow him into the NHL. His acknowledgment that his success was partly due to a goalie coach led to the goalie coach "explosion" of the 1990s.

In 1986, he was a rookie leading a young, but solid, team to victory. In 1993, he was the key to victory for an average Canadiens team. His overtime clutch-goaltending heroics in 1986 and 1993 were some of the most spectacular in NHL history.

In 1993, 11 of the 20 playoff games Montreal played went into overtime. Montreal won the last ten, a Stanley Cup record that may never be broken. Roy's attitude toward the overtimes was comforting if you were a Canadiens fan, cocky if you weren't. "I don't mind going into overtime. I knew my teammates were going to score if I gave them some time."

Despite his clutch reputation, Roy could be all too human on some nights.

Roy's most memorable bad game was also the last game he played for Montreal. On December 2, 1995, the feud that had been simmering between Roy and rookie Canadiens coach Mario Tremblay boiled over. Roy turned in a stinker that night, giving up nine goals in about half a game to the Detroit Red Wings. Until the ninth goal, Tremblay had refused to pull Roy, even though it was obvious that Patrick simply didn't have it that night.

When Patrick finally came off the ice, he glared at Tremblay, walked past him to where Canadiens president Ronald Corey was sitting behind the bench, and told Corey that he had played his last game for Montreal.

Roy did not change his mind, and Montreal general manager Réjean Houle decided that he could not choose his goalie over his coach. Four days after the game, Roy was dealt to Colorado and the Avalanche, who had never come close to a Cup before, won one that season. Montreal went into a downward spiral over the next several years, and Roy was still tending goal for the Avalanche long after Tremblay and Houle had been fired.

Roy had two advantages that allowed him to overcome the biggest issues with the butterfly. Because a butterfly goaltender goes down on his knees, he should be vulnerable up high. However, Roy's long torso, combined with a quick glove hand, enabled him to cover the top of the net extremely well. Also, when many goalies move across the ice on their knees, they open up the 5-hole between their legs. Most goals scored on butterfly goalies are scored through the 5-hole. Roy's legs and knees were

so flexible that he could put his legs together at practically 90-degree angles, "like two L's back-to-back," noted former goalie Chico Resch. Roy knew it, too; he often deliberately opened the 5-hole to entice players to shoot, and then snapped it shut to make the save.

Roy had one more weapon in his arsenal that made him technically and mentally strong: his long association with goalie coach François Allaire. Roy worked with Allaire from Junior through his first ten seasons with the Canadiens. Allaire's firing by Montreal was at least part of the problem that led to the explosion between Roy and Tremblay.

Roy's open acknowledgment of the role Allaire played in his development helped the NHL rethink their position on goalie coaches, who became standard personnel on teams at all levels of hockey by the mid 1990s. Some worked exclusively with the NHL club, but many, like Vladislav Tretiak of the Chicago Blackhawks, spent most of their time with prospects, preparing them for a possible NHL future.

So was Roy the best goalie of his generation? John Davidson, former Rangers goaltender, may have answered it best in the mid 1990s: "Name me one who has been any better in the past twenty years."

LINDY RUFF

BORN: Warburg, Alberta, February 17, 1960
POSITION: Defenseman/Left Wing, Buffalo Sabres, 1979–89; New York Rangers, 1989–91; Coach, Buffalo Sabres, 1997–

Most hockey experts suggest that an NHL coach must be a disciplinarian or a "players' coach." Lindy Ruff was a rare example of a bench boss who mastered both roles.

As a player, Lindy was drafted by Buffalo in the second round in 1979 and made the team as a defenseman during his first training camp. Three seasons later, Ruff was converted to forward and became a dependable, rugged left-winger for the Sabres.

After Ruff ended his playing career, one of his old coaches called for his help. When former Sabres and Rangers coach Roger Neilson was hired as the first coach of the Florida Panthers, Ruff was asked to join the expansion franchise as an assistant. Ruff played a vital role in instilling an overachieving attitude in Florida that led the Panthers to the Stanley Cup finals in 1996 and led Ruff to a head coaching position in Buffalo.

As a coach, Ruff built an almost impenetrable defensive team, backstopped by all-world goaltender Dominik Hasek, with an insatiable work ethic and accountability. With the unique experience of playing both forward and defense at the NHL level, Ruff could relate to all the players on his roster. The Sabres quickly responded to Ruff and he became the second coach ever to lead his team to the Conference finals in each of his first two seasons behind an NHL bench, including a trip to the Stanley Cup finals in 1999 that ended with Brett Hull's controversial overtime goal.

Despite the departure of Hasek and Michael Peca in the summer of 2001, Ruff continued to forge the foundations of a young Buffalo team.

JIM RUTHERFORD

BORN: Beeton, Ontario, February 17, 1949
POSITION: Goaltender, Detroit Red Wings, 1970–71, 1974–80, 1982; Pittsburgh Penguins, 1971–74; Toronto Maple Leafs, 1980–81; Los Angeles Kings, 1981–82; General Manager, Hartford Whalers/Carolina Hurricanes, 1994–

When the Carolina Hurricanes reached the finals of the Stanley Cup playoffs in 2002 for the first time in franchise history, Jim Rutherford had amply demonstrated his value as one of the most perceptive NHL executives.

A veteran of 13 NHL seasons, Rutherford began his professional goaltending career in 1969 as a first-round selection of the Detroit Red Wings. While playing for Pittsburgh,

Toronto, Los Angeles, and Detroit, Rutherford played in 457 games and collected 14 career shutouts. For five seasons, he also served as the Red Wings' player representative. Rutherford played for Team Canada in the World Championships in Vienna in 1977 and Moscow in 1979.

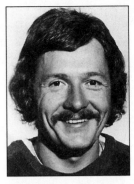

Jimmy Rutherford, when he was a goaltender for Detroit

Jim became the first team president–general manager in professional sports to oversee a franchise move in just three months, as the Whalers relocated to Raleigh. The Hurricanes captured the franchise's first division championship since 1987, when Carolina won the Southeast Division in the 1998–99 season.

Heading into the 2001–02 season, Rutherford stocked the club with seven current and former NHL All-Stars through the Entry Draft, free agency, and trades including Ron Francis, Rod Brind'Amour, Tom Barasso, Arturs Irbe, Sami Kapanen, Sandis Ozolinsh, and Glen Wesley. Rutherford also had a proven history of success in the NHL Entry Draft.

With his first draft choice in 1994, Rutherford chose Jeff O'Neill, later the first team member to score 40 goals for the franchise since it relocated to North Carolina. While draft selections like O'Neill, Kapanen, Shane Willis, David Tanabe, and Josef Vasicek formed the core of the current Hurricanes, other Rutherford draftees were rapidly becoming top level prospects, such as Erik Cole, Jaroslav Svoboda, and Igor Knyazev.

Rutherford's astute handling enabled the Hurricanes to reach their highest level in the spring of 2002. After gaining a playoff berth, Carolina defeated New Jersey, Montreal, and Toronto before losing to the Detroit Red Wings in a stirring final round.

JOE SAKIC

BORN: Burnaby, British Columbia, July 7, 1969
POSITION: Center; Quebec Nordiques,
1988–95; Colorado Avalanche, 1995–
AWARDS/HONORS: Conn Smythe Trophy,
1996; Hart Memorial Trophy, 2001; Lester B.
Pearson Award, 2001; Lady Byng Memorial Trophy,
2001; NHL First Team All-Star, 2001; NHL All-Star
Game, 1990–94, 1996, 1998, 2000–02

The best advertise-
ment for Joe
Sakic, superstar, was
displayed during the
2000–01 Stanley Cup
playoffs, particularly
in the finals against
the New Jersey Devils.

Captain of the
Colorado Avalanche,
and operating with-
out Peter Forsberg,
Sakic guided the Avs
to the Stanley Cup.

Joe Sakic

This surprised no one, since the Avs ace had
already won the Conn Smythe Trophy in 1996
when Colorado won its first Cup.

Sakic was Quebec's second choice (15th
overall) in the 1987 Entry Draft and recorded
23 goals and 39 assists in his rookie season
with the Nordiques (1988–89). Sakic's numbers
grew steadily, including 102 as a sophomore,
and 109 the following year.

He became captain of the Nordiques in
1992, when they made their first playoff
appearance that spring after five years of last-
place finishes and franchise-seeding number
one picks. When the Nords moved to Colorado
for the 1995–96 stanza, Sakic recorded the
highest numbers of his career (120) and drove
to his Conn Smythe performance.

Speedy, with a deadly wrist shot and world-
class offensive skills, the five-feet-eleven, 185-
pound center had a stunning 18-goal, 16-assist
1996 postseason, setting a record for the most
game-winning goals during the playoffs with six.

During the 2000–01 season, Sakic recorded
a career-high 54 goals and once again took the
Stanley Cup after an indomitable drive to
attain the first Cup win for fellow Avalanche
and ex-Boston Bruin star Raymond Bourque.

Joe later won the 2001 Hart, Lady Byng,
and Lester Patrick Trophies, and became the
all-time franchise leader for the Colorado
Avalanche in goals, assists, and points while
appearing in eight consecutive All-Star games.
An Olympian in the 1998 Winter Games in
Nagano, Sakic reprised the honor at the 2002
Winter Games in Salt Lake City, where he
teamed on a dream line with Mario Lemieux
and Paul Kariya and won the gold medal for
Team Canada over Team USA.

Joe's Hall of Fame credentials fueled
Colorado's continued prominence in 2001–02,
as they again finished first in the Northwest
Division. However, after defeating first the
Kings and then the Sharks in seven games, Sakic
and his Avs were bested by Detroit in the seventh game of the Western Conference finals.

BORJE SALMING

BORN: Kiruna, Sweden, April 17, 1951
POSITION: Defenseman, Toronto Maple Leafs, 1973–89; Detroit Red Wings, 1989-90
AWARDS/HONORS: NHL First Team All-Star, 1977; NHL Second Team All-Star, 1975–76, 1978–80; NHL Challenge Cup All-Star, 1979; NHL All-Star Game, 1976–78; Hockey Hall of Fame, 1996

One of the best European hockey players to make the trip across the Atlantic, Borje Salming was the steadiest defenseman on the struggling Maple Leafs during the 1970s.

Borje Salming

Formerly a member of the Swedish National Team with Maple Leaf teammate Inge Hammarstrom, Salming was so impressive in his rookie season (1973–74) that he finished third in the balloting for the Calder Trophy. A defensive defenseman, Salming nonetheless scored 76 points in his first two campaigns with the Leafs. Borje eclipsed the mark in 1976–77 with a breakthrough 78-point campaign.

Salming was widely acknowledged as one of the most talented backliners in the NHL, when an eye injury stopped him in the 1978 Stanley Cup playoffs against the New York Islanders. His great popularity and worth were evident by the thousands of get-well cards that poured into the Swede's hospital room from all over the world.

Salming bounced back in the 1978–79 season, tallying 73 points and continued to courageously defy the "soft" stereotype of European players, inspiring scores of his countrymen to work their way to the NHL. For 16 seasons, Salming remained a durable defenseman on the Toronto back line, and his 1,344 career penalty minutes show he was not intimidated by the North American game.

Borje would never win a Cup, but his legacy as a Leaf emerged in the team scoring annals as their third all-time leading scorer, with 768 points, and top all-time assist leader, with 620.

He finished his brilliant career in 1989–90 as a Detroit Red Wing, but his fame never diminished in Toronto, and he returned to his adopted city when elected to the Hall of Fame in 1996.

TOMMY SALO

BORN: Surahammar, Sweden, February 1, 1971
POSITION: Goaltender, New York Islanders, 1994–99; Edmonton Oilers, 1999–
AWARDS/HONORS: NHL All-Star Game, 2000, 2002

Tommy Salo's most famous save did not take place in a National Hockey League game. It occurred during the 1998 Olympics.

The sensational stop, along with numerous International Hockey League awards including Most Valuable Player (1995) and Rookie of the Year (1995), appeared at the time to be the prelude to a long and successful National Hockey League career. However, when Salo became a member of the New York Islanders, the team was in a state of disarray and he soon became involved in a series of clashes with general manager Mike Milbury. The feuding eventually led to Salo's being dealt to the Edmonton Oilers where his career was successfully revived.

In 2000-01, Salo posted a 36–25–12 record with a 2.46 goals-against average and eight shutouts as the Oilers finished the season with their highest win total (39) since their last Stanley Cup win 11 years earlier. Salo was most successful playing low in the net and had one of the strongest glove hands in the league. His career 2.59 goals-against average warranted respect going into the subsequent season as Edmonton's key to playoff fortune.

However, Salo continued to suffer misfortune. During the 2002 Olympics, his favored Swedish team was unceremoniously upset by Belarus when a shot hit Salo's mask, bounced over him and into the net for a goal that eliminated Sweden from medal competition. Subsequently, through no fault of Salo's, the Oilers failed to make the playoffs in 2001–02.

ULF SAMUELSSON

BORN: Fagersta, Sweden, March 26, 1964
POSITION: Defenseman, Hartford Whalers, 1984–91; Pittsburgh Penguins, 1991–95; New York Rangers, 1995–99; Detroit Red Wings, 1999; Philadelphia Flyers, 1999–2000

Ulf Samuelsson hit hard and often. At six feet one, 205 pounds, the Swedish defenseman had the size to do so, plus a knack for getting the opposition's goat with devastating nastiness.

It was Samuelsson's infamous 1991 knee-on-knee check against Cam Neely of the Boston Bruins that effectively ended Neely's career, while augmenting Ulf's reputation as a master of the quasi-legal hit.

One of The Game's most hated players and a true all-time bad boy, Ulf totaled 2,453 penalty minutes, peaking in 1993–94 with a whopping 249 minutes in only 77 games. But his 52 career goals and 265 assists showed he could play the puck when he wasn't playing villain.

Samuelsson drew fire from all angles but that of his teammates, including frequent bursts of criticism from *Hockey Night in Canada*'s Don Cherry, and unanimous regard as the league's dirtiest player for his late hits, stickwork, and borderline tactics, especially on the opposition's best skaters. When once asked about casting a vote for the league's dirtiest player, he asked, semijokingly, if he could vote for himself.

The gritty defenseman began his career with the Hartford Whalers, where he played for seven seasons, then continued to Pittsburgh, along with Ron Francis and Grant Jennings, in exchange for John Cullen and Zarley Zalapski, in 1991. His penalty minutes skyrocketed from that point on, but he helped the Penguins win two straight Stanley Cups in 1991 and 1992.

Samuelsson was then part of a deal in which he was sent to New York along with Luc Robitaille for Sergei Zubov and Petr Nedved, and endeared himself to the raucous Madison Square Garden crowd with his belligerent style. A goal-crease sucker punch from the Maple Leafs' Tie Domi during a 1996–97 match softened his bite thereafter, as Ulf's Rangers began slipping regularly from the playoff picture.

At the trading deadline in 1999, Ulf joined an active Red Wings team that had also acquired Chris Chelios, Wendel Clark, and Bill Ranford for a Cup run, but Detroit was ousted in the second round.

Ulf's playing days came to an end with the Philadelphia Flyers in 1999–2000, after nagging injuries forced him out of hockey after 49 games. Many in the hockey world were relieved.

DEREK SANDERSON

BORN: Niagara Falls, Ontario, June 16, 1946
POSITION: Center/Left Wing, Boston Bruins, 1965–72, 1973–74; Philadelphia Blazers (WHA), 1972; New York Rangers, 1974–75; St. Louis Blues, 1975–77; Vancouver Canucks, 1977–78; Pittsburgh Penguins, 1978
AWARDS/HONORS: Calder Memorial Trophy, 1968

If media coverage could be translated into talent, Derek Sanderson would have been the most gifted player ever to lace on a pair of skates. Combining a lusty sex appeal with considerable talent and a penchant for saying outrageous things to the press, Sanderson was featured in such publications as *Esquire, Life,* and *Sports Illustrated* while more talented team-mates were overlooked.

Derek began skating at the tender age of five and soon climbed up the amateur hockey ladder, ultimately landing with the Niagara Falls Flyers, a powerful club in the Ontario Hockey Association, Junior A Division. In September 1967, an outstanding Boston Bruins' training camp convinced everyone that Sanderson was good enough for the NHL, and tough enough, too.

The Bruins knew Sanderson had a surplus of guts when he ran at defenseman Ted Green, the Boston jawbreaker. Derek hit Green once, twice. Whop! Green's stick slashed at Sanderson's head. Undaunted, Sanderson slashed back. Green's thin, slit-like eyes bore through Derek like laser beams. "Listen, kid," snapped the veteran. "I hit you. But you don't hit me. You got that straight? You don't ever hit me or you won't be playing in this league very long."

Normally, Green would wither a rookie with such a knifelike assertion. Sanderson stared right back at the Bruins bully. "The next time you do that," said Derek, "I'm gonna crush your face."

An unspoken armistice had been declared, but it was clear that Sanderson had won something few others ever had from Green. Not long after the episode Green approached Derek. "Y'know, kid," he said, "I like you. You've got guts."

It is doubtful the Bruins would have given Sanderson a full turn at center in his rookie season if he couldn't play his position as well as he could handle his dukes. But he was a superb center, scored 24 goals, and was voted the Calder Trophy as NHL Rookie of the Year.

Derek helped the Bruins to a Stanley Cup victory in 1970 and again in 1972.

Some critics believed Sanderson was finished when he said good-bye to the Bruins in the summer of 1972 and signed a ten-year $2.5 million contract with the Philadelphia Blazers of the World Hockey Association.

However, Sanderson's failure to lead, score, or fight for the Blazers proved a huge disappointment, and Sanderson returned to the Bruins, and in no time at all the team began winning again, with Derek in the forefront, antagonizing and shocking the world as usual. Then, in midseason, all hell broke loose. Sanderson and teammate Terry O'Reilly engaged in a bitter fistfight during a game in Oakland, and Sanderson was suspended after missing the team flight back to Boston following the clubhouse clash.

In May 1974, Derek was traded to the New York Rangers. He was an effective performer, scoring 50 points during his first season with the Rangers. Then accused of being a disruptive influence on the younger, more naive Ranger players, Derek was banished to St. Louis.

Sanderson quit hockey after wandering through several more NHL and minor-league clubs in 1978. By that time, he was flat broke. He lost all of his money in a haze of alcoholism and poor investments. In 1980, Derek checked into an Ontario rehab clinic and got his life back in order.

Clean and sober, Derek landed on his feet and joined the Bruins in the broadcast booth from 1987 to 1997. In March 1998, Sanderson and colleague Phil Kenner opened a special fund catering to professional athletes and coaches, and began promulgating his ideas and experiences to teams, players, and agents around the country.

MIROSLAV SATAN

BORN: Topolcany, Czechoslovakia, October 22, 1974
POSITION: Left Wing, Edmonton Oilers, 1995–97; Buffalo Sabres, 1997–
AWARDS/HONORS: NHL All-Star Game, 2000

The era of Czech players starring in the National Hockey League began with Peter Stastny during the 1980s and was carried on by the likes of Jaromir Jagr and a speedy wing named Miroslav Satan.

When the Edmonton Oilers drafted him 111th overall in 1993, the six-feet-three, 192-pounder was a total unknown.

After bouncing around the International Hockey League, from Cape Breton to the Detroit Vipers to the San Diego Gulls, Satan finally made it to the NHL in 1995–96 when he totaled 35 points (18 goals, 17 assists) in 62 games with the Edmonton Oilers.

After two years with Edmonton, he was traded to Buffalo for Barrie Moore and Craig Millar.

It was one of the Sabres' best exchanges. Satan became a 40-goal scorer in 1998–99 and by 2000–01, had become Buffalo's go-to guy after learning to play the game in both zones and using his speed to his advantage.

A deft stickhandler, Satan also showed he could deliver in clutch playoff games. Limited to only 12 postseason contests when the Sabres reached the Stanley Cup finals in 1999, Satan potted eight points, including a double-overtime tally against Ottawa in Game Two of the opening round. In 13 contests during the 2001 postseason, he scored three goals and 10 assists for a total of 13 points. With the rebuilding Sabres missing out on the 2002 playoffs by just a few points, Satan remained their primary offensive weapon for any resurgence the franchise would make.

GLEN SATHER

BORN: High River, Alberta, September 2, 1943
POSITION: Left Wing, Boston Bruins, 1966–69; Pittsburgh Penguins, 1969–71; New York Rangers, 1971–74; St. Louis Blues, 1974–75; Montreal Canadiens, 1974–75; Minnesota North Stars, 1975–76; Edmonton Oilers (WHA), 1976–77; Coach, Edmonton Oilers, 1979–89, 1993–94; General Manager, Edmonton Oilers, 1980–2000; New York Rangers, 2000–
AWARDS/HONORS: Jack Adams Award, 1986; Hockey Hall of Fame, 1997

Once a member of Boston's Big Bad Bruins, Glen Sather plodded through a foot soldier's career spiced with a gung ho style that compensated for many of his deficiencies.

But in 1977, he became coach of the Edmonton Oilers of the World Hockey Association, a stint that would lead him to the epicenter of the hockey world in the 1980s.

The Oilers entered the NHL in 1979, and Sather was appointed president and general manager. Building around a core of young breakthrough talent—which included Kevin Lowe, Grant Fuhr, Jari Kurri, Paul Coffey, Mark Messier, and a free-agent phenom named Wayne Gretzky—"Slats" schooled his team in the ways of winning.

Edmonton turned into an NHL power-house, with Sather as the mastermind behind five Stanley Cup championships between 1984 and 1990, numerous division titles and team scoring records, not to mention the career of the record-shattering Gretzky. Sather's .706 winning percentage in the Stanley Cup play-offs as a coach is one of the highest in league history. Undaunted, he stepped down as Edmonton coach in 1989 to concentrate on general managing duties.

The cigar-chomping Sather became an astute executive, one of the league's most shrewd, especially after Edmonton's dynastic days ended with the team struggling to stay afloat as a Canadian small-market team in the expanding NHL. Among the moves he made to strengthen the organization was the 1993 trade of an aging Esa Tikkanen for center Doug Weight, the preeminent playmaking Oilers star of the 1990s, generally acknowledged as one of hockey's all-time steals.

His keen sense of team building also led him to berths as Team Canada's general manager and coach for the 1994 Canada Cup and the 1996 World Cup of Hockey.

In 1997, Sather was inducted into the Hockey Hall of Fame, but his tenure took another turn shortly afterward. After 24 years with the Oilers organization, Glen stepped down in 2000 to become president and general manager of the New York Rangers, with whom he had played in the mid 1970s, with protégé Kevin Lowe taking over in Edmonton. One of Sather's first, and by far the most popular, moves was bringing back old reliable former Oiler and ex-Ranger Stanley Cup–winning captain Messier to lead the Blueshirts. But the 2000–01 Rangers could not make the playoffs.

One of the most influential power brokers in The Game, Sather's task of redefining the Ranger franchise began in earnest during the summer of 2001, when he acquired controversial, oft-concussed superstar Eric Lindros and a conditional first-round pick for Jan Hlavac, Kim Johnsson, Pavel Brendl, and a third-round pick. When the team struggled down the stretch of the 2001–02 season, Slats's magic worked again with the March 2002 trade for goal-scoring machine Pavel Bure from Florida, sending two prospects and little-used defenseman Igor Ulanov, plus picks. But for the fifth straight year, the Rangers did not get into the postseason, with Sather primed to further revamp the Blueshirts over the off-season, starting with the hiring of ex-rival Bryan Trottier as head coach.

DENIS SAVARD

BORN: Pointe Gatineau, Quebec, February 4, 1961
POSITION: Center; Chicago Blackhawks, 1980–90, 1995–97; Montreal Canadiens, 1990–93; Tampa Bay Lightning, 1993–95; Assistant Coach, Chicago Blackhawks, 1997–
AWARDS/HONORS: NHL Second Team All-Star, 1983; NHL All-Star Game, 1982–84, 1986, 1988, 1991, 1996; Hockey Hall of Fame, 2000

Among the most outstanding French-Canadian hockey players, following in the steps of Jean Beliveau, Henri Richard, and Bernie Geoffrion, was Denis Savard.

Combining superior skating skills with exceptional stickhandling and an accurate shot, Savard emerged as one of the best draft picks in Chicago Blackhawk history.

The year was 1980. Ironically, the Montreal Canadiens always chose French-Canadian talents over their English-Canadian counterparts, but in this year, for inexplicable reasons the Habs—who owned the first pick—bypassed Savard and instead chose Doug Wickenheiser. When Winnipeg went for a defenseman with Dave Babych, it was left to Chicago, exercising the third overall pick, to opt for Savard.

For many years, Chicago fans gloated over the Montreal mistake. Savard rapidly blossomed into a major offensive threat, while Wickenheiser proved nothing better than a checking forward with minimum offensive skills.

Veteran Chicago hockey observers compared Savard's jackrabbit skating style to an earlier Windy City hockey hero, Hall of Famer Max Bentley, otherwise known as the Dipsy Doodle Dandy.

Most Chicagoans considered Savard a permanent fixture at Chicago Stadium, but in 1990, the popular Blackhawk was dealt to the Montreal Canadiens for Chris Chelios and a draft pick. In francophone Montreal, he went on to compile 179 points in 210 games and was a member of the 1993 Stanley Cup champions.

Following that season, Savard signed with the Tampa Bay Lightning, but was traded back to Chicago in 1995. Rejuvenated by his return to Chicago, Savard went on to lead the Blackhawks to the Conference finals, leading the team with 18 points in the postseason. He played two more seasons before retiring as a Blackhawk in 1997. The fifth jersey ever retired by the Blackhawks, Savard's 18 was lifted to the rafters in 1998.

In June 2000, Denis Savard was extended the ultimate hockey honor, induction into the Hockey Hall of Fame, joining the likes of Stan Mikita, Bobby Hull, Glenn Hall, and Tony Esposito as the only Blackhawks to have their number retired and to achieve the Hall of Fame.

SERGE SAVARD

BORN: Montreal, Quebec, January 22, 1946
POSITION: Defense, Montreal Canadiens, 1966–81; Winnipeg Jets, 1981–83
AWARDS/HONORS: Conn Smythe Trophy, 1969; Bill Masterton Memorial Trophy, 1979; Team Canada, 1972; NHL Second Team All-Star, 1979; NHL Challenge Cup All-Star, 1979; NHL All-Star Game, 1970, 1973, 1977–78; Hockey Hall of Fame, 1986

A star Canadiens blueliner during the 1970s, Serge Savard had to fight his way through a number of crippling injuries, which might have ended the careers of other athletes.

After a brilliant rookie season in 1968–69, when he was the recipient of the Conn Smythe Trophy for the most valuable player in the Stanley Cup playoffs, Savard missed the final weeks of the following season with a fractured left leg. That injury also caused him to sit out parts of the next two years as well, as he refractured the leg, and complications set in.

Following 1972–73, however, Serge remained healthy, and, in 1975, had an incredible offensive year—for him—scoring 20 goals and

adding 40 assists. The following year, with the veteran defenseman's scoring totals down closer to his norm at 47 points, Les Canadiens won their first of four consecutive Stanley Cups while sporting an All-Star defense that included Guy Lapointe, Larry Robinson, and Savard. Serge slowed down, and was claimed by Winnipeg in the 1981 Waiver Draft, and finished his playing career two years later.

Savard replaced Irving Grundman as Habs general manager in 1983, and proceeded to fortify the Montreal core. His drafting of goalie Patrick Roy in 1984 proved to be the foundation of the Adams Division title on four occasions as well as Cup championships in 1986 and 1993. Savard's one blunder may have been dealing John LeClair, Eric Desjardins, and Gilbert Dionne for Mark Recchi, as the raw LeClair went on to become a perennial 50-goal scorer with the Philadelphia Flyers.

Réjean Houle took over for Savard in 1995.

TERRY SAWCHUK

BORN: Winnipeg, Manitoba, December 28, 1929
DIED: May 31, 1970
POSITION: Goaltender, Detroit Red Wings, 1950–55, 1957–64, 1968–69; Boston Bruins, 1955–57; Toronto Maple Leafs, 1964–67; Los Angeles Kings, 1967–68; New York Rangers, 1969–70
AWARDS/HONORS: Calder Memorial Trophy, 1951; Vezina Trophy, 1952–53, 1955, 1965 (shared with Johnny Bower); Lester Patrick Trophy, 1971; NHL First Team All-Star, 1951–53; NHL Second Team All-Star, 1954–55, 1959, 1963; NHL All-Star Game, 1950–56, 1959, 1963–64, 1968; Hockey Hall of Fame, 1971

One of the greatest and most tragic players ever to grace a major-league hockey rink was Terry Sawchuk. Quite possibly the best goaltender ever to strap on the tools of his trade, he was a moody, brooding figure who was a physical and mental wreck of a man when he met his untimely death in 1970.

His 20-year career in big-league hockey included tours of duty with the Detroit Red Wings, Boston Bruins, Toronto Maple Leafs, Los Angeles Kings, and New York Rangers. Terry broke into the majors with the Wings, making First Team All-Star during his maiden season and copping the Calder Trophy as the NHL's rookie of the year.

Terry Sawchuk as a Red Wing

Incredibly, his goals-against average never topped 2.00 during his first five years with Detroit, a stretch that saw him rack up 56 shutouts. He finished his up-and-down career with an amazing 103 career shutouts, a record that would stand for decades. Sawchuk insisted that the finest moment of his career came with the 1966–67 Toronto Maple Leafs, when he dramatically guided the Leafs to an upset Stanley Cup victory.

It was said of Terry Sawchuk that he wasn't a whole man; rather, he was stitched together, held in place by catgut and surgical tape. He suffered a painful shoulder injury early in his career that for the rest of his playing days restricted lifting his stick hand any higher than chest level. A full-page photo of Terry once appeared in a national magazine, illustrating each stitch he had taken in his ruined face. The shocking picture could easily have passed for a horror-movie publicity shot.

An enigmatic, bitter man to the end, Terry died as a result of injuries received in a scuffle with teammate Ron Stewart on the lawn of his home in Long Island.

MILT SCHMIDT

BORN: Kitchener, Ontario, March 5, 1918
POSITION: Center, Boston Bruins, 1937–42, 1945–55; Coach, Boston Bruins, 1955–62, 1963–66; General Manager, Boston Bruins, 1967–73; General Manager, Washington Capitals, 1974–76; Coach, Washington Capitals, 1975–76
AWARDS/HONORS: Hart Memorial Trophy, 1951; Art Ross Trophy, 1940; NHL First Team All-Star, 1940, 1947, 1951; NHL Second Team All-Star, 1952; NHL All-Star Game, 1947–48, 1951–52; Hockey Hall of Fame, 1961; Lester Patrick Trophy, 1996

The saddest part of Milt Schmidt's career was that the majestic center excelled in the National Hockey League in the pretelevision era.

Comparable to Gordie Howe in style, Milt's fearlessness and multiple talents escaped the realm of videotape, but not legend.

Best known as the center for the famed Kraut Line of the Boston Bruins in the 1930s, Schmidt played pivot for Woody Dumart and Bobby Bauer, and was a prime force in the Bruins' Stanley Cup championships of 1939 and 1941. In 1940, Schmidt won the Art Ross Trophy as the NHL's leading scorer

Milt Schmidt, captain of the Bruins, circa 1946

and became the policeman of the Bruins' forward corps.

Although Schmidt's career began unfortunately with a broken jaw, keeping him out for four weeks in 1938, and a painful ankle injury, keeping him on the sidelines again for the 1939 season, he recovered to lead the Bruins in playoff scoring. He, along with Bauer and Dumart, joined the Royal Canadian Air Force during World War II, and returned to the ice four years later in 1946–47 not missing a beat; Schmidt won the Hart Trophy in 1951 as league MVP.

In 1955, Schmidt resigned from active duty and was given the coaching reins of a struggling Boston hockey club. He stayed on until 1962–63, when Phil Watson was called in to take charge. But Watson could not rejuvenate the Bruins, and Schmidt took over again in the middle of the 1962–1963 season.

He stayed atop the Bruin organization as general manager from 1966 until 1973 and saw his club win two Stanley Cups with help from trades that he masterminded.

But it was during Schmidt's tenure that the B's drafted young Bobby Orr, arguably the greatest offensive defenseman of the modern era. Perhaps the greatest coup of Schmidt's managerial career was engineering that famous—or infamous—trade between the Bruins and Blackhawks in which Chicago got goalie Jack Norris, defenseman Gilles Marotte, and center Pit Martin in return for forwards Ken Hodge, Fred Stanfield, and Phil Esposito. Hodge, Stanfield, and Esposito formed the backbone of the feared Bruins' power play that enabled them to walk away with the Stanley Cup in 1970 and again in 1972.

When the National Hockey League expanded in 1974 to 18 teams, Schmidt accepted the position of general manager of the new Washington Capitals. Beset by a lack of talent due mostly to the slim pickings in the expansion draft, the Caps finished with the worst record in National Hockey League history, leaving Schmidt the unenviable task of trying to build a contending hockey club from the ashes of a disaster. But the Caps, under his administration, never became competitive and Schmidt eventually left the disaster scene, returning to Boston, where he went to work for the Bruins in the ticket-selling department, and then ran the Boston Garden Club.

Schmidt remained a fixture around Boston Garden through the 1990s, always upright, always reflecting the greatness of his past.

JIM SCHOENFELD

BORN: Galt, Ontario, September 4, 1952
POSITION: Defenseman, Buffalo Sabres, 1972–81; Detroit Red Wings, 1981–83; Boston Bruins, 1983–84; Buffalo Sabres, 1984–85; Coach, Buffalo Sabres, 1985–86; New Jersey Devils, 1987–90; Washington Capitals, 1993–97; Phoenix Coyotes, 1997–99
AWARDS/HONORS: NHL Second Team All-Star, 1980; NHL All-Star Game, 1977, 1980

Jim Schoenfeld caught the injury jinx during his first NHL season, and through his entire playing career the strapping—but somewhat delicate—redhead would never once play every game in a season. Still, it evolved into a 14-year career.

The rugged blueliner, who originally was a Buffalo first-round pick in 1972, had his best season in 1979–80, with a plus-60 rating and 36 points, enjoying a ten-year run as the Sabres' defensive sage. He captained the team until his trade to Detroit—along with Danny Gare and Derek Smith for Dale McCourt, Mike Foligno, and Brent Peterson—in 1981, before a swan song return in 1984–85 and subsequent coaching stint that lasted for 43 games and a .500 record in 1985–86.

A passionate performer, Schoenfeld guided an upstart 1987–88 New Jersey Devils team to the Eastern Conference finals against the Boston Bruins in his first year behind the bench. After Game Three of the series, which Boston won 6–1, Schoenfeld berated referee

Don Koharski, resulting in a semiscuffle infamously recorded on video that ended with Koharski falling awkwardly while Schoenfeld shouted, "Have another doughnut, you fat pig!" He was allowed to coach in the following Game Four after a legal appeal by the Devils, and Schoenfeld's skaters won the game, 3–1, with off-ice officials substituting for striking referees, but ultimately lost the series.

Jim failed to get the Devils into the playoffs in 1988–89, and was fired 14 games into 1989–90. During 1993–94, the Washington Capitals hired Schoenfeld in midseason to replace Terry Murray. The Capitals won 113 games for Jim through 1997, but couldn't muster a Conference final berth in that period, and missed the postseason dance in 1996–97.

Schoenfeld forged on in his coaching endeavors the very next season with the Phoenix Coyotes, and overcame a team decimated by injuries to his top players for an 82-point stanza, followed by a hard-fought loss to the Detroit Red Wings in round one of the postseason tournament. A 90-point season followed, but again, Jim endured another first-round loss and another firing.

Following his Phoenix experience, Schoenfeld served as an affable, insightful hockey analyst for ESPN broadcasts, while still topping many executives' lists as a coaching candidate, until he was hired by the Rangers as an assistant coach in the summer of 2002.

SWEENEY SCHRINER

BORN: Calgary, Alberta, November 30, 1911
DIED: July 4, 1990
POSITION: Left Wing, New York Americans, 1934–39; Toronto Maple Leafs, 1939–43, 1944–46
AWARDS/HONORS: Calder Memorial Trophy, 1935; Art Ross Trophy, 1936–37; NHL First Team All-Star, 1936, 1941; NHL Second Team All-Star, 1937; NHL All-Star Game, 1937; Hockey Hall of Fame, 1962

There have been few forwards in NHL history more exciting than Dave "Sweeney" Schriner, who was named Rookie of the Year when he broke in with the New York Americans in 1934–35. A season later, Schriner led the NHL in scoring and repeated the feat a year after that. After five seasons with the Amerks, the left-winger was traded to the Maple Leafs in 1939–40.

Sweeney continued to shine and played a pivotal role in the Leafs' comeback in the 1942 Stanley Cup finals with the Red Wings when they trailed three games to none. Prior to the fourth game, Schriner was especially moved by a letter written to the Toronto club by a 14-year-old-girl. Before taking the ice, Sweeney rose in the dressing room, looked over at coach Hap Day, and shouted, "Don't worry about this one, Skipper. We'll win this one for the little girl!" The Leafs, thanks to Schriner's scoring, won the next four straight games. With Toronto behind, 1–0, in the seventh and final game, Schriner tied the score. Pete Langelle put Toronto ahead, 2–1, and then Sweeney scored the clincher as the Leafs won, 3–1. He starred again in April 1945, when the Leafs again whipped the Red Wings in seven games. Schriner ended his NHL career a year later with the Leafs.

DAVE SCHULTZ

BORN: Waldheim, Saskatchewan, October 14, 1949
POSITION: Left Wing, Philadelphia Flyers, 1971–76; Los Angeles Kings, 1976–77; Pittsburgh Penguins, 1977–79; Buffalo Sabres, 1979–80

No athlete ever received more media attention for less talent than Dave Schultz, a pugnacious forward who burst onto the NHL scene in 1971–72 for one game and became a regular a season later. A key member of the ferocious Flyers when they were bringing home the Stanley Cup regularly, Schultz worked hard to earn his nickname— "the Hammer."

He led the NHL in penalty minutes during the 1972–73, 1973–74, and 1974–75 seasons (garnering an astronomical record-breaking 472 minutes in 1974–75), and in his first eight seasons as a pro, spent the equivalent of 57 games in the penalty box.

In addition to his fistic ability, Schultz honed his hockey skills and accumulated 20 goals in 1973–74.

Unfortunately for Schultz, with a growing awareness around the NHL of excessive violence and with the "intimidation" game becoming passé, the Hammer became expendable and was dealt to the Los Angeles Kings in 1976. Schultz became somewhat of a journeyman hockey player, going to the Pittsburgh Penguins in 1977, and then to the Buffalo Sabres in 1979.

Schultz retired in 1980, then went into coaching, holding various minor-league jobs, before moving to the business realm in the Philadelphia area, where he retained high popularity.

TEEMU SELANNE

BORN: Helsinki, Finland, July 3, 1970
POSITION: Right Wing, Winnipeg Jets, 1992–96; Anaheim Mighty Ducks, 1996–2001; San Jose Sharks, 2001–
AWARDS/HONORS: Calder Memorial Trophy, 1993; Maurice "Rocket" Richard Trophy, 1999; NHL First Team All-Star, 1993, 1997; NHL All-Rookie Team, 1993; NHL Second Team All-Star, 1998–99; NHL All-Star Game, 1993–94, 1996–2000, 2002

Known as "The Finnish Flash," Teemu Selanne was among the league's most exciting players of the 1990s, and for good reason. He came barreling into the NHL with the Winnipeg Jets, scoring a rookie-record 76 goals in his first National Hockey League season (1992–93).

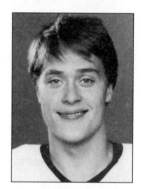

Teemu Selanne as a Winnipeg Jet

Selanne's scoring touch and charismatic performances, along with speed and a deadly accurate shot, became instant trademarks.

A severed tendon injury hindered his sophomore campaign, but he returned to form for Winnipeg in 1994–95 with 48 points in 45 games, mostly paired with Alexei Zhamnov and Keith Tkachuk. Selanne had already amassed 72 points in 51 games of 1995–96 when he was traded to Anaheim, where he immediately went on a line with Paul Kariya. The two were instantly and hugely successful.

Teemu finished that 1995–96 season with 40 goals, and accelerated his game as Kariya's linemate the following season with a 51-goal, 109-point outburst. The inseparable pair seemed to read each other's thoughts on the ice, connecting for one highlight reel goal after

another, while propelling the Mighty Ducks
to their only franchise playoff-round victory
against the Phoenix Coyotes. Selanne scored
the first playoff goal in Anaheim history in
Game One of that quarterfinal series.

As a Lady Byng and Hart Trophy finalist in
1997–98, the affable Selanne also helped his
native Finland attain the bronze medal at the
1998 Olympic Games at Nagano, and appeared
destined for further greatness by carrying a
thin Anaheim team with 86 points without
Kariya, who played only 22 games due to injury.

Despite a 107-point season in 1998–99, in
which he exploded for 77 points over 49
games, Selanne and his Ducks were swept in
the opening round of the playoffs by the
Detroit Red Wings. It appeared the Ducks
were going nowhere fast, with no players of
note to supplement Selanne and Kariya.

A financially strapped Anaheim organization knew Selanne would soon be a restricted
free agent, thus a deal was made in March
2001, after Selanne's goal output slipped to
26 in 61 games. The San Jose Sharks acquired
Teemu to enhance their offense in the playoffs, sending young speedster Jeff Friesen and
goalie Steve Shields to the Ducks in return.
Selanne finally meshed with coach Darryl
Sutter's team system and contributed two
assists in six playoff matches against eventual-
winner St. Louis in spite of a broken thumb
suffered in Game One of the series.

On Sutter's deep, defensive-minded Sharks,
Selanne recorded just 54 points in 2001–02, but
the team finished first in the Pacific Division,
and, to many critics, had the best chance of
usurping Western powers Detroit and Colorado
for a berth in the Stanley Cup finals. Alas, it
was not to be. Although Selanne played well
and San Jose made it to the second round, they
were overcome by the Stanley Cup–defending
Avalanche in seven games of round two.

FRANK SELKE SR.

BORN: Kitchener, Ontario, May 7, 1893
DIED: July 3, 1985
AWARDS/HONORS: Hockey Hall of Fame,
1960; Trophy in His Name, 1978

Few men have been more steeped in hockey
lore than Frank Selke Sr., the little man
from Berlin (now Kitchener), Ontario. Selke
broke into the hockey business like most
Canadians, as a player. Until hockey permanently intruded, Frank was an electrician. But
he became more and more enamored of the
game, and when old-time Montreal Wanderers
star Hod Stuart presented him with a gift stick
at the end of a game in Berlin, young Selke
was hooked for keeps. By 1912, he was managing City League teams and he continued
climbing the hockey ladder while working
non-ice jobs on the side.

Selke eventually made his way to Toronto,
where he came into contact with Conn
Smythe. In time, Smythe appointed Selke his
aide-de-camp, and when Smythe went overseas
with the Canadian Armed Forces in World
War II, it was Selke who filled the breach and
guided the Toronto sextet. However, one of
Selke's smartest moves in Toronto led to his
downfall as a member of the Leaf hierarchy
and his "deportation" to Montreal.

The *coup de grace* was rooted in a decision
Selke made in 1944 while Smythe was overseas. The Leafs had signed Frankie Eddolls, a
young defenseman who learned his hockey in
Verdun, not far from where Rocket Richard
played his junior games. Montreal coach Dick
Irvin saw Eddolls play and liked what he had
seen. Since Dick was on speaking terms with
Selke, he mentioned he wouldn't mind having
the Montreal lad in the Canadiens' system.

Selke's mind was turning. He knew that Les
Canadiens had the rights to a tenacious center
playing in nearby Port Colborne, Ontario.
"We'll let you have Eddolls," said Selke, "if you
give up Ted Kennedy."

At last, the parties agreed to the swap and Ted Kennedy put on the royal blue and white uniform of the Maple Leafs. In time, young "Teeder" would become the darling of Toronto hockey fans, one of the most proficient centers in NHL history, and the captain of the Leafs.

There was only one thing wrong. In his haste to complete the deal, Selke neglected to obtain the green light from Smythe, who happened to be in war-torn France at the time. When the vitriolic Smythe finally learned about the trade, he made nearly as much noise as the cannons that were booming around him. He promptly cabled Maple Leaf Gardens demanding that the deal be erased and Eddolls returned to the Toronto fold. This, of course, could not be arranged, and when Smythe was so advised he blasted off again to no avail.

The wisdom of Selke's decision would be underlined in years to come. Eddolls eventually became a member of the Canadiens, but only as a mediocre defenseman soon traded to the Rangers. Kennedy was eventually voted into the Hockey Hall of Fame.

Smythe's return to Toronto at war's end generated open warfare at Maple Leaf Gardens. He publicly roasted Selke for the Leafs' demise in the 1945–46 season, overlooking the fact that Toronto had annexed the Stanley Cup the previous year. Smythe still rankled over the Kennedy deal, and the Major, a stern advocate of discipline, drove Selke to resign from the Maple Leaf organization in May 1946. By autumn, Selke had obtained a job with Montreal.

In time, Selke became the architect of the great Canadiens dynasties of the late '40s, through the '50s, and the early '60s. The Canadiens won nine Stanley Cups from 1950 to 1966, including five in a row from 1956 to 1960. Selke retired in the early '60s. He was honored in 1978 when an award for the NHL's best defensive forward was named for him. Montreal's Bob Gainey was the first recipient of the Frank J. Selke Trophy.

EDDIE SHACK

BORN: Sudbury, Ontario, February 11, 1937
POSITION: Left Wing, New York Rangers, 1958–60; Toronto Maple Leafs, 1960–67, 1973–75; Boston Bruins, 1967–69; Los Angeles Kings, 1969–70; Buffalo Sabres, 1970–72; Pittsburgh Penguins, 1972–73
AWARDS/HONORS: NHL All-Star Game, 1962–64

Clear the track—here comes Shack!" That used to be Eddie "the Entertainer" Shack's calling card as he as he came into his own with the Toronto Maple Leafs during the mid 1960s. Eddie, a left-winger by trade, was known for mad dashes up, down, and across hockey rinks whenever the mood happened to seize him.

Shack broke into the NHL in 1958 with the New York Rangers and played for five other NHL clubs before being bought by the Toronto Maple Leafs in 1973.

Apart from the immense physical strength that enabled him to trade body checks with the biggest foe, Shack possessed a hard shot and a delightful sense of humor. His most successful season was 1972–73, when he scored 25 goals and 20 assists for 45 points in 74 games with the Pittsburgh Penguins. Once the hero of Toronto fandom, Shack became a bench-warmer in 1974–75 with the Maple Leafs, playing in only 26 games.

He retired in 1975 and enjoyed several successful business ventures in the Toronto area.

BRENDAN SHANAHAN

BORN: Mimico, Ontario, January 23, 1969
POSITION: Left Wing, New Jersey Devils, 1987–91; St. Louis Blues, 1991–95; Hartford Whalers, 1995–96; Detroit Red Wings, 1996–
AWARDS/HONORS: NHL First Team All-Star, 1994, 2000; NHL All-Star Game, 1994, 1996–2000, 2002

As the 1980s progressed, the position of power forward was dominated by big, strong, agile players who had shots like cannons and could crash the net on a nightly basis. Some of the first players to define the position included Clark Gillies of the New York Islanders, Cam Neely of the Boston Bruins, and Rick Tocchet of the Philadelphia Flyers. In 1987, Brendan Shanahan joined the ranks of this rare breed.

After the Buffalo Sabres selected Pierre Turgeon with the first overall pick in the 1987 NHL Entry Draft, Brendan was chosen by the New Jersey Devils. The Devils' brass loved Shanahan's aggressive style, and felt he was a perfect fit for a team on the verge of making its first serious playoff run later that season. But Brendan immediately felt enormous pressure to perform and did not produce as much nor as rapidly as expected. His ice time diminished; his confidence wavered.

Seeing his role become one of spectator, Brendan drastically changed his game, taking on all comers and finishing his first season as a pro with 131 penalty minutes in 65 games. But Brendan's paltry six goals that season didn't exactly endear him to his New Jersey coaches.

It all began to change, as Shanahan signed as a free agent with St. Louis in July 1991. The long-awaited goal scorer suddenly appeared, as Brendan produced two seasons of 50-plus goals scored for the Blues.

However, Brendan was developing a "rep." He'd play a few seasons for a team, his goal-production would slack off after a couple, his

team would begin dangling Shanahan as seductive trade bait. The Blues traded him to Hartford (now Carolina) in the off-season of 1995, for up-and-coming Goliath defenseman Chris Pronger. Brendan whipped up 44 goals for Hartford in 1995–96, then was traded again.

In October 1996, the Detroit Red Wings acquired Shanahan and defenseman Brian Glynn from the Whalers in exchange for Keith Primeau, Paul Coffey, and a first-round pick in the 1997 Entry Draft. Some felt the Red Wings paid too steep a price for Brendan, but the Mimico native soon changed naysayers' opinions.

The trade produced the perfect marriage between Brendan Shanahan's undisputed skills and the Detroit Red Wings' need for a chunk or two more of talent in order to produce a Stanley Cup for the first time since 1955.

In Detroit, Shanahan exploded offensively during the 1996–97 season, leading the team in points, with 46 goals and 41 assists on a team that had dominated the regular season on a consistent basis, but faltered in the playoffs. Brendan was exactly what the doctor ordered. The Wings had always been low on grit and toughness, but Shanahan's physical presence began to create open ice for freewheeling skaters Sergei Fedorov and Slava Kozlov.

The Red Wings swept the Philadelphia Flyers in the 1997 Stanley Cup finals, four games to none. Shanahan was everything and everywhere on the ice during his team's playoff run. He led the team in goals and game-winning goals. And he drank from the silver chalice for the first time in his career.

In 1998, Shanahan ended the year with only 28 goals, failing to score 30 goals for the first time since 1990–91. Only 12 of his tallies came during even strength situations, the fewest since his 1987–88 rookie season. But Shanahan rebounded with a vengeance during the 1998 Stanley Cup playoffs. In Game Six of Detroit's first-round matchup with Phoenix, Brendan scored two power-play goals, including the series winner. Facing St. Louis in the second round, Shanahan again came up with a clutch performance, tallying two game-winning goals during the series, including the overtime winner in Game Three.

Brendan and his Detroit teammates eliminated Ken Hitchcock's Stars in the 1998 Western Conference finals to secure their second-straight berth in the Stanley Cup finals. Their opponent was the Washington Capitals, led by behemoth goaltender Olaf Kolzig.

The Caps were no contest against the determined group wearing red and white. Leading three games to none, Shanahan took his pregame nap before Game Four and dreamt that he and his teammates were going to hoist the Cup for the second straight year later that evening. And after the Red Wings defeated the Capitals by a score of 4–1, Brendan's pregame fantasy became a reality.

Shanahan signed a four-year contract extension with the Red Wings right before the playoffs began in 1999, after finishing the season with 40 or more goals for the fifth time in his career.

Shanahan was well on his way to recording 500 goals and 1,000 points in his illustrious career. Plus, with a core of Red Wings in their peak—such as free-agent signees Dominik Hasek, Brett Hull, and Luc Robitaille—the 2001–02 edition, led by Shanahan's opening night hat trick, steamrolled to a Stanley Cup victory again.

FRED SHERO

BORN: Winnipeg, Manitoba, October 23, 1925
DIED: November 1990
POSITION: Defenseman, New York Rangers, 1947–50; Coach, Philadelphia Flyers, 1971–78; New York Rangers, 1978–81; General Manager, New York Rangers, 1978–80
AWARDS/HONORS: Jack Adams Award, 1974; Lester Patrick Trophy, 1980

Fred Shero, Flyers coach

Called everything from the Casey Stengel of hockey to a latter-day W. C. Fields, Shero was a mystery man to the Philadelphia and New York sportswriters, his players, and even his family.

Even after great wins, Shero liked to sit by himself, perhaps concentrating, and conquering his emotions so they wouldn't be visible to the outside world. Shero often expressed himself with a personal note placed in a player's locker or a handwritten quote on the locker room blackboard. After the Flyers once came back from a 4–1 deficit to defeat the New York Rangers (ironically, his future coaching assignment), Shero scribbled the score in the locker room with a sign reading: "This game will never be forgotten by me. Money doesn't live forever. But great moments do."

Bernie Parent, the former Flyers' amazing goalie, was named the 1974 Stanley Cup's Most Valuable Player, after Bobby Clarke, the other prime contender, announced that no one but Parent deserved the award. At the official presentation, Parent took the key to the car that went along with the prize, said he needed 23 more for his teammates, and handed it to his mentor, Fred Shero. That morning, Shero did show emotion, allowing more tears to flow than perhaps ever before during his reign in Philadelphia.

The Flyers responded to their perfectionist coach with dogged determination, tough drive, and two consecutive Stanley Cups. When Fred came to New York in 1978, the reputed "fat cat" Rangers responded just as enthusiastically to their new coach, surprising the hockey world by diligently backchecking and forechecking their way past tough opponents such as Montreal and Philadelphia during the regular season. The Blueshirts were just as impressive in the 1978–79 playoffs, scoring a record five shorthanded goals against the familiar Flyers as the Rangers took the quarterfinal series four games to one and marched to the Cup finals, where they lost.

For 13 years, starting in 1957, Shero had coached minor-league teams in St. Paul, Omaha, and Buffalo. Prior to that time he had played for the New York Rangers. As a coach, he led six teams to first-place finishes and five to playoff championships. Surprisingly, Shero was ignored by NHL teams like the North Stars and the Sabres, which had opportunities to assess his value.

Finally, in 1971, Ed Snider gave Shero a group of loosely organized men who just hadn't made it with the big-boy teams. Equipped with a system based on the discipline of Russia's National team, Shero constructed two winners in Philadelphia, but never stopped searching for new ideas, new techniques for his perfectionism. He was credited with finally incorporating European concepts in the North American game, as well as the use of assistant coaches and video.

The Flyers, 24 years after his departure, still had not found a true replacement for Fred Shero, having gone through myriad coaches and team squabbles. Fred's .642 winning percentage and 48 playoff wins stood high and above Philadelphia coaching annals. Shero continued his loyalty to the Flyers when he returned as a community relations adviser in 1990, before succumbing to a long battle with cancer in November of that year.

ALEX SHIBICKY

BORN: Winnipeg, Manitoba, May 19, 1914
POSITION: Center, New York Rangers, 1935–42, 1945–46

Among the lesser but nonetheless superb lines of pre–World War II NHL hockey, the Rangers' unit of Neil Colville, Mac Colville, and Alex Shibicky ranks in the unsung category. "The line," according to then-coach Frank Boucher, "patterned themselves on our old Cook-Boucher-Cook line, each knowing his routine perfectly, the three swooping over the ice with the precision of a flying circus."

Of the three, Shibicky was the talker and the hardest shooter. He became a Ranger in 1935–36 and played on Broadway until 1946, with a three-year interruption for wartime duties with the Canadian Armed Forces.

A strong skater who played a vital part on the Rangers' 1940 Stanley Cup championship team, Shibicky betrayed one quasi-serious flaw; he'd often hold on to the puck too long when he had a grand opportunity for a shot on goal. He thereby created a humorous response from the Rangers' bench as his frustrated teammates watched him in agony. As Alex waited and waited, the response went: "Shoot, Shibicky . . . Shoot Shibicky . . . Ah, *shit*, Shibicky!"

EDDIE SHORE

BORN: Fort Qu'Appelle-Cupar, Saskatchewan, November 25, 1902
DIED: March 16, 1985
POSITION: Defenseman, Boston Bruins, 1926–40; New York Americans, 1940
AWARDS/HONORS: Hart Memorial Trophy, 1933, 1935–36, 1938; Lester Patrick Trophy, 1970; NHL First Team All-Star, 1931–33, 1935–36, 1938–39; NHL Second Team All-Star, 1934; NHL All-Star Game, 1934, 1937, 1939; Hockey Hall of Fame, 1945

The old Pacific Coast Hockey League, directed by Frank and Lester Patrick, had run aground in 1925 and the Patricks were auctioning off some excellent players at reduced prices, including Eddie Shore, Harry Oliver, and Perk Galbraith. Charles F. Adams, the Bruins' owner, had the money, and for $50,000 he purchased Shore, Duke Keats, and Frank Boucher in a seven-man package. Boucher, in turn, was sold to the newly organized Rangers. Others were dealt to the new Detroit team that had also joined the league.

Nobody really knew it that summer, but the first Boston hockey dynasty had begun to form, and Eddie Shore was to be its general. Until Shore came along, the Bruins lacked a definitive image. They were both amusing and pathetic, effervescent and fumbling, but if you tried to find an adjective that would adequately describe them, you wound up with nothing.

Shore changed that! From the moment he tugged on the gold, white, and black jersey, the Bruin adjective was "tough." With very rare exceptions it was to remain the most singular characteristic of the team, even in the days when it appeared to be loaded with lightweights.

Ironically, manager Art Ross wasn't convinced that Shore belonged on the Bruins when Eddie reported to training camp in the autumn of 1926. This was surprising because Shore, at 24, had already created a Bunyanesque aura about himself in western Canada. Sure, Eddie had demonstrated his toughness in the minor leagues out West, but Ross wasn't so sure the big fellow with the slicked-back hair could make it with the big-leaguers.

He needn't have wondered, as Shore was brash beyond belief and just as mayhem-oriented. In his second NHL season, Shore set a league penalty record with 166 minutes' worth of fouls. The boisterousness that personified Shore was immediately translated to the Boston crowd, until it was impossible to determine which was the catalyst for mania, the frenetic Bruins audience or the player, Shore.

Shore's continual clashes with the Montreal Maroons were legendary. Several of the Montreal players decided that Shore was too liberal in his manhandling of them. During one game, one of them tore open Eddie's cheek with his stick blade, and another sliced his chin. With trip-hammer consistency, the Maroons clobbered Shore, and in the waning minutes of the game Shore was felled by a clout in the mouth, tossed by a Maroon, which removed several teeth and knocked him so cold he had to be carried from the rink after lying unconscious on the ice for 14 minutes. In that one game, Shore had accumulated wounds that many players avoid in a lifetime. He had a broken nose, three broken teeth, two black eyes, a gashed cheekbone, and a two-inch cut over the left eye.

He returned to action in the next Bruin game. And when friends tried to commiserate with him, he dismissed their platitudes abruptly. "This is all part of hockey," he replied. "I'll pay off."

His high-speed collision with a goal post at Madison Square Garden left the steel upright intact, but cost Shore three broken ribs. The damage was so severe that the Bruins left Shore in the care of a physician and entrained for a game in Montreal. The doctor eventually escorted Eddie to a nearby hotel and left momentarily to register Shore at a hospital. "Now, Eddie," the doctor cautioned, "I want you to stay in your room until I can come back and take you over to the hospital."

The doctor, who should have known better, assumed that Shore's lack of response indicated compliance. He left the hotel, signed up for a hospital room, and returned to Shore's room to escort the wounded player to the infirmary. But he found the door wide open and no trace of the player or his baggage. Eddie had stumbled to the lobby and had hailed a cab for Grand Central Station, where he purchased a ticket for the late train to Montreal. He arrived in time for the game with the Canadiens and scored two goals and an assist. Such exploits did much to erase Eddie's image as a ruthless, insensitive player.

Ross, on the other hand, was never one to permit sentimentality to stand in the way of a good deal. He realized by 1939 that Shore had only a couple of years left, and despite what Eddie had done for the Boston franchise, Ross was prepared to trade him to any high bidder. The New York Americans indicated they would make a handsome offer, and Ross seemed interested when they suggested a $25,000 tab.

While Ross was mulling this over, Shore was doing some business of his own and finally announced he had purchased the Springfield Indians of the International-American League for $42,000.

Ross was livid when he learned of Shore's purchase, but the two finally agreed that Eddie would play with the Bruins after December 15, 1939, in case of emergency, but would continue to play for and manage the Springfield sextet also.

Eddie played in three games and scored his final goal as a Bruin on December 5, 1939. Shore revealed he would no longer play for Boston because the club wouldn't permit him to fulfill his obligations in Springfield. Ross wasn't about to quit. It took the stubborn Scot a month to realize he no longer could dominate the man who had made hockey in Boston. At last, on January 14, 1940, Ross called a press conference and made the following announcement: "Shore has a heavy investment with his Springfield club and we want to give him a hand." Within two weeks of this altruistic declaration, Ross had traded Shore to the New York Americans for Eddie Wiseman and cash, thus ending the Shore era in Boston. Shore would play only 10 games for the Amerks before retiring.

BABE SIEBERT

BORN: Plattsville, Ontario, January 14, 1904
DIED: August 25, 1939
POSITION: Left Wing/Defenseman, Montreal Maroons, 1925–32; New York Rangers, 1932–34; Boston Bruins, 1934–36; Montreal Canadiens, 1936–39
AWARDS/HONORS: Hart Memorial Trophy, 1937; NHL First Team All-Star, 1936–38; NHL All-Star Game, 1937; Hockey Hall of Fame, 1964

Albert "Babe" Siebert broke into the professional hockey wars in 1925 with the Montreal Maroons. He was a high-scoring left-winger during his rookie season and promptly helped the Maroons storm to the Stanley Cup.

Babe's thirst for body contact was instantly appreciated by Eddie Gerard, the Maroons' coach, and soon the strapping Siebert was shuttling back and forth from defense to the forward line. In 1930, Babe moved up as a permanent portsider with the formation of the Big S Line. Skating with Nels Stewart and Hooley Smith, this unholy trio was the scourge of the league, averaging well over 200 penalty minutes for the next three seasons.

Sold to the New York Rangers in 1932, Siebert was moved back to defense, where he was paired with the great Ching Johnson. This defensive duo decimated opposing wingers and once again Siebert found himself on a Cup-winning squad (1933).

The following season found Babe on the move again. This time he was off to Boston, where he was hastily pressed into service as a replacement for Eddie Shore. Shore had been suspended by the league following a brutal encounter with Ace Bailey. After Shore's reinstatement, he and Siebert formed one of the most feared blue line patrols in the entire league.

Babe was traded to the Montreal Canadiens in 1936–37, where he collected the Hart Trophy as the league's most valuable player. Siebert played two more seasons with the Habs, captaining the 1939 squad. He was named coach of the Frenchmen for the coming season, but that was never to be. Tragically, Babe Siebert died in a drowning mishap that summer.

CHARLIE SIMMER

BORN: Terrace Bay, Ontario, March 20, 1954
POSITION: Left Wing, California Golden Seals, 1974–76; Cleveland Barons, 1976–77; Los Angeles Kings, 1977–85; Boston Bruins, 1985–87; Pittsburgh Penguins, 1987–88
AWARDS/HONORS: Bill Masterton Trophy, 1986; NHL First Team All-Star, 1980–81; NHL Second Team All-Star, 1978; NHL All-Star Game, 1981, 1984

For many years, Charlie Simmer was considered a third-liner with no particular assets to catapult him to stardom. But when the Kings' general staff placed him on a line with Marcel Dionne and Dave Taylor in the 1978–79 season, the three hockey gears meshed perfectly.

The formation of the Triple Crown Line turned the Kings into a major threat, and Simmer in turn, became a star.

Simmer played in the NHL for 14 years with the Oakland Seals, Cleveland Barons, Los Angeles Kings, Pittsburgh Penguins, and Boston Bruins. His best numbers occurred when he was with the Kings from 1977–85, highlighted by two 56-goal seasons (1979–80 and 1980–81). He also participated in three NHL All-Star games and ranked eighth on the Kings' all-time leading scorers list with 222-244-466 totals in 384 games. Simmer was also a two-time NHL First Team All-Star.

With Boston in 1986, Simmer won the prestigious Masterton Trophy, given to the NHL player who best exemplifies the qualities of perseverance, sportsmanship, and dedication to hockey. He was traded from Boston to Pittsburgh and spent the 1987–88 season as a Penguin, before ending his NHL career with over 700 points (342-369-711).

Simmer played one season in Frankfurt, Germany, before retiring in 1989. The following season, he joined the San Diego Gulls (IHL) as an assistant coach. Simmer then worked three seasons as the radio color analyst for the Anaheim Mighty Ducks, and moved on to be color analyst for the Gretzky-owned Phoenix Coyotes in 2001–02.

CRAIG SIMPSON

BORN: London, Ontario, February 15, 1967
POSITION: Left Wing, Pittsburgh Penguins, 1985–87; Edmonton Oilers, 1987–93; Buffalo Sabres, 1993–95

What should have been a much longer and more illustrious career was cut short by injury after Craig Simpson had established his credentials as a major offensive threat.

Pittsburgh's first choice (seventh overall) in the 1985 Entry Draft, Simpson played two years for Michigan State before signing on with Pittsburgh.

His career took a major turn when the Penguins traded him to Edmonton with Dave Hannan, Moe Mantha, and Chris Joseph for Paul Coffey, Dave Hunter, and Wayne Van Dorp.

From the 1987–88 season until the 1992–93 season, Simpson scored no fewer than 24 goals and 46 points in any season. The culmination was during the Oilers' Cup run in the 1990 playoffs, when Simpson ignited his team with 16 goals (three game-winners) and 31 points in 22 playoff games as Edmonton won its first Stanley Cup in the post-Gretzky era.

Before the start of the 1993 season, Simpson was dealt to Buffalo in exchange for Jozef Cierny and the Sabres' fourth-round draft pick. Injuries prematurely curtailed his career, and he retired after the 1994–95 season. Craig turned to broadcasting and became a successful analyst on Canadian television.

HARRY SINDEN

BORN: Toronto, Ontario, September 14, 1932
POSITION: Coach, Boston Bruins, 1966–70, 1979–80, 1984–85; General Manager, Boston Bruins, 1972–2000; President, Boston Bruins, 1988–
AWARDS/HONORS: Lester Patrick Trophy, 1999; Hockey Hall of Fame, 1983

Harry Sinden was the right man in the right place at the right time when the Boston Bruins handed him its coaching reins at the start of the 1966–67 campaign. The Bruins had finished dead last five times in the previous six seasons and the city was hungry for a winner. It didn't happen immediately. The Bruins finished sixth in Harry's first year on the job, but a hotshot rookie named Bobby Orr provided plenty of consolation. A year later Derek Sanderson arrived, along with Phil Esposito, Kenny Hodge, and Fred Stanfield, and suddenly nobody laughed at the Bruins anymore. For the first time in eight years, they made the playoffs, and two seasons later they captured Boston's first Stanley Cup in 29 years.

The whole town was just wild about Harry. In the midst of that grand celebration, Sinden abruptly quit Boston—publicly charging the brass with underpaying him—and began a new career in the modular home industry. But at the start of the 1972–73 season, the firm he was working for went bankrupt. Meanwhile the Bruins, who added another Stanley Cup in his absence, were rapidly coming apart at the seams. Defections to the upstart World Hockey Association, injuries to veterans, and below par performances by formerly dependable players all took a toll on the Bruins.

When a new owner bought the Bruins, his first move was to bring Sinden back, hoping he was the man to put Humpty Dumpty together again in 1972–73. Just three years after he had left town as a conquering hero of sorts, Harry returned to a less than heartwarming welcome. He was introduced as the team's managing director, a title that did not hide the fact that he was replacing one of the most popular personalities on the Boston sports front, Milt Schmidt.

Schmidt, who had been general manager during Harry's successful coaching stint, was given the new title of executive director, but everybody knew Milt had been relegated to mere window-dressing in the front office. Sinden caught the full force of backlash from the sympathy extended to Schmidt by both the press and the public. Understandably, Harry was slow to assert himself.

Except for replacing coach Tom Johnson with Bep Guidolin, Harry walked softly through his first year at the post. After a 1974 playoff loss to Philadelphia, Sinden dropped Guidolin and hired Don Cherry as coach. But, as manager, Sinden still had not proven he was as competent as he had been as coach. His Bruins were rapidly wiped out of the playoffs in 1975.

In November 1975, Sinden made possibly his most daring move as a general manager; he engineered "The Trade," sending Boston's beloved Phil Esposito and defenseman Carol Vadnais to the New York Rangers for Brad Park (a hated man in the Hub), Jean Ratelle, and Joe Zanussi. Later, the Rangers were trading partners again when Ken Hodge was sent to join Esposito on Broadway—where the former flopped—and ace center Rick Middleton arrived in return and stayed over a decade. Sinden proved a prophet when Bobby Orr headed to Chicago to wind up his career and Park quarterbacked the Bruins to two Stanley Cup finals in 1977 and 1978.

But after coming so close to the chalice, Boston was rattled even further by the clashing of Sinden's and Cherry's egos, which ended in an irrevocable Cherry departure. Sinden weathered the storm and twice went behind the bench himself until he could hire a coach in whom he believed. In the meantime, a young Raymond Bourque was fast becoming the cornerstone defenseman to sustain the Boston backline legacy upon his drafting in 1979.

A member of the Hockey Hall of Fame in the Builder's category, Sinden managed to procure a young power forward named Cam Neely from the Vancouver Canucks in 1986. Neely went on to become one of the most beloved athletes in Boston sports history for his inspired play and superstar-level grit. By 1988, Harry earned the role of team president while retaining the general manager's portfolio—a position he would hold until 2000. Harry invited loyal lifetime B's Terry O'Reilly and Mike Milbury to coach the team with excellent results; both alumni got their teams to the Stanley Cup finals, O'Reilly in 1988, Milbury in 1990.

The course remained steady and sure until Sinden found his Bruins out of the playoffs in 1997, for the first time in 30 years. Number one overall draft pick Joe Thornton and fellow first-rounder Sergei Samsonov were selected in the ensuing Entry Draft and both came into their own by the new century's beginning. Sinden handed the reins of general manager over to his protégé, Mike O'Connell, at the start of the 2000–01 season, while remaining as president and alternate governor of the vaunted Bruins franchise.

DARRYL SITTLER

BORN: Kitchener, Ontario, September 18, 1950
POSITION: Center, Toronto Maple Leafs, 1970–82; Philadelphia Flyers, 1982–84; Detroit Red Wings, 1984–85
AWARDS/HONORS: NHL Second Team All-Star, 1978; NHL All-Star Game, 1975, 1978, 1980, 1983; Canada Cup All-Star Team, 1976; Hockey Hall of Fame, 1989

From the moment the Toronto Maple Leafs were born, their hallmark was an abundance of quality centermen. Check the Hockey Hall of Fame: Joe Primeau, Syl Apps Sr., Ted Kennedy, and Max Bentley. Each of them contributed to former Leafs boss Conn Smythe's theory that the secret of winning hockey teams is "strength through the center." During Toronto's last spate of Stanley Cup–winning years under Punch Imlach, the key Leaf pivots were George Armstrong, Bob Pulford, and Dave Keon. During the 1970s, the Leafs looked to Darryl Sittler as their superstar center.

In his first three National Hockey League seasons, Sittler's point total climbed from 18 (in 1970–71) to 32 to 77, and he hit 100 in 1975–76. But his team-leading 117 points—45 goals, 72 assists—in the 1977–78 season was his best of all, and confirmed the Toronto organization's faith in the six-feet, 190-pound farm boy.

Toronto finished fourth in 1973–74 after lodging in sixth the previous year, and Darryl clearly was the top center on the club. He finished 15 points ahead of veteran pivot Norm Ullman and an embarrassing—but not for Darryl—31 points ahead of onetime ace center Keon.

After playing in the shadow of Swedish ace Borje Salming for a number of years, Sittler finally burst into stardom with magnificent, record-shattering scoring performances.

In February 1976, Sittler scored a whopping 10 points in a game against the Boston Bruins, collecting 4 goals and 6 assists. Later, in the postseason playoffs against the Philadelphia Flyers, he posted five goals in one night, breaking another scoring record. As an encore, to cement his position in hockey history, Sittler electrified hockey fans around the world with a dramatic overtime goal to defeat Czechoslovakia in the 1976 Canada Cup.

The Maple Leafs' all-time leader in goals (389) and points (916) was dealt to the Philadelphia Flyers in 1982, after a salary dispute with Leafs owner Harold Ballard, and united with Bill Barber and Ilkka Sinisalo for an effective trio that added an 83-point season to Darryl's résumé in 1982–83. But the Flyers could not get out the first round of postseason play, and Sittler was dealt again, finishing his career with the Detroit Red Wings in 1985.

Darryl returned to the Maple Leafs organization in August 1991, assisting in the areas of marketing, community relations, and alumni relations.

J. COOPER SMEATON

BORN: Carleton Place, Ontario, 1890
DIED: October 3, 1978
POSITION: Referee, NHA, 1913–16; General Manager, Philadelphia Quakers, 1930–31; Referee in Chief, NHL, 1931–37
AWARDS/HONORS: Hockey Hall of Fame, 1961

J. Cooper Smeaton moved to Montreal as a young lad and became involved in several sports—baseball, football, hockey, and basketball. His hockey ability was such that he twice refused offers to turn professional.

But it is for refereeing the game that Smeaton gained immortality as a member of the Hockey Hall of Fame. He began officiating in the amateur leagues before being appointed to the National Hockey Association by Frank Calder in 1913. He called the shots for several Stanley and Allan Cup series.

Smeaton tried his hand at managing with the Philadelphia Quakers of the NHL in 1930–31, but returned to refereeing the following season, after the Philadelphia franchise folded. He was then made referee in chief of the league until his retirement in 1937.

Smeaton, a World War I winner of the Military Medal, was appointed a trustee of the Stanley Cup in 1946.

BILLY SMITH

BORN: Perth, Ontario, December 12, 1950
POSITION: Goaltender, Los Angeles Kings, 1972; New York Islanders, 1972–89
AWARDS/HONORS: Vezina Trophy, 1982; Conn Smythe Trophy, 1983; William M. Jennings Trophy (shared with Roland Melanson), 1983; NHL First Team All-Star, 1982; NHL All-Star Game, 1978; Hockey Hall of Fame, 1993

The last three dynasties in the NHL all had their money goaltenders. The 1976–79 Canadiens had Ken Dryden, the 1984–88 Oilers had Grant Fuhr, and the 1980–83 Islanders had Battlin' Billy Smith.

Billy Smith in goal for the Islanders, 1987–88

Smith provided quality goaltending for the Islanders from the time he was claimed from the Kings in the 1972 Expansion Draft. He played well in tandem with Chico Resch as the Islanders climbed from expansion team to respectability to contenders, and then continued to shine after the Cup runs were over until his retirement in 1989.

However, Smith's spectacular playoff performances are his legacy, plus his legendary unfriendliness toward anyone who dared to invade his crease. The challenge of the playoffs improved Smith's concentration, and he consistently raised his game in the postseason. Islanders coach Al Arbour called Smith "our Mr. April and Mr. May" in honor of his outstanding playoff performances.

Some of the highlights included the 1975 upset of the heavily favored Ranger team, and an amazing stonewall of the Flyers in Game Six of the Stanley Cup finals, when Smith had to hold off the Flyer onslaught until the cup-winning goal was scored by Bob Nystrom in overtime.

However, Smith's performance against Wayne Gretzky and the Edmonton Oilers in the 1983 finals was his finest hour. In Game One in Edmonton, Smith shut out the high-flying Oilers offense 2–0, despite being under continual siege from wave after wave of Oilers. The Islanders proceeded to complete a four-game sweep of the Oilers for their fourth and last Cup. Smith won the Conn Smythe Trophy as playoff MVP. Oilers defenseman Kevin Lowe described Smith's performance this way; "Bill Smith was out of his mind."

Lowe might have been referring to more than Smith's actual puckstopping ability, as the Oilers, and the entire city of Edmonton, were screaming for Smith's head due to his slash on Glenn Anderson's ankle during Game One. This behavior was nothing new for Smith, who was notorious for this type of behavior well before he ever saw an Oiler uniform approaching his crease. He had even gone after teammates during practice if he didn't like the shots they took on him. He wasn't known as "Battlin' Billy" and "Samurai Billy" for nothing.

The Oilers also objected to Smith's slash on superstar Wayne Gretzky, who should have been more worried about his inability to score during the 1983 finals than about where Smith was putting his goalstick.

Perhaps the strangest incident in his entire career came in 1979, when he became the first goalie credited with a goal in an NHL game, when he was the last Islander to touch the puck before Rob Ramage of the Colorado Rockies shot it into his own net.

Smith won other individual honors, including the 1981–82 Vezina Trophy, the Jennings Trophy (shared with Roland Melanson) in 1982–83, and, finally, the retirement of his sweater number 31 by the Islanders. He was inducted into the Hockey Hall of Fame in 1993 with 305 regular season wins and 88 career playoff victories.

Smith entered the goaltender coaching ranks, first with old boss Bill Torrey in Florida during the 1990s, and then with his familiar Islanders in 2001.

BOBBY SMITH

BORN: North Sydney, Nova Scotia, February 12, 1958
POSITION: Center, Minnesota North Stars, 1978–83, 1990–93; Montreal Canadiens, 1983–90
AWARDS/HONORS: Calder Memorial Trophy, 1979; NHL All-Star Game, 1981–82, 1989, 1991

Bobby Smith," said Minnesota North Stars witty coach, Glen Sonmor, "is going to put a lot of people in our seats because he is the type of player who will bring people off their seats."

Bobby Smith was tagged "superstar" long before he came into the league in 1978 as Minnesota's number one draft choice, after compiling 69 goals and 123 assists in his last year of juniors.

The quiet rookie started poorly in the NHL but came on late in the season to lead the North Stars in scoring, with 30 goals and 74 points in 1978–79. Smith's point total was the best by far among rookies in 1979 and earned him the Calder Trophy.

Six feet four and smart on the puck, Smith led Minnesota four times, including 1981–82, his finest campaign, with 114 points. Just the season before, Smith lived up to Sonmor's billing with a 25-point barrage in the 19 playoff games that saw the North Stars reach the

Stanley Cup finals, which were lost to the surging New York Islanders.

Upon his trade to the Montreal Canadiens in 1983, Smith lasted seven seasons and enjoyed the thrill of hoisting the Stanley Cup in 1986 upon scoring the Cup-winning goal in Game Five. His quest for another Cup in 1991—this time as a returning member of the North Stars—was squelched, however, by the Pittsburgh Penguins.

An active member of the NHL Players' Association thoughout his career, including a tenure as vice president, Smith retired in 1993. Armed with two degrees from the University of Minnesota, Bobby returned to the hockey world with the new Phoenix Coyotes in 1996, and worked his way into the general manager's role. His tenure yielded two 90-point seasons and little trade activity other than the acquisition of popular star center Jeremy Roenick from Chicago for Alexei Zhamnov in 1996 before the inaugural season in Phoenix began.

The arrival of Wayne Gretzky as the team's managing partner in 2000 spelled certain doom for Smith. When The Great One decided to forge his own team, Smith was fired shortly after.

HOOLEY SMITH

BORN: Toronto, Ontario, January 7, 1903
DIED: August 24, 1963
POSITION: Center/Right Wing, Ottawa Senators, 1925–27; Montreal Maroons, 1927–36; Boston Bruins, 1936–37; New York Americans, 1937–41
AWARDS/HONORS: NHL First Team All-Star, 1936; NHL Second Team All-Star, 1932; NHL All-Star Game, 1934; Hockey Hall of Fame, 1972

A Hall of Famer, Hooley Smith played both forward and defense, starring first for the Ottawa Senators, then the Montreal Maroons—where he teamed with Nels Stewart and Babe Siebert to form the famed S Line— the Boston Bruins, and finally the New York Americans. He was nicknamed Hooley by his father after the then-popular comics character Happy Hooligan. Beside his hockey talents, Smith also excelled as an oarsman, rugby player, and boxer. Hooley's best years were spent with the Maroons, who obtained him from Ottawa in 1927 for Punch Broadbent and $22,500. His final NHL season, with the Americans, was 1940–41, when he scored 2 goals and 7 assists.

NEIL SMITH

BORN: Toronto, Ontario, January 9, 1954
POSITION: General Manager, New York Rangers, 1989–2000

Neil Smith would always be remembered affectionately by New Yorkers as the man who managed the Rangers to the Stanley Cup in 1994—the first time the Broadway Blueshirts had achieved that distinction in 54 years.

Ironically, Smith's professional hockey career was launched by the rival New York Islanders, who originally hired him as an administrative assistant. When former Isles assistant general manager Jimmy Devellano became general manager of the Detroit Red Wings in 1982, he brought Smith to the Motor City. With Devellano as his mentor, Smith climbed in the organization, rising to the position of general manager of the Adirondack Wings, Detroit's farm club.

When he joined the Rangers in 1989, Smith artfully obtained top-notch established talent to electrify the Madison Square Garden crowd each season.

In 1991–92, Smith made the most significant moves of his career when he acquired former Edmonton Oilers Mark Messier and Adam Graves to infuse leadership, Stanley Cup know-how, and gritty offensive skill. The talented Alexei Kovalev was drafted 15th overall in the June Entry Draft, the highest ever for a Russian player at that time. All three would play crucial roles on the ice for the Blueshirts in 1994.

For that year, Smith hired the mercurial Mike Keenan as the coach to drive the final stake through the 54-year curse. Smith had added help for Messier with Mike Gartner, Esa Tikkanen, and Steve Larmer and an enviable crop of impact youngsters with Tony Amonte, Sergei Zubov, and superstar Brian Leetch. But Keenan needed even more grit for the playoffs. Smith pulled out all the stops, and on the last trading deadline day, engineered four trades that brought in role players Craig MacTavish, Brian Noonan, and Stephane Matteau (for Amonte), and Glenn Anderson (for Gartner). The Rangers steamrolled into the finals, and took the Cup in seven games over the Vancouver Canucks.

In the aftermath, Keenan lost a power struggle with Smith and landed in St. Louis. Smith remained in control of the Blueshirts, bringing in Colin Campbell, and eventually John Muckler, as coach. For the next few years, Smith pursued every available free agent he could to help the Rangers. Deals were made for Luc Robitaille, Ulf Samuelsson, and, the ultimate prize, Wayne Gretzky for 1996–97, but the Rangers fell in the Eastern Conference finals to the Philadelphia Flyers that spring. Messier bolted for unrestricted free agency, and joined the Canucks in the off-season.

Smith endured public backlash for not keeping the beloved Ranger captain, as well as for not obtaining a high-scoring winger to play with Gretzky. With youth a thin commodity in New York, Neil scoured the free-agent market in 1999 signing six players, including Theoren Fleury and Valeri Kamensky. But all the new blood, especially Fleury, flopped, and the Rangers missed the playoffs for the second straight year.

After Smith and coach Muckler feuded publicly about the usage of Smith's prize draft pick, Manny Malhotra, the stage was set for their dual firing in 2000.

Smith then joined the Anaheim Mighty Ducks as a consultant, and graced the airwaves as a hockey analyst for ESPN.

STEVE SMITH

BORN: Glasgow, Scotland, April 30, 1963
POSITION: Defenseman, Edmonton Oilers, 1984–91; Chicago Blackhawks, 1991–97; Calgary Flames, 1998–2001
AWARDS/HONORS: NHL All-Star Game, 1991

Among the all-time blunders that befell NHL players over the years, few would match Steve Smith's playoff mishap during Game Seven of the 1986 Smythe Division finals, between his Edmonton Oilers and the Calgary Flames.

Helping protect his goaltender Grant Fuhr, Smith accidentally made a clearing pass through the crease that bounced off the goalie and into the net. Although the bonehead play happened early in the game, it would result in Edmonton losing the game and the series.

The accident, avenged the following season when Edmonton recaptured the Cup (with Smith the first to hoist it), marred an otherwise commendable career that began in 1985 with Edmonton and ended with Calgary in 2001.

The mobile Smith, the archetypical defensive defenseman, played a tough but not dirty game. An All-Star in 1991, Smith was not known for his goal-scoring ability but was able to support his forwards on the offensive end with the occasional goal and racked up over 40 assists three times over his 16 NHL seasons. In 702 career regular season games, Smith finished his tenure with 2,179 penalty minutes.

Injuries slowed Steve down through much of the 1990s, when he teamed with Chris Chelios for a bruising blueline tandem in Chicago after a trade with Edmonton for Dave Manson. When a neck injury forced Smith out for most of the 1999–2000 season, he became an assistant coach for his Flames.

RYAN SMYTH

BORN: Banff, Alberta, February 21, 1976
POSITION: Left Wing, Edmonton Oilers, 1994–

As Edmonton's second first-round pick in the 1994 NHL draft, Ryan Smyth, drafted sixth overall, turned out to be what Jason Bonsignore, drafted fourth overall, failed to become: a solid, two-way, heart and soul forward integral to the team's young nucleus. Smyth's tenacious play, leadership, his ability to screen goalies and score rebound/deflection goals on the edge of the crease were what NHL general managers crave on draft day.

His first full 82-game season showed the potential of the gritty, gutsy Smyth. His 39 goals (39–22–61) were good for 13th in the league in 1996–97 and 20 of those goals were on the power play, which tied him for first in that category that year with Detroit's Brendan Shanahan. Those 20 power-play goals also tied Wayne Gretzky's team record, set back in the high-flying season of 1983–84.

Smyth's first playoff experience with Edmonton included five goals and ten points as the upstart Oilers upset the Dallas Stars in the 1997 Western Conference quarterfinals in seven games before falling in the semis to the Colorado Avalanche in five games.

Ryan averaged 22 goals his next five seasons, three of which were cut short by injuries, and was a constant team leader for the sometimes overmatched, but always highly competitive Oilers.

In 2002, despite suffering a severe ankle fracture early in the NHL season, Smyth recovered in time to win a gold medal in the Salt Lake City Olympics with Team Canada, playing on a ferocious line with Owen Nolan and Eric Lindros.

CONN SMYTHE

BORN: Toronto, Ontario, February 1, 1895
DIED: November 18, 1980
AWARDS/HONORS: Hockey Hall of Fame, 1958; Trophy in His Name

One of the most influential and colorful characters associated with the National Hockey League, Conn Smythe first gained notice in the months following the start of World War I. At the time, Smythe played center and captained the University of Toronto's varsity hockey club while majoring in engineering. Smythe's team did the unprecedented when they won the Ontario Hockey Association's Junior championship. After that, hockey players enlisted en masse in the Canadian Armed Forces, and Smythe was sent overseas, where he served with distinction.

Upon his return from the war, Smythe headed straight for the university, where he obtained his degree in applied science and continued to stay in close touch with the varsity hockey team as unofficial manager, promoter, and all-round rah-rah leader. In time, this association would be the catalyst for Smythe's success in the professional hockey ranks.

The much-decorated World War I veteran gained acclaim in college hockey circles for his superb stewardship of the University of Toronto hockey clubs. Each year, Smythe would shepherd his varsity sextet to Boston, where the Toronto skaters wowed Beantown fans on the ice while young Smythe impressed newspaper editors with his flamboyant prose and knack for headline-grabbing, a trait he refined with age. Charles F. Adams, owner of the Bruins, was fascinated by Smythe's deportment and remembered him when Colonel John Hammond, president of the Rangers, asked for a recommendation for a man to organize a group of players to be Hammond's NHL entry. "Conn Smythe is your man," said Adams. "You won't find any better."

With customary vigor, Smythe spent the summer of 1926 signing players for the rookie Rangers franchise. His selections were impeccably sharp, and before the season had begun, Smythe had signed such stickhandlers as Frank Boucher, Bill and Bun Cook, Ching Johnson, Murray Murdoch, and Bill Boyd.

When the players gathered at a Toronto hotel for preseason training, Smythe felt content. His team, he believed, with good reason, would be indomitable. One night, after convening at the training hotel, Smythe chose to take the night off to go to a movie with his wife. It was a reasonable plan, so Smythe was flabbergasted when Colonel Hammond accosted him in the lobby upon his return. "Where have you been?" Colonel Hammond demanded.

When Smythe revealed that he and his wife had enjoyed a leisurely dinner and a good movie, Colonel Hammond bristled with anger: "Well, that night out has just cost us one of the greatest players in the game. St. Pats just sold Babe Dye to Chicago. We could have had him for $14,000."

Smythe was unimpressed, and he told Colonel Hammond so. "I wouldn't want Babe Dye on my team, no matter what the price," snapped Smythe with the brand of finality that either convinces an employer or causes a man to lose his job. "He's not the type of player we need."

Smythe was not about to be fired on the spot; the Colonel wanted more evidence, and for a one-dollar phone call he got it. Hammond phoned Barney Stanley, coach of the Blackhawks, and pointedly mentioned young Smythe's opinion of Dye. Stanley's guffaws could be heard across the continent. When he stopped laughing, the Blackhawks' coach sputtered: "Smythe wouldn't want Dye on his team? Why that man must be crazy. It only proves how little he knows about hockey players. I can't understand, Colonel, why you keep a man like that when there's an outstanding hockey man like Lester Patrick loose and ready to be signed."

The Colonel didn't understand it either. Smythe was promptly summoned to the Colonel's office and given his discharge papers before the season even began.

"Unwittingly," wrote former Toronto hockey publicist Ed Fitkin, "Babe Dye was mainly responsible for the formation of the Toronto Maple Leafs, because Smythe, angered by the Rangers' rebuff, decided he'd get into pro hockey or bust. Within a year he was back in the NHL, this time to stay."

Conn went about the business of trying to purchase the Toronto St. Patricks so that he could proudly reenter the NHL. It took one year from the time the Rangers had fired him for Conn to come through the front door of the major leagues again. The momentous day in Toronto hockey history was February 27, 1927, when an NHL governor's meeting was held in Toronto. Smythe was elected, the name St. Patricks was officially dropped, and from then on, the team would be known as the Toronto Maple Leafs.

It was too late to salvage the 1926–27 season, and Smythe realized that only a five-year plan to build a new hockey empire would be realistic. To do so he would have to wheel and deal as never before in league history.

Smythe decided to build his team around a couple of young aces with rare promise. One of them was Hap Day, a forward who converted to defense on the night the newly christened Maple Leafs won their first game; the other was Joe Primeau.

Primeau and Day would not be enough for a winning team, and Smythe knew it. After the club finished last in the Canadian Division in 1926-27, Smythe rebuilt the team with youngsters from the Marlboros Senior team and some wily veterans, forming a dynasty in Toronto to coincide with the opening of his hockey palace, Maple Leaf Gardens, in November 1931. His deals—especially the one that brought colorful defenseman King Clancy to Toronto—usually had a touch of genius, and in 1932, the Maple Leafs won their first Stanley Cup for Smythe.

His club was regarded as the Gashouse Gang of the NHL because of such robust characters as Charlie Conacher, Red Homer, Hap Day, Baldy Cotton, Busher Jackson, Joe Primeau, and the irrepressible Clancy. Always, though, Smythe was the leader and with each season he managed to gain more importance within the NHL hierarchy itself. When his Gashouse Gang sagged in the mid 1930s, Conn built a new empire around gifted center Syl Apps and goalie Turk Broda. They won the Stanley Cup in April 1942 in a seven-game series with Detroit in which the Maple Leafs fell behind, three games to none, and then won the next four straight matches—a feat unprecedented in NHL history.

While Smythe was overseas serving in the Canadian Armed Forces in World War II, his Leafs won another Cup in 1945 with Franke Selke presiding while Conn was away. When his club disintegrated the following season, Smythe returned from Europe to engineer another rebuilding of the club. Accenting youth, he produced the best Maple Leaf clubs in history. With Hap Day coaching, the Leafs won the Stanley Cup in 1947, 1948, and 1949, a three-straight sweep that had never before been accomplished. They missed in 1950, but with new coach Joe Primeau behind the bench in 1951 they won the Cup again. Although he was president and managing director of Maple Leaf Gardens, Conn became less active on the hockey front and finally retired in 1961, while son Stafford gradually took over.

The elder Smythe, however, continued in the news, frequently orating on some subject that would create headlines. In June 1971, he did just that, resigning from the NHL Hall of Fame Committee in protest over the selection of one of his own Cup-winning stalwarts of the 1932 Leafs, Busher Jackson. Until his death, Smythe frequently surfaced to lambaste the commercialism of the modern game, as colorful and quotable as ever.

STAFFORD SMYTHE

BORN: March 15, 1921
DIED: October 13, 1971

One of the most colorful and, at once, tragic figures in modern professional hockey, Stafford Smythe often was regarded as a chip off the old block—father Conn Smythe. Like his dad, Staff was groomed in the hockey wars at an early age, learning the stickhandling business at Maple Leaf Gardens before he was out of knickers. But Stafford had a tough act to follow, though follow it he did. He was bombastic like Conn and equally as quotable. It was considered inevitable that Staff eventually would move into a position of NHL power as soon as his father would permit such a move.

At the age of 60, Conn Smythe retired as the manager of the Maple Leafs in favor of former coach Hap Day, but retained the presidency of the team. Bereft of ability, the Toronto brass turned to slogans. With King Clancy coaching the team in 1955–56, Day promised a team with "guts, goals, and glamour." They had only a smidgen of each, however, and dropped from fourth to fifth with

Stafford Smythe, second from right. Others (left to right), Arthur Wirtz, David Molson, William Jennings, Bruce Norris, Weston Adams. To the right of Smythe, NHL president Clarence Campbell. This was the board of governors for the original six teams, just prior to expansion in 1967–68.

Howie Meeker doing the coaching. Amid this confusion a power struggle developed for control of Maple Leaf Gardens and the hockey club. A group led by Stafford spearheaded the revolution, and soon Conn's "little boy" was running the show.

A coach and manager as an 11-year-old while playing minor hockey, a coach and manager during student days at the University of Toronto, and a manager with the Marlboro Juniors, Stafford alternately lauded and fought his father.

"My dad gave me lots of rope and lots to do," said Stafford. "When I was thirty I was ten years ahead of everybody, and at forty I was ten years behind everybody." Stafford meant that after his father allowed him to learn so much so soon, Conn continued to regard him as an employee and refused to permit him to make significant decisions even when he had reached the age of 40. As a result, Stafford decided he had to challenge his father, no matter what the reaction, public or private.

"The people my father respects," said Stafford, "are those who stand up to him and fight. After I learned to do this, he respected me, but we had plenty of scraps."

In 1957, Conn Smythe appointed Stafford chairman of a new Maple Leafs' hockey committee. Stafford Smythe gradually laid the groundwork for a revitalization of the Maple Leafs' machine, in much the way his father had done so 30 years earlier.

On November 23, 1961, Stafford—along with Harold Ballard and John Bassett—bought Conn Smythe's stock at $40 a share with a $2 million bank loan that was repaid in four years.

Stafford and Harold Ballard, his friend and business associate of 25 years, were arrested on June 17, 1971, Smythe was charged with defrauding Maple Leaf Gardens and stealing cash and securities from the Gardens, as was Ballard. Both were also charged under the Canadian Income Tax Act with evading income taxes.

On October 31, 1971, just 12 days before he was scheduled for trial on the tax charges, Stafford Smythe died of complications arising from bleeding stomach ulcers. He was 50 years old. The news sent Toronto into a state of shock. "No," wrote *Toronto Star* sports columnist Milt Dunnell, "it wouldn't be in order to break out the orchids for Stafford Smythe now that he is dead. Maybe he didn't deserve orchids. At any rate, he didn't want them. One thing is sure: he got more nettles than he deserved—but he didn't seem to mind that either."

ED SNIDER

BORN: Washington, D.C., January 6, 1933
AWARDS/HONORS: Lester Patrick Trophy, 1980; Hockey Hall of Fame, 1988

Ed Snider was the chairman of the board of the Philadelphia Flyers and one of the original people who spearheaded a drive to bring big-league hockey to the Philadelphia area.

He was one of the more dynamic owners in the NHL, and according to the people who knew him, was as much a fan as an owner. In 1974, when the Flyers became the first expansion team to win the Stanley Cup, Snider said it was the "thrill of a lifetime." He said it again in 1975.

Praised by colleagues as one of the NHL's most progressive owners, Snider was one of the main reasons why the Flyers became a loyal, close-knit organization.

As the veterans of the Flyers' glory years began to fade, Snider showed his hockey instinct by orchestrating, along with general manager Keith Allen, a series of trades that brought youth and vitality back to a tired Philadelphia squad. Though they showed poorly in the 1979 Stanley Cup quarterfinals, dropping out in five games, the rebuilding process was definitely under way. With Snider at the helm, the once-powerful Flyers looked to regain their old form, without ever losing stride. Snider made two moves in that direction during the 1978–79 season. His coach, Fred Shero, was courted by the rival Rangers. Snider allowed Shero to go to New York only after obtaining Bobby Clarke-like center Ken Linseman as compensation for Shero's signing with the Flyers' Patrick Division enemy. Then, he hired Pat Quinn as coach.

Snider's passion for hockey kept pace with his many business successes, and by the 1990s, he ranked among the top NHL power brokers.

Unfortunately, that success did not transcend into another Philadelphia Stanley Cup, as Snider went through a succession of coaches and managers in a futile attempt to bring a title back to Broad Street.

His most significant moves were obtaining Eric Lindros in a complicated deal with the Quebec Nordiques in 1992, and returning to his favorite player, Bobby Clarke, as general manager in 1994. The Snider-Clarke axis remained tight, and in 1997, their Flyers reached the Stanley Cup finals before bowing to Detroit in four straight games.

From that point on, the Flyers endured a series of playoff disappointments through the 2001–02 season, when, after the Philadelphia team won its division title, it suffered a first-round playoff loss in five games to the underdog Ottawa Senators. Snider ordered the firing of coach Bill Barber, allowing Clarke to remain as general manager. Ken Hitchcock was installed as Barber's replacement. On the plus side, the Flyers sold out every game at their home rink, the First Union Center.

GARTH SNOW

BORN: Wrentham, Massachusetts, July 28, 1969
POSITION: Goaltender, Quebec Nordiques, 1993–95; Philadelphia Flyers, 1995–98; Vancouver Canucks, 1998–2000; Pittsburgh Penguins, 2000–01; New York Islanders, 2001–

The swashbuckling, rugged brand of goaltending epitomized by Billy Smith in the 1980s and later by Ron Hextall, impressed many young netminders of the time. One of them was Garth Snow, a star with the University of Maine, who became an NHL regular with the Flyers, after two brief tryouts with the Quebec Nordiques.

A big man in the crease, Snow had no compunctions about using his stick—or fists, if need be—to intimidate opponents. He was also a pretty good goaltender.

In the summer before the 2001–02 NHL season, Snow was acquired by the New York Islanders and was preparing to be the team's starting goalie when October rolled around. After all, the feisty netminder had a lot of experience, including a trip to the Stanley Cup finals with Philadelphia in 1997. However, just weeks before the 82-game journey began, the Isles were able to pick up Detroit Red Wings star goaltender Chris Osgood off waivers.

Snow graciously assumed his role as backup netminder, determined to keep Chris Osgood on his toes by helping him prepare for every game.

Snow, a former Masterton Trophy nominee (for perseverance, sportsmanship, and dedication to hockey), was not only a helpful backup, but, playing in a flurry of games, had important victories throughout the season.

GLEN SONMOR

BORN: Moose Jaw, Saskatchewan, April 22, 1929
POSITION: Left Wing, New York Rangers, 1953–55; Coach, Minnesota North Stars, 1978–87

As a player, Glen Sonmor was regarded more for his pugilistic ability than his goal-scoring. He played parts of two seasons (1953–54, 1954–55) with the New York Rangers and earned the applause of Madison Square Garden fans by decking Detroit Red Wings ace Marty Pavelich for the count. After his second season in the NHL, Sonmor was dispatched to the American League, where he suffered a serious injury to his left eye in 1955 when butt-ended by an enemy stick. He drifted into coaching; first in junior hockey, then the minor leagues, with collegiate stints at Ohio State and the University of Minnesota.

From 1972 through 1977, Sonmor was general manager–coach of the WHA Minnesota Fighting Saints. During the 1977–78 season, he coached the Birmingham Bulls. He began the following year as chief scout of the NHL Minnesota North Stars but replaced Harry Howell in November 1978 as head coach. In 1978–79, under Sonmor's orchestration, the North Stars enjoyed a renaissance, but still failed to make the playoffs. Sonmor's team made the Stanley Cup finals in 1980–81, but lost to the defending champion New York Islanders. Sonmor's coaching career ended in 1987, but he remained close to the game in a scouting capacity. When the Wild returned NHL hockey to Minnesota in 2000–01, Sonmor became a scout for the expansion club.

ALLAN STANLEY

BORN: Timmins, Ontario, March 1, 1926
POSITION: Defenseman, New York Rangers, 1948–54; Chicago Blackhawks, 1954–56; Boston Bruins, 1956–58; Toronto Maple Leafs, 1958–68; Philadelphia Flyers, 1968–69
AWARDS/HONORS: NHL Second Team All-Star, 1960–61, 1966; NHL All-Star Game, 1955, 1957, 1960, 1962–63, 1967–68; Hockey Hall of Fame, 1981

When the Rangers needed defensemen in the years following World War II, Allan Stanley, the property of the Providence Reds, was acquired by Rangers boss Frank Boucher.

Stanley disappointed the Garden faithful, who booed him unmercifully. Boucher, however, appreciated Allan's talents and was upset by the fans' reaction. He decided to spare Stanley by playing him only in away games. But that just left the Rangers with a rusty defenseman, and further increased fan hostility.

The agony endured for six years, with one brief break when the Blueshirts took the Detroit Red Wings to the seventh game of the 1950 Stanley Cup finals before losing. Lynn Patrick was the New York coach at the time and called Stanley his most valuable Ranger.

Allan Stanley as a Maple Leaf

Stanley's agony went on until 1954, when Boucher traded Stanley and forward Nick Mickoski to the Chicago Blackhawks for Bill Gadsby, a high-quality defenseman, and Pete Conacher, a forward. The trade was sensational, since Gadsby was considered a potential star.

Big Allan played two seasons in Chicago, until the Bruins bought him from Chicago for less than the waiver price of $15,000. It was one of the best buys since the NHL was created. Stanley's impact was immediate and powerful. One season, Boston was a fifth-place team in the six-team NHL; a year later, with Stanley a starting Bruins blueliner, the club climbed to first place. Bruins general manager Lynn Patrick claimed Big Allan was "one of the main reasons" for the resurgence.

Stanley played two seasons in Boston, after which the Bruins traded him to Toronto for Jim Morrison. But Stanley was far from finished. Skating for Punch Imlach in Toronto, Stanley was as good as he had been in his Boston prime, playing before a sophisticated Maple Leaf Gardens audience who appreciated his defensive gifts.

It was no coincidence that the Leafs annexed four Stanley Cups with the big guy snowshoeing behind the blue line. Stanley's play had a blend of majesty and intelligence that was both hard and clean, and he finished his career in 1969 with the Philadelphia Flyers after 1,244 NHL games.

In 1981, the longevity and quiet defensive genius of Allan Stanley was rewarded by induction into the Hockey Hall of Fame.

PAT "WHITEY" STAPLETON

BORN: Sarnia, Ontario, July 4, 1940
POSITION: Defenseman, Boston Bruins, 1961–63, Chicago Blackhawks, 1965–73
AWARDS/HONORS: NHL Second Team All-Star, 1966, 1971–72; NHL All-Star Game, 1967, 1969, 1971–72

The Chicago Blackhawks had the good fortune of icing two of the best small defensemen during the 1960s, when Pat Stapleton and Pierre Pilote patrolled the blue line in the Windy City. Originally a product of the Boston Bruins, Stapleton played two seasons in Beantown (1961–62, 1962–63) before returning to the minors. His big-league career took a turn for the better when he was acquired by Chicago in 1965, and from the 1966–67 season until 1972–73, Stapleton was one of the NHL's top blueliners.

When the World Hockey Association entered the scene in 1972, it began raiding NHL teams. The Blackhawks lost superstar Bobby Hull in 1972 and a year later, Stapleton signed with the WHA's Chicago Cougars. He remained with them until the 1974–75 season.

Rather than return to the NHL as other WHA players would, Stapleton finished his career in the renegade league, first with the Indianapolis Racers and finally the Cincinnati Stingers in the 1977–78 season.

Stapleton's career year was 1968–69, when he scored 6 goals and 50 assists in 75 games with the Blackhawks.

ANTON STASTNY

BORN: Bratislava, Czechoslovakia, August 5, 1959
POSITION: Left Wing, Quebec Nordiques, 1980–89

Hidden behind the exploits of his older brother Peter, Anton Stastny never received acclaim during his years in the National Hockey League.

Anton developed his hockey skills with his brothers, Peter and Marian, while playing in what then was Czechoslovakia. Working on a line together, they developed an anticipation of each others' moves that dazzled enemy defenses.

Anton made an instant impact in the NHL in the 1980–81 season, scoring 39 goals and 85 points in 80 games for the Quebec Nordiques. The Philadelphia Flyers had originally drafted the youngest Stastny in 1978, but he reentered the NHL draft in 1979 and was picked by Quebec with the 83rd overall pick that year. He starred alongside Peter for several years.

Anton piled up 252 goals and 636 points in 680 NHL games. The closest he came to matching his rookie season total of 39 goals was in the 1984–85 campaign, when he put up 38.

The four-time, 30-plus goal scorer never played in an NHL All-Star game, and finished his NHL career in 1989. He then went on to play in European leagues until the 1993–94 season.

MARIAN STASTNY

BORN: Bratislava, Czechslovakia, January 8, 1953
POSITION: Right Wing, Quebec Nordiques, 1981–85; Toronto Maple Leafs, 1985–86
AWARDS/HONORS: NHL All-Star Game, 1983

The least-known of the famed hockey-playing Stastny brothers, Marian played adequately in his short major-league stint.

Signed by the Quebec Nordiques in 1980, after defecting from Soviet-controlled Czechoslovakia, Marian reached the 35-goal plateau in his first two seasons. His rookie season (1981–82), Stastny came out flying with his brothers, Anton and Peter, and finished with 35 goals and 89 points in 74 games played. The next season was equally as stellar as he netted 36 goals and 79 points in 60 games and appeared in the 1983 All-Star game.

The next two years with Quebec were dismal, as he only managed 27 goals and 73 points in 118 games. Marian moved on to Toronto, leaving his brothers and the Nordiques behind, and totaled 53 points in 70 games in his only season with the Maple Leafs.

PETER STASTNY

BORN: Bratislava, Czechoslovakia, September 18, 1956
POSITION: Center, Quebec Nordiques, 1980–90; New Jersey Devils, 1990–93; St. Louis Blues, 1994–95
AWARDS/HONORS: Calder Memorial Trophy, 1981; NHL All-Star Game, 1981–84, 1986, 1988; Hockey Hall of Fame, 1998

A living legend in Europe before he signed as a pro in the National Hockey League, the Czechoslovakian-born Peter Stastny was a dominant center in the majors for 15 years. His NHL record for assists by a rookie in one season (70) still stood at the close of the 2001–02 season.

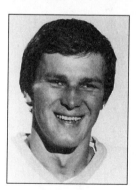

Czech-born Hall of Famer Peter Stastny

Stastny helped turn the Quebec Nordiques into a competitive playoff team in the early 1980s and at one time worked on a line with his brothers Anton and Marian.

Peter played the game the North American way—hitting hard and asking questions later. He stickhandled with the best and delivered many a clutch goal, including one that thrust the Nordiques over the Canadiens in the seventh game of the 1985 series.

Teamed with Michel Goulet on left wing, Stastny enjoyed his most productive years as a pro in the early 1980s, with over 100 points in six consecutive and seven out of eight seasons—including a whopping 139-point sophomore effort in 1981–82. He remained a Nordique until 1990, when the team began to decline. Peter was then dealt to the New Jersey Devils for Craig Wolanin and Randy Velischek.

Stastny had lost a step after his decade in Quebec but still helped improve a Devils team on the rise and remained one of the best players on the club until he returned to his native Czechoslovakia for 1993–94.

Peter had one last big-league stint in 1994–95 with the St. Louis Blues before retiring in 1995.

As one of the pioneering Czechslovakian stars in the NHL, Stastny fully deserved his Hockey Hall of Fame nomination in 1998 and managed the Slovakian National Team in the 2002 Winter Olympic Games at Salt Lake.

PETE STEMKOWSKI

BORN: Winnipeg, Manitoba, August 25, 1943
POSITION: Center, Toronto Maple Leafs, 1963–68; Detroit Red Wings, 1968–70; New York Rangers, 1970–77; Los Angeles Kings, 1977–78
AWARDS/HONORS: NHL All-Star Game, 1968

He was known as the Polish Prince of the NHL. Peter Stemkowski, once compared to comedian Rich Little for his hilarious impressions, Jimmy Durante for his protruding proboscis, and the Goodyear blimp for his awesome girth, conducted his center-ice business in the NHL for 15 years.

It was Stemmer's devil-may-care attitude that sent him packing from the floundering Detroit Red Wings in 1970. The impish Stemkowski decided that the Ivy League disciplinary tactics employed by ex-Cornell coach Ned Harkness were a bit much, and after somehow impounding Harkness's beloved Cornell windbreaker and baseball cap, Pete entertained the weary troops with his patented Harkness imitation.

"Okay guys, gimme a C," Pete gleefully ordered. The howling Red Wings responded with a booming "C!!"

"Gimme an O," continued Stemmer. "Gimme an R!"

Suddenly, the Red Wing dressing room fell silent. Looming behind Stemkowski was a not-at-all-amused Ned Harkness. Without missing a beat, Stemkowski removed the coach's beloved outfit and handed it over. "Okay coach, take over," he said soberly, "I've got 'em warmed up for you." Needless to say, Stemmer's days at Detroit were numbered after the cheerleading incident. Traded to the New York Rangers, Stemkowski settled in as the regular checking center, penalty killer, and emergency left-winger.

Although a notoriously slow starter during the regular season, Stemmer was always a valuable clutch performer for the Rangers, usually saving his best efforts for the Stanley Cup playoffs.

Stemkowski was caught in the Blueshirts' housecleaning efforts of the 1970s, winding up on the West Coast with the Los Angeles Kings. The heavy center had slowed to nearly a standstill by 1978, and was assigned to the Springfield Indians of the American Hockey League.

Following his playing career, Stemkowski briefly coached in the AHL before moving into the broadcasting realm.

KEVIN STEVENS

BORN: Brockton, Massachusetts, April 15, 1965
POSITION: Left Wing, Pittsburgh Penguins
1988–95, 2001–; Boston Bruins, 1995–96; Los
Angeles, 1996–97; New York Rangers,
1997–2000; Philadelphia Flyers, 2000–01
AWARDS/HONORS: NHL First Team All-Star,
1992; NHL Second Team All-Star, 1991, 1993;
NHL All-Star Game, 1991–93

SCOTT STEVENS

BORN: Kitchener, Ontario, April 1, 1964
POSITION: Defenseman, Washington Capitals,
1982–90; St. Louis Blues, 1990–91; New Jersey
Devils, 1991–
AWARDS/HONORS: Alka-Seltzer Plus Award,
1994; Conn Smythe Trophy, 2000; NHL All-Rookie
Team, 1983; NHL First Team All-Star, 1988,
1994; NHL Second Team All-Star, 1992, 1997,
2001; NHL All-Star Game, 1985, 1989, 1991–94,
1996–2001

Having already played in the Olympics before entering the NHL, Kevin Stevens rose up the hockey stardom chart quickly.

After playing parts of two campaigns in 1987–88 and 1988–89, Stevens scored 70 points to go along with 171 penalty minutes in his first full NHL season with the Mario Lemieux–led Pittsburgh Penguins. A preeminent power forward by that time, he helped the Pens win the Stanley Cup in 1991 with an outstanding 17 playoff goals. Stevens's numbers peaked in his next two seasons, over which he scored 109 goals and 125 assists, winning the Cup again in 1992.

But Kevin was never the same player after a collision in Game Seven of the 1993 Conference finals against the New York Islanders. After charging Isles defenseman Rich Pilon, Stevens bounced off the Islander, hit his head on the ice and was knocked unconscious. The fact that he hit the ice face-first, resulted in gruesome facial injuries. Kevin would net 88 points the following season, but never scored above 43 points in eight subsequent seasons.

After being traded to Boston and Los Angeles, Stevens finally found a home on Broadway playing for the Rangers. He played two full seasons with the team, but never again with his old scoring touch. By the 1999–2000 season, Stevens often found himself on the bench.

In 2000, Stevens signed with the Flyers and was later traded back to Pittsburgh, where he reunited with old linemate and friend, Lemieux. With his playing time diminished in 2001–02, Stevens's NHL career appeared to be over.

Open-ice hitting became an infrequent occurrence as the modern era of hockey gave way to an emphasis on speed and team systems. But for over 20 years in the National Hockey League, Scott Stevens made the open-ice hit one of his calling cards.

Scott Stevens as a Washington Capital

His clean, but fog-inducing blue line hit on Detroit's Slava Kozlov in the 1995 Stanley Cup finals stunned the Red Wings and signaled his warriorship in the New Jersey Devils' Cup drive. In Game Seven of the 2000 Eastern Conference finals against Philadelphia, an oft-concussed Eric Lindros—who sought to inspire his sinking team with a defiant comeback—crossed into the Devils' zone and was absolutely shoulder-crunched with a Stevens check in mid-ice that demoralized the Flyers, and sent Lindros into another sabbatical. The Devils then marched to the Stanley Cup over Dallas.

One season later, Stevens struck again in the playoffs by knocking the Carolina Hurricanes' Shane Willis and Ron Francis out of games with concussions, courtesy of two more devastating hits.

Ferocious and feared, Stevens was a team leader, a big-game player and robust defenseman for the New Jersey Devils, leading them to 1995 and 2000 Stanley Cup championships.

Stevens started out as a talented, but temperamental, Washington Capitals blueliner, who could fight as much as he could score, as evidenced by his career-high 21 goals and 221 penalty minutes in his third NHL season, 1984–85. In Washington, Stevens scored over 50 points five seasons in a row, including a 61-assist season in 1988–89. On the side of penalty minutes, Stevens maintained that part of his game, but toned down his brawling ways as his skills as a premier defensive player bloomed.

Following eight seasons with the Capitals, in which deep postseason play was somewhat scarce, Scott signed with the St. Louis Blues to captain the team in 1990–91. But the following year, Stevens was awarded to the Devils as compensation for the Blues' signing of Brendan Shanahan in the fall of 1991. Scott soon became the anchor of the Devils' defense and captain of the New Jersey sextet, helping to cultivate the hard-nosed, in-your-face style of play that came to symbolize the Devils.

Despite the decline of Stevens's offensive skills, the six-feet-two defenseman became a regular at every NHL All-Star game during every season in his Devils tenure, except for 2002. He also managed to prevent the puck from going in the net. Through the 2001–02 stanza, he never had a negative plus/minus ratio, an astounding feat for such an aggressive player.

Stevens came close to captaining another Devils Stanley Cup–winning team in 2001, only to lose a heartbreaking seven-game finals series to the Colorado Avalanche, who gunned out the first and only Cup victory for Stevens's contemporary and chief Norris Trophy rival, Raymond Bourque.

Though near the end of his career in 2001–02, Stevens still loomed as a powerful force for the Devils despite a tough opening-round loss to the Carolina Hurricanes. An impact player in the figurative and literal sense, Stevens surprisingly never won the Norris Trophy, yet certainly had the credentials for, if not the Norris, the Hall of Fame.

BLACK JACK STEWART

BORN: Pilot Mound, Manitoba, May 6, 1917
DIED: May 25, 1983
POSITION: Defenseman, Detroit Red Wings, 1938–50; Chicago Blackhawks, 1950–52
AWARDS/HONORS: NHL First Team All-Star, 1943, 1948–49; NHL Second Team All-Star, 1946–47; NHL All-Star Game, 1947–50; Hockey Hall of Fame, 1964

When veteran hockey writers hark back to "old-time defensemen" who played the frontier-style game, John Stewart is the prototype they have in mind.

In fact, his nickname says it all: Black Jack.

Black Jack, as in Black Jack Pershing, commanding general of the American Army in France during World War I; and Black Jack Stewart as in the roughest, toughest backliner the Red Wings ever owned.

Opponents both hated and respected him at the same time.

"He wasn't dirty," Hall of Fame defenseman King Clancy once explained, "but Black Jack Stewart was the roughest son-of-a-gun you ever would want to meet."

A Detroit Red Wing for most of his career, Stewart played on two Stanley Cup winners and three first-place clubs. Along the way, he accumulated 50 scars and 220 stitches, but never missed a minute because of it during his first ten years in the bigs. "Sew fast, Doc," Stewart would tell the medics who were repairing his injuries, "I'm due back on the ice."

Stewart was as brave as any pro and once played an entire season with a broken hand. A special device attached to his stick and wrist enabled him to firm up his grip."

Like the Rangers' legendary Ching Johnson,

Stewart took a joyous delight in bodychecking. "He was a mean individual," said ex-Wing Ted Lindsay, "but when he was mean he had a big smile on his face. When he had that smile, it was time for the opposition to look out.

"Once Gordie Howe and I decided we'd take this old guy into the corner during practice and rough him up. Jack took his left arm and pinned me across the chest against the screen and then he lifted Howe off the ice by the shirt. Then, he just smiled at both of us."

One of Stewart's toughest battles was with Johnny Mariucci, the brawling Chicago defenseman. They once battled for 15 minutes on the ice, then continued the brawl in the penalty box. At worst, it was a draw; Stewart rarely lost a fight.

As much as he revered Stewart, Adams realized by the start of the 1950s that his thumping warrior was approaching the end of his career. Adams soon included Stewart with goalie Harry Lumley, defenseman Al Dewsbury, and forwards Pete Babando and Don Morrison in a blockbuster deal with the Chicago Blackhawks. The Red Wings received goalie Jim Henry, forwards Metro Prystai and Gaye Stewart, and defenseman Bob Goldham in return.

Black Jack was playing capably for Chicago when he suffered a ruptured spinal disc. He was 34 and doctors said he should be grateful if he could walk again, without a cane or crutch. Stewart listened to their advice, applied some of his own willpower and returned to the lineup.

Unfortunately, the fickle finger of fate was working against him. During a game against the Rangers, Stewart and Clare Martin were paired on defense. They liked to line up an onrushing forward and put him in a human vise as the enemy tried to split their defense. On this night, the eel-like Edgar Laprade was moved into the Chicago zone. Stewart and Martin figured Laprade was coming through and closed the trap. But the little Ranger eluded them and instead Martin rammed his partner to the ice, as one observer noted, "colder than a mackerel."

Black Jack was hospitalized and required 21 stitches to close his wounds. After spending two weeks in the hospital, he announced his retirement. Then, to the amazement of all, he returned to the ice and played two more games for Chicago.

Stewart concluded his career after the 1951–52 season and 566 regular-season games, then went into coaching, starting with Chatham in the Ontario Hockey Association's Senior League. He then coached two years at the Junior level with Kitchener before moving up to the high pro ranks with Pittsburgh of the American League. Stewart gave up coaching for good in 1963, but remained active as a horse trainer.

NELS "OLD POISON" STEWART

BORN: Montreal, Quebec, December 29, 1902
DIED: August 21, 1957
POSITION: Center, Montreal Maroons, 1925–32; Boston Bruins, 1932–35, 1936; New York Americans, 1935–36, 1937–40
AWARDS/HONORS: Hart Memorial Trophy, 1926, 1930; Art Ross Trophy, 1926; NHL All-Star Game, 1934; Hockey Hall of Fame, 1962

Nels Stewart, a strapping centerman, broke into the NHL with the Montreal Maroons in dynamic fashion. During Nels's maiden season, he led the league in scoring

Nels "Old Poison" Stewart of the Montreal Maroons

and copped the Hart Trophy as the league's most valuable player while leading the Maroons to the coveted Stanley Cup.

A big, rough player with a deadly accurate shot, Stewart was the pivot man for the Maroons' infamous Big S Line with Hooley Smith and Babe Siebert. As a unit they were the roughest and readiest forward line in the entire league. Stewart often would chew tobacco, produce juice, and then spit it, blindingly, in the enemy goalie's eyes before shooting and scoring.

After seven seasons with the Maroons, Nels was sold to Boston, where he centered a line with Dit Clapper and Red Beattie. He continued his scoring heroics in Beantown, picking up his 200th career goal as well as maintaining his bully boy image. In 1935, he was suspended for fighting just before being peddled to the New York Americans. Stewart played five years with the Americans, collecting his 300th career goal in 1938 and finally retiring from hockey in 1940.

RON STEWART

BORN: Calgary, Alberta, July 11, 1932
POSITION: Center, Toronto Maple Leafs, 1952-65; Boston Bruins, 1965-67; St. Louis Blues, 1967; New York Rangers, 1967-71, 1972; Vancouver Canucks, 1971-72; New York Islanders, 1972-73
AWARDS/HONORS: NHL ALL-Star Game, 1955, 1962-64

Sadly, a long and distinguished NHL career that began in 1952 and ended 21 years later was marred by an incident during the offseason in the twilight of Ron Stewart's NHL life.

Following the 1969-70 season, Stewart shared an apartment on Long Island with Hall of Fame goalie Terry Sawchuk. The teammates had completed the 1969-70 season with the New York Rangers and were looking forward to another campaign under the Blueshirts' leader Emile Francis.

Late one afternoon, Stewart and Sawchuk became involved in an imbroglio in front of their house. Sawchuk fell over a barbeque pit, injuring himself. The accident sent Sawchuk to the hospital for what seemed to be routine treatment but his condition worsened and he was eventually moved to a Manhattan hospital where he died of complications on May 31, 1970.

Stewart, who was never indicted, continued his playing career for three more seasons before retiring. But Ron's best years had been with the Toronto Maple Leafs, whom he helped win Stanley Cups in 1962, 1963, and 1964. A defensive forward who also could play defense, Stewart also toiled for the Boston Bruins and St. Louis Blues.

MARTIN STRAKA

BORN: Plzen, Czechoslovakia, September 3, 1972
POSITION: Center/Left Wing, Pittsburgh Penguins, 1992-95, 1997–; Ottawa Senators, 1995-96; New York Islanders, 1996; Florida Panthers, 1996-97
AWARDS/HONORS: NHL All-Star Game, 1999

Beginning his major league career on November 7, 1992, with Pittsburgh, Martin Straka went from mere survivor in the NHL to scoring star.

After netting 64 points in his sophomore year, Straka's game went into serious decline, as he bounced around three teams in two seasons. The New York Islanders let him go on waivers in 1996 after landing him as part of a major deal for defenseman Bryan Berard.

But when he returned to Pittsburgh as a free agent in 1997, Martin maximized his chances and impressively rebounded into a key figure and Penguins all-star when he exploded for 35 goals and 48 assists in 1998-99.

Though only five feet nine, Straka became a giant performer. Playing wing on a line that included fellow Czech Robert Lang at center and Alexei Kovalev on the right, he became a major scoring force in 2000–01, collecting a career-high 95 points.

Straka would excel where it counted most—in the playoffs—netting two humongous Game Six overtime goals, including a series clincher against Washington. Unfortunately, the normally durable Straka would miss most of the 2001–02 season with an assortment of injuries. With Straka out of the lineup, the Penguins missed the playoffs.

Straka enjoyed success on international ice as well, winning a gold medal at the Nagano Olympic Games (1998) skating for his native Czech Republic.

MATS SUNDIN

BORN: Bromma, Sweden, February 13, 1971
POSITION: Center, Quebec Nordiques, 1990–94; Toronto Maple Leafs, 1995–
AWARDS/HONORS: NHL All-Star Game, 1996–2002

Few Swedish stars have had a greater impact on the NHL than Mats Sundin.

A native of Bromma, a suburb of Stockholm, Sundin started playing on frozen ponds. His father was a goalie and both his brothers played hockey. By the 1988–89 season, Sundin was playing for a Swedish League team, when he realized that he had a good chance of being drafted by the National Hockey League.

It was a Sundin-Saturday in June 1989 at the NHL Entry Draft, when Mats was the first European to be drafted first overall. The Quebec Nordiques incorporated Sundin into their impressive, but very green, collection of young talent, which included Joe Sakic and Owen Nolan. He spent four years with the club, his best season coming when he skated in 80 games and scored 47 goals and 67 assists for 114 points in 1992–93.

In June 1994, however, Sundin was traded to Toronto for Wendel Clark, the eternal favorite son of Maple Leaf fans everywhere.

Sundin had to prove himself, and was accepted by the fans slowly but surely.

The lockout season of 1994–95, his first with the team, saw the six-feet-four, 220-pound center lead the Leafs in points (47) and goals (23). The big Swede continued to create outstanding numbers on offense, and exhibited more of a leader's attitude. Despite his 94 points in 1996–97, the Leafs could not make the playoffs under coach Mike Murphy. Sundin became captain during the 1997–98 season, following the departure of crowd-pleasing captain Doug Gilmour.

More than ever, the pressure was on Sundin to lift his game. The perception of some Swedish players as "soft" began to disappear in the NHL. Sundin certainly had grit.

With a move to the Eastern Conference and the arrival of Pat Quinn as Leafs' coach and general manager in 1998, credibility was restored. But despite consistently solid seasons and a heightened sense of the captaincy, Mats's postseason performances needed to be upgraded. Sundin delivered a commendable 16 points in 17 playoff games in the 1998–99 playoffs, as the Leafs went to the Conference finals against Buffalo. And for two straight years in the 2000 and 2001 Eastern Conference semifinals, Sundin would be matched up with the hard-checking New Jersey Devils. Mats's gallant nine-point effort in the seven-game 2001 semifinals silenced naysayers, with his increased propensity to play mean, physical, and in more traffic.

A five-time All-Star and two-time Olympian, Sundin was definitely a presence in the NHL, agile on his feet and almost perfecting the art of goal-scoring and true leadership for a gritty, veteran-laden Toronto team. After another 80-plus point season in 2001–02, Sundin fractured his wrist in Game One of the Eastern Conference quarterfinals against the New York Islanders, but played through pain for two games before stepping aside to allow his Leafs to win the seven-game series without him.

CAPTAIN JAMES T. SUTHERLAND

BORN: October 10, 1870
DIED: September 30, 1955

Sometimes referred to as "the father of hockey," this member of the Hockey Hall of Fame (1947) made Kingston, Ontario, a hotbed of the game prior to World War I.

Sutherland coached the Kingston Frontenac Juniors to several championships and later became president of the OHA from 1915 to 1917. Returning from the war, he became president of the CAHA for two years, in 1919. He died in 1955.

BRENT "PUP" SUTTER

BORN: Viking, Alberta, June 10, 1962
POSITION: Center, New York Islanders, 1980–91; Chicago Blackhawks, 1991–98
AWARDS/HONORS: NHL All-Star Game, 1985

Of the six Sutter brothers who played in the National Hockey League (Brent, Brian, Darryl, Duane, Rich, and Ron), Brent accomplished more with less fanfare than any in his family of skaters.

Brent Sutter as captain of the Islanders in 1988–89

Teaming with brother Duane, Brent was a member of New York Islanders Stanley Cup winners in 1982 and 1983. But perhaps his most noteworthy individual achievement occurred in the opening round of the 1988 Stanley Cup playoffs between the Islanders and the New Jersey Devils. In Game Four, Sutter scored a rare shorthanded sudden-death goal that tied the series at two for the Islanders.

A better skater than most of his brothers, Brent possessed a deadly shot and the ability to play a physical, as well as an artistic, game. Picked 17th overall in the 1980 draft, Brent was elevated to the Island in January of the 1981–82 season and fit right into the lineup with his intensity and all-around grit (in true Sutter fashion). He led the team with 114 penalty minutes in only 43 games, but also chipped in 21 goals and 22 assists.

After he experienced the last half of the Islanders four-Cup run, Brent's game rounded itself out. He exploded for a career-high 102 points in 72 games in 1984–85, and eased into a young leader's role (along with Pat Flatley and Pat LaFontaine) as the dynastic team was being dismantled.

When Denis Potvin announced that the 1987–88 season would be his last, his captaincy was handed to Sutter. His ability to deliver in the clutch was proven again when he scored a goal in double overtime at home against the Rangers in the 1990 Patrick Division semifinals. But Sutter's leadership and all-around play would not be enough to sustain the rebuilding franchise.

When the Islanders missed the playoffs for the second time in three years, general manager Bill Torrey transformed the team by dealing his two top players, Sutter and LaFontaine, in separate trades on October 25, 1991.

In Chicago, Brent absorbed the role of a checking center who would come in handy during the playoffs. After running into an unstoppable Mario Lemieux–led Pittsburgh team in the 1992 Stanley Cup finals, Brent's Blackhawks were swept in four straight.

After the 1997–98 season, Hawks missed the postseason for the first time since 1969, and with injuries and age limiting his effectiveness, Sutter finally hung up his skates with more points and accolades than any of his brothers.

Additionally, his Islander tenure landed him on the team's top ten all-time lists for every major category, a grand feat considering the number of franchise players in their rich history.

BRIAN SUTTER

BORN: Viking, Alberta, October 7, 1956
POSITION: Left Wing, St. Louis Blues,
1976–88; Coach, St. Louis Blues, 1988–92;
Boston Bruins, 1992–95; Calgary Flames,
1997–2000; Chicago Blackhawks, 2001–
AWARDS/HONORS: Jack Adams Award,
1991; NHL All-Star Game, 1982–83, 1985

Pioneer of a brand of hockey player identifiable by his last name, Brian Sutter was the first of the six brothers from Viking, Alberta, to play in the NHL, and may have been the best.

Admired for his rugged play, Sutter became the cornerstone of the St. Louis Blues' Kid Line along with Wayne Babych and Bernie Federko in the late 1970s. St. Louis's second choice in the 1976 Junior Draft, Sutter was regarded as one of the essential cogs in the rebuilding of the Blues' hockey machine, and captained the team from 1979 to 1988.

In time, Sutter became one of the most popular hockey personalities in St. Louis, and the man who led them in their greatest playoff moment during the sixth game of the 1986 Conference finals with the Calgary Flames. With St. Louis trailing 5–2 and about to be eliminated, Sutter's inspired goal at 8:08 of the third period sparked a rally that resulted in the Blues coming from behind to tie the game 5–5 and win in overtime, although Calgary eventually won the series.

It was a fiery love of winning that enabled Sutter to quest for more after retiring as a player in 1988 with 636 points to his credit. His number 11 retired by the team, Brian voraciously jumped right behind the St. Louis bench and into the coaching realm the following season, guiding his Blues to the postseason in each of his four years and grabbing a Jack Adams Award in 1991.

The Boston Bruins later hired Sutter to coach the team in 1992–93, but the famous Sutter intensity and work ethic did not translate to Brian's teams at all times. Despite strong regular seasons in Boston, including a 109-point debut in 1992–93, Sutter could not get his team past the second round of the playoffs, and was fired after 1994–95.

Always content to work on the Sutter family farm, Brian remained out of hockey until the Calgary Flames, of his native province of Alberta, came calling with an offer to coach in 1997–98. The small-market, youthful team could not make the playoffs during Sutter's three-year tenure, an event as unfamiliar to him as his losing record of 87–122–37 with the Flames.

Following another two-year sabbatical, Sutter triumphantly returned to the NHL in 2001–02 as coach of the Chicago Blackhawks, marking the rare occurrence of three brothers coaching in the NHL simultaneously, with Darryl guiding the San Jose Sharks, and Duane leading the Florida Panthers. Brian's Hawks surprised everyone with a 96-point season, and breakthrough performances from Eric Dazé, Jocelyn Thibault, and veteran Phil Housley. Despite a first-round loss to his alma mater, the St. Louis Blues, in five games, Brian received a nomination for the Jack Adams Award, as coach of the year.

DARRYL SUTTER

BORN: Viking, Alberta, August 19, 1958
POSITION: Left Wing, Chicago Blackhawks,
1979–87; Coach, Chicago Blackhawks, 1992–95;
San Jose Sharks, 1997–

If anyone could be considered the middle-of-the-road Sutter among the six hockey-playing brothers, Darryl would be the one.

Not as well-known as older brother Brian, nor a Cup winner like younger brothers Brent and Duane, Darryl nevertheless was a significant hockey personality, as both player and coach, who never failed to reach the postseason.

As a left-winger, Sutter featured all the hard-nosed qualities of Brian and Duane, plus talent and finesse sufficient to net 161 goals over eight seasons.

Captaining the Hawks throughout his brief NHL career, Darryl showed the same determination and tenacity as his five brothers who played at the NHL level. Darryl's playing career was relatively short. Injuries forced him to retire at the tender age of 29 following the 1986–87 season.

He currently holds the Chicago record for most goals scored in a playoff year, with 12 goals in 15 games during the 1985 playoffs.

Following his playing career, Sutter jumped straight into coaching, spending the 1987–88 campaign as an associate coach under Mike Keenan, and later becoming Chicago's head coach for three years (1992–95), reaching the Western Conference finals in 1995.

Sutter would then bring his coaching expertise to the West Coast with the San Jose Sharks organization, starting in the summer of 1997. Sutter powered his veteran Sharks troops into one of the top teams in the west with his Sutter-like workmanship and demanding style. Through the 2001–02 stanza, Darryl's 184 wins with the Sharks were a franchise-high, with a steady increase in points over each season.

DUANE "DOG" SUTTER

BORN: Viking, Alberta, March 16, 1960
POSITION: Right Wing, New York Islanders, 1979–87; Chicago Blackhawks, 1987–90

When the New York Islanders dynasty came into being during the early 1980s, two Sutter brothers proved pivotal to the club's success.

Duane—alias "Dog"—was the first to make it big, closely followed by younger brother Brent.

Like another of the six NHL-playing Sutters, older brother Brian, Duane played a bristling game that often put him on the edge but mostly in control.

Duane could check effectively and occasionally came up with big goals, particularly during the final game of the 1980 Stanley Cup playoffs, when he netted a goal to help power the Islanders over the Philadelphia Flyers to win their first Stanley Cup.

His best playoffs, however, was during the 1983 tournament, while playing on a line with brother Brent and Bob Bourne. Duane went on to score 9 goals and 12 assists, while also leading the team in penalty minutes with 43.

Against the New York Rangers in the Patrick Division final, Duane scored his first NHL hat trick and finished the series with 10 points, scoring 5 goals and 5 assists.

During the Stanley Cup finals of that same year, he put on a show against Edmonton for both Islanders fans and fans of his nearby hometown of Viking, scoring 2 goals and 5 assists for 7 points, as the Isles went on to take the series, winning their fourth straight Stanley Cup with a four-game sweep of the Oilers.

"Dog" remained a key Islander throughout the club's Stanley Cup reign. His best statistical season as an Islander was 1985–86, when he scored 20 goals and 33 assists for 53 points.

Sutter completed his playing career tallying 11 NHL seasons—eight with the Islanders and three with Chicago, where he retired after the 1989–90 season.

Like brother Brian, Duane went into coaching, first as an assistant with the Florida Panthers, and eventually as head coach of the team during the 2000–01 season, after Terry Murray was fired. Sutter lasted until early in the 2001–02 campaign, when he was replaced by Mike Keenan.

RICH SUTTER

BORN: Viking, Alberta, December 2, 1963
POSITION: Right Wing, Pittsburgh Penguins, 1982–83; Philadelphia Flyers, 1983–86; Vancouver Canucks, 1986–90; St. Louis Blues, 1990–93; Chicago Blackhawks, 1993–95; Tampa Bay Lightning, 1995; Toronto Maple Leafs, 1995

By the time four Sutter brothers, Brent, Brian, Darryl, and Duane, had become meaningful NHL personalities, two more Sutters were on the way, twins Ron and Rich.

A first-round selection (tenth overall) of the Pittsburgh Penguins in the 1982 Amateur Draft, at a time when the Sutter name was magic throughout the National Hockey League, Rich was under enormous pressure.

As it happened, twin brother Ron proved the more successful of the pair, with Rich the least successful of the entire sibling sextet. No matter where he played, his numbers were under the Sutter standards for success.

Known for his work along the boards and in the corners, Rich played a physical game. A hard worker throughout his career, as were all six of the Sutter brothers, Rich would eventually play for six NHL teams. He teamed briefly with brother Ron in Philadelphia in 1983, and enjoyed a 39-point season in 1985–86. On October 30, 1983, Rich helped make NHL history by teaming with Ron against brothers Duane and Brent, who were on Philly's Patrick Division rival, the New York Islanders—marking the first time four brothers played in one game.

After a 42-point effort for Vancouver in 1986–87, Rich's numbers spiraled downward, and he bounced around from St. Louis to Chicago to Tampa Bay, finishing his career in Toronto after 1994–95. He then became a scout for the Minnesota Wild.

RON SUTTER

BORN: Viking, Alberta, December 2, 1963
POSITION: Center, Philadelphia Flyers, 1981–91; St. Louis Blues, 1991–94; Quebec Nordiques, 1994; New York Islanders, 1994–95; Boston Bruins, 1995–96; San Jose Sharks, 1996–2000; Calgary Flames, 2000–01

Disturb should have been his middle name. If not that, then Hustle, since Ron Sutter did both very well.

In between, he scored a fair amount of goals, set up many more, and for nearly a decade gave the Flyers a brand of center ice pizzazz that only one of the Sutter clan could bestow upon a team.

That Ron was a special breed was as obvious as his surname. Each of the big-league Sutters was special. Ron and twin brother Rich starred together for Lethbridge in the Western Hockey League and each was drafted in 1982. Ron was drafted in the first round, fourth overall, by the Flyers.

Never before had five brothers scored an NHL goal in the same season. In fact, never before had five brothers all played in NHL games during one season, until the Sutters accomplished that feat when Ron played his first game with the Flyers.

Ron became a full-time Flyer in 1983–84 and immediately won accolades for his strong, two-way play. Sutter delivered 19 goals and 32 assists for 51 points in 79 games during his first full season.

Ron played some of his best hockey in the late 1980s and accompanied Philadelphia to the Stanley Cup finals in 1987. During the 1988–89 playoffs, he totaled 10 points in 19 playoff games. Ron remained in the Flyers lineup until September 1991, when he was traded to St. Louis with Murray Baron for Dan Quinn and Rod Brind'Amour.

Sutter's production decreased and he eventually bounced around to Quebec City, then to Long Island, Boston, San Jose, and finally

Calgary. Nevertheless, his trademarks—perseverance, determination, tenacity—remained intact. He was the last Sutter to play in the NHL, retiring after the 2000–01 season.

PETR SVOBODA

BORN: Most, Czechoslovakia, February 14, 1966
POSITION: Defenseman, Montreal Canadiens, 1984–92; Buffalo Sabres, 1992–95; Philadelphia Flyers, 1995–99; Tampa Bay Lightning, 1999–2002
AWARDS/HONORS: NHL All-Star Game, 2000

An exceptionally positive career ended on a terribly negative note in the spring of 2002, when Petr Svoboda announced his retirement. The victim of a concussion on December 14, 2000, at Phoenix, Svoboda was the star defenseman on the Tampa Bay Lightning, having played 15 years in the majors. Hopes for recovery were dashed when recurring headaches and other side effects bedeviled the Czech native throughout the 2001–02 campaign.

Originally drafted by the Montreal Canadiens as their first choice (fifth overall) in 1984, Svoboda was projected to be a superstar before he ever entered the NHL. Although he never reached such lofty heights, he did star for the Canadiens from 1984–85 into the 1991–92 season, when he was dealt to Buffalo for Kevin Haller. After three seasons with the Sabres, he was traded to Philadelphia for Garry Galley. Svoboda had some of his best years on Broad Street, helping the Flyers to the Stanley Cup finals in 1996–97. In December 1998, he was acquired from Philadelphia for Karl Dykhuis by the Tampa Bay Lightning.

Svoboda was the backbone of the Tampa Bay defense into the 2000–01 season. He appeared in 19 games before his career was ended by the concussion. Petr retired in 2002 and became a player agent.

PETR SYKORA

BORN: Plzen, Czechoslovakia, December 21, 1978
POSITION: Right Wing, New Jersey Devils, 1995–2002; Anaheim Mighty Ducks, 2002–
AWARDS/HONORS: NHL All-Rookie Team, 1996

At age 17, Petr Sykora made a powerful impact on American hockey. He left his homeland to play for the Cleveland Lumberjacks before moving on to the Detroit Vipers of the International Hockey League, his talent catching the attention of NHL scouts as a surefire impact player.

A shoulder injury appeared to hurt Sykora's chances of being selected high in the June 1995 NHL Entry Draft, but New Jersey Devils general manager Lou Lamoriello decided to gamble and it paid off in spades. Sykora joined the Stanley Cup–champion Devils the following autumn, playing like a seasoned veteran after learning the North American game in the IHL. He tallied 18 goals and 24 assists as a rookie, earning an NHL All-Rookie team nod, but could not help the Devils make the playoffs to defend their Cup title in 1996. A groin injury would sideline him for most of 1996–97, but he would bounce back mightily.

By 1998–99, Petr accelerated his game under coach Robbie Ftorek, and erected a 72-point season, tops on the first-place Devs. His success was due to the creation of one of 1990s' most vaunted lines, the A-Line, which united Sykora on right wing with countryman Patrick Elias on the left and center Jason Arnott. The team would come up short in ensuing playoffs, but the A-Line would carry the club to a monster 2000–01 campaign with a combined 232 points and plus-104 rating.

After a four-point effort in Game One of the 2000 Stanley Cup playoffs against the Dallas Stars, Sykora would help the Devils win the Cup despite being hospitalized in the clinching Game Six by a vicious Derian

Hatcher hit. Coach Larry Robinson, who replaced Ftorek late in the season, donned Sykora's number 17 jersey during the skating of the prize around the rink, and the team visited the fallen star in the hospital immediately following the victory.

Petr enjoyed his finest point-total in 2000–01 with 81 points, but the Devils finished short of a second consecutive Cup in a seven-game loss to the Colorado Avalanche in the finals. An ankle injury limited Sykora's action

in the following 2001–02 season, as the heralded A-Line was broken up by the trading of Arnott to Dallas. New Jersey, weakened by various infirmities involving Sykora, newly-acquired Joe Nieuwendyk, and Stephane Richer, were beaten by the Carolina Hurricanes in six games to open the postseason. In July 2002, Sykora was traded to Anaheim with Mike Commodore and goalie J. F. Damphousse for forward Jeff Friesen and blueliner Oleg Tverdovsky.

JEAN-GUY TALBOT

BORN: Cap-de-La-Madeleine, Quebec, July 11, 1932
POSITION: Defenseman, Montreal Canadiens, 1954–67; Minnesota North Stars, 1967; Detroit Red Wings, 1967–68; St. Louis Blues, 1968–70; Buffalo Sabres, 1970–71
AWARDS/HONORS: NHL First Team All-Star, 1962; NHL All-Star Game, 1956–58, 1960, 1962, 1965, 1967

During the Montreal Canadiens' dynastic run of five consecutive Stanley Cups, from 1956 through 1960, one of the least heralded heroes was defenseman Jean-Guy Talbot. A product of the Quebec Junior League, Talbot gained a measure of infamy by being suspended for an entire season for inflicting a career-ending head injury on an opposing Junior player named Scott Bowman, who later became the NHL's winningest coach.

After his suspension, Talbot graduated to the NHL Canadiens—along with another rookie, Henri Richard—for the 1955–56 season. When Hall of Famer Emile Bouchard was injured, Talbot became a regular, outlasting legends such as Doug Harvey and Tom Johnson.

In Dick Irvin's oral history of the Canadiens, *The Habs,* Talbot explained: "The Canadiens always made sure they had a lot of good defensemen. Even when they were winning five Stanley Cups they traded Dollard St. Laurent. Then after they won five Cups they traded Harvey. Then they traded Johnson and Bob Turner. I was the only one left. I wondered what I was doing there. I went to Minnesota when the expansion came in 1967."

Talbot also played for the Detroit Red Wings, St. Louis Blues, and Buffalo Sabres before concluding his career in 1970–71. He turned to coaching with St. Louis in 1972–73—ironically, following Scott Bowman—and stayed with the Blues for two seasons.

When John Ferguson took over as New York Rangers general manager, he hired Talbot for the 1977–78 season. Jean-Guy's only imprint on the Manhattan hockey scene was the fact that he wore a sweat suit behind the bench instead of a jacket and a tie in the traditional manner. After one season with the Rangers, Talbot was finished as a big-league coach.

ALEX TANGUAY

BORN: Ste.-Justine, Quebec, November 21, 1979
POSITION: Center/Left Wing, Colorado Avalanche, 1999–

Alex Tanguay was another of the Colorado Avalanche's young prospects to turn into a budding superstar. Following in the steps of fellow Avs youngsters Milan Hejduk and Chris Drury, Alex helped the Avs return to league supremacy in 2001.

Often complementing superstar Joe Sakic on the Avs' first line, Tanguay possessed tremendous speed and deft hands. He finished his rookie season of 1999–2000 with a splash when he ranked second among all freshmen in scoring with 51 points.

However, the best was yet to come. His sensational 2000–01 campaign, which included a team-high 11-game point scoring streak, a plus-35 ranking, and a 27-goal, 50-assist breakthrough helped set the stage for Alex's playoff heroics. In the decisive Game Seven of the Stanley Cup finals that spring against the New Jersey Devils, Tanguay scored two goals, including the game-winner, to clinch the Cup for Colorado. Not bad for a 21-year-old!

Tanguay's pace diminished in the 2001–02 season, but his 200 NHL points after three seasons signaled promise for the talent-rich Avalanche.

CYCLONE TAYLOR

BORN: Tara, Ontario, June 23, 1883
DIED: June 10, 1979
POSITION: Defenseman/Rover/Center, Ottawa Senators (ECAHA, ECHA), 1908–09; Renfrew Millionaires (NHA), 1910–11; Vancouver Millionaires (PCHL), 1913–21, 1923
AWARDS/HONORS: Hockey Hall of Fame, 1945

One of the first hockey superstars, Fred "Cyclone" Taylor was a talented, high-scoring rover/centerman who played for nine successful seasons with the Vancouver Millionaires of the PCHA. His reputation as a scorer, however, as well as his flamboyant nickname, was earned back east, where he broke into hockey as one of the game's earliest rushing defensemen.

Fred Taylor earned the handle "Cyclone" with the 1908 and 1909 Ottawa squads, scoring 17 goals in 21 games and helping his team to the 1909 Stanley Cup. The following year saw the newly formed Renfrew club vying for

Taylor's services and, after much controversy, Taylor had found a new home.

This began one of the fiercest rivalries in big-league hockey history and also started Taylor on the road to becoming a Canadian folklore legend. Quite naturally, contests between Renfrew and Ottawa took on warlike dimensions with Taylor being scorned as a turncoat and traitor in his old hometown. It didn't help matters much when, on a bet, Cyclone brashly announced that in the two teams' first meeting, he would skate backward through the entire Ottawa squad and score a goal.

Fact and legend become muddled at this point, but it is on record that Taylor did in fact, skate backward for "about five yards" before lifting a blistering backhander into the Ottawa cage. The fact that Renfrew lost the game was beside the point. Soon, Cyclone Taylor stories abounded all the way to Medicine Hat and back.

Renfrew's franchise floundered after two seasons and Cyclone made his way west to Vancouver, where he remained until his retirement in 1921. The old warrior couldn't get the game out of his blood that easily, however, and returned for one last game in 1923.

He retired to Vancouver where his legend remained intact.

DAVE TAYLOR

BORN: Levack, Ontario, December 4, 1955
POSITION: Right Wing, Los Angeles Kings, 1977–94; General Manager, Los Angeles Kings, 1997–
AWARDS/HONORS: Bill Masterton Memorial Trophy, 1991; King Clancy Trophy, 1991; NHL Second Team All-Star, 1981; NHL All-Star Game, 1981, 1982, 1986, 1994

The ascendancy of Dave Taylor from an insignificant 43-point scorer in his rookie season (1977–78) to a 91-point man (43 goals, 48 assists) a year later was a highlight of the Los Angeles Kings' pursuit of NHL respectability.

Hockey's first superstar, Fred "Cyclone" Taylor

Taylor was a major find for Los Angeles, since he was the 210th player chosen in the 1975 Amateur Draft and the Kings' 15th choice. At the time, Taylor was playing for Clarkson College in Potsdam, New York, where he set a four-year scoring record. In his senior year (1976–77), Taylor led the NCAA in scoring with 41 goals and 108 points.

As a player, the hardworking Taylor reached his peak working with Marcel Dionne and Charlie Simmer on the Kings' highly successful Triple Crown Line. Gritty and nonspectacular, Taylor's boardwork made room for Dionne's magic and Simmer's shot, and the undeniable chemistry spurred the Kings' ascendance. Dave's best season was a 112-point masterpiece in 1980–81 consisting of 47 goals and 65 assists. A consistent performer with numerous All-Star nods, Taylor reached at least 21 goals 12 of his 17 NHL seasons, earning the honor of his number 18 sweater's retirement in 1995. A stutterer when he arrived in the NHL, Taylor worked hard at his problem and soon was able to conduct interviews.

Taylor hung up his skates after the 1993–94 season, one year removed from his only Stanley Cup finals appearance, in which the Wayne Gretzky–led Kings were beaten by the Montreal Canadiens in five games. By this time, Dave had become a Los Angeles sports favorite, and parlayed that into a front office job, becoming general manager of the Kings in 1997. His hiring of enthusiastic rookie coach Andy Murray in 1999 proved a major step in reviving the franchise.

But Taylor's moves—such as the acquisitions of Ziggy Palffy, Mathieu Schneider, Felix Potvin, Adam Deadmarsh, and Jason Allison without depleting too much of his roster over the course of two years—were a key element in the Kings' emergence in the Western Conference. A 2001 Stanley Cup playoff upset over the Detroit Red Wings to open the tournament proved the Kings' might, as well as a tense seven-game loss to the eventual Cup-winning Colorado Avalanche. Taylor's Kings

were a dark horse playoff team again in 2002, but were knocked down in seven by Colorado after coming back from a three-games-to-one deficit.

JOSÉ THÉODORE

BORN: Laval, Quebec, September 13, 1976
POSITION: Goaltender, Montreal Canadiens, 1996–
AWARDS/HONORS: Vezina Trophy, 2002; Hart Memorial Trophy, 2002

During the first round of the 1997 Stanley Cup playoffs, the Montreal Canadiens fell desperately behind, three games to none, versus the New Jersey Devils. Goaler Jocelyn Thibault was not cutting it for the Habs and in a desperate move, Coach Mario Tremblay inserted a raw rookie, José Théodore, between the pipes. Poised, if not perfect, Théodore effectively stopped the Devils streak and, in a sudden-death performance, outdueled veteran Martin Brodeur to give the Habs a 4–3 victory.

It didn't guarantee a full-time job immediately, but by the 2001–02 season, Théodore reached a level of maturity that was reflected in his improved play. Thanks to José the Habs were able to withstand a crippling series of injuries, yet remain in the playoff hunt through the home stretch.

A quick-footed workhorse of Greek descent who could be relied upon to steal games, the 44th overall selection in the 1994 draft helped to ease the pain of the goaltending woes that plagued the Canadiens following the abrupt departure of the legendary Patrick Roy in 1995.

In the 2001–02 season, Théodore solidified his position among elite, young goaltenders in the league. With Montreal expected to fall short of a playoff berth, and with captain Saku Koivu battling cancer, Jose stood on his head for the duration of the season and earned a nomination for both the Hart and Vezina Trophies. Standing tall behind a shaky defense, Théodore's goals-against average (2.11) and save percentage (.911) remained outstanding on a team that regularly allowed over 40 shots on goal per game. In stunning fashion, not only did Théodore's Habs make the playoffs, but they then beat the top-seeded Boston Bruins in seven games to open the tournament, thanks largely to Théodore's sparkling play late in Game Seven.

Théodore became the sixth goaltender to record a regular season goal, and the first to score a goal while simultaneously racking up a shutout on January 2, 2001, in a 3–0 blanking of the New York Islanders. At season's end, José was the Molson Cup winner, a trophy awarded annually (since 1972) to the Canadiens player with the most three-star selections of the season. Topping off the season, Théodore also won both the Vezina Trophy and Hart Trophy.

STEVE THOMAS

BORN: Stockport, England, July 15, 1963
POSITION: Left Wing, Toronto Maple Leafs, 1984–87; 1998–2001; Chicago Blackhawks, 1987–91, 2001–; New York Islanders, 1991–95; New Jersey Devils, 1995–98

Among the league's best clutch players of his time, Steve "Stumpy" Thomas was the type of player that every hockey team needed to win. With Thomas came the complete package: a wicked shot, scoring ability, tremendous speed, and punishing play on the boards, despite his five-feet-ten frame.

Thomas originally made a name for himself with the Maple Leafs in the late 1980s before being dealt to Chicago. But he became a true star on the Islanders, starting in 1991. Thomas and center Pierre Turgeon led an exciting Islanders playoff run in 1992–93.

Feared by enemy goalies for scoring in overtimes and in the playoffs, Thomas became the NHL's all-time regular season overtime goals leader with 11 and ranked second all-time

in overtime points (11–10–21) behind Mark Messier (8–15–23).

A 42-goal scorer with the New York Islanders in 1993–94, Thomas was a player who gave 100 percent each night. It was Thomas's two goals in a 2–0 victory over Tampa Bay in the final week of the 1993–94 schedule that enabled the Islanders to clinch a playoff berth.

Dealt to New Jersey in 1995, Steve had trouble fitting in with the Devils' defensive style. He was dealt back to Toronto in 1998 and enjoyed a career revival with the Leafs. Despite leading Toronto in playoff goals with six during the 2001 playoffs, Thomas was considered expendable. The Maple Leafs brass made it obvious to him the following summer that he was no longer a part of their plans. It was a devastating year for Thomas, both from a team standpoint and personally. Playing the first half of the season with an aggravated knee injury before finally opting for surgery in midseason, Stumpy came back with a strong playoff performance. But it wasn't enough to vault the Leafs over the defending Stanley Cup–champion New Jersey Devils.

In July 2001, Steve re-signed with Chicago for his second stint. Under new coach Brian Sutter, Thomas hoped to help a revitalized Blackhawks squad, but a series of injuries limited his action. However, Thomas returned late in the 2001–02 season, helping the Hawks reach a playoff berth.

His tenacity and speed assured him a longer career than most veterans.

TINY THOMPSON

BORN: Sandon, Alberta, May 31, 1905
DIED: February 11, 1981
POSITION: Goaltender, Boston Bruins, 1928–38; Detroit Red Wings, 1938–40
AWARDS/HONORS: Vezina Trophy, 1930, 1933, 1936, 1938; NHL First Team All-Star, 1936, 1938; NHL Second Team All-Star, 1931, 1935; NHL All-Star Game, 1937; Hockey Hall of Fame, 1959

One of the National Hockey League's most accomplished goaltenders, Cecil "Tiny" Thompson won the Vezina Trophy four times in 12 NHL seasons. His rookie year, 1928–29, saw him produce an astonishing 1.18 goals-against average with the Boston Bruins and 12 shutouts. Boston

Cecil "Tiny" Thompson, Boston Bruin goalie, in mid 1930s

also won the Stanley Cup that season. With Tiny in the nets, Boston finished first and won the Prince of Wales Trophy in 1929, 1930, 1931, 1933, 1935, and 1938. Thompson was prepared to continue in the Bruins' goal, but Boston had discovered sensational young Frankie Brimsek and decided to trade Tiny to the Detroit Red Wings.

Thompson completed his NHL career after the 1939–40 season in Detroit. He later became the chief scout of western Canada for the Chicago Blackhawks, a position he maintained until his death in 1981. Tiny was enshrined as a member of the Hockey Hall of Fame in 1959.

JOE THORNTON

BORN: London, Ontario, July 2, 1979
POSITION: Center, Boston Bruins, 1997–
AWARDS/HONORS: NHL All-Star Game, 2002

If ever there was an example of patience on the part of management paying huge, long-term dividends, it was the case of the Boston Bruins and Joe Thornton.

Selected first overall in the 1997 Entry Draft, Thornton had all the physical and artistic equipment to be an instant star, or so the critics thought.

But when Thornton stumbled from the gate, he was ridiculed by the media and fans alike. The raw 18-year-old straight out of junior hockey only played 55 games for the B's and had three goals. Even in his second year with the Bruins, Thornton showed little improvement, and was considered by many to be a dud. They were wrong.

By 1999, Joe found himself and the latent skills and mean streak suddenly emerged. He recorded 9 points in 11 playoff games that spring and began playing the way a top draft pick had been expected to perform. Boston coaches Pat Burns and, later, Mike Keenan, challenged the six-feet-four, 220-pound Thornton to maximize his talent and develop a rugged style similar to Eric Lindros. The result was a tremendous breakthrough performance in 2000–01, as Thornton developed a power game for the young Bruins and pelted the National Hockey League with a 37-goal, 34-assist, 107-penalty minute season.

As the 2001–02 Olympic season trudged along, Thornton was among the top five scorers at midpoint, but injuries limited his action in the second half. Although he wasn't selected by Wayne Gretzky for the Salt Lake City Canadian Olympic team, The Great One all but said Thornton's name would have been the first on the back of a red-and-white jersey had injuries beset the team. His fame was further enhanced by a national television commercial. Many critics believed that Thornton would be one of the NHL's most popular figures of the new century.

ESA TIKKANEN

BORN: Helsinki, Finland, January 25, 1965
POSITION: Left Wing, Edmonton Oilers, 1985–93; New York Rangers, 1993–94, 1997, 1998–99; St. Louis Blues, 1994–95; New Jersey Devils, 1995; Vancouver Canucks, 1995–97; Florida Panthers, 1997–98; Washington Capitals, 1998

Few players could combine the elements of talent and ability to annoy the opposition as well as Finnish-born Esa Tikkanen. From the time he arrived in Edmonton in 1985, Esa proved a major asset to an Oilers team that would go on to win Stanley Cups that year, in 1987, 1988, and finally again in 1990.

Tikkanen's scoring ability was evident, particularly in his early years, when he scored 362 points over his first five full seasons. However, Esa's best scoring performances came during the playoffs, as he scored 27 points in 19 games in the 1988 postseason, 24 points in 22 games while going for the Cup in 1990, and 20 points in 19 games in the spring of 1991. In total, Tikkanen scored 72 goals and 60 assists in 186 playoff games, a much better percentage than during the regular season play.

Tikkanen was therefore sought for playoff help by several teams. The New York Rangers traded away Doug Weight for the Finn's services in 1993, followed by the Vancouver Canucks, Rangers again, and finally the Washington Capitals. Tikkanen helped propel the Capitals to the finals in 1998, and also was a member of the Rangers' Stanley Cup–winning team in 1994.

The pesky Finn finished his playing career back in Finland after parting ways with the Rangers in 1999.

DAVE TIPPETT

BORN: Moosomin, Saskatchewan, August 25, 1961
POSITION: Left Wing, Hartford Whalers, 1983–90; Washington Capitals, 1990–92; Pittsburgh Penguins, 1992–93; Philadelphia Flyers, 1993–94; Coach, Los Angeles Kings, 2002–

During his 11 NHL seasons, Dave Tippett ranked among the most noble workers as a tenacious defensive forward with Hartford, Washington, Pittsburgh, and Philadelphia. A heady performer, Tippett impressed his employers despite the fact that his highest scoring season was 1988-89, with 17 goals and 24 assists in 80 games.

"He was one of the best players I ever had in every way," said former Hartford Whalers president Howard Baldwin. "Every team needs a player like a Dave Tippett." He also was one of the smartest and carried that wisdom into the coaching ranks.

Following the conclusion of his playing career in 1995 with the International League's Houston Aeros, Tippett became a coach, first in the IHL as a head coach in Houston and then as an assistant with the Los Angeles Kings. He worked three years as an aide in Los Angeles, turning one of the worst power plays into the best by the 2001-02 season.

In May 2002, Tippett was hired to be head coach of the Dallas Stars by Stars general manager Doug Armstrong. "When you're in charge of a power-play unit, you're obviously working with the top players on the team," said Armstrong. "He was able to take that group and mold them into the best power play in the NHL. In the NHL, you have to have your best players be your best players every night."

KEITH TKACHUK

BORN: Melrose, Massachusetts, March 28, 1972
POSITION: Left Wing, Winnipeg Jets, 1991–96; Phoenix Coyotes, 1996–2001; St. Louis Blues, 2001–
AWARDS/HONORS: NHL Second Team All-Star, 1995, 1998; NHL All-Star Game, 1997–99

Like Clark Gillies and Cam Neely before him, Keith Tkachuk was a dominating "power forward" at the NHL level, combining size, skill, and strength.

With 225 pounds behind his muscular six-feet-two-inch frame, Tkachuk gave opposing players a choice: to either move out of his way or be crushed. His aggressiveness was exemplified in penalty minute totals, which surpassed 200 minutes per season three times in his career, the most coming in the 1993–94 season with Winnipeg, when he sat for 255 minutes.

But the bruising Tkachuk was a popular and prolific scorer throughout his career. Captain of the Winnipeg Jets and protector of finesse linemates Alex Zhamnov and Teemu Selanne, Keith gradually learned the NHL style after arriving in 1992 following his Team USA berth at the Olympic games. A 41-goal, 255-penalty minute stanza in 1993–94 announced his arrival in the NHL as a major force. He went on to score 50 goals in his final season in Winnipeg, and after the team moved to Phoenix the following season, he potted 52 goals, a league high that year.

Usually paired with Jeremy Roenick in Phoenix, Tkachuk's goal-scoring tailed off somewhat after 1997–98, but many claim he became a better all-around player by cutting down on his penalties and improving his skating.

Tkachuk was traded from Phoenix in 2001, when Wayne Gretzky bought the team and restructured the fiscal model. Arriving in St. Louis for Michal Handzus, Jeff Taffe, Ladislav Nagy, and a first-round draft choice, Tkachuk eventually found his game with the contending Blues, and helped in their drive to the 2001 Conference finals.

With a bounce-back season of 38 goals, Tkachuk remained healthy for most of 2001–02, and, paired with newly-acquired Doug Weight, sought to help the Blues achieve supremacy. In Game Three of the Western Conference semifinals against the powerful Detroit Red Wings, a Tkachuk hat trick helped ignite a St. Louis revival. He was unable to sustain his offensive effort and, once again, the Blues—and Tkachuk—were out of the playoffs. Nevertheless, the club rewarded Keith with a new long-term contract.

WALT TKACZUK

BORN: Emstedetten, Germany, September 29, 1947
POSITION: Center, New York Rangers, 1967–81
AWARDS/HONORS: NHL All-Star Game, 1970

Possessing an iron constitution and an alphabet-soup surname, Walt Tkaczuk was generally acknowledged around the NHL as one of hockey's most underrated players.

Never a consistently high-point man, Tkaczuk developed into a sparkling defensive specialist, excelling as a penalty killer. He was not noticeable when one first looked at him out on the ice, but Tkaczuk had brute strength and, when skating at full steam, was practically immovable.

Tkaczuk never lived up to his advance billing as a superstar, and finally retired after the 1981 season. An active member of the Rangers' alumni association, he also stayed busy in the rink business through the 2001–02 season.

RICK TOCCHET

BORN: Scarborough, Ontario, April 9, 1964
POSITION: Right Wing, Philadelphia Flyers,
1984–92, 2000–; Pittsburgh Penguins,
1992–94; Los Angeles Kings, 1994–96; Boston
Bruins, 1996; Washington Capitals, 1996–97;
Phoenix Coyotes, 1997–2000
AWARDS/HONORS: NHL All-Star Game,
1989–91, 1993

When Rick Tocchet arrived in Philadelphia in 1984, he was rough around the edges but showed definite signs of pending power-forward superstardom. He brought vim, vigor, and vitality to the sport, as well as a zest for fighting. While never a goon, Tocchet was never choosy about his opponents and battled some of the NHL's best fighters. He was encouraged to fight by then-coach Mike Keenan and racked up 284 penalty minutes in the 1985–86 season, and 288 in the following season.

A change in strategy led to a 45-goal season with 183 penalty minutes in 1988–89. Rick had achieved a better balance and continued with some of the same delightful digits in the next two campaigns. Tocchet was named captain of the Flyers in 1990 and was then dealt to Pittsburgh in 1992 with Kjell Samuelsson and Ken Wregget for Mark Recchi, Brian Benning, and a draft choice.

Rick also played for Los Angeles, Boston, Washington, and Phoenix, and finally came back to his original starting point, Philadelphia, in 2000. After more than a decade and a half of major-league hockey, he remained a force and a desirable commodity for any team.

Despite his many NHL stops, Tocchet always was known as a Flyer. He was one of only two players in NHL history, Pat Verbeek being the other, to collect 400 goals and 2,000 penalty minutes during his career. A four-time participant in the NHL All-Star game Rick battled back from the brink of retirement in 2001–02 to help the Flyers maintain their Atlantic Division title.

JOHN TONELLI

BORN: Milton, Ontario, March 23, 1957
POSITION: Left Wing, New York Islanders,
1978–86; Calgary Flames, 1986–88; Los Angeles
Kings, 1988–91; Chicago Blackhawks, 1991–92;
Quebec Nordiques, 1992
AWARDS/HONORS: NHL Second Team All-
Star, 1982, 1985; NHL All-Star Game, 1982,
1985; Canada Cup MVP, 1984

Ask any Islander who played on the four-consecutive-Stanley Cup dynasty about unsung heroes, and chances are the name John Tonelli will be heard. Although not a member of the Hockey Hall of Fame, Tonelli's value to the Islanders transcended goals, of which he scored many, and assists. He was, in fact, one of the cleanest, most effective power forwards of the post-Expansion era.

In the mid 1970s, the Toronto native learned his trade in the WHA, displaying tenacity along the boards and in the corners. Islanders architect Bill Torrey drafted him in the second round of the 1977 Entry Draft, with an eye on adding that grit to his team's offense. Tonelli arrived in 1978–79 to bolster the Isles' depth, as well as instill emotion and spirit into the emerging team. A veritable whirling dervish on skates, the burly left wing not only had a keen eye for the net, but a relentless work ethic that soothed the heart of demanding coach Al Arbour.

It was Tonelli who used his speed to draw two Flyers defensemen on a two-on-two and saucer a perfect pass to Bob Nystrom for the Isles' 1980 Game Six overtime victory, clinching the Stanley Cup. It was Tonelli who scored a late third-period slap shot goal against the Colorado Rockies, to lift the 1982 Islanders into the record books for what was then an NHL all-time best 15 consecutive victories.

One of the greatest comebacks in a playoff game came courtesy of Tonelli's trademark workmanship. The Islanders trailed 3–1 in Game Five of the Patrick Division semifinals of 1982 with just over five minutes to play. With their dynasty in grave danger, the Isles ended up tying the game at 17:39 when Tonelli pounced on a loose puck that hopped over Pens defensman Randy Carlyle's stick and drove it by goaltender Michel Dion.

With the crowd in a frenzy, Tonelli seized the momentum in the ensuing overtime period. After the Islanders weathered a Pittsburgh attack, Tonelli sprang on a breakaway. His shot was stopped, but after a flurry of rebounds, he finally jabbed the puck behind Dion for the magical win.

Long Island fans embraced the tenacious Tonelli—who still holds Islander records for goals (42) and points (100) in a season by a left-winger—as an all-time favorite. But when the dynasty was being disassembled in the late 1980s, Tonelli was dealt to Calgary, saddening the Coliseum fans who marked his return visit with signs that read "Thanks, J.T." Clearly, his verve was a big part of the team's soul.

Tonelli brought his intensity to the Los Angeles Kings, Chicago Blackhawks, and Quebec Nordiques in his twilight years, but those stops never erased the warm association between Tonelli and the Islanders.

BILL TORREY

BORN: Montreal, Quebec, June 23, 1934
POSITION: General Manager, Oakland Seals, 1967–72; New York Islanders, 1972–93; Florida Panthers, 2000–02; President, Florida Panthers, 1993–2002
AWARDS/HONORS: Hockey Hall of Fame, 1995

Never a pro iceman himself, Bill Torrey, a general manager for the Oakland Seals, the Florida Panthers, and—most prominently—the New York Islanders, was actively involved in hockey since his collegiate playing days at St. Lawrence University in New York.

Torrey's climb up hockey's managerial ladder began in 1960 with the AHL's Pittsburgh

Hornets, where he served for five years as publicity director and business manager. In 1968, Torrey moved out west as executive vice president of the Oakland Seals. Four years later, he was appointed general manager of the Islanders.

Islanders' dynasty builder, Bill "Bowtie" Torrey

After a weak start, the Islanders made the playoffs in 1975 and upset the Rangers and Penguins. Torrey was voted Manager of the Year by the *Sporting News*. When the bow-tied Torrey became the Islanders' manager, he said he hoped the club would be contenders within five years. The Isles not only were on schedule but made the Stanley Cup semifinals four times by the end of the 1978–79 season. Time and again, Torrey's selections for building a winner turned out to be gems. Denis Potvin ripened into one of the NHL's best defensemen, Bryan Trottier became a premier center, and Mike Bossy blossomed as one of the most prolific scorers major-league hockey has known. When the Islanders suffered a financial setback during the summer of 1978, Torrey—with the aid of new owner John Pickett—reorganized and stabilized the club's fiscal foundation.

Meanwhile, Torrey continued to make prudent acquisitions. He signed left wing John Tonelli, formerly with Houston of the WHA, and Tonelli instantly established himself as a productive workhorse. As a team, the Islanders improved each year on their previous record and achieved a new measure of excellence in 1979 when they annexed the Prince of Wales Trophy as the club with the most points in the entire league. In addition, Torrey organized and directed the NHL All-Star squad which competed against the Soviet National team in February 1979. Most objective hockey analysts regarded Torrey as one of the brightest executives in the game. In 1980, with the Islanders ready for a major push, Torrey made a signature move that set a trading deadline precedent, when he acquired center Butch Goring from the Los Angeles Kings as the final piece of what would become a champion.

Torrey's creativity paid off when the Islanders won four consecutive Stanley Cups from 1980 through 1983. It marked the first time an American franchise had ever accomplished such a feat; only the Montreal Canadiens had ever won four Cups in a row. In addition, the Islanders had won 17 straight playoff series. No team has ever matched that feat. The Islanders remained a premier franchise through the late 1980s, but Torrey left the general manager's duties to Don Maloney in 1993, and when Florida was added to the NHL in the fall of that same year, he became president of the Panthers.

A Hockey Hall of Fame inductee in 1995, Bill was honored by his alma mater, the Islanders, in 2001 with a commemorative banner, depicting his trademark bow tie, to hang from the Nassau Coliseum rafters along with retired jerseys and Stanley Cup banners.

Torrey's new team followed a similar blueprint to that of his Long Island success, as the Panthers organized a collection of veterans sprinkled with youth and hot goaltending. The inaugural Panthers team broke a record for expansion teams with 33 wins and 83 points, and reached the Stanley Cup finals against the Colorado Avalanche in 1996, in just their third year of existence. Working constantly to raise awareness of the sport in a new market like Florida, Torrey found his job was made easier by the enormous success early on, as well as the acquisition of superstar Pavel Bure in 1999.

Torrey took over from Bryan Murray as Panthers general manager in December 2000, after the team faltered, but was relieved of his managerial duties during the 2001–02 season,

although he stayed on in an administrative role. Chuck Fletcher, Torrey's aide, temporarily replaced him as general manager while Mike Keenan took over as coach. Rick Dudley became the new general manager in the summer of 2002.

There's little question that Torrey will go down in hockey history as the general manager's general manager.

GILLES TREMBLAY

BORN: Montmorency, Quebec, December 17, 1938
POSITION: Left Wing, Montreal Canadiens, 1960–69
AWARDS/HONORS: NHL ALL-Star Game, 1965, 1967

One of the most promising players ever to grace the NHL had his career cut short by a respiratory ailment, just when he appeared to be en route to stardom. Gilles Tremblay graduated to the Montreal Canadiens from Junior ranks and earned a regular berth in the 1960–61 season, playing 45 games at left wing. The NHL was a six-team league in those days and it was difficult for youngsters to remain a regular unless they had the goods.

Tremblay knew he was in the NHL to stay when he lined up against tough Gordie Howe of the Detroit Red Wings. "Howe tested me a couple of times at the beginning of the game," recalled Tremblay. "But afterwards he told me that as soon as he saw how I reacted in that game, he knew I was in the league for good."

The 1961–62 season was Tremblay's first full year with the Habs. Managing director Frank Selke Sr. signed Tremblay to a $7,500 contract. "Mr. Selke told me at Christmastime not to worry about money," said Tremblay, "that he would fix me up at the end of the year. He kept his promise and gave me a bonus of $3,500. I scored thirty-two goals and got the same bonus as Bernie Geoffrion when he scored fifty."

Tremblay never broke the 30-goal mark again, but he did play for Montreal's Stanley Cup winners in 1965–66 and 1967–68. He played part of the 1968–69 season but missed the playoffs and retired because of his ailment. He remained close to hockey as a Montreal hockey broadcast analyst for many years.

J. C. TREMBLAY

BORN: Bagotville, Quebec, January 22, 1939
DIED: Date unknown
POSITION: Defenseman, Montreal Canadiens, 1959–72; Quebec Nordiques (WHA), 1972–79
AWARDS/HONORS: NHL First Team All-Star, 1971; NHL Second Team All-Star, 1968; NHL All-Star Game, 1959, 1965, 1967–69, 1971–72; First Team All-Star (WHA), 1973, 1975–76; Second Team All-Star (WHA), 1974; Outstanding Defenseman (WHA), 1973, 1975

Among the many top defensemen to adorn the Montreal Canadiens' roster during their Cup-winning years of the late 1950s and 1960s, Jean Claude Tremblay was among the least-appreciated. After a lengthy Montreal career, Tremblay was the most sought-after player when the World Hockey Association's Quebec Nordiques were formed in 1972. The popular Canadiens' defenseman was often referred to as "J. C. Superstar," after the Broadway show of the same name.

J.C. was one of the highest-scoring defensemen in the NHL during the 1970–71 and 1971–72 seasons, and won a berth on the First All-Star Team in 1971. He played brilliantly after joining the WHA, being named to the All-Star First Team three times, the Second Team twice, and as the outstanding defenseman on two occasions. One of the best mild-mannered defensemen of the post–World War II era, Tremblay retired in 1979 as a member of the WHA Quebec Nordiques at the age of forty.

BRYAN TROTTIER

BORN: Val Marie, Saskatchewan, July 17, 1956
POSITION: Center, New York Islanders, 1975–90; Pittsburgh Penguins, 1990–94; Coach, New York Rangers, 2002
AWARDS/HONORS: King Clancy Memorial Trophy, 1989; Calder Memorial Trophy, 1976; Art Ross Trophy, 1979; Hart Memorial Trophy, 1979; Conn Smythe Trophy, 1980; Bud Man of the Year Award, 1988; NHL First Team All-Star, 1978–79; NHL Second Team All-Star, 1982, 1984; NHL Plus/Minus Leader, 1979; NHL All-Star Game, 1976, 1978, 1980, 1982–83, 1985–86, 1992; Hockey Hall of Fame, 1997

Arguably the best two-way center of the post-Expansion era, Bryan Trottier was once described by Hall of Fame referee Bill Chadwick as "greatest player of all time."

Trottier—along with fellow Hall of Famers Mike Bossy, Denis Potvin, and Bill Smith—provided the skill and energy

Bryan Trottier as an Islander in 1987–88

to propel the New York Islanders to four consecutive Stanley Cups and no less than 19 straight playoff victories from 1980 through 1984.

Arriving on Long Island in 1975, Trottier made the difficult jump from junior hockey to the NHL without missing a beat.

Although the high command of general manager Bill Torrey and coach Al Arbour had thought of sending Trottier to the minors, Bryan was so dominant in training camp, 1975, that he virtually forced himself on the varsity.

His style embodied the best features of old-time and modern hockey. He could bodycheck with the very best hitters, was a crafty passer, and, as any goalie will tell you, one of the best shooters in the game.

"I can use Bryan in any situation," said Arbour. "It didn't matter whether he was killing a penalty, working the power play, or taking a regular turn; Bryan was always at the top of his game."

Two years after Trottier had become an Islander, the Islanders drafted Mike Bossy as a right wing. With Trottier at center and Bossy on the right, the Islanders had the best one-two scoring combination of the late 1970s and into the 1980s.

Eventually, Clark Gillies became a fixture on the left and El Trio Grande emerged as the dominant line for the Islanders through their dynastic years.

Trottier excelled at defense as well as offense. In two separate playoffs against the Edmonton Oilers, he completely stifled Wayne Gretzky en route to Stanley Cup victories. During the 1983 finals, Trottier sparked New York to a four-straight sweep of Gretzky's Oilers.

His baby face masked a mean streak, and Trottier delivered some of the hardest body checks any forward ever tossed at an opponent. During the 1984 playoff against the Montreal Canadiens, a Trottier hit knocked the powerful Bob Gainey to the ice where he lay unconscious for several minutes.

Bryan often excelled in critical playoff games against the Rangers. In one series, during which it appeared that the favorite Isles might be knocked out by the Blueshirts, Trottier turned the series in the Isles' favor with an overtime goal against Eddie Mio.

Trottier spent 15 seasons on Long Island before moving on to Pittsburgh, where he helped win Stanley Cups for the Penguins in 1991 and 1992. After retiring in 1994, Trottier became an assistant coach with Pittsburgh, head coach of Portland in the AHL, and assistant coach for Colorado. After failing to gain a head coaching position for a few years, Trottier was finally named head coach of the Rangers in 2002.

PIERRE TURGEON

BORN: Rouyn, Quebec, August 28, 1969
POSITION: Center, Buffalo Sabres, 1987–91; New York Islanders, 1991–95; Montreal Canadiens, 1995–96; St. Louis Blues, 1996–2001; Dallas Stars, 2001–
AWARDS/HONORS: Lady Byng Memorial Trophy, 1993; NHL All-Star Game, 1990, 1993, 1994, 1996

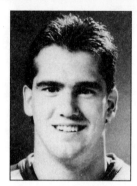

Pierre Turgeon

Few first-round draft picks (first overall in 1987) fulfill their expectations as well as Pierre Turgeon did, starting with the Buffalo Sabres, and later the Islanders, Canadiens, Blues, and, to a much lesser extent, the Stars.

After a successful four years in Buffalo, Turgeon was part of a major trade that sent Pat LaFontaine from the Islanders to the Sabres. Replacing a fan favorite like LaFontaine was challenging, but in the 1992–93 season, Pierre rose to the occasion with several dramatic moves. One of them was a goal against the Rangers at Madison Square Garden that clinched an Islander playoff berth.

Turgeon finished that season with 132 points, a career high, and then starred in an upset of the Washington Capitals in the first round. However, in the clinching game at the Nassau Veterans Memorial Coliseum, Turgeon was struck viciously from behind by Dale Hunter when the Frenchman scored the back-breaking goal. A brawl ensued, Hunter received what then was a record 21-game suspension, and Turgeon's shoulder was separated.

But the Islanders would dethrone the Stanley Cup champion Pittsburgh Penguins in the second round without Turgeon's services, only to lose in five straight to Montreal in the Conference finals.

With Turgeon's deft playmaking and timely scoring, the Islanders seemed set for years up on their top line. But concerns over Turgeon's lack of grit, durability, and intensity prompted then–general manager Don Maloney to abruptly deal Pierre, along with Vladimir Malakhov, to the Montreal Canadiens for Kirk Muller, Mathieu Schneider, and Craig Darby in 1995.

In Turgeon, the Canadiens had another French-flavored offensive superstar, in the tradition of Guy LaFleur and Maurice Richard, to build around. He recorded a 96-point season in 1995–96 and was named captain of the Habs in their last season at the Montreal Forum.

Shockingly, Pierre was dealt again one month into the following season to the St. Louis Blues, where he teamed with a succession of high-scoring wingers in Brett Hull, Scott Young, and Pavol Demitra. In just five seasons, Turgeon amassed 355 points in just 327 games, good for seventh all-time on the Blues' list.

Though his numbers would always be more than adequate, Turgeon never seemed to carry a team on his shoulders through the playoffs until the spring of 2001. St. Louis made it past the second round for the first time since 1986, and battled the eventual-champ Colorado Avalanche to five games in the Western Conference finals. Turgeon, due to become an unrestricted free agent, led the Blues valiantly, potting nine points in a first-round win over the San Jose Sharks, and finishing with 15 points to lead the team.

But, again, the Blues, feeling that they needed more grit and leadership from the center ice position, traded for Doug Weight in the summer of 2001. With playmakers at a premium, the Dallas Stars added Turgeon to their stable of top centers. Never shown the respect he deserved for the numbers he delivered, Pierre joined two-way Mike Modano and Joe Nieuwendyk on a defense-oriented team to prove he could produce in any circumstance. Unexpectedly, the Stars never even made it to the postseason, and Turgeon had trouble scoring. For the first time in his career, Pierre appeared to be slowing down.

FRANK UDVARI

BORN: Yugoslavia, January 2, 1924
POSITION: Referee, NHL, 1951–66
AWARDS/HONORS: Hockey Hall of Fame, 1973

One of the few referees ever inducted into the Hockey Hall of Fame, Frank Udvari was a less effective official than his Hall of Fame induction would indicate. Udvari was more of an establishment official who, unlike Dalton MacArthur, Eddie Powers, or Red Storey, rarely criticized NHL management. An uncertain referee when he began his career, Udvari did mature into a competent whistle-blower. He was rewarded for his efforts after retirement when the NHL named him one of the league's supervisors of officials.

In 1972, with the inception of the World Hockey Association, the NHL lost many top referees to the rival league. Criticism of NHL officiating reached hysterical proportions during the 1978–79 season, as violent incidents became a game-by-game occurrence, and Udvari was forced to spend many interviewing hours defending his refereeing corps.

Once, during a game at Nassau Coliseum, Udvari, who had become supervisor of NHL officials in 1966, was watching from the press box, when the regular referee was injured and had to leave the game. Udvari borrowed a pair of skates and a striped referee's sweater, although he still wore his suit pants. He officiated the rest of the game, and showed he had not lost his refereeing touch.

NORM ULLMAN

BORN: Provost, Alberta, December 26, 1935
POSITION: Center, Detroit Red Wings, 1955–68; Toronto Maple Leafs, 1968–75
AWARDS/HONORS: NHL First Team All-Star, 1965; NHL Second Team All-Star, 1967; NHL All-Star Game, 1955, 1960–65, 1967–69, 1974; Hockey Hall of Fame, 1982

When discussions about the top Detroit centers of all time take place, names like Sid Abel, Alex Delvecchio, and Steve Yzerman inevitably emerge.

But over the years, there has been another cadre of peerless pivots headed by Norman Ullman, who served the Red Wings nobly for more than a decade starting in the 1955–56 season.

Ullman's job was a difficult one, to say the least. He was called upon to center Gordie Howe and Ted Lindsay, who were two-thirds of the original Production Line.

The center who had originally set the standard was Sid Abel, who helped the Red Wings win the Stanley Cup in 1950. After Abel left Detroit in 1952, he was succeeded by Delvecchio. When Red Wings general manager Jack Adams decided that Delvecchio would be more useful

Hall of Fame referee Frank Udvari (left), with other former officials, Bill Chadwick (middle) and Cooper Smeaton (right)

on another line, others auditioned with Howe and Lindsay. Norm Ullman to the rescue.

Ullman had been skating for the Red Wings farm team in Edmonton and was summoned to the big club in 1955. Once he got the feel of the NHL, Norm was placed between Howe and Lindsay and turned out to be as reliable as Abel and Delvecchio before him. Nobody knew it at the time, but Ullman had begun what was to be a distinguished 20-year career as a major-leaguer.

Playing between Howe and Lindsay, Ullman became one of the most unobtrusive high scorers in NHL annals. In the 1964–65 season, for instance, Ullman scored 42 goals, topped only by Chicago's Golden Jet Bobby Hull and Norm's teammate, Mr. Hockey himself, Gordie Howe.

In the view of some observers, Ullman operated on the ice with computer-like efficiency. Ullman went out, backchecked, forechecked, and scored with perfection. In his first decade with the Red Wings, Ullman amassed 237 goals and 324 assists for 561 points, putting him in a tie with Syd Howe for fourth place among all-time Detroit scorers. During that tenth season, 1964–65, he was the Red Wings' high point (83) man, team MVP, a First Team All-Star, and a runner-up for the Hart Trophy as League MVP.

But exactly because he shunned publicity, avoided public appearances, and gave the impression he'd rather play hockey in private, few people knew Norm Ullman existed, outside of the then-highly provincial confines of the hockey world.

When the Red Wings played the Chicago Blackhawks in the March 1964 Stanley Cup semifinals, coach Billy Reay acknowledged that Ullman was the key to the Red Wings' success.

Ullman confirmed Reay's fears by scoring hat tricks in two of Detroit's victories over Chicago, tying a league record.

Ullman's first nomination to the All-Stars resulted in a nod over Stan Mikita, and in balloting for the most valuable player, he was runner-up—103-96—to Bobby Hull. But in the

second half vote for the Hart Trophy, Ullman routed Hull, 74–15.

Still, for all his recognized skills, he remained largely ignored by fans and press. "He won hockey games," said one NHL veteran, "but he didn't sell tickets."

But Ullman was unconcerned about this lack of attention. "If you looked around the league," he said, "you'll find that the better players were not the guys who fooled around and made all the noise. The better ones were the more serious types. To be very honest, I'd rather stay the way I am."

Ullman finished the 1963–64 season with 21 goals. The leap to 42 in 1964–65 indicated that Ullman must have been doing something right, but he was not sure exactly what it was, except possibly playing on a line with Floyd Smith, whose digging style blended well with Ullman's *modus operandi*.

If Ullman had a weakness, it was his shot, which lacked the speed of Hull or Howe's. But Hull said that Ullman penetrated so deeply behind enemy lines he'd be able to score with a shot of just average velocity. "He got in close enough, then he shot for the corners," Hull said, "and often got them."

Because of his strength and tenacity, Ullman was practically indestructible. Once, a

One of the most underrated forwards of all time, Norm Ullman as a Maple Leaf, 1974–75

tendon in his left foot was so badly bruised that doctors mummified it with bandages and insisted Ullman use crutches. He used the crutches to get himself to the dressing room. Then he parked them in a corner, removed the bandages from his foot, and played the game as if nothing was the matter.

This had been the Ullman philosophy since playing organized hockey for the Red Wing–sponsored Maple Leaf A.C. in Edmonton at the age of ten. He quit high school at the age of 17 to devote himself to hockey.

Ullman played 13 full seasons for the Red-and-White, becoming a household word in the Motor City—although it was a word more whispered than shouted.

Then it happened.

Ullman was dealt to the Maple Leafs with Floyd Smith and Paul Henderson for Frank Mahovlich, Pete Stemkowski, Garry Unger, and the rights to Carl Brewer on March 3, 1968. Ullman would go on to play seven full seasons for Toronto, often distinguishing himself as he had done with the Red Wings, with massive efficiency and no fanfare.

Norm closed his career in Edmonton, his hometown, playing two seasons for the Edmonton Oilers before calling it a career.

GARRY UNGER

BORN: Calgary, Alberta, December 7, 1947
POSITION: Center, Toronto Maple Leafs, 1967–68; Detroit Red Wings, 1968–71; St. Louis Blues, 1971–79; Atlanta Flames, 1979–80; Los Angeles Kings, 1980–81; Edmonton Oilers, 1981–83
AWARDS/HONORS: NHL All-Star Game, 1972–78

It was to have been a glorious career for Garry Unger in Detroit. In some ways, he could have been an early day Steve Yzerman. All the ingredients were there—speed, radar-shot, smarts, and drive.

As it happened, his career in the Motor City

was short-lived. Nevertheless, while he was in Detroit, Unger demonstrated the ingredients that eventually would enable him to play starry hockey for 16 seasons.

Unger's arrival in Detroit was a surprise in itself. He had already been earmarked as a future Toronto Maple Leafs ace during his teenage years and made his National Hockey League debut with Toronto in 1967-68. No doubt he would have remained a Leaf, had the Red Wings not made an offer that the Leafs' high command could not refuse. On March 3, 1968, Toronto obtained Norm Ullman, Paul Henderson, and Floyd Smith. For that package, the Leafs relinquished Unger along with Frank Mahovlich, Pete Stemkowski, and the rights to Carl Brewer.

Coach Bill Gadsby placed him on a line with Gordie Howe at right wing and Alex Delvecchio at center, and nobody was more impressed than Garry himself. Superior centers were driven to distraction trying to orchestrate plays for Howe because Howe was the one who did the conducting. But for new center Unger it was less than a disaster.

"I remember the first time I played with Gordie. They put me on his line and right away we got a two-on-one breakaway. I kind of pulled the defenseman to one side and flipped the puck to Gordie. It wasn't a very good pass. In fact, it was a pretty bad one. But he leaned back and got it and—wham!—the puck was in the net for a goal. I remember thinking to myself as I skated behind the net, 'God, I'm going to get 900 assists this season.'"

Garry played 13 games for Detroit in the latter portion of the 1967-68 season and had all the credentials of a whiz-bang center. With five goals as well as ten assists, he was being tabbed a star by some writers.

Coach Sid Abel watched in disgust as Garry began frittering away the 1968-69 campaign, his first full year with the Red Wings. Instead of averaging a point a game, Unger was hard pressed to produce 44 points in 76 contests. But at the end of the 1969-70 season, Unger had established himself as one of hockey's brightest stars, scoring 42 goals—just one less than league-leader Phil Esposito—and this in only his second full NHL season.

In 1969–70, Ned Harkness came to Detroit as coach, and was a disaster. On January 8, 1971, Harkness was fired as coach; but instead of being released by Red Wings owner Bruce Norris, he was elevated to the managership of the Detroit club.

Unger was indicted by Harkness for his mod lifestyle and long hair. But a Harkness-Unger *détente* was never achieved. By far the most outstanding issue was hair. Unger flatly rejected Harkness's specifications for thatches. "Once," said Garry, "he even drew a sketch illustrating how he wanted my hair. I balked at that. I'm just not the kind of person who could submit to that type of regimentation."

By the middle of the 1970–71 season, Harkness was quite willing to forget that he had once placed an "untouchable" tag on his blond center. "Unger," said Harkness, "has not been doing anything to help this club. He's been more downhill than uphill."

The time had come for Garry to reverse the trend. Ironically, it was his nemesis, Ned Harkness, who would catapult Unger back into the galaxy of stars. The wondering, as far as Detroit fans were concerned, ended when Unger was dispatched to St. Louis along with Wayne Connelly for Red Berenson and Tim Ecclestone. There, Garry was told he could let his hair grow down to his ankles, if he wanted, as long as he scored goals. He did score goals, although not at record-breaking levels, but it was there under the Golden Arch that Unger became the "Iron Man" of hockey.

Unger broke Andy Hebenton's then-record of 630 consecutive NHL games played during the 1975–76 season, and stretched his "iron man" streak to 914 games before injuries forced him out of the lineup in December 1979. His streak remained the second-longest in league history, behind the 964 games played by Doug Jarvis.

After departing the NHL in 1983, Unger played four years in Great Britain before retiring in 1987. He moved into coaching, and by 2001–02, guided the CHL Tulsa Oilers.

ROGIE VACHON

BORN: Palmarolle, Quebec, September 8, 1945
POSITION: Goaltender, Montreal Canadiens, 1966–71; Los Angeles Kings, 1971–78; Detroit Red Wings, 1978–80; Boston Bruins, 1980–82; Coach, Los Angeles Kings, 1983–84, 1987–88, 1994–95; General Manager, Los Angeles Kings, 1984–92
AWARDS/HONORS: Vezina Trophy (shared with Lorne Worsley), 1968; NHL Second Team All-Star, 1975, 1977; NHL All-Star Game, 1973, 1975, 1978; Canada Cup All-Star Team, 1976

After having a hand in three Montreal Canadiens Stanley Cup seasons, Rogatien "Rogie" Vachon was traded to the Los Angeles Kings in 1971. With the number one job in goal his for the taking, Vachon settled into his sunny new surroundings by becoming one of the most exciting goaltenders in the NHL.

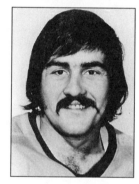

Rogie Vachon goaltending the Kings in 1974–75

A tiny netminder at five feet seven, 160 pounds, Vachon was a superb reflex goalie who used his catlike reactions to offset his lack of bulk. Vachon had no trouble adjusting to the West Coast's balmy weather and free and easy lifestyle. Soon after he joined the Beverly Hills sextet, Vachon sprouted a droopy Fu Manchu mustache and an even woollier pair of muttonchop sideburns. Asked about his newfound tonsorial tastes, the free-spirit backstop responded, "Zee sideburns, zey are good for zee balance."

After seven superb seasons with the Kings—in which he was named Player of the Year by the *Hockey News* in 1975–76—Rogie became a free agent in 1978 and opted to sign a lucrative long-term contract with the Detroit Red Wings, who, at the time, appeared to be only a quality goaltender away from becoming Cup contenders.

Rogie, whose track record had earned him a spot among the top goalies in the league, had nothing but trouble in his first year in the Motor City. With little or no defense in front of him, he soon crumbled. His incredible acrobatics in net often went for naught as the rest of the team was unable to give any assistance, and his goals-against average skyrocketed to 3.90.

In order to save face, impatient Detroit general manager Ted Lindsay attempted to shake Vachon, making the All-Star goalie available to any team that could come up with the $30,000 waiver price.

Though no team in the league could doubt Rogie's value, no club could afford to pick up his hefty contract. Consequently, Vachon spent the remainder of the year warming the bench and watching the futile Red Wings conclude another losing season.

Vachon spent his last two seasons with the Bruins, and while he posted a high goals-against average, he won the majority of his games before he retired in 1982 after 16 seasons and 355 wins, good for tenth all-time coming into the new century.

The ex-goaler and fan-favorite went on to make a name for himself in management, serving the Kings in various capacities until becoming general manager of the Kings in 1984, through the Wayne Gretzky years, and into 1992. The seeds of his reign would bear fruit in 1993, when the Kings made their one and only Stanley Cup finals appearance.

During his run, Los Angeles enjoyed its best season in 1990–91 with a 102-point campaign, good enough for first place in the Smythe Division. He lasted in the LA post until stepping up in a team presidential role during the late 1990s, representing the Kings to the community at large.

CAROL VADNAIS

BORN: Montreal, Quebec, September 25, 1945
POSITION: Left Wing/Defenseman, Montreal Canadiens, 1966–68; California Seals, 1968–70; California Golden Seals, 1970–72; Boston Bruins, 1972–75; New York Rangers, 1975–82; New Jersey Devils, 1982–83
AWARDS/HONORS: NHL All-Star Game, 1969–70, 1972, 1975–76, 1978

Just prior to the NHL's expansion from six to 12 teams in 1967–68, the Montreal Canadiens' farm system spawned a pair of promising young defensemen, Carol Vadnais and Serge Savard. The latter became a Montreal icon while Vadnais traveled all over the league.

Boston Bruins officials predicted big things for Vadnais when they acquired him from California midway through the 1971–72 season, because, after all, he had been selected to the NHL's West Division midyear All-Star team in each of the three previous seasons. They paid a steep price to get this high-scoring defenseman, and that was the beginning of Carol's problems. Popular spare defenseman Rick Smith, brawling Bob Stewart, and top draft pick Reggie Leach were all dispatched to the Golden Seals as payment for Vadnais. The hotly partisan Boston fans were incensed, especially since Smith and Stewart had become crowd favorites. To make matters worse, Vadnais replaced longtime Bruins star Teddy Green, perhaps the best-loved of all the Boston skaters.

It was an uncomfortable situation, compounded by the fact that Vadnais had no chance to learn the Bruins' system before playing in front of the Boston audience. Predictably, he was roasted. He was not as good as Boston fans thought he would be, but he certainly wasn't as bad as they claimed he was. Fellow teammates, sizing up the situation, offered moral support. "Every time someone scored, they'd all skate past me and tap me with their sticks, like I had done something to help them," he smiled. "I couldn't wait to contribute." After contributing in the 1972 Stanley Cup playoffs with three goals, Vadnais became a bona fide Bruin, his popularity growing each year.

Then in November 1975, the dream ended abruptly as Vadnais, in what was referred to as "The Trade," was sent to the New York Rangers with Phil Esposito in exchange for Brad Park, Jean Ratelle, and Joe Zanussi.

It took the Ranger fans awhile to get used to the offensive-minded Vadnais, but with the change in management, and the arrival of defensive specialist Fred Shero in New York, Carol became a conscientious defensive defenseman, a solid veteran among a crop of young blueliners.

The cigar-smoking backliner retired after the 1982–83 season as a member of the New Jersey Devils with a 587-point career to his credit.

JOHN VANBIESBROUCK

BORN: Detroit, Michigan, September 4, 1963
POSITION: Goaltender, New York Rangers, 1981–93; Florida Panthers, 1993–98; Philadelphia Flyers, 1998–2000; New York Islanders, 2000–01; New Jersey Devils, 2001–02
AWARDS/HONORS: Vezina Trophy, 1986; NHL First Team All-Star, 1986; NHL Second Team All-Star, 1994; NHL All-Star Game, 1994, 1996–97

Few goaltenders enjoyed as long and successful a career as John Vanbiesbrouck, whose tenure spanned two decades and counting.

Originally drafted by the New York Rangers, Vanbiesbrouck starred on Broadway for more than ten seasons. The 1986 Vezina Trophy winner was eventually eclipsed between the pipes by a young Mike Richter, resulting in the Florida Panthers claiming him (via Vancouver) in the 1993 Expansion Draft, and, to this day, it remains the best thing that ever happened to hockey in Miami.

With Vanbiesbrouck guarding the crease, the Panthers emerged as a playoff threat in the first year of the franchise and, incredibly, marched all the way to the Stanley Cup finals in June 1996 before bowing to the heavily favored Colorado Avalanche. Most of the credit belonged to Beezer, as he was known throughout the National Hockey League, who stood among the best half-dozen goalies in the league.

When playing on the Midget level, Beezer had doubts about his professional potential. He was back in school sitting in a classroom while the Entry Draft was being held. A broadcast of the draft was hooked up to the school loudspeaker system. Suddenly, the announcer proclaimed, "Selected in the fourth round, John Vanbiesbrouck of the New York Rangers."

In 1984–85, after playing in the Canadian Hockey League and being voted co-Most Valuable Player (along with Bruce Affleck) and Minor League Player of the Year by the *Hockey News,* Beezer moved up to the bigs. He finished his rookie season at 12–24–3 and managed to dispel the "sophomore jinx" in the 1985–86 season, winning the Vezina Trophy as the NHL's best goalie, contributing to upset playoff victories over Washington and Philadelphia.

When then-Rangers general manager Neil Smith eventually had to make a decision between either Beezer or the newly-acquired Mike Richter, Smith opted for the kid and John was on his way south to Miami. Beezer's goaltending was never better than the period from mid March 1996 through the Stanley Cup finals. He remained a strong member of the Panthers club until the 1998–99 season, when he was signed as a free agent by

Philadelphia right after he played on the American team for the Olympics.

He recorded career highs in shutouts, save percentages, and games played with the Flyers, but after two seasons was traded to the New York Islanders. He spent a productive year (2000–01) on Long Island and at the trade deadline was shipped to New Jersey, as a backup to Martin Brodeur. At the beginning of the 2001–02 season, the Beezer retired, but decided to rejoin the Devils for the playoff run. After the 2001–02 campaign, Vanbiesbrouck permanently retired to run an amateur team in Sault Ste. Marie, Ontario, of which he was part owner.

ED VAN IMPE

BORN: Saskatoon, Saskatchewan, May 27, 1940
POSITION: Defenseman, Chicago Blackhawks, 1966–67; Philadelphia Flyers, 1967–76; Pittsburgh Penguins, 1976–77
AWARDS/HONORS: NHL All-Star Game, 1969, 1974–75

Ed Van Impe, defenseman on the Philadelphia Flyers, Stanley Cup winners of 1974 and 1975

In an era when slashing was tolerated more than it is in contemporary hockey, Ed Van Impe was one of the most feared stickmen in the NHL.

Originally property of the Chicago Blackhawks before the NHL expanded, Van Impe was claimed in the 1967 Expansion Draft by the brand new Philadelphia Flyers.

General manager Bud Poile was more than satisfied with his acquisition. After helping the Flyers to the

West Division title in their opening campaign, Van Impe was named captain the next year.

Ed's willingness to take the team's younger players aside and patiently instruct them contributed to his captaincy. His reputation was another story. A horror story, if you listened to some opponents. Those who drifted to Van Impe's side of the rink were apt to feel the swing of lumber, as in cross-check, high stick, or butt end. He was not particular and his message was clear. Beware, brother, beware!

"I didn't want other teams to push us around," he said. "It was my belief that opposing forwards had to respect us. I had to keep them wondering what I might do."

Van Impe was a major defensive component of the Broad Street Bullies who won Stanley Cup championships in 1973–74 and 1974–75 while under coach Fred Shero. His career wound down as he was traded to the Pittsburgh Penguins with Bobby Taylor for Gary Inness and future considerations. His final season was 1976–77, when he played only ten games for Pittsburgh.

MOOSE VASKO

BORN: Duparquet, Quebec, December 11, 1935
POSITION: Defenseman, Chicago Blackhawks, 1956–66; Minnesota North Stars, 1967–70
AWARDS/HONORS: NHL Second Team All-Star, 1963–64; NHL All-Star Game, 1961, 1963–64, 1969

It was the perfect Mutt and Jeff combination for a decade in Chicago Stadium: the hulking "Moose" Vasko teaming with the petit Pierre Pilote on the Blackhawk blueline.

Vasko performed his defensive skills with an even-tempered geniality that belied his size, six feet three and 210 pounds, and the nickname "Ferdinand the Bull" would have been more appropriate than the "Moooooooooooose" that bounced around the arena each time he took the ice.

As a rookie, Vasko was expected to be the defenseman for the coming era, but his basically gentle heart was a downfall. He finished quietly in 1970 with the expansion Minnesota North Stars, then disappeared into suburban Illinois, where he took to coaching a bantam team and selling hockey sticks.

PAT VERBEEK

BORN: Sarnia, Ontario, May 24, 1964
POSITION: Right Wing, New Jersey Devils, 1982–89; Hartford Whalers, 1989–95; New York Rangers, 1995–96; Dallas Stars, 1996–99, 2001–02; Detroit Red Wings, 1999–2001
AWARDS/HONORS: NHL All-Star Game, 1991, 1996

"Toughness," said former Dallas coach Ken Hitchcock, "is only good if the guy can play."

Pat Verbeek proved it by surviving in the NHL for two full decades. Verbeek could score, agitate, dig, needle opponents, and, if the spirit moved, fight. Verbeek did tours of duty with the Devils, Whalers, Rangers, and Stars, who, in 1997–98 won the President's Trophy as the National Hockey League team with the most points.

Verbeek's gritty style had been evident since his earliest days, when he beat up Rangers defenseman Brian Leetch at the Meadowlands in 1988. A native of smalltown Wyoming, Ontario, Verbeek was drafted to the Ontario Hockey League at 16 and became the rookie of the year. He impressed scouts with his play and was drafted by New Jersey in 1982.

After developing for seven years with the Devils under veterans Ron Low, Don Lever, and Mel Bridgman, Verbeek was traded to Hartford, where he racked up three straight seasons of 200-plus penalty minutes, but also led his Whalers in scoring during the 1990–91 and 1993–94 seasons.

Verbeek bounced around from Jersey to Hartford to New York to Dallas to Detroit then back to Dallas, but in his 21-plus years with the NHL, never changed his style from his rookie days in Jersey. His game was played on the edge, to be agitating to the enemy so they were distracted from play, or to be so aggressive that he would have to take the penalties. An agitator and fighter, Verbeek knew the lines between talent and goon, and he used this knowledge to be the best aggressor possible. He also scored over 40 goals four times—twice for the Whalers (1989–90, 1990–91), once for the Devils (1987–88), and once for the Rangers (1995–96).

Pat had 515 career goals coming into 2001–02, when he returned to his familiar Dallas. But the Stars unexpectedly missed the playoffs. Verbeek also provided insightful commentary on the popular *NHL 2Nite* telecasts once the regular season ended.

MIKE VERNON

BORN: Calgary, Alberta, February 24, 1963
POSITION: Goaltender, Calgary Flames, 1982–94, 2000–02; Detroit Red Wings, 1994–97; San Jose Sharks, 1997–99; Florida Panthers, 1999–2000
AWARDS/HONORS: William M. Jennings Trophy (shared with Chris Osgood), 1996; Conn Smythe Trophy, 1997; NHL Second Team All-Star, 1989; NHL All-Star Game, 1988–91, 1993

One of the most traveled—and most competent—goalies of the late 1980s through the new century, Mike Vernon was a nonpareil competitor. Among his many accomplishments is the role Vernon played in the Red Wings finally breaking the 42-year-old

Mike Vernon as a Calgary goaltender

Stanley Cup hex that had been on their franchise since last winning the Stanley Cup back in 1955.

A quick-footed goalkeeper who didn't back down from anyone larger or smaller than his five-feet-nine frame, Vernon was the backbone of a Calgary powerhouse, which boasted future Hall of Fame scorers Lanny McDonald and Doug Gilmour. From 1986 to 1989, Mike had 116 wins, including a league-leading 37 in the Stanley Cup–winning stanza of 1988–89. Then, Detroit traded Steve Chiasson for him on June 29, 1994.

He was acquired for one reason specifically: to help bring a Stanley Cup back to the Motor City.

Vernon would also share the number one goaltender duties with younger netminder Chris Osgood. They would take turns starting games during the regular season and then Detroit coach Scotty Bowman would usually decide to play Vernon once they made the playoffs. Vernon had the experience that Bowman preferred. Mike also had to teach his fellow netminder and teammate Osgood how to deal with adversity.

In Vernon's first year with Detroit (1994–95), the Red Wings went to the Stanley Cup finals. But once they got there, they were no match for the New Jersey Devils, who swept them in four straight.

The following year, Vernon and Osgood would once again split the netminding duties, with Osgood playing the majority of the games during a regular season that saw him win a remarkable 39 games in 50 tries. Vernon also did well in his time by winning 21 games and posting a 2.26 goals-against average.

This time, Osgood got the nod over Vernon for the playoffs. Vernon played the role of backup and cheered on his talented understudy. But the Red Wings' record-breaking 131-point season went down the drain with a bitter Conference final upset loss to the eventual-champion Colorado Avalanche.

It was back to the drawing board for Vernon and his Red Wings in 1996–97. Vernon got the nod over Osgood from head coach Scotty Bowman and soon after that, Detroit would finally fulfill its dream of the Stanley Cup returning to the Motor City.

Lifted by Vernon's performance against St. Louis and the Anaheim Mighty Ducks, the Red Wings would be facing an all too familiar opponent in the defending 1996 Stanley Cup champion Colorado Avalanche in the Western Conference final.

After Colorado won the opener, the Red Wings responded by taking the next three games, with Games Two and Three having a lot to do with Vernon's heroics. He was spectacular in those games and seemed to get into some of the Avalanche players' heads. In Game Four, the frustration finally mounted when the Avalanche were buried by Detroit in a 6–0 rout in front of a sold-out capacity Motor City crowd that loved every vengeful minute of it.

After Colorado returned the favor with a 6–0 victory of its own to stave off elimination and chase Vernon, Mike and the Wings finished off the defending champions back home in Detroit with a 3–1 win to take the series.

Detroit thoroughly outclassed Philadelphia in the Stanley Cup finals, taking the first two games in Philadelphia by identical 4–2 scores and hammering them 6–1 in front of the home folks. Detroit was now one win away from the Stanley Cup and Game Four was Vernon's.

Mike proved he was up to the task by stoning the Flyers and even taking a shutout into the last minute of the game. But with Detroit ahead, 2–0, the Flyers would not go quietly. Eric Lindros scored his only goal of the series to make it a 2–1 game. That was all the Flyers would get as Vernon's Detroit teammates played terrific defense in front of him to secure the Stanley Cup.

To the surprise of few, Vernon was named the Conn Smythe Trophy winner as playoff MVP.

However, Vernon would be traded to San Jose because the Detroit hierarchy felt that Osgood was finally ready to be the number one goalie on his own. They would be proven right a year later in 1997–98, when Osgood led the Wings to a repeat Cup victory.

As for Vernon, he would spend time in San Jose—the Sharks also had Cup designs with Vernon in mind—and Florida before winding up back where his career started, in Calgary. Mentoring newly-acquired Roman Turek, Vernon saw little action in 2001–02, which included a surprising stint in the minors once the Flames began to lose their grip on their season after a hot start. Vernon ended his long NHL career by announcing his retirement in September 2002.

GEORGES VEZINA

BORN: Chicoutimi, Quebec, January 21, 1887
DIED: March 27, 1926
POSITION: Goaltender, Montreal Canadiens, 1917–26
AWARDS/HONORS: Vezina Trophy named in his honor, 1926–27 season; Hockey Hall of Fame, 1945

Georges Vezina, "the Chicoutimi Cucumber," as well as being a superb goalie, was the acme of gentility on the ice. He also had a philosophic nature and once penned a short essay entitled "Sport, Creator of Unity."

Few were aware of Vezina's capacity for philosophy. The fans cared about only one thing, whether or not he was a good goaltender, and through the early 1920s there was no doubt about his excellence. He proved his mettle in the 1922–23 season in several episodes, some of which were defaced with blood.

During a game at Hamilton, his former teammate Bert Corbeau smashed into Vezina with such force that the goaltender's head was cut open and his nose was broken. Vezina continued playing despite the wounds and continued to excel. A few games later he led the Canadiens to a win over Ottawa, allowing the

Senators only one goal, although 79 shots were hurled at him.

"After the game," wrote Canadian author Ron McAllister, "he left the rink a solemn, plodding figure, in sharp contrast to the wild hilarity of his teammates, who were already celebrating the victory that Vezina had won for them."

Another reporter observed, "Georges has a calmness not of this world." The commentary was more prophetic than the writer had realized, for Georges Vezina's body was being tortured by the early symptoms of tuberculosis. Whether or not Vezina himself was aware of the gravity of his condition is debatable. One thing is certain, and that was his determination to continue in the nets for Les Canadiens. There was no outward suggestion that Vezina was faltering.

Although the Canadiens finished second to Ottawa in the 1923–24 season, Vezina allowed only 48 goals in 24 games, including three shutouts, for a goals-against average of 2.00. He then blanked Ottawa, 1–0, in the NHL playoff opener and sparkled as Les Canadiens swept the series, 4–2, in the second game, thus qualifying to meet a representative from one of the two western professional leagues.

A squabble between officials of the Western Canada Hockey League and the Pacific Coast Hockey Association resulted in a bizarre turn of events. Instead of one team coming east to challenge Montreal for the Stanley Cup, both Calgary and Vancouver showed up. Les Canadiens really weren't overly extended. They first dispatched Vancouver by scores of 3–2 and 2–1 and routed Calgary, 6–1 and 3–0. The final game was switched to Ottawa because of poor ice conditions in Montreal, but Vezina was never better. His Stanley Cup record was six goals against in six games for a perfect 1.00 average.

Proof that Vezina was outfighting his ailment was provided by his uncanny performance in the 1924–25 season. Les Canadiens finished in third place behind Hamilton and Toronto, but Georges's 1.90 goals-against

average was easily the best in the league. His teammates rallied behind him in the first round of the playoffs to oust Toronto, 3–2 and 2–0, but Vezina enjoyed only one good game, a 4–2 win at Victoria as the western champs dispatched Les Canadiens by scores of 5–2, 3–1, and 6–1 to win the Stanley Cup, the last time for a western professional team. The Pacific Coast League folded and the Stanley Cup was competed for by NHL teams only since 1926.

The 1925–26 season was truly momentous for the National Hockey League. It had expanded into the United States, first accepting Boston the previous year, and now embracing New York and Pittsburgh as well. A second team, the Maroons, had been added to Montreal to provide an English-speaking club as the natural rivals for the Canadiens. Needless to say, the outstanding attraction in the American cities among Montreal players was the redoubtable Vezina. But Vezina was beginning to betray signs of fatigue.

Pittsburgh, one of the new entries, provided the opposition for Les Canadiens in the season opener on November 28, 1925, at Mount Royal Arena. There were 6,000 spectators in the stands on that rainy night who had come to see the great Vezina, ignorant of the fact that the lean goalie was suffering enormous discomfort as he took the ice for the opening face-off.

"No one knew," wrote McAllister, "that the great goaltender had struggled to the arena in spite of a temperature of 105 degrees. A death-like chill settled over him; but with Pittsburgh forcing the play from the face-off, Vezina functioned throughout the entire first period with his usual dexterous ease, deflecting shot after shot. In the dressing room he suffered a severe arterial hemorrhage, but the opening of the second period found him at his accustomed place in goal."

Fighting desperately against the fatigue and fever that completely throttled his body, the great Vezina could no longer see the puck as it was skimmed from one side of the rink to the other. Suddenly, a collective gasp engulfed the arena. Vezina had collapsed in his goal crease! "In the stricken arena," said one observer, "all was silent as the limp form of the greatest of goalies was carried slowly from the ice."

It was the end of the trail for Georges and he knew it. At his request he was taken home to his native Chicoutimi where doctors diagnosed his case as advanced tuberculosis. On March 24, 1926, a week after the Canadiens had been eliminated from a playoff berth, Georges Vezina passed away.

An enormous funeral, held in the old cathedral at Chicoutimi, saw players and fans from all parts of the country deliver their final tribute to the gallant goaltender. A year later, the Canadiens' owners donated a trophy in his honor that is given now to the goaltender with the best goals-against average in the NHL.

CARL VOSS

BORN: Chelsea, Massachusetts, January 6, 1907
DIED: September 13, 1973
POSITION: Forward, Toronto Maple Leafs, 1926–27, 1928–29; New York Rangers/Detroit Falcons, 1932–33; Detroit Red Wings/Ottawa Senators, 1933–34; St. Louis Eagles, 1934–35; New York Americans, 1935–36; Montreal Maroons, 1936–37; Chicago Blackhawks, 1937–38
AWARDS/HONORS: NHL Rookie of the Year, 1933; Hockey Hall of Fame, 1974

There have been few American-born players in the NHL more accomplished than Carl Voss, who broke into the majors with the New York Rangers (1932–33), was immediately dealt to the Detroit Red Wings, then the Ottawa Senators (1933–34), the St. Louis Blues (1934–35), the New York Americans (1935–36), the Montreal Maroons (1936–37), and finally the Chicago Blackhawks, where he gained most of his fame.

Coach (and major-league baseball umpire) Bill Stewart of the Blackhawks overruled club owner Major Frederic McLaughlin over Voss. The Major insisted Voss be cut from the squad as an obvious loser. Stewart was adamant. Voss would stay. He not only stayed but played a vital part in Chicago's most stirring hockey triumph, winning the Stanley Cup in 1938. In 10 playoff games, Voss scored 3 big goals and 2 assists. Yet, he left the majors after that season and gained renown later in life as referee in chief of the NHL under president Clarence Campbell. In that position, Voss was frequently criticized as a puppet of the clubowners. He eventually retired and was replaced by Scotty Morrison.

FRED WAGHORNE

BORN: Tunbridge Wells, England, 1866
DIED: 1956
POSITION: Referee, Several leagues prior to NHL
AWARDS/HONORS: Hockey Hall of Fame, 1961

This Hall of Fame member was a referee for more than 50 years, was one of the founders of the Toronto Hockey League, and introduced several innovations, sometimes in the middle of a game!

Fred Waghorne began the practice of dropping the puck for face-offs rather than placing the puck on the ice between the two sticks. "Wag" also introduced the whistle for stoppage of play rather than the bell, which must have lightened the referee's load considerably.

Hockey pucks were originally two pieces of material glued together, and it was Waghorne who ruled "no goal" one night when a puck split in two, one piece entering the net and one flying into the boards. Waghorne ruled the legal size had not entered the net.

RYAN WALTER

BORN: New Westminster, British Columbia, April 23, 1958
POSITION: Center/Left Wing, Washington Capitals, 1978–82; Montreal Canadiens, 1982–91; Vancouver Canucks, 1991–93
AWARDS/HONORS: NHL All-Star Game, 1983; Bud Man of the Year Award, 1992

Speed and savvy were two qualities Ryan Walter parlayed into a 15-year NHL career. Selected second overall in the 1978 Entry Draft by the Washington Capitals, Walter was expected to be among big-league hockey's elite forwards. While he did play consistently well for most of his NHL stewardship, he ultimately fell short of expectations. "Reliable" became the operative word for Walter.

Among his most notable moments was Walter's involvement in a major trade. It happened in 1982, when the Caps dealt Ryan—who had just achieved a career-best 38 goals and 87 points as the Caps' captain—and defenseman Rick Green to the Montreal Canadiens for Rod Langway, Brian Engblom, Doug Jarvis, and Craig Laughlin.

The trade did wonders for Washington, and Walter solidified the Canadiens' middle, culminating in the 1986 Stanley Cup victory over Calgary. Ryan, who had major knee surgery during that season, still brought a workmanlike element to his game, but his numbers slipped thereafter. He played another five years as a Canadien before signing as a free agent with the Vancouver Canucks. After 25 games, three goals, and no playoffs in 1992–93, Walter retired and moved into the Vancouver broadcasting booth.

A father of five, Walter also authored a inspirational book connecting hockey and life principles entitled *Off the Bench . . . and Into the Game,* and traveled North America giving motivational speeches to hockey players and businesses.

MIKE WALTON

BORN: Kirkland Lake, Ontario, January 3, 1945
POSITION: Center, Toronto Maple Leafs,
1966–71; Boston Bruins, 1971–73, 1978–79;
Minnesota Fighting Saints (WHA), 1973–76;
Vancouver Canucks, 1976–78; St. Louis Blues,
1978–79; Chicago Blackhawks, 1979
AWARDS/HONORS: NHL All-Star Game, 1968;
Bill Hunter Trophy (WHA Leading Scorer), 1974;
Second Team All-Star (WHA), 1974; WHA Team
Canada, 1974

Mike Walton signed with the Toronto Maple Leafs as an NHL rookie in 1966–67, and became an integral part of the Leafs' family—in more ways than one. He married Candy Hoult, granddaughter of Conn Smythe, Leafs' founder and president, and niece of Stafford Smythe, Conn's son and successor. One would have thought these credentials would cement his relationship with the Leafs, but by February 1969 it was clear this was just not the case. After doing more bench-sitting for Punch Imlach than he believed he deserved, Mike walked out on Toronto in the homestretch of their desperate playoff drive. It took the mediation of Mike's attorney, Alan Eagleson, to achieve a truce and return Mike to the team, which then gained a playoff berth.

Still, the Leafs were humiliated in the Stanley Cup round by the Bruins, and in the wake of the four-game defeat, Imlach was fired. But this was not to be the end of Walton's woes. Under coach John McLellan, Walton moved up and down faster than a yo-yo.

By late November 1970, Walton was terribly depressed, and after watching one too many Maple Leafs' victories from the sidelines, he again walked out on the team.

He refused to rejoin the Leafs, and was suspended. In the depths of his despair, and with his livelihood in jeopardy, Mike visited an NHL-sanctioned psychiatrist. The doctor reported that Mike's depressive illness, complicated by his family relationship to the team,

would attain serious proportions if he remained with the Leafs.

Finally, on February 1, 1971, Walton was traded to the Philadelphia Flyers, and then to the Bruins as part of a complicated three-way deal. Although Mike skated hesitantly for the Bruins at first, he regained his confidence and a year later helped Boston win the 1972 Stanley Cup.

Just when he seemed to be sitting on top of the hockey world, the nomadic center jumped to the WHA's Minnesota Fighting Saints, signing a three-year contract that included, among other provisions, hefty scoring bonuses and an option to return to the NHL after his first WHA season. Not so coincidentally, Mike's kid brother, Rob, also was signed by the Saints, which turned out to be a mixed blessing. Both Waltons played mediocre hockey through December 1973 and the Fighting Saints went nowhere. Then Rob was traded to the Vancouver Blazers, and Mike and the Saints went into orbit. The five-feet-nine, 170-pound Walton sped past the pack—including former WHA scoring pacesetters Andre Lacroix, Gordie Howe, and Wayne Carleton—and finished the season with 117 points on 57 goals and 60 assists, as well as the WHA scoring title.

Amid rumors he might skip back to the NHL, Walton signed a new Saints' contract that purportedly made him one of the three highest-paid players in the game at the time, courtesy of Eagleson. Despite the lucrative contract, Walton jumped back to the NHL with the Vancouver Canucks in 1976; a smart move, because the Saints folded a couple of seasons later.

Walton saw action with three NHL clubs during the 1978–79 season, finishing out the year and his career by taking a regular shift with the Chicago Blackhawks.

GRANT WARWICK

BORN: Regina, Saskatchewan, October 11, 1921
POSITION: Forward, New York Rangers, 1941–48; Boston Bruins, 1948–49; Montreal Canadiens, 1949–50
AWARDS/HONORS: Calder Memorial Trophy, 1942; NHL All-Star Game, 1947

Prior to Uncle Sam's entry into World War II, the Rangers featured a contending team with many young characters. One of them was forward Grant Warwick. Nicknamed "Knobby," Warwick played a robust and efficient brand of offensive hockey for the Rangers from 1941–42 until he was dealt to Boston in 1947–48. He finished his NHL career in 1949–50 with the Canadiens, but his chief source of fame was yet to come. Knobby received his "amateur" reinstatement and played for the Penticton, British Columbia, V's, a senior division club that won the Allan Cup in 1954. Surrounded by a hard-bitten crew, Knobby, along with his brothers, Bill and Dick, skated for Penticton in the World Amateur Hockey championships in 1955 at Krefeld, Germany. The Canadians brought a boisterous, gashouse-gang style of hockey to the championships. Paced by the galvanic Warwick brothers, Penticton reached the finals against a favored Russian sextet and whipped the Soviet club, 5–0. The Warwicks, but particularly Knobby, were hailed as national heroes.

Kid brother Billy Warwick starred for the New York Rovers and had a brief fling with the parent Rangers.

HARRY WATSON

BORN: Saskatoon, Saskatchewan, May 6, 1923
POSITION: Left Wing, Brooklyn Americans, 1941–42; Detroit Red Wings, 1942–43, 1945–46; Toronto Maple Leafs, 1946–55; Chicago Blackhawks, 1955–57
AWARDS/HONORS: NHL All-Star Game, 1947–49, 1951–53, 1955; Hockey Hall of Fame, 1994

One of the strongest and least publicized lines in NHL history comprised Toronto's Syl Apps Sr. (center), Bill Ezinicki (right wing), and the least-known forward of the trio, left-winger Harry Watson. A onetime Brooklyn American, Watson skated powerfully, shot hard and true, and, unknown to most, was one of the kindest yet toughest forwards ever to patrol the majors. Watson, Apps, and Ezinicki powered the Leafs to Stanley Cups in 1947 and 1948. Watson, who was nicknamed "Whipper," once broke Boston defenseman Murray Henderson's nose with one punch after the Bruin taunted him into a fight.

Every NHL skater respected Watson's fighting ability although he frequently was a candidate for the Lady Byng Trophy for sportsmanlike play. Once, during a Leafs–Red Wings Pier Six brawl, Watson found himself confronted by defenseman Bill Quackenbush, himself a Byng candidate. While everyone else was pushing and shoving, Quackenbush grabbed Watson by the shoulder. "Shall we waltz?" he asked, grinning. "No," Watson grinned back, "let's get in the middle and start shoving a bit. I think they're going to take pictures!"

Watson was a surprise nomination to the Hall of Fame in 1994. A Toronto resident, he was an active member of the Maple Leafs alumni association.

JIMMY WATSON

BORN: Smithers, British Columbia, August 19, 1952
POSITION: Defenseman, Philadelphia Flyers, 1972–82
AWARDS/HONORS: NHL Plus-Minus Leader, 1980; NHL All-Star Game, 1975–78, 1980

The name Watson—as in defensemen Joe and Jimmy—became a household word in Philadelphia when the Flyers of the late 1970s were notorious as the Broad Street Bullies.

The junior member of the duet was Jim. Showing the cool for which his sibling Joe was renowned, Jim played solidly when the Flyers captured the Stanley Cup in 1974 and 1975.

Watson played his end of the rink exquisitely, but also could launch the counterattack and create goal-scoring opportunities. Jimmy did it so well that it caused coach Fred Shero to comment, "He is one of the best and most underrated defensemen in the NHL." Which was pure fact.

As a member of Team Canada during the 1976 International Canada Cup tournament, Watson received a serious eye injury when he got in the way of a blast by teammate Gary Sargent. Jimmy spent the following season getting used to playing with a protective mask, but continued to be the Flyers' steadiest blueliner.

Watson had what was by far his best season in 1979–80, when he scored 23 points and had a plus-minus rating of plus-53. His unfailing steadiness got him into five NHL All-Star games and no one could dispute his place as a major component in the Flyers' machine.

Watson wound down at the end of the decade, playing only 18 games in 1980–81. He retired after a 76-game season in 1981–82.

PHIL WATSON

BORN: Montreal, Quebec, October 24, 1914
DIED: February 1, 1991
POSITION: Center, New York Rangers, 1935–43, 1944–48; Montreal Canadiens, 1943–44; Coach, New York Rangers, 1955–60; Boston Bruins, 1961–62; Philadelphia Blazers (WHA), 1972–73; Vancouver Blazers, 1973–74
AWARDS/HONORS: NHL Second Team All-Star, 1942

A French-Canadian with an English name, Phil Watson was as volatile a player—and later coach—on the ice as he was off. Mostly, Watson was a classy center for the Rangers and architect for Bryan Hextall on right wing and Lynn Patrick on the left. Together, they comprised the Rangers' top line in the late '30s and early '40s until World War II disrupted them.

Watson never served in the armed forces. After the 1942–43 season, he was "loaned" to the Montreal Canadiens. Phil purportedly took a job in a war plant, was exempted from the draft, and was able to play a full season with the Canadiens. It was a curious state of affairs but questioned by few. He returned to New York in 1944–45 and finished his career with the Rangers in 1947–48.

A battler who rarely won a fight, Watson played his last game as a Ranger in the semifinals of the Stanley Cup playoffs against the Red Wings. Detroit wiped out the Rangers in the series, the final game of which was played at Madison Square Garden. Watson squared off with Jimmy McFadden of the Red Wings, who rarely won a fight. This time McFadden won.

Watson turned to coaching, first with the New York Rovers of the Eastern League and eventually the Rangers in 1955–56. He inherited a team developed by Frank Boucher, his former mentor, and guided it to a playoff berth in his rookie coaching season. His flamboyant style appealed to New York newsmen and he became the darling of the press—until he started losing.

By the 1958–59 season, his players had become disenchanted with Watson's antics. Although the Rangers had been playing well, Watson ordered brutal practices. Once, immediately after a loss at Madison Square Garden, Watson ordered his skaters back on to Garden ice and put them through an energy-sapping workout.

On March 11, 1959, the Rangers had a seven-point lead over fifth-place Toronto. Watson's practices had drained the Rangers and they blew the lead, finishing fifth on the final night of the season in what was one of the biggest collapses in sports.

Watson's days were numbered in New York. He soon was fired, later surfacing as head coach in Boston where he also failed. When the WHA was organized, Watson popped up again, this time with the Philadelphia Blazers. When the Blazers moved to Vancouver, Watson went with them. However, he soon left the club and retired from pro hockey.

DOUG WEIGHT

BORN: Warren, Michigan, January 21, 1971
POSITION: Center, New York Rangers, 1991–93; Edmonton Oilers, 1993–2001; St. Louis Blues, 2001–
AWARDS/HONORS: NHL All-Star Game, 1996, 1998, 2001

When Doug Weight was traded to the Edmonton Oilers for Esa Tikkanen, few expected him to become an impact player. But after eight seasons with the Edmonton Oilers, the swift center matured into one of the more accomplished and productive big-league forwards. In fact, Weight became the leader of the high-speed Edmonton Oilers offense.

The five-feet-eleven, 196-pound center was drafted by the New York Rangers (second choice, 34th overall) in the 1990 Entry Draft. He played with the club for less than two seasons before being traded to Edmonton for what would prove to be an over-the-hill Tikkanen. But the trade proved fruitful and the lesser-known Michigan native was named both Chrysler Canada MVP and Oilers' most popular player during the 1995–96 season.

Bringing a rare combination of speed, play-making ability, and gritty leadership to the ice, Weight was a member of the gold-winning Team USA at the 1996 World Cup of Hockey, and played for Team USA at the 1993 and 1994 IIHF World Hockey Championships. He also played on the silver-medal Team USA in the 2002 Winter Olympics at Salt Lake City.

By the 2000–01 season, Doug became the sixth player in Oilers history to score over 500 points and led the Oilers in scoring, finishing eighth in the NHL. He ranked 12th in career assists by U.S.-born players, and was sixth in the NHL with most assists since 1996.

Due to the team's inability to keep fiscal pace with large-market teams and pay Weight his fair-market value, Edmonton general manager Kevin Lowe was forced in 2001 to let go of the power player, dealing him to St. Louis with Michel Riesen for Marty Reasoner, Jochen Hecht, and Jan Horacek. The Blues had expected to lose center Pierre Turgeon to unrestricted free agency and looked for a replacement to feed skilled wingers Keith Tkachuk and Pavol Demitra.

Weight's positive chemistry with his new team emerged by the middle of the 2001–02 season, helping the Blues storm into the play-offs. However, a late season injury hampered Doug in the 2002 playoffs.

COONEY WEILAND

BORN: Seaforth, Ontario, November 5, 1904
DIED: July 3, 1985
POSITION: Center, Boston Bruins, 1928–32, 1935–39; Ottawa Senators, 1932–34; Detroit Red Wings, 1934–35; Coach, Boston Bruins, 1939–41
AWARDS/HONORS: Art Ross Trophy, 1930; Lester Patrick Trophy, 1972; NHL First Team All-Star (as coach), 1941; NHL Second Team All-Star, 1935; Hockey Hall of Fame, 1971

Boston's premier all-time hockey heroes include Bobby Orr, Eddie Shore, Frankie Brimsek, and Phil Esposito. But there have been others in the upper tier, including Ralph "Cooney" Weiland.

"Cooney" centered the Bruins' Dynamite Trio, playing between Dit Clapper and Dutch Gainor when Boston won its first Stanley Cup in 1929. He scored 43 times in 44 games that season. Weiland led the Hubmen to another title in 1939. He then coached the Bruins to the NHL regular-season championship in 1939–40 and the Stanley Cup in 1940–41.

A winner of the Lester Patrick Trophy for "outstanding service to hockey in the United States," Weiland coached Harvard's Ivy League powerhouses from 1950–71.

Weiland, as a coach, didn't approve completely of hockey as it had changed.

"Years ago," he said, "you could always see great man-to-man showdowns, one-on-one with the goaltender. Now, you are never sure who scored the goal and how it's scored. There are so many people in front of the goaltender, jockeying for position and slapping at the puck.

"There's no bodychecking in hockey today, either," Weiland continued.

"They call it bodychecking, but it's really boardchecking, which isn't the same. I'm talking about rocking the guy at mid-ice."

As a coach, Cooney always stressed defensive hockey. "Any championship team has to have a sound defense. They have to know when to play defense and how to check each man, keep his man under control."

ED WESTFALL

BORN: Belleville, Ontario, September 19, 1940
POSITION: Right Wing, Boston Bruins, 1961–72; New York Islanders, 1972–79
AWARDS/HONORS: Bill Masterton Memorial Trophy, 1977; NHL All-Star Game, 1971, 1973–75

If the National Hockey League had an award for "Most Versatile Forward," unquestionably Ed Westfall would have won it. Originally a defenseman when he broke into the bigs (1961), Westfall later became a quality two-way forward and top-of-the-line—along with

Islanders original captain, Eddie Westfall

Derek Sanderson—penalty killer for the Boston Bruins.

Westfall was overshadowed in Boston by the likes of Bobby Orr and Phil Esposito.

Ralph "Cooney" Weiland, a top Bruin player, who turned coach, seen behind the bench talking to Milt Schmidt

But when he moved to Long Island, Westfall reached center stage. It took 11 seasons, but Eddie finally became a team leader, even if it was because of seniority, on the Islanders. Westfall had been plucked in the 1972 Expansion Draft by the Isles.

Named captain of the fledgling sextet, Westie's veteran savvy proved to be a steadying influence on the improving Isles' performance. Within three years of its birth, the team was making a respectable showing in the playoffs under the aegis of "Captain Eddie," a star in the 1975 quarterfinals against the Pittsburgh Penguins with his game-winning goal in a tense 1–0 Game Seven.

Westfall, later dubbed "18" for his sweater number, continued to improve with age, both as a penalty killer and utility forward. In 1977, he voluntarily relinquished the team captaincy, which was assumed by Clark Gillies. Nevertheless, Westfall remained a valuable cog in the Islanders' juggernaut, assisting them to first place in the Patrick Divison in 1978 and first place in overall points in 1979.

In the spring of 1979, Westfall announced that he would retire as an active player. Moving into the Islanders broadcasting booth as an analyst, he teamed for years with Jiggs McDonald, and later with Howie Rose and Joe Micheletti through the new century.

An expert golfer, Westfall also made a name for himself in the business world while retaining his television identity.

HARRY WESTWICK

BORN: Ottawa, Ontario, April 23, 1876
DIED: April 3, 1957
POSITION: Goaltender/Rover, Ottawa Silver Seven, 1895–1908
AWARDS/HONORS: Hockey Hall of Fame, 1962

Harry Westwick broke into hockey in 1895 with the legendary Ottawa Silver Seven. "Rat," as he was known, was a goalie by trade in those days, but after only two games in the nets, some insightful observer suggested that he switch to the forward line. It was no sooner said than done and Westwick became the Silver Seven's regular rover for the next 12 seasons, bagging better than a goal per game over his lengthy career.

Harry played on three consecutive Stanley Cup winners with the Seven.

TIGER WILLIAMS

BORN: Weyburn, Saskatchewan, February 3, 1954
POSITION: Left Wing, Toronto Maple Leafs, 1974–80; Vancouver Canucks, 1980–84; Detroit Red Wings, 1984–85; Los Angeles Kings, 1985–87; Hartford Whalers, 1987–88
AWARDS/HONORS: NHL All-Star Game, 1981

Though Dave "Tiger" Williams may not have shared the hockey skills of a Darryl Sittler, Lanny McDonald, or Borje Salming, he was an equally important element on the Toronto Maple Leafs of the late 1970s with his tenacious checking, fast skating, and overall aggressive play.

In 1975–76, when the Leafs were busy setting new club records for scoring, Tiger Williams was setting a new Toronto team record for penalty minutes with 306. The following season, 1976–77, he broke his own mark with 338. In 1977–78, he once again topped his previous high with 351 minutes in the sin bin. He dropped off in 1978–79, both in scoring and in penalty minutes, with a comparatively calm though league-leading 298 minutes. Nevertheless, Williams emerged as not only the Leafs', but perhaps the league's, premier policeman. His combination of skating, hitting, and scoring elevated him from the ranks of goondom.

How did he get that way? At the age of 15, while in the tenth grade, Tiger was given a guidance test to help determine future career possibilities. His ambition to become a pro hockey player was obvious even then, when he merely wrote "NHL" across the page. What became a total dedication to the game and to his team was misinterpreted by some who put a "bad sportsman" rap on Williams. One case in point was his history of snubbing opposing players during post–Stanley Cup handshaking ceremonies. "I can't go out here and pretend to be friendly to those guys after spending so much time trying to beat 'em. It's phony," he explained.

After Williams moved on from the Maple Leafs, he continued to score and total penalty minutes in long stretches with the Canucks and the Kings. He again had an NHL and career-high 358 penalty minutes in 1986–87 with Los Angeles, while netting 34 points. Williams finished his career with 3,966 minutes in the penalty box, the most ever in the NHL. He retired to become a successful businessman in the Vancouver area and was often seen at Canucks home games.

TOMMY WILLIAMS

BORN: Duluth, Minnesota, April 17, 1940
DIED: February 8, 1992
POSITION: Right Wing, Boston Bruins, 1961–69; Minnesota North Stars, 1969–71; California Golden Seals, 1971–72; New England Whalers (WHA), 1972–74; Washington Capitals, 1974–76

While most Americans consider the 1980 gold-medal victory at Lake Placid the one and only miracle on ice for Uncle Sam, a few critics point to an earlier gold-medal triumph at Squaw Valley in 1960 as of equal value as a major upset.

Paced by Jack McCartan's outstanding work in goal, the Americans scored stunning victories over Canada and Russia before edging Czechoslovakia to take the championship. One of the best forwards on that team was Duluth, Minnesota, native Tommy Williams, who signed with the Boston Bruins after Squaw Valley and immediately became a news item.

In those days of the six-team NHL, it was most unusual for an American to play in the NHL; therefore, Williams became a curio of sorts. First, Boston sent him to its Kingston

1960 U.S. Olympic hero Tommy Williams as a Bruin

affiliate in the Eastern Pro League in 1960–61 before calling him up to The Show. The likeable blond caught on immediately and played eight seasons in Beantown before continuing his pro career with the Minnesota North Stars, California Golden Seals, and New England Whalers of the World Hockey Association.

He completed his NHL career with the Washington Capitals in 1975–76, having opened the gates for other Americans to play major-league hockey. Over his 15-year pro career (playoffs included) Williams amassed 546 points in 831 games.

DOUG WILSON

BORN: Ottawa, Ontario, July 5, 1957
POSITION: Defenseman, Chicago Blackhawks, 1977–91; San Jose Sharks, 1991–93
AWARDS/HONORS: James Norris Memorial Trophy, 1982; NHL First Team All-Star, 1982; NHL Second Team All-Star, 1985, 1990; NHL All-Star Game, 1982–86, 1990, 1992

Tall and lanky, Doug Wilson ranged somewhere between the top-level and next-best as a defenseman, depending on the team and the season. Yet somehow, his overall accomplishments tend to have been overlooked by critics.

An excellent point man on the power play, he proved to be a better all-around player than older brother Murray, who played in the Montreal Canadiens' system.

Originally, Doug made an impact with the Chicago Blackhawks in the 1977–78 season. At the end of a long NHL career, which saw him play in 1,024 games over 16 seasons, Wilson played for the expansion San Jose Sharks for two seasons (1991–93), serving as their first captain.

Wilson had one breakout season in the opposing zone (1981–82), in which he, as a defenseman, scored 39 goals and added 46 assists for a total of 85 points. One of the top blueliners in the National Hockey League

in his heyday, Doug was rewarded for his accomplishments with seven All-Star game appearances and a Norris Trophy in 1982.

The top-scoring defenseman in Blackhawks history retired into an active hockey afterlife, serving as a coordinator of business development for the NHL Players' Association and on the NHL Alumni Board of Directors. When director of pro development for the Sharks, Wilson used his experience to help cultivate a solid hockey environment in San Jose.

JOHNNY WILSON

BORN: Kincardine, Ontario, June 14, 1929
POSITION: Left Wing, Detroit Red Wings, 1949–55, 1957–59; Chicago Blackhawks, 1955–57; Toronto Maple Leafs, 1959–61; New York Rangers, 1961–62; Coach, Los Angeles Kings, 1970; Detroit Red Wings, 1972–73; Michigan Stags/Baltimore Blades (WHA), 1974–75; Cleveland Crusaders (WHA), 1975–76; Colorado Rockies, 1976–77; Pittsburgh Penguins, 1977–80
AWARDS/HONORS: NHL All-Star Game, 1954, 1956

Johnny Wilson's 11-year NHL career included an iron man string of 580 consecutive regular-season games, a record he set in 1960 while playing for the Toronto Maple Leafs. That record was broken by Andy Hebenton of the Rangers in 1964.

Wilson broke into hockey with his brother Larry, and played alongside him for several campaigns with Detroit and Chicago. John became a star in Detroit as an all-around player.

Although never a big scorer, Wilson nonetheless collected 23 goals in 1952–53 with Detroit, and 24 in 1955–56 with Chicago, for the best seasons of his career.

The end of his career was hastened by a broken collarbone suffered in training camp in the fall of 1961. Wilson turned to coaching and found a home in the World Hockey Association.

The Michigan Stags/Baltimore Blades gained his coaching services in 1974. In 1975, he signed to coach the WHA Cleveland Crusaders.

Soon after, Wilson left the Crusaders for the hapless and hopeless Colorado Rockies of the NHL. The Rockies, formerly the Kansas City Scouts, never blossomed as expected under Wilson's tutorage, and the coach packed his bags for a new club at the end of the 1976–77 season. He later would coach in Denver, Pittsburgh, Detroit, and Los Angeles.

Wilson joined the Penguins in 1977–78, and his coaching tactics worked with the Steel City club. The Pens barely missed the 1978 playoffs, but a year later they pieced together a new team with intelligent trades and posted 85 points, good for a playoff berth in the Stanley Cup quarterfinals.

Wilson left Pittsburgh in 1980 and retired from bench work in 1980. His nephew, Ron Wilson, continued the family tradition, coaching the inaugural Anaheim Mighty Ducks and the Washington Capitals (with whom he reached the Stanley Cup finals in 1998).

RON WILSON

BORN: Windsor, Ontario, May 28, 1955
POSITION: Defenseman, Toronto Maple Leafs, 1977–80; Minnesota North Stars, 1984–88; Coach, Anaheim Mighty Ducks, 1993–97; Team USA, World Cup of Hockey, 1996; United States Olympic Team, 1998; Washington Capitals, 1997–2002

Every so often, a successful coach is victimized by political machinations in the front office. Such was the case with cerebral Ron Wilson, who was an instant hit with the Anaheim Mighty Ducks after taking over in 1993. Previously, he had played for Providence College as well as in the NHL. In 1990, he had become assistant coach of the Vancouver Canucks. But he gained attention after moving to Anaheim.

Under Wilson's sharp baton, the expansion franchise gained immediate legitimacy, compiling a 120–145–31 record through 1996–97. Despite such commendable results, Wilson was dismissed after a disagreement with the general staff in 1997, a move that was sharply criticized by the California media.

However, the coach landed on his feet and thrived. His next coaching job was with the Washington Capitals, and he promptly led them to a 40-win, 32-loss record and a 1998 Stanley Cup finals berth against the Detroit Red Wings. He registered two more seasons of 40 or more wins with the Caps (1999–2000, 2000–01), but could not get out of the first round of the postseason.

By 2001–02, the Caps obtained high-priced superstar Jaromir Jagr, but suffered crippling early season injuries that set back the team for the first half of the year. Wilson got the team back on track, but by then, it was too late to wrest the last playoff berth from a resurgent Montreal. Eventually it cost Wilson his job, as the Caps fired him in May 2002.

BILL WIRTZ

BORN: Chicago, Illinois, October 5, 1929

Dean of the National Hockey League's Board of Governors, Bill Wirtz was the son of Arthur M. Wirtz, credited by some with saving the NHL during its fiscal floundering of the early 1950s. It was Arthur Wirtz who bought the Chicago Blackhawks in 1954, and rejuvenated the team to a Stanley Cup championship in 1961, the last time Chicago won a Stanley Cup.

After graduating from Ivy League Brown University, Wirtz and brother Michael helped their father strengthen the franchise in the 1960s. In 1966, Bill took over as Blackhawks president, and the team finished first in its division for the first time in its history.

Beloved by almost all owners for his straightforward demeanor, Wirtz was elected as chairman of the board of governors nine times. He served in the role for 18 years, resigning after the 1991–92 season.

As a league power broker, Wirtz worked hand-in-hand with NHL president John Ziegler during the late 1970s and early 1980s.

Ill health diminished Wirtz's work schedule in the late 1990s, but the well-built leader maintained his position with the club, and by the 2001–02 season, had become active again.

Wirtz always was a believer in fiscal responsibility. During the 2001–02 season, he explained his philosophy: "We're going to operate within a budget. That's cast in iron. If you have to sell stocks to support a loss, you have no business being in sports.

"I answer to stockholders. My deceased brother Mike's family and his children are stockholders. Whenever people write, 'The Wirtzes aren't interested in hockey, they're just interested in money,' that hurts. We started out in 1941 with a 48 percent interest in the Detroit Red Wings with the Norris family and we're still here. We must have done something right because we're the oldest family in sports continuously."

GUMP WORSLEY

BORN: Montreal, Quebec, May 14, 1929
POSITION: Goaltender, New York Rangers, 1952-53, 1954-63; Montreal Canadiens, 1963-70; Minnesota North Stars, 1970-74
AWARDS/HONORS: Calder Memorial Trophy, 1953; Vezina Trophy, 1966 (shared with Charlie Hodge), 1968 (shared with Rogatien Vachon); NHL First Team All-Star, 1968; NHL Second Team All-Star, 1966; NHL All-Star Game, 1961-62, 1965, 1972; Hockey Hall of Fame, 1980

Gump Worsley was one of the most competent, colorful, cantankerous, and stubborn characters in hockey. The nomadic netminder saw duty with ten clubs in five different leagues over a 24-year professional career, leaving a hilarious trail of Worsley

anecdotes wherever he parked his pudgy frame. It took 24 years before Gump gave in and agreed to wear a mask while tending goal. He thus became the last outstanding NHL goalie to put on a face-covering, yet he never overcame his intense fear of flying. It was said to be written into Gump's contract that he be allowed to fly in the pilot's cockpit so he could be sure the plane's skipper was paying attention.

He was nicknamed Gump from a comic strip character called Andy Gump, who resembled Worsley. Originally the property of the New York Rangers, Gump came to the NHL with the 1952 Broadway team. Worsley was the diamond in the rough on this conglomeration of underachievers. His fearless performances while facing as many as 50 shots per game earned him the Calder Trophy as the NHL's rookie of the year. Yet, inexplicably, Gump was promptly sent to the minors (Vancouver) for the 1953–54 season, replaced by John Bower.

Gump's round, jowled face and watery, hound-dog eyes sometimes gave the impression of complete nonchalance as he flopped around the ice covering up for his teammates' many blunders.

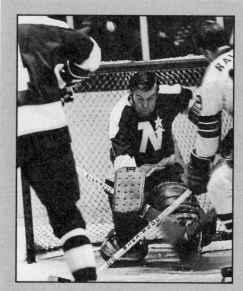

Lorne "Gump" Worsley as the last unmasked goalie, here with the Minnesota North Stars

Worsley's comic-strip form became a fixture for New York's hockey community until the summer of 1963. At the annual league meetings in Montreal, Worsley was traded to the Montreal Canadiens.

Gump was 34 years old when traded to the Habs, and although few knew it at the time, Worsley had been reborn. It wasn't easy at first—Charlie Hodge had inherited the Hab netminding chores—so Gump found himself gathering splinters on the Canadiens bench or laboring for the minor-league Quebec Aces. But the 1964–65 playoffs found Gump carrying the brunt of the Canadiens netminding, as the Habs rolled to the Stanley Cup. Worsley, supposedly in the twilight of his career, posted a 1.68 goals-against average, including two shutouts, to lead all playoff netminders.

Gump was a Canadiens fixture for the next four seasons, steering them to three more Stanley Cups and twice winning the coveted Vezina Trophy, awarded annually to the loop's top netminder. Midway through the 1969–70 season, Worsley, then almost 40 years old, was sold to the expansion Minnesota North Stars. Teamed with another veteran, tall Cesare Maniago, this Mutt and Jeff pair of backstops proved they still had some good games left as they steered the Stars into the playoffs for the next five consecutive campaigns.

After the 1972–73 season had ended, Gump, for the umpteenth time, announced his retirement from pro hockey. He returned to his home to watch the Stanley Cup finals before settling down to a life of leisure. The final round that year pitted his old Montreal Canadiens against the powerful Chicago Blackhawks. The series was being billed as a "battle of the goaltenders" as Hab Ken Dryden and Hawk Tony Esposito reigned as the loop's top two stoppers.

When the smoke had cleared after the highest scoring slugfest of a final round in recent history, Gump showed that his retirement age had not mellowed him one bit. "If those two guys are supposed to be the best," he observed acidly, "then I know I can play at least one more year."

He did just that at the age of 45, playing one more season with Minnesota before hanging up his goaler's pads for good. Worsley continued his hockey career for years as a scout, before retiring to his native Montreal.

Many still remembered Worsley for his wit as well as his puckstopping.

Once, while playing for a terrible Rangers team in 1954–55, Gump was interviewed by a magazine writer.

"Which NHL team gives you the most trouble?" Worsley was asked.

"That's easy," dead-panned the Gumper, "the Rangers!"

ROY WORTERS

BORN: Toronto, Ontario, October 19, 1900
DIED: November 7, 1957
POSITION: Goaltender, Pittsburgh Pirates, 1926–28; Montreal Canadiens, 1930; New York Americans, 1928–29, 1930–37
AWARDS/HONORS: Hart Memorial Trophy, 1929; Vezina Trophy, 1931; NHL Second Team All-Star, 1932, 1934; Hockey Hall of Fame, 1969

Roy "Shrimp" Worters, one of the tiniest goaltenders in hockey history, broke into pro shinny with the Pittsburgh Yellowjackets of the USAHA. When the Pittsburgh Pirates were granted an NHL franchise in 1926, little Roy was signed as their netminder.

Roy "Shrimp" Worters as a New York Americans goalie

After three steady years with the Bucs, Roy got into a bitter contract dispute with the club's brass and was suspended by league president Frank Calder. The New York Americans, who had finished their season in the NHL's cellar, were in desperate need of a goalie with Roy's credentials. A deal was hastily worked out between the two clubs and in 1929 Roy was decked out in the red, white, and blue spangled jerseys of the Amerks.

Worters played so well that first year with the New Yorkers, that he lifted his club out of the league basement and into the playoffs. For his heroics, Roy was awarded the Hart Trophy as the league's most valuable player. It was the first time the honor had been bestowed on a backstop.

Shrimp's finest season was 1931, when he racked up a stingy 1.68 goals-against average and won the Vezina Trophy as the loop's top stopper. There was one small problem though; the Americans' forwards sometimes seemed unable to score any goals. Despite Roy's artful acrobatics in goal, the Americans failed to make the playoffs.

Worters played six more years with the punchless Americans, performing admirably, but unable to single-handedly carry his club to the playoffs. He finally retired in 1937.

ALEXEI YASHIN

BORN: Sverdlovsk, USSR, November 5, 1973
POSITION: Center, Ottawa Senators, 1993–2001; New York Islanders, 2001–
AWARDS/HONORS: NHL Second Team All-Star, 1999; NHL All-Star Game, 1994, 1999, 2002

As the Russian population of the National Hockey League increased in the 1990s, one of the most intriguing ex-Soviet Union skaters to make an immediate impact on North American hockey was Alexei Yashin.

The son of a highly-respected Russian engineer (father) and an Olympic volleyball star (mother), Yashin was drafted as a first-round pick, second overall, by the Ottawa Senators in 1992.

Overshadowed by over-hyped Ottawa's number one draft pick Alexandre Daigle, Alexei nonetheless made an immediate and positive impact the following year in his rookie season, 1993–94, leading all rookies in assists and ranking second in points for the otherwise hapless Senators. He was also the only rookie to play in the All-Star game. In following years, he consecutively led Ottawa in either goals and/or points, and was a finalist in 1998 for the Hart Trophy and the Lester B. Pearson Award as most valuable player with 44 goals and 54 assists for 94 points. By this time, the more-than-disappointing Daigle had departed hockey altogether.

Yashin played for the Russian team in the 1998 Olympics, bringing back a silver medal and recording six points in six games. He represented Russia in the World Championships six times, and twice in the World Junior Championships.

Yashin's sojourn with the Senators would become pockmarked with controversy, however.

After leading the Senators to an upset playoff victory over the Devils in 1998, topping the team in power-play goals, game-winning goals, and shots on goal, Yashin and his agent Mark Gandler collided with the Senators' management. The lanky Russian finally sat out the entire 1999–2000 season.

After it was decided in court that Yashin was obligated to play out his contract with Ottawa, he returned to the lineup for the 2000–01 season, bouncing back amid boos by reaching the 40-goal plateau for the second time in his career, and tying for second place in the NHL for game-winning goals, tenth in goals, and eleventh in points. He appeared in all 82 games for the club, which he had also done in the three previous seasons he played.

But on June 23, 2001, Yashin was quickly snatched up by the cellar-dwelling New York Islanders. Armed with an abundance of young assets as well as cash resources from new owners Charles Wang and Sanjay Kumar, Islanders general manager Mike Milbury wanted to make a turnaround statement at the NHL Entry Draft. In exchange for Zdeno Chara, Bill Muckalt, and the Isles' 2001 first-round pick (Jason Spezza), Yashin came to Long Island as a legitimate number one center and star the once-proud franchise could build around. An unprecedented—and much questioned—ten-year contract solidified Yashin's commitment to the reborn franchise.

Coupled with the good fortune of acquiring Michael Peca and Chris Osgood, the Islanders benefitted from Yashin's presence, which helped electrify Long Island fans, who were happy to see NHL-caliber talent in their barn. The Isles got off to an 11–1–1 start and a playoff berth for the first time since 1994. Strong on the puck with deceptive skills and size, Yashin finished the 2001–02 season with 75 points despite having no consistent linemates.

His playoff effectiveness, continuously questioned after dismal production as the Senators' top gun during the 1998–99 and 2000–01 postseasons, sharply rebounded. Against the Toronto Maple Leafs, Yashin's seven points in seven games led the team, as the brutal series came down to a barrage of Yashin-led Islander scrambles in the third period of Game Seven, nearly tying the cliffhanger before Toronto held on to win, 4–2. Yashin had found peace on Long Island unlike his tumultuous years in Ottawa.

MIKE YORK

BORN: Waterford, Michigan, January 3, 1978
POSITION: Center/Left Wing, New York Rangers, 1999–2002; Edmonton Oilers, 2002–
AWARDS/HONORS: NHL All-Rookie Team, 2000

Every so often an untouted player comes along and, by pure force of drive and talent, is able to make a name for himself. Such was the case with Michigan State graduate Mike York. Small by NHL standards, standing five feet ten and weighing 185 pounds, York nevertheless earned a spot on the New York Rangers during the 1999–2000 season and proceeded to win the hearts of New York fans with his relentless play and at the same time compel management to give him increased duty.

The results almost produced a Calder Trophy for the U.S. native. In his freshman year, York tallied 26 goals and 36 assists playing in all 82 games. By the 2001–02 season, he was a Rangers mainstay on a high-flying top line featuring Eric Lindros at center and Theoren Fleury on right wing. The trio's play vaulted the Rangers into first place, but the constant battering and punishment meted out to the smallish York appeared to tire him out during the second half of the season, and his production markedly decreased, as did the rest of the team's.

In March 2002, Rangers general manager Glenn Sather made a trade deadline move, sending York to Edmonton for Rem Murray and Tom Poti. The trade disappointed Rangers fans, who enjoyed York's enthusiastic play; but he fit in perfectly with the Oilers' fleet, offensive style.

DMITRY YUSHKEVICH

BORN: Yaroslavl, USSR, November 19, 1971
POSITION: Defenseman, Philadelphia Flyers, 1992–95; Toronto Maple Leafs, 1995–02; Florida Panthers, 2002–
AWARDS/HONORS: NHL All-Star Game, 2000

Ever since the late Cold War years, the Philadelphia Flyers tended to avoid involving themselves with Russian players. But after Slava Fetisov broke the hockey Iron Curtain and signed with the New Jersey Devils in 1989, the Flyers took a more liberal view of players from the former Soviet Union.

In the 1991 Entry Draft, they demonstrated the change of policy by making Dmitry Yushkevich their sixth choice (122nd overall) and starting with the 1992–93 season, the rugged backliner made the move pay dividends. Tough, effective on the attack, and smart behind his blue line, Yushkevich played three effective seasons for the Flyers before being dealt to Toronto in August 1995.

Yushkevich wasted no time becoming a hero in Toronto and the best all-around defender coach Pat Quinn iced, night in and night out. After playing 81 games in the 2000–01 season—the most he ever played in one big-league campaign—Yushkevich had reached a higher rung on the ladder and appeared ready for bigger and better things.

However, a late-season injury a year later ruined the homestretch for Dmitry's 2001–02 season and he was forced to miss the playoffs as well.

STEVE YZERMAN

BORN: Cranbrook, British Columbia, May 9, 1965
POSITION: Center, Detroit Red Wings, 1983–
AWARDS/HONORS: Lester B. Pearson Award, 1989; Conn Smythe Trophy, 1998; NHL All-Rookie Team, 1984; Frank J. Selke Trophy, 2000; NHL First Team All-Star, 2000; NHL All-Star Game, 1984, 1988–1993, 1997, 2000

Playing in an era when hockey players quickly bolted teams that drafted them for bigger money elsewhere, Steve Yzerman was an exception. He never wavered from his undying spirit and loyalty for his one and only team, the Detroit Red Wings.

The youngest captain in Detroit history, Steve Yzerman

"I love playing in Detroit," said Yzerman. "I feel honored to play for an Original Six team that has so much tradition both on and off the ice. To play my whole career here is something that I want to do."

But "Captain Cup," as he was referred to by his adoring fans in Detroit, suffered through some horrible and downtrodden times while he ascended to greatness.

Steve set the Red Wing record for most goals (39) and most points (87) by a rookie in 1983–84. He finished second to Tom Barrasso in the Calder Trophy voting for rookie of the year honors, and was selected to the NHL All-Rookie team in 1984. In the summer of 1984, 19-year-old Yzerman was selected to play for Team Canada in that year's Canada Cup Tournament with the likes of Wayne Gretzky and Raymond Bourque.

But in the opening game of the tournament, Yzerman crashed heavily into the boards at the old Montreal Forum. The collision resulted in a hip pointer, and knocked the youngster out of the game. After the contest, Yzerman was barely able to walk, and his status for the rest of the tournament was in jeopardy.

Showing the determination and fortitude that would become his trademark, Yzerman bounced back after missing just four games. He returned to the lineup to help Team Canada win the event.

In March 1988, Yzerman tore ligaments in his right knee in the same game in which he scored his 50th goal of the season. He ended up missing the final 15 games of the regular season as well as the first two rounds of the playoffs. Again, the heart and soul of the club returned, but was unable to spur his team to victory, playing at barely 50 percent.

On April 14, 1994, Yzerman sprained his right knee on the final night of the regular season, with two minutes remaining in the contest. The Red Wings collected 100 points that season, and had high hopes heading into the playoffs. But Yzerman's injury hindered the team's chances of hoisting the Stanley Cup. He missed the first four games of the round-one playoff series against the San Jose Sharks, who were huge underdogs. The Wings felt they could defeat the young team without the help of their captain. Stunningly, the Red Wings were upset by the upstart Sharks in seven games.

When the Red Wings made him their captain at the tender age of 21, Yzerman carried the weight of a franchise that hadn't won a Cup in decades. And after the five years of spectacular regular seasons, Yzerman and his Red Wings continually flopped in the playoffs.

To get them over that proverbial hump, the Wings hired Scotty Bowman as coach in 1993. Bowman brought six Stanley Cup rings when he was hired by owner Mike Ilitch to change the style of play that had developed in Detroit under former coaches Bryan Murray and Jacques Demers.

Bowman immediately instituted a more defensive-style of system, much to the chagrin of captain Yzerman, always considered more of an offensive player, who had notched 50 or more goals six times in the ten years prior to Bowman's arrival.

But Bowman decided to change the way the captain played. He knew Yzerman had the offensive skill, but for the team to succeed and take their game to another level, they needed Yzerman to become a smart, disciplined player.

In the 1994–95 lockout season, Detroit came out of the gate quickly and won 33 of the 48 games played in the abbreviated season. They marched into the playoffs and reached the Stanley Cup finals for the first time since 1966, looking to win their first Stanley Cup since 1955.

At the age of 30, Steve Yzerman had finally led his team to the promised land.

Their opponent was the Eastern Conference New Jersey Devils. The Devils, employing a clever style of play devised by their coach Jacques Lemaire, called "The Trap," beat Detroit at every facet of the game, promptly sweeping the Wings.

Undaunted, Yzerman and the Red Wings reached the Stanley Cup finals for the second time in three years in 1997. Their opponent was the Eric Lindros-led Philadelphia Flyers.

Before the series, pundits salivated over the matchup between the disciplined style of Steve Yzerman and the Red Wings versus the physical style of the Flyers. But going in, everyone knew who the key was for Detroit.

The elusive ring was just four wins away.

Yzerman led his team to a four-game sweep of the Flyers, capturing Lord Stanley's Cup for Detroit for the first time since 1955.

Motivated by the previous summer's tragic accident that crippled both team masseuse Sergei Mnatsakanov and defenseman Vladamir Konstantinov, Yzerman and his team dedicated the following season to their fallen friends, and carried the club to their second straight Stanley Cup finals in the fall of 1998.

That year's opponents were the Washington Capitals. Again, the Red Wings trounced their opponent en route to a second straight finals round sweep. Yzerman was absolutely brilliant, scoring two goals that sparked a Detroit comeback from a 3–1 deficit in Game Two. He led all scorers with 24 points in 22 games, and won the Conn Smythe Trophy as Most Valuable Player in the playoffs.

At the urging of his teammates, Yzerman handed the mug to Konstantinov in one of the most emotional and touching moments ever witnessed at a championship celebration. If the world didn't know what type of person Steve Yzerman was before that instant, they did now.

With the Conn Smythe Trophy, Steve Yzerman joined a select few in the annals of professional hockey and gained the respect so lacking early in his brilliant career. As he was playing in the same era as two of the greatest centers that ever laced on a pair of skates—Wayne Gretzky and Mario Lemieux—Yzerman's offensive presence on the rink never got as much publicity as it should have.

Among Yzerman's personal milestones was an electrifying 65-goal and 90-assist season in 1988–89 which earned him the Lester B. Pearson Award as the top performer in the league as voted by his peers. Both marks were Red Wing franchise records. Besides Yzerman, only three other players had ever topped the 150-point barrier: Lemieux, Gretzky, and Phil Esposito.

Yzerman's class always touched every teammate that he ever played with and every coach that he ever played for. When he finally won his first Stanley Cup in 1997, his critics began to be hushed. But when he won his second the following year, along with the Conn Smythe Trophy, he became the critics' darling.

By 2001–02, Detroit—fresh from a first-round upset at the hands of the Los Angeles Kings the previous spring—remained a Cup favorite, thanks in part to a summer shopping spree, netting a trio of future Hall of Famers:

Luc Robitaille, Brett Hull, and Dominik Hasek. It was clear Yzerman's leadership helped silence the talk of the Wings' age as they finished with 116 points and the President's Trophy.

Despite injuries that cramped his style, Yzerman courageously played on. Thanks to his leadership, Detroit marched to the Stanley Cup finals, defeating Carolina to win the title.

"Steve doesn't take a second off," Bowman once said. "There's a select few players who show up for every game and every practice. That's why they get to where they are. [Wayne] Gretzky is like that. Bobby Orr was like that. [Guy] Lafleur was like that in Montreal."

LARRY ZEIDEL

BORN: Montreal, Quebec, June 1, 1928
POSITION: Defenseman, Detroit Red Wings,
1951–53; Chicago Blackhawks, 1953–54;
Philadelphia Flyers, 1967–69

Few sports comebacks have ever been laced with the flair produced by defenseman Larry Zeidel in the summer of 1967. Zeidel was one of the few Jewish players in professional hockey, and in Yiddish there's a word for what he did. It's chutzpah.

A rugged, hard-hitting type who was known as a good fighter, Zeidel played briefly in the NHL for Detroit and Chicago before being demoted to the minors in 1954, where he played until 1967 when the National Hockey League expanded from six to 12 teams. In that year, Zeidel, aged 39, compiled a flashy résumé complete with a letter from a doctor stating he had the heart of a 22-year-old and sent the brochure to everybody important on each of the 12 NHL teams.

Every club but one said "thanks—but no thanks." The Philadelphia Flyers were willing to take a chance. Manager Bud Poile signed

Larry "The Rock" Zeidel, defenseman on the original Philadelphia Flyers, 1967–68

Zeidel and started him alongside Joe Watson. The Flyers began winning and Larry appeared to be playing better hockey than he had with the Cup champion Red Wings or the Blackhawks (1953–54).

On November 4, 1967, the Flyers were scheduled to meet tougher competition than they had met in their expansion division: the Montreal Canadiens. That afternoon, Bernie Parent, then a young goalie, and Zeidel were in their hotel room where Parent had a bad case of the shakes. But Zeidel encouraged him to think "positive" and to have confidence in his ability.

Five hours later, the game was over—Philadelphia 4, Montreal 1. Bernie Parent had thought "positive." A week later, Philadelphia went to Boston and defeated the Bruins. A week after that, Philadelphia defeated the Rangers. Zeidel started every game with Watson at his side.

The Flyers finished first, winning the Clarence Campbell Bowl, and Zeidel was among the best players on the club. Although the Flyers were eliminated from the playoffs, Zeidel appeared to be a fixture with the Flyers. But he fought with Poile in the 1968–69 season. Poile wanted Zeidel to play in Quebec of the American League, but Zeidel refused. He retired from hockey in 1969 and went into the investment counseling business.

The Rock's unquenchable desire to win was reflected in later years when he played for—and later coached—Flyers alumni teams.

PETER ZEZEL

BORN: Toronto, Ontario, April 22, 1965
POSITION: Center, Philadelphia Flyers, 1984–88;
St. Louis Blues, 1988–90, 1995–97; Washington
Capitals, 1990–91; Toronto Maple Leafs,
1991–94; Dallas Stars, 1994–95; New Jersey
Devils, 1997–98; Vancouver Canucks, 1998–99

Peter Zezel enjoyed one of the most upbeat relationships with local fans of anyone who skated at The Spectrum as a Philadelphia Flyer.

Part of the Toronto native's appeal was his enduring work ethic, another part was his delightful personality, a third, probably his dark-maned good looks.

He was the Flyers' first choice—41st overall—in the 1983 Entry Draft, and made the team one year later, drawing comparisons to New York Islanders ace Bryan Trottier. Employing footwork in his game as a result of expert soccer skills, Peter scored 15 goals and 46 assists as a rookie.

Admiring the youngster's team-first attitude, Flyers coach Mike Keenan thrust Zezel into a pivotal role during their march to the 1985 Stanley Cup finals. His overall ice presence and grit impressed the coach, and Zezel played more during his sophomore year of 1985–86. By his third season, 1986–87, Zezel improved his consistency and zoomed to a career-high 72 points, helping the Flyers make another run to the Stanley Cup finals.

However, Zezel's production dropped dramatically, and he was shipped to the St. Louis Blues for Mike Bullard in November 1988. He duplicated his career-high 72 points in 1989–90, but struggled to attain anything like earlier numbers afterward. He was part of the high-flying Maple Leafs teams of 1993 and 1994 that made the Eastern Conference finals, but like a tennis ball, Peter bounced from team to team—including stops in Washington, Dallas, St. Louis again, New Jersey, and Vancouver—until his retirement in 1999.

He was likeable wherever he played, but never more so than when he wore the orange and black at The Spectrum.

ALEXEI ZHAMNOV

BORN: Moscow, USSR, October 1, 1970
POSITION: Center, Winnipeg Jets, 1992–96;
Chicago Blackhawks, 1996–
AWARDS/HONORS: NHL Second Team All-Star, 1995; NHL All-Star Game, 2002

When Mike Smith was general manager of the Winnipeg Jets, he beat several of his colleagues to the punch in signing Russian stars. Among the most prized acquisitions was Alexei Zhamnov, who kept the Jets competitive from the moment he arrived until the franchise was moved to Phoenix, Arizona.

Drafted in 1990, Alexei debuted on November 10, 1992, against the Detroit Red Wings, recording his first NHL assist. Centering fellow freshman Teemu Selanne, Zhamnov used his skills and smarts for not only a 25-goal breakout performance, but also a league-leading, record-shattering 76 goals for linemate Selanne.

The first Russian to ever be nominated for the Lady Byng Trophy, Zhamnov scored an astounding five goals in a 7–7 tie against the Los Angeles Kings in 1995. But his numbers, although commendable, would decline upon being dealt to the Chicago Blackhawks in a 1996 deal for fan-favorite Jeremy Roenick.

In his first season as a Blackhawk, he would lead the team in assists with 42 and record 62 points, while replacing the popular Roenick. But injuries, including a fractured larynx in 2001, and inconsistency marred his production in subsequent years, despite playing with sniper Tony Amonte. Still, Zhamnov developed into a reliable two-way performer, capable of timely playmaking, and was rewarded with an assistant captainship in 2000.

With Brian Sutter's arrival in Chicago as coach for 2001–02, Zhamnov's production escalated, earning him his first All-Star berth.

JOHN ZIEGLER

The last president of the National Hockey League in June 1977, following the retirement of long-time prexy Clarence Campbell, John A. Ziegler found himself at the helm of a ship that went through many storms but came through intact.

The former lawyer for the Detroit Red Wings organization was confronted with such crises as the arrest of New York Ranger Don Murdoch for cocaine possession. He handled that with considerable leniency, suspending Murdoch for only the 1978–79 season, then commuting that sentence to merely the first half of the season. Many thought Murdoch got off easy.

As one of the biggest merger advocates, Ziegler struggled relentlessly against the powerful antimerger bloc (a minority among NHL owners) until March 1979, when an agreement of consolidation was finally reached between the NHL and WHA.

Ziegler's reign as president reached a peak in the early 1980s. The league prospered following its merger and the emergence of an American team, the New York Islanders, as four-time Stanley Cup champions from 1980 through 1983.

Ziegler's rule was abetted by Chicago Blackhawks owner Bill Wirtz, then chairman of the powerful board of governors. A minority of owners, led by Harry Ornest of St. Louis and John McMullen of the New Jersey Devils, were sharply critical of Ziegler in the mid 1980s, but it wasn't until late in the decade that Ziegler came under fire for his disappearance during a critical period of the 1988 playoffs between the Devils and the Boston Bruins.

"Where I was is my personal business," he insisted. "I answer to the board and nobody else." The media were astonished by this arrogant and obdurate comment.

But Ziegler's downfall had more to do with the labor war between management and the NHL Players' Association. When Bob Goodenow replaced Eagleson as NHLPA boss, Goodenow took a much tougher stance. The confrontation led to a players' strike, and what many observers believed was Ziegler's capitulation.

Right or wrong, Ziegler was considered by ownership to be sufficiently weakened in the eyes of management to have to be replaced. Ziegler finally resigned as NHL president in June 1992.

Following his departure from the NHL, Ziegler resumed his law practice. When Gary Bettman became chief executive of the NHL in 1993, the title "President," which Ziegler held, was changed to "Commissioner."

SERGEI ZUBOV

BORN: Moscow, Russia, July 22, 1970
POSITION: Defense, New York Rangers, 1992–95; Pittsburgh Penguins, 1995–96; Dallas Stars, 1996–
AWARDS/HONORS: NHL All-Star Game, 1998–2000

The value of Sergei Zubov could be pinpointed in several ways:

- He was a key member of the Rangers' 1994 Stanley Cup-winning team.

- When he left New York in a trade with Pittsburgh, the Rangers began plummeting.

- After joining the Dallas Stars, he became an integral part of their Cup-winning team in 1999.

Zubov's armament included a dynamically accurate shot, superior playmaking ability, and solid defense. With over 700 games of National Hockey League experience, the dependable Zubov—a draft gem at 85th overall by the New York Rangers in 1990—had scored more than 500 points in the NHL through 2001–02.

One of the best point men on the power play, the smooth-skating Russian led his team in scoring as a defenseman (89 points) with the 1993–94 President's Trophy–winning Rangers. While Zubov could score he also protected his end of the ice, finishing no lower than minus-two in any season and accumulating just over 200 career penalty minutes as a top-four blueliner.

Sergei was a major asset to the Stars in the late 1990s but was often overlooked as one of the game's better defensemen. The Stars plummeted out of the playoffs in 2001–02, but Zubov remained at the top of his game.

About the Authors

Stan Fischler is the preeminent hockey author in North America, as well as a major historian in the field of transportation. A broadcaster and former university professor, Stan has written more than 100 books on hockey, including several best-sellers.

Some of his more notable books include the definitive *Hockey Encyclopedia,* coauthored with his wife, Shirley; *Metro Ice,* a collection of photos and stories about the history of New York metro area hockey; *Cracked Ice,* with stories and anecdotes about the game's strangest events; and *Grapes,* the autobiography of Canada's notorious Don Cherry.

Stan, 70, hosts pregame and between-periods programs for New York Islanders and New Jersey Devils telecasts. He frequently appears on radio and television talk shows in his role as hockey historian.

In 1988, Stan won an Emmy Award for his participation in New York Islanders and New Jersey Devils telecasts for SportsChannel. He won a second Emmy in 1999 for his work with Fox Sports.

His journalism career began in 1954 when he became a publicist for the New York Rangers. In 1955 he was hired as a columnist by the *New York Journal-American,* then the nation's leading afternoon newspaper. During his 11 years at the *J-A,* Stan covered city hall, Broadway, entertainment, sports, and transportation.

In 1967, Stan authored his first book, *Gordie Howe,* the biography of the NHL immortal. He has collaborated with such Hall of Famers as Denis Potvin *(Power on Ice),*

Rod Gilbert *(Goal)*, Brad Park *(Play the Man)*, Derek Sanderson *(I've Got to Be Me)*, and Kevin Lowe *(Champions)*.

Stan's work has also appeared in the *New York Times, Sports Illustrated, Inside Sports, Maclean's,* and the *Toronto Star,* for whom he was the New York bureau chief for 12 years.

He also writes a syndicated column for MSG.com. In addition, Stan and Shirley author hockey's only 52-week-a-year newsletter, the *Fischler Report,* the insider's tribune of the industry.

Shirley Walton married Stan in February of 1968, largely because the New York Rangers hockey team was on the road, giving the newlyweds a whole week to honeymoon—and ski—in Stowe, Vermont. The two then settled into their new apartment on Manhattan's Upper West Side, where they remain to this day.

After interviewing several Rangers' wives, then submitting to Stan's editorial expertise, Shirley—who had never been to a live NHL game until the previous fall—had her first hockey piece published, in the *Toronto Star,* in April 1968. She's been writing about the game ever since.

Between raising two boys, doing a weekly local radio show, and operating a women's bookstore in Greenwich Village, Shirley also found time for a couple of "firsts." She took Madison Square Garden, the Rangers, and the Professional Hockey Writers' Association to the New York City Human Rights Commision in the summer of 1971, after being refused admittance to the Garden press box during the Stanley

Cup playoffs. As the 1971–72 season began, there were women in an NHL press box for the first time.

Shirley then became the first woman to do TV color commentary for a major league hockey team, when she and Stan performed that function for the New England Whalers of the World Hockey Association in the 1973–74 season.

Most recently Shirley joined the electronic revolution, writing daily hockey squibs and columns for an on-line sports content provider for three seasons. She also made multiple contributions to the NHL's *Total Hockey* encyclopedia, 1999 and 2000 editions.